CONSTITUTIONAL FUNCTIONS AND CONSTITUTIONAL PROBLEMS OF INTERNATIONAL ECONOMIC LAW

Progress and Undercurrents
in Public International Law
PUPIL

Edited by
Detlev Chr. Dicke

Volume 3

PUPIL Progress and Undercurrents in Public International Law 3

CONSTITUTIONAL FUNCTIONS AND CONSTITUTIONAL PROBLEMS OF INTERNATIONAL ECONOMIC LAW

International and Domestic Foreign Trade Law and Foreign Trade Policy in the United States, the European Community and Switzerland

By
DR. ERNST-ULRICH PETERSMANN
Professor of International,
European and Swiss Public Law
at the University of St. Gallen,
Switzerland

Routledge
Taylor & Francis Group
LONDON AND NEW YORK

First published 1991 by Westview Press

Published 2018 by Routledge
52 Vanderbilt Avenue, New York, NY 10017
2 Park Square, Milton Park, Abingdon, Oxon OX14 4RN

Routledge is an imprint of the Taylor & Francis Group, an informa business

ISBN 13: 978-0-367-00440-8 (hbk)

ISBN 13: 978-0-367-15427-1 (pbk)

"All government, specially if democratic, should be limited. The reason is that democratic government, if nominally omnipotent, becomes as a result of unlimited powers exceedingly weak, the playball of all the separate interests it has to satisfy to secure majority support".

F.A. v. Hayek[1]

"An economic constitution is not complete without a theory of foreign economic policy and the legal control of it".

J. Tumlir[2]

---

1 F.A. v.Hayek, Law, Legislation and Liberty, Volume 3, 1979/1982, p. 99.

2 J. Tumlir, Franz Böhm and the Development of Economic-Constitutional Analysis (unpublished paper 1985).

CONTENTS

Abbreviations

AJIL	:	American Journal of International Law
ALR	:	American Law Reports
BIS	:	Bank for International Settlement
BISD	:	GATT Basic Instruments and Selected Documents
COCOM	:	Coordinating Committee for East-West Trade
Cong.	:	Congress of the USA
COMECON	:	Council for Mutual Economic Cooperation
EC	:	European Communities
ECJ	:	Court of Justice of the EC
ECOSOC	:	Economic and Social Council of the UN
ECR	:	European Court Reports
ECSC	:	European Coal and Steel Community
EEC	:	European Economic Community
EFTA	:	European Free Trade Area
EURATOM	:	European Atomic Energy Community
F	:	Federal Reporter of US court decisions
F 2d	:	Federal Reporter Second Series (since 1924)
F.Suppl.	:	Federal Supplement of US court decisions
GATT	:	General Agreement on Tariffs and Trade
IATA	:	International Air Transport Association
IBRD	:	International Bank for Reconstruction and Development
ICAO	:	International Civil Aviation Organization
ICM	:	International Committee for Migration
ICSID	:	International Center for the Settlement of Investment Disputes
IFC	:	International Finance Corporation
ILM	:	International Legal Materials

ILO	:	International Labour Organization
IMCO	:	Inter-Governmental Maritime Consultative Organization
IMF	:	International Monetary Fund
ITC	:	International Trade Commission
ITU	:	International Telecommunication Union
JWTL	:	Journal of World Trade Law
LDC	:	Less Developed Country
MFA	:	Multifibre Agreement (= International Textiles Agreement 1973)
MFN	:	Most-Favoured Nation
MIGA	:	Multilateral Investment Guarantee Agency
MTN	:	Multilateral Trade Negotiations
OECD	:	Organization of Economic Cooperation and Development
O.J.	:	Official Journal of the EC
OMA	:	Orderly Marketing Agreement
OPEC	:	Organization of Petroleum Exporting Countries
OPIC	:	Overseas Private Investment Corporation
S.Rep.	:	Senate Reports
UN	:	United Nations
UNCTAD	:	United Nations Conference on Trade and Development
UNESCO	:	United Nations Educational, Scientific and Cultural Organization
UNIDO	:	United Nations Industrial Development Organization
US(A)	:	United States (of America)
USC(A)	:	United States Code (Annotated)
VER	:	Voluntary Export Restraint
VRA	:	Voluntary Restraint Arrangement
WIPO	:	World Intellectual Property Organization
ZaöRV	:	Zeitschrift für ausländisches öffentliches Recht und Völkerrecht

ACKNOWLEDGEMENTS

This book was submitted to, and accepted by, the Faculty of Law of the University of Fribourg (Switzerland) as a post-doctoral 'Habilitationsschrift' (habilitation thesis) in 1989. I am much indebted to Professor Rudolf Bernhardt (Director of the Heidelberg Max-Planck-Institute for Public Comparative Law and International Law and Judge at the European Court of Human Rights at Strasbourg), Professor Herrmann Mosler (former Director of the Heidelberg Max-Planck-Institute and former Judge at the International Court of Justice at The Hague) and to Professor Detlev Chr. Dicke (University of Fribourg), without whose support and encouragement this book would never have been completed. I am also grateful to the Director-General of GATT, Mr. Arthur Dunkel, who generously allowed me a leave of absence from my work as legal counsellor in the GATT Secretariat, and to the German Research Society (Deutsche Forschungsgemeinschaft) for its financial assistance which enabled me to write most of this study during my leave without pay from the GATT Secretariat. Thanks are also due to Christopher Prins of the UN Economic Commission for Europe for reading the manuscript and correcting my imperfect English and to Mrs. Patricia Bongard-Ragonesi and Mrs. Sandra Eberle for the typing work. But most of all, I am indebted to my wife and four children for their patience, love and serenity in spite of my often unreasonable demands in connection with this study.

I dedicate this study to my friends and former colleagues in the Legal Division of the GATT secretariat, with whom I could discuss many of the issues analyzed in this book and who are often confronted, in GATT negotiations and GATT dispute settlement proceedings, with the 'constitutional problems' of international and domestic foreign trade law.

INTRODUCTION AND SUMMARY

> "It might be said that since the end of the Second World War, we ... have lived under an economic constitution ... Since its adoption, we have had 40 years of a prosperity more widely shared and more generous than the world has ever known ... I am speaking of the collection of postwar international economic agreements that created the IMF, the World Bank, and the GATT. Today, each of those agreements and institutions has come to a turning point" ...
>
> R. Reagan[1]

1. Approaches to the Study of International Economic Law

Writing a book on international economic law is "like trying to describe a landscape while looking out the window of a moving train - events tend to move faster than one can describe them".[2] This is particularly true for an area like foreign trade law which has evolved into the most densely regulated area of international economic relations and is determined by an intricate interplay of national and international legal, political and economic processes. At the same time, the comprehensive renegotiation of the basic rules of the "international trading system" in the context of the current "Uruguay Round" of multilateral trade negotiations within the General Agreement on Tariffs and Trade (GATT), and the various proposals for a "GATT for services" and a "GATT for investments", have increased the need for an analysis focusing on the "constitutional problems" of national and international economic law, without losing sight of the individual "trees" constituting the overall "wood" of regulatory systems.[3]

---

1 US President R. Reagan, in his speech to the annual meeting of the IMF Board of Governors 1986, in: IMF Survey 1986, p. 326.

2 J.H. Jackson, Legal Problems of International Economic Relations, 1977, p. XV.

3 For two recent analyses of the GATT's "Uruguay Round" from the point of view of international law and economics see: E.U. Petersmann/M. Hilf (eds.), The New GATT Round of Multilateral Trade Negotiations. Legal and Economic Problems, 1988; D. Dicke/E.U. Petersmann (eds.), Foreign Trade in the Present and in a New International Economic Order, 1988.

The completion of this attempt at an integrated economic, political, historical, legal and constitutional analysis of national and international foreign trade law was complicated by yet another constraint: Most of the manuscript had to be written in the course of a 1-year "academic leave" from the GATT Secretariat, during which I taught international economic law at the University of Fribourg (Switzerland) and at the Europa-Institute of the University of the Saarland (Germany).

But this time constraint had also one advantage. The few lawyers, who dared to write a book on the broad and constantly changing subject of national and international economic law, frequently ended up with more than 1000 pages[4] - yet, often without addressing the "constitutional problem" analyzed in this book: How must the discretionary trade policy powers of governments be constitutionally restrained in order to protect the equal freedoms and property rights of domestic citizens, and how can these necessary constitutional restraints be actually brought about? Students of law and economics shun lengthy legal treatises and may read them without understanding the broader "constitutional problems". Encouraged by Dr. Johnson's experience that "when a man knows he will hang in a fortnight, it concentrates his mind wonderfully", the limited time available made it necessary to confine this study from the outset to a deliberately selective enquiry.

The plan to write this book emerged first from discussions during the late 1970s with Professor Dr. Dr. H. Mosler, former judge at the International Court of Justice at the Hague as well as at the European Court of Human Rights at Strasbourg, who had supervised my Ph. D. thesis at the University of Heidelberg and encouraged my plans to write a "Habilitationsschrift" on interrelationships between German, European and international foreign trade law. My interest in this subject had been triggered by the historical phenomenon of the apparent, gradual breakdown of the liberal international trade and monetary order, so successfully designed and implemented after World War II, since about the

4 See: J.H. Jackson/W.J. Davey, Legal Problems of International Economic Relations, 2nd edition, 1986; W. Fikentscher, Wirtschaftsrecht, 2 Vols. 1983; P. Picone/G. Sacerdoti, Diritto Internazionale Dell' Economia, 1983; P. Verloren van Themaat (ed.), Studies over Internationaal Economisch Recht, 2 Vols. 1977/1979; A.F. Lowenfeld, International Economic Law, 6 Vols. (1977 ff). The pertinent French books comprise more than 600 pages each: Carreau/Flory/Juillard, Droit International Economique, 2nd ed. 1980; Bollecker-Stern/Dahan/Kopelmanas, Droit Economique, 1980; Blanc/Rigaux, Droit Economique II, 1980. Two shorter books are highly recommendable: G. Erler, Grundprobleme des Internationalen Wirtschaftsrechts, 1956; P. Verloren van Themaat, The Changing Structure of International Economic Law, 1981.

worldwide economic crisis of 1973/74. As a research fellow in charge of "international economic law" at the Heidelberg Max-Planck-Institute for Comparative Public Law and International Law during the years 1972-1978, I had described these changing structures of international trade, monetary and investment law in more than 20 articles[5] and published a comparative study of the law of regional economic integration in Europe, Africa, Latin America and Asia.[6] My experience from this academic research was that the legal analysis of international economic relations from the perspective of public international law could provide only limited insights for a number of reasons:

Firstly, international economic law cannot be understood without a good knowledge of economic theory.[7] For instance, what lawyers tend to describe and analyze as "international trade conflicts" among states are often, from an economic and political perspective, to a large extent conflicts of interests **within** states rather than between states. The economist W. Röpke has explained this insight in the following terms: "In a question of trade policy the interests of the home producers who are in favour of a protective tariff are opposed to the joint interests both of the consumers and of all the other producers of every nation. The alleged international front is thus in reality a home front and every trade concession is not a sacrifice which the entire nation is forced to make in favour of the foreigner, but one which the special group of protection seekers is forced to concede to the rest of the nation. That this actual conflict of interests which cuts through the middle of the nation is disguised as a conflict between home and abroad is only a superficial phenomenon".[8] My own practical experience e.g. in international GATT dispute settlement proceedings fully confirms that governments often gladly accept GATT dispute settlement reports committing them to the use of transparent, non-discriminatory and welfare-increasing trade

5 See, for instance, my regular reports during this period in the quarterly journal published by the Heidelberg Max-Planck-Institute for Comparative Public Law and International Law: Zeitschrift für ausländisches öffentliches Recht und Völkerrecht 1972, pp. 339-393; 1973, pp. 266-311 and 489-502; 1974, pp. 452-502; 1975, 213-281; 1976, pp. 492-550; 1981, pp. 267-328.

6 E.U. Petersmann, Wirtschaftsintegrationsrecht und Investitionsgesetzgebung der Entwicklungsländer, 1974, 253 pages. An English summary was published in: Law and State, Vol. 12 (1975), pp. 17-35

7 For a more detailed explanation see: E.U. Petersmann, International Economic Theory and International Economic Law, in: Macdonald/Johnston (eds.), The Structure and Process of International Law, 1983, pp. 227-261.

8 W. Röpke, International Order and Economic Integration, 1959, p. 15.

policy instruments which they were previously prevented from using by domestic political pressures from powerful protectionist interest groups.

Secondly, liberalism and internationalism must begin at home. This is true not only for the international economic policy objectives of liberal trade and monetary stability laid down in the GATT and in the Articles of Agreement of the International Monetary Fund (IMF), which cannot be achieved unless the major trading countries and monetary areas pursue liberal trade and monetary stability also at the domestic level. But it is also true for the basic legal principles underlying the international trade and monetary law of the GATT and IMF Agreement such as transparent policy-making, use of less-distortive, proportional policy instruments, non-discriminatory market access and protection of individual rights. A liberal international division of labour is not possible among states which prevent decentralized decision-making through national exchange controls and do not protect, in their domestic legal systems, the freedoms and property rights of those engaged in international trade, monetary and investment transactions.

Thirdly, international economic law and practice can not be understood without taking into account the political processes from which they result. Why do governments engage in protectionist trade policies and inflationary monetary policies inconsistent with their self-imposed GATT and IMF obligations in full knowledge that they are economically harmful to their constituencies? And this not only over short periods of time but over several decades, for instance in the case of trade in agricultural and textiles products? Why did the series of international economic conferences after World War I fail to achieve their declared objective of restoring a liberal international trade order, which had operated so successfully during the "liberal era" from the Cobden-Chevalier trade agreement between England and France (1860) to 1914? Neoclassical economics and traditional legal analyses have for a long time ignored the political constraints of economic and legal policies. These analyses have then often produced economic and legal policy recommendations which - because they were based upon the politically unrealistic assumption of "benevolent, omnipotent governments" seeking "public goods" presumed to exist independently of the individual freedom to express one's individual preferences - promoted at best support for liberal trade and for rule of law without addressing the underlying "constitutional problems" and the political hindrances for the actual implementation of liberal policies.

The above academic experiences prompted me in 1978 to work, for a period of 3 years, in the Legal Office of the Foreign Trade Department of the German Federal Ministry of Economy, Bonn, so as to gain a better insight into the practical operation of foreign trade law and policy. This practical experience has been instructive in many respects such as:

- the regular and valuable, but not fully representative, consultations - explicitly stipulated in the internal working procedures for the German Federal Ministries - with the associations of trade and industry as well as with other private representatives of the "public interest";
- the lack of effective parliamentary control of foreign trade policy within the EEC;
- the close collaboration in certain limited fields of trade policy (such as trade embargoes and nuclear exports) with the Foreign Office and the influence of foreign policy considerations on the conduct of this "strategically sensitive" trade policy;
- the ever closer international policy coordination in international institutions (such as EEC, OECD, GATT, UN, COCOM, international commodity agreements) and the frequent "domestic policy functions" of this constant international coordination of domestic policy issues[9];
- the extensive knowledge, talent and goodwill of most public officials in national and international trade administrations, but also their political constraints and dependence on political support, as well as the numerous "protectionist biases" e.g. in the Ministry of Agriculture as well as in the increasing number of other "sectional bureaus" in charge of assisting import-competing producers in certain sectors (e.g. textiles, clothing, steel and steel products).

In 1981, the GATT established for the first time - 34 years after its inception - an "Office of Legal Affairs" and offered me the newly created post of "legal officer" together with the request of elaborating, besides the current work, an "Analytical Index" designed to make GATT law and GATT practice more

9 See on this aspect, for instance: M. Henderson, The OECD as an instrument of national policy, in: International Journal 1981, pp. 793 ff, who notes with respect to the "monitoring function" of the OECD's "country studies" that "not a word appears in the published survey which is not considered acceptable by the government whose policies have been assessed" (p. 798).

transparent again.[10] The day-to-day work in an international trade organization aimed at liberalizing welfare-reducing national trade barriers and promoting "rule-oriented" rather than "power-oriented" trade policies reveals even more clearly the political constraints of trade policy-making and the very limited influence of economic and legal advisers.[11] The surprising strength of GATT rules, in spite of their flimsy institutional underpinning, derives from the fact that observance of the voluntarily accepted GATT obligations for the public choice of transparent, non-discriminatory, less-distortive and welfare-maximizing trade policy **instruments** is in the national self-interest of every state regardless of its stage of development and its domestic economic, political or legal system.[12] Whenever the GATT Contracting Parties have met at ministerial level to deal with international trade and economic crises, they have reaffirmed the lasting validity of the framework of GATT rules and the national self-interest of all states in abiding by the GATT disciplines.[13] In GATT dispute settlement proceedings, more than 70 GATT panel reports establishing the inconsistency of a trade restriction with GATT law have been adopted by the Contracting Parties by means of consensus including the "losing" respondent contracting party which then used the political weight and legal binding character of GATT dispute settlement decisions as a means to overcome domestic pressures from protec-

10 See: E.U. Petersmann, GATT Analytical Index. Notes on the drafting, interpretation and application of the Articles of the General Agreement, loose-leaf edition GATT 1985, 850 pages.

11 The absence of a GATT legal office up to 1981 was due not only to the preference of the first and second Directors-General of the GATT for a "pragmatic management" of GATT matters but also to the political opposition to the creation of a GATT legal office notably from the EEC. If one looks at the more than 100 publications during these years by members of the legal services of the IMF, the World Bank or the European Communities, regularly explaining their respective fields of law and thereby promoting legal transparency, effectiveness of the rules and their support e.g. by national courts, one cannot be surprised by the regrettable fact that GATT law and GATT's "diplomat's jurisprudence" (R.E. Hudec) appear to have become a mystery to lawyers and judges all over the world.

12 See on this point also Th. Flory, Le GATT - Droit International et Commerce Mondial, 1968, p. 276.

13 See, for instance, the GATT Ministerial Declaration of November 1982 in which the then 88 GATT member countries declared themselves to be "conscious of the role of the GATT system in furthering economic well-being and an unprecedented expansion of world trade, and convinced of the lasting validity of the basic principles and objectives of the General Agreement in a world of increasing economic interdependence"; they also decided "to reaffirm their commitment to abide by their GATT obligations and to support and improve the GATT trading system so that it may contribute vigorously to the further liberalization and expansion of trade" ... (full text in: GATT Activities in 1982, GATT 1983, pp. 9 ff, 11). See likewise the most recent "GATT Ministerial Declaration" of September 1986 opening the "Uruguay Round" of multilateral trade negotiations (text in: GATT Activities in 1986, GATT 1987, pp. 15 ff).

tionist interest groups and to remove the trade restrictions concerned in its own national self-interest.[14]

Besides my academic research in national and international economic law and my practical professional experience in the German Federal Ministry of the Economy and as a German representative within a number of international trade organizations (including the EEC, OECD, ECOSOC, various international commodity organizations, COCOM and GATT), two other factors have shaped the approach of this book. The one was my studies in economics under Professor F.A. von Hayek at Freiburg University and Professor Jan Tumlir at the Geneva Graduate Institute of International Studies. Both of them taught economics from a liberal, individualistic perspective and were critical of the authoritarian premises and seemingly scientific mathematization of neoclassical economics. From their liberal perspective, the only source of value is individual preferences which cannot be known without protection of individual rights and decentralized market processes within which people can make choices. Hence, economists cannot define individual utility functions and evaluate an "efficient" allocation of scarce resources independently from the behaviour of persons in the market process. The proper object of economics should therefore be the study of how individual objectives can be furthered by voluntary exchanges and through agreed rules which can turn short-term conflicts of interests into mutually beneficial cooperation. Economic and legal institutions should be designed to allow individuals to interact freely and permit citizens to have equal access to the political decision-making process. Attempts to create "efficient" or "fair" outcomes instead of rules inevitably introduce biases in the economic system by allowing favoured individuals or groups to impose their own value preferences and to influence public policy for their own selfish benefit. As is evident also from the footnotes, the works of Hayek and Tumlir have had a strong bearing not only on the economic premises of this study.

From the legal point of view of national constitutional law, which I taught at the Universities of Hamburg and Heidelberg, it is evident that the principles underlying such a liberal economic approach are identical with those of political and legal liberalism and that the political task of reconstructing a liberal international trade order raises basic constitutional questions. These constitutional

14 On the regular adoption and implementation of GATT dispute settlement decisions under GATT Article XXIII and on the "domestic policy functions" of GATT dispute settlement proceedings see: E.U. Petersmann, Strengthening GATT Procedures for Settling Trade Disputes, in: The World Economy, March 1988, pp. 55-89.

problems of foreign trade policy and foreign trade law in constitutional democracies are the main subject of this book.

The classical liberal economists, such as David Hume, Adam Smith and John Stuart Mill, derived their individualistic value premise from utilitarian ethics. Thus the freedom of the individual was described as beneficial because "every man is the best judge of his own interest" (Jeremy Bentham), or because of "the natural preference which every man has for his own happiness above that of other people" (Adam Smith), or because the diversity of individual opinions and experiments of living generate new knowledge and can help each individual to improve his own imperfect knowledge of what is good for him (John Stuart Mill).[15] Such utilitarian justifications of individual economic freedom with the need to set appropriate incentives, with the use of existing knowledge or with the transmission and accumulation of knowledge are less necessary in democratic societies with liberal constitutions which stipulate that all government power is limited and bound by inalienable human rights (see Article 1 of the German Basic Law of 1949). Here, the case for freedom and individualism must no longer be economically justified or empirically derived from a demonstration of the beneficial consequences of freedom. Hence, from a legal perspective, the constitutional guarantees of individual rights and the constitutional constraints on the exercise of national government powers are the necessary starting point for a legal analysis of **national** trade law and policy. Also the historical evolution of private and public **international** trade law has been strongly influenced by the experiences and constitutional rules of national legal systems.[16] National as well as international constitutions (such as the EEC Treaty and GATT) reflect the historical experiences and wisdom of many generations and are based on principles which gradually emerged in response to "constitutional problems" such as those of the "old mercantilism" between the 15th and the 18th century. The methodological approach traditionally applied at the Heidelberg Max-Planck-Institute for Comparative Public Law and International Law, namely to analyze international legal problems from the perspective of both comparative national public law as well as international law, appears indispensable for any "constitutional analysis" of international economic law and of international economic or-

---

15 For a discussion of the different economic justifications of a free society see: R. Vaubel, The Philosophical Basis of the Free Society, in: ORDO Vol. 37 (1987), pp. 21 ff.

16 See: E.U. Petersmann, Principles of World Trade, in: R. Bernhardt (ed.), Encyclopedia of Public International Law, installment 8 (1985), pp. 530 ff.; J.H. Jackson/ J.V. Louis/ M. Matsushita, Implementing the Tokyo Round. National Constitutions and International Economic Rules, 1984.

der. Economic policy and economic law belong to those areas where "market failures" and "government failures" have been criticized early and persistently since the times of the old mercantilism up to the presence, and which have been the causes for constitutional reforms in many countries.[17]

2. Outline and Major Conclusions of the Book

The book analyzes in four parts constitutional problems of foreign trade policy and foreign trade law in "constitutional democracies" which protect fundamental human rights and effective political equality through constitutional restraints on the exercise of all government powers.

The **first part** on **"International Economic Transactions, International Economic Law and International Economic Order"** (chapters I to IV) begins in **chapter I** with a brief introduction to the different types, functions, principles, rules and interrelationships of international economic and legal transactions (I.1). Economic analysis proceeds from the assumption that, in economic markets, man tends to act as a self-interested "maximizer" of his own interests. From this follows the fundamental economic theorem that, so long as cooperation is voluntary, national as well as international exchanges of goods, services and capital will take place only if each party considers the transaction beneficial to itself (I.2). Voluntary international economic transactions can therefore be characterized as agreements on welfare-increasing exchanges of property rights (I.3). The historical evolution of private and public, national and international liberal economic rules can likewise be understood as resulting from welfare-increasing agreements for the reduction of international transaction costs. Since economic freedoms, property rights and contract law ("pacta sunt servanda") are preconditions of any exchange economy, the same "invisible hand" which leads individuals to pursue their own individual welfare through extensive cooperation and division of labour, tends to promote voluntary social agreement also on legal rules of private and public, national and international law designed to protect the individual freedoms, property rights and welfare-increasing transactions of producers, traders and consumers (I.4). The "international market" is composed of a large number of national markets and different legal jurisdictions. The

17 The elaboration of, for instance, the US Constitution of 1787 and of the Swiss Constitution of 1874 were strongly influenced by the objective of securing freedom of trade within the respective federation of states.

private, governmental and intergovernmental regulation of transnational economic transactions has therefore led to a "stratification of rules" and to a "layered system" of national and international economic law (I.5). The objectives, principles, rules and theories of national and international economic law often involve assumptions about the economic benefits and political feasibility of government measures, which call for a comprehensive legal, economic, political and historical analysis of the law of international economic relations (I.6).

Chapter II analyzes in more detail the **historical evolution of international economic law** into a "stratified order". Decentralized economic and legal systems - such as the international division of labour, private commercial law agreed among independent economic agents, and public international economic law agreed among sovereign states - tend to produce rules with three basic regulatory functions: to constitute and delimit autonomy; to coordinate autonomous specialized activities in a way harmonizing private and social welfare; and to promote legal security. It is shown that the liberal **international** rules, for instance those of GATT, fulfill these functions not only in respect of states and the conduct of government policies, but also in respect of private traders, producers and consumers engaged in international trade and in respect of the implementation of their transnational economic transactions. The **national** constitutions and foreign trade laws in most states tend to limit the governmental foreign economic policy powers in much vaguer terms than the international rules and often do not recognize individual freedoms to engage in international trade (II.1). The historical evolution of national and international economic law (II.3) and of international economic organizations since World War II (II.4) has led to a "stratified legal order" of transnational economic relations, whose properties, subsystems and interrelated "layers" of worldwide, regional, national, public and private law cannot be understood as isolated parts because of the numerous functional interrelationships between private and public, national and international trade and monetary law (II.5).

Chapter III shows that voluntarily agreed, decentralized economic and legal "orders" rest on principles and rules different from those of hierarchically constructed "organizations". Complex "spontaneous orders", such as the international division of labour among more than 170 sovereign states, require general and abstract rules and cannot be combined effectively in any manner one likes with an "organization" of economic activities through specific and concrete regulations (e.g. of traded prices and quantities). Attempts to transform the decentralized international economic system into a deliberate organization of economic activities are likely to give rise to fundamental "constitutional problems" and to remain ineffective for legal, political and economic reasons (III.1). In accordance with the basic "constitutional principles" of the international legal system, such as respect for inalienable human rights and for the national sovereignty and diversity of states, the globally integrated modern world economy continues to be characterized by highly decentralized legal structures and economic decision-making processes, by constantly changing conditions of economic activity, and by the "constitutional ignorance" (v. Hayek) of every individual of most of the particular facts which determine the millions of daily international economic transactions (III.2). Economic theory tends to confirm that, if "economic order" is equated with unobstructed adjustment to continuous change (e.g. in production technologies and consumer demand), the existence of an "international economic order" depends to a large extent on the functioning of the international price mechanism (as a cybernetic information, incentive, coordination and distribution system) and on economic freedoms and property rights enabling economic agents to adjust their decentralized economic activities. Even large multinational corporations and governments usually do not have the power to avoid economic adjustment indefinitely, but can only delay it at increasing adjustment costs (III.3).

The decentralized structures and constant flux of international economic transactions have a strong bearing on the functions and the nature of the rules on which international economic order depends. Market competition is the only information, incentive and coordination mechanism which can effectively combine economic and political freedoms of individuals and of governments as well as decentralized economic planning with extensive cooperation and international division of labour. The extent to which it is necessary to use government (e.g. for correcting "market failures") and international rules (e.g. for limiting "government failures") to accomplish jointly what cannot be accomplished individually through voluntary market transactions, may differ in the various fields of social interaction. Liberal international competition cannot exist without the observance in private and public national laws of a number of "constituent principles" of a competitive order (e.g. monetary stability, open markets, private property rights, freedom of contract, personal liability, steadiness of economic policy) as well as of "regulative principles" for keeping the competitive order working (e.g. competition, monetary and social policies). Economic policies often involve the governmental redistribution of income among domestic groups and can hardly be made without politics and without democratic accountability of policy-makers. National states are therefore likely to continue to remain "optimum jurisdiction areas" for most discretionary rather than "rule-oriented" economic policies. The main function of worldwide liberal trade agreements, such as GATT and the IMF Agreement, is to prohibit the use of mutually harmful trade and monetary policy instruments, to assist governments in increasing the national welfare through voluntary liberalization of national trade and exchange restrictions, and to protect the freedoms and property rights of those engaged in international trade (III.4).

Chapter IV explains in more detail that an "economic analysis" of international economic law can contribute important insights to a better understanding of national and international economic rules. For instance, the rationale of many international trade and monetary rules for the use of "market-conforming" policy instruments cannot be understood without the economic theory of comparative advantage, which teaches that anything preventing prices from expressing freely the conditions of demand or supply distorts the transmission of accurate information and of allocative incentives for the least costly production of goods satisfying consumer preferences. It reduces the potential economic welfare of all countries affected by the price and trade distortions because it directs scarce resources into less efficient uses (IV.1). "Positive economic analysis" - e.g. of the various price effects, consumption effects, production effects, trade effects, government revenue effects, private income and redistribution effects, terms-of-trade and national welfare effects of import restrictions[18] - may be necessary for the application of "result-oriented" rules (such as the prohibition of export subsidies in GATT Article XVI:B if they produce certain trade-distorting effects) and for the examination of the liberal constitutional requirement of proportionality, according to which governmental restrictions of individual rights must be a suitable, necessary and proportionate means for the achievement of the declared policy objective (IV.2). "Normative economic analysis" proceeds from the same value premises as the constitutional guarantees of liberal democracies (e.g. individual freedom of choice and voluntary agreements as values) and is indispensable for understanding the economic and legal ranking of the various economic policy instruments in national and international economic law (IV.3). Economists emphasize that the "incentive function" of prices (i.e. to use scarce resources for the most highly valued purposes) is intimately connected with their "distributive function" (i.e. to determine the distribution of income and to stimulate utility-maximizing economic activities). But they also admit that the

18 For a discussion of the 12 major "economic effects" of an import restriction see: e.g., Glisman/Horn/Nehring/Vaubel, Weltwirtschaftslehre Vol. I, 3rd edition 1986, pp. 23-36.

technical economic definitions of "efficiency" and "value" yield no answer to the question of whether the distribution of income and wealth is "just" and whether individual consumer satisfaction should be the dominant value of economic systems. Such "distributive principles" are to be found in national constitutions and international agreements, which tend to recognize economic efficiency as one among other determinants of "social justice" (IV.4). While an understanding of the economic effects of alternative trade rules is often necessary for fully understanding and correctly applying trade law, chapter IV concludes by recalling the need for separating economic and legal issues because of the different value criteria of welfare economics and law. From a legal perspective, for instance, the greatest benefit of a "spontaneous market order" based upon appropriate "laws and institutions" (Adam Smith) is not its tendency to maximize individual and social economic welfare, but that it tends to maximize individual liberty by enabling all citizens to express their individual preferences, to pursue their diverse ends and to cooperate and benefit each other even though they may be unable to agree on common aims.

The **second part** on "Past and Present Trade Mercantilism as 'Government Failure' and 'Constitutional Failure'" (chapter V and VI) turns to the main problem analyzed in this study. **Chapter V** begins with an explanation of why governments usually cannot directly produce economic wealth, but only a framework of rules which may encourage or impede the creation of wealth, and why trade liberalization has become a universally recognized policy objective endorsed by all states and by all international economic organizations (V.1). Having defined the term "liberal trade" and the various legal forms of "protectionism", the characteristic features of the "new trade mercantilism" are seen in:

- resort to disproportionate, mutually impoverishing and conflict-oriented policy instruments (V.2.A);
- return to "power-oriented" bilateralism and sectoral trade policies on the pattern of the 1930s rather than "rule-oriented", general and market-conforming trade policies in compliance with the multilateral GATT prohibitions of discriminatory "beggar-thy-neighbour" policies (V.2.B);
- administrative "grey area trade restrictions" and "managed trade" without effective parliamentary and judicial control (V.2.C);

- lack of transparent policy-making based on simple rules of general application and of a democratic determination of the "public interest" (V.2.D); and

- use of discriminatory trade restrictions for the arbitrary, surreptitious redistribution of income among domestic groups for the benefit of well organized, protectionist interests groups (V.2.E).

Chapter V.3 then summarizes the various reasons why trade liberalization meets resistance and why trade is not free. The apparent contrast between governments' repeated statements of support for a liberal, non-discriminatory trading system and their increasing resort to bilateral and sectoral trade restrictions illustrates that the economic objective of maximizing economic welfare does not dominate trade policy-making. This striking contradiction between trade theory and trade policy has been convincingly explained by the "public choice theory" which views people in private as well as in "political markets" as self-interested individuals and conceptualizes "politics as exchange". The generally accepted conclusion is that national decision-making processes about trade policy are biased against the public interest in non-discriminatory trade liberalization and in favour of protectionist self-interests of import-competing producers, periodically elected trade policy-makers and administrations assigned to "serve" the industries concerned. Hence, the constitutional task of protecting more effectively the national and individual self-interests in liberal trade (V.3).

In a historical perspective, the problems caused by trade mercantilism and by the strong influence exerted by protectionist interest groups are not new. The premises of the modern economic, political and legal "constitutional theories" in Western democracies were elaborated by the classical liberals during the 18th and 19th century in response to the economic, political and legal problems of the old mercantilism. The GATT was also modelled on long-established standards and principles of bilateral trade agreements for the reciprocal liberalization of mercantilist trade restrictions, and was strongly influenced by the practical experiences and discussions, beginning in the 18th century, of the benefits of trade liberalization. Chapter V includes, therefore, also a brief historical account of the old mercantilism, of its criticism by the classical liberals, and of the continuing relevance of much of this criticism in respect of the "new protectionism" (V.4). Chapter V concludes from the experience with past and present trade mercantilism that trade policy powers should be subjected to the same constitutional safeguards as other government powers of taxation and of economic regulation in order to protect individual rights, define the national self-interest in liberal trade and in rule of law, limit the scope of trade policy powers and regulate the proportionate use of the various trade policy instruments (V.5).

Chapter VI describes the **lack of sufficient constitutional restraints in national laws and in European Community law on the powers of governments to tax and regulate the foreign trade transactions of their own citizens.** Most Western democracies have adopted national constitutions and economic legislation providing for - often stringent - legal disciplines for the exercise of government powers to tax and regulate **domestic** economic activities. By contrast, since about World War I, the national executives in the same states have acquired (e.g. due to the abandonment of the gold standard), or reasserted (e.g. due to the breakdown of the pre-1914 commercial treaty system in Europe), broad discretionary powers to tax and regulate the **transnational** economic activities of their citizens (VI.1). A detailed analysis of foreign trade policies and of foreign trade laws in the United States (VI.2.A) and in the European Community (VI.2.B) seems to confirm that the classical liberal constitutional barriers to arbitrary, welfare-reducing government interferences in the domestic economy - such as equal protection of individual freedoms and property rights, limitation of legislative powers to the enactment of general rules, separation and only limited delegation of powers, effective judicial review of governmental restrictions - no longer prevent the public choice of non-transparent, discriminatory, disproportionate and welfare-reducing government restrictions on **transnational** economic transactions. As foreign economic transactions have an average share of 20 to 30% in the national gross domestic product of OECD states, this "government failure" has a corrosive effect not only on the domestic foreign trade laws but also on the observance of basic constitutional principles of Western democracies (VI.2). An analysis of the various social decision-making processes for the reconciliation of individual interests and the "public interest" - such as the formation of interest groups, democratic, parliamentary, bureaucratic and judicial decision-making - reveals a number of additional "protectionist biases" and a lack in domestic laws of sufficient procedural guarantees for a transparent, non-discriminatory and welfare-increasing exercise of governmental trade policy powers (VI.3).

Since trade protection means helping one industry at the expense of national welfare through inefficient and often ineffective policy instruments, chapter VI concludes that the need for legal constraints on the use of welfare-reducing **foreign** economic policy instruments is even stronger than in respect of the usually less distortive and more precisely regulated **internal** economic policy instruments. The modern trade mercantilism and the insufficient substantive and procedural restraints in domestic laws as well as in European Community law on government powers to tax and restrict the transnational trade transactions of their citizens appear therefore to reflect also a more fundamental "constitutional failure" (VI.4).

How can governments be restrained more effectively from using their broad discretionary trade policy powers to do harm to the general public for the benefit of a few? How can fundamental principles of Western constitutional law - such as protection of equal freedoms and property rights, separation and limited delegation of government powers, parliamentary and judicial review - be more effectively guaranteed in the ever more important field of international trade? How can a justifiable distinction be introduced between foreign policy, which often must be discretionary and eludes strict judicial review (as illustrated by the "act of state"-doctrines of British, French and US courts), and trade policy, which is amenable to and requires regulation by long-term general rules rather than by short-term discretionary government interventions in response to protectionist pressures? Why are precise legal obligations for a transparent, non-discriminatory and welfare-increasing use of the various trade policy instruments to be found only in international trade agreements such as GATT, but not in the autonomous national foreign trade laws of most countries? How can international legal obligations for a transparent, non-discriminatory and welfare-increasing conduct of foreign trade policy, such as those of GATT, be adequately "anchored" in national laws so as to fulfill their "constitutional functions" more effectively? How can "international public goods" - such as legal certainty, open markets and monetary stability - be sufficiently produced without an international government?

The **third part** on **"Constitutional Functions of Liberal International Economic Rules"** (chapter VII) explains why, in the absence of a world government, "public goods" like non-discriminatory access to foreign markets and supplies, monetary stability and international legal certainty can be produced only through liberal international rules with "constitutional functions" (VII.1). The detailed analysis in chapter VII.2, 3 and 4 of the liberal international trade, monetary and investment rules of GATT law and the "Bretton Woods Agreements" shows that their basic principles - such as transparency, non-discrimination, rule of law, use of proportionate policy instruments, fair competition, "due process", judicial review, protection of individual rights, and national sovereignty - correspond to the liberal principles of democratic constitutions for the use of domestic policy instruments of taxation and economic regulation. But the multilaterally agreed guarantees of GATT law go far beyond those of the autonomous domestic foreign trade laws of all countries. The self-imposed liberal international economic obligations can therefore serve "constitutional functions" for a more liberal interpretation, application and agreed extension to foreign trade of the corresponding constitutional principles of democratic societies such as: transparent policy-making ("government by discussion"), non-discriminatory market access, separation and only limited delegation of government powers, public choice of proportionate policy instruments, "due process" and judicial protection of equal freedoms, of competition and property rights in transnational economic transactions. Yet, even though the liberal international trade obligations can operate as a "constitutional restraint" on the government powers to tax and restrict individual freedoms in a welfare-reducing manner, their legal effectiveness tends to be considerably reduced by the lack of adequate constitutional "checks and balances" at the international level and their often weak "domestic law effects" within domestic legal systems (VII.5).

The "paradigm shift" in the transformation of the classical "international law of coexistence" into the modern "international integration law"[19] and its implications for the "constitutional functions" of liberal international rules for the interpretation and application of domestic laws cannot be understood if international economic law continues to be portrayed in the - still widespread - mercantilist tradition as an instrument of "foreign policy" to defend the "national interest" against the "national interest" of other states and to obtain "concessions" at the expense of other contracting parties. This supposedly "realistic" conception of international economic law and policy has been illustrated by A. Shonfield in respect of the "traditional French view that states were in practice bound to seek their exclusive national advantage in any international encounter, and that an adversary relationship was the natural one; treaties simply disguised this fact and should therefore be interpreted in the narrowest possible way in order to minimize the constraints which they imposed on national freedom of manoeuvre".[20] This "power-oriented" rather than "rule-oriented" perception[21] still seems

---

19 See on this point: E.U. Petersmann, Constitutional Functions of Public International Economic Law, in: v.Dijk and others (eds.), Restructuring the International Economic Order, 1987, pp. 49 ff.

20 A. Shonfield, International Economic Relations of the Western World, in: Shonfield (ed.), International Economic Relations of the Western World 1959-1971, Vol. I, 1976, p. 101.

to dominate the "foreign legal policy"[22] of many states and, unfortunately, also the common agricultural and sectoral commercial policy of the European Community. But it is in apparent contrast not only to economic theory which demonstrates that international trade liberalization is a "positive sum game", rather than a "negative sum game", enabling an increase in the national economic welfare of each trading country and offering indeed a "free lunch" which all nations can enjoy. It is also contradicted by legal theory and by the practical experience of the EEC's customs union law pursuant to GATT Article XXIV, which has transformed the GATT prohibitions of tariffs and non-tariff trade barriers into directly applicable individual freedoms and has thereby replaced and "depoliticized" the discretionary national trade policies by "rule-oriented" private liberal trade across national frontiers. About 10 years of practical experience in national and international trade administrations (e.g. consultations with domestic lobbies at the national level and at the international level e.g. in the EEC, OECD, GATT and UN committees) have convinced this author even more of the insight that "foreign" trade policy is to a large extent domestic policy taxing and restricting domestic citizens in response to pressures from powerful domestic interest groups. As long as countries conduct their trade policies in a transparent and non-discriminatory manner in compliance with their self-imposed international GATT obligations, conflicts of interests arise less **among** countries than **within** countries among domestic producers investors, importers, exporters, consumers, competitors and taxpayers. It is usually only when governments give in to the selfish pressures of domestic protectionist interest groups at the expense of national economic welfare and resort to trade restrictions and to export subsidies, that the domestic conflicts of interest spill over into international conflicts between states.

The final **fourth part** on **"Possibilities of 'Constitutionalizing' Foreign Trade policy and Foreign Trade Law in Constitutional Democracies"** (chapters VIII and IX) analyzes in **chapter VIII** the regulation of foreign affairs and foreign trade in the liberal 18th century constitution of the United States, in the liberal 19th century constitution of Switzerland and in the liberal 20th century constitu-

21 On the difference between "power-oriented" and "rule-oriented" foreign economic policies see: J.H. Jackson, The Crumbling Institutions of the Liberal Trade System, in: Journal of World Trade Law 1978, pp. 93, 98 ff.

22 On the need for a "foreign legal policy" see the former legal advisor of the French Foreign Office and judge at the International Court of Justice: G. de Lacharrière, La Politique Juridique Extérieure, 1983, pp. 8, 13 ff, who proceeds, however, from a national "conflict-oriented" perspective of foreign policy and international law.

tion of the Federal Republic of Germany. Chapter VIII begins with a brief discussion and refutation of the classical "incompatibility hypothesis", then prevailing even among the liberal founders of the ideas of "democratic constitutionalism" (such as J. Locke and Ch. de Montesquieu), that rule of law and democracy are incompatible with the particular requirements of foreign policy (VIII.1). The comparative analysis of the constitutional laws and practices of the United States (VIII.2), Switzerland (VIII.3) and Germany (VIII.4) shows, on the one hand, that the respective national constitutions were meant to constitute limited government powers also in respect of the governmental taxation and restriction of the transnational trade transactions of domestic citizens. But, on the other hand, both the substantive constitutional requirements (e.g. of transparent policy-making, limited delegation of powers, equal treatment, proportionality of government restrictions) as well as the procedural constitutional safeguards (e.g. of "due process" and judicial review) are often not effectively applied to "grey area trade policies" and discretionary import relief measures. Even though the precise and unconditional GATT prohibitions of tariffs and non-tariff trade barriers have a direct bearing on the rights and interests of domestic citizens and were designed to be applied by domestic courts (see GATT Article X), the parliaments and domestic courts leave it often to the discretion of the trade policy executives whether they want to tax and restrict the trade transactions of domestic citizens in violation of their self-imposed legal GATT obligations.

Chapter VIII concludes that the internationally agreed legal obligations for the use of transparent, non-discriminatory and proportionate trade policy instruments rest on the same liberal principles as democratic constitutions (VIII.5.A). They are equivalent to "substantive international constitutional rules" in that they prescribe more specific, more precise and more comprehensive obligations for the exercise of discretionary trade policy powers compared to the general requirements of national constitutions for the use of transparent, non-discriminatory and proportionate policy instruments (VIII.5.B). But the liberal international trade rules cannot fulfill their "constitutional functions" unless they are placed into a "constitutional system" of institutional "checks and balances". Since the liberal international trade rules recognize the national sovereignty of states and the diversity of their national economic and legal systems, such a constitutional framework cannot be made effective at the intergovernmental level in the context of worldwide international organizations. Hence the need for integrating the liberal international trade rules into the domestic constitutional systems of the member states (VIII.5.C).

Chapter IX on **"Constitutionalizing Foreign Trade Policy through Liberal International Rules and their Incorporation into Domestic Constitutional Systems"** inquires into how international legal obligations (e.g. of GATT, European Community Law, the EFTA Agreement) and the corresponding national constitutional principles for the use of transparent, non-discriminatory and proportionate policy instruments can be rendered more effective. It begins by emphasizing that international economic and legal integration do not require uniformization of foreign trade and economic laws: Just as there is a strong economic case for maximizing individual and social economic welfare through decentralized market competition, there is also a strong legal case for maximizing individual freedoms, property rights and transnational commercial contracts through private law; but there are also clear limits to international private law as a legal technique of market integration, policy integration and legal integration (IX.1).

Since the emergence of nation states in Europe, kings and governments have invariably asserted broad discretionary trade policy powers as an essential attribute of state sovereignty. The need for constitutionalizing these discretionary trade policy powers derives not only from economic and legal insight and historical evidence that trade restrictions tax domestic citizens, restrict their individual rights and redistribute income among domestic groups in a disproportionate, unnecessarily welfare-reducing manner. History also shows that discretionary government powers of economic regulation are an incentive for "rent-seeking" pressure groups to influence the exercise of these powers for the benefit of their special interests. Due to the lack of adequate constitutional restraints and effective parliamentary and judicial control, the modern "neo-mercantilism" and "grey area trade policies" have in some respects become what they were in the Middle Ages - "an inscrutable power above the people, to be lobbied, petitioned and propitiated for the favours it can dispense".[23] But in a constitutional democracy, government powers must be justifiable in terms of their potential for satisfying individual preferences and maximizing individual rights. The pre-democratic authoritarian assumptions - such as that "the king can do no wrong" or, as up to the present in England, that "parliament can do no wrong" - not only have no place in democratic societies with constitutionally limited government powers, but have also been amply refuted by the history of past and present trade mercantilism. Yet, is it not likely that the same protectionist pressures which prevent liberal trade policies, will also prevent liberal national trade rules restraining the redistributive use of discretionary trade policy powers for the

23 J. Tumlir, Economic Policy as a Constitutional Problem, 1984, p. 19.

benefit of powerful protectionist interest groups? **Chapter IX.2** shows that there are indeed a number of important impediments to constitutionalizing trade policy unilaterally at the national level, such as the traditional political insistence on "external sovereignty" and foreign policy discretion, the persistence of mercantilist thinking, the asymmetries in domestic decision-making processes about trade policy, and the "public good"-character of a liberal international trade order. Hence, even if governments are viewed from a democratic perspective as mere instruments designed for the purpose of supplying "public goods" and meeting individual needs that cannot be readily satisfied through private market exchanges, it remains unlikely that a "constitutional design" of national trade policy powers and procedures can be achieved unilaterally through national constitutional reforms.

But how can a "constitution of trade policy" be then achieved? Can it be realistically expected that those trade politicians who are responsible for the current "constitutional dilemma", in which the liberal international trade rules have been "pragmatically" allowed to erode to the extent that the piecemeal adjustments risk to undermine the whole multilateral trading system, will voluntarily agree to more stringent legal constraints for the current conduct of their trade policies?

The discussion in **chapter IX.3 and 4** of the possibilities of genuine constitutional reform in the trade policy area begins by emphasizing the need for a "constitutional attitude", by which is meant an understanding and appreciation of the fact that freedom of both individuals and governments is possible only under general, effectively enforced rules of law and that the choice of the long-term, basic "constitutional rules" must be separated from the private and public choices and current processes within those rules.[24] As regards the "constitutional choice" of the basic rights and obligations of governments and individuals which establish the constitutional-institutional framework for the "post-constitutional" decisions of governments and individuals,[25] chapter IX.3.A recalls the important insight from chapter VII that liberal international trade rules can also serve democratic constitutional functions if the rules are drafted in a general, non-discriminatory manner and extend and protect individual rights across national frontiers by legally limiting governmental trade restrictions. Chapter

24 See: J.M. Buchanan, Freedom in Constitutional Contract, 1977, pp. 287 ff.

25 On the important differences between the "constitutional choice" of the basic rules and the "post-constitutional choices" of strategies within those rules see: J.M. Buchanan, The Limits of Liberty, 1975, pp. 35 ff.

IX.3.A suggests that, at least in constitutional democracies in which individual liberties and property rights are recognized as constitutional values and as the ultimate aim of all government policies, precise and unconditional international legal prohibitions of tariffs and non-tariff trade barriers must be constitutionally presumed to confer individual rights.

Chapter IX.3.B lists the various reasons why it is politically easier to agree on and specify liberal basic rules for international trade on a reciprocal basis in international agreements rather than unilaterally in national laws. Chapter IX.3.C recalls the often overlooked fact that, while many international agreements (including most human rights conventions) prescribe "minimum standards" for the conduct of national government policies, the liberal international trade rules often go far beyond the constitutional guarantees even of liberal democracies by enlarging and protecting individual rights across national frontiers and by giving a more precise and more comprehensive meaning to the general constitutional principles of equal treatment and proportionality of government restrictions in the trade policy area. Chapter IX.3.D illustrates and confirms this "constitutional insight" by a detailed comparison of the "general principles" of the administrative law of the European Economic Community with the corresponding "general principles" of the foreign trade law of GATT, which are more precise and more comprehensive than those of the foreign trade law of the EEC.

Chapter IX.4 probes the various possibilities of incorporating liberal international trade rules into domestic constitutional systems. It proceeds from the observation that more and more everyday transactions of domestic citizens, including trade and financial transactions, are regulated by international treaties designed to protect individual rights across national frontiers and to limit mutually harmful government restrictions. The traditional international treaty practice of leaving the domestic implementation of such international treaty obligations to the discretion of each contracting party, and of considering international trade agreements as a matter for governments alone, appears as a legal anachronism in respect of the constitutional functions of liberal international trade rules. Likewise, the traditional insistence on "external state sovereignty" and on governmental freedom to restrict private commercial transactions across national frontiers appears as an expression of legal positivism, i.e. an assertion of government powers to define "the law" and individual rights without sufficient regard to the constitutional guarantees of individual liberties and the constitutional limitation of government powers in constitutional democracies. In view of the lack of an effective "trade policy constitution" in the national legal systems, there is a need for more detailed international rules regulating the "domestic law effects" of liberal international trade obligations. While national trade policy executives might be interested in portraying liberal international trade agreements (such as GATT) as "post-constitutional" executive arrangements which the trade politicians may freely disregard in their conduct of trade policy, the legislative and judicial branches of governments should strictly enforce liberal international trade rules in view of their constitutional function. To this end, international trade agreements should include provisions explicitly requiring the incorporation of liberal international trade rules into the respective domestic trade legislation as well as the availability of judicial review by domestic courts (IX.4.A).

The incorporation of liberal international trade rules into domestic constitutional systems and the interaction between different levels of rules and decision-making authorities raise issues similar to those of "federalism". Chapter IX.4.B describes the historical experiences since the establishment of the German Confederation (Deutscher Bund) in 1815 with the progressive constitutionalization of German foreign trade law, first in the context of the German Customs Union (Deutscher Zollverein 1834-1866), then in the context of the North German Confederation (Norddeutscher Bund 1867-1870), later within the German constitutions of 1871 (Reichsverfassung), 1919 (Weimarer Verfassung) and 1949 (Grundgesetz), through the progressive incorporation of the international GATT obligations, since 1951, into German foreign trade law and, since 1958, through the customs union law of the EEC which is based upon and implements GATT Article XXIV. The federal experience, also within the United States and Switzerland, confirms that federal and confederal guarantees of freedom of trade have operated as an effective legal restraint on protectionist abuses of the regulatory powers reserved by the constituent states (cantons). The successful trade liberalization achieved through the EEC Treaty prohibitions of tariffs and non-tariff trade barriers within the EEC, and the protectionist abuses of the discretionary agricultural and commercial policy powers provided for in Articles 41, 43 and 113 of the EEC Treaty without constitutional-institutional safeguards, likewise illustrate the important role of liberal international trade rules and individual freedom of trade in bringing about effective legal restraints on discretionary trade policy powers: States are more likely to agree on liberal trade rules if they have to choose long-term basic rules from behind a "veil of uncertainty" (J.M.Buchanan) which makes it difficult for them to identify the future impact of the rules and makes them more inclined to take into account long-term constitutional principles of non-discrimination and fairness. By contrast, trade policy decisions on short-term policy alternatives (e.g. EC Council decisions on support prices for agricultural products) tend to be influenced much more by short-term interests and "rent-seeking" protectionist group interests.

Chapter IX.4.C describes the contribution which liberal international trade agreements have made to the "legalization", harmonization and "judicialization" of national customs laws, antidumping laws and other areas of foreign trade law. The detailed rules of the 1979 GATT Antidumping Agreement and their incorporation into the domestic antidumping laws of major trading countries and the EEC have restrained the protectionist abuse of antidumping duties and have promoted more transparency, legal certainty, "due process" and judicial review of antidumping proceedings notably within the EEC.

Chapter IX.4.D recalls the refusal of the US Congress to implement the injury requirement and other provisions of the 1967 GATT Antidumping Agreement as an illustration of the need to involve national legislatures in international rule-making. Just as the constitutional allocation of trade policy powers in the United States and the EEC has had a strong impact on the development of the international GATT rules (see the absence of institutional provisions in the General Agreement due to the lack of sufficient negotiating authority of the US executive), the "domestic law effects" of the international GATT rules depend on the taking into account of the constitutional structures of the major trading countries. The "fast track procedures" set out in the US Trade Act of 1974, which made the negotiating authority of the US President as regards non-tariff trade barriers contingent on close consultations with the key committees of the Congress and provided for a "fast track procedure" for the congressional incorporation of the negotiation results into domestic legislation, were the major reason for the prompt approval and implementation of the 1979 GATT Tokyo Round Agreements in the United States.

Chapter IX.4.E turns to the need to involve domestic courts in order to achieve effective constitutional-institutional reforms in the trade policy area. After all, it is the courts that have to enforce the liberal trade rules and protect the individual freedoms of trade against illegal administrative trade protectionism. The interpretation by the EC Court of Justice of the EEC Treaty prohibitions of tariffs and non-tariff barriers as directly applicable individual rights and the EC Court's "constitutional jurisprudence" regarding the autonomy, primacy, direct effects and unwritten general principles and fundamental rights guarantees of European Community law demonstrate the important role of domestic courts in constitutionalizing and enforcing liberal international trade rules. Since the international GATT prohibitions of trade discrimination and non-tariff barriers are more precise and more comprehensive than those of the domestic foreign trade laws of most states as well as of the EEC, the refusal by domestic courts to take into account and observe precise, unconditional international GATT obligations is difficult to justify on legal grounds. The "judicial protectionism" and support for discretionary safeguard measures in manifest violation of international law poses perhaps the most serious impediment to the effective application of the internationally agreed liberal trade rules. While the impact on foreign trade law of the English and French doctrines of parliamentary supremacy and lack of judicial review of parliamentary legislation has been greatly reduced within the EEC due to the "communitarization" of the foreign trade law, it still limits the scope of judicial review of foreign trade law in countries such as Switzerland which recognize judicial review only for cantonal legislation vis-à-vis federal law, but not of federal legislation.

Chapter IX.4 concludes by emphasizing the importance of individual rights for the liberalization of international trade. This not only on grounds of constitutional law because, in constitutional democracies, individual rights and needs are recognized as the highest constitutional values and as the only legitimate objective of the exercise of all government powers. Hence, from the point of view of constitutional law, there are no valid reasons why the individual freedom of trade should be restricted to the choice of domestic trading partners, subject to exceptions on grounds of public policy. But there are also important economic arguments to the effect that decentralized market competition tends to maximize individual as well as social economic welfare only if the individual rights are well defined. Where individual rights are lacking (e.g. rights to a clean environment), private business activities risk to produce goods with more social costs than benefits. Political experience, for instance within the EEC, also confirms that the liberalization of tariffs and non-tariff trade barriers within the EEC could be achieved because the international prohibitions of tariffs and non-tariff barriers were construed as directly applicable individual rights enabling domestic citizens to enforce the liberal trade rules against their own governments. Where such individual rights were not recognized (e.g. vis-à-vis grey area trade restrictions and the observance of the GATT prohibitions of trade discrimination and non-tariff trade barriers), the protectionist self-interests of governments and import-competing producers were allowed to prevail over the constitutionally mandated legal protection of equal freedoms and property rights as the legal prerequisite of welfare-maximizing competition and decentralized "spontaneous order". The recognition of individual freedoms of trade binding all government organs is therefore the most important condition of a "self-enforcing liberal trade constitution". Since the international prohibitions of governmental trade restrictions are not an end in themselves and legally define the public interest in individual freedom of trade (subject to tariffs), they should be seen as an agreed definition of the constitutionally guaranteed freedom of trade and individuals should be entitled to their observance.

3. How to read this book

As is apparent from the preceding summary of conclusions, this book can be read and used in different ways.

- Students of international law, economics and political science might begin with the first part and may find chapters I to IV provide a useful introduction to the law and economics of international economic transactions, international economic law and international economic order. While an understanding of the basic legal and economic concepts and interrelationships explained in the first part is necessary for understanding the following parts of the book, the experienced international economic lawyer might skip over the first part or read only the attempt in chapter III to elaborate a legal theory of international economic order.

- The second part is essentially an introduction to the economic, political and legal problems and historical dimensions of trade protectionism. Lawyers not familiar with economic trade theory, with the characteristic features of trade protectionism and with the "public choice" explanation of why a liberal international trade order does not develop spontaneously, may be interested in reading chapter V. Economists not familiar with the specific legal and constitutional problems posed by non-transparent, discriminatory and disproportionately harmful trade policies may benefit from reading the description in chapter VI of the insufficient substantive and procedural constitutional restraints on the use of discretionary trade policy powers. Admittedly, both chapters V and VI were written in order to illustrate, rather than to analyze in a comprehensive manner, the existing problems posed by trade protectionism.

- The third part describes the constitutional functions of liberal international economic rules and is essential not only to the understanding of the gist of this study but, in the view of this author, also to a better understanding of national and international economic law. This "constitutional analysis" of the international GATT, IMF and World Bank rules and procedures differs from the conventional textbook presentation of international economic obligations as "concessions" which states undertake in order to obtain the benefit of the synallagmatic rights. Since the "constitutional insight" - that liberal international economic rules and other substantive and procedural **international** legal restraints can assist in maintaining constitutional order at the **national** level and apply to the trade policy area the liberal principles of constitutional democracies - is alien to the traditional perception of international economic law,[26] experienced international trade lawyers and economists might prefer to begin reading this book with this third part.

- The fourth part extends the constitutional analysis by a comparative study of the constitutional theory and constitutional regulation of foreign affairs in the United States, Switzerland, Germany and the EEC. Chapter IX then summarizes and applies the conclusions from all the preceding chapters to the concrete policy task of developing improved constitutional rules for trade policy-making - not through a formal amendment of the national constitutions, but through improved international rules and their incorporation into domestic legislation and the more effective judicial protection of individual rights. The informed international economic lawyer and readers with little time may wish to read first the summary and conclusions in chapter IX before deciding whether they wish to read also other parts of this book.

26 "Constitutionalism", a standard vocabulary of political, legal and economic scholars e.g. during the late 18th century, is regrettably rarely encountered in the modern literature on international economic relations.

FIRST PART: INTERNATIONAL ECONOMIC TRANSACTIONS, INTERNATIONAL ECONOMIC LAW AND INTERNATIONAL ECONOMIC ORDER

"I know there are many minds who cannot comprehend and master a proposition in political economy; I believe that study is the highest exercise of the human mind and that the exact sciences require by no means so hard an effort. But barring these two accidents - want of capacity and having a sinister interest - I defy any man to look into this question honestly, and come to any other than one conclusion. Then why should we not agree?"

R. Cobden[1]

"... the rules of just conduct which the lawyer studies serve a kind of order of the character of which the lawyer is largely ignorant; this order is studied chiefly by the economist who in turn is similarly ignorant of the character of the rules of conduct on which the order that he studies rests".

F.A. Hayek[2]

I. INTERNATIONAL ECONOMIC TRANSACTIONS AND INTERNATIONAL ECONOMIC LAW

1. International Economic Transactions: Types and Legal Interrelationships

In the national, regional and worldwide regulation of transnational economic relations, a distinction is frequently made between five major categories of international economic transactions:

a) International movement of goods (usually denoted as "trade");

b) International movement of services (often denoted as "invisible trade") by transactions involving the cross-border supply of the service (e.g.

1 R. Cobden, in his speech against the English Corn Laws on 27 February 1846, in: R. Cobden, Speeches on Public Policy, 1870, Vol. I, p. 383.

2 F.A. v.Hayek, Law, Legislation and Liberty, 1982, Introduction p. 4.

communications) as well as by cross-border movements of consumers of the service (e.g. tourism), cross-border movement of providers of the service (e.g. transports) and the establishment of commercial presence for the production, distribution, sales or delivery of a service (e.g. banking and insurance services);

c) International movement of persons (e.g. freedom of movement for workers, freedom of establishment for self-employed natural and legal persons);

d) International movement of capital, over which the foreign investor may retain direct control ("direct investment", e.g. the setting-up of an enterprise) or not ("portfolio investment" such as the purchase of securities, international loans and development aid);

e) International payments relating to the above-mentioned economic transactions, usually involving the exchange of foreign currencies ("foreign exchange transactions").

Since World War II, decreasing costs of transportation, new communication techniques and the worldwide liberalization of private and governmental restrictions of international economic transactions have led to ever increasing levels of international trade and finance and to a globally integrated world economy, in which more than 150 billion dollars move across national borders every day. Most of these international economic transactions are subject to detailed and mutually interacting legal regulations at three different levels: **first**, private commercial contracts agreed upon between economic agents residing in different countries; **second**, national governmental regulations of international economic transactions; and **third**, international economic rules agreed upon among states or adopted by international economic organizations. The national and international government regulations often set out specific rules differentiating among the main types of international economic transactions. For instance, section 1 of the German Law on Foreign Economic Relations (Aussenwirtschaftsgesetz) of 1961 proceeds from the general principle of freedom of foreign economic transactions: "In principle trade and commerce with foreign economic areas are free as to goods, services, capital, payments or other economic transactions as well as to transactions between residents in foreign assets and gold. Applicable are the restrictions contained in this Law or prescribed by ordinance based on this Law".[3] The law then authorizes the introduction of specific regulations and control procedures, which differentiate according to whether they relate to exports or imports of goods, shipping, air transport, insurance, different types of capital transactions as well as of other international economic transactions.

At the international level, the General Agreement on Tariffs and Trade (GATT) of 1947[4] regulates not only trade in goods and related payments (cf. Article XV), but also certain world-traded services (cf. Articles III: 4, 10, IV, V, VIII, XVII, XXXVII).[5] The Articles of the Agreement of the International Monetary Fund (IMF) of 1944[6] prescribe that, "subject to the provisions of Article VII, Section 3 (b) and Article XIV, Section 2, no member shall, without the approval of the Fund, impose restrictions on the making of payments and transfers for current international transactions" (Article VIII: 2, a). The different rules, procedures and institutional jurisdictions for mutually interdependent international economic transactions and interchangeable policy instruments raise various legal problems.

For instance: While Article XV: 4 of GATT stipulates that "contracting parties shall not, by exchange action, frustrate the intent of the provisions of the (General) Agreement", Article XV: 9,a exempts from all GATT obligations "the use... of exchange controls..., in accordance with the Articles of the Agreement of the International Monetary Fund". Here the question arises whether the general exemption of exchange restrictions authorized by the IMF relieves a GATT contracting party also of its obligation not to frustrate the General Agreement's intent through such exchange actions.[7] Or: A GATT dispute panel had to examine in 1952 whether a "contribution" levied by the Greek Government on certain imported goods was a discriminatory internal tax contrary to Article III: 2 of GATT, a frustration by exchange action of the intent of Article III in contravention of Article XV: 4 of GATT, an import charge within the meaning of GATT Article II or, as contended by the Greek Government, "a charge imposed

3 Aussenwirtschaftsgesetz of 28 April 1961, Bundesgesetzblatt I, p. 481 (as amended in 1980 Bundesgesetzblatt I, p. 1905)

4 See: Text of the General Agreement on Tariffs and Trade, GATT 1986

5 See, e.g.: R.J. Krommenacker, World-Traded Services: The Challenge for the Eighties, 1984, pp. 163 ff

6 See: Articles of Agreement of the International Monetary Fund, IMF 1978

7 For a discussion of this as yet open legal issue see: F. Roessler, Countertrade and the GATT Legal System, in: Journal of World Trade Law 1985, pp. 604, 611 f

on foreign exchange allocated for the importation of goods from abroad equivalent to a multiple currency practice" in conformity with the IMF Agreement."[8] The IMF Agreement defines what is meant by "payments for current transactions" for the purposes of the Articles (see Article XXX, d) and, by implication, regards all other payments and transfers as capital transfers; as a working rule, an international financial transaction is considered a capital transfer if it establishes a claim to foreign currency that is not a claim to prompt payment for goods or services.[9] The EEC Treaty provisions on the free international movement of goods, services, persons, capital and related payments make use of both general definitions of the transactions concerned (e.g. in Articles 48, 52, 60), to be concretized by means of "secondary" Community law and by decisions of the Court of Justice; as well as of lists specifying the transactions concerned (see the "list of invisible transactions referred to in Article 106" in Annex III of the EEC Treaty). The latter method of negotiated lists enumerating the economic transactions has been used in particular in the unpublished lists of embargoed "strategic" goods and services negotiated within the Coordinating Committee for East-West Trade (COCOM), as well as in the Code of Liberalization of Current Invisible Operations and the Code of Liberalization of Capital Movements negotiated within the Organization for Economic Cooperation and Development (OECD).[10]

2. International Economic Transactions as Welfare-Increasing Exchanges of Goods, Services and Capital

Standard economics proceeds from the assumption that the individual is the best judge of his own welfare and, in a world with limited resources in relation to human wants, will tend to act as a rational maximizer of his self-interests. For example, consumers will tend to prefer more to less, and producers will tend to maximize their profits by minimizing their production costs. Individual preferences are assumed to be stable over time so that, for instance, a fall in the price of a good can be expected to improve the economic welfare of consumers of

8 See for further details: E.U. Petersmann, Trade Restrictions for Balance-of-Payments Purposes and the GATT, in: D. Dicke (ed.), Foreign Debts in the Present and in a New International Economic Order, 1986, pp. 181, 203 f.

9 See, e.g., J. Gold, International Capital Movements under the Law of the IMF, 1977

10 Published as separate loose-leaf publications by the OECD. For a survey see: Introduction to the OECD Codes of Liberalization, OECD 1987.

that good (this proposition of empirical positive economics would not be possible without the assumption of stable preferences). The economic value of a good or service is defined by using the "measuring rod of money", i.e. the individual's willingness to pay, either in money or in kind, to acquire the good or service. Value in economics means therefore exchange value and is not necessarily the same as the production costs of goods and services. Economic "costs" are usually thought of as "opportunity costs", i.e. as the opportunities foregone by employing a resource in a way that excludes its most attractive alternative use to which it could be put (e.g. the alternative price of goods and services used in the production of a commodity). "Money" represents only purchasing power. All costs have to be met by someone ("there is no free lunch"), albeit not necessarily by the producer and user of a good or service.

The ultimate objective of voluntary economic activity is mutually beneficial exchange among parties wishing to obtain goods, services, payments or capital on advantageous terms. In national and international economic markets, the activities of buyers and sellers are mediated by market prices which inform producers and consumers about the relative costs and rewards associated with selling and buying different goods, services or capital. Market prices also tend to act as an economic incentive for the allocation of resources and the continuous adjustment of demand and supply until they are in balance. Empirical evidence confirms that there is an inverse relationship between the price of a commodity and the quantity demanded: a rise in the price of a good tends to reduce the quantity of the purchases of and the effective demand for this product by consumers, provided other prices remain unchanged ("law of demand"). And there tends to be a positive relationship between the market prices of goods and their quantity supplied by producers: a rise in the market price will act as an incentive to produce and supply additional goods to the market ("law of supply"). With increased consumption of a good, the satisfaction of consumers from and their willingness to pay for an additional unit of this good will decrease ("diminishing marginal utility"). In a competitive market, the production of a good or service will increase until their price equals the marginal opportunity costs of the resources used to produce them. Undistorted competition among utility-maximizing producers and consumers and the continuous adjustment of market prices, supply and demand tend "to clear the market" by making the decentralized economic plans and activities mutually consistent in a way maximizing the satisfaction of individual consumer preferences, minimizing production costs and equilibrating supply and demand at the level of opportunity costs through a decentralized system of decision-making where everyone is free to choose according to his own preferences and resources.

Economic theory admits the existence of various possible "market failures" which may lead to a less than optimal functioning of the price system. For instance: In the case of increasing returns to scale and restraints of competition (e.g. cartelization, abuse of a dominant position), market competition tends to destroy itself ("paradox of freedom"). Divergences between the total "social costs" involved in producing a good or service and the "private costs" borne by the individual producers concerned (e.g. due to "external costs" generated by environmental pollution) will lead to an "inefficient" pattern of production, because the lack of identity of those benefiting and those carrying the cost will stimulate too much or too little supply. While a market-oriented distribution of income tends to reward efficiency and comparative advantages, the existing distribution of resources and income, or the allocation of resources in response to consumer willingness to pay, may be considered as "unjust". The existence of "market failures" and the political demand for "public goods", that cannot be produced on the open market, may therefore warrant corrective government interventions, such as anti-trust policy (e.g. prohibition of cartels), consumer policy (e.g. prohibition of dangerous products), structural policy (e.g. promotion of "infant industries" and of labour mobility), and social policy (e.g. income redistribution). But corrective government regulations may also fail to produce a superior outcome, because individuals, politicians and interest groups pursue their own interests not only in the economic (market) sphere but also in the political process; and regulatory agencies may also fall under the influence of sectional interest groups (e.g. ministries of agriculture pursuing only the interests of the farmers).[11] Hence, there is always the risk of "government failure" worse than "market failure".[12] Moreover, there is virtually unanimous agreement in international trade theory today, as discussed further below (chapter V.1), that foreign trade restrictions are hardly ever an economically efficient

11 Cf., e.g., G.J. Stigler, The Theory of Economic Regulation, in: The Bell Journal of Economics 2 (1971), pp. 3-21, who gives an economic explanation of the private demand for and political supply of government regulations (e.g. on market access, minimum prices, exemptions from antitrust laws) that serve the private interests of politically influential groups and of the industries regulated (e.g. by permitting price increases above competitive levels) rather than the protection and benefit of the public at large.

12 For a discussion from a legal and an economic perspective see: R. Bowles, Law and the Economy, 1982, pp. 164 ff; R. Posner, Economic Analysis of Law, 2nd edition 1977, pp. 193 ff; B.S. Frey, Democratic Economic Policy, 1983, pp. 58 ff

remedy for correcting these various domestic distortions and "market imperfections" within the national economies.

Since Adam Smith, economists assume that individuals trade in markets because exchange is mutually advantageous and in order to maximize their perceived individual welfare: "Voluntary trade is mutually beneficial (i.e. utility-increasing for both parties). This is the Fundamental Theorem of Exchange".[13] Voluntarily agreed **international** exchanges of goods, services and capital will also take place only if each party considers the exchange advantageous to itself. The reason why each trading partner values the goods differently lies in the different situations of production costs, supply and demand in their respective countries. For instance, if each country specializes in the production of those goods which it can produce at lower cost than its trading partners ("absolute advantage"), then specialization and trade enable each country to obtain more goods than under a system of national autarky. But even if a country enjoys an absolute cost advantage in the production of all goods compared to other countries, it can still gain from specializing in the production and export of those goods which it can produce relatively more efficiently ("comparative advantage"). By trading its comparatively most efficiently produced goods for those most efficiently produced goods of other states, each country can obtain more goods and a higher real national income than if it had attempted to produce all goods at home.[14]

---

13 J. Hirshleifer, Price Theory and Applications, 1976, p. 164

14 Detailed verbal and mathematical explanations of the mutually beneficial exploitation of "absolute advantages" (A. Smith) and "comparative advantages" (D. Ricardo) are to be found in any textbook of international trade theory, see e.g.: G.M. Meier, International Economics, 1980, pp. 14 ff. See also below chapter V.1. Most economists emphasize that "the invention of the law of comparative advantage may be regarded as one of the greatest achievements of economic theory" (F. Machlup, A History of Thought on Economic Integration, 1977, p. 42). As L. Robbins, Political Economy: Past and Present, 1976, concludes: "This analysis must surely be regarded as one of the main triumphs of abstract economic thought, far transcending in importance the problems of international trade to which it was first applied; it ultimately explains, not only the advantages arising here, but also any advantages arising from specialization anywhere where there are unequal differences in potentialities. It establishes, too, principles of action, not only for market economies, but also for any economic organization which aspires to rational allocation of resources. Other things being equal, a purely collectivist economy should organize its resources so as to minimize the comparative opportunity costs of achieving any particular goal." (p. 154). Yet, the Ricardian demonstration that trade is mutually profitable even when one country is absolutely more efficient in the production of every product, continues not to be understood by many people and has been described by Nobel Prize economist P. Samuelson as the one proposition, in all of the social sciences, which is both true and non-trivial (quoted from Meier, above, at p. 28). And even economists sometimes seem to forget that the gains from trade derive not only from absolute advantages in terms of real

3. International Economic Transactions as Agreements on Welfare-Increasing Exchanges of Property Rights

The production and exchange of goods and services require legal rules. Producers must enjoy economic freedoms to produce, sell and purchase goods and services, as well as property rights relating to the production factors used (land, labour, capital, know-how, etc.), to the goods produced and to the means of payment. Traders and consumers must enjoy economic freedoms and property rights as to the purchase and sale of goods and services. In international markets, state-trading enterprises also tend to act as utility-maximizing agents and depend on freedoms and property rights for the implementation of their international trade and financial activities. Economic freedoms, property rights and contract law are legal preconditions for any exchange economy and historically emerged long before they were codified in written rules.

The functioning of markets depends to a large extent on the nature of the property right system, which determines what can be bought and sold and which, by influencing the cost of carrying out various kinds of market transactions, influences also what is, in fact, bought and sold, and by whom.[15] The economic approach to human behaviour - especially "the assumption that man is a rational maximizer of his ends in life, his satisfactions - what we call his self-interest"[16] - suggests that also "the creation and specification of property rights... takes place in response to the desire of the interacting persons for more utility".[17] The eco-

---

resources used at home compared to abroad, but also from comparative cost advantages relative to alternative uses of resources within the national economy.

15 See: R.H. Coase, Economics and Contiguous Disciplines, reprinted in: Ogus/Veljanowski (eds.), Readings in the Economics of Law and Regulation, 1984, pp. 3, 7. A.A. Alchian, Some Economics of Property Rights, in: Alchian, Economic Forces at Work, 1977, pp. 127 ff, 130: "By a system of property rights I mean a method of assigning to particular individuals the 'authority' to select, for specific goods, any use from a nonprohibited class of uses". "A property right for me means some protection against other people's choosing against my will one of the uses of resources, said to be 'mine'".

16 Posner (note 12), p. 3. That individuals tend to act efficiently in their own interests is the "credo" of the so-called Chicago School of Law and Economics as exemplified by the work of Posner, G.J. Stigler (e.g. The Citizen and the State, 1975) and G.S. Becker (e.g. The Economic Approach to Human Behaviour, 1976).

17 S. Pejovich, Towards an Economic Theory of the Creation and Specification of Property Rights, reprinted in Ogus/Veljanowski (note 15), pp. 53, 54. On the very broad scope and uncertain limits of the economic concept of "property rights" see: A.A. Schmid, Property, Power and Public Choice, 1978, p. 5. Furobotn/Pejovich (eds.), The Economics of Property Rights, 1974, understand "property rights" as "the sanctioned behavioural relations among men that arise from the existence of goods and pertain to their use. These relations specify

nomic theory of property rights assumes "that (i) from the social point of view the creation of property rights assignments is a powerful and possibly necessary condition for more efficient allocation and use of resources, and (ii) from the individual's point of view the specification of property rights is associated with his search for more utility".[18] The purpose of trade is to exchange property rights relating to the goods and services that are exchanged. The value of the traded goods and services (e.g. a patent) depends on the content of the "property rights" in those goods and services. Property rights assignments tend to affect the allocation and use of resources in a specific and often predictable way. For instance, the absence of property rights assignments tends to stimulate a less efficient and possibly wasteful use of non-owned resources (e.g. catch of whales and other fishes in the high seas) compared to a situation where transferable property rights are established in the respective good. Property rights act as an incentive for taking into account adverse long-term effects of a short-term over-exploitation of the resources.[19] Legal uncertainty as regards property rights tends to increase international transaction costs and to reduce the quantity and time horizon of foreign trade and investments, since investors will feel less confident that they will be able to capture the expected future profits of foreign trade and investment transactions. In the absence of legal rules protecting the enforcement of entitlements **in specie** (e.g. **restitutio in integrum** of illegally expropriated foreign investments), agreement on liability rules (e.g. rights to adequate compensation) can act as a substitute promoting welfare-increasing exchanges of property rights.[20]

---

the norms of behaviour with respect to goods that each and every person must observe in his daily interactions with other persons, or bear the cost of nonobservance".

18 Pejovich (note 17), p. 55 f

19 See: H. Demsetz, Towards a Theory of Property Rights, 57 American Economic Review 1967 (Proc.), pp. 347 ff, who demonstrates (with the example of fur hunters) how the absence of private property rights may lead to an overutilization of natural resources, because those exploiting the resource do not take account of the future social costs arising from the depletion of the resource. The establishment of a private property right in the resource acts as an incentive for its owner to take into account the costs and benefits also of the resource's future uses.

20 That adverse "external effects" (e.g. environmental pollution) can be efficiently corrected not only by imposing a tax on the externality-creating activity (as suggested by traditional "welfare economics" such as Pigou, The Economics of Welfare, 4th edition 1932), but also by means of property rules, liability rules and private contracts without government intervention, was demonstrated by R.H. Coase, The Problem of Social Cost, in: Journal of Law and Economics 1960, pp. 1 ff; G. Calabresi/A.D. Melamed, Property Rules, Liability Rules and Inalienability, in: Harvard Law Review 1972, pp. 1089 ff

From a legal perspective, international economic transactions usually consist of contractual arrangements for the sale, carriage, delivery and payment of goods, services or capital, as well as of agreed exchanges of property rights (e.g. legal titles to own the purchased goods and the agreed payment). Governmental restrictions of international trade and economic transactions usually operate by restricting the freedoms and property rights of the traders and other persons involved (e.g. the freedom to purchase and sell goods in the best foreign markets). Even if governmental restrictions of international economic transactions do not impair the **existence** of property rights (e.g. by rendering the agreed implementation of a commercial contract impossible and thereby invalidating the existence of the contractual obligations concerned), they are likely to affect their economic **value.** Thus an import tariff imposes a tax on domestic importers and consumers and may decrease the value of their property rights in the taxed import goods. A quantitative import restriction enables importers to raise the domestic resale price of the restricted product (scarcity rent) and may increase the value of import licenses. A "voluntary export restraint" (VER) enables exporters to raise their export prices and may decrease the value of import licenses.

4. National and International Liberal Economic Rules as Welfare-Increasing Agreements for the Reduction of International Transaction Costs

According to F.A. v. Hayek,[21] the process of cultural evolution and the emergence of an international division of labour are due to the human urge for maximizing the satisfaction of human desires by economizing the limited resources. The transition from the social life in small hunting and gathering groups, that were based on a "socialist morality" of collective pursuit of common ends through hierarchically organized groups and solidary sharing among known people, to an "extended society" of peaceful cooperation among people without common purposes and often without knowing each other was made possible through the gradual recognition of a "new morality" based on abstract rules. In particular "the toleration of bartering with the outsider, the recognition of delimited private property, especially in land, the enforcement of contractual obligations, the competition with fellow craftsmen in the same trade, the variability

21 See, e.g.: F.A. v.Hayek, Law, Legislation and Liberty, Vol. II, 1976, pp. 107 ff; idem, The Fatal Conceit, 1989.

of initially customary prices, the lending of money, particularly at interest",[22] made possible an exchange economy and acted as an incentive for saving, investments, specialization, greater efficiency and the production of complex goods which no individual could have made for himself. Those groups and communities that followed the new rules and thereby promoted individual utility and profit maximization, became more prosperous than other groups. The new traditions of abstract rules gradually became the basis of the pluralist Western civilization and of an international division of labour which made possible ever increasing specialization, efficiency, economic wealth and population growth. The decentralized economic activities of millions of dispersed individuals and the division of labour were coordinated spontaneously through market prices, which act as a financial incentive for the continuous adaptation of supply and demand; as a self-regulating information-processing mechanism, market prices enable to overcome the "constitutional ignorance" (v. Hayek) of everybody of most of the particular facts which determine the daily course of the international division of labour.

Regardless of the validity of Hayek's theory of cultural evolution, it is a fact that the behaviour of any individual is constrained by the behaviour of others and by the limitation of available resources. Any society that progresses beyond the stage of "every man for himself" will see the need for rules enabling cooperative behaviour and regulating the assignment ("allocation") of available resources through the recognition of property rights.[23] The production of goods for the satisfaction of consumer demand and the division of labour require the regulation and reconciliation of conflicting claims over limited resources. Property rights and other rules were established because human societies very early became aware that agreement on such rules increases their welfare and that a legal framework for the exchange of property rights enables them to be attracted into

22 F.A. v.Hayek, Law, Legislation and Liberty, Vol. III, 1979, p. 161

23 See, e.g.: D. K. Whynes/R.A. Bowles, The Economic Theory of the State, 1981, pp. 11 ff, who argue that "the emergence of property rights in historical terms may be viewed as a response to scarcity" and "that the most efficient form that cooperation can take is for a system of private property rights to be devised" (p. 33). This is in line with the widely referred to "Coase theorem" (by R. Coase, note 20) that the legal definition of property rights and subsequent private adjustments to the pattern of these rights tend to maximize the value of output. In addition to these purely economic rationales for the existence of property rights, there are, of course, additional arguments in support of private property rights or particular allocations, such as John Locke's value judgment that individuals have an inalienable right of "ownership" of their own persons and, therefore, also rights in any items produced by them.

their socially most productive uses.[24] From time immemorial, international trade among private merchants has given rise to uniform commercial usages, principles and rules serving the common commercial needs of participants in international trade transactions. Particular rules for the interregional commerce of ancient times were already present in the Babylonian Code of Hammurabi, in the laws of the Greek cities and in Roman law. The recognition of private property, freedom of contract and **pacta sunt servanda** led to the emergence of an international exchange economy and of an essentially individualist private law already in classical antiquity. By promoting legal certainty and enabling economic agents to form reasonably correct expectations regarding future economic transactions, the largely spontaneously evolved private commercial law contributed also to the reduction of international transaction costs. The ancient Greek cities and the Roman State largely confined themselves to the model of the "minimalist state" in economic affairs: allocation of rights and obligations, the establishment of general rules promoting international commerce, and the provision of general procedures for the settlement of disputes arising from disagreements over contracts between individuals.

The emergence of new sovereign states in Europe since about the 16th century and their coexistence and active foreign trade policies necessitated new rules of national and international public economic law. Most states considered the provision of a stable means of payment, a well-ordered legal system promoting legal security and protecting private rights, as well as the "mercantilist" regulation of economic activities to be important regulatory tasks. Since the exports from one country are the imports of another country, and since no state can unilaterally protect the freedoms and property rights of its national traders and investors in foreign jurisdictions, there arose an increasing need for the conclusion of bilateral international trade agreements on the mutual liberalization of national trade barriers. Many national foreign economic policy measures (e.g. export subsidies, the determination of the value of the national currency, promotion of foreign investments) risk to remain ineffective without a legal framework limiting offsetting countermeasures by other states. From an economic perspective,

---

24 On the various conditions for the emergence of general rules by way of social consensus (e.g. importance of uncertainty as to the future effects of the rules on individual positions), and on the potential conflicts between the general interest in welfare-increasing rules and individual self-interests in breaking such rules (e.g. "prisoner's dilemma"), see: B.S. Frey (note 12), pp. 23 ff, 31 ff.

J. Buchanan[25] has described a nation's stock of observed laws protecting economic freedoms, contracts and property rights as a sort of "public capital" which, if properly maintained, yields increasing returns over time.

Thus not only private but also public national and international economic law emerged because they were considered to contribute to welfare. Not only trade between two nations but also a voluntary international trade agreement was to confer gains to both of them. International trade was also seen as a means of reducing political conflicts. In the words of J.St. Mill: "Commerce first taught nations to see with good will the wealth and prosperity of one another. Before, the patriot, unless sufficiently advanced in culture to feel his world his country, wished all countries weak, poor, and ill-governed, but his own. He now sees in their wealth and progress a direct source of wealth and progress to his own country. It is commerce which is rendering war obsolete, by strengthening and multiplying the personal interests which are in natural opposition to it."[26]

Productive economic activity presupposes a consensus about the basic rules of a society. A voluntary agreement on such rules will come about only if each participant expects such an agreement to be profitable for himself and acts in a state of uncertainty ("behind a veil of ignorance") as regards the future effects of the agreement. The willingness of states to agree to welfare-maximizing general international trade and economic rules rather than to pursue possible individual advantages outside general rules, was largely absent as long as the mercantilist doctrines and practices of states during the 15th to the 18th centuries identified national "wealth" with the accumulation of gold and silver by means of export promotion, import restrictions and the conquest of foreign colonies. The mercantilist view of the economy as a static "zero sum game", in which "what is given to someone, has to be taken away from somebody else" (J.B. Colbert, French minister of finance under Louis XIV), and its nationalistic perception of international economic relations as a struggle among rival sovereigns for national "power" and balance of trade surpluses, ran counter to the idea of multilateral international trade agreements and intergovernmental economic organizations.

25 J.M. Buchanan, The Limits of Liberty: Between Anarchy and Leviathan, 1975, chapter 7 ("Law as Public Capital")

26 J. St.Mill, Principles of Political Economy, 5th edition 1864, p. 136. It is noteworthy also that the classical Greek word for bartering or exchanging - katalattein - meant also "to admit into the community" and "to change from enemy into friend", see: v.Hayek, New Studies in Philosophy, Politics, Economics and the History of Ideas, 1978, p. 60

The liberal economists from Adam Smith onwards, by demonstrating that the liberalization of mercantilist trade restrictions was in the national self-interest because it enabled each country to maximize its national consumption possibilities (then considered as the real wealth of nations) beyond its domestic production possibilities, laid down the theoretical basis for the liberal international economy that arose during the second half of the 19th century. This liberal economic order rested on the shared perception of liberal trade as a dynamic "positive sum game". The European commercial treaty system between 1860 and 1914 rested on an interrelated network of long-term bilateral trade agreements interlinked through most-favoured-nation obligations, and was supplemented by multilateral agreements establishing customs unions, international administrative unions for the common administration of certain resources (e.g. international river commissions), and by functional intergovernmental organizations for the coordination of certain technical and legal activities (e.g. International Telecommunication Union, Universal Postal Union) as well as of certain economic activities (e.g. the Paris Sugar Convention of 1864). The legal certainty and economic gains made possible by these trade and monetary arrangements (e.g. the Latin Monetary Union of 1865 to 1921) may be illustrated by the example of the German Customs Union (Zollverein) of 1833 to 1866: In 1790, what later became Germany had 1,700 tariff boundaries and 300 rulers levying tolls as they pleased,[27] thereby making impossible the exploitation of the gains from trade to any reasonable degree. The coming into force of the common customs legislation of the German Zollverein on 1 January 1834 resulted in the formation of a customs union without internal customs duties and contributed to an economic upswing and dynamic economic integration in Germany. The correct perception of the national gains to be derived from trade acted as an incentive for most European states during the second half of the 19th century to participate in international agreements on the liberalization of trade barriers.

The post-1914 transition to systematic governmental economic interventions into the national economies and the emergence of modern "welfare states" after World War II, which perceive "welfare" in terms of full employment (rather than in terms of maximum consumption possibilities) and pursue a "conservative social welfare function" aimed at avoiding "any significant absolute reductions in real incomes of any significant section of the community",[28] engendered an increasing regulatory need for the international coordination of the external ef-

27 C.P. Kindleberger, Government and International Trade, 1978, p. 5

28 Cf. W.M. Corden, Trade Policy and Economic Welfare, 1974, pp. 107 ff.

fects of state interventions. The abandonment of the gold standard, which had been practiced unilaterally by national governments and central banks, made necessary multilateral rules and institutions for the regulation of the value of national currencies, exchange rates, balances of payments, foreign exchange restrictions and international liquidity. The trade protectionism of the inter-war period demonstrated that the reaping of the gains from liberal trade and from an international division of labour required also multilateral rules and institutions for non-discriminatory trade liberalization, coordination of trade policies and the settlement of international trade disputes. Since the mere liberalization of tariffs and payments may not suffice to bring about an improved resource allocation if other policy-induced domestic distortions exist, and the gains from the reduction of such non-tariff distortions may be as great as those to be derived from tariff liberalization, it was also found to be in the national interest of states to harmonize their economic policies in other areas such as competition policies, traffic and industrial policies (e.g. industrial standards), monetary, commercial, fiscal and social policies (e.g. health regulations).

Since World War II, the increasingly felt necessity to coordinate the external effects of national economic interventions and to address a number of problems which - because of their transnational nature - can be satisfactorily solved only by international cooperation, has led to the establishment of an ever increasing number of worldwide and regional international economic organizations in the field of international trade in goods, services, payments and monetary matters, capital transfers and international movement of persons.[29] The welfare effects of multilateral rules for transparent, non-discriminatory and market-conforming trade and monetary policies, such as the GATT and IMF rules, manifest themselves, inter alia, in the considerable reduction of public and private transaction costs (such as: reduced information costs concerning foreign trade barriers, reduced negotiation costs for multilateral trade liberalization and dispute settlement, reduced uncertainty for private investments and trade transactions, improved specialization and allocational efficiency through international market competition, and depoliticization of trade policies).[30] For instance, the lack of the most-favoured-nation obligation of Article I GATT would necessitate more

29 For a survey of the numerous international economic organizations and of the pertinent literature see: E.U. Petersmann, International Economic Organizations and Groups, in: R. Bernhardt, Encyclopedia of Public International Law, Installment 8 (1985), pp. 161-167

30 See, e.g.: U. Müller, Welfare Effects of the GATT System, in: Intereconomics 1982, pp. 173 ff

than 15,000 bilateral agreements among the 125 countries participating in the GATT (1987) to achieve the same effect.

In contrast to the economic proposition by B. Balassa for the distinction between five stages of progressive economic integration - to be ranked from the lowest to the highest forms starting from preferential tariff systems to free trade areas (abolition of substantially all internal tariffs and quantitative restrictions), customs unions (addition of a common external tariff), common markets (additional removal of all barriers to movements of production factors among member States) and to economic unions (additional integration of all economic policies among members) -, the actual process of integration among "mixed economies" has led to the emergence of numerous additional types and stages of economic integration. There are also many combinations of various degrees of "market integration" (as the main determinant for the allocation of available resources) with gradually evolving "policy integration" (with respect to macroeconomic stabilization and selective redistributive measures).[31] International economic cooperation and international agreements proved difficult to reach in the field of "global commons" (e.g. deep seabed mining, whaling, pollution of the seas), where badly defined property rights and the unhampered pursuit of sectional interests lead to the risk of inefficient use of resources.[32]

5. "International Economic Law" as a Layered System

The spontaneous historical evolution of the international economy has led to a "stratification of rules of conduct"[33] not only at the levels of private and public national and international economic law, but also in the form of legally non-mandatory principles, usages, informal "declarations of principles", "codes of conduct" and other arrangements.[34] All these principles and rules are designed

31 Cf. B. Balassa, A Theory of Economic Integration; 1962; E.U. Petersmann, Wirtschaftsintegrationsrecht und Investitionsgesetzgebung der Entwicklungsländer, 1974; J. Pelkmans, The institutional economics of European integration, in: Capelletti/Seccombe/Weiler (eds), Integration through Law, 1985, Vol. I 1, pp. 318 ff.

32 Cf.B. Frey, International Political Economics, 1984, pp. 122 ff

33 Cf. F.A. v.Hayek, Law, Legislation and Liberty, Vol. III, 1979, p. 159

34 Cf. F.Roessler, Law, De Facto Agreements and Declarations of Principle in International Economic Relations, in: 21 German Yearbook of International Law (1978) pp. 27 ff; E.U. Petersmann, Codes of Conduct, in: R. Bernhardt (ed.), Encyclopedia of Public International Law, Installment 7 (1984), pp. 28 ff

to influence individual behaviour and to promote "spontaneous order" or deliberately created "directed orders" so as to enable economic agents to form reasonably correct expectations regarding the future behaviour of individuals (including government officials) in the economic sphere. Hardly any other area of the international economy has such a detailed national, regional and worldwide international legal framework as foreign trade. The various "legal layers" may mutually strengthen and reinforce each other following the "plywood principle".[35]

But they may also conflict with each other and cause economic disintegration. This may arise in particular because "spontaneous orders", which emerge from rule-oriented free actions, and "organizations", which are based on rules and commands for the performance of assigned tasks, cannot be mixed in any manner one likes.[36] The basic policy choices between a deliberate agreement upon, or a spontaneous evolution of, principles and rules (e.g. the evolution of "pragmatic GATT practices" outside the general GATT rules, the exchange arrangements in contravention of the old Article IV of the IMF Agreement after the breakdown of the IMF system of fixed parties in 1971), between legally binding rules or non-mandatory "declarations" (e.g. of the OECD) and "recommendations" (e.g. of the UN General Assembly), or between general principles (e.g. in the 1974 UN Charter of Economic Rights and Duties of States) and more precise rules, are perennial themes in international economic negotiations and require different answers depending on the concrete circumstances.[37] The structure of the modern international economy and of "international economic law" has become so complex not through a "grand design", but because it evolved as a largely spontaneous and self-generating order.

From a legal perspective, the international economic order is characterized by a highly decentralized legal structure. The international law principle of the "sovereign equality" (Article 2: 1 UN Charter) of today's more than 170 sovereign states protects the national freedom to choose the national economic, political and legal system. The principles of parliamentary democracy, enshrined in the national constitutional law of the 24 OECD countries which account for more

35 Cf. J. Tumlir, International Economic Order and Democratic Constitutionalism, in: Ordo Jahrbuch 33 (1983), pp. 71, 80

36 Cf. F.A. v.Hayek, Law, Legislation and Liberty, Vol. I, 1979, pp. 48 ff

37 Cf. F. Roessler (note 34) for a discussion of the various proposed "management approaches", "common law approaches" or "legalist approaches" to the regulation of international economic relations.

than 60% of world trade and finance, require political accountability and appear to stand in the way of transferring comprehensive regulatory powers in the economic field to worldwide bodies unrestrained by parliamentary control and by judicial protection of individual rights. Communist countries insist on central economic planning at the national level and are also opposed to transferring mandatory planning powers to international bodies. The constitutional guarantees of economic freedoms and property rights in OECD countries protect also the more than 20,000 transnational enterprises resident in these countries, which manage vast economic resources through globally integrated corporate strategies transforming over a third of world trade and finance into "intra-corporate business". The international banks operating on the "Euro-money market" also elude effective international supervision and transfer daily billions of dollars around the globe in response to temporary price changes (e.g. of interest rates and exchange rates). The history of economic "government failure" is full of examples (e.g. as regards the "steering" of international agricultural, commodity and capital markets) illustrating that international economic coordination through multilateral political negotiations cannot process and disseminate the economic informations of the millions of economic agents as efficiently as decentralized markets continuously do. It also shows that utility-maximizing private economic agents do not react to government policies in a "Pavlovian manner" but on carefully considered decisions of their own and in often unexpected ways (as illustrated by the frequent emergence of "black markets" or "voting by feet").

The decentralized legal and economic structures of the international economy are not likely to change. The legal principle of national economic sovereignty requires that international economic law remains based on the respect for national freedom and for national diversity. Theories of international economic order and of international economic law, which presuppose or aim at the elimination of the differences among the more than 170 national economic and legal systems, may therefore prove to be of little practical value and to remain utopian. The non-ratification of the 1948 Havana Charter for an International Trade Organization and the little practical impact of the majoritarian adoption of the 1974 UN Recommendation for a "Charter of Economic Rights and Duties of States" bear witness to the interdependence between national and international systems and to the need for consensus on international trade and economic rules.

In the absence of consensus on precise substantive rules, international economic law will often have to confine itself to agreed general objectives, principles and procedures (e.g. for the promotion of "public goods" such as international trade liberalization and stable exchange rates), the prohibition of mutually harmful policy instruments with adverse external effects (e.g. trade discrimination, trade-distorting export subsidies, confiscation of foreign property), and "minimum standards" and general framework rules with decentralized decision-making. In view of the "constitutional ignorance" of everybody of most of the particular facts which determine the daily course of the worldwide division of labour, it would - also from an economic point of view - amount to "intellectual hubris" to pretend that the self-regulatory information-processing mechanism of decentralized market prices could be effectively replaced by worldwide economic planning and "constructivist rationalism".[38] The incurable ignorance of everybody of the plans and actions of a large number of economic agents, of their economic effects and of the overall economic processes makes the rational recognition of the limits of individual reasoning an important task. Man cannot acquire the full knowledge necessary for a rational and efficient central steering of the constantly changing developments in the world economy. A far-reaching international division of labour among billions of people is possible only by relying, to a large extent, on the informations conveyed by spontaneous market prices (as a cybernetic feedback mechanism) and on the free efforts of millions of people guided by general framework rules of private and public national and international law.

6. Need for a Comprehensive Analysis of the Law of International Economic Relations

A) Need for a Comprehensive Legal Analysis of "International Economic Law"

The stratified structures and interdependences of the globally integrated modern world economy and the requirements of national constitutional laws for the conduct of foreign economic policies imply that many legal problems of the international economic order cannot be adequately analyzed if - as proposed by

38 Cf. F.A. v.Hayek, The Errors of Constructivism, in: v.Hayek, New Studies in Philosophy, Politics, Economics and the History of Ideas, 1978, pp. 3 ff

some lawyers including Schwarzenberger,[39] Carreau/Juillard/Flory[40] and Verloren van Themaat[41] - the study of "international economic law" is confined to the field of public international economic law. The international law principle of national economic sovereignty and the decentralized economic activities based on private and public national law suggest to proceed rather from a "principle of subsidiarity" in the legal search for the "optimal level of legal regulation" of international economic relations.

Thus, contrary to Professor J. Tinbergen's proposals for the setting-up of a large number of new international economic organizations at a world level so as to secure an "optimum level of decision-making where external effects are negligible",[42] the search for alternative decentralized solutions at the level of private and public national law may prove politically inevitable, legally more effective and, in the end, economically also more efficient. Individuals, enterprises and states will remain the most important agents in the international economy, and they are likely to prefer decentralized legal solutions and to consent only to those international legal disciplines that respect their autonomous freedoms as far as possible (e.g. individual economic freedoms and property rights of producers, traders and consumers, maintenance of competition, "sovereign equality" of states). The decentralized coordination and steering of international economic activities through market competition and through private and public national law are likely to remain of far greater importance than public international economic law which, due to the necessary respect for national economic so-

39 G. Schwarzenberger, The Principles and Standards of International Economic Law, Recueil des Cours 1966, I, pp. 5 ff; 7: "International economic law is the branch of public international law which is concerned with (1) the ownership and exploitation of natural resources; (2) the production and distribution of goods; (3) invisible international transactions of an economic or financial character; (4) currency and finance; (5) related services and (6) the status and organization of those engaged in such activities".

40 Carreau/Juillard/Flory, Droit International Economique, 1978, p. 11: "Le Droit International Economique est cette branche du droit international qui règlemente, d'une part l'installation sur le territoire des Etats des divers facteurs de production (personnes et capitaux) en provenance de l'étranger et, d'autre part, les transactions internationales portant sur les biens, les services et les capitaux".

41 P. Verloren van Themaat, The Changing Structure of International Economic Law, 1981, pp. 9 ff: "For the purposes of this study international economic law can be described in overall terms as the total range of norms (directly or indirectly based on treaties) of public international law with regard to transnational economic relations". But Verloren van Themaat also adds: "Admittedly norms of public national law concerned with international economic relations form an important part of the totality of norms regulating international economic relations seen from an economic point of view" (p. 11).

42 J. Tinbergen, Reshaping the International Order, 1976, p. 82

vereignty, will have to confine itself in many areas to general framework rules, procedures and institutions with decentralized decision-making. The possible advantages from legally "decentralized" solutions, rather than worldwide uniform solutions at the level of global multilateral agreements among states, are similar to those of market competition among firms or political competition among political parties: there is greater scope for taking into account different preferences of states and economic agents, and "legal competition" may offer better possibilities for innovation, experimentation and decentralized information-processing.

The "law of the international economy"[43] may be systematized according to the main economic sectors and to the "legal layers" of national and international economic law, as illustrated by the following chart:

43 Such a broader definition, which does not focus on the origin of the norms but on their object of regulating international economic transactions, is used, inter alia, by G. Erler, Grundprobleme des Internationalen Wirtschaftsrechts, 1956, pp. 9 ff; J.H. Jackson, Legal Problems of International Economic Relations, 1977, pp. XIX ff; W. Fikentscher, Wirtschaftsrecht Band I (1983), pp. 49 ff.

Regulation of transnational movements of	through national economic law (private and public)	through international economic law and organizations (private and public)
Goods	e.g. trade law competition law tax law	e.g. GATT, UNCTAD, OECD, MFA, Commodity Agreements, EEC, EFTA, private cartels
Services	e.g. banking law insurance law patent law transport law	e.g. ICAO, IATA, IMCO, WIPO, ITU, EEC, OECD, private shipping conferences
Persons	e.g. labour law social welfare law, right of establishment	e.g. ILO, UNESCO, ICM, EEC, Association Agreements, codes of conduct
Capital	e.g. company law, investment law, capital market regulations	e.g. IMF, World Bank Group, ICSID, MIGA, OPIC, OECD, EEC, private and public investment agreements
Payments	e.g. monetary law, exchange restrictions	e.g. IMF, BIS, GATT, EEC, EFTA, 'Euro-dollar banks'

There are numerous interrelationships between these various kinds of international economic transactions and their legal regulation. For example: Trade in goods is frequently related to supplementary services (e.g. transport, insurance, banking, sales promotion, supply of know-how) and necessitates international payments and foreign exchange transactions; foreign investments often take place as a substitute for foreign trade in order to overcome foreign trade barriers; additional foreign exchange earnings from trade prove to be an indispensable prerequisite for the repayment of the high foreign debts of developing countries; freedom of establishment in foreign countries and other foreign investments require the liberalization of international capital transfers. The history of international economic relations provides numerous examples for the interaction between, and mutual interchangeability of, private and public national and international economic regulations. For instance: Restrictive business practices in the form of private law (e.g. private cartels) are often used as a substitute for governmental trade regulations in the form of public law (e.g. "voluntary" restraint agreements), and **vice versa** (e.g. regulation by public national and international law of private international shipping conferences, prohibition in Article VIII: 2,b IMF Agreement of the enforcement of certain private exchange contracts). The contents, interpretation and application of national foreign trade and economic laws (e.g. antidumping and countervailing duty legislations, extraterritorial application of national antitrust laws) are to an ever increasing extent dependent upon international agreements on the respective subject matters.

"International economic law" can be systematized from various points of view and in many different ways. Following the system used by the Roman lawyer Gaius, the distinction among "**personae, res, actiones**" could serve as a basis for the systematization of national and international economic law: Who are the actors of international economic relations (e.g. natural and legal private persons, states and other public national agencies, international organizations)? What are the objects and legal relationships regulated by international economic law (e.g. sales, purchases and ownership of goods, services, capital and payments, etc)? What are the major problem areas of international economic relations[44] and the major objectives, principles, rules, procedures and institutional characteristics of national foreign economic policies and of international economic organizations?[45] To what extent may the systematizations used by economic theory - for instance, the "triptych of public economic functions" (allocation, stabilization, distribution), the above-mentioned "stages of economic integration", the subdivision of the chief foreign economic policy instruments into price mechanism devices (e.g. tariffs, import deposits, internal taxes, subsidies, multiple exchange rates, variable levies, minimum prices) and direct controls (e.g. prohibitions, directives, quantitative restrictions) - be helpful for the systematization of international economic law? The "functional unity" of the international division of labour and the need for more legal certainty and consistency in the national as well as international regulation of transnational economic activities are the main reasons why the traditional separation of legal disciplines (such as private commercial law,

---

44 Cf. the list of major problem areas of a "new international economic order" by Verloren van Themaat (note 41), p. 1 ff

45 For a thorough comparative legal analysis of international economic organizations see: P. Verloren van Themaat (note 41) and, more specifically confined to the problem of international supervision: P. v.Dijk (ed.), Supervisory Mechanisms in International Economic Organizations, 1984

conflicts of law, national foreign trade law, public international law) needs to be transcended by integrating the pertinent rules, procedures and other coordinating mechanisms into a more coherent "international economic law" Yet, no generally accepted theory of international economic law has been developed so far. The definitions, theories and models suggested by individual authors depend ultimately not on what is "scientifically right or wrong", but rather on the practical purposes of the analysis and on the utility of the methods used for the purpose.

B) Need for an Economic Analysis of International Economic Law

Market competition, the private commercial law for the regulation of economic transactions among independent private economic agents, and the public international economic law agreed among sovereign states present similar "horizontal structures" and pursue similar objectives (e.g. efficient allocation of resources) through the legal protection of equal freedoms under general rules of law.[46] They all presuppose decentralized economic planning and take account of both "market failures" as well as "government failures", which are recognized to constitute important regulatory tasks of national and international economic law. This objective of regulating national and international economic processes in a way which will harmonize, and if possible maximize, individual and social welfare often cannot be met without an "economic analysis" of economic law. The legal requirement of the proportionality of government restrictions of individual rights, for instance, makes it necessary to take account of the economic effects of alternative legal instruments (e.g. import tariffs, quantitative import restrictions, or voluntary export restraints) by examining questions such as the following:

- What are the respective costs and economic benefits of the government intervention?

- Who pays and who benefits?

---

46 Models of utility-maximizing behaviour and of market competition are applied for purposes of legal analysis especially by the lawyers belonging to the "Chicago School of Law and Economics", such as R. Posner (note 12) who describes participants in the legal process as rational maximizers of their satisfactions and explains many doctrines (e.g. on the meaning of "justice") and institutions of the legal system (e.g. the judicial development of common law) as efforts to promote the efficient allocation of resources; see also: R. Posner, The Economics of Justice, 1981.

- Do the national benefits outweigh the national costs?
- Does the government intervention distort competition?
- Are there less-distortive, alternative means of government intervention?
- Is there scope for "deregulation" and more decentralized decision-making?
- Does the legal limitation of economic freedoms risk stimulating the creation of "black markets"?
- Who ought to decide these questions and subject to what kind of procedural safeguards?

For a thorough understanding and effective application of many provisions of international economic law (such as GATT Article XVI: B on export subsidies or GATT Article XXIV on free trade areas and customs unions), it seems necessary to grasp also the economic objectives and rationale of the rules concerned. For instance, government interventions designed "to make the market work" (e.g. by means of competition rules), or the interpretation of the GATT prohibition of export subsidies "which result in that contracting party having more than an equitable share of world export trade in that product" (Article XVI: 3), may require a good knowledge not only of the legal but also of the economic problems involved. The legal principle of proportionality, which forms part of the national constitutional laws of most Western democracies as well as of European Community law, requires confining restrictions of individual freedoms and property rights to the minimum necessary to obtain the objective which justifies those restrictions; hence, it is arguable that an analysis of the economic efficiency and effects of alternative legal regulations is a legal obligation and a logical prerequisite for the examination of what is required and proportionate to achieve the objective without unnecessary restriction of individual liberties.[47]

47 For a detailed discussion of the concept and problems of "economic analysis of law" see below chapter IV.

C) Need for a Political Analysis of International Economic Law

From a political perspective, the apparent contrast between the economic consensus on the gains from trade liberalization and the actual practice of trade protectionism shows that politicians face important "political constraints" in their decision-making about foreign economic policies. They may be guided not so much by economic rationality or by the requirements of international economic law as by a desire to maximize political support and to minimize political opposition.[48] The important legal task of devising "constitutional constraints" for the often broad and vaguely defined foreign economic policy powers of governments in order to restrain periodically elected politicians from using the various foreign economic policy instruments to do harm to the general public for the benefit of a few, cannot be resolved without a political analysis of the "public choice" among the various legal instruments of foreign economic policy. Just as, according to v.Hayek, "an economist who is only an economist cannot even be a good economist",[49] a lawyer analyzing national and international economic law from a purely legalistic perspective runs the risk of missing a major part of the practical problems.[50]

---

48 Cf. A. Downs, An Economic Theory of Democracy, 1957, p. 52. See also: A. Breton, The Economic Theory of Representative Government, 1974.

49 F.A. v.Hayek, Reflections on Constitutional Economics, in: R.B. McKenzie (ed), Constitutional Economics, 1984, pp. 235 f

50 For a detailed political analysis of trade protectionism see below chapters V and VI. The analyses of trade protectionism by international economic organizations (such as GATT, the IMF, the World Bank, UNCTAD, OECD) are unanimous in their emphasis on the political causes and welfare-reducing effects of trade protectionism. Lawyers often continue to be reluctant to take note of the economic and political dimensions of international trade laws. See, on the one hand, K.M. Meessen, Vom Anti-Protektionismus zur Fortentwicklung der internationalen Wirtschaftsordnung, in: Neuer Protektionismus in der Weltwirtschaft und EG-Handelspolitik, 1985, pp. 81, 82, according to whom lawyers have no "scientific" competence for foreign trade policy and should restrain themselves to the role of a notary public in this respect. See, on the other hand, the rule-oriented "policy of the law" advocated by the former legal advisor of the International Labour Organization, W. Jenks, Legal Advisers and International Organizations, 1966, p. 5. On the impact of the diplomatic process on the interpretation and application of GATT law see the former GATT Director-General: O. Long, Law and its Limitations in the GATT Multilateral Trade System, 1985, e.g. pp. 107 ff. For a rather radical policy-oriented approach to international economic law see: Judge M. Bedjaoui, Pour un Nouvel Ordre Economique International, 1979, e.g. p. 254.

II. HISTORICAL EVOLUTION OF INTERNATIONAL ECONOMIC LAW INTO A "STRATIFIED ORDER"

1. Basic Functions of International Economic Rules

In each economy, regular interaction of individuals and organizations engenders legal or extra-legal principles and rules with three regulatory functions[1]: to constitute and delimit autonomy; to coordinate autonomous specialized activities in a way which harmonizes private and social advantage; and to promote continuity and "relative stability". The rules may serve several functions at the same time. Property rights, and the markets arising from transactions in such rights, not only establish and delimit freedoms but, by assigning potential profits and the risks of loss, also permit and promote decentralized adjustment and coordination which, in a world of continuous change, is a condition of the overall "dynamic stability" of the international economy.

Autonomy, coordination and continuity are promoted by the international economic rules with regard to both states and private economic agents. The GATT rules, for instance, are designed to protect not only member states from "power-oriented", discriminatory trade policies by other states as well as from protectionist pressures by domestic interest groups aimed at selective trade protection at the expense of national welfare. But the GATT guarantees of non-discriminatory market access (e.g. in Articles I:1, II, III, XI, XIII), by prohibiting non-tariff trade barriers and the taxation of international trade transactions in excess of tariff bindings, are designed to protect also the economic freedoms of traders, producers and consumers in GATT member countries to purchase and sell goods in the best foreign markets. The GATT rules for the use of transparent, non-discriminatory and market-conforming trade policy instruments (i.e. tariffs) purport to coordinate not only national foreign trade and monetary policies (cf. Article XV). They are ultimately aimed at the creation and maintenance of non-discriminatory and undistorted market competition as the most efficient mechanism for the decentralized coordination of specialized economic activities.[2] The

1 Cf. e.g.: J. Tumlir, Can the International Economic Order be saved?, in: The World Economy 1977, pp. 3, 5 f; E.U. Petersmann, Trade Policy as a Constitutional Problem, in: Aussenwirtschaft 1986, pp. 405, 424 ff.

2 The importance of international market prices also for the communist GATT member countries (e.g. Czechoslovakia, Hungary, Poland, Romania and Yugoslavia) has been em-

multilateral framework of general GATT rules of unlimited duration enhances legal certainty and continuity not only for the trade policies of governments but also for the private expectations, transactions and investment decisions of traders, producers and consumers.

Thomas Hobbes, in his classic treatise "Leviathan" (1651), proceeded from the assumption that selfish individuals operating in a "state of nature", unconstrained by a framework of laws, would steal from each other producing a "war of all against all". In order to progress from this stage of "every man for himself", a society needs "constitutional rules" establishing and delimiting the rights of individuals, the limits of state power and the basic rules of the economic and legal order. The state acting as a "protective state" (J.M. Buchanan) for the protection of individual rights is indispensable for a free society. But should governments also interfere with the production and distribution of goods and services in private markets? Legal and economic "constitutional theory"[3] emphasize that the "productive state" (J.M. Buchanan) concerned with the political "allocation" of available resources to specific uses, with the "stabilization" of macroeconomic processes (e.g. business cycles, inflation) and with the redistribution of income (e.g. between the generations or between regions), should be used only under constitutional safeguards preventing a misuse of collective power and of majority rule (e.g. separation of powers, limited delegation of powers, rule of law).

Today, all governments enjoy broad powers for the regulation of national and international economic relations. Yet, since the worldwide "stagflation" experi-

---

phasized by J. Tumlir, GATT Rules and Community Law - A Comparison of their economic and legal functions, in: Hilf/Jacobs/ Petersmann (eds.), European Community and GATT, 1986, pp. 2 ff. On the general proposition that hierarchically created and managed "organizations" can properly function only in a broader context of "spontaneous order" see: M. Polanyi, The Determinants of Social Action, in: Streissler/Haberler/Lutz/Machlup (eds.), Roads to Freedom, Essays in Honor of F.A. v.Hayek, 1969. Since GATT was designed primarily for market economies, the protocols for the accession of Hungary, Poland and Romania to the GATT include special safeguard provisions to accommodate the special trading problems caused by the foreign trade monopolies of non-market economies.

3 See, e.g.: F.A. v.Hayek, The Constitution of Liberty, 1960, as well as his description of a "model constitution" in: F.A. v.Hayek, Law, Legislation and Liberty, Vol. 3 (1979), pp. 105 ff, where v.Hayek argues for the "dethronement of politics" through constitutional rules designed to secure an effective separation of the power of legislation from the executive and judicial powers of government by means of a two-chamber-constitution (providing for a Legislative Assembly, a Governmental Assembly and a Constitutional Court but not for a list of specially protected fundamental rights, since v.Hayek considers any such separate enumeration of individual rights "unnecessary", p. 110). See also: J.M. Buchanan, Freedom in Constitutional Contract, 1978; J.M. Buchanan et al., The Economics of Politics, 1978; G. Brennan/J.M. Buchanan, The Power of Tax, 1980; R.B. McKenzie (ed.), Constitutional Economics. Containing the Economic Powers of Government, 1984.

enced after 1973, there is increasing awareness of the limited possibilities of "Keynesian fiscal policies" aimed at the deliberate macroeconomic steering of business fluctuations, full employment and economic growth. In economics, there has been a noticeable shift away from "quantitative economics" aimed at maximizing social welfare through mathematical techniques of optimization. Modern "constitutional economics" emphasizes the need to reconsider the constitutional constraints on the taxing, spending, money-issuing and regulatory powers of government in the light of "government failure" and to protect more effectively economic liberties and property rights from state interference. This new version of the broad "political economy approach" of the classical economists has suggested various constitutional reforms for containing the economic powers of government (e.g. "balanced budget"- and "tax-limitations"-amendments to the US Constitution) and for promoting "deregulation" (e.g. in the United Kingdom and Germany), which in some states (e.g. within the USA) have already led to far-reaching changes of national economic law.[4] That the "power to tax" is a "power to destroy", and that governments can redistribute society's wealth not only through taxation but also through regulation, is true for both domestic and foreign economic policy. But the legal restraints on the foreign economic policy powers of governments are in most states only vaguely defined by national law.

The regulatory function of **international** rules has traditionally been seen in the protection of the "national interest" against the interests of other states and in the provision of international "public goods" (such as peace). It is only a relatively recent insight that international economic rules can also serve important "domestic policy functions" for the protection of **domestic** competition and individual rights, the legal limitation of the abuse of discretionary government powers and the enhancement of their parliamentary and judicial control (see below chapter VII). International trade competition gives rise to conflicts of interests not only between traders, producers and consumers residing in different countries (for instance, if a state differentiates between domestic and foreign competing firms through tariffs, internal taxes or subsidies). It also gives rise to purely domestic conflicts of interest **within** the trading countries. Economic theory shows, for example, that an import tariff taxes domestic importers, consumers and export industries for the benefit of domestic import-competing producers (see below chapter V.1 and 3). The liberal international GATT rules for the use of transparent, non-discriminatory and less-distortive trade policy in-

4 See: McKenzie (note 3), Introduction, at p. 2

struments regulate these **domestic** conflicts of interests in a more precise manner than the usually vague autonomous foreign trade regulations of domestic laws (see below chapters VII and VIII). They protect thereby the freedoms and property rights of domestic traders, producers and consumers and legally define the national self-interest in liberal trade and in the use of transparent, non-discriminatory and proportionate trade policy **instruments** for whatever trade policy objectives a country decides to pursue. They limit the discretionary trade policy powers of periodically elected governments, politicians and bureaucracies and can serve as a constraint on the various asymmetries in domestic decision-making processes about trade policy (see below chapters V.3 and VI.3). The liberal international trade rules extend the freedom of trade across national frontiers by limiting the admissible degree, instruments and public policy reasons of national trade restrictions and by protecting non-discriminatory access to foreign markets also abroad vis-à-vis foreign governments.

2. Taxonomy of Trade Policy Instruments

The chief economic policy instruments used for the regulation of transnational economic relations may be subdivided into price-mechanism devices (e.g. tariffs, exchange rates, internal taxes, subsidies, minimum prices, variable levies, import deposits) and direct controls (e.g. prohibitions, directives, quantitative restrictions). Governments can intervene in transnational economic relations through **internal or external measures**; these can be of a **general nature** (i.e. affecting all transactions such as an increase in the money supply or a change in the exchange rate) or of a **selective nature** (i.e. affecting only some transactions such as trade policy border measures or internal trade regulation by means of taxes, subsidies and government procurement rules).[5] Selective internal measures can be aimed at either the consumption or at the production of goods and services (e.g. a consumption tax, production subsidies). Selective external measures can be aimed either at import transactions or export transactions. All selective foreign economic policy measures can be applied either in a discriminatory manner (i.e. relating only to certain exports or imports) or in a non-discriminatory fashion. They can be implemented by regulating either the "real transfer" of

5 For a useful discussion of this taxonomy of trade and monetary policies see: F. Roessler, Trade Policy and International Trade Arrangements, in: SEANZA Lectures, The Monetary Authority of Singapore, 1982, pp. 456, 474 f; idem, Selective Balance-of-Payments Adjustment Measures Affecting Trade: The Roles of the GATT and the IMF, in: JWTL 1975, pp. 622 f.

goods, services or capital, or by exchange measures regulating the related payments.

From a legal perspective, most foreign economic policy measures operate through legal statutes, regulations and administrative measures specifying, restricting or enlarging individual freedoms and property rights of importers, exporters, producers or consumers. For instance, import restrictions limit the rights of domestic importers and consumers to import and consume the restricted foreign goods and, by distorting domestic relative prices compared to world market prices, act as an incentive for the protected domestic producers to increase their production and prices. In addition, import restrictions discriminating between supplier countries are likely to entail discrimination and competitive distortions also between competing domestic traders and producers (e.g. processing industries) importing from these countries. Many domestic "market failures" (e.g. cartels) and "government failures" (e.g. economically unjustified subsidies) can persist only because they are sheltered from international competition through restrictions on international economic transactions.[6] International economic rules prescribing the use of transparent, non-discriminatory and welfare-increasing instruments of economic policy limit the scope for both "market failures" as well as "government failures" and protect thereby individual freedoms, property rights and "public goods" such as undistorted competition.[7]

3. Historical Evolution of International Economic Law: A Brief Survey

International economic law evolved to a large extent spontaneously from decentralized law-creating processes in which the fittest norms often survived. Its historical development may be subdivided into three stages.

The first was characterized by the evolution of private international commercial law up to the period of the medieval law merchant. The ancient Greek and Roman trade had already given rise to particular commercial usages and customs (**ubi commercium, ibi jus**), and the Roman **jus gentium** was applicable also to foreigners and sometimes conceived of as an expression of **naturalis ratio** common to all people. The mercantile customs and trading institutions of

6 This has often been emphasized, see e.g.: Competition and Trade Policies, Their Interaction, OECD 1984, pp. 85 ff

7 On the economic notion of "public goods" see e.g.: B.S. Frey, Modern Political Economy, 1978, pp. 4, 24 f

the Middle Ages - such as the fair, the rise of banking, and joint-stock and regulated companies - contributed to the emergence of an uniform law merchant in Europe which was not only a **jus mercatorum** but often became customary law approved by governmental authorities and administered by special commercial courts. This old **lex mercatoria** was characterized by its emphasis on freedom of contract, freedom of alienability of movable property, abrogation of legal technicalities, and decision of cases **ex aequo et bono**. It evolved rules and concepts, some remaining of great importance to the present day (e.g. the bill of exchange, the principle of assignability and negotiability, the charterparty and the bill of lading), which often differred markedly from those of Roman law or of the ordinary local laws.

The second stage in the legal evolution of the international economic order began with the development of public international economic law prompted by the coexistence and foreign trade of the newly emerging sovereign states in Europe since the end of the Middle Ages. Political nationalism and economic mercantilism led to the incorporation of the law merchant into national codifications of law. The state's prerogative over the regulation of money and of foreign trade were considered essential elements of sovereignty. International commerce became subjected to governmental trade regulations such as customs duties, quantitative restrictions, state trading, shipping monopolies and preferential arrangements for trade with overseas colonies. The legal insecurity, economic costs and political frictions caused by mercantilist foreign trade interventions gave rise to the conclusion of bilateral commercial treaties aimed at coordinating and liberalizing the respective national trade regulations on a reciprocal basis. The increasing use of most-favoured-nation clauses contributed to the gradual coming into being of a more "rule-oriented" multilateral trading system. The numerous long-term bilateral trade agreements concluded among European countries since the 1860 Cobden-Chevalier treaty of commerce between England and France were interlinked through unconditional most-favoured-nation clauses. They also often provided for "national treatment", "freedom of commerce" between the territories of the contracting parties, reciprocal protection of personal and property rights of their nationals, and the admission of consuls who assisted in promoting international trade. With multilateralized trade liberalization, freedom of contract and of payments at stable exchange rates based on the gold standard, freedom of international capital movements, protection of property rights and other widely accepted rules of international good behaviour, this non-discriminatory long-term "commercial treaty system" operated economically like a multilateral trading order. Hence it became more rational to negotiate further-reaching multilateral liberalization and integration measures, as well as to supplement bilateral trade agreements by multilateral agreements in the fields of international trade (e.g. the international sugar conventions of 1864 and 1902), monetary relations (e.g. the Latin Monetary Union of 1865), international transport (e.g. the Rhine Navigation Acts of 1831 and 1868) and industrial property rights (e.g. the 1883 Paris Convention on the Protection of Industrial Property).

The outbreak of World War I in 1914 marked the end of the classical liberal era and, in many states, the coming into being of modern national public economic law, large governmental bureaucracies for the administration of economic policy and an ever increasing "politicization" of the economy. The centre of economic power shifted from England to the United States. However, notwithstanding President Wilson's pledge for "removal, so far as possible, of all economic barriers and the establishment of an equality of trade conditions among all nations" (point 3 of Wilson's Fourteen Points), the United States was not prepared to follow the British tradition of free trade and to engage in multilateral trade negotiations; this obstructed repayment of the international loans in the only way they could be repaid. The League of Nations Covenant provided only for a general commitment to the objectives of freedom of communications and of transit as well as of equitable treatment of the commerce of all League members (Art. 23(e)). The five major international trade and monetary conferences convened during the 1920s produced only minor results and failed to restore the pre-war liberal trading order.

The Wall Street stock exchange crash of 1929 and the ensuing Great Depression led to the abandonment of the gold standard, a decline in world trade by more than 50 per cent within a few years, widespread "beggar-thy-neighbour" policies characterized by protectionist tariff increases (Smoot-Hawley Tariff Act of 1930 in the United States), pervasive trade restrictions, exchange controls, competitive devaluations and nationalization of foreign property. The United States Reciprocal Trade Agreements Act of 1934, which led to the conclusion of thirty-two trade agreements with unconditional most-favoured-nation clauses between 1935 and 1945, aimed at re-establishing multilateral trade. But it could not reverse the widespread resort to discriminatory bilateral trade and payments agreements. The 1936 Tripartite Monetary Agreement between the United States, the United Kingdom and France was again a step in the right direction, but it was already overshadowed by the threat of war.

The third stage in the legal evolution of the international economic order began with the Atlantic Charter of 1941. It is characterized by the determination to avoid a recurrence of the experience of the 1930s through use of deliberate multilateral regulation and liberalization of international monetary, financial and trade relations in the framework of mutually supporting multilateral agreements and universal, intercontinental and regional economic organizations. The United Nations Charter proceeds from the "principle of the sovereign equality of all its Members" (Article 2:1). It sets out rules and procedures for "international economic and social cooperation" (Chap. IX) based on general principles of cooperation (Article 56) and "good neighbourliness" (Article 74). Such cooperation is to be coordinated by the United Nations General Assembly (Article 60), the United Nations Economic and Social Council (Chap.X) and "various specialized agencies established by intergovernmental agreement" (Articles 57 and 63).

The 1944 Agreement establishing the IMF provides for stable exchange rates reflecting countries' competitiveness in international trade (Art. IV), avoidance of exchange restrictions on current payments for international trade in goods and services (Article VIII), financial assistance to overcome temporary balance of payments difficulties (Article V), national freedom to control international capital transfers (Article VI) and a great deal of autonomy for national economic policies in pursuit of agreed "primary objectives of economic policy" (Article I) such as full employment, economic growth and price stability. The World Bank was created for the purpose of supplementing private lending and capital flows by public long-term loans so as to meet the financing needs of the war-torn and underdeveloped countries.

The Havana Charter for an International Trade Organization having failed to attract the necessary ratifications to bring it into force, the GATT has remained the only multilateral agreement setting out general rules and procedures for non-discriminatory trade liberalization between its 125 participating states (as of 1987). The mutually supporting monetary, financial and trade rules are supplemented by a large number of international agreements regulating other fields of economic cooperation such as international commodity trade, restrictive business practices, free trade areas, customs unions and other international economic organizations and groups, foreign investments, international taxation and avoidance of double taxation, capital movements, loans, economic and technical aid and international financial cooperation.

4. Legal Evolution of International Economic Organizations since World War II: Some Comparative Legal Aspects

The "age of integration" since 1945 is characterized by numerous multilateral attempts to achieve trade liberalization simultaneously with a well-ordered monetary system and development financing in a framework of worldwide, transcontinental, regional and sectoral economic organizations and groups. At the worldwide level, the GATT[8] is the only international agreement that lays down a framework of multilateral rules for a worldwide liberalization of trade barriers, for the harmonization of trade policies and for a forum for continuous discussions on trade policy matters, negotiations on the reduction of trade barriers and the settlement of international trade disputes. It is supplemented by various sectoral trade organizations, such as international commodity organizations (e.g. for wheat, sugar, tin, coffee, olive oil, cocoa, jute, tropical timber, natural rubber),[9] as well as by functional trade organizations, such as the Customs Cooperation Council. The United Nations Conference on Trade and Development (UNCTAD) was designed to fill part of the void resulting from the repeated failures to set up a more comprehensive International Trade Organization, and addresses itself mainly to trade and development issues of particular importance to developing countries.[10]

The functioning of the multilateral rules and institutions for trade in goods and services depends on complementary rules and institutions for the free flow of payments for current international transactions and for predictable currency exchange rates as the monetary prerequisite of an international price system and competition. The essential objective of international monetary institutions,

8 Out of the vast literature on GATT, see especially: J.H. Jackson, World Trade and the Law of GATT, 1969; K.W. Dam, The GATT. Law and International Economic Organization, 1970; R.E. Hudec, The GATT Legal System and World Trade Diplomacy, 1975; O. Long, Law and its Limitations in the GATT Multilateral Trading System, 1985; E. McGovern, International Trade Regulation, 2nd edition, 1986; R. Senti, GATT, System der Welthandelsordnung, 1986; E.U. Petersmann, GATT - Analytical Index - Notes on the Drafting, Interpretation and Application of the GATT, 1986.

9 For a survey of the law of international commodity agreements see, with further references to the literature: C. Tomuschat, Commodities, International Regulation of Production and Trade, in: R. Bernhardt (ed.), Encyclopedia of Public International Law, Installment 8 (1985) pp. 94 ff.

10 On UNCTAD see, with further references to the literature: M.Z. Cutajar (ed.), UNCTAD and the South-North Dialogue. The first twenty years, 1985; Final Act of UNCTAD VII, UN 1987.

such as the IMF,[11] is to support a well-functioning international monetary system and to assist in overcoming temporary balance of payments deficits which could impede the exchange of goods, services and capital among countries. The World Bank Group[12] and the numerous Regional Development Banks serve the complementary task of mobilizing and lending resources for the financing of productive investments in particular in developing countries. In addition to the various international trade and financial organizations or looser economic groups, such as the "Group of Ten" and the "Group of Twenty-Four" in the monetary field, there exist numerous other worldwide international organizations concerned with international economic relations, including the various UN bodies (e.g. ECOSOC) and UN specialized agencies (e.g. the United Nations Industrial Development Organization, the Food and Agriculture Organization).[13]

Regional economic organizations and groups have been established in increasing number and at various levels. At present, there exist more than a dozen agreements establishing free trade areas, customs unions or common markets in Western Europe, including the Benelux Economic Union, the European Communities, the European Free Trade Area (EFTA) and free trade areas among the EEC and each of the six EFTA member countries. The UN Economic Commission for Europe, the OECD and the Council for Mutual Economic Cooperation (COMECON) are interregional economic organizations, in which countries outside Europe also participate. The EEC is linked by additional agreements aiming at the progressive establishment of free trade areas or customs unions with 12 Mediterranean countries as well as with 64 African, Caribbean and Pacific Countries. But by far the largest number of regional economic organizations and groups has been agreed upon among developing countries in Africa, Latin America, the Caribbean, Asia and the Pacific. In addition to the various regional economic organizations among developing countries, there

---

11 On the IMF see, e.g.: J. Gold, Legal and Institutional Aspects of the IMF, Vol. I 1979, Vol. II 1984

12 On the World Bank see, e.g.: H. Golsong, International Bank for Reconstruction and Development, in: R. Bernhardt (ed.), Encyclopedia of Public International Law, Installment 5 (1983), pp. 58 ff; H.G. Petersmann, The World Bank's Contribution to the Law of International Finance and Development (1944-1984), in: Archiv des Völkerrechts 1985, pp. 241 ff

13 For a survey see, e.g.: H.G. Schermers et alii (eds.), International Organization and Integration. Annotated Basic Documents and Descriptive Directory of International Organizations and Arrangements, 4 volumes 1981-1983

exist also several interregional economic organizations and groups between developing countries not belonging to the same geographic region.[14]

The law and institutions of international economic organizations present numerous parallels and are confronted with similar problems. Most international economic organizations pursue the same objectives of promoting economic growth and stability by liberalizing integration methods and/or by coordination of economic interventions and planning. The liberalization of trade and of production factors is carried out on the basis of agreed multilateral substantive principles and rules. These usually make use of the classical standards of international economic law, such as the most-favoured-nation clause or the standard of "national treatment", which can be applied to states with divergent national economic and legal systems and form part of the law of most international economic organizations. The basic norms of substantive law consist of variations of principles of freedom, equality and solidarity, and display an increasing trend to complement the principles of freedom and formal equality by principles of substantive equality (e.g. preferential treatment of developing countries) and solidarity (e.g. obligations for mutual assistance and for mutual cooperation in policy areas with external effects for other states).[15] Organizations primarily aimed at coordinating domestic economic steering policies usually have only few permanent substantive legal principles and rules and rely rather on legal procedures and the setting up of institutions for discretionary policy coordination.

The functions and competences of international economic organizations typically comprise fact finding functions, limited rule-making functions (e.g. as regards implementing regulations and dispute settlement), operational, administrative and/or supervisory functions. Economic steering measures of international organizations usually go no further than the exchange of information, consultation procedures, indicative advice and planning, as well as financial incentives and conditions attached to it. Common policies, as they are typical of the EC, and the adoption of implementing rules may, however, also lead to "international legislation" enacted by economic organizations. The institutional structure is usually characterized by the following types of organs: the "general assembly"; the board-type "council" with a limited composition; the "secretariat";

---

14 For a survey see, with further references to the literature: E.U. Petersmann, International Economic Organizations and Groups, in: R. Bernhardt (ed.), Encyclopedia of Public International Law, Installment 8 (1985), pp. 161 ff

15 Cf. P. Verloren van Themaat, The Changing Structure of International Economic Law, 1981, pp. 239 ff

specialized organs and, in a few organizations, inter-parliamentary and judicial organs. The decision-making processes of the various organs reveal certain legal and institutional tendencies: the "pre-negotiation" of resolutions within and among informal groups; a trend to unanimity or "consensus" in the adoption of binding international regulations or of economic steering measures; a proliferation of subsidiary and auxiliary organs dealing with the international coordination of national economic interventions with external effects; the increasingly varied character of legal instruments used; and a considerable increase in the direct effects of international measures with regard to private persons. The administrative and operational expenses of international economic organizations are traditionally financed by contributions from the member states or, as in the case of international financial organizations and the EC, by income from own means or by international loans.

There is no "general law" of international economic organizations, but each organization has its own legal system.[16] The law of the worldwide and regional economic organizations does, however, often interact and is influenced by a certain "expansive logic" ("spill-over") of economic integration processes. Customs unions and common markets like the EEC, for example, can hardly pursue their common policies without participating in other international economic organizations such as GATT, which itself contains special provisions for free trade areas and customs unions (Article XXIV).[17] The various efficiency advantages of monetary cooperation (e.g. reduction of transaction costs and of exchange risks) have prompted most member countries of customs unions or common markets to participate also in (sub)regional monetary and financial arrangements. The progression to higher stages of economic integration may make it possible to redress regulatory deficiencies of lower forms of integration, such as the need to maintain internal trade controls within free trade areas so as to avoid "trade deflection" through imports from third countries via low-tariff members of the free trade area. But it also gives rise to additional regulatory needs. Thus, international competition rules for preventing private trade restrictions, which were not taken over from the Havana Charter (Articles 46 ff) into the GATT, were considered necessary in free trade areas (e.g. Article 15 EFTA Agreement) and even more so in common markets (e.g. Articles 85 ff EEC Treaty). The greater homogeneity of the economic and legal systems of member

---

16 Cf. H.G. Schermers, International Institutional Law, 1980; D.W. Bowett, The Law of International Institutions, 1982

17 Cf. e.g. E.U. Petersmann, Participation of the EC in GATT: International Law and Community Law Aspects, in: O'Keefe/Schermers (eds.), Mixed Agreements, 1983, pp. 167 ff

states of regional organizations may also facilitate progress beyond sectoral co-operation or mere "trade integration" by providing also for "production factor integration" and/or "economic policy integration" in the framework of the same organization. The estimate that more than a third of intra-EEC trade resulted from "net trade creation" (replacement of domestic by partner-country sources of supply) and that there seems to have been only a minor amount of "trade diversion" (replacement of foreign by partner-country sources) at the expense of third states,[18] bears out the legally recognized fact (cf. GATT Article XXIV:4) that the formation of regional economic groups need not necessarily have a negative impact on the worldwide economic system.

The achievement of the objectives of international economic organizations depends on whether their objectives, principles, rules, procedures, institutions and steering instruments form a mutually coherent system which must also be consistent with the domestic economic and legal structures of their member states. A comparative legal analysis of these "infrastructural principles", objectives, substantive legal principles and rules, steering instruments, institutions, scope of operation, dispute settlement procedures and mutual coordination reveals important shortcomings in the law of many international economic organizations. The legal gaps (e.g. for the protection of market competition), lack of coordination and insufficient conflict-solving mechanisms show that the elaboration of a more coherent worldwide "economic integration law" remains a major policy task.[19]

5. International Economic Law as a "Stratified Order"

The historical evolution of "spontaneous order" and deliberately created "directed orders" and "organizations" has led to a "stratification of rules of conduct".[20] International economic law developed first on the level of private commercial law, then on the level of public national law, and even later on the level of international bilateral and multilateral agreements among states and international organizations. Yet, the main political authority remains vested in the sovereign

18 Cf. e.g. R.C. Hine, The Political Economy of European Trade, 1985, p. 53 f; J. Pelkmans, Market Integration in the European Community, 1984, pp. 18 ff

19 See especially the study by Verloren van Themaat (supra note 15), who suggests the elaboration of a "Charter of Economic Rights and Duties of States and of their nationals" (cf. chapter V).

20 Cf. F.A. v.Hayek, Law, Legislation and Liberty, Vol. 3 (1979), p. 159 f

states. Legal guarantees for the use of transparent, non-discriminatory and proportionate policy instruments are to be found in both national and international law. This raises the question as to the relationship between these different levels of legal obligations. Like the international covenants on the protection of human rights and on the prohibition of the use of force which, in general, protect only international "minimum standards", the international legal commitments undertaken by states for the use of transparent and non-discriminatory foreign economic policy instruments can be conceived of as "essentially a reflection of national constitutional control" and "as the second line of national constitutional entrenchment".[21] In the words of J. Tumlir:

> "Reciprocal relations between national, regional and international systems of rules and orderly political processes increase the resiliency of the whole by a compound factor, on the 'plywood principle'. Broadly speaking, the closer adjustment of international and national economic order can only be brought about by securing a firmer grounding in national law for the economic-political engagements governments undertake internationally. In this way, foreign economic policy would become an explicit and systematic concern of constitutional jurisprudence. This would also imply a gradual restoration of constitutional oversight in domestic economic matters. All this would amount to a reversal, or at least substantial change, of several jurisprudential traditions of long standing. In particular, constitutional jurisprudence would have to abandon its traditional reluctance to pronounce on matters of foreign policy... foreign policy issues have become largely economic, and economic issues demand regulation by law."[22]

The present movement away from general "rule-oriented" trade and monetary policies to short-term administrative "management" of prices, market shares, exchange rates and foreign debts in a way no longer transparent to the general public, and the accompanying rise of individual and collective insecurity in international economic relations, can be seen as signs of "constitutional failure"[23] not only at the level of the international rules but also at the level of domestic legal systems. They indicate that international economic rules are often not ef-

---

21 J. Tumlir, International Economic Order and Democratic Constitutionalism, in: Ordo Jahrbuch 33 (1983), pp. 71, 80

22 Tumlir (note 21), p. 80

23 See below chapter VI and, e.g.: J. Tumlir, Clash of Security and Progress: The Constitutional Resolution, in: Ordo Jahrbuch 36 (1985), pp. 3, 8

fectively "anchored" in domestic legal systems; and that the discretionary use of "grey area trade policies" outside the agreed rules for purposes of surreptitious income redistribution is not effectively controlled by domestic legislatures and courts.[24] Yet, in spite of these mutual inconsistencies between trade practices and trade law, there is hardly any other area of international economic relations with a "stratified legal order" as dense and detailed as international trade. This "stratified nature" of the legal framework of international trade and economic relations may be illustrated with a few examples of interdependences between private and public national and international trade law.

A) Interdependences between Private and Public National Trade Law: A Historical Retrospective

The economic costs of legal uncertainty in international trade have prompted traders and governments ever since to reduce international transaction costs through general rules of law. The performance of foreign trade transactions usually requires the allocation of a large number of commercial risks which are typically regulated in contracts of sale and arrangements for the carriage, insurance, delivery and payment of goods. If sellers and buyers reside in different countries, they often prefer to avail themselves of generally recognized legal principles - such as freedom of contract, good faith, pacta sunt servanda, the applicability of commercial customs, the use of commercial corporations with separate legal personality, the resort to commercial arbitration and the recognition of commercial arbitral awards - so as to apply customary commercial and contract practices to their contractual relations rather than submitting the contract exclusively to the municipal law and domestic courts of one party to the possible disadvantage of the other foreign party. Despite wide differences among national legal systems, contract practices for the export and import of goods exhibit a high degree of uniformity and, with the legal recognition of them as optional rules in national domestic laws, have given rise to uniform principles of private transnational commercial law.[25]

The widespread cartelization of world trade between the two world wars by means of private market-regulating agreements, as well as the risks of abuses

24 On the redistributive nature of trade policy as a means of surreptitious income redistribution see, e.g.: G. Banks/J. Tumlir, The Political Problem of Adjustment, in: The World Economy 1986, pp. 141 ff

25 Cf., e.g.: N. Horn/C. Schmitthoff (eds.), The Transnational Law of International Commercial Transactions, 1982

inherent in privately agreed applicable law clauses and in forum or arbitration clauses as a means for escaping domestic contract laws, corporation, tax or industrial property laws, illustrate, however, also the need to limit private party autonomy by mandatory rules of national and international public order (ordre public). In medieval Europe, the commercial customs (coutumes) evolved into international uniform principles of equity and mercantile law often administered by merchants themselves in speedy and informal procedures and derived from various elements: usages and customs of the large international fairs which were regularly held throughout Europe; the rise of banking, foreign exchange and commercial arbitration; the institution of the "staple" which channelled commerce through governmentally-controlled staple places; the commercial leagues of cities such as the Hanseatic League which included over 70 cities; the general codes regulating maritime law, e.g. the laws of Oleron (circa 1150), Wisby (circa 1350) and the Consolato del Mare of Barcelona (14th century); and, from the 16th century onwards, the dominance of about a hundred joint-stock and chartered companies carrying out international trade (such as the English, Dutch and French East India companies), often vested with sovereign powers, trade monopolies or privileges and functionally operating as a substitute for a governmental trade policy.

From about the 17th century, the medieval **lex mercatoria**, which had not only been a **jus mercatorum** but often also customary law approved by governmental authorities, became increasingly "nationalized" and incorporated into the national codifications of commercial laws in several European countries, such as Colbert's Ordonnance sur le commerce (1673) and the Ordonnance de la marine (1681) in France. In England, the law merchant continued to be recognized as a universal body of law separate from common law and equity until 1756 when, under Lord Mansfield Chief Justice of the King's Bench and specially created juries of merchants, the customary merchant and maritime law was recognized as an integral part of English common law. Various kinds of systematic codifications emerged from the 18th century onwards: partial codifications such as the English Bills of Exchange Act (1882) and the Sale of Goods Act (1893); comprehensive codifications of commercial law such as the French Code de commerce (1807) and the German Allgemeines Deutsches Handelsgesetzbuch (1861); or systematic civil law codifications, such as the Swiss Obligationenrecht (1910), which regulate commercial transactions as part of civil law. The national commercial laws often elaborated on the contents of the old law merchant and on established international commercial customs.[26]

Modern private transnational commercial law is characterized by new types of commercial customs and standard contracts, by an increasing number of national foreign trade legislation and government procurement practices prescribing the terms of the contracts, and the influence of intergovernmental and private "formulating agencies" of international trade law, such as the United Nations Commission on International Trade Law or the International Chamber of Commerce, which elaborate international conventions, standard contracts, model laws and commercial usages relating to the international sale of goods, international payments and credits, arbitration and shipping regulations.[27] The largely depoliticized principles of transnational law, founded on the principle of the autonomy of the parties' will and its recognition as optional law in the various national legal systems, increasingly replace the traditional national rules of private international law in the conflict of laws sense (which aim at "nationalizing" the dispute by localizing the "seat of the obligation" and consigning the case to one single municipal law system) by uniform substantive principles of commercial law and arbitration.

B) Interdependences between Public National and International Trade Law

The foreign economic policy instruments used by states during the time of mercantilism included not only tariffs but also a variety of non-tariff trade barriers such as trade monopolies, state-trading enterprises, variable import levies, quantitative restrictions, navigation acts and "power-oriented" colonial policies. Yet, during the liberal trade era between the Cobden-Chevalier trade agreement between England and France and the outbreak of World War I, tariffs were the main trade policy instrument used by most European states. Quantitative trade restrictions were rather rare. The first world war led in many European states to the introduction of non-tariff trade barriers and to the establishment of large governmental bureaucracies for the regulation and administration of foreign economic policies. The non-tariff trade barriers were often maintained after the end of the war, and were intensified throughout the 1930s.[28]

---

26 Cf.,e.g.: C.M. Schmitthoff, Commercial Law in a Changing Economic Climate, 1981, p. 6 f

27 Cf., e.g.: C.M. Schmitthoff (note 26), pp. 24 ff

28 For a historical survey see, e.g.: G. Curzon, Multilateral Commercial Diplomacy, 1965, pp. 20 ff

Systematic national foreign trade legislation committing states to the use of transparent, non-discriminatory and economically efficient trade policy instruments without harmful effects on other countries was introduced in most states only after their accession to the GATT in the context of the implementation of their GATT obligations. Under the influence of the United States, many GATT provisions were drafted on the basis of provisions which had been used in the national foreign trade legislation of the United States as well as in the more than 30 trade agreements concluded by the United States under the authority granted in the US Reciprocal Trade Agreements Act of 1934. While the GATT was negotiated and accepted by the United States under the 1945 renewal of this Reciprocal Trade Agreements Act, its international acceptance and incorporation into the domestic law of the United States has had a far-reaching impact on US foreign trade law and on the respective roles of the US Congress and the US President in the conduct of US foreign trade policy. According to J. Jackson,[29] the conduct of foreign trade policy in the framework of GATT as the only worldwide multilateral trade agreement resulted in a substantial shift of trade policy power away from Congress to the US President. Within US domestic law, Parts I and III of GATT are considered to be superior to pre-GATT federal legislation. GATT law is considered directly applicable to state and local governments in the United States, and to supersede all state and local law.[30] In the European Community, the international GATT obligations of the EEC are recognized to form an "integral part of European Community law", thereby taking precedence over inconsistent national foreign trade regulations of EEC member states.[31] The various general EEC regulations on the common customs tariff, on the valuation of goods for customs purposes, on common rules for imports and exports, for the protection against dumped or subsidized imports as well as on other trade protective measures are explicitly designed to implement GATT law and to incorporate the relevant GATT rules into European foreign trade law.[32]

---

29 J.H. Jackson in: Jackson/Louis/Matsushita, Implementing the Tokyo Round. National Constitutions and International Economic Rules, 1984, p. 145

30 See: J.H. Jackson, The General Agreement on Tariffs and Trade in United States Domestic Law, in: Michigan Law Review 1967, pp. 250, 312

31 Cf., e.g., U. Everling, Das Recht in den internationalen Wirtschaftsbeziehungen der EWG, p. 187, and C.D. Ehlermann, Die innergemeinschaftliche Anwendung der Regeln des GATT in der Praxis der EG, p. 220, in: Hilf/Petersmann (eds.), GATT und Europäische Gemeinschaft, 1985

32 Cf. E.U. Petersmann, International and European Foreign Trade Law: GATT Dispute Settlement Proceedings Against the EEC, in: Common Market Law Review 1985, pp. 441, 463 f

The many interrelationships between national and international public trade and economic law are particularly evident in the law of regional economic organizations. Verloren van Themaat's comparative analysis of the law of international economic organizations has shown close interrelations between the objectives and legal principles of regional economic organizations and the economic and legal systems of their member states.[33] For example, the centralized national economic planning in COMECON member states inevitably leads to emphasis on national economic sovereignty and to the rejection of legally binding majority decisions by international organizations with regard to subject matters regulated by national central planning. The market economies and parliamentary democracies of EEC member states are reflected in EEC law in permanent legal guarantees for the "five economic freedoms" (in trade, services, movement of persons, payments and capital transfers), in the European competition law, the independent supranational EC Commission and parliamentary and judicial Community organs, as well as in the fact that countries without a parliamentary democracy are excluded from membership. The less developed economic, political and legal infrastructures of developing countries often led to a fragile legal and institutional suprastructure of their regional economic organizations, which are not merely aimed at promoting mutual trade and industrialization but are often motivated also by political considerations such as "collective self-reliance" and the strengthening of the bargaining power of developing countries. Differences in the law and institutions of economic organizations are thus often explainable in terms of differences in their respective national infrastructure, especially as regards the domestic legal, economic and political systems of their respective member states.

C) Interdependences between Private and Public International Trade Law

During the 1930s, between 30 and 40% of world trade were estimated to be influenced by cartels.[34] This development of extensive "international private economic orders" (H. Kronstein) and the cartelization of international commerce were accomplished primarily through the use of the international and national law of contracts, the choice of forum (e.g. courts of hospitable countries like England and Germany) and arbitration courts, the use of international cor-

33 See: Verloren van Themaat (note 15), pp. 327 ff

34 Cf. J.A. Rahl, pp. 246 ff, in: Schachter/Hellawell (eds.), Competition in International Business, 1981

poration law and of the national and international law of industrial property.[35] Many of these private market regulations, such as export cartels, private "voluntary export restraints" (VERs) or cartelistic practices of shipping conferences, were induced or tolerated by governments and explicitly exempted from the US antitrust laws.[36] After World War II, formal private world cartels of the pre-war type rapidly declined in number primarily because of the impact of US antitrust law, German and EEC competition law.[37]

Chapter V of the Havana Charter for an International Trade Organization of 1948 explicitly condemned "business practices affecting international trade which restrain competition, limit access to markets, or foster monopolistic control", as specified in Article 46, and set out detailed obligations of member states to prevent such restrictive business practices. But the Havana Charter never entered into force, and the GATT provisions did not explicitly deal with restrictive business practices. The GATT arrangements adopted in 1960 for consultations on restrictive business practices[38] were hardly ever applied. The OECD Council Recommendation of 1978 concerning action against restrictive business practices affecting international trade explicitly recognized "that the solution to these difficulties cannot at present be found in an international convention establishing control of restrictive business practices affecting international trade owing mainly to the still differing attitudes adopted by countries towards restrictive business practices and in particular to their varying national legislations in this field".[39] Also the "Set of Multilaterally Agreed Equitable Principles and Rules for the Control of Restrictive Business Practices", negotiated in a UN Conference on Restrictive Business Practices, was adopted only in the legally non-mandatory form of a recommendation by the UN General Assembly of 1980.[40]

Notwithstanding the explicit objective of this UN "Code" to "ensure that restrictive business practices do not impede or negate the realization of benefits that should arise from the liberalization of tariff and non-tariff barriers affecting

---

35 Cf. H. Kronstein, The Law of International Cartels, 1973, pp. 4, 447 ff

36 Cf. Kronstein (note 35), pp. 9 ff, 30

37 Cf. J.A. Rahl (note 34), pp. 247 ff

38 See: GATT Basic Instruments and Selected Documents 9th Supplement, 1961, pp. 28 f, 170 ff

39 Text in: OECD, International Investment and Multinational Enterprises, 1979, pp. 65 ff

40 Text in: UN Doc. TD/RBP/10, Rev. 1 (1981)

world trade",[41] the Code exempted "intergovernmental agreements or restrictive business practices directly caused by such agreements" (section B, para. 9) and has not prevented "the growing use of restrictive business practices as a protectionist device in international trade transactions".[42] The national antitrust laws, especially of the United States and Germany, as well as the competition law of the EEC, remain the major and most effective methods for eliminating those restrictive business practices that are not supported by governments.[43] Even though, according to the "territoriality principle" of international law, the binding force of legislative, executive and judicial acts of a state is confined to the territory of the state that issues them, American, German and European competition law assert jurisdiction also for their "extraterritorial" application to international restraints of competition with anticompetitive effects on their domestic economic order. For instance, in the decision by the EC Commission on the dyestuffs cartel,[44] which was subsequently confirmed by the European Court of Justice, the Commission has applied the prohibition of cartels in Article 85 of the EEC Treaty to a concerting of prices between EC firms and non-EC firms although the concerting had taken place outside the EEC (but related to prices charged within the EEC).

The "extraterritorial" application of domestic antitrust laws and related law enforcement measures have given rise to legal controversies in both national and international law over whether, and to what extent, the "effects principle" or other legal principles (e.g. the "principle of active nationality") can actually justify such antitrust jurisdiction and subject to what limits (e.g. respect for prevailing foreign interests). Most authors recognize today, and state practice seems to confirm, that the right of several states to regulate the same international restrictive business practice entails a legal obligation under customary international law to balance the interests of all states involved.[45] Both the OECD

41 See: Section A - Objectives (note 40), p. 6

42 See: Report of the UN Conference to Review all Aspects of the Set of Multilaterally Agreed Equitable Principles and Rules for the Control of Restrictive Business Practices, UN 1985, p. 8

43 For a survey of government-supported restraints of competition (such as VERs and national export cartels) see: Competition and Trade Policies. Their Interaction, OECD 1984, pp. 85 ff

44 The decision is published in the official journal of the EC No. L 195 of 7 August 1969, p. 11

45 Cf. e.g. K.M. Meessen, Antitrust Jurisdiction under Customary International Law, in: American Journal of International Law 1984, pp. 783 ff; W. Meng, Admissibility and Limits of Extraterritorial Jurisdiction under Public International Law, in: Zeitschrift für ausländi-

Recommendation and the UN Code for Restrictive Business Practices appear to corroborate this interest balancing requirement and may help in resolving such jurisdictional conflicts and the regulatory problems resulting from the discrepancy between the territorial limits of state jurisdiction and the worldwide reach of transnational enterprises. As an expression of internationally agreed principles and rules, even legally non-binding international "codes of conduct" may effectively contribute to the resolution of "conflicts of law" relating to international business practices. The draft UN Code of Conduct for the Transfer of Technology goes even a step further in providing not only for framework rules for the conduct of governments and for antitrust rules aimed at protecting market competition, but also for international minimum standards for the content of private contracts for transfer of technology.[46] Since the protection and regulation of economic markets and of legal contracts are complementary objectives, this regulatory approach is in principle to be welcomed. Yet, after more than 10 years of negotiations on this UN Code, many provisions of the present draft (notably in chapter 4 on restrictive business practices and in chapter 9 on applicable law and settlement of disputes) continue to be controversial.[47]

sches öffentliches Recht und Völkerrecht 1984, pp. 675 ff (in German with English Summary)

46 For the most recent text see: Un Doc. TD/CODE/TOT/47 (1985).

47 See: Negotiations on a Draft International Code of Conduct on the Transfer of Technology, TD/CODE/TOT/51 (1987); A. Yusuf, The UN Code of Conduct on Transfer of Technology, in: D. Dicke/E.U. Petersmann (eds.), Foreign Trade in the Present and a new International Economic Order, 1988.

III. INTERNATIONAL ECONOMIC ORDER AND INTERNATIONAL ECONOMIC LAW

1. Different Kinds of "Order" and of Law

In a general sense, an "order" may be described by the regularity of the interactions among its elements and by the possibility to form reasonably correct expectations regarding their future behaviour.[1] The existence of two different kinds of social order and of the risk of disorder, because the two different kinds of order cannot be mixed in any manner one likes, was illustrated by Adam Smith with the following example:

> "The man of system... seems to imagine that he can arrange the different members of a great society with as much ease as the hand arranges the different pieces upon a chessboard. He does not consider that the pieces upon the chessboard have no other principle of motion besides that which the hand impresses upon them; but that, in the great chessboard of human society, every single piece has a principle of motion of its own, altogether different from that which the legislature might choose to impress upon it. If those two principles coincide and act in the same direction, the game of human society will go on easily and harmoniously, and is very likely to be happy and successful. If they are opposite or different, the game will go on miserably and human society must be at all times in the highest degree of disorder."[2]

Political, economic and legal liberalism proceed from the discovery of self-generating "spontaneous orders" in social affairs, which result from rule-oriented free actions of individuals and make it possible to use their individual knowledge and utility-maximizing abilities to a much greater extent than would be possible through any deliberate "organization" designed to direct individual activities according to the plan and commands of a central authority. In every society, "spontaneous orders" (e.g. economic and political markets) and deliberate "organizations" (e.g. the family, the farm, firms, the government) will regularly coexist (e.g. "black markets" in communist countries). But their respective

1 Cf. F.A. v.Hayek, Law, Legislation and Liberty, Vol. I (1979), p. 36: "By 'order' we shall throughout describe a state of affairs in which a multiplicity of elements of various kinds are so related to each other that we may learn from our acquaintance with some spatial or temporal part of the whole to form correct expectations concerning the rest, or at least expectations which have a good chance of proving correct."

2 A. Smith, The Theory of Moral Sentiment (1759), Part 6, chapter 2, penultimate paragraph.

rules and regulatory functions are different and may mutually conflict with each other. Adam Smith emphasized already that the spontaneous order of a liberal society, which leaves individuals free to use their own knowledge for their own purposes, requires the legal protection of equal freedoms and property rights of citizens and, in addition to this "law enforcement function" of constitutionally limited governments, the supply of certain "public goods" (as defense, public works and schools, administration of justice).[3] Rules governing a "spontaneous order" must be abstract (i.e. independent of a concrete purpose), general (i.e. applicable to an unknown number of persons and instances) and aimed at an order, the particular contents and results are not known by anyone because of the individual freedom of action and of the individual adaptation to a large number of particular facts which are not known in their totality to anyone. In contrast to the general rules of such spontaneous "invisible hand order", which is "the result of human action, but not of human design" (v.Hayek), rules of "organization" are characterized by commands determining the common purposes to be achieved, the function to be performed by each member, and rules for the performance of assigned tasks.[4]

Any endeavour to turn all or part of a spontaneous market order into a deliberate organization of economic activities serving agreed common ends (e.g. "stable and remunerative commodity prices") is therefore confronted with serious "organizational problems" at the level of both national and international law, such as:

a) Will it be possible to overcome the **legal problems** of imposing on the economic agents concrete common purposes and obligations for particular actions and to limit their individual freedoms and property rights accordingly (e.g. worldwide enforcement of production and trade quotas for the stabilization of a commodity price)?

b) Will it be possible to overcome the **political problems** of establishing and controlling such regulatory powers in compliance with the constitutional requirements of the parliamentary democracies of OECD States,

3 Cf. A. Smith, An Inquiry into the Nature and Causes of the Wealth of Nations (1776), Modern Library Edition 1965, p. 651. On A. Smith's concept of constitutional democracy see, e.g.: E.G. West, in: G.P. O'Driscoll (ed.), Adam Smith and Modern Political Economy, 1979, pp. 132 ff; E.J. Mestmäcker, Die sichtbare Hand des Rechts, 1978, pp. 139 ff.

4 Cf. v.Hayek (note 1), p. 49; v.Hayek, Studies in Philosophy, Politics and Economics, 1967, pp. 96 ff; E.J. Mestmäcker, Regelbildung und Rechtsschutz in Marktwirtschaftlichen Ordnungen, 1985, S. 5 ff.

which account for more than 60% of international economic activities (e.g. parliamentary and judicial control of the international management of commodity prices and buffer stocks)?

c) Will it be possible to overcome **the information processing problems** resulting from the fact that only spontaneous market prices can constantly process all the individual knowledge dispersed among all market participants, which is not given to any "organizer" in its totality (as illustrated by the bankruptcy in 1985 of the international buffer stock for tin), and that "price stabilization" renders ineffective the various economic functions of prices to inform about incipient scarcities or surpluses anywhere in the world, to ensure that goods are produced in the most efficient and least costly way practicable, and to act as an incentive for adjusting and balancing supply and demand in response to constantly changing conditions?[5]

d) Will it be possible to overcome the **behavioural problem of any "social engineering"** that individual economic agents do not react to (inter)governmental policies in a "Pavlovian manner" but on utility-maximizing decisions of their own, so that the actual behavioural incentives, effects and repercussions of e.g. foreign trade and monetary regulations are often very different from those intended (see the frequent circumvention of trade embargoes and trade quotas prescribed by commodity agreements)?[6]

e) Will the particular "organization" of economic activities meet the **general systemic problem** that the effectiveness of any organization depends

5 Cf. F.A. v.Hayek, The Use of Knowledge in Society, in: American Economic Review XXXV (1945) pp. 519 f: "The peculiar character of the problem of a rational economic order is determined precisely by the fact that the knowledge of the circumstances of which we must make use, never exists in concentrated or integrated form but solely as the dispersed bits of incomplete and frequently contradictory knowledge which all the separate individuals possess. The economic problem of society is thus not merely a problem of how to allocate 'given' resources - if 'given' is taken to mean given to a single mind which deliberately solves the problem set by these 'data'. It is rather a problem of how to secure the best use of resources known to any of the members of society for ends whose relative importance only these individuals know. Or, to put it briefly, it is a problem of the utilization of knowledge which is not given to anyone in its totality."

6 On the game-theoretical nature of the relations between governments and laws, on the one side, and utility-maximizing private economic agents, on the other side, who react to changes in economic conditions or in legal regulations not only in the economic market (as producers, consumers, traders) but also in the "political market" (as voter, lobbies etc), see e.g.: B.S. Frey, Democratic Economic Policy, 1983.

on its compatibility with the overall, predominantly decentralized "spontaneous order" of the world economy (e.g. high price guarantees for natural commodities as an economic incentive for synthetic substitute products)?

2. The Notion of "International Economic Order"

The international exchange of goods, services and capital requires an order that permits private and public economic actors to form reasonably correct expectations regarding future economic transactions and government interventions in the economy. **"Spontaneous orders"** grow out of practices without an initial overall design. The international monetary system of the gold standard before 1914, for instance, rested upon autonomous national regulations in the principal trading nations and - through free convertibility of currencies into gold and freedom of payments and capital transfers - provided for stable exchange rates and balance of payments adjustments. **"Directed orders"** are deliberately created by agreements, such as the agreements establishing the IMF, the World Bank and the GATT. The distinction between "spontaneous" and "directed" economic orders is blurred due to the fact that even carefully negotiated multilateral treaty systems, like the IMF and the GATT, often evolve by pragmatic rule adaptations in response to changing circumstances and rely on spontaneous market coordination between autonomous specialized activities.

Attempts to direct the international economy deliberately may be made through long-term principles, rules and institutions (**"framework policy"**) or short-term flexible steering instruments and discretionary decisions aimed at influencing prices and quantitative developments (**"process policy"**). They may be undertaken by private and public actors and may make use of a variety of legal and extra-legal instruments. These include private international law, such as the old **lex mercatoria** within the Hanseatic League of cities in the 13th century, or the modern law merchant of Eurocurrency transactions; public national law and governmental measures, whose application to transnational economic activities may give rise to "conflicts of law" and "countervailing measures" by adversely affected states which make necessary rules on the limits of extraterritorial jurisdiction; international agreements, institutions or informal arrangements aimed at reconciling conflicting national interests and at enabling governments to pursue their economic and other self-interests in an interdependent world economy.

The law of the "international economic order" can thus be viewed as a **three-tiered regulatory structure** on the levels of private law, national public law and international public law for the steering of international trade in goods and services, international movements of production factors (labour, "capital", transfer of technology) and the exchange of national currencies. The term "international economic order" may be used as a factual concept referring to the reality and interacting elements of the international economy, such as actual patterns of production, consumption and distribution. As a legal concept, the term international economic order relates to the legal principles, rules and institutions which shape the factual international economic order and which, by promoting legal security and reducing international transaction costs, contribute to an efficient allocation of resources. Since the factual international economic order and its legal framework are never perfect, the term international economic order is also used to denote ideal orders or theories of a satisfactorily functioning international economy, that may permit improvements in the factual and legal international economic order so that it forms a coherent system capable of achieving agreed objectives in an orderly fashion.

The central problem of all social orders can be seen in the problem of how dynamic change and disorder on the small scale can be made compatible with order on the large scale, in time and in space. Constant change in supply, demand, technology and in the relative efficiency of competing suppliers are a fundamental fact of the modern world economy. Most economic problems arise because something changes (e.g. the supply of a commodity or the discovery of new uses for it) and because adjustments have to be made in the constantly moving world economy even though neither producers nor governments have complete knowledge of all relevant facts. Economic growth consists essentially of innovation and adjustment to it permitting a continuous movement of resources from lower to higher productivity uses. "Dynamic stability" of any social order depends on its capacity to accommodate orderly change. The main function of the international price system and market competition is to act as decentralized information, coordination and incentive systems for directing resources into their most productive uses and, thereby, to create "order" in the sense of continuous adjustment to change. A main function of international trade and monetary restrictions can be seen as the prevention of the adjustment pressures generated from market competition, or their reduction to politically acceptable levels. The major function of the liberal international economic agreements (such as GATT, the IMF and the World Bank Agreement) can be seen in assisting governments in the pursuit of transparent, non-discriminatory and welfare-increasing foreign economic policies promoting the continuous adjustment of national economies to the ever changing international division of labour. Due to the many "horizontal" and "vertical" interdependences among national and international economic rules and processes, the national and international trade and monetary rules have to be closely adjusted to each other; for the various instruments of trade and payments restrictions are largely interchangeable.

3. Basic Elements of an Economic Theory of International Economic Order

A) Need for Decentralized Regulatory Mechanisms

The 1970s were a decade of almost continuous multilateral negotiations on reforms of the international economic order. They showed that, in contrast to the relatively stable international economic order existing before 1914 and in part reconstructed during the 1940s, neither states nor economists continued to agree on how to devise and actually implement an economically rational overall order of the world economy. Just as the efforts during the 1920s to restore the liberal pre-war international economic order were unsuccessful, the decade of inflation, unemployment and stagnation after 1973 revealed an increasing inability of states to maintain and respect the legal disciplines of the liberal "GATT-IMF system" which, up to 1973, had enabled a quarter-century of unprecedented economic growth and prosperity of the international economy. The breakdown of the IMF system of fixed parities and exchange rates indicated that, among countries without national monetary stability and with high and differing rates of inflation, stable exchange rates and international monetary stability are no longer feasible. The inflation and exchange rate fluctuations also reduced the value of international prices as an information-mechanism indicating relative scarcities and investment opportunities. The basic GATT rules on non-discrimination (e.g. Articles I:1, XIII, XXIV), prohibition of quantitative restrictions (e.g. Articles XI) as well as of export subsidies (Article XVI:B) were increasingly ignored or evaded. Government support for export cartels and "orderly marketing arrangements" increased, reflecting a mercantilist identification of governments with "their" export industries; and, as Jan Tumlir remarked, the increasing concern of national competition authorities and international commercial diplomacy about "just prices" seems to take up a search which the catholic church had to give up at the end of the middle ages.[7]

Today, the ambitious idea of "global negotiations" on a global strategy for a "New International Economic Order" is widely recognized as unrealistic in view of the different national economic and legal systems of the more than 170 sovereign states.[8] Due to the international law principle of national sovereignty, each individual state will have to decide autonomously on what international legal disciplines it is willing to voluntarily accept as being in its national self-interest. Economic theory does not provide a practicable theory for a "global management" of the world economy. Yet, it can usefully assist each state in its decision-making on its national foreign economic policy.

Thus, there is today broad agreement among economists that each nation, regardless of its national economic system and stage of development, can benefit from exploiting the economic gains from - multilateral or even unilateral - trade liberalization.[9] Economists also tend to agree that the mutually welfare-improving gains from the liberalization of barriers to trade in goods - such as more efficient production enabling increased output and wider consumer choice - will arise in a similar manner also from freer trade in services.[10] The opening of a new "GATT Round" of multilateral trade negotiations in September 1986 for the liberalization of trade in goods and services and its political support in the Final Act of UNCTAD VII adopted in August 1987 reflect a renewed worldwide political commitment to translate these economic insights into political action. Like all voluntary exchanges, international movements of production factors (labour, capital) take place voluntarily only if they are considered to be be-

---

7 See: J. Tumlir, Die Weltwirtschaftsordnung heute, in: Zwischenbilanz der Diskussion über eine neue Weltwirtschaftsordnung, 1981, pp. 9 ff 18.

8 On the inconsistencies and regulatory gaps of the 1974 "Charter of Economic Rights and Duties of States" and its controversial adoption by a majority resolution of the UN General Assembly see for instance: E.U. Petersmann, Charter of Economic Rights and Duties of States, in: R. Bernhardt (ed.), Encyclopedia of Public International Law, Installment 8 (1985), pp. 71 ff.

9 See, for instance, the contributions (especially by M. Corden, A.O. Krueger and R.E. Baldwin) to: Jones/Kenen, Handbook of International Economics, Vol. I 1984, and the contributions (notably by M. Wolf) to: Finger/Olechowski (eds.), The Uruguay Round. A Handbook on the Multilateral Trade Negotiations, The World Bank 1987.

10 See, e.g.: J. Bhagwati, International Trade in Services and its Relevance for Economic Development, 1986, p. 25 f; R.J. Krommenacker, World-Traded Services: The Challenge of the Eighties, 1984, pp. 33 ff ("most trade theorists take it for granted that comparative advantage applies equally to goods and services").

neficial to all partners involved in the transaction.[11] There is also broad agreement among economists that fixed exchange rates are not feasible in the presence of divergent national monetary policies and inflation rates, and that large international capital movements are a necessary condition of a dynamic equilibrium in a world economy with large national balance-of-payments imbalances and different stages of national development. Yet, there is less agreement among economists on whether, since a country's exchange rate can be considered as the relative price of different national monies, freely floating[12] or "managed"[13] exchange rates represent the optimal **market-conforming system** for both developed and developing countries; and to what extent capital controls, even if detrimental to world economic welfare, may be beneficial to the national economic welfare of individual countries;[14] and to what extent not only "market integration" but also "policy integration" may be expected to increase the national economic welfare (e.g. in terms of consumption levels of domestic citizens) of participating countries.[15]

---

11 See, e.g.: M.B. Krauss, The New Protectionism, 1978, p. 43: "Since guest workers can be thought of as but another way in which countries trade with one another, the neoclassical idea of the 'gains from trade' can be applied to the guest worker phenomenon." D. Lal, A Liberal International Economic Order: The International Monetary System and Economic Development, 1980, p. 4: "If nationals are willing without coercion to exchange their rights from local assets for those from foreign assets, both sides to the bargain have presumably gained. Hence, from an economic viewpoint, the fear of foreigners' buying up local assets would not be rational."

12 In this sense: Lal (note 11), p. 2.

13 See: W.M. Corden, The Logic of the International Monetary Non-System, in: F. Machlup et alii (eds.), Reflections on a Troubled World Economy. Essays in Honours of H. Giersch, 1983, pp. 59, 71 ff: "The current laissez-faire international monetary system is simply a market system which coordinates the decentralized decisions reached by private and public actors and is likely to be as efficient in this as the market system is within the domestic economy. In formal terms one might make the assumption that when governments intervene in the foreign exchange market and when they practice their monetary and fiscal policies they are trying to maximize a national social welfare function in the same way as households are presumed to be maximizing a utility function and firms are presumed to be efficiently maximizing profits".

14 Cf., e.g.: A. Lamfalussy, Changing attitudes towards capital movements, in: A. Cairncross (ed.), Changing Perceptions of Economic Policy, 1981, pp. 194 ff.

15 See, e.g.: H.G. Johnson in: Johnson/Wonnacott/Shibata, Harmonization of National Economic Policies under Free Trade, 1968, who concludes "that the need for harmonization additional to what is already required of countries extensively engaged in world trade is relatively slight". On the economic and political advantages of "competition among economic policies" see e.g.: R. Vaubel, Coordination or Competition Among National Macro-Economic Policies? in: F. Machlup et alii (note 13), pp. 3 ff, who argues that "competition among national stabilization policies is in fact preferable to coordination because competition provides a public good which coordination fails to provide" (p. 15)... "rational politicians and bureaucrats have an incentive and the power in a democracy to act against the

B) The Economic Theory of "Optimal Intervention"

From the **national perspective** of maximizing the national economic welfare, the economic theory of "optimal intervention" teaches that a country's alternative corrective policies for remedying a distortion in its national economy can be ranked according to their efficiency in correcting the "market imperfection" (e.g. a monopoly, "external effects") or the policy-induced market distortions (e.g. inflation).[16] There is broad agreement among economists today that "the link between the case for free trade and the case for laissez-faire has been broken":[17] If a government intervention in the national economy is called for - be it to eliminate domestic market distortions or to pursue political objectives considered more important than market efficiency - domestic interventions directly at, or as close as possible to, the relevant distortion usually achieve the goal more efficiently than import restrictions, which reduce the national gains from trade and introduce additional macroeconomic distortions. Thus a production subsidy should deal with a production distortion (e.g. in case of "infant industries), a consumption tax with a consumption distortion (e.g. in case of "external effects" or socially undesirable luxury goods), and competition policy with competitive distortions (e.g. monopolies). Standard economic analysis recognizes only a few narrowly defined exceptions where "optimal tariffs", "infant industry protection" or "strategic protection" of oligopolistic industry might theoretically improve national welfare. But these exceptional conditions are difficult to establish in practice and are hardly ever actually ascertained in decision-making about trade.[18] As Professor Jan Tumlir from the GATT Secretariat

interest of the majority of their voters, let alone the welfare of society at large. What is only gradually coming to be known is that international collusion strengthens this power" (p. 18). R. Komiya, Is International Coordination of National Economic Policies Necessary? in: P. Oppenheimer (ed.), Issues in International Economics, 1980, pp. 16, 32, concludes: "Decisions to set national targets for rates of economic growth, unemployment and inflation should be regarded as a matter lying outside the domain of international coordination, since they depend crucially on domestic political and social factors with which other governments or a multilateral body are not familiar, and the latter are not responsible for the political consequences of choosing a particular set of targets".

16 See, e.g.: H.G. Johnson, Optimal Trade Intervention in the Presence of Domestic Distortions, in: R. Baldwin et alii (eds.), Trade, Growth and the Balance of Payments, 1965; J.N. Bhagwati, The Generalized Theory of Distortions and Welfare, in: J. Bhagwati et alii, Trade, Balance of Payments and Growth, 1971; W.M. Corden, Trade Policy and Economic Welfare, 1974; Blackhurst/Marian/Tumlir, Trade Liberalization, Protectionism and Interdependence, GATT 1977, pp. 29 ff.

17 Corden (note 16), p. 4.

18 See, e.g.: A.O. Krueger, Foreign Trade Regimes and Economic Development: Liberalization Attempts and Consequences, 1978; W.M. Corden, Policies Towards Market Disturbance, in: R.H. Snape (ed.), Issues in World Trade Policy, 1986, pp. 121 ff.

put it, all economic arguments for trade protection "are essentially theoretical curiosities. Not only that the conditions postulated appear... to be exceedingly rare. They are impossible to ascertain, in the predictive sense, with any degree of reliability in practice".[19]

C) Efficient Allocation of Resources

From the **global perspective** of the efficiency and proper functioning of the international economy as a whole, the regulatory tasks of the international economic order may be subdivided - in accordance with the traditional distinction of "allocation", "stabilization" and "distribution" - into: (a) promotion of an efficient allocation of the world's scarce resources of manpower, capital and natural resources so as to maximize the satisfaction of consumer preferences by minimizing costs; (b) coordination of decentralized economic activities without excessive price fluctuations and business cycles that may adversely affect the allocative efficiency of market prices; and (c) an equitable distribution of benefits and costs. The two value judgments underlying these three broad objectives - the need for economic efficiency and distributive equity - have been universally recognized in numerous legal instruments and UN resolutions. Given the decentralized legal structure of the international economic order with its more than 170 sovereign states and millions of private economic actors, the central regulatory task consists in establishing incentives and disincentives to guide the self-interested conduct of individuals, enterprises and states in a way conducive to the achievement of these economic objectives.

According to economic theory, undistorted competition is the most efficient allocator of society's resources unless there are "market imperfections" (such as monopolies and "external effects") or a demand for "public goods" that cannot be produced on the open market. Even though in reality "perfect competition" hardly ever exists, many advantages of the spontaneous price mechanism and of competition as a discovery procedure do not rest on their being "perfect" in any way. No country is rich enough to disregard economic efficiency or renounce the economic gains from liberal trade. Whereas sovereign states have different perceptions as to their internal national economic regulations and policies, the external policy objective of expansion and gradual liberalization of international trade and payments has become universally recognized since 1944 (Article I of

19 J. Tumlir, GATT Rules and Community Law - A comparison of their economic and legal functions, in: Hilf/Jacobs/Petersmann (eds.), European Community and GATT, 1986, p. 3.

the IMF Agreement, preamble of the GATT). Its pursuit requires two sets of trade and monetary rules that must be carefully dovetailed, since trade and monetary restrictions are largely interchangeable (cf. Article XV of GATT). The international trade and monetary rules should be non-discriminatory so as to prevent the allocation of resources pursuant to comparative advantages from being distorted for the benefit of less productive interest groups (Articles I, III, XIII and XVII of GATT). From an economic point of view, an optimal worldwide exploitation of the gains from the international division of labour would require free movement of goods, services, persons, freedom of payments and capital transfers, as well as guarantees of other "constitutive legal principles" of market competition such as antitrust rules, private property, freedom of contract, freedom of profession, personal liability, non-discrimination and monetary stability.

D) Coordination and "Dynamic Stability"

If economic order is equated with unobstructed adjustment to continuously changing economic conditions, the international economic order cannot efficiently function unless it is based on essentially liberal principles. For only where the price system quickly transmits information about incipient scarcities or surpluses anywhere in the world and the economic actors dispose of economic freedoms and property rights enabling them to engage in a continuous process of innovation and adjustment, can the world economy remain in a state of "dynamic stability". Liberal trade and currency convertibility connect national price systems into an international price system which is an information-processing mechanism and a decentralized coordination and sanctioning system indispensable for the economic efficiency and stability of the international economic order. The history of "government failure", for instance in the steering of international agricultural markets, confirms that governmental bureaucracies and international economic coordination through political negotiations cannot process, disseminate and bring to bear the economic informations from the millions of international economic actors as efficiently as decentralized markets continuously do.

Market competition cannot function without legal guarantees of economic freedoms, property rights and contract law as legal prerequisites of voluntary economic exchange. The existence of "market failures" and "government failures" also necessitates legal rules preventing the abuse of these rights and protecting competition against both private and governmental restraints. From the worldwide perspective of the international economic order, there is increasing awareness that neither macroeconomic theory nor "intergovernmental management without economic theory" offer satisfactory solutions for macroeconomic stabilization policies, and that microeconomic market coordination remains of decisive importance also for macroeconomic regulatory tasks. The system of floating rates of exchange, which emerged unplanned out of the breakdown in 1973 of the Bretton Woods system of agreed fixed rates of exchange, reflects the view that the millions of private and public participants in international money and capital markets are the best judges of their own interests and that, also in the monetary field, market prices, i.e. floating exchange rates and interest rates, may coordinate and "stabilize" the millions of decentralized decisions more efficiently than political negotiations among government bureaucracies. At the same time, the IMF continues to assist member countries in overcoming temporary balance of payments imbalances without resort to restrictions detrimental to their national welfare. The "Set of Multilaterally Agreed Equitable Principles and Rules for the Control of Restrictive Business Practices", which was recommended by the UN General Assembly in December, 1980, also reflects a focus on the regulatory task of "making the market work". The various international arrangements aimed at stabilizing commodity prices by means of export quotas (e.g. for cocoa, coffee, sugar and tin), buffer stocks (e.g. for cocoa, natural rubber, sugar and tin), multilateral contract systems (e.g. for wheat), or by the 1980 Agreement Establishing the Common Fund for Commodities, have met with only limited success up to now.

E) Equitable Distribution

"Equitable commodity prices" and a "new international economic order" have become universally recognized objectives of international economic policy. Yet views about the appropriate policy instruments for achieving these objectives continue to differ. They are influenced by value judgments on "social justice" which, in the economic field, necessarily depend on conceptions of the equity of a market-oriented distribution of benefits (which rewards not only superior skills and comparative advantages but also the existing distribution of resources) and of governments' capacity to steer the world economy deliberately. Moreover, "social justice" is an attribute of relations between individuals and, as a policy objective, has to be determined politically by each society concerned.[20]

20 See also: F.A. v.Hayek, The Principles of a Liberal Social Order, in: Nishiyama/Leube (eds.), The Essence of Hayek, 1984, pp. 363, 375 ff: "It ought to be freely admitted that the

It lacks a precise meaning in relations among governments. From an economic point of view, direct financial transfers are a more efficient instrument of income redistribution than interference with market prices or with non-discriminatory competition rules.[21] Rule-oriented market policies may enable more economic growth and equally distributed welfare than many redistributive governmental policies in the name of "social justice" which inhibit economic growth and often entail arbitrary distributive effects.

4. Basic Elements of a Legal Theory of International Economic Order

The problem of a rational economic order cannot be properly discussed without an examination of its legal requirements. The importance which the classical liberal economists, such as Adam Smith, attached to the protection of equal freedoms and property rights, rule of law and constitutional government, the powers of which had to be limited for the sake of the freedom of the individual, is based on the insight that such legal rules are an essential condition for the maintenance of a self-generating "invisible hand order" capable of harmonizing individual and social welfare. The classical liberals (such as John Locke, David

market order does not bring about any close correspondence between subjective merit or individual needs and rewards. It operates on the principle of a combined game of skill and chance in which the results for each individual may be as much determined by circumstances wholly beyond his control as by his skill or effort. Each is remunerated according to the value his particular services have to the particular people to whom he renders them, and this value of his services stands in no necessary relation to anything which we would appropriately call his merits and still less to his needs."... "More than by anything else the market order has been distorted by efforts to protect groups from a decline from their former position; and when government interference is demanded in the name of 'social justice' this now means, more often than not, the demand for the protection of the existing relative position of some group. 'Social justice' has thus become little more than a demand for the protection of vested interests and the creation of new privilege, such as when in the name of social justice the farmer is assured 'parity' with the industrial workers."... "In a market order the fact that a group of persons has achieved a certain relative position cannot give them a claim in justice to maintain it, because this cannot be defended by a rule which could be equally applied to all..." "There is of course no reason why a society which, thanks to the market, is as rich as modern society should not provide outside the market a minimum security for all who in the market fall below a certain standard. Our point was merely that considerations of justice provide no justification for 'correcting' the results of the market and that justice, in the sense of treatment under the same rules, requires that each takes what a market provides in which every participant behaves fairly. There is only a justice of individual conduct but not a separate 'social justice'."

21 For the economic argument that it is more efficient to pursue distributional goals through direct taxes and social welfare benefits rather than indirectly through interferences with market prices or through property rights see: M. Friedman, Capitalism and Freedom, 1962, pp. 190 ff; E.K. Browning, Redistribution and the Welfare System, 1975.

Hume, Adam Smith, Immanuel Kant) did not assume a natural harmony of interests, but emphasized that the divergent individual interests could be reconciled only by the observance of general rules. According to David Hume, social peace and an exchange economy were made possible only through "the three fundamental laws of nature, that of stability of possession, of its transference by consent, and of the performance of promises".[22] Adam Smith emphasized that the proper functioning of markets depended on the proper assignment of individual freedoms and property rights, which were seen not only as an incentive for private productive economic activities but also as a safeguard against the arbitrary mercantilist government restrictions of individual freedoms. Undistorted competition (not only in the economic but also in the political process) and the mutual adjustment of individual economic plans in a way maximizing social welfare were considered to be only possible in a mutually consistent legal framework of general freedoms, property rights, contract law and limited government. Freedom for all could be achieved, according to Immanuel Kant, only under a law which ensured that the freedom of each did not extend further than was compatible with an equal freedom for all others. According to Kant, the "justice" of the rules depended on their "universalizability", i.e. the possibility of generally applying the rule to all similar situations and to make it a maxim of general legislation ("categorical imperative"). In order to overcome the "Hobbesian war of each against all", these basic principles of law and justice had to be respected in both the public international law relations among equal sovereign states as well as in the private law relations among legally equal, free citizens. And because private and public, national and international law should strive to reconcile the individual freedom - of citizens as of states - with the equal freedoms of all others under general rules of law, I.Kant emphasized in his essay "Towards eternal peace" (1795) that public international law rules could be applicable also by private citizens.[23]

22 D. Hume, Treatise, Works II, p. 293 (quoted from F.A. v.Hayek, Law, Legislation and Liberty, vol. II, 1976, p. 40).

23 On Kant's legal philosophy see the two recent analyses by G. Dietze, Kant und Rechtsstaat, 1982, and P. Koslowski, Staat und Gesellschaft bei Kant, 1985. On Adam Smith's legal philosophy see for instance: E.J. Mestmäcker, Die sichtbare Hand des Rechts, 1978, S. 139 ff.

A) Need for an "Economic Constitution": The "Constituent" and "Regulative" Principles Proposed by the "Freiburg School" of "Ordo-liberalism"

In response to the apparent failures and partial breakdown of national and international economic and legal systems during the 1930s, economists and lawyers - especially those belonging to the "**School of Ordo-Liberalism**" at Freiburg university, to the "**Chicago School**" of "law and economics" and to the "**Virginia School**" of "public choice"[24] - have addressed anew the question of whether one should rely primarily on private markets or on governments for the provision and distribution of goods and services and how to promote undistorted competition through legal rules and procedures.

The economists (e.g. W. Eucken) and lawyers (e.g. F. Böhm) at Freiburg began their analysis at the "Archimedian point", as Eucken called it, that "plans are the starting point for every economic activity" and that "in an economy with extensive division of labour, the individual can see only parts of the economic process. But then, how does the direction of the whole process come about? It is the economic order that is decisive. It is the task of the economic order to bring about the interlocking of the hours of work performed by everyone who is in employment and the physical means of production so numerous as to prevent any overview of them being gained, in such a way that economic scarcity is eliminated as far as possible".[25] In view of this limited "problem-solving capacity" of the individual and the existence of "market failures" (e.g. monopolies and cartels) as well as "government failures" so evident during the "time of experiments" of the 1920s and 1930s, the development of the economic order cannot be left to itself but has to be created through a consistent "order policy" ("Ordnungspolitik") by the state. The various economic, political, legal and other social processes are interrelated. Each act of government intervention must therefore be seen in connection with the total process and overall economic order so as to ensure the "system conformity of measures". The state should "take an overall

24 For a survey of the "Freiburg School", especially the writings of the economist W. Eucken and the lawyer F. Böhm, see: D. Schmidtchen, German "Ordnungspolitik" as Institutional Choice, in: Zeitschrift für die Gesamte Staatswissenschaft 1984, pp. 54 ff; E.U. Petersmann, Trade Policy as a Constitutional Problem, in: Aussenwirtschaft (Swiss Review of International Economic Relations) 1986, pp. 405 ff. The "Chicago School" is exemplified by the writings of the lawyer Posner, the economists Stigler and Becker, and the "Journal of Law and Economics" and "Journal of Legal Studies" published by the University of Chicago. On the "Virginia School" see the numerous publications by J.M. Buchanan (e.g. Liberty, Market and State: Political Economy in the 1980s, 1986) and the journal "Public Choice" edited by Buchanan and others.

25 W. Eucken, Grundsätze der Wirtschaftspolitik, 1952, p. 6 f, 21.

political decision on the system and thus bring together the individual parts of its economic policy in a rational way".[26] Yet, the state should not attempt to conduct the economic processes itself but rather make use of decentralized planning of economic activity. Hence, "the creation of a properly-functioning price system based on complete competition is the essential criterion for assessing every economic policy measure. This is the basic principle of economic constitutional law".[27]

In order to create and safeguard such a mutually consistent "economic constitution", Eucken and Böhm set out "to translate the philosophy of the classical economists into the language of the law": "The principles which should underlie the economic order (or system) need to be developed so that their pursuit will ensure the unity of this economic policy".[28] According to Eucken, the proper functioning of the price system and the unity of economic policy can be ensured only if the following six "constituent principles" for a system of rules of a competitive order, and a number of "regulative principles" for keeping the competitive order working, were observed:[29]

a) Monetary stability secured through a self-regulating system functioning "as automatically as possible".

b) Open markets so as to avoid restraints of competition.

c) Private ownership of the means of production so as to enable flexibility in the decentralized planning of the economic process.

d) Freedom of contract as a precondition of the freedom of producers, traders and consumers to choose.

e) Liability according to the principle: "Whoever is responsible for the plans and actions of enterprises (firms) and households bears liability".[30]

f) Steadiness of economic policy in order to promote investment security and the calculability of economic decisions.

---

26 W. Eucken, Unser Zeitalter der Misserfolge, 1951, p. 72.

27 Eucken (note 25), p. 254.

28 Eucken (note 26), p. 71.

29 Eucken (note 25), pp. 254 ff.

30 Eucken (note 25), p. 281.

Yet the application of the "constituent principles" alone is not enough to prevent "market failures" as well as "government failures", such as abuse of private or governmental power, "external effects" and an "unjust" income distribution. Eucken consequently emphasized that the "constituent principles" of the "economic constitution", without which undistorted market competition cannot unfold, must be supplemented by "process policies" based on mutually consistent "regulative principles". Thus, antitrust legislation and an antitrust authority were considered necessary "to make those who wield economic power behave as if there were complete competition";[31] and an anti-cyclical stabilization policy as well as a social policy (e.g. for the old or unemployed) were also called for.[32]

The "constitutional theory" of the neo-liberal Freiburg School has been criticized on various grounds. For instance, the various economic and legal "constitutional theories" elaborated by members of the "Freiburg School", the "Chicago School" or the "Virginia School" appear to overlook that "an economic constitution is not complete without a theory of foreign economic policy and the legal control of it".[33] There are also doubts as to whether the notions of "choosing an economic order" (Eucken) and of deliberately determining its structure and development through an "economic constitution" can be extended beyond specific situations such as the constitutional choice which Germany faced right after the war. Economists belonging to the "Virginia School" of "public choice" emphasize the importance of uncertainty over future positions as an incentive for individuals (or states) to voluntarily agree to long-term constitutional rules which are more likely to reflect their long-term interests in general rules of law and justice compared to short-term rules and policy alternatives with predictable short-term effects for the benefit of identifiable special interests.[34] Such uncertainty over the future impact of rules on individual positions existed not only in some of the war-torn states after World War II, but also at the international level during the 1940s in the negotiations on the reconstruction of the international economic order as well as in the 1950s during the negotiations on the treaties establishing the European Communities. It is interesting to examine the - actual and potential - contribution of the neoliberal theories of "economic constitutions" to the

31 Eucken (note 25), p. 295. For Eucken, "complete competition" does not mean what is often called "perfect competition", see: Schmidtchen (note 23), p. 60.

32 See: Eucken (note 24), pp. 308 ff, 321 ff.

33 J. Tumlir, quoted from an unpublished manuscript. For a discussion of these various "constitutional theories" see: Petersmann (note 23).

34 Cf. J.M. Buchanan/G. Tullock, The Calculus of Consent, 1962, pp. 78 ff.

past and present search for a legal "constitutional theory" of the international economic order.

B) "Constituent" and "Regulative" Legal Principles of the International Economic Order

History shows that a centrally administered economy can be combined also with private ownership of the means of production (e.g. in Nazi Germany). Eucken saw the classifying feature of an economic system, therefore, not in the collective or private ownership of the means of production, but in the distribution of the real planning power and the rights of disposal.[35] From this perspective, an international economy composed of more than 170 sovereign states with predominantly market-oriented national economic systems and with more than 20'000 transnational enterprises constitutes an international market with a high degree of decentralized economic planning. It is remarkable that the worldwide economic agreements, such as GATT and the IMF Agreement, explicitly recognize or implicitly assume, at least in principle, the need for virtually all six "constituent principles" mentioned by Eucken as prerequisites of the proper functioning of a market economy. For example:

a) The IMF Agreement sets out obligations of the 149 (1986) IMF member states, inter alia, for the maintenance of "financial and economic stability", a "stable system of exchange rates", "reasonable price stability", and "a monetary system that does not tend to produce erratic disruptions" (Article IV:1 of the IMF Agreement).

b) The GATT sets out obligations of the 125 (1987) states participating in the GATT for the maintenance of non-discriminatory market access (e.g. Articles I, III, XIII, XVII) and for the use of market-conforming trade policy instruments (e.g. Articles XI, XV-XVII of the GATT).

c) The World Bank Agreement prescribes obligations of the 149 (1986) World Bank member countries for the promotion and protection of private foreign investments and for the granting of financial assistance "to supplement private investment" (e.g Article I of the World Bank Agreement). The IMF Agreement and GATT (e.g. Article XVII) also proceed from the assumption that state enterprises are an exception to

35 Cf. W. Eucken (note 25), p. 104 f.

the general existence of private enterprises and of commercial competition undistorted by discriminatory government interferences.

d) Freedom of contract, albeit to a limited extent in the case of state-trading enterprises, is the legal basis of almost all international economic transactions and of related contracts for the international sale of goods, the modes of payment and of securing payment (e.g. bank and export credit guarantees), or transport and insurance contracts.

e) The principle of "legal liability" (e.g. pacta sunt servanda) is recognized in international economic law with regard to both private commercial contracts and investments, as well as principles of state responsibility for the compliance with international legal obligations.

f) Eucken's call for "steadiness of economic policy" is the underlying economic rationale of many rules of international economic law, e.g. as regards stable exchange rates (Article IV of the IMF Agreement), financial assistance from the IMF so as to enable member countries "to correct maladjustments in their balance of payments without resorting to measures destructive of national or international prosperity" (Articles I, V), obligations for the avoidance of restrictions on current payments and of discriminatory currency practices (Article VIII), the legal "binding" of trade liberalization measures (Article II of the GATT) and the prohibition of non-tariff trade barriers (e.g. Articles V to XI of the GATT), the protection of foreign investments and the granting of development assistance (e.g. Article I of the World Bank Agreement).

As regards Eucken's "regulative principles" for the proper functioning of a market economy over time, it is again remarkable that Eucken's call for a competition policy, an anticyclical stabilization policy and a social policy is, at least in principle, also recognized in international economic relations and international economic law. The "Set of Multilaterally Agreed Equitable Principles and Rules for the Control of Restrictive Business Practices", adopted by the UN General Assembly on 5 December 1980, pursues the explicit objective of "greater efficiency in international trade and development ... through: (a) The creation, encouragement and protection of competition; (b) Control of the concentration of capital and/or economic power; (c) Encouragement of innovation".[36] The im-

36 See: part "A. Objectives" in: The Set of Multilaterally Agreed Equitable Principles and Rules for the Control of Restrictive Business Practices, UN 1981, p. 7.

portance of an international "stabilization policy" is reflected in the provisions of the IMF Agreement (e.g. Articles XV ff on "special drawing rights" to "meet the long-term global need, as and when it arises, to supplement existing reserve assets in such manner as will ... avoid economic stagnation and deflation as well as excess demand and inflation in the world", cf. Article XVIII:1). It is likewise reflected in various GATT provisions (e.g. Articles XII, XVIII:B on "restrictions to safeguard the balance of payments", Articles XXXVI ff e.g. on "measures designed to attain stable, equitable and remunerative prices" for primary products of less-developed countries and "measures designed to stabilize and improve conditions of world markets", cf. Articles XXXVI:4, XXXVIII:2); as well as in the agreements establishing the World Bank Group (e.g. Article I of the World Bank Agreement: "to promote the long-range balanced growth of international trade and the maintenance of equilibrium in balances of payments by encouraging international investment"); and, above all, in the practice of international economic organizations and various groups of states (e.g. "management" of foreign debts in the "Paris Club", anticyclical policies initiated on the annual "world economic summit meetings" of the major industrialized countries). Finally, "social policy", as advocated by Eucken, is also a recognized objective of a large number of international agreements and organizations (e.g. the International Labour Organization, the UN Development Programme, the UN High Commissioner for Refugees, etc.).

C) Conclusions: A Pluralistic International Economic Order must be Based on Liberal Principles

The preceding, brief comparison of the neo-liberal proposals for a mutually consistent "economic constitution" of a market economy with the present multilateral legal framework of the world economy suggests four preliminary conclusions for an economically rational legal theory of international economic order:

First, due to its highly decentralized economic planning and decentralized legal structures, the international division of labour among the more than 170 separate national economies with billions of consumers and millions of producers and traders will continue to be shaped primarily by market competition and continuously changing prices (including, for the time being, interest rates and exchange rates), to which individual sellers, buyers, investors and consumers in the various countries will react and adjust their economic plans accordingly. Most international economic transactions will continue to be effectuated by means of private commercial and financial contracts. And most international decisions of intergovernmental economic organizations will continue to be implemented by means of national economic law. International "market integration" is largely possible on the basis of general framework rules with decentralized decision-making. Also international "economic policy coordination" may often be easier to achieve at a decentralized level. Thus, international cartels might be prevented more effectively by means of a coordinated extraterritorial application of the existing domestic antitrust laws of the USA, the EEC and a few other OECD countries than through international measures in the context of the UN principles and rules for restrictive business practices. GATT practice shows that liberal international "prohibitive rules" are not considered sufficient in respect of state trading countries, which regulate their foreign economic relations through state monopolies and do not recognize the liberal separation of public economic law and private economic planning by means of private law. Liberal international prohibitive rules are further considered insufficient whenever there are other market distortions caused by private enterprises (e.g. GATT Article VI: dumping) or by government interferences (e.g. GATT Articles VI, XVI: subsidies).

Second, the present multilateral legal framework of the international division of labour recognizes the need for "constitutive principles" and "regulative principles" for the proper functioning of international market competition. The economic logic of market competition has a strong bearing on the contents of many rules of international economic law (see e.g. GATT Articles VI, XVI on anti-dumping and subsidies). There is also worldwide recognition that many objectives of national economic policies can no longer be achieved without international economic organizations, in which the external effects of national economic interventions can be continuously coordinated and a number of problems be addressed which - because of their transnational nature - can be satisfactorily solved only by international cooperation. States perceive international economic organizations as agreed frameworks for the multilateral pursuit of national interests in an interdependent world economy and as a prerequisite for maintaining their national economic order as it interacts with foreign economies. But there are only very few international economic organization (e.g. the EEC), to which states have been willing to delegate international regulatory powers to determine, even against the will of individual states, international prices, market shares or production quotas. In accordance with the principle of "sovereign equality of States" (Article 2:1 of the UN Charter), the worldwide economic agreements recognize the national freedom of member states to decide autonomously on their national level of trade protection (see GATT Articles II,

XXVIII), on their national exchange rate system (Article IV of the IMF Agreement), on the convertibility of their national currency (Articles VIII, XIV of the IMF Agreement), or on their national system for the ownership of the means of production (see also Article 222 of the EEC Treaty). An international "steering" of international economic processes is, therefore, often possible only through general framework rules negotiated and accepted among interested states with decentralized decision-making. "Conduct-oriented" rules (e.g. on non-discriminatory treatment and prohibition of non-tariff trade barriers) have proven to be much more effective for the achievement of commonly agreed objectives than "result-oriented" obligations (e.g. in GATT Article XVI:3 prohibiting export subsidies "which result in that contracting party having more than an equitable share of world export trade in that product", Article XXXVI:4 GATT relating to "stable, equitable and remunerative prices" of primary commodities of developing countries). This tends to confirm the neoliberal insight that outcomes emerge from the interaction of individuals acting within the constraints established by rules and often cannot be decided about.

Third, the more than 170 sovereign states will continue to have differring views on the precise content, economic desirability and political acceptability of multilaterally agreed international "constitutive principles" and "regulative principles" of international economic cooperation. Attempts at worldwide uniform solutions may prove impractical in view of the principle of "sovereign equality" of states. Competition among national economic and legal policies has also the advantage of promoting diversified processes of discovery, learning and adjustment. For instance, the strengthening of the general GATT rules by additional multilateral agreements between interested contracting parties has proven beneficial also to third GATT contracting parties and has attracted an increasing number of accessions to the 1979 Tokyo Round Agreements on non-tariff trade barriers. The emergence of dissenting views on general legal principles, such as the international minimum standard for the protection of foreign property, may prompt "legal competition" as well on the level of national public and private law (e.g. a reorientation of foreign private investment to host countries offering more legal security). This may also foster decentralized international law-creation processes, such as the conclusion of the more than 200 bilateral investment protection agreements since 1945, which could also strengthen or redefine the general rules.[37] The legal evolution of the international economic order

37 For a comparative analysis of these bilateral investment protection agreements see: Verwey/Schrijver, The Taking of Foreign Property under International Law: A New Legal Perspective? in: Netherlands Yearbook of International Law 1984, pp. 3 ff:

shows, on the one hand, a surprising continuity: The classical principles and standards of international treaty practice - such as most-favoured-nation treatment, national treatment, preferential treatment, fair treatment, reciprocity and the minimum standard - continue to form part of many international economic treaties and organizations. Owing to their applicability to states with different economic systems, they reconcile the need for international cooperation with the diversity of national economic and legal systems. On the other hand, the various levels of private and public national and international economic law are slowly being integrated into a comprehensive "international economic law" with mutually interacting and complementary structures and developments, such as the distinct tendency in both national and international economic law to supplement the classical principles of freedom and formal equality by new principles of substantive equality and solidarity.

Fourth, the elaboration of a more coherent international "economic integration law" may prove feasible only in international agreements and organizations limited to states with homogeneous national economic, political and legal systems. Thus the "constitutional guarantees" of European Community law for free international movement of goods, services, persons, capital and payments, non-discrimination, undistorted competition and judicial protection of individual rights presuppose the existence of market economies and parliamentary democracies at the national level. The agreed objectives and principles for the establishment of a common market based on undistorted competition have enabled the European Court of Justice to construe various EEC Treaty provisions - e.g. on the prohibition of quantitative trade restrictions (Articles 30, 34, 36) - in a more liberal way than it has been possible with regard to the corresponding and almost identically worded GATT prohibitions. And the common traditions of the national constitutional laws of EEC member states have enabled the Court to recognize in its case-law the existence of fundamental individual freedoms and other individual rights as an integral part of the general principles of Community law, and to protect these rights from interferences by the Communities and member states.[38] The law and practice of other international economic organizations also confirms a frequent need for territorial, functional and legal differentiations (e.g. acceptability of "weighted voting rights" in international fi-

---

Peters/Schrijver/de Waart: Permanent Sovereignty, foreign investment and state practice, in: Hossain/Roy Chowdhury (eds.), Permanent Sovereignty over Natural Resources in International Law, 1984, pp. 8 ff.

38 See, e.g.: M.A. Dauses, The Protection of Fundamental Rights in the Community Legal Order, in: European Law Review 1985, pp. 398 ff.

nancial organizations and in international commodity organizations). P. Verloren van Themaat's comparative legal analysis of international economic organizations has shown that differences in the objectives, principles, rules, procedures and institutions of international economic organizations are often due to the different economic and political systems of their respective member states.[39]

39 Cf. Verloren van Themaat, The Changing Structure of International Economic Law, 1981, e.g. pp. 143 ff.

IV. NEED FOR AN ECONOMIC ANALYSIS OF INTERNATIONAL ECONOMIC LAW

1. Economic Analysis of Law: Concepts and Problems

Economists disagree on the defining characteristics of economic science. According to Robbins, "economics is the science which studies human behaviour as a relationship between ends and scarce means which have alternative uses".[1] This comprehensive conception of economics as a science applicable to all human behaviour and to all human choice in situations of scarcity has prompted many economists, over the past two decades, to go beyond the narrow neoclassical restriction of economics to the study of markets and material welfare and to apply economic analysis, especially the economic assessment of the costs and benefits of alternative choices, also to law, political science ("public choice") and other fields of human and institutional behaviour (see J. Bentham's statement: "madmen also calculate"). Other economists perceive Adam Smith's proof of the gains from trade and of division of labour through voluntary, mutually beneficial market transactions as the bedrock of all economic theory and, from this "contractarian paradigm" (J. Buchanan), emphasize the need for economic analysis of the contracts and transaction costs underlying market exchanges.[2] The economic theory of property rights emphasizes the dependence of the use of resources and of every division of labour on the assignment and specification of property rights, and infers from this assumption the need for an economic analysis of law. All these modern economic approaches represent attempts to make economic analysis more relevant in practice by integrating the economic impact of legal, political and institutional systems into economic theory, as it was done already in the "political economy approach" of the classical economists during the 18th century.

---

1 L. Robbins, An Essay on the Nature and Significance of Economic Science, 1932, p. 15, who continues: "When time and the means for achieving ends are limited and capable of being distinguished in order of importance, then behaviour necessarily assumes the form of choice ... it has an economic aspect".

2 See, e.g.: J. Buchanan, A Contractarian Paradigm for Applying Economic Theory, in: American Economic Review 65 (1975), pp. 225 ff, 229; O.E. Williamson, Transaction-Cost-Economics: The Governance of Contractual Relations, in: Journal of Law and Economics 1979, pp. 233 ff. The term "transaction costs" refers to the costs of specifying and enforcing the contracts underlying exchanges including all the costs of the political and legal organization of the division of labour.

Lawyers often continue to view economics as one of "the softest" of all sciences and are sceptical about the potential contribution of economics to a better understanding and to a more effective application of law even in the classical areas of competition law and competition policy. While it is recognized that models must always abstract from reality and simplify it in order to make possible a better understanding of the real world, the empirical predictions of positive economic models are frequently criticized as being unreliable and of little practical value because they are based on too unrealistic assumptions (e.g. "perfect competition") or on pretense of knowledge (e.g. as to the promotion of "workable competition" and the correction of "market failures").[3] The economist's model of "economic man" as a merely self-interested egotist and rational maximizer of his individual preferences (i.e. choosing consistently the subjectively preferred alternatives from those available to him) is sometimes criticized as too simplistic a fiction of the complexity of decision-making, because people are not generally selfish; yet, if this model is confined to the self-interested behaviour of participants in economic and political markets, it has proven useful for the assessment of the effectiveness and implications of economic regulations and of individual reactions to changes in the benefits and costs of regulations or contracts. Given the existence of individual freedoms and property rights, lawyers tend to be sceptical of "quantitative economics".[4] Lawyers also emphasize the technical nature of the definition by welfare economics of the

---

3 See, for instance D. Schmidtchen, Property Rights, Freiheit und Wettbewerbspolitik, 1983, p. 5: "Praktische Wettbewerbspolitik vollzieht sich - was leider von vielen Oekonomen, die sich mit Wettbewerbstheorie und Wettbewerbspolitik befassen, immer wieder übersehen wird - in erster Linie im Wege staatlicher Rechtsetzung und Rechtsanwendung ... So bestechend die Modelle der reinen Oekonomie auch aussehen mögen - einen Bezug zur Rechtswissenschaft und Rechtspraxis besitzen sie nicht. Und es ist auch fraglich, ob sie angesichts ihres ökonomischen Grundzuges überhaupt in juristische Kategorien umgesetzt oder mit solchen angereichert werden können."

4 On the need for economists to be content with "pattern prediction" or "prediction of the principle" see F.A. v.Hayek. Knowledge, Evolution and Society, 1983, p. 21 ff: "Being scientific involves in this connection a frank admission of how limited our powers of prediction really are" ..."I doubt whether microeconomic theory has ever discovered any new facts. Decreasing returns, decreasing marginal productivity or marginal utility, decreasing marginal rates of substitution were of course all phenomena familiar to ordinary people even if they did not call them by that name. In fact, it is only because ordinary people knew these facts, long before economists discovered their importance, that they have always been among the determinants of how the market actually functions. What the economic theorists found out was merely the relevance of these particular facts for the decisions of individuals in their interactions with other persons". See further Hayek's criticism of the "misconception of equilibrium" (p. 22 f), the "lure of false measurement" (p. 23 f) and the "errors of macroeconomics" (pp. 24 ff) in neglecting that "the concrete course of the process of adaptation to unknown circumstances cannot be predicted. All we can predict is certain abstract features of the process, not its concrete manifestations" (p. 26).

concepts of "value" and "efficiency" in terms of willingness to pay,[5] and the frequent economic neglect of the relationship between social efficiency and the distribution of income and wealth. Since "willingness to pay" and, therefore, also "value" and "efficiency" depend on the existing distribution of income and other resources,

> "economics yields no answer to the question whether the existing distribution of income and wealth is good or bad, just or unjust, neither does it yield an answer to the ultimate question whether an efficient allocation of resources would be good, just, or otherwise socially or ethically desirable. Nor can the economist tell us whether, assuming the existing distribution of income and wealth is just, consumer satisfaction should be the dominant value of society. The economist's competence in a discussion of the legal system thus is strictly limited. He can predict the effect of legal rules and arrangements on value and efficiency, in their strict technical senses, and on the existing distribution of income and wealth. He cannot prescribe social change".[6]

Allocative efficiency is defined by economics either as a situation in which the welfare of one individual cannot be improved without reducing the welfare of any other member of society ("Pareto efficiency"), or as a policy whose social benefits exceed its social costs independent of whether those suffering losses are actually being compensated ("Kaldor-Hicks efficiency").[7] Since most policy changes are likely to diminish at least one person's perceived individual welfare, the "Pareto criterion" appears to be of little practical relevance for questions of legal policy. The social cost-benefit analysis underlying the concept of "Kaldor-Hicks-efficiency" disregards the redistributive implications of "efficient" legal reforms on individuals and has therefore less ethical appeal than the "Pareto criterion".

The reality of national and international economies is characterized by the existence of "market failures" (e.g. monopolies, external costs, imperfect information) implying divergences between social and private costs or benefits. These are - the famous "Coarse theorem" notwithstanding - often unlikely to be corrected through decentralized bargaining and market competition.[8] Such market

5 See R.A. Posner, Economic Analysis of Law, 2nd ed. 1977, p. 10: "Efficiency means exploiting resources in such a way that 'value' - human satisfaction as measured by aggregate consumer willingness to pay for goods and services - is maximized".

6 Posner (note 5), p. 10

7 For a critical discussion of these two concepts see: Veljanowski, in: Ogus/Veljanowski (eds.), Readings in the Economics of Law and Regulation, 1984, p. 19 f.

8 While R. Coarse, The Problem of Social Cost, in: Journal of Law and Economics 1960, p. 1 ff, has demonstrated that perfectly competitive markets could ensure that harmful activities

failures may provide an efficiency rationale for statutory and other legal corrective measures (e.g. placing liability on the "cheapest cost avoider" as proposed by Calabresi).[9] Much of national and international economic law (e.g. antitrust law, GATT and the IMF Agreement) is rationalized in terms of economic efficiency as being justified in order to narrow the gap between private and social costs or benefits and to avoid economic distortions. The long history of "government failures" and of the abuse of government regulations for the surreptitious redistribution of income for the benefit of powerful interest groups has, however, also demonstrated that the frequent economic assumption of the existence of benevolent, omnipotent governments correcting market imperfections via informed interventions is usually unrealistic. Moreover, the economic theory of "second best" shows that, if some sectors of the economy deviate from efficiency, fostering efficiency piecemeal in other sectors will not necessarily bring about a more efficient allocation of resources in the overall economy. The desirability of corrective government interventions aimed at social efficiency presupposes also a value judgment that the initial distribution of resources and of legal rights in them, which determine in part the economic value and "efficient" allocation of resources in an economy, is desirable and just.[10]

A lawyer will therefore look not for economics and for the "measuring rod of money" but for the respective national and international constitutional law as a moral and legal basis for such value judgments and for the legal assessment of individual rights and redistributive government measures. Contrary to positive and normative economics, constitutional law does provide and legally rank value judgments which may justify requirements of "efficiency" (e.g. a cost-benefit-

---

(e.g. pollution) do not generate socially inefficient "external costs", his analysis relies on highly restrictive assumptions (e.g. no "transaction costs" of the voluntary bargaining between polluter and victims on the damage costs and abatement costs) that are unlikely to exist in the real world of imperfect information and uncertainty.

9 See G. Calabresi/Hirschoff, Toward a Test for Strict Liability in Torts, in: Yale Law Journal 81 (1971), pp. 1054 ff, who define the "cheapest cost avoider" as "which of the parties to the accident is in the best position to make the cost benefit analysis between accident and accident avoidance and to act on that decision once it is made" (p. 1060).

10 Depending on the initial distribution of resources and property rights, there can be an infinite number of socially efficient outcomes. Hence: "To say that a situation is allocatively efficient is to say only that all the (potential or actual) gains from trade have been exhausted, given the initial distribution of wealth among individuals. If the wealth in society were redistributed then there would be a different efficient allocation of resources. To take a rather extreme example, if wealth is concentrated in the hands of a few rich landowners who buy Rolls Royces and caviar, then allocative efficiency will be consistent with the poor starving and the economy's productive activity channelled into the manufacture of these luxury items. If wealth were to be distributed more equitably, less Rolls Royces and caviar and more of the necessities of life would be produced" (Veljanowski, note 7, p. 22).

analysis required by the constitutional law principle of proportionality between ends and means of government restrictions of individual rights) as well as of economic "inefficiency" (e.g. parliamentary authorization of redistributive measures so as to meet the "social guarantees" of constitutional law). Constitutional guarantees and legal processes are important determinants of "welfare", for which individuals are willing to pay even if they cause economic inefficiencies. Hence, it would be misleading not to incorporate into economic efficiency calculations the value people place on constitutional principles and processes.[11] The economist's advice on the economic rationale, consistency, costs, benefits and other effects of alternative legal regulations or contracts are important for lawyers in order to increase the effectiveness of economic regulations in achieving their goals and to avoid incentives for individual circumvention of the rules. But the final legal decisions must be based on rule-oriented principles (e.g. equal freedoms, proportionality of government restriction, "due process") and not on result-oriented economic estimates of the efficiency of outcomes. Only to the extent constitutional law justifies or requires considerations of efficiency (as it actually does in democratic societies), can efficient outcomes be recognized to be also desirable. If the initial distribution of rights and "distributive justice" (in the sense of the socially accepted degree of economic inequality) have been constitutionally determined and justified, even Posner's proposal of defining "justice" as "efficiency" and "injustice" as immoral waste of scarce resources may be legally acceptable.[12]

2. Positive "Result-oriented" Economic Analysis of International Economic Law

Many provisions of national and international economic law contain prohibitions whose legal effects are conditional on the ascertainment of specified economic effects. Article XVI:3 of GATT, for instance, prescribes that "if a contracting party grants directly or indirectly any form of subsidy which operates to increase the export of any primary product from its territory, such subsidy shall not be applied in a manner which results in that contracting party having more than an equitable share of world export trade in that product, account being taken of the shares of the contracting parties in such trade in the product

11 See: Burrows/Veljanowski, The Economic Approach to Law, 1981, pp. 17.

12 See R.A. Posner, The Economic Approach to Law, in: Ogus/Veljanowski (note 7), pp 43, 45.

during a previous representative period, and any special factors which may have affected or may be affecting such trade in the product". In order to determine a "more than equitable market share", GATT Panels established for the settlement of disputes over the interpretation and application of Article XVI:3 have tended to insist on positive empirical economic evidence of "market displacement" or "price undercutting" in individual markets caused by export subsidies, rather than to rely on a legal presumption that export subsidies causing a considerable increase in the share of world exports must be assumed to result in "more than an equitable share".[13] By contrast, the requirement of GATT Article XVI:4 that "contracting parties shall cease to grant either directly or indirectly any form of subsidy on the export of any product other than a primary product which subsidy results in the sale of such product for export at a price lower than the comparable price charged for the like product to buyers in the domestic market", has been applied by GATT Panels by relying on a legal presumption, based also on GATT Article XVI:2, that export subsidies can usually be presumed to result in "double pricing".[14]

Lawyers tend to be reluctant to make the application of legal rules dependent on "result-oriented interpretations" and empirical economic findings. The 1983 Panel report on EEC subsidies for the export of wheat flour[15] concluded, for instance, that, although the EEC world market share had increased from 24% (1963/66) up to 62% (1978/81), there was no empirical evidence either of "market displacement" or "price undercutting" in the 17 markets examined by the Panel. The Panel found it was unable to conclude as to whether the increased market share had resulted in "more than an equitable share" given the highly artificial levels and conditions of trade in wheat flour, the complexity of market developments and the difficulties inherent in the concept of "more than equitable share". Mainly due to this legally exceptional and unsatisfactory "non liquet" and to the Panel's disregard of the legal presumption in GATT Article XVI:2 of harmful effects of export subsidies, adoption of this Panel report was blocked by various GATT contracting parties. Lawyers, aware of the prohibition

13 For a detailed description of GATT practice since 1947 relating to Article XVI see: E.U. Petersmann, GATT - Analytical Index - Notes on the drafting, interpretation and application of the Articles of the General Agreement, GATT 1986, section Article XVI.

14 See above note 13 for references to GATT practice.

15 The Panel report (SCM/42) has not yet been adopted by the GATT Subsidy Committee.

of denial of justice and of its underlying rationale,[16] will be critical of such politically motivated "non liquet findings" rationalized with the imperfections of empirical economics. The terms of reference and functions of GATT Panels are "to examine the matter in the light of the relevant GATT provisions",[17] and the "political filtering" of GATT Panel reports is a task deliberately conferred not on GATT Panels but on the political GATT bodies, which have to "adopt" Panel reports submitted to them. Hence, it is to be welcomed that GATT Panels have tended to construe other GATT provisions in a "rule-oriented" rather than "result-oriented" manner. For example, discriminatory treatment of imported and domestic goods by internal taxation (Article III:2 GATT) or other internal regulations (e.g. Article III:4, 5) have been presumed "to afford protection to domestic production" (Article III:1); the prohibition of export subsidies on processed products (Article XVI:4) has been construed to justify the legal assumption that export subsidies result in "bi-level pricing"; the violation of GATT Articles is presumed to cause "nullification or impairment of benefits accruing under the General Agreement" (Article XXIII); and, contrary to the suggestion made e.g. by K. Dam[18] to construe the exception clauses in Article XXIV (permitting customs unions and free trade areas) by relying on an empirical economic finding that their respective "trade creating effects" are larger than their "trade distorting effects", GATT practice has tended to apply also Article XXIV in a "rule-oriented" rather than "result-oriented" manner.[19]

The judicial review by domestic courts of the actual use of discretionary trade policy powers may likewise necessitate empirical economic analyses of the actual effects of legal regulations. For instance, the recognized legal principle that

16 See Article 4 of the French Code Civil: "Le juge qui refusera de juger, sous prétexte du silence, de l'obscurité ou de l'insuffisance de la loi, pourra être poursuivi comme coupable de déni de justice."

17 Standard wording of the terms of references of GATT Panels.

18 K. Dam, Regional Arrangements and the GATT: The Legacy of a Misconception, in: The University of Chicago Law Review 1963, pp. 615 ff, who shows that the drafting and principles of Article XXIV suffer from various economic misconceptions, and that the present Article XXIV does not ensure that regional arrangements lead to an improvement in the allocation of world resources. Yet, Dam's praise of the use of empirical product-by-product studies (e.g. by the GATT Working Party examining the EEC Treaty in 1957) so as to bring down "the discussion .. from lofty legalistic peaks to an expert, technical study of the concrete effects to be expected of the arrangements" (p. 649) appears to underrate the legal and political rationale of some of the concepts used in Article XXIV (e.g. need for legal certainty and political admissibility of regional integration, need for criteria applicable ex ante and not only ex post).

19 For detailed references to GATT practice relating to these GATT Articles see Petersmann (note 13), section Article XXIII.

the EEC Treaty must be interpreted systematically in order to ensure conditions which are as close as possible to those prevailing in an internal market, has prompted the Court of Justice of the EC to adopt a broad interpretation of the prohibition of "measures having equivalent effect" to quantitative import restrictions (Article 30).[20] The case-law of the Court relating to the EEC Treaty principle of nondiscrimination includes cases where the Court declared illegal provisions because of their trade-distorting discriminatory effects.[21] The constitutional principle of proportionality requires to limit restrictions on individual rights and freedoms to the minimum necessary to attain the constitutionally authorized objective which justifies those restrictions. In the skimmed-milk powder cases, for instance, the Court of Justice declared invalid purchase requirements imposed on producers of feeding-stuffs for animals, because the Court found the high price level fixed and the purchase requirements disproportionate to attain the objective in view (i.e. disposal of surplus stocks of skimmed milk powder).[22]

As regards foreign trade policy vis-à-vis third countries, it is noteworthy that the Court appears never to have proceeded to an empirical assessment of the various "price effects", "production effects", "trade effects", "consumption effects" and "income redistribution effects" of foreign trade restrictions, even if they had been imposed in a discriminatory way and in manifest violation of the legally binding GATT prohibitions of trade discrimination. Both empirical and normative economics demonstrate that import restrictions can hardly ever give net protection to the national economy as a whole; only particular industries can be protected at the expense of other industries, consumers and taxpayers. Since protection is usually granted to the relatively less productive industries, any trade protection imposes costs on three main groups within the restricting economy:[23] **consumers** will be harmed not only by higher prices and a reduced variety of consumer goods, but also as a result of the reduced productivity in the restricting country and over time reduced real income of consumers; domestic

---

20 See e.g. case 120/78 - "Cassis de Dijon" - (1979) E.C.R. 649; case 27/80 - "Fietje" - (1980) E.C.R. 3839; case 270/80 - "Polydor" - (1982) E.C.R. 329.

21 See e.g. Cases 124/76 and 20/77 - "Maize groats and meal" - (1977) E.C.R. 1795, where the Court declared illegal a provision of Regulation No 120/67 on the common organization of the market in cereals, which maintained production refunds for maize intended for the manufacture of maize starch, but withheld refunds for groats and maize converted into groats or meal for the brewing industry.

22 Case 114/76 - "Skimmed milk powder" - (1977) E.C.R. 1211.

23 For a detailed analysis see: R. Blackhurst, The Economic Effects of Different Types of Trade Measures and their Impact on Consumers, in: International Trade and the Consumer, OECD 1986, pp. 94 ff.

producers will be harmed even if they are not using the restricted imports as an input, because the ultimate effect of import restrictions is to tax exports ("a tax on imports is a tax on exports") by increasing domestic production costs and reducing foreign demand;[24] and domestic **taxpayers** will be harmed whenever import protection is not granted by means of production subsidies or import tariffs, but in the form of quantitative import restrictions or VERs which transform the potential tariff revenue into private "quota rents" of importers or, in the case of a VER, of exporters abroad.[25]

3. Normative "Rule-oriented" Economic Analysis: The Ranking of Foreign Trade Policy Instruments

Positive economics seeks to make testable predictions that can be falsified by empirical evidence. Normative or welfare economics seeks to establish criteria for the promotion of allocative efficiency and distributive justice. International agreements, such as GATT and the IMF Agreement, rank the various trade and monetary policy instruments according to their respective economic efficiency and prohibit only the use of non-transparent, discriminatory and mutually harmful policy instruments.

GATT permits production subsidies (Article XVI:1) because they usually do not distort the relative prices of traded goods and are considered by economic theory as the least inefficient way of protecting import competing industries.[26] If a country wants to use trade policy border measures, GATT law prescribes the use of transparent and non-discriminatory tariffs (Articles I, XI) because they do not interrupt the price mechanism completely, generate government revenue and are comparatively easy to administer and to liberalize. Non-tariff trade barriers, such as a global quota or quotas allocated to individual supplier countries, are generally prohibited because of their greater economic costs (e.g. due to the interruption of the international price mechanism and the loss of alternative tariff revenue unless licenses are auctioned) and their greater scope for protectio-

24 For a detailed explanation of why import-competing producers are always protected at the expense of domestic exporters see: Clements/Sjaastad, How Protection Taxes Exporters, 1984.

25 For details see Blackhurst (note 23)

26 On the very stringent and hardly ever satisfied conditions for an economic justification of subsidies on economic efficiency grounds see Blackhurst (note 23), p. 97; R. Blackhurst, The Twilight of Domestic Economic Policies, in: The World Economy 1981, pp 366 ff.

nist abuse (e.g. discriminatory allocation of quotas). Bilateral quantitative restrictions administered from the export side (e.g. VERs) cause additional economic distortions and costs (e.g. export cartelization, distortion of world prices, discrimination, transfer of the "quota rents" from the importing to the exporting country, lack of transparency) and are generally prohibited under Articles I, XI, XIII of GATT.

A similar ranking of alternative economic policy instruments according to their economic efficiency can be found in many other international agreements on the liberalization of international economic relations. The law and practice of the IMF likewise promote the use of transparent, non-discriminatory and market-conforming policy instruments that tend to increase national economic welfare (e.g. flexible and realistic exchange rates, avoidance of discriminatory currency practices, financial balance-of-payments assistance rather than trade restrictions, non-inflationary money policies). The law and practice of the World Bank Group promote the efficient use and legal protection of foreign capital in borrowing countries. And the EEC Treaty aims at undistorted competition within the common market.

The interpretation and application of private and public, national and international economic law must take account not only of the effects of the respective rules of law, but also of their economic rationale and functions in order to assess the economic advantages and detriments of alternative courses of action. Since individual economic agents tend to act as rational and self-interested "utility-maximizers", private international commercial contracts and international economic agreements among states can often be explained as efforts to reduce international "transaction costs" of economic exchanges and to promote the efficient allocation of resources by specifying economic freedoms, conditions of market access, property rights and their transferability across national frontiers. For example, without the multilateral unconditional most-favoured-nation obligation of GATT Art. I, the 125 states participating in the GATT legal system would have to conclude 15,500 bilateral trade agreements amongst each other in order to secure economic and legal effects equivalent to those deriving from Art. I of GATT. Since trade theory demonstrates that trade restrictions are a "negative-sum-process" which does not increase the resources available in the restricting economy and reduces the international division of labour and potential national product,

> "analysis of the economics of protection casts doubt on the fundamental assumption that the governments of trading nations act to maximize national economic welfare. In most

> cases the way to maximize welfare is to eliminate trade barriers, yet governments persist in imposing such barriers. In a few cases, the way to maximize welfare is to impose an optimal tariff, yet governments normally do not do so. In other cases, trade barriers can increase national welfare by shifting profits to domestic firms or offsetting domestic market distortions, yet much if not most protectionist activity appears more an effort to protect the incomes of particular segments of a community than an effort to correct or exploit market failures."[27]

Hence, economic analysis suggests that the primary regulatory function of the GATT rules for transparent and economically efficient policy-making and non-discriminatory foreign trade competition does not consist in the resolution of **international** conflicts of interests among states, but in the transparent, non-discriminatory and welfare-increasing resolution of **domestic** conflicts of interests **within** GATT member countries among individual producers, importers, exporters and consumers. It is only when governments resort to welfare-reducing trade policy instruments prohibited by GATT law, that the primarily domestic conflicts spill over into "secondary trade conflicts" among governments. Given these "domestic policy functions" of GATT rules,[28] it has rightly been concluded that "part of the analysis of restrictive trade policies should be carried out in an income redistribution framework"[29] and with due regard to the interference of trade restrictions with individual freedoms and property rights.[30]

The negotiation of and agreement on the "constitutive" and "regulative" principles of an economy by means of public national and international economic law are ultimately aimed at regulating the relationships between economic freedoms, property rights and other incentives for the economic behaviour of producers, investors, traders and consumers. Any change in these legal regulations (e.g. foreign exchange restrictions) can change also the incentives and disincentives for millions of individuals, who will react to the changes not only in the economic markets (as sellers, buyers, producers etc.) but also in the political

27 K.W. Abbot, The Trading Nation's Dilemma: The Functions of the Law of International Trade, in: Harvard International Law Journal 1985, pp. 501, 513. See also: E.U. Petersmann, The European Communities and GATT. On the economic and legal functions of GATT rules, in: Legal Issues on European Integration, 1984, pp. 37, 44 ff.

28 See: E.U. Petersmann, Trade Policy as a Constitutional Problem. On the "domestic policy functions" of International Trade Rules, in: Aussenwirtschaft 1986, pp 405 ff, and H. Hauser, Domestic Policy Foundation and Domestic Policy Function of International Trade Rules, ibidem, pp. 171 ff.

29 Blackhurst (note 23), p. 94

30 See below chapter VIII, sections 2 and 3.

markets (e.g. as voters, interest groups) in often unpredictable ways and with possibly unforeseen social results.

The preceding survey of international economic theory has shown that some international economic rules (e.g. of GATT) can build on a broad consensus in economic theory; other international economic rules (e.g. on fixed exchange rates) had to be changed (in favour of floating exchange rates) in response to unforeseen but inevitable market developments; and there are also international economic rules and "administered prices" whose rationale is political without economic justification (e.g. discriminatory trade protection). An evaluation of the potential effectiveness of international economic rules must therefore take account of the extent to which the legal, economic and political rationales of the respective rules coincide. It must examine which rule may best reconcile the various legal, economic and political private and public interests involved and which economic policy objective must be given priority in case of a policy conflict (e.g. transition to floating exchange rates after 1973 in order to maintain the convertibility of currencies). The frequent emergence of "black markets" in response to governmental restraints of economic freedoms and property rights shows that government regulations cannot manipulate at will the self-interested conduct of producers, traders and consumers. Economic and legal theory have shown the existence of a large number of alternative legal remedies of private law (e.g. voluntary bargaining, private insurances, judicial proceedings among interested private parties) as well as of public law (e.g. corrective taxes, liability rules, reassignment of property rights) for the correction of "market failures", and have demonstrated the different social costs of the respective legal techniques. But the "theory of economic regulation" has also shown and empirically confirmed that government regulations (e.g. on market access, minimum prices, exemptions from antitrust laws) are often designed to serve private interest groups and the industries regulated (e.g. by permitting price increases above competitive levels) at the expense of the national welfare.[31]

31 See: G.J. Stigler, The Theory of Economic Regulation, in: The Bell Journal of Economics, 1971, pp. 3 ff; R.A. Posner, Theories of Economic Regulation, in: The Bell Journal of Economics, 1974, pp. 335 ff. Referring to the traditional "public interest theory", which holds that government economic regulation is supplied in response to the demand of the public for the correction of inefficient or inequitable market practices, Posner comments: "Were this theory of regulation correct, we would find regulation imposed mainly in highly concentrated industries (where the danger of monopoly is greatest) and in industries that generate substantial external costs or benefits. We do not. Some fifteen years of theoretical and empirical research, conducted mainly by economists, have demonstrated that regulation is not positively correlated with the presence of external economies or diseconomies or with monopolistic market structure... The conception of government as a costless and de-

4. "Social Justice" and the "New International Economic Order"

That economic "value" and the "efficiency" of the allocation of resources are a function of, and vary according to, the existing distribution of resources and property rights, has been emphasized already. Consequently, "each different distribution of wealth generates a different pattern of demand, a different set of prices and different production decisions".[32] Hence, the "efficiency" of market processes or of policies can be recognized to be socially desirable only if it is consistent with a society's distributional principles. Today, most states (except Israel, New Zealand and the United Kingdom) have adopted written constitutions determining the fundamental principles, rights, distributive processes, the socially acceptable degree of economic inequality and, thus, the basic elements of "justice", if the term is used in the sense of J. Rawls: "For us the primary subject of justice is the basic structure of society, or more exactly, the way in which the major social institutions distribute fundamental rights and duties and determine the division of advantages from social cooperation. By major institutions I understand the political constitution and the principal economic and social arrangements".[33] Multilateral international treaties such as the UN Charter, GATT, the IMF Agreement, the World Bank Convention, the various international human rights conventions with their guarantees of civil, political, economic, social and cultural freedoms and other rights including property rights,[34] or the treaties establishing the European Communities can be perceived as an additional international "constitutional entrenchment" of basic legal principles and determinants of "social justice".

These principles, such as the constitutional requirement of the proportionality between the ends and means of government restrictions of individual freedoms

---

pendably effective instrument for altering market behavior has also gone by the boards. Theoretical revision has both stimulated and been reinforced by a growing body of case studies demonstrating that particular schemes of government regulation cannot be explained on the ground that they increase the wealth or, by any widely accepted standard of equity or fairness, the justice of the society." (p. 336) On the economic inefficiency of many antitrust regulations see C.K. Rowley, Antitrust and Economic Efficiency, 1973, pp. 72 ff.

32 Veljanowski (note 7), p. 22.

33 J. Rawls, A Theory of Justice, 1971, p. 7.

34 Property rights are expressly guaranteed e.g. in the Universal Declaration of Human Rights of 1948, in the American Declaration of the Rights and Duties of Man of 1948, in the First Protocol to the European Convention for the Protection of Human Rights of 1950, in the American Convention of Human Rights of 1969, and in the African Charter on Human and Peoples' Rights of 1981.

and property rights, appear to confirm the view of R. Posner that "a second meaning of 'justice' and the most common I would argue, is simply 'efficiency'" and the avoidance of unnecessary waste of scarce resources.[35] Hence, the concern for economic "efficiency", namely whether the existing distribution and productive allocation of resources can be rearranged in a way improving society's production and consumption possibilities given the existing and constitutionally protected distribution of wealth, is not only a technocratic question but incorporates also a value judgment. As R. Nurkse put it, "the world is not rich enough to be able to despise efficiency".[36] And as K. Dam has concluded: "The goal of increased efficiency through international trade is sufficiently important (although in many cases outweighed by goals of distributive justice, equality of opportunity, and avoidance of undue social hardship) that in considering most international trade problems it is highly useful to identify the prospective policy that would maximize efficiency before preferring some other policy".[37]

"Social justice" is a recognized policy objective in the national economic laws of many "social market economies", in European Community law, as well as in international resolutions on a "new international economic order".[38] For instance, when the European Coal and Steel Community (ECSC) introduced in 1981 a steel production quota system in an attempt to adjust steel supply to the decline in demand, the European Court of Justice exercised considerable restraint in its judicial review of the numerous complaints by adversely affected European producers and interpreted the ECSC Treaty provisions expansively in deference to the EC Commission's power of discretion and in the interest of "European solidarity".[39] According to the Court, "Article 58 (of the ECSC Treaty) does not in any way require the Commission to guarantee each individual undertaking a minimum level of production determined in accordance with the undertaking's own criteria of profitability and development. The aim of Ar-

35 Posner (note 12), p. 45, who continues: "There may be, however, more to notions of justice than a concern with efficiency, for many types of conduct widely condemned as unjust may well be efficient"... "no rational society can ignore the costs of its public policies... The demand for justice is not independent of its price" (p. 46)

36 R. Nurkse, International Trade Theory and Development Policy, in: Ellis (ed.), Economic Development for Latin America, 1961, p. 234.

37 K. Dam, The GATT: Law and International Economic Organization, 1970, p. 8.

38 Cf. E.U. Petersmann, The New International Economic Order: Principles, Policies and International Law, in: Mcdonald (ed.), The International Law and Policy of Human Welfare, 1978, pp. 449 ff.

39 For a survey see: E. Grabitz/Hanlon, A Review of the Steel Quota Cases: Judicial Endorsement of ECSC Crisis Management, in: Common Market Law Review 1984, pp. 163 ff.

ticle 58 is to spread in the most equitable manner possible amongst all undertakings the reductions required by the economic situation and not to guarantee undertakings a minimum level of employment proportionate to their capacity".[40] Yet, the "constitutional justification" of why the Commission's administrative perception of "equity" and "solidarity" should take precedence over the fundamental constitutional principles of equal freedoms and property rights of European steel producers, of undistorted competition (Article 4 ECSC Treaty) and only "a limited measure of intervention" (Article 5 ECSC Treaty), remained vague and doubtful in the Court's judgments, for instance when the Court justified the Commission's disregard, in the elaboration of the quota system, of illegally granted subsidies and of their distortive effects on the ground that the quota system had to be established quickly.[41]

During the 1950s, economists like G.Myrdal, the first Secretary of the UN Economic Commission for Europe, and R.Prebisch, the first Secretary of the UN Conference on Trade and Development (UNCTAD), disputed the traditional "Heckscher-Ohlin-Samuelson-theorem" that free trade tends to equalize production factor prices in different trading countries. In their view, developing countries tend to gain less from international trade than developed countries.[42] The various UN resolutions on the establishment of a "New International Economic Order" and a "Charter of Economic Rights and Duties of States" recommended to replace the traditionally general and abstract rules of international economic law by new principles for the reform of North-South relations with a view to bridging the economic gap between developed and developing countries, including principles of "promotion of international social justice" and "generalized preferential, non-reciprocal and non-discriminatory treatment of developing countries in those fields of international economic co-operation where

40 See Case No 119/81 - Klöckner Werke A.G. v. Commission, - E.C.R. 1982, pp. 2627, 2650 f.

41 See Case No. 119/81 (note 40), at p. 2652.

42 For a discussion of the Prebisch thesis that the prices of primary commodities from developing countries are continuously declining relatively to the prices of manufactured exports, see, e.g.: A.I. MacBean/P.N. Snowden, International Institutions in Trade and Finance, 1983, pp. 95 ff, who conclude: "The empirical evidence advanced in support of this view that the commodity terms of trade have shifted against primaries or against developing countries cannot in fact sustain that judgment" (p. 95)... "The theoretical arguments advanced in support of an inevitable tendency for a worsening in developing countries' terms of trade are equally unconvincing" (p. 96)... The average annual growth of gross domestic product in developing countries as a group was higher between 1960-1982 than in industrial market economies (see: World Bank Annual Report 1985, p. 38).

it may be feasible".[43] These and other "principles", such as an "extension of active assistance to developing countries by the whole international community, free of any political or military conditions",[44] were justified by developing countries not only as a matter of charity and on grounds of need, but as a matter of "social justice" and as an entitlement to be embodied in a new "international law of development".[45]

Legal obligations to grant trade preferences, financial and technical development assistance have been voluntarily accepted in numerous bilateral and multilateral international agreements (e.g. the World Bank Agreement, the Lomé Conventions, Articles 131-136 EEC Treaty). But can redistributive claims and obligations for development assistance evolve into customary international law in spite of the lack of a generally agreed definition of the term "developing countries"? Can moral claims based on individual needs justify a legal right of governments to receive assistance free of any conditions? Is it contradictory for aid-receiving countries to claim international obligations to assist their poor people and to insist, at the same time, that "substantive equality" within their own country (e.g. treatment of their poor people) is their own sovereign internal affair? Do donor countries impinge on the sovereignty of receiving countries when they make the granting of aid conditional on its efficient use and on the promotion of development through protection of human rights? Can governments, by proclaiming a "right to development", actually promote development and strengthen the protection of human rights as a constitutive element of "development" and of individual welfare?

Since Aristotle's elaboration of the idea of "proportionate equality", all philosophies and theories of "justice" have consisted of variations on the theme of equality. The concepts of "formal equality" (**iustitia commutativa**) and of "procedural justice" are rule-oriented (e.g. equality of individual rights, "sovereign equality" of states, observance of agreed procedures as criteria of "justice"). The

43 The two principles are set out in Chapter I, paragraph m, and in Article 19 of the 1974 Charter of Economic Rights and Duties of States, see: International Legal Materials 1975, pp. 251 ff.

44 This principle was enunciated in paragraph 4, k of the 1974 UN "Declaration on the Establishment of a New International Economic Order", in: International Legal Materials 1974, pp. 715, 718.

45 See: O. Schachter, Sharing the World's resources, 1977, pp. 1 ff; E.U. Petersmann, International Economic Development Law, Droit International du Développement, Entwicklungsvölkerrecht - Myth or Reality?, in German Yearbook of International Law 1974, pp. 145 ff.

contents of "substantive equality", "distributive justice" and "equity" (in the original legal sense of special relief from formal justice) tend to be result-oriented. For the liberal philosopher Immanuel Kant, the test of the morality and "justice" of a rule was its "universalizability", i.e. whether its universal application is possible and desirable ("categoric imperative"). Since freedom for all can be achieved only if the freedom of each does not extend further than is compatible with an equal freedom for all others, "justice" in the sense of Kant is equal freedom under general rules of law. "Welfare, however, has no principle, neither for him who receives it, nor for him who distributes it (one will place it here and another there); because it depends on the material content of the will, which is dependent upon particular facts and therefore incapable of a general rule".[46]

Adam Smith, whose demands for a "system of natural liberty" were based on considerations of both economic efficiency and justice,[47] and many liberal economists ever since justify the rule-oriented interpretation of "justice" also on grounds of economic efficiency: Market competition makes it possible to maximize not only the equal "natural liberties" of citizens (e.g. their individual freedom to produce and trade goods and services), but also the total satisfaction of their individual consumer preferences and the rule-oriented redistribution of income in a way rewarding particular efforts and skills. The fact that the application of equal rules to factually different individuals will produce unequal results and that market outcomes remain unpredictable for all competitors, has led to the recognition within and among states of the need to limit the economic inequality by redistributing part of the maximized social welfare outside the market for the benefit of unsuccessful competitors.[48] But the liberal, rule- and efficiency-oriented definition of "justice" does not support claims to particular market outcomes or to the maintenance of relative market positions, since such claims interfere with the equal liberties of citizens, distort competition and unnecessarily waste scarce resources.[49] Empirical evidence seems to confirm

46 I. Kant, Der Streit der Fakultäten, 1798, sect. 2, para. 6, note 2.

47 Cf. A. Smith, The Theory of Moral Sentiments (Liberty Classics Edition Indianapolis 1976, p. 167): "Justice is the main pillar that upholds the whole edifice. If it is removed, the immense fabric of human society... must in a moment crumble into atoms".

48 For a detailed statement of this position see, e.g.: F.A. v.Hayek, "Social" or Distributive Justice, in: Nishiyama/Leube (eds.), The Essence of Hayek, 1984, pp. 62 ff, 373 ff. See also: R. Posner, The Economics of Justice, 1981, Part I (especially pp. 88 ff).

49 See: v.Hayek (note 48), pp. 102 ff. For a discussion of the applicability of the liberal theories of "justice" developed by J. Rawls (A Theory of Justice, 1971) and R. Nozick (Anarchy, State and Utopia, 1974), which both start from the inviolability of human rights but reach different conclusions as to whether the state has a right to coerce individuals to aid others,

that, outside close family relationships, there are no universally agreed customary rules defining specific rights and obligations of individuals or governments for income redistribution according to merits or to individual needs.

In modern "welfare states", redistributive policies are usually implemented by means of public law (e.g. taxation, subsidies) which specifies redistributional rights and legal duties of individual citizens. In "horizontal" legal relationships, such as private law or unorganized public international law, voluntary agreement on specific rights and obligations for result-oriented income redistribution ("social justice") is difficult to secure over time.[50] The factual and moral basis for redistributive claims (e.g. poverty, "equality in results"), and the resources available for redistribution, are likely to change over time. The preservation of the particular pattern of any supposedly "just" end-state distribution would therefore require continuous adjustment through government interventions in individual rights. While states have the power to coerce some of their own citizens to aid others and to limit individual property rights accordingly for the sake of an agreed concept of "social justice", states have no similar powers and common views of "international social justice" on the international level. "Substantive equality" among governments is no generally accepted objective (e.g. should all governments have nuclear weapons?). Making international aid dependent on "substantive equality" within the receiving country (e.g. protection of equal freedoms and assistance to the poor) is often rejected as an infringement on the sovereignty of the receiving country. Aid-granting states will therefore reserve

---

with regard to international economic relations see: I.M.D. Little, Distributive Justice and the new International Economic Order, in: P. Oppenheimer (ed.), Issues in International Economics 1980, pp. 37 ff. According to the entitlement theory of Nozick, any end-state is just if it is arrived at by "just" historical processes (including exchange contracts, gifts, taking possession of anything that was not scarce); the distribution of world income would be "unjust" only, and justify claims to "rectification", in so far as property was obtained by aggression or fraud in the past. Rawls's "difference principle" of justice, according to which social and economic inequalities are to be arranged so that they are to the greatest benefit of the least advantaged (p. 83), can hardly be transferred to the intergovernmental relations among sovereign states (see Little, p. 46).

50 See: D. Hubbard, The International Law Commission and the New International Economic Order, in: German Yearbook of International Law 1979, pp. 80 ff., according to whom "the essential aspects of the New International Economic Order could not be reflected in international customary law. The realization of this order in a legal framework would require the partial replacement of customary law by international organizational legislation" (p. 96)... "the basic principles of the New International Economic Order can only be implemented through changes in existing treaties by political bodies and not through the progressive development of international law by an independent commission of legal experts" (p. 98).

the right as to whom and under what conditions they are willing to grant assistance.

Some countries are "developed" in one area (e.g. OPEC countries as donors of financial aid), but "less-developed" in another area (e.g. OPEC countries as beneficiaries of non-reciprocal tariff preferences for developing countries). In its 1978 report on the most-favoured-nation clause, the International Law Commission concluded that there is at present "no general agreement among states concerning the concepts of developed and developing states".[51] According to D. Hubbard, the lack of agreement on the beneficiary countries and on a "just" distribution of the global product logically excludes the emergence of specific rights and obligations under customary international law favouring poor countries.[52] International consensus on redistributive rights and obligations has been possible to reach only in the context of international agreements and organizations (e.g. the World Bank Group, the Lomé Convention, the European Communities), and also then only subject to limitations in time, various conditions and procedural safeguards. But the increasing use in international treaty practice of differentiated agreed standards of "substantive equality", "solidarity" and legal responsibility for the actual extraterritorial effects of national economic regulations (as opposed to their legal effects limited to the national territorial jurisdiction) contributes to the gradual evolution of general legal principles of "substantive equality", "good neighbourliness" and "solidarity" in the sense of obligations to prevent adverse external effects of domestic policies and to take into account the interests of other states and of their citizens.[53] In this sense, there seems to be indeed a parallel between the principles underlying the "liberal revolution" in western democracies ("liberté, égalité, fraternité") and the increasing recognition of agreed principles of substantive equality and solidarity in international law.

---

51 Report of the International Law Commission on the Work of its Thirtieth Session, UN Doc. A/33/10 (1979), p. 162. For a critical discussion of this report see Hubbard (note 50). On the various legal definitions of the term "developing country" in international treaty practice see also: E.U. Petersmann, The Third World and International Economic Law. "Developing Country" as a privileged legal status, in: Zeitschrift für ausländisches öffentliches Recht und Völkerrecht 1976, pp. 492, 536 ff (in German with English summary).

52 See: Hubbard (note 50), pp. 92 ff.

53 On the evolution of such principles of "solidarity" see P. Verloren van Themaat, The Changing Structure of International Economic Law, 1981, pp. 240 ff.

5. Separating Economic and Legal Issues

National and international trade law are not an end in themselves but a means of promoting other economic, political and legal objectives. Economic, political and legal liberalism tend to proceed from the same value premise that equal individual liberties are valued either directly in their own right or, from a utilitarian perspective, as a means for achieving important economic, political and legal goals (e.g. economic welfare, limitation of government power, free use of knowledge and freedom of opinion). Notably economists emphasize the close interrelationships that exist e.g. between economic, political and legal freedoms, and increasingly recognize that "every economic problem can be regarded as a problem of finding an optimum set of rules of action" and "how different rules of action would work out".[54] They freely admit that the mere existence of trade protectionism shows that "the pursuit of (global or national) economic welfare is not the dominant motivation for foreign trade policies. If this were the case, a liberal international trade order should evolve spontaneously without a strong need for international coordination".[55]

Economists and lawyers do, however, often use different criteria for evaluating alternative rules and procedures. From an economic perspective it is easy to point to many legal rules and court judgments vindicating the dictum (attributed to Justice Brandeis) that "a lawyer who has not studied economics ... is very apt to become a public enemy". For instance, the political and legal practice of describing the legal freedom of developing countries to use trade distortions as "preferential treatment" is strongly criticized by many economists on the ground that such a legal freedom might actually harm developing countries by inviting protectionist "rent-seeking" and by inhibiting rule-oriented policies.[56] Or, the legal justification by the EC Court of Justice of GATT-inconsistent, discriminatory "voluntary restraint arrangements" (in lieu of GATT-conforming import relief measures) on the ground of the "principle of proportionality"[57] will be criticized by economists as turning the economic ranking of proportionate trade po-

54 R. Vining, Economics in the United States of America, 1956, p. 11.

55 H. Hauser, Foreign Trade Policy and the Function of Rules for Trade Policy Making, in: D. Dicke/E.U. Petersmann (eds.), Foreign Trade in the Present and in a New International Economic Order, 1988, pp. 18, 36.

56 See: R. Hudec, Developing Countries in the GATT Legal System, 1987, p. 140 f.

57 See: Case 245/81 - Edeka v. Federal Republic of Germany - ECR 1982, pp. 2745, 2756 f.

licy instruments on its head.[58] The economic analysis of law can thereby show that legal policies may not be capable of attaining their declared policy objectives.

Lawyers must emphasize that national and international trade regulations often pursue also important legal objectives. For instance, the GATT principles of transparent policymaking, rule of law, non-discrimination and judicial review correspond to general legal principles to be found in the national constitutions of most liberal democracies (see below chapters VII and VIII). The taking into account in GATT law of the economic ranking of the various alternative trade policy instruments according to their respective economic costs and trade distortions can be construed as reflecting the general legal principle of proportionality, i.e. the legal requirement recognized in many national constitutional laws to choose the least restrictive means (e.g. of alternative trade policy instruments) needed to achieve a legitimate government policy objective. Lawyers also may value the objective of liberal trade less on economic efficiency grounds than on the legal ground that open markets enlarge and protect individual freedoms and property rights (e.g. the freedom to buy scientific books from abroad). And they may criticize economic policies also on purely legal grounds, for instance by pointing out that GATT's current policy of exempting developing countries from the main GATT obligations (e.g. non-discrimination, reciprocity, prohibition of non-tariff trade barriers) and of authorizing developed countries to grant non-reciprocal trade preferences to LDCs cannot secure legal certainty and non-discriminatory market access inter alia because "the role of international legal obligations as a form of self-imposed restraint is perhaps their most important function in the trade-policy area"[59] and one-sided welfare-type recommendations cannot secure legal certainty in international trade.[60]

The analysis in the remaining chapters of this book of the "constitutional problems" posed by the "new protectionism" is not so much concerned with the economic efficiency gains from free trade or the "social injustices" involved in the "power-oriented" governmental distribution of "trade protection rents" for the benefit of "rent-seeking" protectionist interest groups. Even though the histori-

58 See, e.g., Blackhurst (note 23) pp. 94 ff.

59 Hudec above (note 56), at p. 129.

60 See, e.g., Hauser (above note 55), at p. 35: "Not asking for reciprocal commitments means that governments will not offer rule-oriented behaviour. Waiving the reciprocity requirement for developing countries destroyed an important incentive for domestic groups within these countries to seek rule-oriented behaviour of their governments."

cal, economic and political origins and effects of mercantilist trade policies are taken into account, the following Parts II to IV focus on the "constitutional problem" of how the liberal constitutional guarantees of economic liberty, equality, transparent policymaking, proportionality of government restrictions, limited delegation of powers, "due process" and judicial review can be rendered more effective in the trade policy area in constitutional democracies such as the United States, the EEC and EFTA countries which together account for more than half of world trade.

SECOND PART: "GOVERNMENT FAILURES" AND "CONSTITUTIONAL FAILURES" OF PAST AND PRESENT TRADE MERCANTILISM

"There is a fundamental antagonism between the seller and the buyer. The former wants the goods on the market to be scarce, in short supply, and expensive. The latter wants them abundant, in plentiful supply, and cheap.
Our laws, which should at least be neutral, take the side of the seller against the buyer, of the producer against the consumer, of high prices against low prices, of scarcity against abundance. They operate, if not intentionally, at least logically, on the assumption that a nation is rich when it is lacking in everything."

F. Bastiat[1]

"No one has a vested right to trade with foreign nations"

United States v.
Yoshida Int.Inc.,
US Court of Customs
and Patent Appeals[2]

1 F. Bastiat, Economic Sophism, 1850, p. 14

2 United States Court of Customs and Patent Appeals, 1975, 526 F.2d 560.

V. NEED FOR CONSTITUTIONAL RESTRAINTS ON GOVERNMENT POWERS TO TAX AND RESTRICT THE FOREIGN TRADE TRANSACTIONS OF DOMESTIC CITIZENS: TRADE MERCANTILISM AS "GOVERNMENT FAILURE"

1. The National Self-Interest in Trade Liberalization

There is broad agreement among economists "that the rate of economic growth is the outcome of the rate of resource accumulation, the efficiency with which additional resources are used, and the rate of increase of efficiency in resource utilization".[3] Why is it that countries rich in natural resources, such as Argentina and Zaire, continue to have low rates of production of goods and services, whereas countries less favoured with natural riches, like Japan and Switzerland, have evolved into members of the group of the world's wealthiest and most industrialized nations? Since the publication of Adam Smith's "Inquiry into the Nature and Causes of the Wealth of Nations" in 1776, economists tend to agree on two broad answers to this question: First, the individual incentives for the production of goods and services, for saving and for human effort and ingenuity depend to a large extent on the evolution of political, legal and social institutions that protect individual freedoms and property rights. Governments usually cannot directly produce economic wealth, but only a framework of rules that may encourage or impede the creation of wealth.[4] Second, in accordance with Adam Smith's famous theorem that "the division of labour is limited by the extent of the market", there is considerable empirical evidence to show that trade liberalization can and has acted as an "engine of growth", for instance during the unprecedented period of international economic growth between 1950-1973, and especially in trade-oriented developing countries (such as South Korea, Singapore, Hong Kong, Taiwan, Brazil and Colombia) compared to those with

---

3 A.O. Krueger, Protectionism and Growth, in: Protectionism and Growth, EFTA 1985, pp 11, 12 ff.

4 See, e.g.: K. Brunner, The Poverty of Nations, in: Cato Journal 1985, pp. 37 ff; D.C. Mueller (ed.), The Political Economy of Growth 1983; M. Olson, The Rise and Decline of Nations: Economic Growth, Stagflation and Social Rigidities, 1982. For an empirical analysis of a developing country economy from this perspective see, e.g.: J. Röpke, Die unterentwickelte Freiheit. Wirtschaftliche Entwicklung und unternehmerisches Handeln in Indonesien, 1982.

high levels of protection and import-substitution policies (e.g. India, whose exports exceeded those of Japan as late as 1952).[5]

Many discussions on international trade policy and international trade law suffer from the fact that international trade often continues to be viewed not as a means of making better use of domestic resources, but as a matter of national rivalry and supposed conflicts among national interests. One of Adam Smith's achievements was to demonstrate that a mercantilist trade policy of trying to maximize a country's gold reserves through export expansion and import restrictions would impoverish rather than enrich the country that followed it. Since then, the evolution of post-mercantilist trade theory and trade law can, rather crudely, be classified into three stages:[6]

In the first stage, during the nineteenth century, the gains from trade came to be appreciated, leading to a gradual liberalization of the mercantilist trade laws and to the European "commercial treaty system" based on bilateral long-term agreements interlinked through unconditional most-favoured-nation commitments.

In the second stage, between the first and second world war, more and more qualifications to laissez-faire and complete free trade were developed, promoting in many European countries the establishment of large government bureaucracies for the administration of economic policy, an ever increasing public sector, the 'politicisation' of the economy, trade restrictions and discrimination in international trade.

In the third stage, the period since World War II, "the link between the case for free trade and the case for laissez-faire has been broken" on the ground that trade interventions are hardly ever an 'optimal policy' for dealing with 'domestic distortions'. Almost any national economic policy objective can be achieved more efficiently and more effectively by internal government interventions (e.g.

5 For detailed analyses see: Krueger, Foreign Trade Regimes and Economic Development: Liberalization Attempts and Consequences, 1978; Bhagwati, Foreign Trade Regimes and Economic Development: Anatomy and Consequences of Exchange Control Regimes, 1978; Krueger, Trade and Employment in Developing Countries, Vols. 1-3, 1981-1983; Agarwala, Price Distortions and Growth, World Bank 1984.

6 See: W.M. Corden, Trade Policy and Economic Welfare, 1974, pp. 2 ff.

taxation, subsidies, competition policy, labour legislation) than by foreign trade restrictions with their adverse economic distortions.[7]

Today, hardly any economic policy commands greater agreement among economists and virtually all states than does the desirability of trade liberalization: "The intellectual consensus in this area is in fact quite rare, at least within the realm of economic policy; Keynesians, monetarists, so-called supply-siders, and virtually all other schools of thought agree on the virtues of open trade".[8] Also in state practice since World War II, the expansion and progressive liberalization of international trade have become universally recognized policy objectives laid down in numerous international agreements and UN resolutions. The GATT preamble states that trade liberalization and the elimination of discriminatory treatment in international commerce enable a higher real income, more employment and the full use of resources in all countries. While the individual and national gains from trade may be distributed unequally, every trading country is likely to improve its national welfare by engaging in foreign trade in accordance with its comparative advantages. The complete liberalization of tariffs and quantitative trade restrictions within free trade areas (like EFTA) and customs unions (like the EEC) is an even more perfect legal expression of the economic assumption that the advantages of liberal trade and rule of law within nations are not different in nature from the advantages of liberal trade and rule of law between nations. Just as no country seems to believe that the erection of trade barriers within its national economy could increase its national economic welfare, the advantages of global trade liberalization would be maximized if the political frontiers among states ceased to be trade barriers.

---

7 On this economic theory of "optimal intervention" see, in addition to the literature already mentioned in Chapter III.3 (notes 9 and 16), also: R.E. Baldwin, The Inefficacy of Trade Policy, 1982. While the "theory of second best" (see: Lipsey/Lancaster, The General Theory of Second Best, in: The Review of Economic Studies 1956/57, pp. 11 ff) has shown that partial trade liberalization may have under certain conditions also adverse effects, these exceptions are widely considered as "silly-clever... exceptions that are best confined to the classroom" (J. Bhagwati, International Trade in Services and its Relevance for Economic Development, 1986, p. 26). The economic studies on the optimal ranking of government policies to achieve non-economic objectives also show that trade policy is often an ineffective means of achieving the desired objective; see, e.g.: R.E. Baldwin, Ineffectiveness of Protection in Promoting Social Goals, in: The World Economy 1985, pp. 109 ff.

8 C.F. Bergsten/W.R. Cline, Trade Policy in the 1980s: An Overview, in: W.R. Cline (ed.), Trade Policy in the 1980s, 1983, pp. 59, 96.

Trade liberalization offers each trading country national economic gains in six important areas:[9]

a) Liberal trade enables consumers to obtain cheaper, better and a larger variety of goods than it would be possible without trade. It increases thereby not only the individual real income of consumers but these consumption gains involve also a net gain to the liberalizing country as a whole.

b) Trade liberalization offers important production gains by acting as an incentive for replacing inefficient domestic production by imports and for reallocating domestic resources (land, labour and capital) into more productive uses in those industries in which the country has a comparative advantage (as described by David Ricardo). The international price mechanism allows producers to make use of a maximum amount of information dispersed among millions of economic agents all over the world (e.g. information about supply conditions, available production processes and consumer preferences). Prices inform producers how much labour and skill it is worth putting into a product, and price competition ensures that goods are produced in the most efficient and least costly way practicable. Economic theory shows that the costs of adjustment to import competition are lower than the production gains from liberal trade or the "costs of not adjusting".

c) Trade liberalization benefits each country also through various "economies of scale gains" because it enables producers to exploit increasing returns to scale in a larger market, as Adam Smith emphasized (e.g. economies of larger scale plants and of intra-industry specialization).

d) Enlargement of the national market via trade liberalization brings also gains from a more competitive domestic economy because import competition increases domestic competition, encourages innovation and technological progress, reduces the extent and abuse of market power (e.g. by acting as an anti-

9 For a detailed discussion of the national benefits of trade liberalization see: Blackhurst/Marian/Tumlir, Trade Liberalization, Protectionism and Interdependence, GATT 1977, pp. 23-42; Bergsten/Cline, (note 6), pp. 66 ff; Trade Policies for a Better Future, GATT 1985, pp. 23-24; M. Wolf, Why Trade Liberalization is a Good Idea, in: The Uruguay Round. A Handbook on the Multilateral Trade Negotiations, World Bank 1987, pp. 14 ff;, Corden/Little/Scott, Import Controls versus Devaluation and Britain's Economic Prospects, 1975. For a discussion of the widely held view "that our current economic difficulties, such as stagflation, are primarily a reflection of governments' failure to apply liberal economic principles consistently, rather than a failure of the liberal economic order" (p. 4), see the introduction of and contributions to: Amacher/Haberler/Willet (eds.), Challenges To A Liberal International Economic Order, 1979.

trust device against domestic oligopolistic industries), and can also break down other institutional obstacles to change.

e) Trade liberalization further contributes to domestic price stability since imports tend to reduce price and wage pressures.

f) Trade liberalization, especially if it is carried out through multilateral trade agreements such as GATT, promotes the use of less-distortive economic policy instruments and limits the abuse of government discretion not only in the trade policy area, but also in related fields (e.g. competition and industrial policy). The economic theory of optimal intervention (above chapter III.3.B) emphasizes that almost all economic policy objectives can be achieved more efficiently and more effectively through internal government interventions (permitted under GATT law) than through foreign trade restrictions which almost invariably reduce the potential national economic welfare. And the economic ranking of the various trade policy instruments (above chapter IV.3) demonstrates that GATT law prohibits only the use of non-transparent, discriminatory and disproportionately harmful policy instruments which cannot constitute first-best policies for anything that is thought to require a government policy.

From a liberal perspective, the national gains from multilateral, bilateral or unilateral trade liberalization come primarily from the ability to import cheaper or better foreign goods and services, from replacing high-cost domestic production by low-cost foreign production, and from reallocating domestic production factors into comparatively more advantageous uses. Exports are beneficial and necessary only to the extent that they enable an economy to finance the imports it needs. Foreign exchange and "money" earned by exports are valued by most economists only to the extent that they represent purchasing power to be exchanged for goods and services.

2. Characteristic Features of the "New Protectionism"

Liberalization is about the relative roles of voluntary market transaction and government restrictions. "Liberal trade" can be defined as exchanges between firms which are exposed to competition on both sides of the transaction which itself encounters, if at all, only tariffs and non-discriminatory internal taxes and other regulations but no non-tariff trade barriers imposed by the importing country. During the liberal era between the Cobden-Chevalier trade agreement between England and France (1860) and the beginning of World War I, almost all international trade among European countries was "liberal" in this sense.[10] Non-tariff trade barriers became widespread only during and between the two wars. The quarter-century after World War II was characterized by the gradual liberalization of tariffs and non-tariff trade barriers and was more prosperous than ever before. The multilateral GATT rules are liberal in the sense that they promote the use of transparent, non-discriminatory and market-conforming trade policy instruments (i.e. tariffs) and prohibit nontransparent, discriminatory and market-disrupting trade policy instruments that thwart privately agreed international trade transactions. Since the economic crisis in 1973/74, protectionist non-tariff trade barriers have increased and economic growth has slowed dramatically.

The term "protectionism" is used for high tariffs, non-tariff trade barriers, export subsidies and other governmental interferences in international market competition designed to introduce market distortions for the benefit of domestic producers. From an economic point of view, an important distinction is between "market-conforming" instruments of trade protection (e.g. production subsidies, import tariffs, import surcharges and prior deposit schemes) that do not completely suspend the interrelationship between the international and the national prices of the protected good, and other forms that disconnect national and international price developments (e.g. quantitative restrictions); and between across-the-board restrictions, such as general import restrictions for balance-of-payments reasons introduced mainly by developing countries, and sectoral trade protective measures designed to protect specific industries (e.g. subsidies, preferential treatment of domestic firms in government procurement). From a legal viewpoint, the various forms of trade protection may be subdivided into three categories:

(a) Trade protection that is introduced in a transparent and lawful manner in conformity with the international legal obligations of GATT contracting parties. GATT law leaves it to each individual contracting party to decide autonomously on its own national level of tariff protection (Articles II, XXVIII). GATT also includes generously drafted safeguard clauses which allow each contracting party to maintain or introduce unilaterally tariffs, subsidies, quantitative restrictions, state-trading enterprises and other non-tariff barriers for almost every conceivably legitimate economic or non-economic policy objective (see e.g. Ar-

10 For details see: J. Forman-Peck, A History of the World Economy. International Economic Relations since 1850, 1983

ticles IV, VI, XI:2, XII, XV, XVI-XXI, XXIV, XXXV), provided the measures are introduced in a transparent manner (see e.g. Articles XVI:1, XIX:2) and in conformity with the procedural and substantive requirements of GATT law (see e.g. Articles VI: 6,a, XII:4, XIII, XVII:1, XVIII-XXI, XXIV).

(b) Trade protection that is introduced in violation of the obligations of contracting parties under the GATT, such as tariffs and other "charges of any kind" in excess of tariff bindings (Article II), quantitative import or export restrictions not permitted under any of the exception clauses of GATT (Article XI), discriminatory internal taxation and regulation (Article III), export subsidies (Article XVI:B) and other non-tariff trade restrictions (e.g. Articles VI-XI, XV, XVII). This category of illegal trade protection includes also most "grey area trade restrictions", such as VERs and orderly marketing agreements (OMAs) in violation of Articles XI and XIII of GATT, unless they have been authorized by all GATT contracting parties (e.g. VERs under the International Textiles Agreement of 1974).

(c) Private restraints of international trade and competition, subject to domestic antitrust laws and competition policy, but frequently induced or supported by governments (e.g. private export cartels, OMAs, countertrade arrangements, restrictions relating to industrial property rights, collusive pricing practices). GATT law permits governmental countervailing measures in response to private trade distortions (see Article VI: antidumping duties). But it is subject to legal controversy whether, and to what extent, government support for private restraints of international trade competition can be legally challenged under other GATT provisions.

The purpose of GATT rules and procedures is to promote the realization of the benefits from trade liberalization (e.g. increase of the national gains from trade, avoidance of "nullification or impairment" of tariff concessions, protection of the international price mechanism, structural adjustment in response to import competition) and to assist governments in the implementation of transparent, nondiscriminatory and welfare-increasing trade policies. The "new protectionism", a term frequently used in the media and in academic writings since the mid-1970s,[11] refers not only to an increase in the quantity of protectionism practiced but also to the differences in the forms and the broader, systemic implica-

11 From an economic perspective see, e.g.: M.B. Krauss, The New Protectionism. The Welfare State and International Trade, 1978. From a legal perspective see, e.g.: C.J. Green, The New Protectionism, in: Northwestern Journal of International Law and Business 1981, pp. 1 ff.

tions of protectionist measures. Characteristic features of the "new protectionism" are, inter alia:

A) Recourse to Disproportionate, Mutually Harmful Policy Instruments

The liberal trade premises underlying GATT law - that governments are negotiating about the rules of trade and will conduct their trade policies in a rule-oriented manner leaving market prices and competition to settle the outcomes in a way maximizing individual and social welfare - are politically less and less accepted by the modern "welfare states". International trade offers only an opportunity of increasing national welfare. The actual exploitation of this opportunity requires that production factors are mobile and can be shifted from low-productivity uses to alternative high productivity uses identified by market prices. In the modern "redistributive states",[12] a major objective of many government interventions into the private economy is to provide "social security" by shielding individual citizens and groups from individually adverse pressures to adjust to import competition. For instance, European producers and employees in the farm, textiles, clothing, shoe, steel and other industries are systematically supported not only by "market-conforming" protective instruments (such as production subsidies and import tariffs) but also by quantitative import restrictions, "administered prices", export subsidies and other policy instruments which, according to economic theory (see above Chapter III.3 and IV.3), are unnecessarily harmful and mutually impoverishing (e.g. export cartels).

Import protection keeps labour and capital in low-productivity uses, retards their adjustment to international competition and acts as a "tax on exports" to the detriment of the export industries of the restricting country.[13] In order to offset the reduced competitiveness of the protected producers and to support the continued exportation of their uncompetitive products, the import restrictions are often supplemented by export subsidies, international market-sharing arrangements and other external "beggar-thy-neighbour" policies, by which governments attempt to solve their domestic economic problems at the expense of foreign countries. The common agricultural policy of the EEC, which has transformed the EEC from a net-importer of agricultural products into the world's

12 On the historical emergence of the "redistributive state" which sees one of its main functions in redistributing the income and wealth of its citizens, see: J. Tumlir, Economic Policy as a Constitutional Problem, 1984.

13 For an economic explanation of why "a tax on imports is a tax on exports" see, e.g.: International Trade 1981/82, GATT 1982, pp. 15-18.

largest exporter by means of systematic import restrictions and export subsidies, is a case in point. Such trade-distorting measures tend to impair production, trade and competition also outside the restricting country.[14] They are "conflict-oriented" in the sense of the Kantian "universalizability" criterion because their underlying principles cannot be equally applied by all countries and tend to discriminate notably against exports from developing countries (e.g. in the area of agricultural products, textiles, shoes, steel, consumer electronics).

B) Return to "Power-oriented", Bilateral and Sectoral Trade Policies

Diplomatic techniques and other social decision-making systems can be roughly categorized into "power-oriented" and "rule-oriented" techniques.[15] The history of international economic cooperation, and of civilization at large, may be described as a gradual evolution from a power-oriented towards a rule-oriented approach.[16] A power-oriented approach seeks to assert the power which a negotiator wields or represents, either openly (e.g. promise of a trade concession or of development aid) or subtly (e.g. voting in the IMF or World Bank, withholding of military aid). The preferred power-oriented techniques are bilateral negotiations, unilateral threats, executive discretion and secrecy, which allow the negotiator to bring to bear the power of his nation and to negotiate ad hoc compromises. A rule-oriented approach, by way of contrast, seeks to establish long-term and generally acceptable principles and rules which, because of their longer-range reconciliation of the interests involved and the voluntary agreement of the parties concerned, offer important advantages such as: a higher degree of stability and perceived fairness of the rules due to less reliance on raw power; more predictability and more scope for decentralized decision-making by private economic agents; more transparent policy-making with enhanced possibilities for parliamentary control and citizen participation; more regard to mutual long-term interests rather than unilateral ad hoc short-term interests;

14 While a production subsidy applies to all production regardless of where the goods will be consumed, an export subsidy creates a divergence between domestic and world market prices. An export subsidy may benefit individual domestic exporters and foreign consumers, but it imposes costs on the exporting country (budget costs, deterioration of the national terms of trade as a result of reduced export prices) and on competing foreign producers due to the distortion of international competition (unless the export subsidy merely compensated extra costs caused by domestic distortions).

15 See: J.H. Jackson, The Crumbling Institutions of the Liberal Trade System, in: Journal of World Trade Law 1978, pp. 93, 98 ff.

16 Jackson (note 15), p. 99; L. Henkins, How Nations Behave, Law and Foreign Policy, 2nd edition 1979, p. 1.

more scope for multilaterally acceptable rules and procedures and for the reduction of transaction costs made possible through multilateralism; more consistency with the values and principles of national constitutional laws for the exercise and limitation of government powers (e.g. transparency, non-discrimination, "due process", constitutionally limited government powers).

Representatives of large trading nations or of powerful protectionist interest groups often favour bilateral negotiations and other power-oriented techniques (e.g. non-transparent policy-making, executive discretion), which enable them to bring to bear their respective power to win advantage in particular negotiations. Small countries and members of unorganized groups, by way of contrast, tend to be more inclined to rule-oriented methods for the settlement of conflicts of interests (i.e. elaboration of generally beneficial rules, procedures and institutions designed to ensure adherence to the agreed rules). The "new protectionism" reflects a clear trend away from the general GATT rules and from non-discriminatory competition with decentralized decision-making (e.g. of producers, traders and consumers) towards bilateral and sectoral trade restrictions imposed for the benefit of powerful interest groups. The increasing reliance on unilateral or bilateral VERs, sectoral OMAs, discriminatory import restrictions, and on government-supported private national and international cartel arrangements is incompatible with the GATT objectives and GATT rules for non-discriminatory trade competition.[17] The trade discrimination and trade distortions created thereby underlay most of the current problems of the multilateral trading system based on GATT. The European Community, followed by the United States, is the most frequent user of bilateral market-sharing arrangements which often evade the legal requirements of the GATT's safeguard clauses (Articles VI and XIX) and violate the GATT's prohibitions of quantitative restrictions (Article XI) and trade discrimination (Articles I and XIII).[18] Empirical evi-

17 For a survey of the various kinds of restraints of competition see, e.g.: Green (note 11) pp. 3 ff; Competition and Trade Policy - Their Interaction, OECD 1984, pp. 27 ff; M. Kostecki, Export-restraint Arrangements and Trade Liberalization, in: The World Economy 1987, pp. 425 ff. On the inconsistency with GATT of governmental discriminatory quantitative trade restrictions see also: E.U. Petersmann, Grey Area Trade Policy and the Rule of Law, in: Journal of World Trade Law April 1988.

18 Kostecki (note 17) lists 139 bilateral export restraint arrangements applied in 1986 - without bilateral VERs concluded under the International Textiles Agreement -, of which 68 protect the EEC market, 45 the US market and 10 the Canadian market. The products affected include steel and steel products (44), agricultural products (25), machine tools (6), automobiles and transport equipment (15), textiles (25 arrangements with countries not participating in the International Textiles Agreement), consumer electronics products (10) and footwear (81).

dence confirms that this most dangerous form of the "new protectionism" has also an inherent tendency to expand, for instance due to circumvention and "trade deflection" of bilateral trade deals, the creation of vested interests, the force of precedent, and the competitive distortions of import restrictions on intermediate products (e.g. textiles, steel, agricultural raw materials) for processing industries (e.g. clothing, automobiles, agricultural industries).[19] Trade in textiles, clothing, agricultural products, steel and certain electronic products is increasingly regulated outside the general GATT rules through "power-oriented" sectoral deals imposed mainly by the USA and by the EEC. Especially the worldwide network of bilateral trade arrangements for textiles and steel has led to a "global management" of trade in these products. In 1985, at least 10% of world trade was covered by bilateral export restraint arrangements.

C) Administrative "Grey Area Trade Restrictions" without Effective Parliamentary and Judicial Control

Since the 1970's, the welfare-increasing effects of the successful liberalization of tariffs and non-tariff barriers within GATT are increasingly being undermined by recourse to "grey area trade restrictions" such as private or public unilateral "voluntary export restraints" (VERs) or bilateral "voluntary restraint agreements" (VRAs). Their distinctive legal features are that they result from bilateral arrangements between importing and exporting countries (usually in the form of minimum price undertakings, quantitative restrictions, surveillance systems or export forecasts), involve the use of private and/or public discriminatory export restraints for selected products, and are deliberately used by government executives as a means to circumvent basic principles of international and domestic trade and competition laws. A recent GATT document listing 135 export restraint arrangement practiced in 1986/87 suggests that the bulk of these measures are concentrated on relatively few sectors (steel: 38, textiles not covered by the MFA: 28, agriculture: 21, transport equipment: 14, electronics: 11, footwear: 8, machine tools: 7) and involve relatively few GATT contracting parties on both the importing side (EEC: 69, USA: 4, Canada: 7) as well as on the exporting side (Japan: 25, Korea: 24, EEC: 7). Many of these trade arrangements involve quantitative trade restrictions and other non-tariff trade barriers inconsistent with GATT Article XI:1; trade discrimination incon-

19 For a discussion of the various economic, political and legal reasons of the "expansive logic" of bilateral VERs see, e.g.: Kostecki (note 17), pp. 10 ff; C. Pearson, Emergency Protection in the Footwear Industry, 1983, p. 30 f.

sistent with GATT Articles I:1, XIII or XVII:1; or government-supported export cartels for the implementation of VERs or other "crisis cartels" (e.g. for steel and synthetic fibres in the EEC), many of which appear to be inconsistent with the competition laws of the importing countries concerned.[20] The public choice by government executives of non-transparent and unlawful forms of trade protection raises also broader legal issues because neither in the United States nor in the EEC do the executive branches enjoy a general statutory authority to enter into VERs inconsistent with their international GATT obligations and to induce private firms to set up private export cartels inconsistent with the respective competition laws in the United Sates and the EEC respectively.

As a result of this bilateral and sectoral approach to trade policy, the GATT objective of general trade policy based upon non-discriminatory tariffs, to be liberalized and legally bound in successive "GATT rounds" and laid down in transparent tariff legislation of general application, has increasingly been undermined. Another reason for this shift from a "tariff-centred" trade policy by relatively simple instruments to "administered trade" by a variety of complicated, discretionary and discriminatory protective measures is the dramatic increase in recent years of antidumping, countervailing duty and other safeguard proceedings in OECD countries. These are often viewed as a protectionist abuse through "legal harassment" in view of the considerable uncertainties, legal complexities, costs and protectionist bases of these procedures.[21] Following a precedent set in the US Trade Act of 1974 and taken over into the 1979 GATT Subsidy Code, most antidumping and countervailing duty laws now permit "voluntary" export restraints as an alternative to antidumping or countervailing duties and are increasingly used as a legal basis for the imposition of VERs.[22] Due to their frequent secrecy and administration abroad, such VERs curtail the

---

20 See, e.g. E.J. Mestmäcker, The Applicability of the ECSC-Cartel Prohibition (Article 65) During A "Manifest Crisis", in: Michigan Law Review 1984, pp. 1399 ff, according to whom the EC Commission's support of price-fixing agreements among steel undertakings violates Article 65 of the ECSC Treaty and exceeds the limited powers of the EC Commission under the ECSC Treaty. See also: E.U. Petersmann (note 17 above).

21 See, e.g.: Green (note 11), pp. 11 ff; Trade and Development Report 1984, UNCTAD 1985, p. 74; R. de C. Grey, The Decay of the Trade Relations System, in: R.H. Snape (ed.), Issues in World Trade Policy, 1986, pp. 17 ff, according to whom the number of antidumping and countervailing duty activities in OECD countries increased from 124 in 1979 to 405 in 1982 (p. 29).

22 In the EEC, for instance, more than 50% of all antidumping cases have been terminated as the result of acceptance by the EC Commission of price revision undertakings, see: van Bael/Bellis, International Trade Law and Practice of the European Community. EEC Anti-Dumping and other Trade Protection Laws, 1985, p. 98.

legal and judicial remedies available for adversely affected domestic importers. If exporting countries do not accept to impose VERs, importing countries frequently resort to alternative protective measures on the import side. For example: France continues to keep Japanese automobile imports to less than 3% of its market through the administrative manipulation of type-approval procedures.[23] The French limitation of the importation of Japanese videorecorders was made effective by the so-called "Poitiers measures" whereby all customs clearance formalities for imports of videorecorders had to be fulfilled in the small town of Poitiers. Most of the various selective trade protection measures are hardly ever openly discussed and authorized in national parliaments, and their judicial review is largely confined to the control of the observance of procedural rules without substantive review of the broad trade policy discretion of government executives (see below chapter VI.2 and 3).

D) Lack of Transparent Democratic Policy-making in the "Public Interest"

According to the democratic ideal of Abraham Lincoln's "government of the people, by the people, for the people", governments are established with limited powers that must be exercised in a transparent and representative manner so as to protect and promote the equal rights of their citizens. GATT law commits governments to tax and regulate the trade transactions of their citizens by means of tariffs (i.e. a transparent price mechanism) rather than quantitative restrictions (except in limited and defined circumstances), and to publish all governmental trade regulations "promptly in such a manner as to enable governments and traders to become acquainted with them" (Article X:1). It also requires GATT contracting parties to observe certain liberal principles in the exercise of their trade policy powers - such as non-discrimination, use of less-distortive policy instruments and "due process" in the administration of foreign trade regulations - which correspond to basic constitutional principles of liberal democracies and can be easily understood by domestic citizens. The GATT rules for non-discriminatory trade competition imply that production and trade should be determined in a decentralized ("democratic") manner by the citizens themselves (i.e. through their private demand and supply in response to market signals) and that governmental trade policies should aim at maximizing individual market access and freedom of choice.

---

23 For details see: M.C.E.J. Bronckers, Selective Safeguard Measures in Multilateral Trade Relations, 1985, p. 124 f.

A distinct feature of the "new protectionism" is the secrecy of many grey area trade restrictions and the lack of transparency of the administrative "management" of trade by means of hundreds of frequently changing "administered prices", quantitative production or trade quotas, and various degrees of trade preferences. For instance, most VERs and VRAs are not published. The 21 common agricultural market organizations of the EEC and the thousands of annually changing trade quotas allocated by the EC bureaucracies for textiles, clothes, steel and other products are regulated every year in over 3'000 EEC regulations, directives and decisions, which even "agricultural experts" or "textiles experts" find impossible to read and fully comprehend.[24] This makes an informed public discussion on the "protection costs" involved all but impossible. And also the trade bureaucracies themselves tend to be neither willing nor capable of examing the various price, production, trade and welfare effects of the various trade restrictions in a comprehensive manner, thus making it impossible to take a balanced and representative decision with due regard to all affected interests on whether the trade restriction is required by the "public interest".[25]

Recent studies of the costs and benefits of protection conclude that the spread of protection has yielded few benefits, but imposed substantial costs. For instance, the economic costs imposed by the EEC's import restrictions on European consumers have been estimated to amount to about 300 billion DM in 1983.[26] For the USA, it has been estimated that US trade restrictions in 1980 imposed an average implicit tax cost of at least 255 Dollars per person.[27] VERs cause considerable additional economic costs because they transfer the private

24 See, e.g.: Glismann/Horn/Nehring/Vaubel, Weltwirtschaftslehre, Vol. I, 3rd edition 1986, p. 12: "Die schiere Zahl der Eingriffe in den Aussenhandel durch die Regierungen... ist in den letzten Jahren derart gestiegen, dass sie auch für Spezialisten unter den Spezialisten nicht mehr überschaubar ist. Beispielsweise gibt es heute wohl kaum einen unter den vielen tausenden von Agrarexperten der Europäischen Gemeinschaft, der mit dem ständig steigenden Output allein der europäischen Agrarbürokratie Schritt zu halten vermöchte... Gar nicht erwähnt ist das Problem der Wirkungen - wie soll man diese erfassen, wenn man nicht einmal über eine Aufzählung aller handelspolitischen Massnahmen verfügt?"

25 See the answer by the EC commission to parliamentary Question No. 1289/84 (O.J. 1985 C 113/4), where the Commission refused to make any cost-benefit analysis of the effects of trade protective measures on consumers.

26 Calculation made by the German Foreign Trade Association of Retailers, in: Frankfurter Allgemeine Zeitung 23.5.1984, p. 13.

27 Challenge, January 1984, p. 54. For detailed estimates of the protection costs see the OECD study: Costs and Benefits of Protection, OECD 1985, 254 pages. See also the examples and literature cited by M. Wolf in the World Bank study above note 7, p. 17 f.

"scarcity rents", which in the case of import restrictions are reaped by domestic importers, abroad to the exporting country. Thus it has been estimated that the VER imposed on imports of Japanese automobiles into the USA led to an annual off-budget transfer of 4 1/2 billion dollars from US consumers to foreign and domestic producers.[28] The economic costs of the VER imposed by the EEC on Japanese videorecorders implied an annual payment of "scarcity rents" in the order of 175 million pounds by EC buyers to Japanese producers[29] - without public discussions, without transparent regulations and outside the rule of law. Even if VERs are published and based on multilaterally agreed rules, their administration usually remains opaque, as evidenced by the more than 3000 annually changing textiles quotas of the EEC under the International Textiles Arrangements. The economic irrationality of "grey area trade restrictions" becomes most obvious by the increasing number of studies showing that the national protection costs (e.g. per job preserved in the protected industry) are often many times higher than the income received by workers in the protected industry, and that the stated objectives of trade protection have rarely been achieved. The "eminent persons report" on "Trade Policies for a Better Future" sees a major reason of the "new protectionism" in the lack of openness and public discussion in the making of trade policy as well as in the "danger of secrecy and administrative discretion":

> "In each country, the making of trade policy should be brought into the open. The costs and benefits of trade policy actions, existing and prospective, should be analysed through a "protection balance sheet". Private and public companies should be required to reveal in their financial statements the amount of any subsidies received. Public support for open trade policies should be fostered."[30]

E) Surreptitious Income Redistribution for the Benefit of Special Interest Groups

Economic theory and the trade policy analyses of international economic organizations are virtually unanimous today in concluding that trade restrictions can hardly ever give net protection to the national economy as a whole and only redistribute income among domestic groups at considerable net cost to the re-

---

28 The Consumer Cost of US Trade Restraints, in: Federal Reserve Bank of New York Quarterly Review, Summer 1985, p. 8.

29 B. Hindley, EC Imports of VCRs from Japan. A Costly Precedent, in: Journal of World Trade Law 1986, pp. 168, 178.

30 Trade Policies for a Better Future, GATT 1985, p. 35 f.

stricting economy. Like much of domestic economic policy, "foreign trade policy, too, is pure redistribution, although here again it is masked by the rhetoric of national interest".[31] Economic theory also teaches that, should countries choose to intervene in trade, production subsidies or price distortions through tariffs are less costly for the restricting country than non-price interventions. Both the redistributional "income transfer effects" as well as the overall "resource misallocation effects" of quantitative trade restrictions are larger compared to a production subsidy (which transfers income directly and distorts only producer prices) and to a tariff (which transfers income indirectly through production and consumer price distortions but generates public revenue).[32]

The fact that "grey area trade policies" redistribute income among domestic groups in a surreptitious manner explains in part the preference of protectionist interest groups (including politicians) for the use of more costly non-tariff trade barriers: Whereas subsidies redistribute income through the public budget and tariffs are also transparent and generate public revenue, alternative non-tariff trade barriers redistribute income indirectly in a more hidden way. Another reason for the "public choice" of grey area trade restrictions rather than safeguard measures permitted under GATT lies in the fact that VERs, government-supported cartels or quantitative import restrictions offer additional "protection rents" to traders and import-competing producers: While import tariffs generate revenue for the public budget, the use of alternative quantitative trade restrictions transfer the "scarcity rents" to those private traders and producers which dispose of the import licenses and can appropriate to themselves the "protection rents" resulting from the increased prices of the restricted goods.

The "new protectionism" thus resolves the conflict between the national economic self-interest in liberal trade and the protectionist group interests within the restricting economy even more for the benefit of special interests at the expense of national welfare. Another important issue in this context is "rent-seeking". In an economy where the government has broad discretionary power to distribute "protection rents" and gives in to the protectionist demands from domestic producers, lobbying for protection will become an important entrepreneurial activity.[33] Lobbying for protection may be more profitable for import competing

31 Banks/Tumlir, The Political Problem of Adjustment, in: The World Economy 1986, pp. 141 ff. See also Krauss (note 9), pp. XVII, 6 ff.

32 See, e.g.: Krauss (note 11), pp. 6 ff.

33 See: A. Krueger, Trade Policies in Developing Countries, in: Jones/Kenen (eds.), Handbook of International Economics. vol. I, 1984, pp. 534 f.

producers than structural adjustment to import competition. And a producer who does not lobby, may risk being driven out of the market by the lobbying of his competitors.

3. Why Trade is Not Free and Why Trade Liberalization Meets Resistance

A) The National Interest in Trade Liberalization vs. Group Interests in Trade Protection

As has been shown, the issue of liberal trade versus protectionism is characterized by the conflict between the public interest and special interests. The national public interest relates, inter alia, to:

- the contribution of liberal trade to the individual and social welfare of domestic citizens not only in terms of economic efficiency and a higher real income but also in terms of larger personal freedom and additional protection against the abuse of private economic as well as government power (see above chapter V.1);

- the contribution of the international market mechanism to a decentralized and depoliticized coordination of the international division of labour among people and nations with diverse interests, notably, the avoidance of mutually impoverishing "beggar-thy-neighbour" policies and of the international conflicts triggered thereby, which contributed to a worldwide economic and political crisis in the 1930s (see above chapter V.2a);

- the national self-interest in a rule-oriented rather than power-oriented conduct of trade policy (above chapter V.2.b) and in the observance of the substantive and procedural requirements of international and domestic foreign trade laws (such as GATT Article VI and XIX) for the introduction and administration of import restrictions (above chapter V.2.c);

- the national self-interest in transparent policy-making (above chapter V.2.d) and in democratic discussion and control of governmental income redistribution among domestic groups (chapter V.2.e).

However, free trade is not best for everyone. While trade liberalization benefits the liberalizing economy as a whole, it is likely to impose adjustment costs on import competing industries and their workers. Given the difficulties of actually redistributing the gains from liberal trade in order to compensate the losers from a potentially "Pareto-optimal" trade liberalization, the benefits and harms from trade liberalization are usually unequally distributed. Hence, there is a built-in opposition to trade liberalization within all states. Import competing industries will strongly resist the removal of the import restrictions on which they have come to rely, and will put pressure on trade policy-makers in support of their demands for the maintenance of trade protection. Governmental trade restrictions can change the "winners" and "losers" from import competition. Protectionist interest groups have therefore strong incentives to seek to change the outcomes of non-discriminatory market competition, as envisaged by GATT, for their individual self-interests: Import-competing producers will individually benefit from subsidies and from "protection rents" made possible by import protection. Periodically elected trade politicians and trade bureaucracies may likewise individually benefit from "serving" their clientèles through the granting of trade protection in exchange for political support. Economic theory shows, however, that the total economic protection costs for domestic consumers (including processing industries) and exporters are necessarily greater than the sum of the protection gains of domestic producers and the government,[34] and that trade protection is a costly and ineffective form of income redistribution among domestic groups.

B. "Protectionist Biases" in Domestic Decision-making about Trade Policy

In liberal democracies of the Western type in which individual freedoms and preferences of the population are respected, economic policy should conform to the will of the people. If economic theory, the trade policy declarations of governments and the economic analyses of virtually all international trade, mone-

---

34 See e.g.: Krauss (note 11), p. 7 ff; M. Kreinin, International Economics: A Policy Approach, 1979, pp. 267 ff; Lindert/Kindleberger, International Economics, 1982, pp. 120 ff. See also: J. Tumlir, International Economic Order: Rules, Cooperation and Sovereignty, in: P. Oppenheimer (ed.), Issues in International Economics, 1980, pp. 1, 6: "If only sub-optimal policies are proscribed by the international rules, it follows that only a sub-group can benefit from its government breaking a rule - at the cost, mainly, of the rest of the society. Here we can generalize the monopoly theorem according to which the loss to society always exceeds the monopolist's gain. So also the costs of a government's interference with the market, when undertaken in defiance of international rules, always exceed the gain of the group on whose behalf the government intervened".

tary and financial organizations - such as GATT,[35] UNCTAD,[36] the IMF,[37] the World Bank[38] and the OECD[39] - unanimously emphasize the national and international welfare gains from trade liberalization: Why then has trade protectionism been on the increase since the 1973 crisis in the world economy? Can governments act against the national economic self-interests of their own countries? Economic history shows that they can. But economic theory,[40] political economics[41] and the analyses of international economic organizations[42] are today also in broad agreement on the economic, political and legal causes of this "government failure" to translate into practice the repeatedly professed attachment to the liberal GATT rules.

The glaring discrepancy between the economic arguments for free trade and the reality of trade protectionism cannot be convincingly explained in terms of lack of information of governments about the welfare-gains from trade liberalization. The governments themselves as well as all international organizations are time and again emphasizing the need for trade liberalization and the economic as well as political dangers of trade protectionism. Most trade policy-makers also

---

35 See, e.g.: Blackhurst/Marian/Tumlir, Trade Liberalization, Protectionism and Interdependence, GATT 1977; idem, Adjustments, Trade and Growth in Developed and Developing Countries, GATT 1978; Trade Policies for a Better Future, GATT 1985.

36 See, e.g., UNCTAD's analysis of the "level, costs and effects of protectionist measures" in: Trade and Development Report 1984, UN 1985, pp. 183 ff; or UNCTAD's policy paper for UNCTAD VI on "Protectionism, trade relations and structural adjustment", TD/274 1983.

37 See, e.g.: World Economic Outlook, IMF October 1985, pp. 28 f; Anjaria/Kirmani/Petersen, Trade Policy Issues and Developments, IMF 1985; Nowzad, The Rise in Protectionism, IMF 1978; M. Corden, Protection and Liberalization: A Review of Analytical Issues, IMF 1987.

38 See, e.g.: World Development Report 1987 (devoted to foreign trade), World Bank 1987; The Uruguay Round. A Handbook on the Multilateral Trade Negotiations, World Bank 1987; Agarwala, Price distortions and growth, World Bank 1984; A. Krueger (Vice-President of the World Bank), Protectionism and Growth, in: Protectionism and Growth, EFTA 1985, pp. 11-30.

39 See, e.g.: Costs and Benefits of Protection, OECD 1984.

40 See, e.g.: R.E. Baldwin, The Political Economy of Protectionism, in: J. Bhagwati (ed.), Import Competition and Response, 1982, pp. 263-292; Finger/Hall/Nelson, The Political Economy of Administered Protection, in: American Economic Review June 1982, pp. 452-466; P.A. Messerlin, Bureaucracies and the Political Economy of Protection, World Bank 1983; V. Cable, Economics and the Politics of Protection, World Bank 1983; B. Hindley/P. Nicolaides, Taking the New Protectionism Seriously, 1983.

41 Cf. B.S. Frey, International Political Economics, 1984, pp. 15 ff, with further references.

42 See, e.g. Blackhurst/Marian/Tumlir, Trade Liberalization (note 35), pp. 43-60; OECD (note 39), pp. 184-200, with further references.

appear to have understood that the economic arguments for liberal trade do not rest on a naive belief in "laissez faire" but on the existence of more efficient and more effective domestic instruments of government intervention for the correction of domestic "market failures", the promotion of "infant industries", or for the management of the national balance of payments. Why then do governments often conduct trade policy against their declared convictions? There is broad agreement today that this "government failure" is due to various "protectionist biases" in domestic decision-making processes about trade policy and to insufficient legal restraints on the discretionary trade policy powers of governments.

a) Unbalanced political representation of the general public interest in liberal trade

An economic analysis of import restrictions shows that their various "import effects", "production effects", "consumption effects" and "redistribution effects" typically entail direct, concentrated and clearly visible benefits for a small number of protected producers and only indirect, widely dispersed and frequently non-transparent costs for consumers and the domestic economy at large. The reduction in the quantity of the restricted imported goods enables the protected producers to raise their prices, output and income accordingly ("protection effect"). The resulting taxation of consumers, processing and export industries is only indirect, occurs at a later point of time and imposes an individually small burden on consumers, who usually do not spend time and money in order to find out and evaluate the causes of the price increase. Import-competing producers have considerably stronger financial incentives and better organizational possibilities for maximizing their income through political demand for trade protection, compared to consumers who have individually little incentive to bear the "information costs" and "organization costs" of lobbying for trade liberalization which, as a "public good", benefits all consumers including those not actively lobbying for liberal trade.[43] Periodically-elected politicians and trade bu-

43 A. Downs, An Economic Theory of Democracy, 1957, explains the more active role of producer interests in the formation of economic and trade policy by the fact that most people earn their income in one area but spend it in many. Hence it is rational for them to remain uninformed on many consumer issues ("rational ignorance") and to invest "information costs" and "organization costs" to exert political influence in their role as income receivers (producers) rather than in their role as income spenders (consumers). While trade theory focuses on the welfare of domestic and foreign consumers, trade policy tends to be influenced much more by producer interests. Also foreign trade law is usually characterized by a distinct "producer bias" (cf. Articles VI, XIX of GATT). See: R.E. Baldwin, The Economics

reaucrats are often considered to be protection-prone because import restrictions allow additional tariff revenue, additional jobs in the public sector, additional discretionary powers and prestige for trade administrators, the discreet distribution of "protection rents" in exchange for political support, and political "success" in helping the import-competing industries and their workers by relieving them temporarily from the pressure to adjust to import-competition.

b) The "political market for protectionism"

In liberal democracies, economic policies are the outcome of complex politico-economic processes. Just as the "spontaneous order" resulting from economic market competition may be economically inefficient due to the existence of "market failures" (e.g. the "order" that emerges when producers dump litter on the beach because it is in their own self-interests),[44] the "spontaneous order" emerging from competition on the "political market" may suffer from "government failures".

Since the 1970s, the economic theory of politics ("public choice theory") has elaborated comprehensive "theories of government failure", comparable to the theory of "market failure", which are used also in the trade policy analyses of international economic organization (such as GATT, the IMF, the World Bank, the OECD).[45] The analysis proceeds from the assumption that individuals act as rational "utility maximizers" and seek to advance their self-interests not only in the economic (market) sphere, but also in the political process. Economic agents react to changes in economic conditions not only in the economic market (as producers, investors, consumers etc.) but also outside the market in the poli-

of the GATT, in: P. Oppenheimer, Issues in International Economics, 1980, pp. 82 ff, who states with regard to the GATT safeguard clause in Article XIX that the "framers of GATT...recognized the pressure-group nature of international economic policy-making and established a safeguards rule as a means of moderating the major source of opposition to trade liberalization" (p. 85). Also the "differential GATT treatment at the border of goods affected by taxes and by subsidies is simply a by-product of the producer bias that affects so many government interventions into domestic markets" (p. 89). But Baldwin concludes: "Since producers (including workers) are more likely to incur significant reductions in real income as a result of changes in trade than are consumers, there is some justification for the producer bias of the GATT on income distribution grounds" (p. 92).

44 For a discussion of this example see: J.M. Buchanan, Law and the Invisible Hand, in: B.H. Siegan (ed.), The Interaction of Economics and the Law, 1977, pp. 127 ff.

45 For a survey of Public Choice Theory see: J.M. Buchanan/R. D. Tollison (eds.), The Theory of Public Choice, 1972; idem, The Theory of Public Choice - II, 1984. For a use of public choice theory in the trade policy analyses of international economic organizations see the literature mentioned in notes 33 to 37.

tical sector (e.g. as voters, lobbies, trade unions, members of political parties). Politicians and bureaucrats condition these two kinds of responses and react to them. The political decision-makers are no longer considered as unitary, impartial "benevolent, omnipotent and omniscient dictators" who maximize social welfare and correct "market failures" via informed interventions. The members of government, public administration, parliament and international organizations are viewed instead as endogenous agents within the politico-economic system, whose actions are influenced by numerous constraints (e.g. lack of information), self-interests and political forces (e.g. private interest groups, political parties, voters). Since the various participants in this "political market" will (also) pursue their own self-interests, just as they do in economic markets, import-competing producers (and their workers) are considered as "demanders" of trade protectionism seeking to maximize the income they can obtain by reducing imports; elected trade politicians are considered as the main "suppliers" of trade protection, who seek to maximize their political support and chances of reelection. The level and structure of trade protection may be explained as a "political price" that equilibrates the "political market for protectionism".[46]

Public choice theory explains not only why free trade, which is optimal from the point of view of national economic welfare, is not actually found in reality. But it also explains why the economically optimal forms of transparent and non-discriminatory trade protection, as prescribed by GATT law, are often not used by trade politicians. Much of what is criticized as economic foolishness in trade policies may be explained as "politically rational" for policy-makers who are less guided by economic rationality than by a desire to maximize political support and to minimize political opposition.

For instance: Since import restrictions cannot give net protection to the national economy as a whole but only redistribute income between different sectors of the domestic economy, trade policy-makers may prefer to use trade policy instruments other than tariffs (e.g. selective non-tariff barriers to trade) whose non-transparent character minimizes consumer opposition and whose redistributive effects may be difficult to identify and to challenge by court action. Less visible and discriminatory trade policy instruments might also prove attractive to governments that want to subsidize indirectly domestic interest groups through selective "trade protection rents" or to circumvent their international legal obligations and the risk of retaliation by other trading countries. The political

46 For a more detailed description of this model see: B.S. Frey, International Political Economics, 1984, pp. 15-39.

choice among the various instruments of trade control may be influenced also by their different procedural characteristics and legal requirements. Changes in import tariffs, domestic taxation and subsidies require time-consuming debate and legislation in many states. By contrast, the administration of import licenses, quantitative restrictions or state trading offer greater administrative flexibility and may enable trade policy-makers to implement trade policies without additional parliamentary debates and legislative acts. Licenses and state trading enable non-transparent politically motivated differentiations among supplier countries, traded products and commercial transactions. The replacement of import restrictions by VERs administered abroad in the exporting country, makes parliamentary and judicial review of such trade policy measures in the importing country even more difficult. Automatically adjustable instruments, such as variable import levies and export restitutions designed to equalize differences between international and domestic prices, offer the administrative advantage of built-in automatic adjustment mechanisms. The choice among the various import relief procedures might be likewise influenced by their different legal requirements and procedures (e.g. the different "injury" requirements set out in Articles VI and XIX GATT). These various examples illustrate that periodically elected governments as well as trade bureaucracies may have strong political, administrative and legal self-interests in modifying the ranking proposed by economic theory for the optimal use of trade policy instruments.

c) The "conservative social welfare function"

Apart from the "political economy explanation" of trade protection in terms of demand for protection from the affected interest groups and supply of protection by the political system, there are a number of other political reasons - including nationalistic, xenophobic and mercantilistic ones - why some degree of protection has traditionally been "the norm" rather than the exception. A helpful concept for understanding the actual trade policies of many countries is the "conservative social welfare function" prevailing in modern welfare states, i.e. the assumption of an implicit value judgment underlying certain trade protective measures. By this is meant the policy aim that "any significant absolute reductions in real incomes of any significant section of the community should be avoided".[47] Policies pursuing such an income distribution target can be descri-

47 W.M. Corden, Trade Policy and Economic Welfare, 1974, p. 107 f. See also: A.V. Deardorff, Safeguards Policy and the Conservative Social Welfare Function, in: H. Kierzkowski (ed.), Essays in honor of W.M. Corden, 1986.

bed as "conservative" because they tilt against the wind of change and seek to protect the existing income distribution, on which not only the maintenance of social peace but also the survival of a government may depend.

The assumption of an implicit "conservative welfare function" supports the view that governments introduce trade protection not only because of political pressures from special groups but also out of concern for the income and adjustment problems of import-competing industries. It can also be seen as a part of a social insurance system protecting against sudden income losses, which is politically accepted because those who will have to bear the "protection costs", are prepared to pay this "insurance premium " in order to benefit from similar help if the need arose. Yet, the "conservative welfare function" is a political argument and does not offer any justification for granting protection by means of trade policy instruments rather than by more efficient, alternative internal policy instruments (such as direct subsidies or adjustment assistance). Furthermore, even as a political principle it is not applied in a non-discriminatory manner: governments do not have the economic means and do not consistently attempt to protect all major groups of constituents from being hurt by economic changes that benefit some at the expense of others (e.g. changes due to domestic competition and technological innovation within the country).

The assumption of a "conservative social welfare function" cannot therefore explain the widespread existence of selective trade protection. With regard to domestic competition, most OECD states pursue competition policies based on the assumption that shifts in demand or supply conditions in the national market will lead to various price, output and income distribution changes which are more likely, in due course, to trigger spontaneous adjustments and efficient market responses than discretionary government interventions that are subject to government failure owing to lack of information, institutional rigidities or self-interested motives of politicians and bureaucrats. Such efficiency and growth-oriented competition policies are usually justified because of their long-term social gains and opportunities for everyone to be better off. Why then are this "social gains argument" and the income distribution effects of the "efficiency approach" politically acceptable in the field of competition policy but not in trade policy? Is there any economic or social justification of the "producer bias" of trade policy to the detriment of consumer interest? Why is income protection granted selectively to certain import-competing industries only and by means of non-transparent, inefficient trade policy instruments which forgo the possibility of tariff revenue in the importing country and allow foreign export firms to appropriate the "protection rents" and implement the restrictions abroad through VERs?

C) How Can the Political Resistance to Trade Liberalization Be Overcome?

Chapter V has argued so far that liberal trade and transparent, non-discriminatory trade policy-making are in the national economic and political self-interest of each country and that the widespread existence of non-transparent, discriminatory trade restrictions is largely the result of various "protectionist biases" in domestic decision-making about trade policy, such as the traditionally weak political representation of the consumer interests in liberal trade and other asymmetries in the "political market for protectionism". How can the obstacles to trade liberalization be overcome? Why do governments not follow the virtually unanimous advice from economic theory that even unilateral trade liberalization yields significant benefits for a country's efficiency and growth? Is it politically realistic and wise to hope for benevolent governments which will better resist the protectionist pressures from import-competing producers (e.g. by subsidizing the adjustment costs of injured firms and workers) and might more successfully activate political support for trade liberalization by impressing on the rest of the population the national gains from liberal trade?

Since World War II, worldwide trade liberalization has been achieved only through multilateral international negotiations and agreements notably in the context of the eight "GATT Rounds". Also prewar trade liberalization was achieved mainly through reciprocal international trade agreements in the context of the US Reciprocal Trade Agreements Programme of 1934 or, during the period from 1860 to 1914, through the European bilateral commercial treaty system. By contrast, the UNCTAD recommendations for unilateral, non-reciprocal trade preferences by developed in favour of developing countries have led to only very little effective trade liberalization because the tariff preferences introduced were largely undermined by the simultaneous introduction or maintenance of non-tariff barriers on developing country exports. This historical experience seems to support the conclusion of chapter V that trade policy decisions are often determined more by the rules and procedures shaping the "political market" than by the good intentions of politicians or by the advice from economic theory.

A recent OECD analysis of "Costs and Benefits of Protection" suggests that changes in domestic and international trade policy be analyzed as a function of the following four factors:[48]

First, the costs and benefits of trade flows for domestic political actors, which shape the demand for and resistance to protection. The report describes in this context the increasing need for structural adjustment, but also the aggravated adjustment costs in a situation of slow economic growth and pervasive rigidities, which encourage interest groups to seek insulation from market forces.

Second, governments' objectives and ability to cope with protectionist pressures, which set the supply of protection. Here the report identifies an increasing permeability of political systems to sectional demands and interest group pressures, and a diminishing range of policy options available to governments for dealing with these demands (e.g. budgetary limitations for direct transfer payments, previous protectionist precedents as arguments for additional protection).

Third, the perceived need for and advantages of international agreements in satisfying government objectives, which set the demand for international action. Trade cooperation on a multilateral rather than bilateral basis reduces considerably the "transactions costs", organization and information costs which countries incur in trade negotiations; it enables a stable multilateral legal framework for commerce, that protects especially the interests of small and weak countries and assists governments in containing pressures from domestic interest groups.

Fourth, international constraints, which impede or facilitate the development of international arrangements. Here, the increasing resort to bilateral bargains outside the general GATT rules and the difficulties experienced in extending GATT rules to other activities (e.g. agriculture, services) have weakened the credibility and perceived usefulness of GATT. "Whether the resistance of the trade policy system to sectional pressures can be increased will be a major factor in determining the future of the multilateral trading system".[49] This applies in particular to the two major trading powers, the EEC and the USA, for - as stated also in a recent GATT report - "an international trade system based on rules

48 Costs and Benefits of Protection, OECD 1985, pp. 184 ff.

49 OECD (note 48), p. 200.

cannot be effective unless the few large trading countries actively support it by their national policies".[50]

4. Lessons from the Past: Common Features of Past and Present Trade Mercantilism

The "new mercantilism"[51] of the 1930s and of the 1970s has brought out the dangers of a retreat into mercantilist policies leading to a gradual erosion of the international economic and legal order as a result of a cumulation of piece-meal decisions, the full implications of which are often not thought through. The economic, political and legal rationale of the international GATT and IMF principles and of their domestic implementing legislation in many countries go back, in part, to the criticism by the classical economists of the "old mercantilism", i.e. the economic doctrines and practices of European states in the period roughly from the 15th to the 18th centuries. Their mournful catalogue of the arbitrariness of the mercantile system provides a useful, and still topical, starting point for the assessment of contemporary trade mercantilism and for devising institutional-legal changes reducing the scope for abuses of the state's power to tax and regulate foreign trade for the benefit of special interests. The liberal economists, politicians and philosophers, during the 18th and 19th century, criticized the old mercantilism already for the same "government failures", for which modern economists blame the "new protectionism":

A) Economic Inefficiency and Waste

According to the old mercantilist doctrine,[52] the two primary objectives of economic foreign policy should be to increase national "power" and the national stock of precious metals through export promotion and import restrictions, whereby a country without gold or silver mines could obtain a continuous net inflow of the precious metals. Two major achievements of Adam Smith's "Inquiry into the Nature and Causes of the Wealth of Nations" (1776) were to demonstrate that mercantilism misspecified the "wealth of nations" and would impoverish

50 International Trade 1980/81, GATT 1981, p. 12.

51 See, e.g.: H.G. Johnson (ed.), The New Mercantilism, 1974.

52 The two "classic" analyses of the "old mercantilism" continue to be: E.F. Heckscher, Mercantilism, 2 Vols. 1931; J. Viner, The Long View and the Short: Studies in Economic Theory and Policy, 1958 (e.g. pp. 277-305).

rather than enrich the country. Moreover, the mercantilist policies proceeded from an authoritarian definition of "public good" as if it can exist separately from the individual freedom of choice and individual preferences of the citizens. What makes a nation rich is not money but the accumulation and efficient use of productive resources through specialization and division of labour maximizing the consumption opportunities of a country's citizens. Trade liberalization enlarges the division of labour beyond national frontiers and thereby permits a more efficient use of domestic resources. A country gains from imports, which increase the quantity of goods available for the domestic citizens, and its exports are the price it has to pay to get imports. Attempts to achieve a perpetual balance-of-payments surplus are likely to be self-defeating in the longer run because of the inflationary effects of the resulting inflow of international money. The fundamental truth that open markets and an international division of labour through trade promote economic efficiency and national welfare continues to be valid to the present day: If goods of the same quality can be produced with more or less costs, it is in the national self-interest of each country to minimize its production costs and to maximize the satisfaction of its consumers by specializing in the production of those goods which it can produce domestically at a comparative cost advantage, and by obtaining other goods through international trade. The "new protectionism" and the use of export subsidies for the "conquest" of foreign markets still remain a welfare-reducing policy instrument as criticized already by Adam Smith.[53]

B) Prevalence of Special Interests over the General Public Interest

Another major theme of Adam Smith's inquiry was to explain the mercantile restrictions as a result from the demand for regulation and for privileges by merchants and manufacturers. According to Smith, "consumption is the sole end and purpose of all production: and the interest of the producer should be attended to only so far as it may be necessary for promoting that of the consumer" ... "But in the mercantile system, the interest of the consumer is almost constantly sacri-

53 On the economic inefficiency of export subsidies see above note 14 and: International Trade 1984/85, GATT 1985, p. 20: "It is evident that, in the absence of market imperfections, export expansion based on subsidies does not contribute to economic growth, since the labour and capital attracted into the export sector by subsidies would be more productive elsewhere in the economy".

ficed to that of the producer; and it seems to consider production, and not consumption, as the ultimate end and object of all industry and commerce".[54]

Adam Smith showed the conflicts between the national economic self-interest in liberal trade and the protectionist self-interests of specific groups which, like the government and private monopolies, may individually gain from tariff revenue or from protection against import competition. Recent economic and historical analyses have explained the old English mercantilism and French mercantilism[55] as "rent-seeking" power politics by domestic economic agents using the public regulatory power and their private economic power for the pursuit of special favours and profits. The covert "capturing" of public regulatory powers by special interest groups,[56] and the social waste and surreptitious income redistribution involved in trade protectionism,[57] continue to be perceived as major problems of contemporary "neomercantilism" necessitating legal-institutional changes in decision-making about trade.[58]

C) Lack of Effective Protection of Individual Freedoms and Property Rights

Hobbes' theory of governmental organization justified an "unbounded state" where "Leviathan" was not subject to constitutional constraints other than his personal responsibility to God. The reality of mercantilism was characterized by excessive government regulation of all foreign trade and exchange transactions. During the period of "bullionism", it strived to ensure that each individual transaction made a net contribution to the national stock of precious metals. The

54 A. Smith, An Inquiry into the Nature and Causes of the Wealth of Nations, 1776 (Modern Library Edition), p. 625.

55 Cf: Baysinger/Ekelund/Tollison, Mercantilism as a Rent-Seeking Society, in: Buchanan/Tollison/Tullock, Toward a Theory of the Rent-Seeking Society, 1980, pp. 235 ff; Ekelund/Tollison, A Rent-Seeking Theory of French Mercantilism, in: Buchanan/Tollison, The Theory of Public Choice II, 1984, pp. 206 ff.

56 On this "capture theory" of wealth redistribution through the regulatory process, according to which economic regulation often does not promote the "general welfare" but rather the private interests of the regulated firms and of the "regulators" themselves, see: G.J. Stigler, The Theory of Economic Regulation, in: The Bell Journal of Economics and Management Science 2 (1971), pp. 3-21; S. Peltzman, Toward a more general Theory of Regulation, in: The Journal of Law and Economics XIX (1976), pp. 211-240.

57 See for instance: B. Hindley/E. Nicolaides, Taking the New Protectionism Seriously, 1983, pp. 7 ff.

58 See, e.g., the suggestions for "the embodiment of liberal principles in regional agreements and in domestic law" in: L. Dunn et alii (eds.), In the Kingdom of the Blind. A Report on Protectionism and the Asian-Pacific Region, 1983, pp. 116 ff.

mercantilist perception of the individual human being took it for granted that the unconstrained pursuit of self-interest would yield the "Hobbesian war of all against all", and that government interferences into individual economic activities were therefore justified.

By contrast, Adam Smith's key insight was that voluntary exchange can benefit both parties and will not take place unless both believe they will benefit from it. Moreover, the "public good" cannot be known unless citizens are free to express their individual preferences in the marketplace. But he emphasized also that the particular property of the price mechanism, namely to maximize and harmonize private advantage and social welfare, was conditional upon the existence of individual freedoms and property rights of producers and consumers and on economic competition. Hence the need for the protection of equal freedoms and property rights through the limitation of government powers to the enforcement of general rules that enable and preserve effective competition and allow individuals to make the best use of their particular capabilities, of which no government could know.

Since the end of absolute monarchy, the main aim of the classical economic and political liberals was to limit all governmental powers and prevent their arbitrary exercise through "constitutional restraints". The concept of individual liberty was based on the political idea of pre-existing individual freedoms. And the concepts of rule of law, separation of powers and limited "government by law, not by men", which arose from the struggle between King and Parliament in England especially during the 17th century and were later taken over into American constitutional law from the 18th century on, proceeded from the idea of pre-existing general principles of common law limiting the legislative powers delegated by the people to the government in order to preserve and enlarge the individual freedoms and property rights by protecting them from restraints and violence from others.

This recognition of individual freedoms and property rights aimed also to place substantive legal limits on mercantilist government interventions into the economy. In the United States, for instance, the US Supreme Court examined federal and state laws dealing with social and economic matters, and - under the "due process of law clauses" of the Fifth and the Fourteenth Amendment - declared several such laws unconstitutional because they deprived a plaintiff of liberty or property without procedural or substantive due process of law.[59] The creation and specification of freedoms and property rights over scarce resources acted as an incentive for the production and exchange of goods and services and for a more efficient allocation of resources (e.g. recognition of patent rights as an incentive for devoting resources to inventions). The allocation of goods and services was no longer decided, as in Hobbes' model of anarchy, on the basis of "might makes right" or on the basis of mercantilist grants by kings and princes of various property rights to merchants and manufacturers, but rather by self-interested and utility-maximizing individual producers, investors, traders and consumers. The economic markets, which emerged from voluntary transactions of property rights, promoted not only efficient resource allocation and market-conforming income distribution. The decentralized structure of private demand and supply and of the "invisible hand" of market competition also tended to decentralize and disperse power and, thereby, to reinforce the protection of freedoms and property rights.

Since the late 1930s, the US Supreme Court has essentially abandoned judicial review of economic and social legislation and upheld such laws unless they are found to violate intellectual, political or other specially protected liberties.[60] As Siegan has demonstrated, this judicial deference to legislative and executive economic regulations considerably reduced the legal and judicial protection of economic freedoms and property rights in the United States. It not only violated the intentions of the framers of the US Constitution, which expected the judiciary effectively to protect economic freedoms and property rights from majoritarian invasion. But, as Siegan has demonstrated with reference to more than fifty studies of the effects of economic government regulations in the United States, it also tolerated economically harmful and discriminatory restraints of economic freedoms and property rights for the benefit of the regulated special interest groups. The lack of effective judicial protection of individual economic liberties weakened also the constitutional doctrine of limited delegation of powers. In the modern "redistributive states", in which legislative bodies claim almost unlimited regulatory powers for the re-allocation of the income of their citizens, there appear no longer to be effective legal limits on the ability of governments to interfere with economic freedoms and redistribute income

59 For a detailed discussion of this case-law see: B.H. Siegan, Economic Liberties and the Constitution, 1980, pp. 24 ff, 110-182.

60 See the case-law discussed and criticized by Siegan (note 59), pp. 184 ff., and J.A. Dorn/H.G. Manne (eds.), Economic Liberties and the Constitution, 1987, pp.1 ff., 39 ff.

through non-transparent and discriminatory "grey area trade policies". As J.Tumlir has shown, "this plenitude of regulatory powers used for surreptitious redistribution implies that private property rights are virtually without effective constitutional protection (that is, they are unprotected against the state)...."[61]

D) "Unjust" Rules

According to Adam Smith, "Justice is the main pillar that upholds the whole edifice. If it is removed, the immense fabric of human society... must in a moment crumble into atoms"...[62] "Commerce and manufactures...can seldom flourish in any state in which there is not a certain degree of confidence in the justice of government".[63] Smith's suggestions for a "system of natural liberty" and for the removal of arbitrary government restrictions of individual freedoms were based on considerations of both economic efficiency and justice. The parallels between Smith's conception of equal rights and competition as necessary prerequisites of rule-oriented "justice", Kant's morally founded "categoric imperative" for applying "universalizable" general rules compatible with the whole system of accepted rules, and Hayek's theory of "general rules of just conduct", cannot be discussed here.[64] But all these different "theories of justice" do emphasize that those "systems either of preference or of restraint", that Adam Smith fought against and that have since reappeared in the form of discriminatory piece-meal

61 J. Tumlir, Protectionism. Trade Policy in Democratic Societies, 1985, pp. 13 ff, 16.

62 A. Smith, The Theory of Moral Sentiments (Liberty Classics edition Indianapolis 1976), p. 167 f.

63 A. Smith (note 62), pp. 328 f.

64 For a discussion see: J.M. Buchanan, The Justice of Natural Liberty, in: O'Driscoll (ed.), Adam Smith and Modern Political Economy, 1979, pp. 117 ff; F.A. v.Hayek, Law, Legislation and Liberty, Vol. II 1976, pp. 27 ff; E.J. Mestmäcker, Die sichtbare Hand des Rechts, 1978, pp. 139-170. See also J. Rawls, A Theory of Justice, 1971, who has developed a rule-oriented theory of "justice as fairness", under which "each person is to have an equal right to the most extensive basic liberty compatible with a similar liberty for others" and "social and economic inequalities are to be arranged so that they are both to the greatest benefit of the least advantaged and attached to offices and positions open to all under conditions of fair equality of opportunity" (pp. 60, 83). Rawls' derives his "principles of justice" from a contractarian model where individuals are asked to step behind a "veil of ignorance" and are thereby led to choose rules and institutions that cannot favour any one individual or group (pp. 11-22, 136-142). Buchanan has inferred from Rawls' theory "that a libertarian position is not inconsistent with an egalitarian one, despite attempts to make these seem contradictory by both the libertarian-antiegalitarians and the collectivist-egalitarians. A strong defense of the liberties of individuals, which can only be secured in an operating market economy, may be joined with an equally strong advocacy for the reform of basic social institutions designed to produce greater equality among individuals in their initial endowments and capacities" (p. 130).

restraints of foreign trade and the administrative dispensation of "protection rents" in favour of protectionist interest groups, are "unjust".[65]

E) Bureaucratic Dirigism, "Pretense of Knowledge" and Non-transparent Policy-making

The classic economists criticized the mercantilist administrative "dirigism" also for its less efficient information-processing compared to the self-regulatory mechanisms of market prices and competition among self-interested producers, investors and consumers. In the words of Adam Smith: "It is not from the benevolence of the butcher, the brewer, or the baker that we expect our dinner, but from their regard to their own interest. We address ourselves not to their humanity but to their self-love, and never talk to them of our own necessities but of their advantages."[66] "By pursuing his own interest he frequently promotes that of the society more effectually than when he really intends to promote it. I have never known much good done by those who affected to trade for the public good".[67] As regards "industrial policy", Smith pointed out:

> "No regulation of commerce can increase the quantity of industry in any society beyond what its capital can maintain. It can only divert a part of it into a direction into which it might not otherwise have gone; and it is by no means certain that this artificial direction is likely to be more advantageous to the society than that into which it would have gone of its own accord. Every individual is continually exerting himself to find out the most advantageous employment for whatever capital he can command. It is his own advantage, indeed, and not that of the society, which he has in view. But the study of his own advantage naturally, or rather necessarily leads him to prefer that employment which is most advantageous to the society."[68]

In view of the allocative efficiency of the spontaneous "invisible hand order", Adam Smith recommended to limit governmental economic policies:

---

65 See also M. and R. Friedman, Free to Choose 1979, pp. 30 ff (note 59), who emphasize that the economic effects of foreign and domestic market competition are not different in nature and "whatever we do should be evenhanded with respect to foreign and domestic trade" ... "any measure to ease the adjustment to sudden changes should be applied evenhandedly to domestic and foreign trade".

66 A. Smith (note 54), p. 14.

67 A. Smith (note 54), p. 423.

68 A. Smith (note 54), p. 421.

"The statesman who should attempt to direct private people in what manner they ought to employ their capitals would not only load himself with a most unnecessary attention, but assume an authority which could safely be trusted, not only to no single person, but to no council or senate whatever, and which would nowhere be so dangerous as in the hands of a man who had folly and presumption enough to fancy himself fit to exercise it."[69]

According to Smith

"the sovereign is completely discharged from a duty, in the attempting to perform which he must always be exposed to innumerable delusions, and for the proper performance of which no human wisdom or knowledge could ever be sufficient: the duty of superintending the industry of private people, and of directing it towards the employments most suitable to the interest of the society".[70] And: "It is the highest impertinence and presumption in kings and ministers, to pretend to watch over the economy of private people, and to restrain their expense, either by sumptuary laws, or by prohibiting the importation of foreign luxuries. They are themselves always, and without any exception, the greatest spendthrifts in the society. Let them look well after their own expense, and they may safely trust private people with theirs. If their own extravagance does not ruin the state, that of their subjects never will."[71]

A comparison of the present literature on the "new protectionism", on "neo-mercantilism" or on what H.Priebe has described as the "subsidized folly"[72] of the EEC's agricultural protectionism with Adam Smith's analysis of the "old mercantilism" shows that the problems identified have little changed and economic waste and arbitrariness continue to be criticized as distinctive features also of the modern administration of e.g. the thousands of administered prices and quotas for trade in agricultural products, textiles, clothes and steel. In today's integrated world economy, the international division of labour depends on autonomous actions of millions of producers, traders, investors and consumers whose individual freedoms entail "the unavoidable imperfection of man's

69 A. Smith (note 54), p. 423.

70 A. Smith (note 54), p. 650 f, where he also states: "Every system which endeavours, either by extraordinary encouragements to draw towards a particular species of industry a greater share of the capital of the society than what would naturally go to it or, by extraordinary restraints, force from a particular species of industry some share of the capital which would otherwise be employed in it, is in reality subversive of the great purpose which it means to promote. It retards, instead of accelerating, the progress of the society towards real wealth and greatness; and diminishes, instead of increasing, the real value of the annual produce of its land and labour."

71 A. Smith (note 54), p. 328 f.

72 See: H. Priebe, Die subventionierte Unvernunft, 1985.

knowledge and the consequent need for a process by which knowledge is constantly communicated and acquired".[73] The essence of classical liberalism is the belief that, within a system of general rules securing and protecting equal liberties, property rights and personal liability, there will arise a spontaneous decentralized market order that enables the use of constantly evolving knowledge and informations dispersed among millions of producers and consumers and "brings about a continuous adaptation of economic effect to millions of particular facts or events which in their totality are not known and cannot be known to anybody".[74]

The mercantilist assumption that government bureaucracies can ascertain and process without delay all the relevant particular facts determining the national and international economy, is rightly criticized as a "pretense of knowledge".[75] It disregards the central problem of rational economic order, namely "the inevitable ignorance of everybody of most of the particular facts which determine this order".[76] A rational and efficient international division of labour must to a large extent rely on general rules and the use of market prices as the most efficient information-processing mechanism. As a "conflict-solving" mechanism, market competition is not dependent on the good intentions of Hobbes' "benevolent dictator", but on the effective performance of the three basic functions of prices to transmit information, to provide an incentive for the use of the least costly production methods and to determine the distribution of market income. Open markets and transparent policy-making also serve important political functions, as emphasized by J.St. Mill in his treatise "On Liberty" (1859): On the "political market" as well are individual liberty, free discussion, transparency and access to all relevant informations the most effective means of improving the quality of "public opinion" and policy-making. Economic and political freedoms are often inseparable. By ensuring that economic activity is <u>not</u> subject to government control, a market economy limits the scope for abuse of government power. Market mechanisms enable a decentralized division of labour among

73 F.A. v.Hayek, The Use of Knowledge in Society, in: American Economic Review Vol. XXXV (1945), pp. 519, 530.

74 F.A. v.Hayek, Knowledge, Evolution and Science, 1983, p. 19.

75 See the Nobel Memorial Lecture by F.A. v.Hayek on "The Pretense of Knowledge", in: F.A. v.Hayek, New Studies in Philosophy, Politics, Economics and the History of Ideas, 1978, p. 23 ff. In his essay on "competition as a discovery procedure" (p. 179 ff), F.A. v.Hayek emphasizes that "competition is valuable only because, and so far as, its results are unpredictable and on the whole different from those which anyone has, or could have, deliberately aimed at" (p. 180).

76 F.A. v.Hayek (note 74), p. 19.

people even if they hate each other and without any need for reaching political consensus on what should be produced and on what tastes should be satisfied.[77]

F) Conflict-oriented Foreign Power Policies

The mercantilist doctrines perceived international economic relations in terms of inherent conflict of interest, power rivalries and struggles for economic advantage. The resort to war, the conquest of colonies, the "Machiavellian" use of economic power, trade discrimination, trade preferences and trade monopolies were distinctive elements of foreign economic policies. Since power is a relative status, economic damage to a rival country was seen as beneficial to one's own country. The mercantilist doctrines - such as the pursuit of a "favourable" balance of trade - were "conflict-oriented" in that they did not meet Kant's "universalizability test" for resolving conflicts of interest through generally applicable rules. The classical economists replaced the mercantilist view of the economy as a static "zero sum game" by the notion of mutually profitable trade transactions that take place because all parties benefit from them. Co-operation, not conflict, should be the rule. The mutual gains from trade and David Hume's theory of the self-equilibrating mechanisms of the balance-of-payments led to the liberal proposition that states should, as far as possible, abstain from direct interference with international trade or finance because liberal trade and competition between states are no less favourable than liberal trade and competition within states.

5. Conclusions: The Need to Tame the Mercantilist Leviathan through Constitutional Rules

The historical, economic and political survey and analysis of past and present trade mercantilism in chapter V has revealed that "government failures" in the trade policy area have been criticized persistently for more than two centuries and that there are important reasons why trade policy powers must be subjected

77 On the interrelationship between economic and political freedom see: M. and R. Friedman, Capitalism and Freedom, 1962, p. 24: "The widespread use of the market reduces the strain on the social fabric by rendering conformity unnecessary with respect to any activities it encompasses. The wider the range of activities covered by the market, the fewer are the issues on which explicitly political decisions are required and hence on which it is necessary to achieve agreement".

to the same constitutional safeguards as other government powers of taxation and economic regulation.

A) The Need to Protect Individual Rights in the Trade Policy Area

Economic theory shows, and economic history confirms, that the economic policy objective of maximizing individual and social welfare through division of labour is identical and does not conflict with the liberal rule of law idea of maximizing the equal freedoms and property rights of people under the rule of law. Economic theory further shows, and economic history confirms as well, that if governments begin treating people as pieces in an economic chess game, the economic and social processes will go on smoothly only as long as the "rules of the game" are observed, i.e. the rules imposed by governments upon individual producers, investors, traders and consumers must respect and be in concord with the inherent rights and "principles of motion" (e.g. self-interest) of the individual economic agent. If governmental trade regulations arbitrarily interfere with the equal freedoms and property rights of domestic citizens, they are likely to produce disorder and to reduce economic welfare.

Trade restrictions operate and become effective by taxing and restricting the freedoms of domestic citizens (e.g. the freedom to buy cheaper foreign goods). They may interfere with private property rights (e.g. by rendering the execution of existing commercial contracts impossible) and may distort competition among domestic traders and producers. They are also an important means for raising government revenue (e.g. tariff income), for indirectly subsidizing import-competing producers (by enabling the latter to raise their prices and profits) and for redistributing income among domestic groups. Due to the close interrelationship between economic and political freedom, trade restrictions as well as exchange restrictions may restrict also the effective exercise of the political freedoms of the citizens (e.g. to inform oneself through imported books, to express one's opinion with the help of imported printing materials, to exercise one's chosen occupation as a trade firm, or to go abroad with foreign exchange).

Trade theory shows that government restrictions on the freedom of domestic citizens to import and export tend to reduce not only their individual welfare (e.g. their effective freedom and real income) but also the national economic welfare of the restricting country. Since almost all economic policy objectives can be achieved more efficiently and more effectively by means of internal government interventions, the proportionality requirements of the constitutional laws of liberal democracies and the voluntarily accepted international GATT obligations provide additional legal arguments for protecting individual freedoms of trade against market-distorting trade restrictions. Economic markets, in which domestic citizens can make daily choices between alternative products and continually select the quantity of each product they desire, enable also a more democratic "government of the people, by the people, for the people" (Abraham Lincoln) than the "political marketplace" where elections may be years apart, votes are taken by majority and only on packages of different policies rather than specific trade policy issues. Hence, at least in liberal democracies, the limited and infrequently available choices in the "political market" compared to national and international economic markets provide also an important political argument for protecting individual freedoms of trade as much as possible from governmental trade restrictions.

B) The Need to Define the National Self-Interest in Liberal Trade and Rule of Law

The liberal English economists and philosophers during the 18th century (such as David Hume, Adam Smith and Adam Ferguson) did not share the belief of the French physiocrats in the natural goodness of man, in a natural harmony of interest and in "laissez faire, laissez aller, le monde va de soi-même". Contrary to the laissez faire-doctrine that the smaller the body of law and the less government intervention there is in society the better it is, the classical English liberals emphasized the importance of legal rules and institutional arrangements for protecting "life, liberty and property" and for transforming conflicts of interest into mutually beneficial cooperation. According to Adam Smith, the English common law guarantees of economic freedom and legal security had been one of the main causes of the economic prosperity in England.[78] The individual was perceived as a selfish maximizer of his own interests, and an important function of the spontaneously evolved common law guarantees of property, contract, honesty and other values was seen in their ability to transforme private self-interested behaviour into (economic) activities that were profitable also to other in-

78 A. Smith (note 54), Book IV, chapter V, p. 42 f: "That security which the laws in Great Britain give to every man that he shall enjoy the fruits of his own labour, is alone sufficient to make any country flourish, notwithstanding twenty other absurd regulations of commerce... The natural effort of every individual to better his own condition, when suffered to exert itself with freedom and security, is so powerful a principle that it is alone, and without any assistance, not only capable of carrying on the society to wealth and prosperity, but of surmounting a hundred impertinent obstructions with which the folly of human laws too often incumbers its operations."

dividuals. According to Adam Smith, the regular supply of the consumers did not depend on the benevolence of the butcher or the baker, but on the pursuit of their self-interests and their protection under the law. Because the assumption of self-interested human behaviour and conflicts of interests was applied also to political agents, the English liberals were much more skeptical of delegating discretionary government powers to political agents than many "rationalist" philosophers (such as Thomas Hobbes and J.J.Rousseau) who sought the guarantee of freedom in enlightened interference by benevolent governments.[79] In the words of David Hume: "In constraining any system of government and fixing the several checks and controls of the constitution, every man ought to be supposed a knave and to have no other end, in all his actions, than private interest".[80]

The survey and comparison in chapter V of the "old" and the "new" mercantilism seems to confirm the "constitutional analysis" of the classical political economists and their presumption of the ubiquity of conflicts among the short-term interests of economic agents which must be constrained and mutually reconciled through long-term legal rules. Like the English common law described by Adam Smith, the private commercial law for the ancient interregional commerce as well as the commercial customs and ius mercatorum in medieval Europe evolved quite spontaneously in a manner protecting and promoting freedom of contract, good faith, fulfillment of contractual obligations ("pacta sunt servanda"), the transfer of property rights among traders, and the reconciliation of the conflicts of interests among sellers and buyers or among competing traders. But these various safeguards of decentralized competition and privately agreed commercial law did not offer effective protection against the centralized government powers and mercantilist trade restrictions of the newly emerging sovereign states in Europe after the end of the Middle Ages. While the "invisible hand" of competition and open markets can effectively constrain abuses of decentralized private economic power, there is no equivalent "invisible hand" in the "political market" effectively containing the abuse of the monopoly of power of governments. The practice and analysis of governmental trade mercantilism

79 On the different traditions in the English and the French concepts of liberty see: F.A. v.Hayek, The Constitution of Liberty, 1960, pp. 54 ff.

80 D. Hume, Of the Independence of Parliament, quoted from: G. Brennan/J.M. Buchanan, The Reason of Rules, 1985, p. 60, who rightly note that the assumption of the self-interested homo economicus for both economic as well as political markets has proven useful even if this model embodies more cynicism about the behaviour of individuals than simple evidence warrants.

over the past 200 years show that the interests of the government (even if democratically elected) and the governmental policies emerging from the complex political processes do not necessarily coincide with the national interest of the country as a whole (see above chapter V.1 and 3). Given the practical difficulties of assessing "market failures" and corrective government action, even unselfish government intervention in the public interest may lead to "government failure" much worse than "market failure". Undistorted market competition as a national "public good" must, therefore, be protected through "constitutional rules" against the abuse of power, private and governmental restraints of competition and unproductive "rent-seeking" activities.

C) The Need to Limit the Scope of Trade Policy Powers

The more than 200 years practical experience with trade mercantilism appears to confirm Lord Acton's observation that "power corrupts, and absolute power corrupts absolutely". Thomas Hobbes, in his classic treatise "Leviathan" (1651), described the life of persons in a society without law and without government as "solitary, poor, nasty, brutish and short". His justification of unlimited state power ("legibus absolutus") to implement laws transforming the unconstrained individual pursuit of self-interest (the Hobbesian "war of all against all") into a rule-ordered society was based on the assumption that the governmental "Leviathan" would respect his accountability to God and would act as a "benevolent dictator". Historical experience with trade mercantilism up to the 18th century showed, however, that the assumption of "benevolent" and "omnipotent" governments was too optimistic and that governmental powers of taxation and economic regulation, if left unconstrained, are likely to be abused by special interest for selfish purposes of redistribution and accumulation of powers. In the search for alternative solutions to the "Hobbesian dilemma", the criticism of the economic and political failures of the "old mercantilism" by liberal writers such as John Locke, David Hume and Adam Smith contributed to the "constitutional attitude" of the framers of the Constitution of the United States in favour of subjecting all governmental powers to permanent constitutional rules with a higher legal ranking than the ordinary legislation and governmental regulation. The chief constitutional principles - such as limited government under the rule of law, separation and only limited delegation of government powers, equal treatment and judicial protection of individual rights - were meant to limit the exercise of all government powers and interferences into individual freedoms and property rights. Government coercion was thought to be admissible only in the general "public interest" and only according to general rules equally applicable to all.

Adam Smith's proposals for "chaining-in Leviathan" were not confined to the "minimal state" as recommended by modern libertarian writers such as R.Nozick,[81] where the function of the state is only to act as referee enforcing the equal rights and general rules of society. Adam Smith's definition of the three duties of a government[82] also comprised the governmental supply of "public goods" (e.g. public schools, a stable monetary system) and the correction of "market failures" (e.g. monopolies), even though Smith regarded these tasks as having a narrow application.[83] Yet, the classical economists did not inquire into the problems of how to maintain the "rule of law" in the foreign economic relations of modern "redistributive welfare states".[84] The analysis in chapter V of the national self-interest in liberal trade (V.1), of the "conflict oriented" and "power-oriented" features of the "new protectionism" (V.2), and of the "protectionist producer bias" in national decision-making processes about trade policy against the interests of consumers and competitive export industries (V.3) led to the conclusion that past and present trade mercantilism has been criticized rightly as "government failure" resulting in economic waste, prevalence of powerful special interests over the general public interest, lack of effective protection of equal freedoms and property rights, and arbitrary exercise of discretionary government powers (V.4). It was shown that there is today virtually un-

81 R. Nozik, Anarchy, State and Utopia, 1974, pp. 26 ff, 333 f.

82 A. Smith,(above note 54), pp. 650, 651 (book II, chapt. III): "According to the system of natural liberty, the sovereign has only three duties to attend to; three duties of great importance, indeed, but plain and intelligible to common understandings: first, the duty of protecting the society from the violence and invasion of other independent societies; secondly, the duty of protecting, as far as possible, every member of the society from the injustice or oppression of every other member of it, or the duty of establishing an exact administration of justice; and, thirdly, the duty of erecting and maintaining certain public works and certain public institutions which it can never be for the interests of any individual, or small number of individuals, to erect and maintain; because the profit could never repay the expense to any individual or small number of individuals, though it may frequently do much more than repay it to a great society." See also A. Smith's definition of "political economy": "Political economy, considered as a branch of the science of a statesman or legislator, proposes two distinct objects: first, to provide a plentiful revenue or subsistence for the people, or more properly to enable them to provide such a revenue or subsistence for themselves; and secondly, to supply the state or commonwealth with a revenue sufficient for the public services. It proposes to enrich both the people and the sovereign." (p. 297).

83 Cf. M. and R. Friedman, Free to Choose, 1979, pp. 30 ff.

84 Cf. Lord Robbins, Political Economy: Past and Present, 1976, p. 186 f.

animous agreement among economists and international economic organizations that trade restrictions almost always reduce the national economic welfare of the restricting country and the individual freedoms of their citizens. And even attempts to justify trade protection on social policy grounds cannot explain the distributive inequities involved in the redistribution of income among domestic groups by means of non-transparent, discriminatory and "power-oriented" grey area trade restrictions for the benefit of well-organized import-competing industries.[85] Hence, there is a strong case supported by economic, legal, political, social and historical arguments for the need of limiting the discretionary trade policy powers of governments through long-term constitutional rules protecting the private and the public interest in liberal trade and individual freedoms under the rule of law.

D) The Need to Regulate the Proportionate Use of Trade Policy Instruments

The economic theory of optimal intervention (chapter III.3.B above) and the economic ranking of alternative trade policy instruments according to their respective economic costs and benefits (chapter IV.3 above) demonstrate that trade restrictions are hardly ever an efficient and effective policy instrument for correcting domestic "market failures" and for increasing national economic welfare. Moreover, the existence of market imperfections does not justify government interventions because the risk of "market failure" must always be weighed against the risk of "government failure" - whether as the result of lack of competence, self-interested behaviour of politicians and bureaucrats, or of the various asymmetries in the political process. The historical survey of past and present mercantilism has shown that the discretionary use of the various trade policy instruments provides numerous opportunities for economic waste, corruption and backroom deals benefiting special interest groups rather than the nation as a whole. Broad discretionary trade policy powers are an invitation to protectionist interest groups to influence the exercise of these powers. Hence there is a need for long-term legal constraints of discretionary trade policy powers requiring the

85 On the distinction between "above board" income redistribution through budgets and "surreptitious" income redistribution through deliberate governmental price distortions (e.g. by means of industrial, agricultural and trade policies), see: J. Tumlir, Economic Policy as a Constitutional Problem, 1984, pp. 8 ff. D. Usher, The Economic Prerequisite to Democracy, 1981, p. 29, distinguishes between redistribution of income among the population at large via progressive taxation, on the one side, and "reassignment" of rights and income among organized interests, on the other side (e.g. through trade policy).

public choice of transparent, non-discriminatory and economically less costly trade policy instruments.

VI. INSUFFICIENT CONSTITUTIONAL RESTRAINTS IN NATIONAL LAWS AND IN EUROPEAN COMMUNITY LAW ON GOVERNMENT POWERS TO TAX AND RESTRICT FOREIGN TRADE: TRADE MERCANTILISM AS "CONSTITUTIONAL FAILURE"

1. The Increase in Government Discretion for the Conduct of Foreign Economic Policy

For the classical liberal economists, equal protection of freedoms and property rights under the rule of law was a necessary prerequisite of the reconciliation of individual and social welfare through market competition and was seen as the major cause of spontaneous economic order and of economic growth. Ever since the early English court decisions in Davenant v. Hurdis (1599), when it was said that "prescription of such nature to induce sole trade or traffic to a company or person, and to exclude all others, is against the law", and in Darcy v. Allein (1603) where the court found that the grant of exclusive rights to produce any article was "against the common law and the liberty of the subject", the demand for the protection of individual liberty through equal laws for all citizens became the main weapon of the English Parliament in its opposition to the kings.[1] After the "Glorious Revolution" of 1688, John Locke, in his "Two Treatises of Government" (1690), supplied the classical statements of these ideas of natural and inalienable liberties and property rights limiting all state powers and of safeguards against the abuse of authority through the separation of powers, the limitation of legislative powers to the enactment of general rules of law, and severe restrictions on the powers of the executive. David Hume, in his "History of England" (1754/1762), interpreted English history as the gradual emergence of the rule of law. And Adam Smith's "Inquiry into the Nature and Causes of the Wealth of Nations" (1776) concluded "that those restrictions on the powers of government which had originated from sheer distrust of all arbitrary power had become the chief cause of Britain's economic prosperity".[2]

In addition to the protection of individual freedoms and the rule of law, the liberal economists recognized that a satisfactory functioning of a market economy

1 For a historical account see: F.A. v.Hayek, The Constitution of Liberty, 1960, pp. 167 ff.

2 F.A. v.Hayek, New Studies in Philosophy, Politics, Economics and the History of Ideas, 1978, p. 125.

required government action in at least two other fields: the provision of a stable monetary system and of antitrust rules designed to preserve competition. The monetary system of the gold standard rested on national legislation in the major countries and, up to 1914, provided an automatic, rule-oriented mechanism for the regulation of the value and supply of money, for exchange rate stability, convertibility and "automatic" balance of payments adjustments in international monetary relations. In view of the English common law concerning monopolies[3] and the pro-competitive effects of the free trade era after 1860, antitrust legislation developed rather late, beginning with the Sherman Act of 1890 in the USA and even later in Western Europe. The Cobden-Chevalier trade agreement of 1860 between England and France was the first of a large number of bilateral long-term commercial treaties, interlinked by most-favoured-nation obligations, which secured the reciprocal liberalization of tariffs and the absence of non-tariff trade barriers. The principle of most-favoured nation treatment promoted not only non-discriminatory access to markets and supplies and, thereby, international trade competition. It also enhanced a transparent, non-discriminatory and welfare-increasing conduct of trade policy and stabilized the levels of trade protection among countries, because a non-discriminatory increase in trade protection would affect several large trading partners capable of effective retaliation. Tariff concessions were withdrawn usually only after the expiry of the long-term bilateral commercial treaties or after negotiations on compensatory concessions designed to maintain the average level of trade protection in spite of a change in the pattern of protection.

The outbreak of World War I marked the beginning of a new era of economic interventionism undermining the existing legal guarantees for liberal and non-discriminatory trade competition. As a consequence of the abandonment of the gold standard (e.g. in England by the Gold Standard Acts of 1925 and 1931), governments acquired far-reaching discretionary powers for the regulation of the value of the national currency, exchange rates, exchange restrictions and budgetary policy. The political acceptance of Keynesian economics legitimized budged deficits and inflationary money policies and destroyed the classical "balanced-budget rule".[4] The termination of the pre-1914 long-term commercial treaty

3 See: W.L. Letwin, The English Common Law concerning monopolies, in: University of Chicago Law Review XXI (1953/54).

4 See: J.M. Buchanan/R.E. Wagner, Democracy in Deficit. The Political Legacy of Lord Keynes, 1977, who criticize the politically naive assumption of Keynesian economics that politicians would create budget surpluses as willingly as they create deficits. Since politicians enjoy spending and do not like to tax, Buchanan and Wagner examine ways and

system removed the legal constraints on tariff increases, on non-tariff trade barriers and on trade discrimination and led to a revival of trade protectionism. In many European countries, the comprehensive trade and economic ministries established during World War I remained in existence after the war and were granted ever more regulatory tasks and powers to interfere in market competition (e.g. for macro-economic monetary, fiscal, full employment and exchange rate policies, income redistribution, etc.). The traditional liberal constitutional barriers to government interferences in the economy - such as equal protection of freedoms and property rights, limitation of legislative powers to the enactment of general rules, separation and only limited delegation of government powers - no longer prevented non-transparent, discriminatory and ineffective "beggar my neighbour policies" regardless of their economic costs. The 1930s witnessed an unprecedented crisis of the international economic order and the emergence of a new kind of "Leviathan state" in various European countries, where the liberal principles of open markets, sound money, limited government, general and non-discriminatory law became increasingly replaced by special-interest legislation, administered prices, cartelization of industries, trade protection, exchange restrictions and other market restrictions. Transborder economic transactions, in addition to the applicable regulations for domestic economic transactions, became subject to an ever increasing number of specific foreign trade, exchange and investment restrictions and discretionary bilateral "management" of transnational economic relations.

In contrast to the "rule of law" idea reflected in the post-war multilateral trade and monetary rules of GATT and of the IMF Agreement, the "new protectionism" since about the 1970s reflects again a proclivity of governments for administrative discretionary "management" of international trade. A particularly disturbing legal feature of the new protectionism is its frequent disregard of the existing international trade and competition rules. The domestic foreign trade laws of many GATT contracting parties (e.g. the USA) explicitly authorize the adoption of non-transparent and discriminatory trade restrictions in violation of GATT law (see below). Discretionary trade protective measures are increasingly being taken in the form of discriminatory quantitative restrictions and VERs, whose implementation is often accompanied by the organization of industries into export cartels and by regular intergovernmental negotiations on "administered prices", market shares and particular investment decisions.

---

means of disciplining the "revenue-grabbing proclivities of governments" through constitutional constraints imposed on tax bases and tax rates.

2. Insufficient Constitutional Guarantees in Domestic Laws for a Transparent, Non-Discriminatory and Proportionate Use of Trade Policy Instruments

Governmental trade policies usually operate through statutes, legal regulations and administrative decisions which specify or redefine the economic freedoms and property rights of traders, producers and consumers. The mercantilist trade policies already made use of most of the present instruments of trade regulation such as tariffs, prohibitions, quantitative restrictions, licences, subsidies, state-trading enterprises, government procurement, monopolies, variable levies and monetary controls. Yet, systematic foreign trade legislation was developed in most states only during the 20th century.

The national constitutions of most states, as well as the EEC Treaty provisions on the common agricultural and commercial policies (see e.g. Articles 29, 30, 40, 110, 113 EEC Treaty), do not, or at least not explicitly, place substantive legal limitations on the conduct of foreign economic policy. The Swiss Federal Constitution is among the very few national constitutions which, in its Article 29 adopted in 1874, places an explicit substantive constitutional constraint on the foreign trade policy powers of the government by imposing an obligation to tax imports (except luxury goods) at a rate "as low as possible" and exports at a rate "as moderate as possible". Foreign trade restrictions other than tariffs were not explicitly authorized by the Swiss Federal Constitution until the introduction of Article 31 **quinquies** in 1978. The Swiss, German and Japanese constitutions appear to be almost unique in that their constitutional guarantees of economic liberties are recognized to protect also the individual right to import and export and to engage in other international economic relations. Whereas most national constitutions subject the exercise of the governmental foreign economic policy powers to formal requirements only (e.g. parliamentary ratification of foreign trade treaties), the Swiss Federal Constitution and the German Federal "Basic Law" of 1949 place also important substantive limitations on the foreign economic policy discretion of the government.

The following section is confined to a brief discussion of the foreign trade law of the two major trading powers: the United States and the European Community. Both the United States and the EEC have succeeded in implementing the liberal ideal of a written constitution guaranteeing limited government and economic freedoms. And yet, the written constitutional guarantees have not prevented the increasing resort by both the USA and the EEC to non-transparent, discriminatory and mutually impoverishing "grey area trade policy instruments" in contravention of international law. The purpose of the following section is not to provide an overall, balanced appraisal of the foreign trade law of the USA and the EEC, whose legal and procedural guarantees (e.g. for judicial review in antidumping and countervailing duty proceedings) can in some respects be considered models for effective legal implementation of GATT obligations. The purpose is rather to show that the increasing circumvention of the international GATT obligations for the use of transparent, non-discriminatory and less distortive trade policy instruments has a corrosive effect not only on the domestic foreign trade laws of GATT contracting parties but also on basic constitutional principles of Western democracies.

A. The Foreign Trade Law of the United States: Some Constitutional Problems

The American "founding fathers" were to a large extent motivated by problems of economic regulation (e.g. their demand for "no taxation without representation"). The framers of the US Constitution were the first to lay down long-term "constitutional rules" for economic and political order as a framework for ordinary legislation and administration. The US Constitution was meant to be a "constitution of liberty"[5] that would protect the individual against all arbitrary coercion by ensuring, as the Bill of Rights preceding the constitution of Massachusetts of 1780 expressed it, "a government of laws, not of men". The commitment to long-term principles and the enumeration, limitation, separation, and "checks and balances" of governmental powers were expected to give the people more control ("sovereignty") over the political order than if decisions were taken successively by legislative majorities without constitutional constraints on the exercise of parliamentary powers, as in England since the claim by the British Parliament in 1767 to unlimited parliamentary sovereignty. These constitutional principles of limited government and separation of powers among the executive, legislative and judicial branches of government were applied also to foreign affairs and to transnational economic relations, albeit to a limited extent (see the detailed analysis below in chapter VII.2).

The US Constitution confers the principal powers of foreign trade regulation on Congress. According to Article I, Section 8, the Congress has the power "to lay and collect taxes, duties, imposts and excises" which must be "uniform through-

5 Cf. v.Hayek's analysis (note 1), pp. 176 ff.

out the United States" (clause 1); under the "commerce clause", Congress has also the power "to regulate commerce with foreign nations and among the several States" (clause 3). The exercise of these powers is subject to a number of general restrictions. Article I, Section 9, affords protection to the states by stipulating that "no tax or duty shall be laid on articles exported from any State" (clause 5), and "no preference shall be given by any regulation of commerce or revenue to the ports of one state over those of another" (clause 6). In accordance with the constitutional principles of a limited government of enumerated powers and of protection of individual freedoms against government interference, the Constitution explicitly reserves certain powers to the states and to the people: "The enumeration in the Constitution of certain rights shall not be construed to deny or disparage others retained by the people" (ninth Amendment); "The powers not delegated to the United States by the Constitution, nor prohibited by it to the States, are reserved to the States respectively, or to the people" (tenth Amendment). The liberty of contract and the liberty to produce and distribute goods and services are protected under the due process clauses of the fifth and fourteenth Amendments. Yet, it seems doubtful whether and to what extent the Constitution protects also individual freedoms to engage in foreign trade and in international economic relations. The "contracts clause" (Article I, Section 10, clause 1) has been construed by the US Supreme Court to apply only to retroactive laws and not to contracts executed subsequent to the adoption of a law.

In accordance with the American propensity to regulate domestic economic behaviour, if at all, through general legislation (e.g. the passage of antitrust laws) and through adjudication of complaints that the general rules of conduct were being violated, Congress has exercised its powers of trade regulation by enacting a multiplicity of tariff acts, trade acts, trade agreements acts and other specific foreign trade legislation. The declared fundamental purposes of these foreign trade laws are, inter alia, to promote "fair trade" and "fair application" of the foreign trade laws.[6] But the passage of the highly protectionist Smoot-Hawley Tariff Act of 1930 - "more an accidental product of political logrolling in the Congress than the planned implementation of a new trade policy"[7] - has demonstrated also that "logrolling", whereby politicians trade policies for mutual sup-

6 For a list of the US foreign trade laws and their policy goals see: J.H. Jackson, Perspectives on Jurisprudence of International Trade: Costs and Benefits of Legal Procedures in the United States, in: Michigan Law Review 1984, pp. 1570, 1574 f. A useful collection of the texts is: A.M. Stowell (ed.), US International Trade Laws, 1986 Edition.

7 Howell/Wolff, The Role of Trade Law in the Making of Trade Policy, in: J.H. Jackson et alii (eds.). International Trade Policy: The Lawyer's Perspective, 1985, pp. 3-1,4.

port, would enable parochial protectionist interest groups to trigger a disastrous chain reaction of reciprocal international trade restrictions. Numerous economic and political analyses have shown that US tariff and trade policy continues to be determined to a large extent by political pressures from protectionist interest groups.[8]

The US Constitution itself, or more precisely its present interpretation and application by US courts, does not appear to offer sufficient substantive and procedural safeguards for protecting the national self-interest in transparent, non-discriminatory and welfare-increasing trade policy-making. The frequent resort by the United States to non-transparent and discriminatory "grey area trade restrictions" (e.g. bilateral restraint agreements) casts doubts on whether the fundamental liberal and democractic principles of the US Constitution continue to be effectively applied in the field of foreign trade policy.

a) Limited government?

The drafting history of the US Constitution and the ninth and tenth Amendments to the US Constitution confirm that it was the intent of the framers of the US Constitution to establish a limited government of enumerated powers by reserving large areas of human conduct for the people and by protecting these individual freedoms against government interference. The framers of the US Constitution had been inspired by the older English liberal conception and common-law tradition of protecting individual liberty through the limitation of all government coercion to the enforcement of general rules of law necessary to safeguard a compelling interest of the state. They had disapproved the later claim of the English Parliament to virtually unlimited powers and "parliamentary sovereignty" (rather than "private sovereignty") in the sense of legislative freedom to do whatever the representatives of the majority find expedient to do. The framers had been aware of the political dangers which majority decisions and the "capture" of legislative powers by special-interest groups could pose to the individual liberties they prized. Their common belief in the inherent limitation of legislative powers and their distrust of expanding legislative powers was reflected also in the establishment of a separate judiciary branch in Article III with authority in constitutional matters, which was considered as an essential

8 See, e.g.: R.E. Baldwin, The Political Economy of US Trade Policy, 1976; R.E. Baldwin/A.O. Krueger (eds.), The Structure and Evolution of Recent US Trade Policy, 1984; Brock/Magee, The Economics of Special Interest Politics: The Case of the Tariff, in: American Economic Review 1978, pp. 246 ff.

counterweight enabling "checks and balances" against possible usurpation of unauthorized powers by other governmental bodies and was part of a program to enlist the support of "men of property" for the Constitution.

Historically, one reason for the convening of the Constitutional Convention had been to secure economic freedoms and property rights in the states of the Confederation. Several constitutional provisions - such as the contracts clause and other prohibitions on the states in Article I, section 10, designed to prevent economic abuses and arbitrary state interferences with individual liberties - clearly reflect this concern of protecting economic liberties. As B.H. Siegan's detailed analysis of the records of the constitutional convention concludes:

"The Framers provided Congress with a limited number of economic powers in addition to the regulation of commerce (some of which would not be needed if the commerce power were very broad). These are the power to tax (but restricted on the basis of population with respect to direct taxes) and spend for constitutional purposes, borrow money, establish uniform bankruptcy laws, coin and regulate the value of money, fix standards of weights and measures, establish post offices and post roads, and grant copyrights and patents... the economic controls the Constitution expressly authorizes are quite modest when compared with those France and England exercised or tried to exercise during the period of mercantilism, from the sixteenth to the middle of the eighteenth century: the fixing of prices, wages, and interest rates, prohibition of forestalling and engrossing, regulating the quality of goods, licensing of labor, programs to increase the population, sumptuary control, monopoly grants and other exclusive rights, incorporation, state enterprise, and the control of foreign trade and finance, including the protection of domestic industries."[9]

Another major concern of the framers had been the erection of trade barriers among states. The framers decided to give Congress exclusive control over commercial relations with foreign countries (foreign commerce) and over the commerce among the states (interstate commerce). Historically, the commerce clause (Article I, section 8, clause 3) seems to have been originally intended to preempt state economic controls and to curb government regulation rather than to confer large commercial and economic powers to the federal government. Yet, since the famous case Gibbons v. Ogden (1824), the US Supreme Court has given a very broad meaning to the term "commerce" to cover the movement

9 B.H. Siegan, Economic Liberties and the Constitution, 1980, p. 102. For a useful account of the drafting of the American Constitution see also Hayek (note 1), chapters 11 and 12.

of practically everything across state borders (e.g. individuals, commodities, livestock) as well as the various methods of movement (e.g. railroads, airplanes, ships, trucks, buses, telephone, telegraph, radio, television).

As regards international trade and economic transactions, the constitutional safeguards of enumerated and limited government powers and of inalienable individual liberties protected by the courts no longer appear to hinder Congress and the executive branch from imposing non-transparent and discriminatory "grey area trade restrictions" (e.g. bilateral quantitative restraint agreements in contravention of GATT law), even if they limit individual freedoms and property righs of those engaged in international trade, tax consumers, indirectly subsidize import-competing producers, distort trade competition and promote foreign export cartels (e.g. for the implementation of VERs). In 1980, for example, the competent International Trade Commission rejected an application by the US automobile industry for import relief on the ground that section 201 of the Trade Act of 1974 did not authorize the granting of import relief in the given situation. This gave rise to various initiatives in Congress to legislate protection for the automobile industry, and in the end prompted the executive branch to negotiate automobile export restraints with Japan resulting in an off-budget transfer of about 4 1/2 billion US dollars from domestic consumers to foreign and domestic automobile producers - without specific legislative authority, outside the general rules for import relief measures, without transparent discussion, without publication of the international accord and in circumvention of US antitrust law and GATT law.[10] The large number of some 45 bilateral VERs introduced at the request of, and supported by, the US executive in 1986/87 for steel and steel products, machine tools, automobiles, textiles and clothing (outside the scope of the MFA), and their surreptitious income redistribution among domestic citizens, are illustrative of the dangers of virtually unlimited trade policy powers in modern democracies, where the ruling majority and even statesmen wholly devoted to the public good cannot remain in power unless they "buy" the political support of particular groups by satisfying special interests.[11]

---

10 For an illustrative case-study see: M.W. Lochmann, The Japanese Voluntary Restraint on Automobile Exports: An Abandonment of the Free Trade Principles of the GATT and the Free Market Principles of US Antitrust Laws, in: Harvard International Law Journal 1986, pp. 99 ff.

11 For a list and a critical discussion of these VERs see: M. Kostecki, Export-Restraint Arrangements and Trade Liberalization, in: The World Economy 1987, pp. 425 ff. On the conflicts between the old liberal ideal of "rule of law" or "government under the law", which the early theorists of representative government (e.g. John Locke)conceived to be limited

The existence of constitutionally guaranteed private rights to engage in international trade was denied in a 1975 decision of the Court of Customs and Patent Appeals, "United States v. Yoshida International Inc.", where the Court ruled that "no one has a vested right to trade with foreign nations".[12] When the first draft of the Export Administration Act of 1979 (S.737) referred to the "right to export", the word "right" was later replaced by the word "ability" so as to avoid the law being "misconstrued" as denoting a constitutional or otherwise legally enforceable right to export free from government restriction".[13] The Export Administration Amendments Act of 1985 explicitly limits the President's authority to impose controls on exports covered by previous contracts or agreements.[14] Yet, as regards Milton Friedman's recent proposals for a "Free Trade Amendment" to the United States Constitution which would guarantee "the right of the people to buy and sell legitimate goods and services at mutually acceptable terms" and would limit the power of the United States Congress to tax and restrict foreign trade, Friedman himself has considered it "visionary to suppose that such an amendment could be enacted now."[15]

b) Separation of powers?

The constitutional principle of separation of law-making powers, executive powers and judicial powers also appears to have ceased to act as an effective constraint on the non-transparent, discriminatory and welfare-reducing use of trade policy powers. In the 1953 case "United States v. Gay W. Capps, Inc.", a US federal court still declared an executive "voluntary restraint agreement" between the United States and Canada "void because it was not authorized by Congress and contravened provisions of a statute dealing with the very matter to which it related".[16] According to this court decision, "the power to regulate foreign

---

to the enforcement of general rules equally applicable to all, and modern "unlimited democracy" and pressure-group politics, where governments with often unlimited powers are constantly forced to secure the continued support of a majority by using their powers in the service of special interests, see: F.A. v.Hayek, Economic Freedom and Representative Government, 1973.

12 526 F.2d 560 (1975). Similar court decisions date back to Buttfield v. Stranahan, 192 U.S. U70, 24 S.Ct. 349, 48 L Ed. 525 (1904)

13 S.Rep. No. 169, 96th Cong., 3rd Sess. 1,3 (1979).

14 The Act is reproduced in: International Legal Materials 1985, pp. 1369 ff. For a discussion of the "contract sanctity clause" added to section 6 see: H. Rept. No. 99-180, 99th Cong., 1st Sess., 58, 59 (1985).

15 See: M. and R. Friedman, Free to Choose, 1979, p. 304 f.

16 204 F.2d 655 (Fourth Circuit, 1953).

commerce is vested in Congress, not in the executive or the courts". "The executive may not by-pass congressional limitations regulating such commerce by entering into an agreement with the foreign country that the regulation be exercised by that country through its control over exports".

The congressional power over "foreign commerce" was thus considered to take precedence over the President's more general "foreign affairs power". Most trade policy matters have, indeed, been claimed by the Congress to be exclusively within its power. That the President has no "inherent" or other undelegated power to impose legally binding foreign trade regulations was confirmed also in the 1974 decision in the case "Consumers Union of U.S., Inc. v.Kissinger", where the US Court of Appeals, District of Columbia, held: "From the wide scope of its legislation regulating trade and governing the circumstances and procedures under which the President is authorized to limit imports, it appears quite likely that Congress has by statute occupied the field of enforceable import restrictions, if it did not, indeed, have exclusive possession thereof by the terms of Article I of the Constitution".[17]

Yet, the latter court decision also found that "there is no potential for conflict between exclusive congressional regulation of foreign commerce - regulation enforced ultimately by halting violative importations at the border - and assurances of voluntary restraint given to the Executive". In spite of a statement made by the President that he would not initiate steps to limit steel imports by law if the volume of such imports remained within certain limits, the Court found "the question of congressional preemption is simply not pertinent to executive action of this sort". Only the dissenting Judge Leventhal held the "solemn negotiated bilateral understandings" to be inconsistent with "Congress's exercise of its plenary authority over the regulation of foreign commerce through passage, over the past forty years, of legislation establishing a comprehensive scheme occupying the field of import restraints". According to this convincing dissenting opinion, "Congress has made the exercise of executive authority over import restraints dependent on public ventilation of the issues and has prescribed a procedure with safeguards and right of comment by affected interests. The President has concededly not followed that procedure, and this course cannot stand consistently with the statutory pattern".

The majority decision in "Consumers Union of U.S., Inc. v. Kissinger" is based on a legalistic narrow conception of trade policy and of congressional action in

17 506 F.2d 136, cert. denied, 421 U.S. 1004.

this field: "Congress acts by making laws binding, if valid, on their objects and the President, whose duty it is faithfully to execute the laws". According to this majority opinion, "the formality and specificity with which the undertakings are expressed does not alter their essentially precatory nature insofar as the Executive Branch is concerned". Since the VERs were found to be without legally binding effect, the negotiation of the VER was considered not to encroach upon the congressional competence for foreign trade and upon the congressional legislation for mandatory import controls. By implication, the President's independent "foreign affairs power" was held to encompass a broad discretionary power to negotiate and impose trade restrictions in the most harmful, non-transparent and discriminatory manner without observing the substantive and procedural requirements laid down in the congressional foreign trade legislation. As a consequence, the most dangerous instrument of modern "grey area trade policy" undermining national and international foreign trade law, namely VERs negotiated by the executive branch without legislative authority and outside the legislative rules and procedures for restrictions on the freedom of trade of domestic citizens, continues to elude effective legislative and judicial control in the United States.

While Congress has delegated to the President numerous specific powers of trade regulation, the 1974 Trade Act, the 1979 Trade Agreements Act and the 1984 Trade and Tariff Act reflect a tendency towards greater congressional reassertion of its own trade policy powers. There is also a considerable number of trade acts which Congress has enacted in "sovereign" disregard of its international GATT obligations. The 1954 enactment of restrictions on agricultural imports contrary to Article XI:2 of GATT, the 1964 and 1979 Meat Import Acts imposing restrictions on meat imports contrary to GATT Article XI:2, the 1971 enactment of export subsidies for Domestic International Sales Corporations (DISC) in violation of GATT Article XVI:4, the 1974 revision of the US escape clause legislation in deviation of Article XIX of GATT, the congressional imposition of trade discrimination contrary to Article I GATT (e.g. in the 1979 Trade Agreements Act), the suspension of certain requirements of GATT Article VI in the Trade and Tariff Act of 1984, or the numerous "bills" introduced regularly in Congress threatening sweeping statutory trade restrictions in violation of GATT rules, are illustrative also of another continuing "constitutional problem": There are still no sufficient legal safeguards against a repetition of the historical experience of the Smoot-Hawley Tariff Act of 1930, namely "the realization that the Congress was not able to act on imports for the benefit of the general public interest".[18]

c) Limited delegation of powers?

The doctrine of "limited delegation of powers", first advocated by J. Locke as a principle of constitutional law and as a necessary supplement of the principle of separation of powers, is recognized to form part of US constitutional law. But the jurisprudence of the US Supreme Court suggests that "the history of the delegation doctrine was one of ever-expanding permissiveness toward ever-expanding and increasingly vague delegations".[19] In the field of foreign trade and economic regulation, the congressional delegation of legislative powers often remained unguided and unconstrained concerning subsequent regulatory policies. The "delegation doctrine" seems to have never been used by the Supreme Court for invalidating congressional delegations of foreign trade regulatory powers to the President.[20]

Professor Hudec's detailed analysis of the US foreign trade law concludes that the courts have almost invariably deferred to, and have held constitutional, even very broad delegations of extensive discretionary powers in the field of foreign trade and have given the executive branch every benefit of doubt as to whether the statutory criteria had been met and whether the President should exercise his "foreign affairs powers" in compliance with or in violation of the international GATT obligations. For example, when an importer challenged the imposition in 1971 by the President of a ten per cent surcharge on imports for balance-

18 Jackson (note 6), p. 1573. The GATT-inconsistency of the above-mentioned congressional legislation is discussed in: R. Hudec, The Legal Status of GATT in the Domestic Law of the United States, in: Hilf/Jacobs/Petersmann (eds.), The European Community and GATT, 1986, pp. 187, 239 f.

19 P.H. Aranson, Constitutionalizing the Regulatory Process, in: McKenzie (ed.), Constitutional Economics, 1984, pp. 187, 195; Aranson/Gellhorn/Robinson, A Theory of Legislative Delegation, in: Cornell Law Review 1982, pp. 1-67; S.A. Barber, The Constitution and the Delegation of Congressional Power, 1975.

20 In the Supreme Court decision of 23 June 1983 in the Chadha Case (Immigration and Naturalization Service v. Chadha, 462 US 919, 1983), the Supreme Court has, however, declared unconstitutional the frequently used device of delegating congressional powers to the President subject to a "legislative veto". For a discussion of this decision and of its impact on the legislative veto provisions contained in 15 major foreign affairs laws see: Franck/Bob, The Return of Humpty-Dumpty: Foreign Relations Law after the Chadha Case, in: American Journal of International Law 1985, pp. 912 ff.; Koh, Congressional Controls on Presidential Trade Policymaking after I.N.S. v. Chadha, in: New York University Journal of International Law, 1986, pp. 1189 ff.

of-payments reasons contrary to GATT Articles II and XII, the Court of Customs and Patent Appeals agreed with the President's claim of authority under section 5 (b) of the 1917 Trading with the Enemy Act (as amended) to "regulate... importation... of any property in which any foreign country or a national thereof has any interest" during times of "national emergency". The mere requirement that the discretionary imposition of trade restrictions must have a reasonable relation to a "national emergency" proclaimed by the President, was considered sufficient by the Court to render this sweeping delegation of authority constitutional.[21] In the case "Federal Energy Administration v. Algonquin SNG, Inc.",[22] the Supreme Court held a similarly broad delegation of powers to impose trade restrictions for national security reasons to be constitutional on the ground that the required "national security" purpose provided a sufficiently limiting criterion. As Hudec has shown,[23] the US foreign trade law is rich in other examples of broad delegation of trade policy powers unconstrained by any substantive criteria, which have been held constitutional by the courts. Due to the lack of a democratically responsible parliamentary discussion and of substantive guidelines for the exercise of the delegated powers, the constitutional objectives of the principle of limited delegation of powers - such as to require the legislator itself to discuss and decide the main policy issues in a transparent manner and to formulate generally applicable criteria for the administration of the rules and for their judicial control - are no longer achieved. The resultant discretion of uninstructed agencies increases the risk of "government failure" and of the abuse of regulatory powers for producing private benefits at collective cost.

d) Effective judicial review?

Prompted also by the economic depression of 1974 and 1979, the number of formal and informal trade restrictions introduced by the United States has rapidly increased over the past years: "between the Trade Act of 1974 and the end of 1984 there have been over 47 Section 301 cases, 62 escape clause (Section 201 and 406) cases and 182 Section 337 cases. Just since the Trade Agreements Act of 1979, from 1980 through 1984 there have been over 450 antidumping and countervailing duty cases".[24] The complexity of the 14 different major US im-

---

21 United States v. Yoshida International Inc., see above note 12.

22 426 US 548 (1976).

23 Hudec (note 18), pp. 242 ff.

24 Jackson, Introduction, (note 7), p. XI.

port regulations,[25] and the often broad executive discretion to impose trade restrictions even in violation of GATT law, are frequently criticized as lending themselves to protectionist abuse.[26]

Even though government regulation of imports has become the most regulated section of the US economy, Hudec's detailed analysis of US court decisions relating to GATT has come to the conclusion that, in general, "United States courts have not been disposed to apply meaningful legal controls on Executive Branch actions in the field of foreign trade".[27] Only the various trade regulating laws subject to the jurisdiction of the International Trade Commission (an independent regulatory agency) - especially the antidumping, countervailing duty and escape clause laws - appear to provide substantive criteria and procedural safeguards enabling effective judicial review. But, as the 1981 VER imposed on Japanese automobiles has shown, even a formal decision under the escape clause law (sections 201 and 203 of the Trade Act of 1974), holding that emergency safeguards were not warranted, is no guarantee against the negotiation of VERs outside the legal rules and procedures mandated by this escape clause law. As pointed out by M.W. Lochmann:

> "In the short term, the Auto VER was economically indistinguishable from a direct consumption tax and multibillion dollar subsidy to United States and foreign automakers, but the implementation of the VER by Japan effectively obviated the American democratic process. No one was held politically accountable for the VER or the increased prices it caused. No vote was ever taken in Congress on the amount or duration of the Auto VER; no negotiating position was ever publicly defended by the President; and no challenge can be effectively brought in United States courts."[28]

This circumvention by the executive of the legal criteria established by Congress in the escape clause law would hardly have been possible without the tacit toleration of such trade restrictions by Congress and by the courts. But, in the 1974 case "Consumers Union vs. Kissinger", the courts had already decided that the President's "foreign affairs" powers may justify the negotiation of a VER even if

25 For a survey see: Jackson (note 6), pp. 1584 ff.

26 For a discussion of the risks of manipulation and "harassment" of the legalistic US import regulatory system see: Jackson (note 6), pp. 1579 ff.

27 Hudec (note 18), p. 215.

28 Lochmann (note 10), p. 151, who concludes his detailed analysis of this VER by saying: "The implementation of the Auto VER cost United States consumers billions of dollars and was achieved in a way that circumvented the safeguard procedures of the GATT and the Trade Act of 1974. Through such legerdemain, the Auto VER was implemented without anyone in the United States being held politically accountable" (p. 157).

the President failed to comply with the legal requirements for the imposition of VERs and OMAs stipulated in the escape clause law.[29] The judicial endorsement of the "trigger price mechanism", based on the announcement by the US Treasury Department in 1977 that it would initiate expedited antidumping proceedings against any steel imports priced below a certain "trigger price", is another illustration of how "the Executive Branch was able to create what amounted to a minimum price order without actually using any legally reviewable power".[30]

e) Federalism

The constitutional principles of federalism, i.e. the division of governmental powers between the federal government and the regional state governments, have been clarified with regard to international trade, inter alia, by the provisions of Article I, Section 10: "No State shall, without the consent of the Congress, lay any imposts or duties on imports or exports, except what may be absolutely necessary for executing its inspection laws"... (clause 2); and "No State shall, without the consent of Congress, lay any duty or tonnage" (i.e. may not tax shipping) or "enter into any agreement with another State or with a foreign power" (clause 3). The broad federal powers under the "commerce clause" significantly restrict and largely preempt the powers of the states for the regulation of international trade. Foreign commerce aspects may arise in particular in the context of taxation, government procurement and regulation of technical standards by individual states. But it is an established constitutional principle that federal law (e.g. foreign trade legislation) invalidates and preempts conflicting state laws. In GATT Article XXIV:12, the US government has committed itself also on the level of international law to "take such reasonable measures as may be available to it to ensure observance of the provisions of this Agreement by the regional and local governments and authorities within its territory". It is noteworthy that, so far, the US courts appear to have effectively applied and enforced the international GATT obligations of the USA vis-à-vis the states and local governments within the USA.[31]

29 For a critical discussion of these court decisions see: Hudec (note 18), p. 244; Lochmann (note 10), p. 128 f, who also examines the Japanese automaker's antitrust liability under the Sherman Act (pp. 133 ff).

30 Hudec (note 18), p. 245, with a brief discussion of the pertinent decision of a US District Court in Davis Walker Corp. v. Blumenthal, 460 F. Supp. 283 (DDC, 1978).

31 See the court decisions discussed by Hudec (note 18), p. 221 f. But see also the erosion of the "federal state clause" of GATT Article XXIV:12 in recent GATT practice discussed by:

B. The Foreign Trade Law of the European Community: Some Constitutional Problems

According to the case-law of the Court of Justice of the European Communities (EC), Article 113 of the EEC Treaty establishes an exclusive Community competence for a "common commercial policy". The Community may apply not only the trade policy instruments explicitly mentioned in Article 113 but also "any other process intended to regulate external trade".[32] According to the Court, the "proper functioning of the customs union justifies a wide interpretation of Articles 9, 27, 28, 111 and 113 of the Treaty and of the powers which these provisions confer on the institutions to allow them thoroughly to control external trade by measures taken both independently and by agreement".[33] The content of commercial policy is the same "whether it is applied in the context of the international action of a State or that of the Community".[34] A "restrictive interpretation of the concept of common commercial policy would risk causing disturbances in intra-Community trade by reason of the disparity which would then exist in certain sectors of economic relations with non-member countries".[35] The common commercial policy can be gradually developed by both internal and external measures and "shall be based on uniform principles" (Article 113 para 1). "Measures of commercial policy of a national character are only permissible after the end of the transitional period by virtue of specific authorization by the Community".[36] Yet, most autonomous and conventional trade policy measures of the EEC depend for their implementation on supplementary measures taken by the national administrations in the EEC member states in the forms of their respective national laws and subject to the control of their national courts.

The various "constitutional guarantees" of European Community law have not prevented the EEC from using trade discrimination and "grey area trade restrictions" in contravention of GATT Articles XI and XIII more frequently than other major trading powers and from taxing and restricting thereby European

E.U. Petersmann, in: E.U. Petersmann/M. Hilf (eds.), The New GATT Round of Multilateral Trade Negotiations, 1988, pp. 93-97.

32 Opinion 1/78 of 4 October 1979 (International Agreement on Natural Rubber), (1979) E.C.R. 2871, (para. 45).

33 Case 8/73, Hauptzollamt Bremen v. Massey-Ferguson, (1973) E.C.R. 897, 908.

34 Opinion 1/75 of 11 November 1975 (Understanding on Local Cost Standard), (1975) E.C.R. 1355, 1362 f.

35 Opinion 1/78 (note 32), pp. 2912 f.

36 Case 41/76, Donckerwolcke v.Procureur de la République (1976) E.C.R. 1921 (para. 32).

producers, traders and consumers in a surreptitious manner. The EEC's "new protectionism" and its increasing use for a "power-oriented" redistribution of income and of production and trade shares of European industries (e.g. by means of EC production and trade quotas for European producers of agricultural and steel products) have been widely criticized[37] and are reminiscent of the welfare-reducing "government failures" of the "old mercantilism". They reflect a lack of sufficient legal guarantees in European Community law for a transparent, non-discriminatory and welfare-increasing use of the EEC's broad discretionary commercial policy powers.

a) Limited powers?

Unlike states, the European Communities do not have unlimited jurisdiction and are not "sovereign". As other international organizations, they possess merely derived powers ("compétence d'attribution"). These limited powers are enumerated in the various treaties establishing the European Communities. According to Article 3 of the EEC Treaty, the common commercial policy must be implemented "as provided in this Treaty" (Article 3 EEC Treaty), and "each institution shall act within the limits of the powers conferred upon it by this Treaty" (Article 4 EEC Treaty). The objective of the common commercial policy must be "to contribute, in the common interest, to the harmonious development of world trade, the progressive abolition of restrictions on international trade and the lowering of customs barriers" (Article 110 EEC Treaty). Moreover, "the common commercial policy shall be based on uniform principles" (Article 113 EEC Treaty).

The EC Council has adopted various general regulations establishing common rules of unlimited duration for the common customs tariff, customs legislation, for import and export restrictions and procedures, anti-dumping measures and countervailing duties, other protective measures (e.g. against "unfair" trade prac-

---

37 See, e.g.: R.C. Hine, The Political Economy of European Trade, 1985, pp. 95 ff, 254 ff; J. Tumlir, GATT Rules and Community Law, in: Hilf/Jacobs/Petersmann (note 18), pp. 1,15 ff; E. Verreydt/J. Waelbroeck, European Community Protection against Manufactured Imports from Developing Countries, World Bank Staff Working Papers no. 432, 1980; M. Wolf, The European Communitiy's trade policy, in: R. Jenkins (ed.), Britain and the EEC, 1983; V. Curzon-Price, The European Community-Friend or Foe of the Market Economy ? in: Ordo-Jahrbuch 1983, pp. 85 ff: Bénard et alii, A Europe open to the world - A Report on Protectionism and the EC, 1984.

tices), and export credits.[38] Most of these regulations explicitly state that they are designed to implement the relevant GATT obligations of the Community, and emphasize that the Community may take only "commercial policy measures... which are compatible with existing international obligations and procedures".[39] The general principles of law recognized by the Court of Justice as part of Community law - such as non-discrimination and equal treatment, legal certainty and rule of law, proportionality, good faith, protection of legitimate expectations and of acquired rights, the right to be heard and other principles of "due process" and fair application of the law[40] - entail additional limitations of the commercial policy powers of the Community. Thus, the "Council, having adopted a general regulation with a view to implementing one of the objectives laid down in Article 113 of the Treaty, cannot derogate from the rules laid down in applying those rules to specific cases without interfering with the legislative system of the Community and destroying the equality before the law of those to whom the law applies".[41] International agreements binding upon the EEC, including GATT law, are recognized to form an "integral part of the Community legal system" and take precedence over secondary Community law.[42] An infringement of such international obligations by an EC organ or an EC member state constitutes therefore a breach also of a superior norm of Community law.[43]

The "constitutional limitation" of the EEC's commercial policy powers to the use of transparent, non-discriminatory and less-distortive trade policy instruments as required by GATT law (at least vis-à-vis GATT contracting parties)

38 For a useful compilation of the major customs and foreign trade regulations of the EC see: E.L.M. Völker/J. Steenbergen, Leading Cases and Materials on the External Relations Law of the EC, 1985, pp. 82 ff.

39 See, for instance the preamble and Article 10 para.3 of Council Regulation (EEC) No. 2641/84 of 17 September 1984 on the strengthening of the common commercial policy, O.J. L 252/1 (20.9.1984).

40 For a survey of these and other general principles of European Community law see: H.G. Schermers, Judicial Protection in the European Communities , 3rd ed. 1983, pp. 35 ff.; J. Schwarze, Europäisches Verwaltungsrecht, 1988.

41 Case 113/77 - NTN Toyo Company v.Council - (1979) E.C.R. 1185.

42 See, e.g.: U. Everling, The Law in the External Economic Relations of the European Community, in: Hilf/Jacobs/Petersmann (note 18), pp. 85, 87, 94; C.D. Ehlermann, Application of GATT Rules in the European Community, in: Hilf/Jacobs/Petersmann (note 18), pp. 127, 131, 138.

43 See, e.g., Everling (note 42), p. 94, and E.U. Petersmann, Commentary on Article 234 of the EEC Treaty, in: Groeben/Boeckh/Thiesing/Ehlermann (eds.), EWG-Vertrag Kommentar, Artikel 234, 4th edition 1990.

has not prevented the European Community from introducing discriminatory quantitative import and export restrictions, subsidies and "grey area trade restrictions" in violation of GATT law. Many of these quantitative restrictions were adopted on an **ad hoc** basis (e.g. directly based on Article 113 EEC Treaty) outside the "common principles" and general rules for importation and exportation laid down in the EEC's foreign trade regulations. For instance, the EEC has concluded numerous bilateral agreements restricting imports[44] or exports[45] in a discriminatory manner inconsistent with GATT Article XIII.[46] Even though many of these VERs were not published,[47] they appear to have often been concluded outside the general rules for safeguard measures laid down in the various foreign trade regulations of the EEC.[48]

In some cases, the EC Commission decided to replace protective measures lawfully introduced under Regulation No. 288/82 in conformity with GATT Article XIX by economically more disadvantageous unilateral VERs in contravention of GATT Article XIII, notwithstanding the legal challenge by Germany of the Commission's power to accept a VER.[49] In other cases, the high additional economic costs imposed by VERs on European consumers may have contributed to the replacement of an illegal VER by a subsequent import tariff lawfully introduced in conformity with GATT Law and with European Community law. For instance, the VER on exports of video cassette recorders, negotiated and announced by the EEC and Japan in February 1983, was replaced by an increased import tariff of 14% in 1986, after having imposed on European consumers additional costs of "at least half a billion pounds by the end of 1985" and having failed to encourage European manufacturers of video cassette recorders

44 See, e.g., Council Decision of 8 May 1984 relating to voluntary restraint agreements on mutton, lamb and goatmeat, O.J. EC No. L 154/36 (9.6.1984).

45 See, e.g., Council Regulation (EEC) No. 59/85 of 9 January 1985 on the restriction of exports of steel pipes and tubes to the USA, O.J. EC No. L 9/1 (10.1.1985).

46 The inconsistency of VERs with GATT law has been recognized in a resolution on "International Trade Law" adopted by the International Law Association in August 1988 (see the text in: D. Dicke/E.U. Petersmann (eds.), Foreign Trade in the Present and a New International Economic Order, 1988 pp. 425 f.)

47 Cf., e.g., I. van Bael/J.F. Bellis, International Trade Law and Practice of the EC, 1985, p. 136, as to the annually renewed restraint agreements with 15 steel exporting countries which "differ from one third country to another and are not publicly available".

48 The agreements referred to above (notes 44 and 45), as well as other bilateral restraint agreements (see e.g. O.J. EC No. L 18/11 of 22.1.1985), were based on Article 113 EEC Treaty instead of on the safeguard provisions in the various EEC foreign trade regulations.

49 See, e.g., the "stoneware case" (VER by Korea), discussed by van Bael/Bellis (above note 47) at p. 185 f.

to increase their output and productivity.[50] The EC's bilateral restraint agreements for steel had to be progressively extended to fifteen supplier countries, and the number of supplier countries covered by bilateral restraint agreements of the EEC increased from thirty-three under the International Textiles Agreement of 1974 (MFA I) to 43 under MFA III of 1981, while the number of categories specified went from 23 to 48.[51] The production and trade distortions created by the EEC's high domestic support prices for agricultural products have frequently prompted the EEC to introduce further import restrictions and export subsidies trying to offset the decreasing international competitiveness of European producers by imposing additional distortions on other countries.[52] According to informations supplied by members of the EC Commission, also private and public VERs negotiated, induced or tolerated by individual EC member states in contravention of European Community law are "again tolerated by the Community, in spite of a formal protest by the Commission in 1976".[53]

b) Trade liberalization "in the common interest" (Article 110 EEC Treaty)?

The EEC Treaty defines the objectives of the common agricultural policy and of the common commercial policy only in vague terms leaving a wide margin of discretion to the EC institutions. The judicial review by the EC Court of Justice of the exercise of this broad trade policy discretion of the EC Commission and EC Council has therefore been largely confined to the observance of procedural requirements, of a "manifest error of appraisal" or a "misuse of powers". But can it still be convincingly argued that the objective of the EEC's agricultural policy is "to stabilise markets", "to ensure that supplies reach consumers at reasonable

50 See: B. Hindley, EC Imports of VCRs from Japan. A Costly Precedent, in: Journal of World Trade Law 1986, pp. 168, 179, according to whom the VER was used by European manufacturers to reduce their own output and raise their own prices and profits without any threat from import competition. In the end, the European manufacturers bought a licence for the manufacture of the Japanese video cassette recorders.

51 OECD, Costs and Benefits of Protection, 1985, p. 13.

52 See, e.g.: H. Corbet, Excesses of the Common Agricultural Policy and Thailand's Manioc, in: The World Economy 1982, pp. 208 ff, analyzing VERs imposed by the EEC on the exportation of agricultural products from Thailand. Or see the GATT Council decision of 14 March 1978 (BISD 25 S/49, 65) that discriminatory purchase requirements, introduced by Regulation (EEC) No. 563/76 on the compulsory purchase of European skimmed milk powder held by intervention agencies for use in feedingstuffs violated Article III of GATT.

53 W. Ernst/H.F. Beseler, (both members of the EC Commission), in: Groeben/Boeckh/Thiesing/Ehlermann (eds.), Kommentar zum EWG-Vertrag, 3rd edition 1983, at Article 113, section 24.

prices" (Article 39 EEC Treaty), and "to contribute, in the common interest, to the ... progressive abolition of restrictions on international trade" (Article 110 EEC Treaty), even though the EEC's systematic price guarantees above world market levels, minimum import prices and export subsidies have turned the EEC from a net-importer to a self-sufficient net-exporter with regard to an ever increasing number of its subsidized agricultural products (e.g. grains, sugar, beef, poultry, dairy products)? The EEC's legal obligation "to contribute, in the common interest, to the harmonious development of world trade" (Article 113) has been legally defined in the voluntarily undertaken GATT obligations of the EEC in a way prescribing transparent policy-making, non-discriminatory trade competition and the use of efficient trade policy instruments for whatever trade protection the EEC wants to maintain. Is it compatible with this long-term "constitutional limitation" of the permissible trade policy instruments of the EEC to base its commercial policy largely on restrictive policy instruments which have been prohibited under GATT law because they are, compared to tariffs, unnecessarily harmful trade policy instruments (e.g. minimum import prices, systematic export subsidies, VERs, discriminatory import restrictions, selective trade preferences)?

The economic costs imposed on European consumers and taxpayers as a result of the EC's trade restrictions exceed by far the whole budgetary expenditure of the EC.[54] More than 70 per cent of the EC's budget is spent on the subsidization of agricultural surpluses which have transformed the Community, as regards products produced within the EEC, from a net-importer into the world's largest net-exporter systematically displacing competing foreign agricultural products inside and outside the EEC.[55] The EEC's long-standing trade protection for European textiles and steel products also reduces considerably the real income of European consumers,[56] retards the structural adjustment of uncom-

54 According to the "Aussenhandelsvereinigung des Deutschen Einzelhandels", prices in German retail trade could be about 10% lower without the EC's import protectionism. The total economic costs of import protection are estimated at 300 billion DM for Germany alone (see Frankfurter Allgemeine Zeitung 23.5.1984, p. 13, and BAG-Nachrichten 4/1984).

55 For a critical expert analysis see: H. Priebe, Die subventionierte Unvernunft, 1985, e.g. pp. 17 f

56 For instance, the welfare costs to the economy caused by VERs protecting the clothing industry in the EC have been estimated at 1,4 billion dollars (1980), cf. Kalantzopoulos, The Cost of VERs for Selected Industries in the US and the EC, World Bank January 1985. A study by the British Consumers' Association found an average increase of UK clothing retail prices attributable to the MFA of about 20 percent, cf. OECD, Costs and Benefits of Protection, 1985, p. 109.

petitive European industries to import competition from third countries, and necessitates large bureaucracies for the administration of the several thousand annually changing production and trade quotas imposed by the EC.

A basic aim of both GATT and the EEC Treaty provisions on the customs union is to separate trade policy from other foreign policy issues by means of general rules for transparent, non-discriminatory and market-conforming trade competition. Yet, trade preferences and import protection discriminating among GATT supplier countries have become major tools of the EEC's "foreign policy". Whereas the GATT calls for non-discrimination and a multilateral approach to trade issues using market-conforming tariffs as the principal instrument of trade policy, the EEC is widely criticized for its creation of a "pyramid of privileges" through preferential arrangements and for its increasing resort to a bilateral approach, non-tariff measures, "managed trade" and "exploitative interventions" (Deardorff) seeking foreign trade advantages at other countries' expense.[57] The most-favoured-nation tariff negotiated under GATT is used by the EEC as the principal trade policy instrument with regard to only a small minority of GATT contracting parties (essentially Australia, Canada, Japan, New Zealand, South Africa and USA), and even there subject to minimum import prices for agricultural products and discriminatory import restrictions in particular vis-à-vis Japan. The EEC's commercial policy towards all other GATT contracting parties is based on differing degrees of trade preferences and/or selective import restrictions (e.g. under the Generalized System of Preferences, or towards East European countries). Yet, trade preferences are economically worth little unless they are stable, and the frequent changes in the "preferential hierarchy" in favour of one country are bound to upset many other countries. Hence, the lesson drawn in GATT law from the practical experience of the 1930s seems still valid, and corroborated again by the increasing number of international trade conflicts of the EEC with its major allies like the USA, that the use of trade discrimination as an instrument of foreign and domestic policy

57 Cf. P. Mishalami et alii, The Pyramid of Privilege, in: C. Stevens (ed.), EEC and the Third World, 1981; Hine (note 37), pp. 97 ff. On "exploitative trade interventions" (e.g. subsidized exports of domestic agricultural surpluses) at the expense of other trading nations see: Deardorff/Stern, Current Issues in US Trade Policies: An Overview, in part reproduced in: J.H. Jackson/W.J. Davey, Legal Problems of International Economic Relations, 1986, p. 19 f. As an illustration see the "Declaration of Cairns" adopted on 27 August 1986 by 14 agricultural exporting countries which criticizes the agricultural subsidies of the USA and of the EEC as a sort of "trade war" systematically distorting prices and market shares in agricultural trade.

is neither in the economic nor in the political and legal self-interests of the countries concerned.

c) A "system ensuring that competition in the common market is not distorted" (Article 3 EEC Treaty)?

According to Article 3 EEC Treaty, "the activities of the Community shall include... the institution of a system ensuring that competition in the common market is not distorted". The EEC Treaty provisions aimed at establishing such a system of undistorted competition are based on two sets of rules: rules providing for the liberalization of governmental restraints of trade competition such as tariffs (Articles 12 ff), quantitative restrictions (Articles 30 ff), subsidies (Articles 92 ff), tax discrimination (Articles 95 ff) and foreign trade restrictions (Articles 110 ff); and rules applying to private and public undertakings prohibiting restraints of competition (Article 85), the "abuse of a dominant position" (Article 86) affecting trade between member states, and providing for a remedy against dumping (Article 91). These rules are supplemented by various specific and general prohibitions of discriminatory treatment (e.g. Article 7).

Given the high average share of foreign trade in the gross domestic product of the EEC States, undistorted competition within the EEC is not attainable without complementary rules promoting undistorted foreign trade competition. Economists generally agree that import restrictions distort domestic prices (e.g. increase in the domestic price of the protected good and of substitute goods), domestic production patterns (e.g. expansion of the less productive protected industries at the expense of more productive domestic processing and export industries), domestic consumption patterns (e.g. less consumption of the higher priced protected good), and reduce domestic competition and the efficiency of the domestic economy. They restrict the individual freedom to import and consume the cheaper restricted foreign goods, tax domestic consumers and exporters, and indirectly subsidize the protected producers. The functional interrelationships between domestic and foreign trade competition are obvious in the many instances where quantitative import restrictions of the EEC are subdivided into national subquotas or otherwise limited to the national markets of individual EEC member States and, as a result of supplementary protective measures under Article 115 of the EEC Treaty, suspend the free circulation of the restricted products also **within** the EEC.[58]

The interrelationship between external and internal trade discrimination has given rise to complaints before the Court of Justice of the EC in cases of import restrictions of the EEC which discriminated among supplier countries in breach of GATT Article XIII and, thereby, discriminated also among competing European traders importing from the supplier countries concerned. When adversely affected European importers sought judicial protection against such discretionary restraints of trade competition, the Court of Justice upheld the discretion of the EC Commission to introduce trade restrictions discriminating among supplier countries in violation of the non-discrimination requirement of GATT Article XIII,[59] to impose VERs outside the general rules of GATT and the EEC's safeguard regulations,[60] and to supplement external trade restrictions by internal trade restrictions based upon Article 115 of the EEC Treaty.[61] The EC

---

58 On the erosion of internal trade liberalization within the EEC as a result of external trade restrictions see, e.g.: H.G. Krenzler, The Multifibre Arrangement as a Special Regime under GATT, in: Hilf/Jacobs/Petersmann (note 18), pp. 141, 148 ff. The import restrictions instituted under the safeguard clauses of Title V of Regulation No. 288/82 of 5 February 1982 (O.J. EC 1982 L 35/1) have always been limited to one or two EEC member states.

59 In Case 55/75 - Balkan-Import-Export GMBH v. Hauptzollamt Berlin-Packhof, (1976) E.C.R. 19, the Court held that "in the Treaty there exists no general principle obliging the Community, in its external relations, to accord to third countries equal treatment in all respects and in any event traders do not have the right to rely on the existence of such a general principle" (para.14). In Case 245/81 - Edeka AG v. Federal Republic of Germany, (1982) E.C.R. 2745, the Court rejected a private complaint relating to an infringement of the Community law principles of non-discrimination (e.g. Arts. 7, 40(3)) without regard to the apparent illegality of the discriminatory restriction of imports from South Korea under Article XIII of GATT (non-discriminatory application of quantitative restrictions) and without attaching importance to the ensuing distortion of competition among traders within the EEC (paras. 11-20). Advocate-General Sir G. Slynn argued in his opinion to the Court that "in the light of the Court's decision in Case 55/75, Balkan-Import-Export (supra) it does not seem to me that any decision to discriminate between third countries in the amounts offered (= during the negotiation of a VER by the Commission) is unlawful or can invalidate the regulation" (p. 2770). In Case 52/81 - Firma Faust v.Commission - (1982) E.C.R. 3745, the Court confirmed this lack of judicial protection of traders against discretionary discrimination among supplier countries: "There exists in the Treaty no general principle obliging the Community, in its external relations, to accord to non-member countries equal treatment in all respects. If different treatment of non-member countries is compatible with Community law, different treatment accorded to traders within the Community must also be regarded as compatible with Community law, where that different treatment is merely an automatic consequence of the different treatment accorded to non-member countries with which such traders have entered into commercial relations".

60 See e.g. Case 112/80 - Dürbeck v. Hauptzollamt Frankfurt - (1981) E.C.R. 1095.

61 See e.g. Case 242/84 - Tezi B.V. v. Minister for Economic Affairs - (1986) E.C.R. 933-946, where the Court ruled: "Articles 113 and 115 of the Treaty, considered together, must be

Commission has no statutory authority to negotiate VERs contravening GATT law and, in its Decision of November 1974 on the Franco-Japanese ball-bearing restraint agreement,[62] declared that private restraints of exports to the EEC come within the scope of the cartel prohibition of Article 85 EEC Treaty. And yet, the EC Commission has increasingly resorted to VERs as a means for controlling or limiting imports and seems to have never actually applied Article 85 of the EEC Treaty to foreign private VERs.

Non-discrimination and undistorted competition are basic "constitutional principles" of both Community law as well as of GATT law. Since the GATT obligations are recognized to form an "integral part of the Community legal system", the Community law principles of non-discrimination and undistorted competition should be construed in conformity with these self-imposed GATT obligations. Non-discriminatory and undistorted trade competition **within** the EEC cannot be ensured without general rules (such as those of GATT) for non-discriminatory **foreign** trade competition among European importers, exporters and producers. As J.Tumlir has emphasized: Observance of the EEC's GATT obligations for non-discriminatory trade competition would render ineffective many of the **internal** competitive distortions within the EEC, such as subsidies in contravention of Articles 4 ECSC Treaty and 92 EEC Treaty, or restraints of competition in contravention of Articles 65 ECSC Treaty and 85, 86 EEC Treaty. "Without protection against imports, there would not be enough public funds for the subsidization necessary to keep uncompetitive enterprises afloat. Similarly, national cartels unprotected against imports would soon fall apart".[63]

d) Democratic decision-making?

In its judgment of 29 October 1980, the Court of Justice of the EC granted the complaint by a German undertaking and declared void Council Regulation No. 1293/79 concerning agricultural trade on the ground that the consultation of the European Parliament, required under Article 43 of the EEC Treaty, had been insufficient. According to the Court, this participation of the Parliament in the legislative process of the Community "reflects at Community level the funda-

---

interpreted as meaning that, after the conclusion of the Arrangement regarding international trade in textiles and the adoption of Council Regulation (EEC) No. 3589/82 of 23 December 1982, the Commission may still apply Article 115 in relation to trade in textile products subject to the said regulations."

62 O.J. EC No. L 343, 21 December 1974, p. 23.

63 J. Tumlir (note 37), p. 19.

mental democratic principle that the peoples should take part in the exercise of power through the intermediary of a representative assembly. Due consultation of the Parliament in the cases provided for by the Treaty therefore constitutes an essential formality disregard of which means that the measure concerned is void".[64]

The EEC Treaty provisions for the common commercial policy do not provide for any participation of the European Parliament in decision-making about foreign trade. Nor do the various foreign trade regulations of the EEC envisage any parliamentary participation in trade policy decisions (e.g. on safeguard measures, antidumping duties and countervailing duties). Notably the "sectoral" commercial policy of the EEC for the administration of prices, production and trade quotas of agricultural, steel and textiles products is made in an overly bureaucratic way in spite of its far-reaching impact on adversely affected European consumers, processing and export industries. Given the possibility of majority decisions in the EC Council and the rare discussion of the EEC's common commercial policy in national parliaments of EEC member states, the responsibility of national representatives in the Council to their national parliaments does not provide an effective substitute for parliamentary control. Democratic decision-making, in the sense of parliamentary participation in fundamental policy decisions and parliamentary supervision of the ways in which such decisions are carried out, seems no longer to exist in respect of the EEC's common commercial policy despite the latter's importance for economic welfare and for peaceful cooperation not only within the EEC but in the world at large.

According to the "Statement on democracy" issued by the European Council of Heads of State and Government at its meeting on 7/8 April 1978 on the occasion of the first election of the members of the European Parliament by direct universal suffrage, the "principles of representative democracy" must be respected as part of the "European identity" and require "a political system of pluralist democracy which guarantees both the free expression of opinions within the constitutional organization of powers and the procedures necessary for the protection of human rights".[65] This concept of democracy derives from the liberal belief "that more successful solutions of the problems of society are to be expected if we do not rely on the application of anyone's given knowledge, but encourage the interpersonal process of the exchange of opinion from which

64 Case 113/79 - Maizena GmbH v. Council (1980) E.C.R. 3424, para.34.

65 Bulletin EC 3-1978, p. 5.

better knowledge can be expected to emerge".[66] Free discussion and mutual criticism of opinions and of varied individual experiences are assumed to facilitate the discovery of truth and to improve the quality of social decision-making by a process of "trial and error".

If democracy is understood in this sense of "government by discussion", and transparent policy-making is recognized as a prerequisite of democratic "competition in ideas" as the most effective social discovery procedure, an important function of the EEC's GATT obligations for the use of transparent, non-discriminatory and less distortive instruments of trade policy can be seen in promoting an informed, and possibly educative, public discussion on the benefits and costs of trade restrictions. And the main reason why trade politicians often prefer "grey area trade policy instruments" that are among the costliest and least transparent forms of trade protection, seems to consist, as J.Tumlir and other close observers have convincingly shown, in their political self-interests in dissimulating the protection costs, as well as a public discussion of these costs, and in enlarging their discretionary powers by circumventing the rules.[67] The EEC has become the main user of "grey area trade restrictions" circumventing and contravening GATT rules. Out of 137 export-restraint arrangements relating to steel and steel products, machine tools, automobiles and road transport equipment, consumer electronics products, footwear, textiles exported by countries not participating in the Multifibre Agreement (MFA), agricultural and other products, listed in a recent GATT document,[68] more than 68 protect the EEC market. Most of these market-sharing arrangements have not been published. Due to the covertness and secrecy surrounding this "grey area trade policy" outside the general GATT rules, an open and informed public discussion of the "protection costs" involved is hardly possible. Since these trade restrictions are administered abroad in the exporting country, the protection of individual rights is made even more difficult. With regard to the VER imposed by the EC Com-

66 v.Hayek (note 2), p. 148.

67 J. Tumlir, Protectionism-Trade Policy in Democratic Societies, 1985, pp. 43, 48: "The large additional costs that export restraints impose on national economies buy only greater convenience for governments, convenience which consists entirely in short-changing the national political discussion..." "A major part of the additional cost ... is incurred in order to prevent a more thorough political discussion of it." M. Kostecki, Grey Area Trade Policy, 1986, p. 15: "Under grey area arrangements it is the exporting country's, rather than the importing country's, government that bears a major responsibility for implementing the measures. This helps the importing country's government to defuse the political cost of the decision without preventing it from harvesting the political gratitude of the protected domestic industry".

68 See Kostecki (note 11), p. 5, and the VERs listed in the annex to Kostecki's paper.

mission on imports of Japanese video cassette recorders, B. Hindley concluded his detailed case-study with the following comment: "That Europeans should be taxed largely for the benefit of Japanese producers of video cassette recorders but not be able to obtain information on the tax system is, to say the least, curious. This may in the long run be the worst feature of the VER system".[69]

e) Legal certainty and rule of law?

In the struggle for constitutional government during the 19th century, the liberal insistence on the limitation of all government powers and the democratic insistence on (parliamentary) majority decisions came to be closely associated in their common demand that the powers even of the representatives of the majority must be exercised in accordance with generally accepted principles and must not be used to confer on the supporters of the majority special advantages which cannot be similarly offered to all citizens. The principles of limited delegation and separation of powers between a representative assembly with legislative powers, confined to passing general and abstract rules of law, and an executive branch of government with delegated, more specific powers are therefore of importance not only for the protection of legal certainty and rule of law but also for transparent, democratic decision-making in the national interest.

The lack of separation of legislative and executive governmental powers in the EEC, especially in the field of the common agricultural and commercial policies, has born out this liberal concern that the combination of discretionary legislative and executive powers, unconstrained by substantive constitutional principles and effective judicial control, risks to be abused for the sake of coalitions of various organized interests and to lead to the abandonment of liberal principles in favour of discriminatory measures benefiting the various "distributive coalitions" (e.g. agricultural, textiles and steel lobbies in the EEC). The increasing number of bilateral and sectoral special arrangements for trade in agricultural products, textiles, apparel, steel, shipbuilding, synthetic fibres, automobiles, etc., first negotiated with domestic industry lobbies and subsequently on the intergovernmental level, reflect an increasing prevalence of special interests over the general public interest. The Court of Justice has ruled on several occasions that "the general principle of legal certainty" is "a rule of law to be upheld in the application of the Treaty".[70] But can it still be maintained that the EEC's

---

69 B. Hindley (note 50), p. 172.

70 Case 13/61 - Bosch - (1962) E.C.R. 52.

"grey area trade policy" is predictable for private economic agents and transparent to the general public? If "rule of law" is understood in the general sense of "government under the law", whose power must be exercised in a predictable manner based on rules fixed and announced beforehand: Can it still be claimed that the bureaucratic choice of the least transparent and costliest forms of trade protection in contravention of GATT law and, consequently, also in contravention of the foreign trade law of the EEC, is based on the rule of law?[71]

f) Judicial protection of individual freedoms of trade?

Economists rightly point out "that, because it is impossible to give net protection to the economy as a whole (only particular sectors can be protected, at the expense of other sectors), part of the analysis of restrictive trade policies should be carried out in an income redistribution framework".[72] Import restrictions become effective by restricting the freedoms of importers, taxing consumers and exporters, and indirectly subsidizing the protected producers.

European Community law protects these adversely affected individual freedoms and property rights in various ways. The EEC Treaty recognizes the freedom of movement of goods as a directly applicable individual right with regard to the prohibition of customs duties, quantitative restrictions and measures having equivalent effect in trade between the member states of the Community (Arts. 12, 30, 34). Economic freedom, property rights and the freedom to practice a profession are recognized by the Court of Justice also as fundamental human rights "enshrined in the general principles of Community law and protected by the Court".[73] The foreign trade regulations of the EEC explicity denote the freedom to import and export as a "Community principle" subject to the exceptions provided for in Council Regulations (EEC) No 288/82 on common rules for imports and No. 2603/69 establishing common rules for exports.[74] In view of

71 On the status of GATT law as an "integral part of the Community legal system" and the consequence that infringements of GATT rules by an EC institution or an EC member state tend to entail an infringement also of Community law, see below chapter IX.4.

72 R. Blackhurst, The Economic Effects of Different Types of Trade Measures and their Impact on Consumers, in: International Trade and the Consumer, OECD, 1986, pp. 94 ff.

73 See cases 29/69 - Stauder v. City of Ulm - (1969) E.C.R. p. 425; 4/73 - Nold v. Commission - (1974) E.C.R. p. 491; 44/79 - Hauer v. Land Rheinland-Pfalz - (1979) E.C.R. p. 3740; 50-60/74 - Kampfmeyer v.EC Commission - (1976) E.C.R. p. 711.

74 See Preamble and Art.1 of Council Regulation (EEC) No. 288/82 of 5 February 1982 on common rules for imports (O.J. L 35/1 of 9 February 1982) and the Preamble and Art.1 of

"the principles of representative democracy, of the rule of law, of social justice and of respect for human rights", which were recognized in the 1978 "Declaration on democracy" by all EC member states as part of European Community law,[75] it seems reasonable to conclude that this precisely circumscribed "freedom to import and export" confers also directly applicable rights on the private subjects of Community law which must be protected by the courts. As the Court has stated in its van Gend en Loos-judgement, the legal structures of European Community law and the economic logic of the common market demand that "Community law not only imposes obligations on individuals but is also intended to confer upon them rights. These rights arise not only where they are expressly granted by the Treaty, but also by reason of obligations which the Treaty imposes in a clearly defined way upon individuals as well as upon the Member States and upon the institutions of the Community".[76]

In its judicial control of the exercise of the discretionary trade policy powers of the EEC, the Court of Justice of the EC has recognized, for instance in respect of the EEC's antidumping regulations and competition rules, that "where, under a regulation, undertakings wishing to make complaints are accorded procedural guarantees permitting them to request the Commission to find an infringement of Community rules, those undertakings should be able to institute proceedings in order to protect their legitimate interests".[77] But the Court has also confirmed the broad discretion of the EEC as to the substantive contents of its common commercial policy: "although it may be thought that at the time when the Treaty was drafted liberalization of trade was the dominant idea, the Treaty nevertheless does not form a barrier to the possibility of the Community's developing a commercial policy aiming at a regulation of the world market for certain products rather than at a mere liberalization of trade".[78] Whenever European

---

Council Regulation (EEC) No. 2603/69 of 20 December 1969 establishing common rules for exports (O.J. L 324/25 of 27 December 1969).

75 Declaration of 7 and 8 April 1978, Bulletin EC 3-1978, p. 5.

76 Case 26/62 - van Gend en Loos - (1963) E.C.R. 10 (part II.B). According to the Court, provisions expressing a clear, precise and unconditional obligation requiring no implementing measures or leaving no discretionary power to the relevant authorities are capable of creating rights in favour of individuals, who may rely upon them in the national courts. "The fact that ... it is the Member States who are made the subject of the ... obligation does not imply that their nationals cannot benefit from this obligation" (Case 6/64 - Costa v. ENEL - 1964 E.C.R. 1143).

77 Case 169/84 - COFAZ S.A. v. Commission (1986) 391-417.

78 Advisory Opinion 1/78 - International Agreement on Natural Rubber - (1979) E.C.R. 2871, 2913.

traders sought judicial protection against discriminatory restrictions by the EEC of their individual freedoms to import, the EC Commission and EC member states have emphasized before the Court that individual traders, producers and consumers should not be allowed to invoke before the courts the legal GATT obligations of the Community for the maintenance of non-discriminatory trade competition.[79]

Thus, the Court has never reviewed the compatibility with GATT law of non-tariff trade barriers of the EEC even if, prior to the judgement of the Court, the GATT Council had made a legally binding ruling, with the consent of the EEC, under GATT Article XXIII that the measure concerned was inconsistent with GATT law and must be withdrawn.[80] In the Dürbeck-case, for instance, the EC Commission misinformed the Court of Justice on a legally binding decision by the GATT Council establishing the inconsistency with GATT Article XIII of EEC restrictions on imports on apples from Chile; the Court relied on this misinformation in its dismissal of the complaint by an adversely affected German importer against the EEC import restrictions concerned, without judicial examination of the accuracy of the misrepresented facts which the private applicant could not verify at the time of the proceeding.[81] This case was illustrative also of another problem: A right of the EC Commission to unilaterally interpret itself, without parliamentary and judicial control, its own legal obligations under

---

79 See: H.G. Schermers, Strengthening GATT, in: Common Market Law Review 1983, pp. 393, 395; P. Pescatore, Introduction to: Hilf/Jacobs/Petersmann (note 18), pp. XV-XVII; E.U. Petersmann, Application of GATT by the Court of Justice of the EC, in: Common Market Law Review 1983, pp. 397, 405 ff.

80 See, for instance, the GATT Council decision of 10 November 1980 establishing the inconsistency with GATT Article XIII of the Commission Regulation (EEC) No. 687/79 restricting imports of apples from Chile (Basic Instruments and Selected Documents = BISD 27th Supplement pp. 98 ff). In its subsequent preliminary ruling of 5 May 1981 (Case 112/80 - Firma A. Dürbeck v. Hauptzollamt Frankfurt - (1981) E.C.R. 1119), the Court did not take account of this GATT decision but relied on the "uncontested information on this matter supplied by the Commission during the oral procedure (that) the special GATT group charged with examining the conformity of Community measures with the General Agreement found that in adopting the protective measures in issue the Commission did not infringe either Article I or Article II of that Agreement" (para. 46). This information presented by the Commission to the Court was, however, misleading: the GATT Panel had not pronounced on the consistency of the EEC restrictions with GATT Articles I and II because "the Panel considered it more appropriate to examine the matter in the context of Article XIII (and XI)... rather than Article I" (and II), BISD 27th Supplement p. 112. Regrettably, the Court did not apply the maxim "iura novit curia" and, instead of verifying the true content of the GATT decision, was misled by the false information given by the EC Commission.

81 See note 80 above.

GATT law leaves adversely affected European traders, producers and consumers rather defenseless against restrictions of their individual freedoms in violation of GATT law, and seems difficult to reconcile with the notion of "fair trial" in court proceedings.[82] Similar problems of lack of judicial protection against illegal trade restrictions and of unequal access to relevant informations in proceedings before the Court arose whenever adversely affected European traders applied for judicial protection against trade distortions resulting from VERs imposed by the EEC.[83]

GATT Article XIX and Council Regulation (EEC) No. 288/82 of 5 February 1982 on common rules for imports prescribe that any trade protective measures must be applied in a transparent and non-discriminatory manner on the import side pursuant to justiciable substantive criteria and procedures.[84] Since the EEC's foreign trade regulations explicitly recognize that they have to be construed in conformity with the international GATT obligations of the EEC,[85] the legal requirement of transparent and "non-discriminatory" - as defined, inter alia, by GATT law - safeguard measures on the import side applies also in relation to the safeguard clauses of the common organizations of agricultural markets.[86] Yet, according to the Court of Justice, it is within the discretion of the

82 Cf. P. Pescatore, L'Application Judiciaire Des Traités Internationaux dans la Communauté Européenne et dans ses Etats Membres, in: Etudes de Droit des Communautés Européennes. Mélanges offerts à P.H. Teitgen, 1984, pp. 355, 403.

83 See, e.g., the above-mentioned case Edeka AG v. Federal Republic of Germany (note 59), where the Court again ignored the manifest illegality under GATT Article XIII of safeguard measures openly discriminating against the GATT contracting party Korea, and dismissed the complaint of an adversely affected German importer that the unpredictable, sudden and discriminatory import restriction had placed this importer of mushrooms from South Korea at a disadvantage in relation to competing importers of mushrooms from China (to which the South Korean import quota had been transferred).

84 This requirement of non-discrimination has been explicitly recognized by the EC Commission on numerous occasions, e.g. in: Commission Regulation (EEC) No. 3528/82 of 23 December 1982 introducing protective measures in respect of imports of tableware and other articles (O.J. 1982 L 369/27 of 29 December 1982), which explicitly states: "Whereas such protective measures must be compatible with the Community's international obligations; whereas, accordingly, they should apply to imports originating in third countries covered by Regulation (EEC) No. 288/82".

85 See the detailed references in: E.U. Petersmann, International and European Foreign Trade Law, in: Common Market Law Review 1985, pp. 441, 463 f.

86 These safeguard clauses (e.g. in Article 29 of Council Regulation No. 1035/72 on the common organization of the market in fruits and vegetables, O.J. 1972 L 118/1) usually authorize the Commission to take "appropriate measures" if the Community market experiences, or is threatened with, serious disturbances which may endanger the objectives of Article 39 of the EEC Treaty (i.e. the aims of the common agricultural policy).

EC Commission to introduce not only discriminatory import restrictions in manifest violation of GATT law[87] but to agree also to their administration abroad in the exporting country: "The Commission's attempt to secure the agreement of the exporting countries to a voluntary restriction of their exports to the Community before it decided on the temporary suspension of imports from Chile cannot, in view of Article 29, be regarded as unacceptable under Community law since that attempt reflects the Community's endeavour not to adopt except as a last resort coercive measures such as those in issue".[88]

This legalistic reasoning overlooks the fact that discriminatory VERs imposed at the request of the EEC in violation of GATT Articles XI, XIII are no less "coercive measures" and economically much more harmful for the EEC than alternative safeguard measures lawfully introduced by the EEC in a transparent, non-discriminatory and less distortive manner in conformity with the legal GATT obligations of the EEC and subject to the procedural and substantive safeguards of Community law. It is therefore misleading to invoke, as the Court did in the above-mentioned Edeka-case, the Community law principle of proportionality as a legal justification of this least transparent, costliest, discriminatory and illegal form of import protection curtailing the individual rights of adversely affected European traders and consumers:

> "The Commission's attempt, before adopting coercive measures to obtain the agreement of supplier countries on a voluntary restriction of their exports to the Community cannot be regarded as being unacceptable from the point of view of Community law since it demonstrates the Community's effort to refrain from adopting coercive measures unless all else fails." "It follows that the Commission is justified, when adopting protective measures, in taking account of whether or not a non-member country is ready to accept a voluntary restriction of its exports to the Community. It cannot therefore be said that it exceeded the limits of its discretionary power by almost totally prohibiting imports from Taiwan and South Korea, countries which did not agree to such a voluntary restraint, in favour of imports originating in the People's Republic of China, which did accept an agreement of voluntary restraint, even though such a prohibition is capable of bringing about a deflection in the flow of imports from Taiwan and South Korea to the People's Republic of China" (ground 23).

The open judicial support of discriminatory "grey area trade policies" in violation of GATT law and in circumvention of the procedural and substantive re-

87 See the above-mentioned Dürbeck case (note 60) and Edeka case (note 59), where the Court upheld the validity of discriminatory import restrictions violating GATT Article XIII.

88 Ground 39 of the Court's judgement in the Dürbeck case (note 60).

quirements of the foreign trade law of the EEC is regrettable not only from an economic but also from a legal point of view. It appears to be influenced by a misunderstanding of GATT law as well as of its economic and political rationale.[89] The Court has recognized that the EEC Treaty provisions (e.g. Articles 12, 30, 34, 95) on freedom of trade **within** the EEC, which implement the corresponding GATT prohibitions on tariffs, quantitative restrictions and tax discrimination (e.g. Articles II, III, V, XI:1, XXIV), are precise and unconditional enough to confer directly applicable rights on European traders, producers and consumers. Corresponding prohibitions in the free trade agreements between the EEC and EFTA countries, which are likewise almost literally based on the pertinent general GATT prohibitions, were also recognized to be precise and unconditional enough to be directly applied by the Court of Justice of the EC.[90] By contrast, the no less precise and unconditional GATT prohibitions of trade discrimination and non-tariff trade barriers in trade with **third** GATT contracting parties have never been directly applied and reviewed by the Court of Justice. The Court seems to view these GATT legal disciplines for foreign trade competition with third GATT contracting parties from a mercantilist perspective as a "concession", whose judicial application might render the EEC "defenceless", rather than, like the corresponding GATT rules for trade liberalization **within** the EEC, as guarantees of undistorted competition and equal freedoms in the interest of European traders, producers and consumers. The other assigned "guardian of the rule of law" within the EEC, the Commission (cf. Article 155 EEC Treaty), also seems to have never used its supervisory powers under the EEC Treaty in order to ensure the fulfilment of the EEC's GATT obligations. As stated by the Director-General of its Legal Service, "it dislikes the idea of using specifically Community provisions to do non-member countries' business for them".[91]

---

89 See, e.g., judge Everling's arguments (above note 42, p. 97) against judicial application of GATT rules - e.g. that "respect for the provisions of GATT by the Contracting Parties depends above all upon the fact that each can count upon the others' observing the agreement only if it does so itself" and that the Community will be "defenceless if its partners know that its conduct is already dictated by its own courts" - which reveal a regrettable misunderstanding of the unconditional nature of GATT obligations and of their regulatory function to regulate **domestic** conflicts of interests among traders, producers and consumers in the importing country in a non-discriminatory manner maximizing equal freedoms, undistorted competition and social welfare within the importing country itself.

90 See: G. Bebr, Agreements concluded by the Community an their possible Direct Effect, in: Common Market Law Review 1983, pp. 35 ff.

91 C.D. Ehlermann (note 42), p. 139.

But: Is the maintenance of the rule of law and of non-discriminatory competition in international trade transactions of European traders really the "business" only of other states? Are the protection by the EC Commission and by the Court of equal rights and undistorted competition in trade relations with third states less important or less advantageous than in trade relations among EEC states? Would it not be in the interest also of the EEC and its citizens to ensure, as mandated by Articles 155 and 164 of the EEC Treaty, the observance of the precise and unconditional GATT obligations of the EEC for the use of transparent, non-discriminatory and least distortive trade policy instruments? Whose interests are being served by the case-law of the Court that the EC Commission enjoys broad discretion to resort also to the most distortive, costliest, non-transparent and discriminatory instruments of trade protection in violation of its GATT obligations? Why are the general principles of Community law - such as the principles of non-discrimination or the principle of proportionality[92] - not being construed by the Court in conformity with the EEC's GATT obligations for the use of non-discriminatory and least distortive trade policy instruments? Why are the EEC Treaty provisions on commercial policy and competition policy not construed in a mutually consistent manner to the effect that the EC Commission lacks both discretionary commercial policy powers to impose VERs contravening GATT law as well as discretionary competition policy powers to exempt private foreign export cartels, which are frequently established for the implementation of VERs, from the applicable EEC Treaty prohibitions of restraints of competition (Article 85)? Since, as the Court held, "the vigilance of individuals concerned to protect their rights amounts to an effective supervision in addition to the supervision entrusted by Articles 169 and 170 to the diligence of the Commission and of the Member States":[93] Why are the EC Commission and the Court of Justice opposed to such an additional "effective supervision" by EC citizens of non-discriminatory foreign trade competition in compliance with the EEC's precise and unconditional GATT obligations recognized to form an "integral part of Community law"? Do non-transparent, discriminatory and illegal "grey area restrictions" of individual freedoms of trade and "judicial protectionism" not ultimately risk eroding the liberal and democratic objectives and principles of Community law, such as that "Community law not only

92 See ground 22 of the judgement of the Court in the Edeka case, quoted above (note 59), as well as the judgements of the Court referred to above in note 59.

93 Case 26/62 - van Gend en Loos v. Netherlands Fiscal Administration - (1963) E.C.R. 10.

imposes obligations on individuals but is also intended to confer upon them rights which become part of their legal heritage"?[94]

3. Insufficient Procedural Guarantees in US Domestic Laws and in European Community Law for the Public Choice of Transparent, Non-Discriminatory and Proportionate Trade Policy Instruments

A) Social Decision-making Processes for the Reconciliation of Individual Interests and the "Public Interest" in Pluralist Democracies

The constitutional guarantees of fundamental freedoms and of other basic human rights, at least in the national constitutions of the 24 OECD countries as well as in European Community law which together account for more than 60% of international trade and finance, imply a constitutional recognition of the value premisses of welfare economics that the individual is the best judge of his own welfare and that the welfare of society depends on the welfare of the individuals that comprise it. The national constitutional and foreign trade laws of several states (e.g. Germany, Japan, Switzerland) and European Community law explicitly recognize that the individual freedoms of private traders, producers, investors, banks, consumers, sellers and buyers to pursue their individual interests extend also to the ever more important field of international economic transactions. These individual self-interests may conflict with each other. For instance, the interests of domestic processing industries and consumers in the importation of cheap foreign goods may conflict with the self-interests of import-competing producers and their workers in import restrictions which enable an increase in domestic consumer prices and, thereby, of the income of import-competing producers (see chapter V.1 and 3.A above). The main regulatory function of national and international foreign trade law is to reconcile these conflicts of interests in a way maximizing individual and social welfare. The national constitutions lay down fundamental values (e.g. protection of individual freedoms, property rights, equal treatment), principles for the mutual balancing of these values (e.g. proportionality and non-retroactivity of restrictions), and principles for the organization of the government (e.g. separation of powers) and for the conduct of government policies (e.g. transparent policy-making). They determine, thereby, also legally binding standards for the definition of the

94 Case 26/62 (note 93 above).

"public interest" in international trade, for domestic foreign trade legislation and for the domestic decision-making processes about trade policy.

The modern "pluralist democracies" are characterized by the organization of individuals into political parties, trade unions, federations of industries and other interest groups. Their very function is to influence the process of social and political decision-making in a way benefiting their respective group members. Most modern national constitutions explicitly recognize the freedom of individuals to organize into such interest groups (e.g. Articles 9 and 21 of the "Basic Law" of the Federal Republic of Germany). The social legitimacy and even necessity of the formation of such interest groups is today generally acknowledged. The political election of representative assemblies would hardly be possible without political parties, and also trade unions, federations of industries and other interest groups serve important social functions (e.g. supply of information, coordination and collective presentation of interests, mutual social "checks and balances" among these "pouvoirs intermédiaires"). Yet, their one-sided focus on their respective "group interests" may also pose risks to the general "public interest". Hence, the need for rules - also in the field of international economic relations and international economic policy - to prevent the abuse of the power of such interest groups and to channel their conduct in a way beneficial to the general "public interest" (B below).

All national constitutions define the "public interest" and "social welfare" not only in terms of substantive constitutional principles but also by constitutional rules and procedures for governmental institutions and governmental decision-making processes. But, in contrast to the constitutional theories of absolutism that all government powers derived from the king ("l'état c'est moi"), modern liberal constitutions aiming at "government of the people, for the people and by the people" (Article 2 of the French Constitution of 1958) also make it clear (e.g. in the Preamble of the French Constitution, in the Preamble and Amendments 9 and 10 of the US Constitution, Article 1 of the German Basic Law) that the rationale and only legitimate objective of all government activity is to protect the human rights and interests of their citizens. Whereas individuals and groups are legally free to pursue their own interests, "civil servants" and other holders of government offices are legally bound to promote the "public interest" as defined in their respective constitutional laws and procedures. This presents an important **legal** difference between, on the one side, the power-oriented efforts of private individuals and groups at promoting their own sectional self-interests by influencing public decision-making (e.g. trade policy) and, on the other side, the constitutionally limited and rule-oriented public decision-making processes of legislatures (C below), executives (D below) and judicatures (E below). This legal distinction between the legal freedoms of private individuals and groups and the legal restraints of government members appears important notwithstanding the fact that parliamentarians, judges and government officials may actually use their delegated powers not only for the promotion of the "public interest" (in the sense of the sum of the constitutionally protected private interests of all citizens), but also for the promotion of their own personal self-interests.

The emergence of an ever increasing number of multilateral international conventions recognizing and protecting inherent and inalienable human rights[95] reflects to some extent this liberal and democratic assumption that "states" are mere instruments for the promotion of individual interests and "governments" are ultimately no more than the aggregates of the individuals who compose them. Even those rules of public international law, which are formally addressed to sovereign states or to intergovernmental organizations, are ultimately always addressed to individuals and can become effective only by influencing individual conduct. While the international IMF and GATT rules for the use of transparent, non-discriminatory and economically efficient policy instruments may be legally binding only for the members of the legislative, executive and judicial branches of the governments of the contracting parties, their ultimate objectives (e.g. legal certainty, international division of labour, undistorted prices and competition, peaceful change) are to promote the individual interests of all citizens and to regulate private conflicts of interests in a way maximizing national social welfare. Also the **procedural** guarantees of both national constitutions and international agreements for the transparent and non-discriminatory exercise of government powers (e.g. GATT Article XIX: safeguard measures against an unforeseen increase in injurious imports by means of transparent, non-discriminatory and temporary trade restrictions on the import side) purport to promote "due process" and, thereby, "just results" in the "public interest". Private and governmental decision-making processes suffering from procedural deficiencies risk to produce also deficient outcomes. Hence, the dangers resulting for the "public interest" in welfare-increasing trade policies from the "protectionist biases" in the various social decision-making processes discussed below.

95 For a survey see, e.g.: P. Sieghart, The International Law of Human Rights, 1983; I. Brownlie, Basic Documents on Human Rights, 1981.

B) Protectionist Biases in the Organization and Political Influence of Domestic Interest Groups: Empirical Evidence

The economic theory of politics ("public choice") proceeds from the assumption that individuals and groups tend to maximize their own perceived self-interests. In the current social processes within the existing rules and institutions, people tend to react to costs and other external constraints according to their own short-range interest in a predictable, systematic way. Public choice theory demonstrates that "not all economic interests can easily be organized", and "stable interest groups can become established only under specific conditions".[96] Accordingly, the political influence of the various domestic economic interest groups differs strongly. According to A. Downs,[97] the prevalence of the interests of producers (compared with those of consumers and taxpayers) in the formation of economic policies is mainly due to the fact that most people earn their income in one area but spend it in many; hence, they are more interested in incurring "information costs" and "organization costs" to exert political influence in their role as income-receivers in a specific position (producers, workers) than in their role as income-spenders (consumers, tax-payers) on a variety of different goods, services, direct and indirect taxes. While trade theory focuses on the consumer gains from trade liberalization, trade policy tends to be influenced much more by producer interests and by various "protectionist biases" in decision-making about trade:

a) The clearly visible and concentrated "adjustment costs" imposed by trade liberalization on a few import-competing producers act as a strong incentive for these producers to oppose politically import liberalization.

b) Since the gains from trade liberalization are less visible and dispersed among millions of consumers as a "public good", individual consumers tend to act as "free-riders" and have little incentives to invest the time and costs of organizing into an effective interest group for trade liberalization.

c) The clearly visible and concentrated "protection rents" made possible by import protection for a few import-competing producers act as a strong

96 See, e.g.: B.S. Frey, Democratic Economic Policy, 1983, pp. 121 ff.

97 A. Downs, An Economic Theory of Democracy, 1957.

incentive for the organization of protectionist interest groups and for "rent-seeking" pressures on trade politicians.

d) Various GATT rules and domestic foreign trade regulations, e.g. on the admissibility of production subsidies and safeguard measures to prevent "injury to domestic producers" (Articles XIX, VI of GATT), also suffer from a one-sided "producer bias" without an adequate balancing against the consumer interest in liberal trade.

e) Periodically elected politicians may have political self-interests in giving-in to protectionist pressures in exchange for political support and in taking on government responsibilities for adjustment problems arising from import competition.

f) Public administrations may also have self-interests in helping the producers and industries they are officially assigned to "serve" by relieving them from the pressures to adjust to import competition, and in expanding their own powers, budgets and staff for the discretionary administration of foreign trade.

g) The superior information of interest groups concerning the facts about their economic sector (e.g. competitiveness of import-competing producers), the often only selective information supplied by them to the government, the non-transparency of "grey area trade policies", and the absence of comprehensive and independent cost-benefit-analyses of trade protective measures further reinforce the various "protectionist biases".

A brief empirical look at the political influence of domestic interest groups on trade policy decision-making in the United States, Germany and in the EEC appears to confirm that "economic competition is increasingly replaced by political competition. Losers in the economic arena seek relief from legislators who have the power to make them winners. One law can offset a score of inefficiencies".[98] Especially in the United States, "the intensity and complexity of the politics surrounding the U.S. trade laws has increased as various groups in American society, manufacturers, importers, exporters, retailers and consumers, compete to promote their interests in the formulation of international economic po-

98 B.H. Siegan, (note 9), p. 331.

licy".[99] During the 1984 election campaign, the democratic party made import protection for American industries an important element of its party platform. R.E. Baldwin's statistical analysis of US Congressmen's voting on the US Trade Act of 1974 came to the conclusion that "workers and management who think they are being adversely affected by imports are apparently able collectively to persuade their congressmen to vote against trade liberalization. However, export-oriented industries are not similarly successful".[100] Empirical case studies of the various interest groups influencing the formation of US trade policy (e.g. sectoral federations of industries, the US Chamber of Commerce, the National Association of Manufacturers, Emergency Committee for American Trade, American Importers Association, AFL-CIO and individual trade unions, consumer groups) emphasize the strong influence of protectionist lobbies especially in the US Congress (where both the Senate and the House of Representatives have established a "textile caucus" as well as a "steel caucus" for the representation of these sectoral industrial interests), but to some extent also on the Department of Commerce and on the International Trade Commission.[101]

Empirical studies of German interest groups point out that sectoral federations of industries and trade unions tend to be more protection-prone than the more comprehensive federations of industry and trade (Bundesverband der Deutschen Industrie, Bundesverband des Gross- und Aussenhandels, Deutscher Industrie- und Handelstag).[102] The political influence of the strong agricultural lobby on the Federal Ministry for Agriculture (the recent German ministers for agriculture were always former representatives of agricultural lobbies) and of the textiles lobbies (including the textiles trade unions) on the Federal Ministry for Economics has had a clear impact on German trade policy decisions.[103] By

99 C.G.B. Fontheim, Conclusion, in: Jackson (note 7), p. 18-1.

100 R.E. Baldwin, The Political Economy of Postwar United States Trade Policy, in: Baldwin/Richardson (eds.), International Trade and Finance. Readings, 1981, pp. 64, 75; R.E. Baldwin, The Political Economy of U.S. Import Policy, 1986; W.E. Brock/S.P. Magee, Tariff Formation in a Democracy, in: Black/Hindley (eds.), Current Issues in Commercial Policy and Diplomacy, 1980, pp. 1 ff (p. 1: "Ironically, the more competitive the political system, the more likely distribution questions will dominate efficiency considerations on special interest-issues"); I.M. Destler, Making Foreign Economic Policy, 1980.

101 See: Müller-Godeffroy and others, Der neue Protektionismus, 1983, pp. 50-79.

102 H. Giesecke, Handelsprotektionismus aus der Sicht der deutschen Wirtschaft, in: Hilf/Petersmann (eds.), GATT und Europäische Gemeinschaft, 1986, pp. 63-71.

103 See the detailed case studies in Müller-Godeffroy (note 101), pp. 82-109. The World Bank has published a series of case studies on the influence of protectionist lobbies in major industrial countries, see, e.g.: Glisman/Weiss, On the Political Economy of Protection in Germany, World Bank Staff Working Paper No. 427, 1980; P.K.M. Tharakan, The Political

contrast, German consumers are not effectively represented in the political decision-making process about trade. The Federal German Parliament and German political parties discuss trade policy questions only rarely, and a parliamentary committee for trade policy, established in 1950, was discontinued in the late 1960s.[104] While a recent parliamentary debate on "protectionism"[105] displayed broad political support by all political parties represented in the Bundestag for a liberal trade policy, the parliamentary debates e.g. on the prolongation of the International Textiles Agreement and on trade protection for European agricultural producers revealed also the strong influence of textiles and agricultural lobbies in the parliament.[106]

The trade policy positions adopted by European federations of industries at Brussels vis-à-vis the EC institutions in charge of trade policy-making has been described as more protectionist compared with the positions taken by German federations of industries at the national level.[107] The Consultative Committee established under Article 18 ECSC Treaty and the Economic and Social Committee established under Article 165 EEC Treaty are advisory bodies consisting of representatives of producers, workers, consumers, dealers and, in the case of the Economic and Social Committee, also of farmers, draftsmen, carriers, professional occupations and the general public. The representatives are appointed in their private capacity and are expressly forbidden to act on any mandate or instructions from the bodies nominating them. Depending on the pertinent provisions of Community law (e.g. Article 198 EEC Treaty), the Committees may or must be consulted by the Council or by the Commission, and their advisory opinions have not been without influence.[108] Following a decision of the Paris Summit in 1972 of the Heads of State or of Government, the Economic and Social Committee has been granted a right of initiative to advise on all matters

Economy of Protection in Belgium, World Bank Staff Working Paper No. 431, 1980; K.A. Koekkoek and others, On protectionism in the Netherlands, World Bank Staff Working Paper No. 493, 1981; v.Cable, Economics and the Politics of Protection (in the United Kingdom), World Bank Staff Working Papers No. 569, 1983.

104 See: K. Tudyka, Parlament und Handelspolitik. Der Bundestag als Vermittler aussenwirtschaftlicher Interessen. In: Politische Vierteljahresschrift 12 (1971), pp. 283-300; H.J. Driehaus, Der Beirat des Bundestages für handelspolitische Vereinbarungen, 1972; C. Sasse, Regierungen, Parlamente, Ministerrat. Entscheidungsprozesse in der EG, 1975, pp. 80 ff.

105 See: Bundestages-Drucksache 10/1700 of 2 July 1984.

106 See e.g. Müller-Godeffroy (note 101), p. 105.

107 Giesecke (note 102), p. 68.

108 Schwaiger/Kirchner, Die Rolle der Europäischen Interessenverbände, 1981.

affecting the Community.[109] The Economc and Social Committee is composed of three groups each representing particular interests - the Employers' Group, the Workers' Group and the General Interests' Group - , whose members tend to vote by group and not by nationality.

The political influence of national and European interest groups on the trade policy of the EEC and its member states is often difficult to ascertain due to the fact that, notwithstanding the exclusive Community competence for the common commercial policy, individual EEC member countries continue to have numerous possibilities to grant trade protection at the national level in conformity with Community law (e.g. certain autonomous quantitative import restrictions) or contrary to Community law (e.g. national VERs, non-tariff import barriers, export subsidies).[110] Existing empirical case studies suggest that most import restrictions imposed by the European Community or by individual member states can be explained as a result of "a political market for protection, where special interest groups seek to pressure policy makers to supply desired measures".[111] The broad discretionary commercial policy powers of the EC executives and the lack of effective parliamentary and judicial review of the EC's "grey area trade policies" act as an incentive for protectionist interest groups to invest in influencing the exercise of these powers. The main channel through which interest groups and voters influence the trade policy of the European Community continues to be the governments of member countries via the Council of Ministers and the various EC Committees composed of representatives of member states.[112] A factor favouring the influence of protectionist interest groups has been the fact that the considerable economic waste, generated e.g. by the high import restrictions on agricultural products and textiles, has not been widely appreciated due to disregard of the invisible transfers implied by price distortions or to the absence of a visible impact on the budget of the EEC (e.g. in the case of the International Textiles Agreement).[113] A comparison of

---

109 See: The Right of Initiative of the Economic and Social Committee, EC 1977.

110 For a detailed analysis see: G. Koopmann, National Protectionism and Common Trade Policy, in: Intereconomics 1984, pp. 103 ff; E. Verreydt/J. Waelbroeck, European Community Protection against Manufactured Imports from Developing Countries: A Case Study in the Political Economy of Protection, in: J.N. Bhagwati (ed.), Import Competition and Response, 1982, pp. 369-399.

111 Verreydt/Waelbroeck (note 110), p. 370. See also the literature referred to above in notes 103 and 110.

112 See Verreydt/Waelbroeck (note 110), p. 377, with various examples.

113 See Verreydt/Waelbroeck (note 110), p. 378.

the highly protectionist textiles policy of the EEC e.g. with Switzerland's avoidance of any import quotas on textiles from developing countries illustrates not only that resistance to protectionist pressures is politically feasible even in high-wage industrial countries, but also that adjustment to import competition is the most effective method of promoting the survival and continued efficiency of import-competing industries.

C) Protectionist Biases in Democratic and Parliamentary Decision-making

The "traditional" theory of economic policy assumes that governments act autonomously to a large extent and aim at maximizing social welfare. By contrast, the modern theories of "public choice" take government to be an endogenous part of the politico-economic system acting not autonomously but under the influence of many different forces (e.g. private interest groups, political parties, government administration). The importance of rules and institutions defining the objectives, principles and procedures of public policy-making, and the strong role of incentives as a determinant of the day-to-day economic policy-making process **within** the rules and institutions established, are emphasized.[114] With regard to the foreign trade policy of the United States, for instance, empirical evidence seems to confirm that the legal changes from conditional to unconditional most-favoured-nation commitments in the Fordney-McCumber Tariff Act of 1922, and from unilateral tariff determination to reciprocal international tariff negotiations provided for in the Reciprocal Trade Agreements Act of 1934, created a framework conducive to the dramatic decline in the level of US tariffs between the 1930s and the 1970s and have altered the political balance between pro- and anti-tariff groups.[115]

In a democracy, economic policy should conform to the will and to the individual interests of the people. Hence, it should also aim at maximizing individual freedom of choice and real income, and thereby national economic welfare, through trade liberalization. Like the "theory of market-failure" that emerged from "welfare economics" since the 1930s, modern public choice theory offers comprehensive "theories of government-failure" explaining why electoral requirements are in themselves insufficient to hold the Leviathan-like proclivities of governments in check, and why democratic majority decisions may lead to logi-

114 See, e.g.: J.M. Buchanan/G. Tullock, The calculus of consent, 1962; D. Mueller, Public Choice, 1979.

115 See, e.g.: R.P. Lavergne, The Political Economy of US Tariffs: An empirical analysis, 1983.

cally inconsistent and socially disadvantageous results. For instance, "vote trading" may lead "cyclical coalitions" to vote "insincerely" on a number of issues, and simple majority votes may not only enable the legislative majority to impose costs on minorities, but may also lead to excessive public spending, whenever the benefits accruing to the interests represented by the majority are exceeded by the losses imposed on those represented by the minitory.[116] Rather than relying on the simplistic assumption (e.g. also of Keynesian economics) that public decision-makers will maximize social welfare following the advice given by economic advisers, "constitutional economics" emphasizes the need to reimpose constitutional limits on governmental powers over and beyond those exercised through periodic democratic elections. Long-term rules and procedures are recognized to be necessary for inducing policy-makers to act according to the preferences of their citizens. In the United States, for instance, various proposals for constitutional restraints on the financing of the budget through borrowing, on the taxing and spending powers of governments, and for additional administrative constraints have led already to constitutional and other legal reforms in various states.[117] Yet, the need for a "constitutional reconstruction" of the legal and institutional framework for foreign economic policy-making has received comparatively little attention up to now.

The preceding section has already described various "protectionist biases" in democratic decision-making processes about foreign trade policy. Legislative assemblies (e.g. the US Congress) and other law-making bodies (e.g. the EC Council) are important targets of protectionist pressures, for "very often, the appeal for protection is an appeal to a government to overturn the established rules because, under those rules, the enterprise or industry calling for protection is losing ground. It is an appeal to governments to create legal and institutional instability for the competing enterprises".[118] On the one side, the requirements of political accountability enshrined in the constitutional laws of Western democracies and the redistributive effects of trade restrictions necessitate the participation of domestic political institutions in international trade policy-making. The non-ratification by the US Congress of various trade arrangements negotiated by the US executive during the Havana Conference in 1948 as well as during the GATT Kennedy Round 1964-1967, and the provisions in the US Trade Act

116 See: R. Sugden, The Political Economy of Public Choice, 1981, pp. 182 ff.

117 See, e.g.: J.A. Dorn, The Principles and Politics of Tax Reform, in: Cato Journal 5 (1985), pp. 361 ff.

118 Bénard and others (note 37), p. 6 f.

of 1974 for close consultations by the executive with Congress and with private industry during the GATT Tokyo Round 1973-1979, show that international economic rules may not become effective without active involvement of domestic political and legislative bodies.[119] On the other side, the enactment by the US Congress of the highly protectionist Smoot-Hawley Tariff Act of 1930, which triggered retaliatory trade restrictions by a large number of foreign countries, demonstrated that, "if parochial domestic interests seeking protection are allowed to prevail, a disastrous chain reaction of reciprocal foreign protectionist moves would be triggered, leading to the collapse of world trade and a drastic fall in our standard of living".[120]

The US Reciprocal Trade Agreements Act of 1934 drew the political consequence from the historical experience of the Smoot-Hawley Tariff Act by delegating to the executive limited negotiating authority for international trade liberalization subject to specified conditions (e.g. international trade agreements providing for reciprocal foreign tariff reductions). Based on the 1945 renewal of this congressional delegation of negotiating authority, the US executive negotiated and accepted the GATT as an "executive agreement" (in terms of US constitutional law), thereby voluntarily subjecting its trade policy discretion to additional international legal disciplines for transparent, non-discriminatory and market-conforming trade policy-making. Moreover, Congress has enacted numerous and increasingly detailed statutes limiting the trade policy discretion of the executive and introducing a large number of legal remedies enabling private producers and traders to petition trade protective measures and to have them reviewed through adjudicative procedures.

And yet, notwithstanding the distinct trend towards "legalization" and "judicialization" of US foreign trade policy and the statutory and international constraints on the delegated executive trade policy powers, Congress itself appears to accept only few, if any, substantive constitutional and international legal restraints on its own trade regulation powers. The formulation and implementation of US competition, monetary, fiscal and trade policies through the passage of laws, enforceable in the federal courts or before quasi-judicial commissions (e.g. Federal Trade Commission, International Trade Commission), continues to be a characteristic feature of the American propensity to regulate economic beha-

119 This is emphasized by: Jackson/Louis/Matsushita, National Constitutions and International Economic Rules, 1984, pp. 1 ff; P.R. Trimble, International Trade and the Rule of Law, in: Michigan Law Review 83 (1985), pp. 1016, 1020, 1025 ff.

120 Howell/Wolff (note 7), p. 3-5.

viour through general rules of conduct and adjudicative procedures. At the same time, however, as described above (chapter VI, 2,A), the increasing number of protectionist legislative **ad hoc** measures outside the framework of the general import relief laws and of the delegation of vaguely defined trade policy powers to the executive (e.g. in the import relief provisions of section 201), including powers to conclude bilateral VERs and OMAs contrary to GATT law, raise doubts as to whether the constitutional safeguards of enumerated and limited government powers, separation and limited delegation of powers, "checks and balances" and equal individual liberties still effectively constrain the exercise of the foreign economic policy powers of Congress itself.

Congress does not recognize the international GATT legal disciplines as a constraint on its power to adopt or induce non-transparent, discriminatory and welfare-reducing protective measures (e.g. bilateral VERs) in contravention of GATT rules. The legislative task of ensuring an open and possibly educative democratic discussion of the objectives, proper means, benefits, costs and other implications of important policy measures, and of deciding between important policy alternatives, is frequently being neglected in the field of international economic relations. Commenting on the Economic Stabilization Act of 1970, on the basis of which President Nixon had introduced far-reaching import and other economic restrictions on 15 August 1971, Jan Tumlir has criticized the proclivity of Congress to delegate regulatory powers unconstrained by clear instructions and justiciable standards:

> "The question of 'how' is seldom discussed in much detail. The job is turned over, so to speak, to a black box in which presumably omniscient and disinterested bureaucrats determine how best to proceed and issue appropriate directives. To take only one example, the statute on the basis of which President Nixon decreed the far-reaching economic measures of August 15, 1971, had provided as follows: 'The President is authorized to issue such orders and regulations as he may deem appropriate to stabilize prices, rents, wages and salaries...'. The full panoply of powers needed for central economic planning had been granted by a careless Congress in twenty-two words."[121]

Non-transparent, discriminatory and welfare-reducing "grey area trade restrictions", often implemented abroad and in secrecy without legal remedies for adversely affected importers and consumers, are not the proper form of political decision-making envisaged by democratic constitutions. Moreover, their increasing number and precedential effects have led to a gradual erosion of the liberal

121 J. Tumlir, International Trade Regimes and Private Property Rights: A U.S. Perspective, in: Hesse/Streissler/Tichy (eds)., Aussenwirtschaft bei Ungewissheit, 1985, pp. 317, 331.

multilateral trading system based upon GATT, which had contributed to an unprecedented period of economic growth and international trade expansion between 1948 and 1973. Hence, as remarked by Jan Tumlir, "Congress' bland unconcern about the practice of economic management by perpetual negotiation is striking. These negotiations continuously create precedents that, too, have binding, legal power. Individually, they may be innocuous, but in their slow accretion they are congealing into extensive arrangements, systems of reciprocal commitments and expected practices that may be as difficult to modify or to repeal as a formal treaty. They are changing national law and it can be strongly argued that they are changing it against the grain of our constitutional philosophy".[122]

Apart from their harmful effects on other states, VERs and other discriminatory quantitative trade restrictions are reducing the economic welfare also of the restricting country itself and are a very costly form of income redistribution among domestic groups. In a democracy, the value judgments underlying this discretionary, surreptitious and discriminatory **ad hoc** income redistribution for the benefit of protectionist pressure groups should be made by representative assemblies.[123] According to Tumlir, "the result of the loosening of legislative constraints can best be described as a refeudalization of the economy. The notion that groups have rights is medieval. In a democracy, groups may have political influence, even a degree of economic power, but only persons have rights. In the redistributive state, government has become what it was in the Middle Ages - an inscrutable power above the people, to be lobbied, petitioned, and propitiated for the favors it can dispense."[124]

In the European Community, the common commercial policy has led to a general shift of power from national parliaments to executive authorities. Due to the lack of direct parliamentary participation in, or parliamentary legitimation and effective control of, the conduct of the common commercial policy of the EEC, the only sources of its legitimacy are the rule of law, the equal protection of individual rights and transparent "government by discussion". Hence, "because the only source of its influence is legitimacy, the Community must be even more careful than governments in respecting the treaties under which it was establi-

122 Tumlir (note 67), p. 55.

123 See: International Trade 1983/84, GATT 1984, p. 21; Tumlir (note 67), p. 19.

124 Tumlir (note 67), p. 16.

shed and the GATT agreements it helped to negotiate".[125] Yet, these "constitutional principles" of Community law no longer seem to determine the decision-making processes about the EEC's trade policy and have not prevented the EEC executives from asserting the power to tax and restrict the transnational trade transactions of EC citizens in manifest violation of its self-imposed international GATT obligations.

D) Protectionist Biases in Bureaucratic Decision-making: The Declining Role of the Limited Delegation Doctrine

In the modern, globally integrated world economy composed of more than 170 sovereign states, legislatures no longer have the time and expertise to conduct foreign economic policy and negotiate international agreements themselves. Hence, as the business of a legislature rises, it must delegate more and more of its work to executive and administrative agencies and to courts. As has been shown, legislatures often do not even find it necessary or possible to select themselves among various economic policy alternatives, let alone to control the actual exercise and implementation of the discretionary powers delegated to bureaucracies. Due to their technical expertise, bureaucracies are often able to influence legislative deliberations and to secure outcomes favourable to their own interests. Voters, interest groups and periodically elected politicians, who are often dependent on the assistance from administrations, have little incentives for efficiently controlling public bureaucracies and their inherent tendencies to try to enlarge their budget, personnel and discretionary powers ("Parkinson's law").[126]

It is recognized today that the "productive function" of modern welfare states is not only to create conditions conducive to maximum production of private goods and services, but also to produce a number of "public goods" (such as legal order, equitable income distribution, prevention of environmental pollution and of inflation). Yet, the large number of empirical studies so far undertaken (e.g. of the costs and benefits of antitrust policies, or of public enterprises) suggest that the regulatory costs are often very high and "public production is more

125 Verreydt/Waelbroeck (note 110), p. 375.

126 See: Frey (note 96), pp. 102 ff, according to whom "public employees can be assumed to maximize their own utility subject to the constraints imposed" (p. 106). "Public officials have little incentive to act in a socially optimal way, because a particular member of the public administration is seldom subjected to the consequences (the benefits and costs) of his decisions" (p. 109).

costly than private production".[127] The perception of "government failures" and "administrative failures" in the discretionary exercise e.g. of governmental fiscal, monetary, competition, agricultural, industrial, social and foreign trade policies - such as the tendency of regulatory agencies to avoid confrontations with powerful interest groups and to **identify with the interests** of "their" sector (e.g. ministries of agriculture and the EC Council of agricultural ministers representing solely the interests of the farmers) - has led to a strong movement in some countries (e.g. the United States) and among economists (e.g. the "monetarists", "supply-side" and "constitutional economists") for reimposing constitutional limits on the executive and administrative regulating powers and for freeing the economy from arbitrary government interventions ("deregulation"). The modern "theory of bureaucracy" even tends to view "governments as exploiters of the citizenry, rather than the means through which the citizenry secures for itself goods and services that can best be provided jointly or collectively. Both the modern analysis and the observed empirical record suggest that governments have, indeed, got out of hand".[128] Hence the need for rules and procedures inducing, assisting and containing executives and administrations to conduct foreign economic policy according to the individual preferences of society at large.

The practice of administrative trade protectionism appears to corroborate findings of the "economic theory of regulation",[129] according to which economic regulation often serves the private interests of the regulated groups rather than the "public interest":

a) Hardly any trade restrictions can be justified as an economically efficient policy instrument to promote the national economic welfare because, from an economic point of view, they generate more social costs than social benefits.[130]

b) Some safeguard measures **might** have been justifiable on grounds of economic efficiency (e.g. antidumping and countervailing duties) or on redistributive political grounds (e.g. the "conservative social welfare

127 See Frey (note 96), pp. 110-113.

128 J.M. Buchanan in: Buchanan/Tollison (eds.), The Theory of Public Choice, Vol. II, 1984, p. 19.

129 See the literature on "economic regulation" cited above (chapter IV, note 31; chapter V, note 54) and in Ogus/Veljanowski (eds.), Readings in the Economics of Law and Regulation, 1984, p. 250.

130 See above chapters III.3 and IV.3.

function"), but they are usually introduced without balancing the "protection benefits" for import-competing producers against the protection costs for the national economy at large and without procuring the evidence necessary for a decision on how to promote best the **national** welfare: In the United States, for instance under section 201 of the Trade Act of 1974, "the investigation conducted by the International Trade Commission (ITC) as the basis for a recommendation on granting protection focuses exclusively on the economic hardship afflicting the import-competing industry. The ITC need never inquire into the potential national gains from increased trade and so cannot balance such gains against the concomitant adjustment costs... Safeguard measures often appear inconsistent with distortions theory in another way as well: they do little or nothing to offset or correct relevant market failures".[131] In the EEC, there has been only one case thus far where "Community interests" have been referred to by the Commission as a ground for refusing safeguard action which might otherwise have been warranted under the safeguard clauses of Regulation No. 288/82.[132]

c) Trade restrictions often do not achieve their desired effect, or do so inefficiently at the expense of social welfare, as illustrated by the self-perpetuating and expanding character of many trade protective measures, such as the transformation of the "Short-term Arrangement Regarding International Trade in Cotton Textiles" (1961) into a "Long-Term Arrangement" (1962) and its extension into an "Arrangement Regarding International Trade in Textiles" (1974) periodically renewed and expanded to cover now more than 80% of world trade in textiles and clothing.[133]

Since the 1920s, the congressional delegation to the executive of negotiating authority for international trade agreements has been subjected to various conditions such as unconditional most-favoured-nation treatment (Fordney-McCumber Tariff Act of 1922), reciprocal international tariff concessions (Re-

131 With regard to the United States see, e.g., K.W. Abbot, The Trading Nation's Dilemma: The Functions of the Law of International Trade, in: Harvard International Law Journal 1985, pp. 501, 512.

132 See for details: Van Bael/Bellis (note 47), p. 179 f.

133 The GATT study on "Textiles and Clothing in the World Economy" (1984) has clearly brought out the lack of an economic justification of the continuation of this protective instrument openly disciminating against developing countries for now more than a quarter century.

ciprocal Trade Agreements Act of 1934), and multilateral legal disciplines negotiated within the GATT framework (Trade Act of 1974). At the same time, however, Congress has frequently mandated, authorized or tolerated executive trade restrictions in violation of GATT rules (see above chapter VI.2.A) and has not accepted the international GATT legal disciplines as an effective legal constraint on the exercise of executive trade policy powers. The US Supreme Court, in the 1936 case "United States v. Curtisswright Export Corporation", also took the view that "congressional legislation, which is to be made effective through negotiation and inquiry within the international field, must often accord to the President a degree of discretion and freedom from statutory restriction which would not be admissible were domestic affairs alone involved".[134]

The additional findings of this judgement, that the constitutional doctrine of enumerated and limited government powers applied only to domestic but not to foreign affairs and that the President enjoyed "plenary and exclusive power ... as the sole organ of the federal government in the field of international relations", have been criticized in view of the manifest intention of the framers of the US Constitution to create a federal government of limited and enumerated powers also with regard to foreign relations.[135] But the Supreme Court, since the late 1930s, has never invalidated a statutory delegation of authority by Congress on the ground of lack of meaningful standards or "intellegible principles" circumscribing the objective, scope and means of the delegated powers. In the 1983 case "Immigration & Naturalization Service v. Chadha", the Supreme Court declared unconstitutional the congressional monitoring device, frequently used since the 1930s, of delegating authority to the executive subject to a "legislative veto".[136] According to some observers, this oversight procedure of congressional veto appears to have been often abused by members of Congress for avoiding a thorough legislative discussion on, and precise legislative standards for, the delegation of powers to regulatory agencies, whose regulatory policies they later tried to influence and control to their own advantage as well as to the advantage

134 299 U.S. 304 (1936).

135 See, e.g., Berger, The Presidential Monopoly of Foreign Relations, 71 Michigan Law Review (1972), pp. 26 ff. In Youngstown Sheet & Tube Co. v. Sawyer, the Supreme Court refuted the idea of implied law-making powers of the President: "The Constitution limits his functions in the lawmaking process to the recommending of laws he thinks wise and the vetoing of laws he thinks bad... The Founders of this Nation entrusted the law-making power to Congress alone in both good and bad times" (343 U.S. 579, 1952). See further the American Court decisions referred to above in notes 16 and 17.

136 See above note 20.

of their client firms and other constituents.[137] Since the late 1930s, the constitutional doctrine of limited delegation of powers, which requires the legislature to specify any delegation of regulatory powers to the executive by justiciable standards for the desired ends and available means, seems to have "never stood as the principal tool for invalidating congressional delegations of legislative authority" in the case law of the Supreme Court.[138]

The delegation doctrine, which historically derives in part from the liberal concept of limited government and in part from the prohibition in agency law of subdelegation (**"delegata potestas non potest delegari"**), serves several important functions: It requires the legislature to discuss thoroughly the objectives, means and possible consequences of the delegated powers and to decide itself among important policy alternatives. This political discussion among the people's representatives can be expected to lead to a more comprehensive and, therefore, possibly more accurate view and political valuation of the desirable ends, means and trade-offs involved, compared with bureaucratic decision-making. Since this "legislative discussion" is more representative and more transparent to the general public, and to possibly disadvantaged parties interested in resisting "special interest legislation", the legislative decision is more likely to be general and abstract in nature (i.e. applicable to an open number of people and situations) and public-regarding rather than to serve only special interests. The legislative standards provide guidance to the executive and to the administration, which have to discuss and examine the policy alternatives anew and to decide on the exercise of the delegated powers. The legislative standards accompanying properly delegated powers are a precondition also for effective judicial review and enable the courts to adjudicate complaints of citizens, whose individual rights might be adversely affected by the exercise of the delegated powers.

137 Aranson (note 19), p. 198.

138 Aranson (note 19), p. 196. But see also Schoenbrod, The Delegation Doctrine: Could the Court give it Substance?, 83 Michigan Law Review (1985), pp. 1223, 1289: "The delegation doctrine is alive, but not well articulated or coherently applied by the Supreme Court. The Court continues to invalidate governmental action out of concern that Congress has delegated decisions that should be made in the legislative process, but under rubrics other than delegation, such as due process or vagueness, or even special, narrow versions of the delegation doctrine, such as a stringent approach to cases involving certain rights or favoring statutory constructions that avoid constitutional clashes. Nowhere has the Court attempted to explain how its various approaches to delegation by Congress relate to one another. Thus, the Court's approach to delegation simultaneously fails to serve the doctrine's purposes and, because it is incoherent, invites judicial usurpation of legislative powers."

The greater legislative specificity, required by the proper delegation doctrine, promotes a democratic process of successive and repeated "legislative, executive, individual and judicial filtering" of regulatory legislation and regulatory policies, which is more likely to detect and correct "market failures" as well as "government failures" than reliance in the benevolent exercise of delegated regulatory powers unguided and unconstrained by legislative justiciable standards. A reinvigoration of the constitutional doctrine of limited delegation of powers could therefore serve as a constitutional constraint on the ability of legislative, executive and administrative regulators to generate private benefits at the expense of social welfare. With regard to foreign trade policy, for instance, empirical evidence clearly shows that "rule-oriented" executive trade policy-making according to legislative rules and justiciable standards (e.g. antidumping and countervailing duty proceedings) are less determined by protectionist special interests compared to discretionary, and therefore more "power-oriented", executive trade policy-making less circumscribed by rules and regulations (e.g. safeguard measures under the "escape clause" in section 201 of the Trade Act of 1974).[139]

It seems to be no coincidence that, parallel to the growing scope of congressional delegations of vaguely circumscribed legislative powers and to the refusal by the courts since the late 1930s to uphold a vigorous application of the delegation doctrine, the Supreme Court has largely abandoned judicial review of economic regulation and has not declared unconstitutional any federal or state law on the ground that it denied a citizen or a corporation individual economic liberties such as to pursue a business, trade, or occupation.[140] According to the "rational basis test" deployed by the Supreme Court, the Court reviews socio-economic legislation no longer from the perspective of the constitutional guarantees of economic liberties and property rights, but only inquires whether there is a rational nexus between the means chosen and the legislative objective and "public interest" as defined by the legislature.[141] Together, the legislative delegation of broad discretionary trade policy powers unconstrained by precise standards and

139 See: Finger/Hall/Nelson, The Political Economy of Administered Protection, in: The American Economic Review 1982, pp. 452 ff, who argue that, even though the detailed statutory US regulations for antidumping and countervailing duty measures are "biased toward protectionism" (p. 466), "this bias is not large" and "their function is to resolve or diffuse complaints about import competition, and all in all they seem to serve this function efficiently" (pp. 464, 466).

140 See the detailed analysis by Siegan (note 9).

141 For a critical analysis see: J.A. Dorn, Economic Liberties and the Judiciary, in: Cato Journal 1985, pp. 661 ff.

the judicial non-application of the constitutional requirements of "limited delegation of powers" and "substantive economic due process" tend to reinforce the various "protectionist biases" in decision-making about trade policy described above. The legislative and judicial toleration of VERs and OMAs has tacitly granted the executive far-reaching discretionary powers to distort competition and redistribute income among domestic groups, to transfer the "protection rents" abroad to foreign exporters and governments, to promote and exempt foreign export cartels from antitrust challenge, to violate international law and to change fundamentally the multilateral trading system based on GATT.[142] The broad and largely uncontrolled executive trade policy discretion for "grey area measures" acts as an incentive for additional protectionist pressures, since import-competing producers may correctly perceive investments in the "political market for protectionism" (e.g. additional lobbying) to be easier and more profitable than investments improving their competitivity in the economic market.

Executive and administrative decision-making about the common commercial policy in the EEC reveals "protectionist biases" similar to those in the United States. For instance:

a) Delegation of broad discretionary trade policy powers to the EC executives without a sufficient definition of the "uniform principles" (Article 113 EEC Treaty) on which the common commercial policy shall be based.

b) Lack of effective parliamentary and judicial control of executive "grey area trade restrictions" imposed or induced by the EEC (e.g. VERs).

c) Frequent use of non-transparent "voluntary export undertakings" as a means to terminate more than 50% of the antidumping duty proceedings of the EEC.[143]

d) Protectionist tendencies in national administrations and in sectional EEC bodies (e.g. the EC Council of agricultural ministers) to supply protection to the economic sectors they are to supervise. The decision-making structures of the EEC have been criticized as being "inherently biased in favour of protectionism", and the EC Council of agricultural

142 Cf. Tumlir (note 67), p. 49.

143 See Van Bael/Bellis (note 47), pp. 98 ff.

ministers has been described by H. von der Groeben as an institutionalized "price cartel of protectionists".[144]

e) Parliamentary and judicial toleration of the erosion of the "rule of law" in foreign trade as a result of national and European "grey area trade restrictions" both outside and also **within** the EEC (e.g. bilateral British, French, Italian, Portugese and Spanish restrictions on Japanese automobile imports, "crisis cartels" for steel and synthetic fibres supported by the EEC).

E) Protectionist Biases in Judicial Decision-making: Judicial Abdication vis-à-vis Discretionary Grey Area Trade Restrictions

The legal obligations of international treaties, including those of GATT and the IMF Agreement, apply not only to the legislative and executive but also to the judicial branches of the governments of contracting parties unless the treaty obligations are confined to certain government organs only. Both GATT (e.g. Article X:3) and the IMF Agreement (e.g. Article VIII: 2,b) contain provisions explicitly requiring the judicial observance of treaty obligations by domestic courts. Prior to the IMF Agreement, domestic courts often refused to apply and enforce the foreign exchange control regulations of other countries on the ground that the regulations were contrary to the public policy ("ordre public") of the forum. Article VIII: 2 (b) of the IMF Agreement obligates the administrative and judicial authorities of each member country not to ignore another member's exchange regulations maintained consistently with the IMF Agreement; it superimposes the law of the country, whose currency is involved, upon the usually applicable conflict of laws rules.[145]

---

144 Cf. Patterson, The European Community as a Threat to the System, in: Cline (ed.), Trade Policy in the 1980s, 1984, pp. 224, 226; H. v. der Groeben, Aufbaujahre der EG, 1982, p. 152 f. See also the case study by P.A. Messerlin, Bureaucracies and the Political Economy of Protection. Reflections of a Continental European, World Bank Staff Working Papers No. 568, 1983, whose analysis of the role of "the bureaus" (bureaucrats) in the supply of protection in France concludes that the "tendency has been for the bureaus to advocate protection, even beyond that advocated by politicians. This tendency seems contradictory to the presumed public interest goals of bureaus, which would be to favor free trade. Moreover, the bureaus have often resorted to complex subsidy programs or hidden non-tariff barriers that are hard to measure, rather than to transparent protection measures" (p. I).

145 As regards court practice relating to Article VIII: 2, b IMF Agreement see: G.B. Schwab, The Unenforceability of International Contracts Violating Foreign Exchange Regulations: Article VIII, Section 2 (b) of the International Monetary Fund Agreement, in: Virginia

According to GATT Article X:3 (b).,

> "Each contracting party shall maintain, or institute as soon as practicable, judicial, arbitral or administrative tribunals or procedures for the purpose, inter alia, of the prompt review and correction of administrative action relating to customs matters. Such tribunals or procedures shall be independent of the agencies entrusted with administrative enforcement and their decisions shall be implemented by, and shall govern the practice of, such agencies unless an appeal is lodged with a court or tribunal of superior jurisdiction within the time prescribed for appeals to be lodged by importers."

The text of GATT Article X: 3(b) relates only to "administrative action". As regards "legislative action", the US Supreme Court appears to have never invalidated a federal trade regulation on the ground of inconsistency with GATT law.[146] Nor has the Court of Justice of the EC ever declared invalid a trade restriction imposed by the EC or by an EC member state on the ground of violation of GATT law.[147]

Judges of the US Supreme Court have on several occasions rightly stated that, as Justice Holmes expressed it in his famous dissent in Lochner v. New York, a "constitution is not intended to embody a particular economic theory, whether of paternalism and the organic relation of the citizen to the State or of **laissez faire**".[148] As Justice Rehnquist expressed it more recently, "there is certainly nothing in the United States Constitution which requires the Virginia Legislature to hew to the teachings of Adam Smith in its legislative decisions".[149] Judges must apply legal rules and protect individual rights. It is not the function of judges to act as economists, nor is it the function of constitutions to prescribe specific economic theories. The effective judicial protection of the liberty of contract and of other economic liberties to produce and distribute goods and services by the US Supreme Court between 1897 and 1937, during which period the Court protected economic and noneconomic liberties alike and annulled a

---

Journal of International Law 1985, pp. 967 ff, who concludes: "Despite the apparent purpose of Article VIII, section 2 (b) to ensure that the courts of Fund members recognize the exchange controls of other members, this goal has been thwarted to a large extent by the adoption of different interpretations of the provision" (p. 1005).

146 For a detailed analysis of the application of GATT by US courts see Hudec (note 18).

147 For a detailed analysis of the application of GATT by the Court of Justice of the EC see: M. Maresceau, The GATT in the Case-Law of the European Court of Justice, in: Hilf/Jacobs/Petersmann (note 18), pp. 107 ff; E.U. Petersmann (note 79).

148 198 U.S. 45, 75 (1905).

149 Virginia Stateboard of Pharmacy v. Virginia Citizens Consumer Council, Inc., 425 U.S. 748, 781 (1976).

considerable amount of economic legislation on the ground that it violated economic liberties protected by the Constitution,[150] was not based on any economic theories but on the common view of the framers of the US Constitution that life, liberty, property and other inalienable rights preexist and contain the legislative powers. In the words of Justice Story: "That government can scarcely be deemed to be free, where the rights of property are left solely dependent upon the will of a legislative body, without any restraint. The fundamental maxims of a free government seem to require, that the rights of personal liberty and private property should be held sacred".[151] Even if it might be true that "protecting such rights will nearly always promote the economically 'correct' results",[152] the Supreme Court was rightly concerned with protecting economic liberties and property rights and not with promulgating economically preferable results.

It is generally acknowledged that, in the case West Coast Hotel Co. v. Parrish (1937), the Court terminated substantive economic due process in reviewing economic legislation. Since then, the Supreme Court has given economic liberties and property rights much less protection than other "fundamental rights", such as freedom of speech or press.[153] According to the Court, "when the legislature has spoken, the public interest has been declared in terms well-high conclusive. In such cases the legislature, not the judiciary is the main guardian of the public needs to be served by social legislation".[154] "If the laws passed are seen to have a reasonable relation to a proper legislative purpose, and are neither arbitrary nor discriminatory, the requirements of due process are satisfied, and judicial determination to that effect renders a court **functus officio**".[155] Whereas the framers regarded the Constitution as a safeguard of preexisting individual rights to be constrained by public-regarding laws only, the Supreme Court's "rational basis test" seems to imply that legislatures are almost free to define the "public interest" and the economic liberties of the citizen: "property rights are no longer considered a constraint on legislation. Instead, the will of

150 See Siegan (note 9), pp. 110 ff.

151 Wilkinson v. Leland, 27 U.S. (2 Pet.) 627, 657 (1829).

152 P.H. Aranson, Judicial Control of the Political Branches: Public Purpose and Public Law, in: Cato Journal 1985, pp. 719, 721.

153 See Siegan (note 9), pp. 145 ff. and, more generally, on the evolution of the "double standard" in the judicial protection of individual rights in the USA: H.J. Abraham, Freedom and the Court, Civil Rights and Liberties in the United Stats, 1988, pp. 11 ff.

154 Berman v. Parker, 348 U.S. 26, 32 (1954).

155 Nebbia v.New York, 291 U.S. 502, 537 (1934).

the legislature... is seen to be the source of property rights".[156] As Siegan observed: "Because every economic regulation serves some purpose..., the rational relation standard essentially presupposes judicial withdrawal".[157] Prior to 1936, American courts accepted the inherent limitation of legislative power, and the Supreme Court provided substantial protection for economic liberties and property rights against legislative interferences.[158] The Court's subsequent "refusal to accept and enforce the theory of property rights inherent in the Constitution - as well as its failure to see that property rights, incentives and economic efficiency are all interrelated - has led to a substantial increase in economic regulation... (which) has imposed significant costs on the economy and has led to the rise of vast bureaucracies" redistributing wealth rather than creating wealth.[159]

The declining role of the judiciary in the protection of economic liberties and property rights, and hence also of self-regulation and spontaneous competition arising from the free exercise of such rights, implied an increased freedom of the political bodies to redetermine and respecify economic liberties and property rights through majoritarian special interest legislation and economic regulation. Due to the Court's dangerous dichotomy between civil liberties, which are recognized as "fundamental rights", and economic liberties relegated to the political determinations of the legislature and executive,[160] there appear to be no longer effective substantive constitutional constraints on protectionist legislation and income redistribution through discriminatory foreign trade restrictions. Nor does the Court review economic regulation on economic grounds, such as considerations of "economic efficiency" (e.g. in the Hayekian sense of voluntary individual plan coordination) or cost-benefit-analysis. While the framers of the US Constitution viewed the legislature as the most dangerous branch of government and emphasized the constitutional constraints imposed on the legislative powers by preexisting and inalienable individual rights, the Court seems to

---

156 Dorn (note 141), p. 663.

157 Siegan (note 9), p. 265.

158 A famous case was Lochner v.New Ypork, 198 U.S. 45 (1905), where the Supreme Court declared unconstitutional a New York statute that set maximum hours for bakery workers. See for details Siegan's description of "the substantive due process era" (note 9), pp. 109 ff.

159 Dorn (note 141), p. 667; Siegan (note 9), pp. 283 ff, who demonstrates with a large number of empirical case studies that economic regulation has increased neither freedom nor efficiency, but has been a major cause of inefficient allocation of resources.

160 On the dangers of this dichotomy between political and economic freedom and the "erroneous belief that there are purely economic ends separate from the other ends of life" (p. 66) see: F.A. v.Hayek, The Road to Serfdom, 1944, pp. 66 ff.

consider the legislature to be almost omnipotent in its redistributionist activities driven by majority rule.

In the field of import relief laws, the legislative activism has made imports the most regulated section of the US economy leading to ever increasing complexity of the rules and to a "legalization" as well as "judicialization" of antidumping, countervailing duty and other import relief measures. Some practitioners have taken the view "that the cost of proceedings has become excessive" and "that litigation is an inappropriate technique for resolving such trade issues", as illustrated by the settlement of the 1976 automobile dumping complaints and the 1977/1982 steel subsidy complaints outside the general statutory framework.[161] The multiplicity of overlapping US import relief regulations with their often vague concepts of "fair trade", designed to counter "unfair" foreign trade practices or to grant temporary import protection during a period of adjustment, and the increasing recourse to judicial review of these import relief laws, are criticized for lending themselves to protectionist abuse ("legal harassment") by petitioning industries.[162] The Customs Court Act of 1980 and the Federal Courts Improvement Act of 1982 strengthened and extended the comprehensive system of judicial reviewability by the Court of International Trade (the successor of the previous Customs Court) and by the Court of Appeals for the Federal Circuit (which basically combines the functions of the former Court of Customs and Patent Appeals and the Court of Claims) not only of virtually each administrative determination in antidumping and countervailing duty investigations, but also of certain other administrative actions which affect imports (e.g. customs matters, complaints to the International Trade Commission about "unfair trade practices" pursuant to section 341 of the Trade Act of 1974).[163] The possibility of contesting preliminary determinations was eliminated by the Trade and Tariff Act of 1984, since the interlocutory appeals had resulted in costly and time-consuming actions in some cases.

The explicit statutory procedural requirements in the various US import regulations - e.g. for citizen complaint initiation, investigations by independent regulatory agencies (especially the International Trade Commission), public hearings, time limits, published official determinations with reasoned opinions, and judi-

161 See e.g. N. Hemmendinger, in: Jackson (note 7), p. 2-3, 4.

162 See: UNCTAD, Antidumping and Countervailing Duty Practices, TD/B/979 (1984), p. 16.

163 See for details: Jackson (note 6), p. 1584 ff; E.A. L.M. Vermulst, Judicial review in trade policy matters in the United States and the European Community: the legalization of international trade law, in: Sociaal Economische Wetgiving 1985, pp. 347 ff.

cial review - are no doubt impressive. As Jackson[164] has shown, they contribute to the transparency and "fairness" of the procedures, allow the presentation of all relevant informations and arguments, make trade policy decisions more predictable, render "back room political deals" more difficult and, despite the unavoidable risk of some abuse of the legalistic procedures for protectionist purposes, may in the end promote also a higher degree of liberal trade access and the fending-off of protectionist pressures. The **economic** cost-benefit analysis of Jackson suggests that the share of the private costs and government agency costs of approximately 1/10th of 1% of the total annual value of US imports does not present an excessive "transaction cost" for a regulatory system with substantial political, legal and economic benefits.

And yet, the judicial review is largely confined to customs, antidumping, countervailing duty procedures and "unfair" trade practices (in terms of section 341 Trade Act of 1974), but does not appear to be available in regard of various other safeguard measures, notably VERs and "grey area trade restrictions" in violation of GATT rules.[165] The judicial review of import restraints is essentially confined to examining whether agency findings of fact are compatible with a "reasonableness test", whether the procedural requirements have been observed, and whether the agency's legal interpretations remain within the usually broad executive discretion, to which the courts tend to defer. The available judicial review does not appear to offer a remedy for the "constitutional problems" mentioned above: any trade restrictions enacted by federal legislation, even if they limit individual freedoms and property rights in open contradiction of the GATT prohibitions of trade discrimination and of disproportionate non-tariff trade barriers, will be applied by the courts;[166] the constitutional doctrine of li-

---

164 Jackson (note 6), pp. 1574 ff.

165 In addition to the 1974 case "Consumers Union v. Kissinger" (above note 17), see also the 1977 case "Sneaker Circus, Inc v.Carter", in which the District Court denied a complaint that a VER on imports of shoes, negotiated by the President, had failed to comply with the "minimum-quantity requirement" of the escape clause statute: "To dispose of plaintiffs' claim, the court need only note that the President's decision is not reviewable not only because it was specifically left to his discretion by Congress, but also because it goes to the substance of the agreements and as such is a political question which is beyond the scope of the remand from the Court of Appeals" (457 F. Suppl. 771, 793, E.D.N.Y. 1978). The "nonjusticiability" of VERs imposed on imports of textiles and apparel was confirmed in a 1984 decision of the Court of International Trade (American Association of Exporters and Importers v. United States, 583 F.Suppl. 591, 598). See further Jackson (note 6), p. 1584; Hudec (note 18), pp. 242 ff; Vermulst (note 163), p. 352.

166 For a detailed recent analysis of the legal status of GATT law in the US legal system see Hudec (note 18), pp. 195 ff. In the 1967 decision of the Court of Claims in the case "Select Tire Salvage Co. v. United States", the Court found: "The GATT does not bind Congress or

mited delegation of powers is not strictly enforced by the courts, which have approved of congressional delegation of extensive discretionary trade policy powers to the executive with few, if any, controls on executive discrection;[167] US courts almost invariably defer to the judgement of the executive as to whether statutory criteria have been met and, according to Hudec, "have not been disposed to apply meaningful legal controls on Executive Branch actions in the field of foreign trade";[168] apart from retroactive interferences with existing contracts, individual economic liberties and property rights are not recognized as constitutional constraints on discriminatory trade restrictions, even though the latter invariably harm some citizens in order to benefit others.

In the European Community, the recent case-law of the Court of Justice has clarified that all participants in an antidumping or countervailing duty procedure have the possibility of attacking administrative determinations before the Court of Justice either by means of "direct complaints" under Article 173 of the EEC Treaty (e.g. by foreign exporters and producers, related importers, Community producers) or by means of "indirect complaints" under Article 177 EEC Treaty

have the status of a treaty, because it has never been ratified. However, it is an agreed code of international behaviour. An unambiguous statutory command, contrary to GATT, would of course prevail, but the one here involved can be construed to harmonize" (386 F. 2d 1008, 1013). In the 1971 case "American Express Co. v. United States", the Customs Court decided, inter alia: "GATT is a trade agreement, which if in conflict with a law of Congress, must yield to the latter" (332 F.Suppl. 191, 200).

167 In the 1955 decision in "Bardwil v. United States" (42 CCPA 118), as well as in its 1975 Yoshida decision (**supra** note 12), the Court of Customs and Patent Appeals construed section 350 of the Reciprocal Trade Agreements Act of 1934 (as extended in 1945), under which the GATT was accepted by the USA, as being essentially free of any justiciable legal restraints. In the 1975 Yoshida case (**supra** note 12), the Court also construed the 1917 Trading with the Enemy Act (as amended) to give the President virtually unlimited powers over foreign trade during any period in which a "national emergency" has been proclaimed by the President, thereby justifying the imposition by the President of a 10% surcharge on imports in August 1971. In the 1976 decision in "Federal Energy Administration v. Algonquin, Inc." (426 US 548), the Supreme Court construed the power delegated to the President to impose trade restrictions for "national security" reasons (section 232 of the Trade Expansion Act of 1962) as being sufficiently limited by the requirement of "national security purposes". Section 204 of the Agricultural Adjustment Act of 1936 (as amended) grants almost unconstrained authority to the President to negotiate VERs on agricultural and textile products "whenever he determines such action appropriate"; this was held constitutional and nonjusticiable in the above-mentioned 1984 decision of the Court of International Trade in "American Association of Exporters and Importers v. United States" (note 165). The complete discretion of the President to withdraw preferences under the Generalized System of Preferences, including discriminatory withdrawals against a particular developing country, was confirmed in a 1984 court decision in "Florsheim Shoe Co. v. United States" (No. 83-1371, 5 BNA IRTD 2385).

168 See Hudec (note 18), pp. 215 ff.

(e.g. by independent importers which must first challenge the national implementing actions before the national courts).[169] With regard to import relief measures under Council Regulation No. 288/82 on common rules for imports, this Regulation does not provide for a private complaint procedure. In the absence of Court decisions, it remains uncertain whether Community industries, importers or exporters involved in safeguard measures imposed under this Regulation can directly challenge under Article 173 the protective measures instituted or the refusal to institute safeguard measures. While importers may challenge safeguard measures indirectly through the preliminary ruling procedure pursuant to Article 177, the case-law of the Court indicates that the Court does not review the compatibility of foreign trade restrictions with the GATT obligations of the EEC in proceedings instituted by private complainants. And only very exceptionally, for instance in case of non-compliance by the EC institutions with the procedural requirements set out in the Regulation or a "serious and manifest error" in the assessment of the facts, will the Court interfere with the EC authorities' broad discretion in determining whether safeguard measures are necessary.[170] From the right of petition against illicit commercial practices granted to Community industries under Article 3 of Council Regulation No. 2641/84 on "the strengthening of the common commercial policy with regard in particular to protection against illicit commercial practices", it can be inferred that private complainants are entitled to bring direct actions under Article 173 against adverse determinations by EC authorities under Regulation No. 2641/84. Other private individuals not participating in these Community procedures may challenge import restraints taken under Regulation No. 2641/84 only indirectly through proceedings in national courts and a referral to the Court of Justice under Article 177.

Unlike private persons, EC institutions and EC member states can directly challenge all trade restrictions imposed by the EC or by individual EC member states before the Court of Justice pursuant to Articles 169, 170 and 173 of the EEC Treaty. Yet, neither an EC institution nor an EC member state have ever instituted such a court proceeding. Due to this "collusion" among EC institutions and EC member states in the field of "grey area trade restrictions", and to the refusal by the Court of Justice to apply and enforce the GATT obligations of the EEC in proceedings instituted by private plaintiffs, a large number of discrimi-

169 For a survey of this case-law see: Van Bael/Bellis (note 47), pp. 127 f; E.A. Vermulst, Antidumping Law and Practice in the United States and the European Communities, 1987, pp. 254 ff.

170 Cf. van Bael/Bellis (note 47), p. 128.

natory trade restrictions imposed by the EC or by individual EC states appear to elude judicial control. As regards antidumping, countervailing duty and other import relief measures, the Court has emphasized that the competent Community authority enjoys a "very wide discretion to decide, in terms of the interests of the Community, any measures to deal with the situation it has established".[171] As stated in the Fediol case, the Court will therefore confine itself to examining whether the procedural safeguards of the respective regulation have been observed, whether there have been manifest errors in the assessment of the facts, whether there has been an omission to consider essential matters, or whether the competent organs have abused their powers.[172]

In the recent analysis of the review by the Court of Justice of the legality of various national and European economic policy measures adopted to deal with the apparent crises e.g. in the EECs agricultural and steel policies, Mertens de Wilmars and J.Steenbergen noted:

> "In the nineteenth century and the first half of the twentieth, judges had acquired a quite remarkable mastery of the legal instruments of the liberal economic system and were never in doubt about their powers and capacity to intervene in the economic relations reflected in the civil codes, inasmuch as they awarded damages, modified property rights or annulled contracts or varied contractual obligations. Similarly, judges and all those who assist in the administration of justice in the second half of the twentieth century must master the new legal instruments of the mixed-economy systems in order to ensure that, in those systems as well, the rule of law is upheld."[173]

The preceding survey suggests that many American and European courts still perceive trade policy as "foreign" policy rather than domestic policy interfering with individual freedoms, property rights and competition of domestic producers, investors, traders and consumers. The economic insight, that economic regulation is a form of taxation[174] and that trade restrictions are a very costly and ineffective instrument for the redistribution of income among domestic groups, still appears to be alien to many lawyers and judges. The judicial deference to almost all kinds of non-transparent, discriminatory, impoverishing and redistributive administrative trade restrictions in manifest violation of GATT law indi-

171 Case 191/82 - FEDIOL v. Commission - (1983) E.C.R. 2913, para. 26.

172 Case 191/82 (note 171), para. 30.

173 Mertens de Wilmars/J. Steenbergen, The Court of Justice of the European Communities and Governance in an Economic Crisis, in: Michigan Law Review 82 (1984), pp. 1377, 1398.

174 See, e.g., R. Posner, Taxation by Regulation, in: The Bell Journal of Economics 2 (1971), pp. 22-50.

cates that courts often attach more importance to the judicial protection of the wide discretionary government powers in economic matters than to the equal protection of individual economic liberties and property rights. This attitude is regrettable also from an economic perspective because the constitutional guarantees of individual liberties coincide with the premisses of welfare economics, namely that the individual is the best judge of his own welfare, that the welfare of society depends on the welfare of the individuals that comprise it, and that social welfare tends to be maximized by undistorted competition based on voluntary, welfare-maximizing transactions of property rights. Economists point therefore out that the judicial protection of individual rights and of welfare-maximizing voluntary transactions will nearly always promote also economic and social welfare[175] ("welfare" being measured in economic terms by individual willingness to pay, or in legal terms by the maximization of equal individual rights). Hence, the legal logic of individual rights, of private law, competition and trade law, and the economic logic of market competition, are mutually supportive. They provide a consistency-ensuring core for the legal and economic systems of liberal democracies which, notably in the common market and competition law of the EEC, has considerably extended the justiciability of economic law and has enabled courts to exercise a substantive review of governmental restraints of economic freedoms.

The EEC Treaty provisions on the free movement of goods and persons and the EEC's competition law owe their success largely to the dual system of public and private enforcement of rights by the independent EC Commission, individual EC member states and private parties, who may directly invoke and enforce these rights in national courts. By contrast, in those areas of Community law where individual economic freedoms and undistorted competition have been curtailed by Community competences for the administrative steering of prices and quantities (e.g. of agricultural, textiles and steel products), the foreign trade régime has been partly transformed from one of rule-oriented competition into one of administrative discretionary redistribution. The judicial review of this sectoral agricultural, textiles, steel and other commercial policy by the Court of Justice has been largely confined to the review of the observance of formal rules and procedures.[176] The practical experience inside and outside the EEC suggests that, if states want to maximize their national welfare and the individual freedoms and property rights of their citizens through non-discrimina-

175 See, e.g., Aranson (note 152), p. 721.

176 See, e.g., R. Boest, Die Agrarmärkte im Recht der EWG, 1984, S. 311 ff.

tory foreign trade competition, this can be achieved most effectively through constitutional guarantees of private rights in non-discriminatory, undistorted foreign trade competition and through their protection by national courts against administrative interferences. An effective judicial protection of individual freedoms and property rights against illegal administrative trade restrictions would make necessary a justiciable legal distinction between the foreign policy and security aspects of foreign trade, which may require executive discretion and judicial deference to its exercise, and the economic aspects of securing undistorted trade competition, which require regulation by law and judicial review.

4. Conclusion: Trade Mercantilism as a "Constitutional Failure" of Representative Democracy

Parallel to the use of the term "market failure" for situations in which the spontaneous, unhampered operation of the price system and market forces do not lead to an optimal allocation of resources that maximizes economic and social well-being (e.g. due to market distortions caused by monopoly power or due to adverse "external effects"), the term "government failure" is used to denote badly functioning policy institutions and distorted democratic decision-making processes which fail to lead to political decisions and legal rules that maximize the equal rights and individual and social welfare of domestic citizens. Chapter V.2 has described the "new protectionism" as "government failure" because the administrative use of non-transparent, discriminatory, disproportionately harmful and conflict-oriented trade policy instruments without effective parliamentary and judicial control reduces not only the economic welfare of domestic citizens (e.g. their real income and non-discriminatory competition) but also their enjoyment of individual freedoms of choice and of other constitutional guarantees.

Chapter V.3 had shown, however, that the "political failure" did not necessarily imply a personal failure of politicians or bureaucrats once the unrealistic assumption is discarded that individual participants in politics seek "public good" and that governments can promote the "public good" like benevolent and omnipotent despots. If the individualist, economic model of human behaviour is applied also to "political markets" and politics is viewed as a complex institutionalized process through which self-interested individuals express their personal preferences on political alternatives with which they are presented, then the individual participants in the "political market" may act rationally in pursuing protectionist policies, just as individual economic agents may act rationally in the case of "market failure". In both cases, failure results from the lack or insufficient effectiveness of, or tolerated disregard for, rules and institutions for structuring and informing the decision-making processes in a way maximizing social welfare. This shows, as J. Tumlir and G. Banks rightly emphasized

> "the essentially constitutional nature of 'political failure', constitutions being rules for the making of rules. Reforms are needed to ensure that collective decisions are made through an adequately informed political discussion. The task is to establish procedural devices which could serve to minimize political failure in the same way that decentralization - competition and private property rights - minimizes market failure."[177]

What reforms of the political rules and institutions are needed to induce the self-interested political agents to exercise their discretionary trade policy powers in a manner that, similar to the self-interested behaviour of private economic market participants, tends to maximize individual and social welfare? The survey in chapter V.4 of the criticism of the "old mercantilism" showed that the main objective of the classical economic and political liberals during the 18th century was to promote individual and social welfare by means of an - in the words of Immanuel Kant - "constitution that achieves the greatest possible freedom by framing the laws in such a way that the freedom of each can coexist with the freedom of all".[178] In their view, the basic principles of democracy and of a "limited constitution" providing institutional safeguards of individual freedom offered the only effective method of making continuous peaceful change in economic as well as political markets possible. The original idea behind the classical doctrine of liberal constitutionalism was that government powers must be legally limited by long-term, higher-ranking constitutional rules and that the actual exercise of government powers in conformity with these constitutional rules must be further restrained and promoted by additional institutional devices such as the division of government powers between the legislature, the administration and the judiciary.

Chapter VI.1 showed that trade policy powers are powers to tax and restrict domestic citizens in a manner that reduces almost always the freedom and economic welfare of the citizens not only in the restricting country but also in foreign trading countries. Hence, there is a strong case for "deregulation" and constitutional limitation of trade policy powers in order to avoid the risk of "go-

177 J. Tumlir/G. Banks, Economic Policy and the Adjustment Problem, 1986, p. 82 f.

178 I. Kant, Critique of Pure Reason, chapt. II.i, p. 1.

vernment failure" in the trade policy area. That trade liberalization is a practical policy and not just an academic proposition so often derided by "practical men", is illustrated by the fact that the prohibition and successful liberalization of all tariffs and quantitative trade restrictions within the EEC in compliance with GATT Article XXIV is usually celebrated as the climax of European statesmanship of this century, just as all countries around the world take pride in having liberalized all trade barriers within their own national jurisdiction.

The survey of the foreign trade laws and practice of the United States and the EEC in chapter VI.2 and 3 concluded that, notwithstanding the repeated statements of US and EC politicians in favour of trade liberalization and of observance of their self-imposed international GATT obligations, trade policy powers are increasingly exercised by government executives in a non-transparent and welfare-reducing manner without effective parliamentary and judicial control. Both the original US Constitution as well as the EEC Treaty established governments with enumerated powers which could do only what the respective constitutions authorized them to do; everything else, as stated in the Tenth Amendment to the US Constitution, was "reserved to the States respectively, or to the people". But this "enumerated powers principle" of American constitutional law as well as of European Community law has not prevented the US and EC trade administrations from using trade policy instruments for limiting the individual rights and welfare of domestic citizens. And the constitutional principles of separation and only limited delegation of powers have not prevented parliaments and courts to leave the "grey area trade policy", and thereby the future of the multilateral GATT trading system which it undermines, to the bureaucracy. So far, the constitutional principle of federalism seems to have been the least affected by the protectionist pressures and grey area trade restrictions (see above VI.2.1.e), presumably due to the strong self-interest of the US federal government and the EC executives in defending their commercial policy competences vis-à-vis the member states. But there are clear tendencies in several federal states (such as the USA and Canada) to re-interpret the "federal state clause" of GATT Article XXIV:12 in a manner limiting the international GATT obligations of federal states (e.g. to exempt regional and local governments from the scope of application of GATT).[179] And there is a similar trend

179 See the opposition by Canada against the adoption of the two recent GATT Panel Reports reconfirming the traditional interpretation of GATT Article XXIV:12 (e.g. GATT document L/5863 of September 1985) and the position of the US government that the corresponding "federal state clause" in the 1979 GATT Agreement on Technical Barriers to Trade does not require the federal government to use its legal powers to prohibit state governments from violating these obligations (see E.U. Petersmann, above note 31).

within the EEC to tolerate national "grey area trade restrictions" by individual EEC member states (e.g. the long-standing VERs of England, France and Italy limiting the market share of Japanese automobiles in these countries) and to reinterpret the temporary safeguard clause of Article 115 of the EEC Treaty in a way allowing the continued maintenance of national import quotas and supplementary trade barriers within the EEC.[180]

180 See the recent "Tezi-judgment" by the EC Court of Justice relating to Article 115 (quoted above in note 61) and, as regards the toleration of national VERs, the literature quoted above in note 53 as well as: M.C.E.J. Bronckers, A Legal Analysis of Protectionist Measures Affecting Japanese Imports into the European Community, in: E. Völker (ed.), Protectionism and the European Community, second edition 1987, pp. 76 ff.

THIRD PART: CONSTITUTIONAL FUNCTIONS OF LIBERAL INTERNATIONAL ECONOMIC RULES

"Perhaps the most difficult question to determine is how much to decide by rule and how much to leave to discretion". "It is an advantage, and not a disadvantage, of the scheme that it invites the member States to abandon that licence to promote indiscipline, disorder and bad-neighbourliness which, to the general disadvantage, they have been free to exercise hitherto".

J.M. Keynes[1]

"Here is an attempt to use what we have learnt from modern experience and modern analysis, not to defeat, but to implement the wisdom of Adam Smith... They (the international agreements) aim, above all, at the restoration of multilateral trade ... The bias of the policies before you is against barter and every kind of discriminatory practice. The separate economic blocs and all the friction and loss of friendship they must bring with them are expedients to which one may be driven in a hostile world, where trade has ceased over wide areas to be co-operative and peaceful and where are forgotten the healthy rules of mutual advantage and equal treatment. But it is surely crazy to prefer that".

J.M. Keynes[2]

---

1 J.M. Keynes, "Proposals for an International Currency or Clearing Union" of 1942, in: J.K. Horsefield (ed.), The International Monetary Fund 1945-1965, IMF 1969, Vol. III, pp. 6,36.

2 J.M. Keynes, in his advocacy in the House of Lords for the acceptance of the post-war US loan, conditions of which were participation in the Bretton-Woods Agreements and in the negotiations for an International Trade Organization, in: J.M. Keynes, The Collected Writings of J.M. Keynes (edited by D. Moggridge), Vol. XXIV, 1979, p. 623 f.

VII. CONSTITUTIONAL FUNCTIONS OF LIBERAL INTERNATIONAL TRADE AND MONETARY RULES

1. Notion and Functions of "Constitutional Rules"

A) The Reason of Rules

The international division of labour among today more than 170 states consists of millions of constantly changing relations between producers, investors, researchers, importers, exporters, consumers and government officials. The particular facts and concrete events which the individual economic agents encounter in their daily pursuits (e.g. a new discovery) and which affect the course of the international division of labour, cannot be known to any individual or government in their entirety. This irremediable ignorance of everyone of most of the particular facts which determine the actions of all the other participants in the international division of labour, can be reduced only by reliance on the information supplied by rules of conduct and market prices which enable individuals to form reasonably correct expectations and induce the international division of labour to constantly adapt itself to the continuous change.

According to F.A. Hayek, most of the rules of conduct governing individual actions, and most of the institutions which arose out of this regularity, are adaptations to this fragmentation and individual limitation of our knowledge. Yet, "it is the utilization of much more knowledge than anyone can possess, and therefore the fact that each moves within a coherent structure most of whose determinants are unknown to him, that constitutes the distinctive feature of all advanced civilizations".[3] According to Hayek's theory of "spontaneous order", many rules of conduct have developed through a process of "learning from experience" and have prevailed because the regularity of certain actions made a group of men successful. Like the spontaneous evolution of human languages or animal societies into complex orders that were not deliberately created, many rules and institutions of private commercial law (such as recognition and transferability of property rights, "pacta sunt servanda") historically evolved and survived because they brought benefits to those groups of people who adopted them. International commerce during more than two thousand years has given rise to systems of

3 F.A. v.Hayek, Law, Legislation and Liberty, Vol.I, 1982 (1973), p. 14.

private commercial law regulating private commercial transactions with much more complex structures than public international trade law regulating the conduct of governmental trade policies.

The need to distinguish spontaneously grown, self-generating "orders" from deliberately constructed "organizations" has been emphasized already (above chapter III.1). Wherever people regularly interact - be it in the polity, in the economy, in road traffic or in social games - rules and procedures of general application are necessary for coordinating the autonomous activities. Spontaneous orders emerge from rule-oriented free actions and are based upon rules protecting and coordinating the autonomous exercise of individual liberties (or "sovereignties") without prescribing specific results or purposes. Organizations are deliberately created to serve a particular purpose and are based upon rules for the performance of assigned tasks so as to achieve the predetermined objectives. Spontaneous orders based upon individual liberty enable the use of more individual knowledge of local events, individual experimentation (based upon "trial and error") and spontaneous, individual adjustment and are therefore capable of much greater complexity than any planned organization, because they draw upon more facts than any central authority can know and continuously adapt to a large number of events unknown in their totality to anyone.[4]

Just as languages may be spoken without conscious knowledge of their grammar rules, the "regularity" of national and international economic orders may be due to rules explicitly known or unknown to those behaving in accordance with the rules. A particular feature of legally binding rules of conduct is that their content can be, and often has been, laid down or modified by law-making agencies and their applicability and meaning in a concrete situation can be determined through ordered procedures and law-applying agencies.[5]

B) Need for and Functions of Constitutional Rules

Freedom and "sovereignty" may be used in a variety of ways not only for the good but also for the bad. Just as life in a society without rules would tend to be "poor, nasty, brutish and short", as Thomas Hobbes pointed out in his

4 That complexity needs freedom is one of v.Hayek's main arguments in favour of a rule-guided liberal order based upon individual liberty, see Volume I of v.Hayek's "Law, Legislation and Liberty" (above note 3).

5 See also: E.J. Mestmäcker, Regelbildung und Rechtsschutz in Marktwirtschaftlichen Ordnungen, 1985, p.6.

"Leviathan" (1651), people and societies all over the world have found it necessary to establish or recognize government organizations in order to protect the equal rights of people and prevent citizens from breaking the rules. The "constitutional rules", by constituting and limiting government powers so that the holders of government powers remain limited and governed by long-term rules of a higher rank, provide a sort of "meta-rules": They contain the "constitutional choice" of the fundamental "rules of the game", determine the long-term institutions of a political system and provide the legal standards against which the "postconstitutional choices" and current processes **within** the constitutional rules are to be judged.[6] The distinctive contribution of American constitutional law was to assert the supremacy of individual rights over governmental powers and, as spelled out in the Declaration of Independence, "that to secure these rights, governments are instituted among men, deriving their just powers from the consent of the governed".

The need for constitutional rules thus derives from the insight that the short-term identifiable self-interests of both private individuals and government officials often come into conflict and that the current social processes do not lead to optimal results unless they are constrained by long-term rules and, if necessary, their collective enforcement. The prospective, general and permanent nature of constitutional rules acts as an incentive for individuals to concentrate on their long-term common interests (the "public interest") rather than on the short-term distributional implications of the rules which, in case of general long-term rules, are more uncertain and more difficult to identify. General constitutional rules induce people to accept generally acceptable criteria of equal treatment, due process and fairness. They make it possible to transform the Hobbesian "social

---

6 On the distinction between "constitutional choice" and "postconstitutional choice" see J.M. Buchanan, The Limits of Liberty, 1975, pp. 35 ff. The word "constitution" is often used in a factual sense to describe the actual situation of an object, an individual or a community (e.g. the physical constitution of a person). But "constitution" is also used as a normative term, for instance in economic theory in order to denote a set of certain "constitutive principles" and "regulative principles" for the proper functioning of national and international market economies (see above chapter III.4). In legal terminology, the concept "constitution" usually refers to the basic long-term legal rules on which a community is based and by which it is bound. This basic law may be codified in whole or in part in a written "formal constitution". But also in the absence of a written constitution, the basic provisions of a community's legal order are often referred to as a "material constitution". The written "formal constitution" may coincide with the "material constitution" of the legal community concerned. But the formal constitutional document may also include less-important or transitional provisions, or it may authorize the legislative body to regulate important "constitutional questions" through the adoption of long-term rules which remain outside the formal constitution but are legally binding upon all members of the community.

dilemma" of mutually conflicting short-term interests into a mutually beneficial "social order" without requiring persons to understand the structure of the overall order and without requiring a higher morality in individual behaviour. The main functions of constitutional rules on the level of private conduct and of private relations among individuals are threefold (see above chapter II.1): to define and delimit equal individual rights and responsibilities in a way promoting the full use of individual abilities; to coordinate the autonomous individual activities through general rules enabling decentralized coordination mechanisms (e.g. market competition, contract law); and to promote legal continuity, rule-oriented "justice as fairness" (J. Rawls) and, thereby, long-term investments and voluntary adjustment to continuous change.

The historical experience of trade mercantilism has shown that, contrary to Thomas Hobbes' assumption that all persons would willingly submit to unlimited government powers in exchange for the personal security ensured by the governmental Leviathan, constitutional safeguards are needed not only in order to prevent the abuse of private power and to reconcile mutually conflicting short-term private self-interests, but also as a restraint on the abuse of government powers. There is a need for constitutional rules establishing government powers in order to protect and, if necessary, enforce individual rights and to provide certain "public goods" which cannot be produced in private markets. But there is also an additional need for constitutional rules limiting the scope and potential abuse of government powers, protecting individual rights against government interferences, defining the "public interest" in a legally binding manner, and constraining government discretion in order to counteract the many "asymmetries" in the representation of private interests in political decision-making processes. Without effective constitutional constraints on the government discretion to tax and regulate private economic activities, special interest groups might find it more profitable to seek artificial "rents" through governmental economic regulations rather than through private economic competition, thereby compelling their competitors to invest likewise in pressure group activities. The discriminatory taxation and regulation of private economic activities, frequently introduced by periodically elected politicians in exchange for political support from special interest groups, redistributes income by means of distorting market prices and competition, and thereby reduces national economic welfare. In such a situation, constitutional rules can enable both governments and private individuals to shift scarce resources from "protective" into economically productive uses. Since government decisions by periodically elected politicians (e.g. on public spending and borrowing) often reflect shorter time horizons than comparable private decisions, constitutional constraints on the governmental taxing, spending, borrowing and regulatory powers are an essential means of inducing governments to pursue policies that are recognized to be in the long-term interest of the community.[7]

The historical evolution of the old law merchant up to the middle ages (see above chapter II.3) confirms that long-term "constitutional rules" (e.g. on the protection of private contracts and property rights) can be agreed upon also in an "unorganized" international society based essentially on private law. The primary "constitutional function" of these private international commercial rules are to protect individual rights from private intrusions and to coordinate the autonomous individual economic activities so as to make possible mutual gains from international trade. The adoption of national "bills of rights" and written constitutions confirms the contractarian assumption that individuals may be led by their own self-interests to agree on constitutional rules establishing government powers for the performance of specified "protective functions" (e.g. law enforcement and maintenance of peace) as well as certain "productive state functions" (e.g. for the provision of "public goods"). But from the liberal perspective of inalienable human rights as the ultimate source of value and of valuation, the delegated powers are always limited in nature, as explicitly stated in the Ninth Amendment of the US Constitution. The ultimate function of all government activities must consist in protecting and promoting the individual rights and individual welfare of their citizens. At least from a liberal contractarian perspective which seeks to derive and legitimize the constitutional rules of political order from the voluntary agreement of the members of the polity, individuals must be presumed to establish governments for the purpose of protecting and promoting their individual rights.

C) Means of Constitutional Constraint

From the liberal perspective where individuals are the ultimate source of value, the valuation of "private goods" and the determination of "public goods" (e.g. governmental income redistribution) are subjective and cannot be determined as an objective external standard independent of individual preferences. Economic markets and democratic politics are institutional processes enabling per-

7 For a discussion of the "high tax trap", the "inflation trap" and the "public debt trap" see: G. Brennan/J.M. Buchanan, The Reason of Rules, 1985, chapter 8. For a discussion of the similar "trade protection trap" see above chapter V.3.

sons to express their own values on the alternatives with which they are confronted. Thus, in a liberal democracy, the "national interest" (e.g. in the field of trade policy) cannot be democratically determined without individual freedoms, transparent policymaking and economic and political competition as means of discovering individual preferences. The recognition in the constitutional laws of democratic societies of inalienable human rights as the highest value implies, moreover, that the enumeration in written constitutions of specific individual rights cannot be regarded as exhaustive and that the sphere of individual freedoms includes all actions not explicitly restricted by a law.[8] Thus, there is no constitutionally recognized reason to assume that the individual freedom of trade is limited to the choice of domestic trading partners and does not also protect transnational trade transactions with foreign trading partners. The constitutional principle of individual "freedom within constraints" has been explicitly recognized in the national constitutions of several states. The Ninth Amendment of the US Constitution makes it explicit that "the enumeration of certain rights in this Constitution shall not be construed to deny or disparage others retained by the people". Or Article 2 of the German Grundgesetz states: "Everyone shall have the right to the free development of his personality in so far as he does not violate the rights of others or offend against the constitutional order or the moral code... These rights may be interfered with only on the basis of a law". And Article 1 of the German Grundgesetz states: "(1) The dignity of man shall be inviolable. To respect and protect it shall be the duty of all state authority. (2) The German people therefore acknowledge inviolable and inalienable human rights as the basis of every community, of peace and of justice in the world. (3) The following basic rights shall bind the legislature, the executive and the judiciary as directly enforceable law".

A major conclusion of chapter VI was, however, that neither the US Constitution nor the EEC Treaty effectively limit and constrain the broad discretionary trade policy powers. Congressional majorities as well as the EC executives feel largely free to use their respective trade policy powers for restricting individual rights and redistributing income among domestic groups as they like. Chapters V.3 and VI.3 further referred to the insight of modern public choice theory that individual liberties, democratic electoral competition and majority rule are not sufficient guarantees to constrain governments to implement "the public interest" and to prevent abuses of the practically unlimited legislative and regulatory

8 See F.A. v.Hayek, The Constitution of Liberty, 1960, p. 216; Z. Giacometti, Die Freiheitsrechtskataloge als Kodifikation der Freiheit, 1955.

powers in the trade policy area. Hence, the need for additional constitutional safeguards.

Most liberal constitutional theories since the 18th century treat the economic and the political system symmetrically as markets in which the outcome is determined by the interaction among individuals pursuing their own and often mutually conflicting self-interests. The same model of the utility-maximizing "homo economicus", applied by the classical economists for their analysis of economic behaviour, is used also for the behaviour of political agents, not because all persons behave in a selfish manner at all times and in all circumstances, but rather because the model reflects inherent tendencies in human behaviour and has proven useful for purposes of "constitutional construction".[9] In order to turn conflict into cooperation and to transform the pursuit of private self-interests into socially beneficial behaviour, there is a need to limit and control the exercise of discretionary government powers through additional constitutional constraints such as:

- rules limiting the domain and admissible instruments of government measures (e.g. limitation of policy powers through the constitutional requirements of "due process" and "proportionality" of policy instruments);
- quantitative and procedural limitations of the government powers to create money, to tax, to borrow, to spend and to redistribute private income (e.g. a "balanced budget requirement" in order to reduce the bias

9 See J. St. Mill, Considerations on Representative Government, in: Essays on Politics and Society, Collected Works, Vol. 19 (1977), p. 505: "The very principle of constitutional government requires it to be assumed that political power will be abused to promote the particular purposes of the holder; not because it always is so, but because such is the natural tendency of things, to guard against which is the especial use of free institutions". This assumption of utility-maximizing selfish behaviour is fully compatible with v.Hayek's (note 8, p. 78) following remark: "There is much confusion of the ideal that a person ought to be allowed to pursue his own aims with the belief that, if left free, he will or ought to pursue solely his selfish aims. The freedom to pursue one's own aims is, however, as important for the most altruistic person, in whose scale of values the needs of other people occupy a very high place, as for any egoist. It is part of the ordinary nature of men (and perhaps still more of women) and one of the main conditions of their happiness that they make the welfare of other people their chief aim. To do so is part of the normal choice open to us and often the decision generally expected of us. By common opinion our chief concern in this respect should, of course, be the welfare of our family. But we also show our appreciation and approval of others by making them our friends and their aims ours. To choose our associates and generally those whose needs we make our concern is an essential part of freedom and of the moral conceptions of a free society."

in governmental decision-making towards public debts and budget deficits);

- rules and "accounting procedures" promoting transparent policy-making and competition in the "political market" (e.g. procedural requirements to calculate and publish the costs of alternative policy measures);

- institutional safeguards and separation of government powers so as to reduce the influence of special interests (e.g. transfer of the government power to create money to an independent central bank);

- procedural safeguards strengthening individual rights vis-à-vis both the coercive functions as well as the service functions and redistributive powers of government (e.g. individual access to courts and judicial reviewability of all trade restrictions);

- rules specifying the general constitutional requirements of rule of law, certainty of law, equal treatment, legally limited administrative discretion, fair application of the law (e.g. proportionality and non-retroactivity of government interferences into individual rights), protection of acquired rights (e.g. "no expropriation without just compensation"), and of procedural safeguards (e.g. habeas corpus).

D) How to Provide International "Public Goods" without International Governments? The Need for Internationally Agreed Restraints on National Policy Instruments with Harmful Effects Abroad

Economics distinguishes between privately produced goods and "public goods" that are not produced privately either because consumers cannot be excluded from their use (e.g. in case of a public road) or because their production involves the government monopoly of power. Adam Smith's definition of the three duties of a government[10] limited the list of national public goods to be provided by governments to national defense, law and order, and a limited number of public works and public institutions which it would not pay individuals to produce for themselves. The modern welfare states have considerably extended the list to include, inter alia, stabilization and a "conservative welfare function" (see above chapter V.3.B.c.). But how can international public goods - such as peace, an open trading system, freedom of communications, monetary stability and le-

10 See above chapter V, note 82.

gal certainty - which are produced domestically by governments, be produced on the international level without a world government or, at least, without a hegemonic world power interested in supplying international public goods (such as Great Britain during the time of "pax britannica" and the USA following World War II)?

States are increasingly aware that, in the modern integrated world economy, many national policy objectives and "public goods" can no longer be achieved without voluntary international cooperation and active participation in international organizations as legal and institutional frameworks for the multilateral pursuit of national interests in an interdependent world. Just as voluntary market exchanges of private goods work as a positive-sum game in which the gain for one participant does not imply a loss for another, reciprocal international exchanges of national public goods (e.g. liberalization of national trade barriers, convertibility of the national currency, national treatment of foreign goods and investments) can create international public goods across national frontiers, which a single government could not achieve unilaterally. International guarantees of transnational freedoms and international prohibitions of national government actions with adverse external effects enable a spontaneous, mutually beneficial division of labour among the citizens of different states and can operate as a substitute for "international legislation" by a world government. The contractarian, voluntarily agreed nature of multilateral rules makes it likely that the international rules will be of a general nature allowing individual governments to pursue their separate courses and diverse preferences within the rules. Hence, international "public goods" (such as international legal certainty and open markets) can be produced also without "international governments" through internationally agreed restraints on national policy instruments with harmful effects on other countries.

E) International and Domestic Constitutional Functions of Liberal International Trade Rules

In public international law, the term "constitution" is either used in a formal sense in order to denote multilateral treaties establishing international organizations with legislative and administrative powers of their own. Or it is used in order to denote the substantive, long-term basic rules ("material constitution") of international organizations or of general public international law (e.g. the basic rules for the creation, change and enforcement of international law, for the legal subjects of international law and international legal responsibility).[11]

Thus, the GATT is sometimes referred to as the "constitution" of the multilateral trading system because the GATT is the only worldwide agreement with general rules of unlimited duration for the liberalization of national trade barriers, the coordination of national trade laws and policies, and the peaceful settlement of international trade disputes. Various GATT rules make it explicitly clear that the basic GATT objective of nondiscriminatory, market-conforming trade competition cannot be achieved unless the basic GATT prohibitions of trade discrimination (e.g. GATT Articles I, II, XII) and of non-tariff trade barriers (e.g. GATT Article XI:1) are observed by all GATT contracting parties. GATT Article XXIII, for instance, grants each individual GATT contracting party the right to initiate a multilateral GATT dispute settlement proceeding and to insist on the withdrawal of any GATT-inconsistent discrimination or non-tariff trade barriers by any other GATT contracting party regardless of whether the trade discrimination or non-tariff trade barrier has actually caused trade damage to the complaining country.[12] The GATT rules serve "constitutional functions" on the international level among states by prohibiting harmful trade policy instruments, by limiting (pursuant to Article 41 of the Vienna Convention on the Law of Treaties) the national freedom of contracting parties to conclude "inter-se-agreements" modifying certain multilateral GATT rules as between themselves alone, and by protecting the consistency of the multilateral GATT legal system through collective dispute settlement and enforcement rules.[13] The conception of the basic GATT rules as a "constitution" assists in analysing the inconsistencies between GATT law and GATT practices not only on a case-by-case basis but also as a possible expression of a broader "constitutional failure".

In international state practice and in the literature on public international law, the advantages of liberal international trade rules are often seen only in the rights which the rules grant to governments vis-à-vis other governments (e.g. GATT rights to non-discriminatory access to foreign markets). Also in GATT law are the synallagmatic GATT obligations described as "concessions" (Article

---

11 See e.g. A. Verdross, Die Verfassung der Völkerrechtsgemeinschaft, 1926; see also above note 6.

12 See E.U. Petersmann, Strengthening GATT Procedures for Settling Trade Disputes, in: The World Economy 1988, pp. 55 ff., 64.

13 See E.U. Petersmann, Grey Area Trade Policy and the Rule of Law, in: Journal of World Trade Law, 1988, pp. 23 ff, 30-35.

II), and exemptions from these GATT obligations are denoted as "preferential treatment" (e.g. for less-developed countries). Economic analysis shows, however (see above chapters IX.3 and V.1), that the national economic gains from international trade come primarily from the liberalisation of a country's own trade barriers and from its own observance of the GATT obligations for the use of transparent, non-discriminatory and proportionate trade policy instruments. A major conclusion of this chapter is that observance of the voluntarily accepted GATT obligations generates also important legal advantages within countries for their own citizens because the GATT legal principles of transparent policy-making, open markets, non-discrimination, proportionality, due process and rule of law are more precise with regard to foreign trade law than the corresponding general requirements of liberal national constitutions. Since international legal commitments for the use of transparent, non-discriminatory and proportionate trade policy instruments meet the duties of constitutional democracies to protect the equal rights of their own citizens in the ever more important foreign trade sectors of the modern "open economies", they serve also important "domestic constitutional functions" and offer a means for "constitutionalizing" the broad discretionary trade policy powers of governments.

This insight, that liberal international trade rules are an expression of, and give precision to, the liberal constitutional obligations of governments towards their own citizens, has implications for the interpretation of international and domestic foreign trade law. It runs counter to the traditional "non-individualistic", "power-oriented" perception of trade policy as a Machiavellian arena where observance of international law is within the discretion of the "sovereign government" and freedom from international legal restraints might be considered to increase the power of the state in the "national interest". If the legal value of international legal guarantees of freedom of trade as well as of other GATT rules derives not only from the rights and duties vis-à-vis foreign governments but also from their constitutional functions for the protection of the individual rights of domestic citizens, liberal international trade rules acquire their "constitutional value" not only from the consent of government representatives but also by virtue of the national constitutional laws of democratic societies. Liberal international trade rules protect and extend individual freedom of trade across national frontiers and, consequently, should be viewed not only as "external obligations" which governments might freely abrogate. Just as, in constitutionally limited democracies, individual freedom of trade is not "granted" to the citizens by governments, liberal international trade rules protecting individual freedom of trade in transnational trade transactions should be viewed as an expression of liberal states' obligations towards their own citizens.

2. Constitutional Functions of Liberal International Trade Rules: Basic Principles of GATT Law

The preceding analysis has shown that the mutual gains from international trade cannot be fully exploited without general rules and without voluntarily undertaken legal restraints on the use of mutually harmful, welfare-reducing trade policy instruments. These can serve a "constitutional function" for the protection of the public good of an international division of labour under the rule of law among different national economic and legal systems, for non-discriminatory access to foreign markets and the avoidance of "market failures" (e.g. domestic cartelization) as well as "government failures" (e.g. arbitrary protectionism). The international trade and monetary rules are designed not only to prevent and resolve conflicts **among** trading nations. They can also serve as a mast against which governments can tie their hands so as to escape the siren-like pressure groups **within** their countries.[14]

The General Agreement and the more than 200 additional side-agreements concluded in the context of GATT have created an extremely complex legal system.[15] US Congressmen have groaned that "anyone who reads GATT is likely to have his sanity impaired".[16] And the presumably small number of people who have ever succeeded in reading the full text of the General Agreement - many provisions of which have been drafted "with Anglo-Saxon discursiveness"[17] (e.g. the 23 paragraphs of Article XVIII extending over 8 narrow-typed pages plus 2 pages Annex) - may have shared the conclusion of one expert that "only the

14 F. Roessler, The Scope, Limits and Functions of the GATT Legal System, in: The World Economy 1985, pp. 287 ff, 298. On the use of pre-commitments as a technique of social regulation see more generally: J. Elster, Ulysses and the Sirens. Studies in Rationality and Irrationality, 1979.

15 See E.U. Petersmann, GATT - Analytical Index - Notes on the Drafting, Interpretation and Application of the General Agreement on Tariffs and Trade, GATT 1985 (loose-leaf edition), 850 pages; GATT, Status of Legal Instruments, GATT 1989.

16 Senator Milliken, at the 1951 hearings on GATT in the US Senate, Senate Finance Committee p. 92, quoted from: J.H. Jackson, World Trade and the Law of GATT, 1969, p. VII.

17 P. Pescatore, Introduction, in: Hilf/Jacobs/Petersmann (eds), The European Community and GATT, 1986, p. XV.

learned can communicate with it, and then only in code".[18] But if one cuts through the legalistic thicket of the detailed and often highly technical GATT rules for tariffs and, in principle, for all kinds of non-tariff trade barriers, one can extract a relatively small number of general principles underlying the bewildering complexity of GATT rules and ensuring the overall consistency of the GATT legal system.

A) The GATT Principle of Transparent Policy-making

GATT law proceeds from the principle that trade policy shall be conducted in the form of tariffs (i.e. a price mechanism) and that non-tariff trade barriers are prohibited (Articles XI:1, XV:4) subject to specified exceptions (e.g. Articles XII, XVIII-XXI). In most OECD countries, tariffs have to be determined in general legislative acts and to be published in the national law gazette. They are more difficult to manipulate by "administrative protectionism" compared to most administrative non-tariff trade barriers. GATT law requires that all general government measures affecting foreign trade must be published before their application "in such a manner as to enable governments and traders to become acquainted with them":

> "Laws, regulations, judicial decisions and administrative rulings of general application, made effective by any contracting party, pertaining to the classification or the valuation of products for customs purposes, or to rates of duty, taxes or other charges, or to requirements, restrictions or prohibitions on imports or exports or on the transfer of payments therefor, or affecting their sale, distribution, transportation, insurance, warehousing, inspection, exhibition, processing, mixing or other use, shall be published promptly in such a manner as to enable governments and traders to become acquainted with them. Agreements affecting international trade policy which are in force between the government or a governmental agency of any contracting party and the government or governmental agency of any other contracting party shall also be published. The provisions of this paragraph shall not require any contracting party to disclose confidential information which would impede law enforcement or otherwise be contrary to the public interest or would prejudice the legitimate commercial interests of particular enterprises, public or private". (Article X:1). "No measure of general application taken by any contracting party effecting an advance in a rate of duty or other charge on imports under an established and uniform practice, or imposing a new or more burdensome requirement, restriction or prohibition on imports, or on the transfer of payments therefor, shall be enforced before such measure has been officially published" (Article X:2).

18 H. Feis, quoted from Jackson (note 16).

Numerous GATT provisions require GATT contracting parties to notify specific trade measures to the GATT (e.g. Articles II, VI, IX-XII, XVI-XVIII, XXII-XXV, XXVIII, XXXVII). The notifications received are promptly published by the GATT and regularly reviewed in periodic meetings of the various competent GATT bodies.[19] "Concessions" legally bound under Article II and published in the respective "schedules" of GATT contracting parties, which are annexed to and thereby incorporated in the General Agreement, may be modified or withdrawn only subject to specified conditions and procedures (see, e.g., Article XXVIII). The transparency and predictability of trade policy measures are further promoted by the GATT principles of non-discriminatory and rule-oriented trade policy-making (see below).

Transparent policy-making ("government by discussion") is a basic constitutional principle of democratic societies in which individual citizens are considered to be the subject and not the mere object of policy-making. Since trade protection is a form of taxation and subsidization of domestic groups, non-transparent trade protection without parliamentary approval amounts to "taxation without representation" - a grievance which, more than 200 years ago, triggered a "constitutional revolution" in the United States. At the national level, politicians and bureaucrats may have little incentive to make the welfare costs and redistributive effects of their own "grey area trade restrictions" fully transparent. The reciprocal international GATT obligations for the use of transparent trade policy instruments facilitate the parliamentary, judicial and democratic control by the citizens themselves of administrative trade protectionism.

Since a major function of rules is to provide information about the behaviour of other actors and to coordinate their independent and possibly conflicting activities, transparency is a prerequisite of the effectiveness of generally applicable rules and of the efficient use of individual freedoms of trade. Transparent and predictable trade measures enable governments and private traders, producers and consumers to reduce their information and transaction costs (e.g. due to greater legal and investment security) and to anticipate more reliably the need for adjustment measures in response to expected changes. They also facilitate international negotiations on the reciprocal liberalization of trade barriers, since tariffs are easier to discern and to quantify as to their trade effects than non-tariff trade barriers. The visibility of trade measures assists governments in fulfilling their "information function" towards their respective electorate, which

19 For a detailed survey of the various notification requirements and GATT surveillance mechanisms see: E.U. Petersmann (note 15), Article X, pp. 3 ff.

is a prerequisite of an informed public understanding and discussion of the costs and benefits of alternative protective measures and of their public scrutiny by all interested parties. Such an informed and possibly educative discussion and public awareness of the welfare-reducing consequences of trade restrictions are in turn a precondition of the democratic control of trade policy, for instance whether it is conducted in the "national interest" or for the benefit of special interests. Effective democratic control and legitimation of transparent trade policies can strengthen governments in resisting protectionist pressures from special interests.

B) The GATT Principle of Rule-oriented Policy-making

GATT law prescribes a large number of detailed rules for the tariffs and, in principle, all non-tariff trade barriers of the 96 (1989) GATT contracting parties. It also provides a multilateral legal framework enabling the adoption of GATT decisions on the interpretation and application of all GATT provisions, the negotiation of additional GATT rules and supplementary trade agreements, and the legally binding settlement of disputes among GATT contracting parties. This "rule of law approach" to international trade emerged after World War II in reaction to the historical experience between and during the wars that the "law of the jungle" in international trade relations and the bureaucratic "management" of prices, quantities and trade shares may lead to "power-oriented" foreign economic policies and to "government failures" much worse than "market failures". GATT law does not proceed from the assumption of benevolent and omnipotent governments capable of correcting market imperfections through informed government interventions. It rather emphasizes the need for precise and justiciable legal limitations of the government powers to tax and regulate foreign trade. As a result of GATT law and of the respective domestic implementing legislation, there exist today few other sectors in the domestic economies of GATT contracting parties where the government powers to tax and regulate the economic activities of their citizens are subject to such precise legal constraints for the use of transparent, non-discriminatory and welfare-increasing policy instruments as those of GATT law.

GATT's rule-of-law-approach to international trade thus proceeds from the "constitutional skepticism" of the 18th century towards the assumption of "benevolent despots". The historical experience of the ingenuity of governments in the use of an almost unlimited variety of non-tariff trade barriers is reflected in the often very detailed GATT regulations, e.g. for the indirect circumvention of concessions (see Articles II, XI), for surreptitious forms of trade discrimination (see Articles III, XIII, XVII), for arbitrary customs valuation procedures (Article VII), excessive fees and formalities (Articles VII, IX), protectionist exchange arrangements (Article XV), or the abuse of trade monopolies (Article XVII). Like constitutional rules, the GATT disciplines legally limit the trade policy powers of GATT contracting parties and provide for institutional supervisory mechanisms at the international level (see, e.g., Articles XII:4, XXIII:2) as well as for judicial review at the domestic level (e.g. Article X:3,b).

The basic requirement of GATT law to conduct trade policy in a rule-oriented manner on the basis of a few, rather simple general principles is but a reflection of the national constitutional principles of limited government, legal certainty and the rule of law. In the trade policy area, additional economic rationales for rule-oriented rather than power-oriented trade policies have been pointed out by economists ever since Adam Smith's important discovery that the economic welfare of England was largely due to its liberal "laws and institutions". General rules promote efficient decentralized economic decision-making, act as an incentive for investments, reduce transaction costs, and are a more effective safeguard against "government failure" than reliance on the good intentions of self-interested trade politicians. GATT's focus **not** on market results (as in the case of international commodity agreements), but rather on general rules that generate market outcomes, greatly facilitates international trade liberalization because the scope for agreement on trade policy **rules** is necessarily wider than the scope for agreement on trade policy **results**. This is due to the fact that general trade policy rules are permanently and equally applicable over time to an unlimited number of states, whereas agreement on trade policy results (e.g. traded prices or market shares) involves directly the particular interests of particular persons and may prove to be unfeasible (e.g. for economic reasons) beyond a limited period of time. The uncertainty of the future effects of general and permanent rules acts as an incentive for states and economic agents to look at their long-term interests rather than at the short-term results of the agreement. General rules and particular outcomes generated under such rules tend to be more easily recognized as "fair" and "just" (in the sense of John Rawls' "justice as fairness") than direct agreements on particular outcomes whose redistributive effects (e.g. due to changes in prices and market shares) may be influenced more by the respective power of the participants than by adherence to general rules and to undistorted economic competition.

General trade policy rules, by promoting principled policies and decentralized decision-making, correspond to the value-premises of market competition (e.g. decentralized definition of individual "utility" and "private goods") and of Western democracies (e.g. individual freedoms and legal equality). By contrast, intergovernmental agreements on prices and market shares proceed from the authoritarian assumption that the allocation, distribution and utility of scarce resources should be determined externally by bureaucrats rather than by the individual market participants themselves. The (inter)governmental determination of market outcomes presupposes a government power - often lacking in Western democracies - to limit and redefine the freedoms and property rights of private traders, producers and consumers according to politically determined values rather than according to the privately expressed individual preferences of market participants.

C) The GATT Principles of Non-discriminatory Market Access

The commercial treaty system among European states before World War I owed its success to the use of tariffs as the major trade policy instrument together with contractual obligations to grant "most favoured nation" (MFN) treatment. The efforts after World War I to restore the pre-1914 system of long-term commercial treaties foundered largely on the unwillingness of major countries (e.g. France and the United States) to accept unconditional MFN commitments.[20] The breakdown of the international trading system during the early 1930s was largely attributed to the failure during the 1920s to reestablish a

20 In September 1918, the French Minister of Commerce, M. Clementel, declared that "the government had denounced all commercial conventions which embody the MFN clause. That clause will not reappear. It will never again poison our tariff policy" (see J. Viner, International Economics, 1951, p. 95). In the following years, France introduced nine different degrees of the French tariff and classified its trading partners according to political considerations into corresponding categories, each receiving a different degree of "trade favour" and being expected to grant reciprocal equivalent favours. The United States continued to base its commercial policy on the principle of conditional MFN treatment until the Tariff Act of 1922. But the conditional MFN clause, as well as the French differentiation among numerous grades of reciprocal tariff preferences, proved unworkable because the condition - i.e. the equivalence of reciprocal trade concessions - could not be defined in the abstract and had to be negotiated bilaterally; thus, "the conditional most-favoured-nation pledge turned out to be no pledge at all because its essential element - the nature of the counterconcessions that have to be made to obtain the benefits of the pledge - cannot be defined in advance" (F. Roessler, Trade Policy and International Trade Arrangements, in: SEANZA Lectures 1982, 1984, pp. 456, 474). Both trade policy stances contributed to the fact that Article 23 of the Covenant of the League of Nations remained confined to the pledge of member States to grant each other's trade "equitable treatment" (rather than the originally proposed "equal treatment").

contractual system of international trade rules guaranteeing non-discriminatory market access. It was against this historical background that the framers of the General Agreement decided to make the principles of unconditional most-favoured-nation treatment of foreign countries (Articles I, II) and of national treatment of imported foreign products (Article III) the cornerstone of the GATT legal system. Both principles are designed to secure non-discriminatory access to markets and supplies. And most substantive GATT provisions purport either to implement these two principles or to specify agreed exceptions from them.

The GATT rules for non-discriminatory market access distinguish between trade policy border measures, internal trade measures applied to foreign goods after they have cleared customs, exchange controls, and government participation in trade through government procurement and state-trading enterprises. The unconditional most-favoured-nation obligation of Article I applies not only to border measures but also to internal measures affecting imports or exports: "any advantage, favour, privilege or immunity granted by any contracting party to any product originating in or destined for any other country shall be accorded immediately and unconditionally to the like product originating in or destined for the territories of all other contracting parties" not only with respect to "customs duties and charges of any kind imposed on or in connection with importation or exportation or imposed on the international transfer of payments for imports or exports, and with respect to the method of levying such duties and charges, and with respect to all rules and formalities in connection with importation and exportation", but also with respect to "all matters referred to in paragraphs 2 and 4 of Article III", namely internal taxes or other internal charges of any kind applied to like domestic products, and "all laws, regulations and requirements affecting (the) internal sale, offering for sale, purchase, transportation, distribution or use" of imported products. The MFN treatment must be extended unconditionally, i.e. without any condition of reciprocal concessions.

Compared to tariffs, the non-discriminatory administration of non-tariff trade barriers is more difficult to ensure and led to additional GATT rules on the non-discriminatory administration of quantitative restrictions (Article XIII), state-trading enterprises (Article XVII:1), government procurement (Article XVII:2 and the 1979 GATT Agreement on Government Procurement), internal controls (Article III) and exchange controls (Articles XIV, XV). While the MFN-obligations relating to trade policy border measures prohibit trade discrimination among imports from and exports to other GATT contracting parties, the national treatment obligation of Article III goes further and requires the equal treatment of imported foreign products and like domestic products as regards internal taxation and regulation. GATT law admits various exceptions to the prohibitions of trade discrimination, especially in favour of certain long-standing historical trade preferences (Article I: 2, 3), protective measures against unfair competition (Article VI), free trade areas and customs unions (Article XXIV), security measures (Article XXI), preferential treatment in favour of, or between, less-developed countries (1979 GATT decision on "Differential and More Favourable Treatment, Reciprocity and Fuller Participation of Developing Countries"), and discriminatory treatment as a result of the non-application of the General Agreement among particular GATT contracting parties (Article XXXV).

The GATT obligations not to discriminate among imports from or exports to foreign markets do not impose any economic sacrifice on GATT member countries. Welfare economics demonstrates that non-discriminatory trade liberalization enables the most efficient use of resources and the exploitation of all gains from trade. The generously drafted GATT exceptions to the non-discrimination obligations also respect the traditional freedom of member states to participate in preferential trade arrangements (e.g. under Article XXIV) and to resort to trade embargoes for political ends (Article XXI). The ultimate function of the GATT prohibitions of trade discrimination is legally to commit the contracting parties to avoid those discriminatory trade restrictions which were generally agreed to have economically, legally and politically harmful effects for all contracting parties.[21]

From an economic point of view, the observance of the GATT prohibitions of trade discrimination tends to promote economic efficiency by avoiding welfare-reducing trade distortions both among and within countries. It enables domestic traders, producers and consumers to buy and sell goods in the best markets. Each country can thereby minimize the economic costs of its national level of trade protection. And goods tend to be produced where the production costs are lowest.

From a legal point of view, the GATT prohibitions of discriminatory trade policy measures protect the economic advantages of concessions granted under Article

21 On the various functions of the MFN principle see: J. Tumlir, GATT Rules and Community Law, in: Hilf/Jacobs/Petersmann (note 17), p. 8 ff.; E.U. Petersmann, Economic, Legal and Political Functions of the Principle of Non-Discrimination, in: The World Economy, 1986, pp.113-120.

II from being impaired by subsequent trade preferences in favour of other countries. The unconditional MFN obligation to extend any trade liberalization to all GATT contracting parties transforms bilateral bargains (e.g. during the regular "GATT Rounds" of trade negotiations) into a multilateral trading system based on generally applicable and transparent rules. It prohibits those forms of trade discrimination (e.g. conditional MFN treatment), which were widely held responsible for the breakdown of the international trading system during the interwar period. The non-discrimination requirement exerts also a detergent effect on the withdrawal of trade concessions (Article XXVIII) or on the use of safeguard measures (e.g. under Article XIX) due to the increased number of adversely affected countries and their combined pressures for either the removal of the trade restrictions or the granting of compensation (see, e.g., Article XXVIII:2). It thus tends to stabilize the level of trade protection, even though the pattern of protection may be renegotiated and varied, and facilitates negotiations to reduce trade barriers. The GATT rules for the non-discriminatory administration of trade policy measures concretize and enlarge the principles of equal treatment and undistorted competition found in the national laws of GATT contracting parties. Because governmental trade discrimination among supplier countries or among export markets entails discrimination also among domestic traders which have entered into trade relations with these countries, the non-discrimination requirements of GATT law prohibit discrimination not only among GATT contracting parties but also among domestic traders importing from or exporting to GATT contracting parties.

From a political point of view, the non-discriminatory treatment of small and large countries alike reduces the scope for power-oriented trade policies and thus contributes to separating trade policy from other foreign policy issues. It protects especially the less-developed countries' trading interests in exploiting their comparative cost advantages through non-discriminatory trade competition and in avoiding the economic costs of trade discrimination, which poor countries can afford least. Non-discriminatory trade policies are transparent, simple to administer, less politicized, easier to understand by the general public and to control by parliaments and domestic courts, and less exposed to protectionist pressures for the surreptitious redistribution of domestic income through selective import protection.

D) The GATT Principle of the Use of Uniform and Proportionate Policy Instruments

The General Agreement proceeds from the general prohibition of all forms of trade protection except customs tariffs (see, e.g., Articles II, III, XI:1) and establishes a procedural framework for regular multilateral negotiations on the liberalization of tariffs and other trade barriers (e.g. Article XXVIII bis). Only under specified circumstances and conditions are certain quantitative restrictions permitted (Articles XI:2 to XIV, XVIII to XXI). The use of uniform trade policy instruments increases the transparency and facilitates the reciprocal liberalization of trade barriers.

The principle of proportionality is one of the basic premises of GATT law. GATT law does not require any contracting party to give up the pursuit of any economic or social policy goal. It only limits the use of non-transparent, discriminatory and particularly harmful instruments for achieving such goals. GATT law ranks the various trade policy instruments according to their respective economic efficiency in almost the same order as economic theory suggests; the more trade-distorting and non-transparent the trade policy instruments are, the more stringent are the legal GATT constraints on their use.[22] But the principle of proportionality underlying GATT law is based not only on economic rationality but also on the basic political and legal requirements for transparent policy-making and due process:

- internal domestic governmental interventions, such as production subsidies (Article XVI:1) or consumption taxes and non-discriminatory internal regulations (Article III), are permitted under GATT and given preference over trade policy border measures such as import restrictions (e.g. Articles II, XI) or export subsidies (Article XVI:2-4) because internal measures can correct domestic market distortions or pursue non-efficiency-related policy objectives without distorting relative consumer prices and without reducing the national gains from trade;

- tariffs (Articles II, XXVIII) are preferred in GATT law to quantitative restrictions (Articles XI, XIII) since they allow the domestic price of the

---

22 On GATT's ranking of the various economic and trade policy instruments in conformity with the "economic theory of optimal intervention" (above chapters III.3.B and IV.3) see J. Tumlir (note 21), p. 4 ff; R. Blackhurst, The Economic Effects of Different Types of Trade Measures and Their Impact on Consumers, in: International Trade and the Consumer, OECD 1986, pp. 94 ff.

protected product to exceed its international price by a given magnitude without completely interrupting the international price mechanism (e.g. the protective effect of the tariff may be offset by a subsequent reduction of the world market price); tariffs also entail government revenue, can be administered in a transparent and non-discriminatory way, and are less subject to administrative abuse since they usually have to be enacted by general legislative acts; however, compared to production subsidies, tariffs distort not only the production pattern but also the consumption pattern once consumers begin to substitute for the protected product;

- quantitative trade restrictions are in principle prohibited (Article XI:1) subject to certain exceptions (Articles XI:2 to XV, XVIII to XXI) because they tend to eliminate the impact of subsequent changes of world market prices on the level of imports as well as on domestic consumer prices; moreover, they forego governmental tariff revenue for the benefit of private "quota rents" by domestic importers (unless import licenses are sold) and are difficult to administer in a non-discriminatory way (see Article XIII); global non-discriminatory quotas are preferred to quotas subdivided among supplying countries (Article XIII:2) because country-allocated quotas entail additional trade discrimination and protection costs;

- bilaterally negotiated quantitative trade restrictions that are administered from the export side (e.g. Voluntary Restraint Agreements = VRAs) are generally prohibited under Articles XI, XIII of GATT because of their incompatibility with a non-discriminatory multilateral trading system: since the discriminatory quantitative restrictions are inconsistent with the GATT objective of non-discriminatory international competition and adversely affect the contractual rights of third GATT contracting parties (as recognized in GATT Article XXIII:1), the general legal principle expressed in Article 41 of the 1969 Vienna Convention on the Law of Treaties would seem to be applicable that such bilateral derogations from the basic "constitutional principles" of a multilateral agreement are incompatible with the law and with the effective execution of the multilateral agreement concerned (i.e. Articles XI, XIII);

- multilateral "orderly marketing agreement" (= OMAs), providing for national quantitative export restrictions, cause additional world market distortions and protection costs;[23] from a legal perspective, the general legal principle expressed in Article 41 of the 1969 Vienna Convention on the Law of Treaties would appear to remain applicable: due to the trade-distorting and legally adverse effects of such market-sharing agreements on third GATT contracting parties, such agreements remain incompatible with the GATT prohibitions of trade discrimination (Articles I, XIII) and quantitative restrictions (Article XI:1) unless all GATT contracting parties consent to such derogations from the central multilateral GATT provisions, as they have done subject to certain conditions in respect of the International Textiles Agreement of 1973.[24]

E) The GATT Principle of Fair Competition

The economic objective, rationale and premisses underlying many GATT rules are those of trade liberalization, market competition and an "ordinary course of trade under fully competitive conditions" (Article VII: 2, b). Most substantive GATT rules are essentially "prohibitive" rules designed to limit the scope for trade-distorting government interferences with private trade transactions. The GATT preamble explicitly spells out the basic assumption that the legal limitation and liberalization of governmental trade barriers is expected to result in a more efficient allocation of resources (through trade) enabling each member country to increase its national economic welfare. While GATT law does not obligate contracting parties to liberalize the level of their national trade protection, it provides a framework and incentives "directed to the substantial reduction of tariffs and other barriers to trade and to the elimination of discriminatory treatment in international commerce" (GATT preamble). The legal obligation to grant any trade protection in the form of market-conforming tariffs, which would be reduced and legally bound against increase in successive negotiations (Articles II, XVIII, XIX:3, XXVIII, XXVIII bis), is aimed at promoting the proper functioning of the international price mechanism as a decentralized information, allocation and coordination mechanism. Once the tariff has been levied, imported goods must be treated within the domestic market no diffe-

23 See, e.g.: J. Tumlir (note 21), p.5.

24 For a more detailed discussion of the incompatibility of discriminatory quantitative restrictions (e.g. VERs and VRAs) with GATT law see: E.U. Petersmann, Grey Area Trade Policy and the Rule of Law (above note 13).

rently from domestic goods. Trade policy instruments paralyzing the price mechanism (e.g. quantitative restrictions) or distorting relative prices (e.g. trade discrimination) are in principle prohibited (e.g. Articles I, III, XI:1, XIII). The admissibility of antidumping and countervailing duties (Article VI) and the prohibition of export subsidies (Article XVI:B) reflect the same premise that the pattern and structure of international trade should be determined by undistorted market competition and that the benefits of trade are maximized if decisions to import or to export are taken by the citizens themselves responding to market forces and informed by market prices.

State-trading enterprises (Article XVII) and state-trading countries (see the GATT protocols of accession for certain COMECON countries) are treated as necessitating exceptional rules to ensure that the general GATT rules and market competititon are not being undermined by the pricing and purchasing practices of state monopolies. Moreover, state-trading enterprises shall make any "purchases or sales involving either imports or exports... solely in accordance with commercial considerations" (see Article XVII:1), and "no contracting party shall prevent **any** enterprise under its jurisdiction from acting in accordance with the(se) principles" (Article XVII:1,c). For example, Articles II:4 and XVII:4 explicitly provide that "import mark-up's", used by import monopolies for the sale of imported products, must not be such as to afford protection in excess of bindings under Article II; and an interpretative note in Annex I of the General Agreement makes clear that "throughout Articles XI, XII, XIII, XIV and XVIII, the terms 'import restrictions' or 'export restrictions' include restrictions made effective through state-trading operations".[25] The Article XIX safeguards clause for "emergency action on imports of particular products" likewise proceeds from the assumption that continuous adjustment to import competition is a prequisite for the proper functioning of the GATT trading system. The GATT dispute settlement system under Article XXIII is based on the premise that trade restrictions violating GATT rules justify an assumption of adverse distortions of trading opportunities ("prima facie nullification or impairment of benefits accruing under the General Agreement") and entitle each GATT contracting party to request the withdrawal of the trade restrictions concerned.[26]

25 Interpretative note ad Articles XI, XII, XIII, XIV and XVIII, see: The text of the General Agreement on Tariffs and Trade, GATT 1986, p. 66.

26 On GATT practice relating to the interpretation and application of the concept of "nullification or impairment of benefits accruing under the General Agreement" (Article XXIII) see E.U. Petersmann (note 15), under Article XXIII, pp. 19-34.

F) The GATT Principles of "Due Process" and Judicial Protection of Individual Rights

Problems in the implementation of **international** trade rules arise mostly at the level of **domestic** trade law and policy-making. For a number of reasons, the effectiveness of international trade rules depends on the modalities and procedures for their implementation within the **domestic** legal systems of contracting parties. GATT law sets out detailed rules and procedures for domestic decision-making processes about trade and about the protection of individual rights of adversely affected traders and producers. For instance:

- the detailed, unconditional and directly applicable GATT rules - e.g. for freedom of transit (Article V), antidumping and countervailing duty procedures (Article VI), customs valuation (Article VII), fees and formalities connected with importation and exportation (Article VIII), marks of origin (Article IX), administration of trade regulations (Article X) and, specifically, of quantitative restrictions (Articles XI and XIII) and state-trading enterprises (Article XVII) - have laid the basis for a largely uniform domestic trade administration law in GATT contracting parties specifying the rights (e.g. freedom of transit) and duties (e.g. customs duties) of those engaged in international trade;

- "each contracting party shall administer in a uniform, impartial and reasonable manner all its laws, regulations, decisions and rulings" and "shall maintain, or institute..., judicial, arbitral or administrative tribunals or procedures for the purpose, inter alia, of the prompt review and correction of administrative action relating to customs matters. Such tribunals or procedures shall be independent of the agencies entrusted with administrative enforcement and their decisions shall be implemented by, and shall govern the practice of, such agencies unless an appeal is lodged with a court or tribunal of superior jurisdiction within the time prescribed for appeals to be lodged by importers" (Article X:3);

- the various 1979 Tokyo Round Agreements on customs valuation, import licensing, antidumping and countervailing duty proceedings, technical barriers to trade, subsidies and government procurement set out additional implementing rules for "due process"[27] in the administration

---

27 The due process of law clauses in the fifth and fourteenth Amendments to the US Constitution - that no person may be deprived of life, liberty or property without "due process of

of the various trade policy instruments. Article 11 of the 1979 Agreement on the Implementation of GATT Article VII (the Customs Valuation Code), for example, specifies the right of appeal in the following terms:

> "1. The legislation of each Party shall provide in regard to a determination of customs value for the right of appeal, without penalty, by the importer or any other person liable for the payment of the duty.
>
> 2. An initial right of appeal without penalty may be to an authority within the customs administration or to an independent body, but the legislation of each Party shall provide for the right of appeal without penalty to a judicial authority.
>
> 3. Notice of the decision on appeal shall be given to the appellant and the reasons for such decision shall be provided in writing. He shall also be informed of his rights of any further appeal."[28]

Article 3,f of the 1979 Agreement on Import Licensing stipulates: "If the licence application is not approved, the applicant shall, on request, be given the reasons therefore and shall have a right of appeal or review in accordance with the domestic legislation or procedures of the importing country". Article VI:5 of the Agreement on Government Procurement likewise recognizes individual rights of information and for the hearing and review of complaints:

> "Entities shall establish a contact point to provide additional information to any unsuccessful tenderer dissatisfied with the explanation for rejection of his tender or who may have further questions about the award of the contract. There shall also be procedures for the hearing and reviewing of complaints arising in connection with any phase of the procurement process, so as to ensure that, to the greatest extent possible, disputes under this Agreement will be equitably and expeditiously resolved between the suppliers and the entities concerned".

---

law" - guarantee procedures which are "due" in light of the circumstances and interests involved (e.g. "fair hearing"), as well as substantive due process of law (e.g. liberty of contract); for details see, e.g.: J.R. Pennock/J.W. Chapman (eds.), Due Process, 1977, pp. 3-68.

28 See: The Texts of the Tokyo Round Agreements, GATT 1986, p. 89.

G) The GATT Principle of National Economic Sovereignty

GATT law does not impose on contracting parties obligations to liberalize trade or to pursue a particular economic policy. Each contracting party is free to decide autonomously on its national level of trade protection and on whether it wants to participate in the regular "GATT rounds" of multilateral trade negotiations (cf. Articles II, XXVIII bis). Trade concessions legally bound under Article II can be modified subject to certain procedures and conditions (Article XXVIII). The generous safeguard and exception clauses of GATT law reserve a broad scope of national freedom to introduce or maintain protective measures for economic or political ends (e.g. Articles VI, XI:2 to XV, XVIII to XXI), such as to avoid that suddenly increasing imports cause "serious injury to domestic producers in that territory of like or directly competitive products" (Article XIX). Contracting parties remain free to intervene into their domestic economies by means of domestic subsidies (Articles III:8,b, XVI:1), internal taxation and regulation (Article III), state-trading enterprises (Article XVII), or trade restrictions for reasons of national "public policy" (Article XX), such as to protect public morals, plant life or human health, or to secure compliance with domestic patent and other laws. And contracting parties also retain broad freedom to use trade restrictions for security reasons (Article XXI), to participate in regional economic integration (Article XXIV), and to grant trade preferences in favour of developing countries (GATT Decision 1979 on "Differential and More Favourable Treatment, Reciprocity and Fuller Participation of Developing Countries").

GATT law thus enables each contracting party to adjust its GATT obligations to its own perceived needs. While most developed GATT contracting parties have legally bound more than 90% of their import tariffs, many less-developed contracting parties have only few or no tariff bindings at all. The less-developed GATT contracting parties have also not accepted the GATT prohibition of export subsidies for manufactured goods (Article XVI:4) and have insisted on an almost unfettered freedom to impose or maintain import restrictions for reasons of infant-industry protection or balance-of-payments protection (see Article XVIII and the 1979 GATT Decision on "Safeguard Action for Development Purposes").[29] The GATT obligations of the contracting parties may also vary as a result of differences in their respective protocols of accession to GATT, which sometimes include broad exemptions from certain GATT obligations (e.g. in fa-

29 Text in: The Texts of the Tokyo Round Agreement, GATT 1986, p. 198.

vour of Swiss agricultural trade restrictions). Other member countries have been granted subsequent "waivers" (Article XXV:5) from certain GATT obligations (e.g. for certain US agricultural trade restrictions). The "grandfather clause" contained in the 1947 Protocol on the Provisional Application of GATT, as well as in all subsequent protocols of accession to GATT, permits the maintenance of certain existing mandatory national legislation inconsistent with Part II of the General Agreement. And Article XXXV of GATT enables member countries to refuse to apply the General Agreement in relation to particular other contracting parties. GATT contracting parties are also free to decide whether they want to participate in the various additional trade agreements negotiated in the context of GATT (e.g. the 1979 Tokyo Round Agreements on the Interpretation and Application of Articles VI, VII, XVI and XXIII GATT). In conclusion, while GATT law does not impose any "sacrifices" on contracting parties (other than the comparatively small budgetary contributions), it considerably enhances the actual capacity of each government to maximize the national gains from trade and to protect itself from "power-oriented" pressures not only by other states but also by its own protectionist domestic interest groups.

H) The GATT Principle of Reciprocity

Expectations of reciprocity continue to be a major determinant of the emergence and application of international law. International legal disciplines are voluntarily undertaken by states in the expectation of equal or equivalent autolimitations by other states and of mutual advantages made possible thereby. This synallagmatic nature of the emergence of international law through reciprocal self-restraints characterizes also its application: Under general international law, for instance, a breach of an international legal obligation by one state may entitle other adversely affected states to reciprocate by means of reprisals or non-performance of treaty obligations (see Article 60 of the 1969 Vienna Convention on the Law of Treaties). International treaties may, however, limit the effect of principles of reciprocity on the contractual rights and obligations of contracting parties. This is also true of multilateral international trade agreements, such as GATT, whose objective is to reduce international legal and business uncertainty through a multilateral framework of rules and of dispute settlement procedures excluding the unilateral resort to reprisals.

The General Agreement refers to the principle of reciprocity explicitly in its preamble and Article XXVIII and implicitly in a number of other GATT provisions. The GATT preamble refers to the objective of "reciprocal and mutually advantageous arrangements directed to the substantial reduction of tariffs and other barriers to trade". The General Agreement reflects the principle of legal reciprocity further in the general applicability of the original GATT provisions to all contracting parties. In case of withdrawal of concessions, "the contracting parties concerned shall endeavour to maintain a general level of reciprocal and mutually advantageous concessions not less favourable to trade than that provided for in this Agreement" (Article XXVIII:2). If agreement cannot be reached in case of renegotiations or in case of a temporary suspension of GATT obligations (e.g. under Article XIX), compensatory withdrawals are to be "substantially equivalent concessions" (Articles XIX:3, XXVIII:3). The central GATT dispute settlement provision of Article XXIII admits also "non-violation complaints" in case of "the application by another contracting party of any measure, whether or not it conflicts with the provisions of this Agreement" (para. 1,b), or in case of "the existence of any other situation" (para. 1,c). A major goal of this provision was to protect the value of tariff concessions against indirect nullification or impairment resulting from trade-distorting measures not prohibited under the GATT (e.g. subsequent introduction of domestic production subsidies on the "concession products" concerned) and, thereby, to ensure "continued reciprocity".[30] Article XXVIII bis declares the intention of the Contracting Parties to sponsor from time to time "negotiations on a reciprocal and mutually advantageous basis, directed to the substantial reduction of the general level of tariffs and other charges on imports and exports" (para. 1). The various possible criteria for measuring "reciprocity" as the basis of such negotiations (e.g. depth of tariff cuts, trade coverage, loss of duties collectable, projected trade impact) were, however, not officially defined in the General Agreement or in GATT practice, apart from the rather imprecise rule of thumb set out in Article XXVIII:2: "The binding against increase of low duties or of duty-free treatment shall, in principle, be recognized as a concession equivalent in value to the reduction of high duties".

Economic theory demonstrates that trade liberalization benefits, first and most, the liberalizing country itself by enabling it to obtain cheaper and better goods and to reallocate its resources into more productive uses. Simultaneous reciprocal trade liberalization generates additional benefits compared to unilateral trade liberalization because it can increase the overall scope, pace and economic gains from trade liberalization and reduces the total adjustment costs. But

30 UN Doc. EPCT/A/PV.6 (1947), at p.5. For the drafting history, interpretation and application of Article XXIII see: E.U. Petersmann (note 15), under Article XXIII.

the national economic gains immediately obtainable through unilateral trade liberalization may be larger than those uncertain benefits possibly resulting from multilateral trade liberalization at some point in the future.[31] Why then do governments seek reciprocity in trade negotiations, if unilateral trade liberalization might be no less or even more beneficial?

Today, there is broad agreement among economists that the original economic arguments for insisting on reciprocity - to ease transitional employment problems caused by import liberalization, to avoid balance-of-payments problems, and to minimize adverse terms-of-trade effects - have lost much of their original validity under floating currencies.[32] The "terms-of-trade argument" in favour of the maintenance of tariffs by a country with monopolistic or monopsonistic market power, which might be able to reduce the world-market price of goods by restricting their importation, is an "essentially theoretical curiosity"[33] fascinating the authors of economic textbooks but "has not had practical relevance in multilateral trade negotiations".[34] The "employment argument" and "balance-of-payments argument" - according to which reciprocal trade liberalization offers the possibility of balancing the employment-reducing effects of, and the additional payments for, increased imports with the employment-creating effects of, and the additional receipts from, increased exports - are less convincing in a monetary system of flexible exchange rates, because governments are free to let exchange rates depreciate and thereby ensure a balanced expansion of the liberalized trade.[35] And the "bargaining chip argument" - which counsels to use import liberalization as a bargaining chip to negotiate reciprocal trade liberalization abroad - only explains why it may be "rational for a given country to insist on reciprocity if its trading partners are ready to lower their import barriers only against counter-concessions; it does not explain why these trading partners

---

31 See: R. Blackhurst, Reciprocity in Trade Negotiations under Flexible Exchange Rates, in: J. Martin/A. Smith (eds.), Trade and Payments Adjustment under Flexible Exchange Rates, 1979, pp. 212, 236.

32 See, e.g.: G. and V. Curzon, The Management of Trade Relations in the GATT, in: A. Shonfield (ed.), International Economic Relations of the Western World 1959-1971, Vol. I (1976), pp. 158 ff; Blackhurst (note 31); R. Roessler, The Rationale for Reciprocity in Trade Negotiations under Floating Currencies, in: Kyklos 1978, pp. 258, 268 f.

33 See J. Tumlir (note 21), p.3.

34 See: R. Roessler (note 32), p. 259.

35 For a detailed exposition of this point see R. Blackhurst (note 31), e.g. p. 235 f, who shows that the compensatory payments and employments effects of depreciation may even ensure a smoother and easier reallocation of domestic resources compared to reciprocal trade liberalization.

should insist on counter-concessions in the first place and hence why there should be reciprocity negotiations at all".[36]

The main reason why governments introduce welfare-reducing import restriction and, having imposed them, proceed to negotiate for their liberalization on a reciprocal basis, lies in the political rather than in the economic sphere. The protectionist "producer bias" in national decision-making about trade policy-making accounts not only for the introduction of most import restrictions, but also for the lack of their unilateral liberalization. Reciprocity negotiations provide visible and strong incentives for the domestic export industries to politically support import liberalization in exchange for international legal guarantees of access to foreign markets. As R. Cooper has put it: "The principle of reciprocity is designed to hold out the promise of export gains to certain sectors of the economy, and thereby to establish a counterweight to those who will be hurt by increased imports. Reciprocity attempts to build pluralistic support for tariff reduction where none would otherwise exist".[37] Or in the words of G. and V. Curzon: "This internal balancing of the economic effects of trade liberalization has a political pay-off, since reciprocity helps to create a constituency for tariff agreements in the export sector, which would not exist if a government proposed to reduce tariffs unilaterally".[38] The switch to flexible exchange rates has enabled trade policy-makers to use exchange rate depreciation as an alternative to the reciprocity principle for attaining the economic objective of reducing adverse employment effects and balance-of-payments effects of unilateral import liberalization. But as H.G. Johnson has pointed out, the "internal politico-economic rationale for reciprocity might become much stronger with floating rates than with fixed rates".[39] The reason is that reciprocal trade agreements produce more obvious and legally more secure export opportunities for particular domestic industries compared to the more diffuse and less identifiable export opportunities resulting from currency depreciation which cannot deliver industry-specific benefits and is influenced by many other macroeconomic factors. Hence, reciprocal trade liberalization will generate stronger politi-

---

36 R. Roessler (note 32), p. 264.

37 R. Cooper, Tariff Issues and the Third World, in: The World Today, 1971, pp. 401, 410. See also H. Hauser, Foreign Trade Policy and the Function of Rules for Trade Policymaking, in: D. Dicke/E.U. Petersmann (eds.), Foreign Trade in the Present and a New International Economic Order, 1988, pp.18, 32 ff.

38 Curzon (note 32), p. 158.

39 H.G. Johnson, Trade Negotiations and the New International Monetary System, 1976, p. 24.

cal support from domestic export industries than the alternative policy of unilateral trade liberalization plus exchange rate depreciation.

I) The GATT Principle of Non-reciprocal and Preferential Treatment of Less-developed Countries

The IMF Agreement and the original 1947 version of the General Agreement were based on the legal principles of "uniformity" and "symmetry" of rights and obligations.[40] Neither the provisions on the rights and obligations of members nor the policies of the IMF and of the GATT discriminated in favour of or against particular classes of countries (e.g. "less-developed contracting parties"). "Uniformity" was not equated with sameness. But the special provisions and any special policies were justified in terms of special problems (e.g. Article XII GATT: restrictions to safeguard the balance of payments, Article XVIII GATT: governmental assistance to economic development and reconstruction). The principle of uniformity of rights and obligations required members to be treated alike in what the law regarded as the same circumstances, and to avoid arbitrary legal differentiations that could not be justified by the subject matter of the right, obligation or policy concerned. The reciprocity principle was designed to promote symmetry in both legal and economic terms. The legal concept of equality of all contracting parties before the law coincided with the liberal economic assumption that stable and realistic exchange rates and an international division of labour (through trade) are beneficial to each country irrespective of its stage of development. Given their low labour costs and the fundamental economic theorem that liberal trade tends to equalize production factor incomes internationally, developing countries could be expected to gain no less from undistorted international trade competition than developed countries. Whenever governments should perceive a need for correcting "market distortions" or for "creating comparative advantages" by government interventions (rather than by private entrepreneurs), the IMF and GATT legal disciplines for the use of transparent, non-discriminatory and least-distortive policy instruments could benefit rich and poor countries alike.

40 See: J. Gold, Uniformity as a Legal Principle of the Fund, in: J. Gold, Legal and Institutional Aspects of the International Monetary System, Vol. I, IMF 1979, pp. 469; J. Gold, Symmetry as a Legal Objective of the International Monetary System, in: J. Gold, Legal and Institutional Aspects of the International Monetary System, Vol. II, IMF 1984, pp. 255 ff.

The law of the IMF continues to be based on the principles of uniformity and symmetry of rights and obligations[41] and has avoided, with minor exceptions in the Second Amendment of the IMF Agreement, the introduction of different rules for "developed" and "developing" member countries.[42] By contrast, GATT law has, since the GATT Review Session of 1955, recognized the distinction between "developed" and "less-developed" contracting parties as being relevant for the scope of application of GATT rules. In response to the demands by developing countries for "non-reciprocal" and "preferential" treatment in their favour, GATT law has introduced additional freedoms of "less-developed" contracting parties to deviate from general GATT obligations as well as additional "commitments" (e.g. in Article XXXVII) on the part of "developed" contracting parties for the promotion of the export interests of the developing contracting parties.

The principle of non-reciprocity has thus been incorporated into GATT law both "negatively" (i.e. affording LDCs additional freedoms from legal disciplines) and "positively" (i.e. providing for additional "commitments" in favour of LDCs e.g. in Article XXXVII).[43] Under GATT Article XVIII, as amended in 1955, "a contracting party the economy of which can only support low standards of living and is in the early stages of development" (para. 4,a) enjoys additional freedoms to modify or withdraw concessions under Article II "in order to promote the establishment of a particular industry with a view to raising the general standard of living of its people" (Section A); to institute, maintain or intensify quantitative import restrictions "to safeguard its external financial position and to ensure a level of reserves adequate for the implementation of its programme of economic development" (Section B); or to introduce other import restrictions "required to promote the establishment of a particular industry with a view to raising the general standard of living of its people" (Section C). The GATT Decision of 1979 on "Safeguard Action for Development Purposes"[44] has extended the scope of application of Article XVIII: Sections A and C to "the development of new or the modification or extension of existing production structures with a view to achieving fuller and more efficient use of resources in accordance with the priorities of their economic development" (para. 1); the Decision provides

41 See J. Gold (note 4)0 and J. Gold, The Rule of Law in the International Monetary Fund, 1980, pp. 70 ff.

42 See J. Gold, Symmetry (note 40), p. 259 ff.

43 See F. Roessler (note 20), p. 476.

44 See: The Texts of the Tokyo Round Agreements, GATT 1986, p. 198.

also for "additional flexibility" as regards the procedural requirements of Article XVIII: Sections A and C.

Article XVIII of GATT reflects the policy of governmental promotion of industrialization through import substitution, which was widespread in developing countries until about the late 1950s. During the 1960s, there was increasing awareness of the lack of success of this policy: Since import restrictions tend to reduce the productivity and competitiveness of the restricting economy, a low standard of living as such does not provide an economic justification for exempting a contracting party from the GATT legal disciplines for import restrictions.[45] The new policy emphasis on the promotion of exports from developing countries ("trade, not aid") was endorsed in the 1958 GATT "Haberler Report"[46] which showed, inter alia, that the reciprocity principle had tended to place countries with small markets at a disadvantage in GATT tariff negotiations.[47] Part IV on "Trade and Development", which was added to the General Agreement in 1965, dealt with this problem in Article XXXVI:8: "The developed contracting parties do not expect reciprocity for commitments made by them in trade negotiations to reduce or remove tariffs and other barriers to the trade of less-developed contracting parties". An interpretative note specifies "that the phrase 'do not expect reciprocity' means... that the less-developed contracting parties should not be expected, in the course of trade negotiations, to make contributions which are inconsistent with their individual development, financial and trade needs, taking into consideration past trade development". This interpretation was subsequently confirmed, and further clarified in respect of the least-developed countries and in respect of the principle of "graduation" of the more developed among the developing countries, in the 1979 GATT Decision on "Differential and More Favourable Treatment, Reciprocity and Fuller

45 For a survey and discussion of economic justifications of trade restrictions in developing countries see, e.g.: A.O. Krüger, Trade Policies in Developing Countries, in: Jones/Kennen (eds.), Handbook of International Economics, Vol. I, 1984, pp. 519 ff.

46 Trends in International Trade. A Report by a Panel of Experts, GATT 1958.

47 In GATT practice, negotiations on reciprocal tariff liberalization have tended to take place among countries supplying 10 per cent or more of the product concerned to a particular market. If a country supplying more than 10 per cent refused to liberalize its tariffs, the other trading partners would often also refrain from tariff liberalization so as to preserve reciprocity and avoid the most-favoured nation obligation to extend their tariff-cuts unilaterally to all other GATT contracting parties (Articles I, II). This can make it difficult for developing countries with small markets to negotiate tariff reductions on items of interest to them.

Participation of Developing Countries".[48] What has been agreed is thus individually graduated reciprocity rather than complete non-reciprocity, which "would exclude the developing countries from active participation in trade negotiations and would as a consequence deprive their governments of the possibility of using such negotiations as a tool for mustering domestic political support for the reduction of the import barriers that no longer serve the national interest".[49]

The GATT obligations relating to less-developed contracting parties have been further modified by the recognition in various GATT decisions, consolidated in the 1979 GATT Decision on "Differential and More Favourable Treatment, Reciprocity and Fuller Participation of Developing Countries", that, "notwithstanding the provisions of Article I of the General Agreement, contracting parties may accord differential and more favourable treatment to developing countries, without according such treatment to other contracting parties", in the following areas:

a) "Preferential tariff treatment accorded by developed contracting parties to products originating in developing countries in accordance with the Generalized System of Preferences;

b) Differential and more favourable treatment with respect to the provisions of the General Agreement concerning non-tariff measures governed by the provisions of instruments multilaterally negotiated under the auspices of the GATT;

c) Regional or global arrangements entered into amongst less-developed contracting parties for the mutual reduction or elimination of tariffs and, in accordance with criteria or conditions which may be prescribed by the CONTRACTING PARTIES, for the mutual reduction or elimination of non-tariff measures, on products imported from one another;

d) Special treatment of the least developed among the developing countries in the context of any general or specific measures in favour of developing countries."[50]

---

48 See: The Texts of the Tokyo Round Agreements, GATT 1986, p. 191 (paras. 3-8).

49 See R. Roessler (note 32), p. 270.

50 See above note 48 (para.2).

3. Constitutional Functions of Liberal International Monetary and Financial Rules: Basic Principles of the Law of the International Monetary Fund and the World Bank

A) The Principle of Separation of Policy Instruments

The General Agreement, the IMF Agreement and the World Bank Agreement explicitly recognize that the tasks and satisfactory operation of the international trade system (e.g. the efficient allocation of current production), the international monetary system (e.g. undistorted international payments and market prices for current trade transactions) and of the international financial system (e.g. efficient allocation of current savings) are interlinked. Thus, Article I of the IMF Agreement declares that one of the purposes of the IMF is "to facilitate the expansion and balanced growth of international trade".[51] The new Article IV of the IMF Agreement, as amended in 1978, states "that the essential purpose of the international monetary system is to provide a framework that facilitates the exchange of goods, services, and capital among countries" (para.1). According to Article I of the World Bank Agreement, the purposes of the Bank include "to promote the long-range balanced growth of international trade and the maintenance of equilibrium in balances of payments by encouraging international investment for the development of the productive resources of members".[52] In a world economy composed of states with differing degrees of economic development, international capital transfers are a prerequisite of the full exploitation of comparative advantages. To the extent that foreign borrowing can only be serviced and repaid by exports, or in foreign exchange earned by exports, international capital movements can be described as "deferred trade".[53]

The international trade, monetary and financial agreements recognize that the respective trade, monetary and financial policy instruments are often interrelated or even interchangeable. Thus it is generally acknowledged among economists that a uniform tariff on all imports combined with a uniform subsidy on all

51 See: Articles of Agreement of the International Monetary Fund, IMF 1985, p.2.

52 See: Articles of Agreement of the International Bank for Reconstruction and Development, World Bank, 1980, p.1.

53 On the interrelationships between trade protectionism and the foreign debt crisis see: E.U. Petersmann, Trade Restrictions for Balance-of-Payments Purposes and the GATT, in: D.Ch. Dicke (ed.), Foreign Debts in the Present and in a New International Economic Order, 1986, pp. 181, 186 ff.

exports has the same economic effect for trade as a devaluation at the same rate. That trade and exchange restrictions can be close substitutes for each other, is explicitly recognized in GATT Article XV which sets out detailed rules and procedures for cooperation between the GATT and the IMF.

Even though trade and monetary measures are often alternatives to achieve the same end, the post-war international economic order is characterized by the coexistence of separate international agreements and international organizations for monetary, financial and trade matters. Just as at the national level most states have enacted separate laws and set up separate ministries for the regulation and administration of monetary, development and trade matters, it was considered preferable also at the international level not to overload the international negotiations and agreements, and to have separate but complementary and mutually supportive specialized international institutions. The Final Act of the 1944 Bretton Woods Conference, which adopted the two treaties establishing the IMF and the World Bank, recommended in its Resolution VII the negotiation of an international trade agreement.[54]

The IMF is confined to an international monetary organization which, although "in the service of international trade" (J. Gold), does not have regulatory powers for requiring, proscribing, validating or invalidating trade practices.[55] And the jurisdiction of the GATT is limited to "tariffs and trade" and circumscribed in order to ensure "a co-ordinated policy with regard to exchange questions within the jurisdiction of the Fund and questions of quantitative restrictions and other trade measures within the jurisdiction of the CONTRACTING PARTIES" (Article XV:1).

Since payment restrictions or exchange restrictions for the purchase of specified imports have a similar effect, so far as the origin and volume of imports are concerned, as a trade restriction on the physical import of those goods, GATT Article XV:4 prescribes that "contracting parties shall not, by exchange action, frustrate the intent of the provisions of this Agreement, nor by trade action, the intent of the provisions of the Articles of Agreement of the International Monetary Fund." In both the IMF Agreement as well as in the 1947 version of the

54 Proceedings and Documents of United Nations Monetary and Financial Conference, Bretton Woods, New Hampshire, July 1-22, 1944, Vol.I, p. 941 (Department of State Publications No. 2866, Washington D.C., 1948).

55 See: J. Gold, Some Legal Aspects of the IMF's Activities in Relation to International Trade, in: Oesterreichische Zeitschrift für Oeffentliches Recht und Völkerrecht 1986, pp. 157, 158.

General Agreement, the inclusion of special rules for developing countries was deliberately avoided due to the insistence, especially by the United States, that the special development problems of the less-developed countries should be addressed by other institutions, such as the UN Economic and Social Council and the World Bank, rather than through trade-distorting monetary and trade rules.[56]

This legal principle of the separation and different legal regulation of the instruments of trade policy, monetary policy and foreign investment and development policy corresponds to a basic principle of the theory of economic policy, first developed by J.Tinbergen,[57] that, if governments wish to attain a set of economic policy objectives efficiently, it is necessary that the number of policy

---

56 See: C. Wilcox, A Charter for World Trade, 1949, p. 141.

57 J. Tinbergen, Economic Policy: Principles and Design, 1956. For an application of Tinbergen's theory to international trade and monetary policy see, e.g.: H.G. Grubel, International Economics, 1981, p. 416 f; Fragen einer Neuen Weltwirtschaftsordnung, Gutachten des Wissenschaftlichen Beirats beim Bundesministerium für Wirtschaft, 1977, p. 14 f: "Nach dem '**Prinzip der Trennung der Aufgabenbereiche**' ist die Ordnung der Weltwirtschaft so zu gestalten, dass die grossen Perspektiven, die dabei zu bedenken sind, deutlich voneinander getrennt, aber gleichwohl aufeinander bezogen werden. Jeweils duch ein Bündel von Regeln und Massnahmen mit den zugehörigen institutionalen Vorkehrungen sind

- eine statisch wie dynamisch international effiziente **Allokation** der knappen Ressourcen anzustreben,

- eine Versorgung mit internationalem Geld und gegebenenfalls eine Abstimmung der nationalen Globalsteuerung derart vorzunehmen, dass der Allokationsmechanismus störungsfrei verlaufen kann und weltweite Inflations- oder Rezessionsgefahren verringert werden (**Stabilisierung**),

- ein partieller Ausgleich der internationalen Wohlstandsunterschiede herbeizuführen und Hilfen in Notfällen zu gewähren (**Distribution**).

Wegen der generellen Interdependenz wirtschaftlicher Tätigkeiten und insbesondere wegen der untrennbaren Verbindung von Faktorallokation und Einkommensverteilung können die drei Bündel von Massnahmen und Regeln sinnvoll nicht unabhängig voneinander, sondern nur in bezug aufeinander entworfen werden. Die Trennung nach Aufgabenbereichen ist notwendig, um die ihnen zugeordneten Teilziele der optimalen Faktorallokation, der Stabilität und der gerechteren Einkommensverteilung mit den jeweils bestgeeigneten Massnahmen zu verwirklichen. Regeln und Massnahmen, die gleichzeitig in bestmöglicher Weise zur Realisierung mehrerer Teilziele führen, lassen sich nur in seltenen Fällen finden. Das bedeutet, dass Massnahmen, die im Hinblick auf ein Teilziel als die bestmöglichen gelten, nicht zur Erreichung eines anderen Teilziels eingesetzt werden sollten. Geschieht es trotzdem, verzichtet man auf höhere Zielerreichungsgrade insgesamt. Das Prinzip der "Trennung der Aufgabenbereiche" sollte auch innerhalb der drei grossen Bereiche beachtet werden. Beispielsweise ist der Allokationsmechanismus so zu ordnen, dass man jeweils eigene, wenn auch aufeinander abgestimmte Regelungen vorsieht für den Welthandel, für den Transfer von Produktionstechniken und für den Transfer von Produktionskapazitäten (optimale Standortwahl)."

instruments equal the number of policy targets. As this economic theory demonstrates, hardly ever does one and the same economic policy instrument provide an optimal means for the efficient realization of two different economic policy objectives. This economic rationale underlies also the legal principle of "uniformity" in the law of the IMF, according to which special provisions and special policies are usually adopted in terms of special problems (e.g. the IMF's "buffer stock financing facility", "oil facility subsidy account") rather than in terms of special rules for a particular class of member countries;[58] and it also accounts for the continued resistance within the IMF to use the "special drawing rights", designed to become the principal reserve asset of the international monetary system, for purposes of income redistribution in favour of developing countries.

B) The Principles of Transparent and Rule-oriented Policy-making

The principles of transparent and rule-oriented policy-making, which have been described as a determinant of GATT law, also underlie the law of the IMF and of the World Bank. The nationalistic monetary "beggar-my-neighbour policies" and the "international monetary non-system" of the 1930s - characterized by mutually impoverishing exchange restrictions, exchange rate manipulation (e.g. competitive devaluations and discriminatory multiple exchange rates) and "power-oriented" bilateral clearing arrangements[59] - showed that national monetary restrictions could reduce and distort the international division of labour no less than national trade restrictions. J.M. Keynes perceived his 1943 "Proposals for an International Clearing Union" as "the beginning of an entirely new stage in the economic organisation of the world".[60] In his view, a multilateral international monetary agreement was necessary not only in order to avoid a re-

58 See J. Gold (note 41), p. 80. On the various forms of financial assistance by the IMF see, e.g.: A.W. Hooke, The International Monetary Fund, IMF 1981, pp. 40 ff.

59 The abuse of clearing agreements for the exploitation of weak by strong countries often operated through the importation of needed primary commodities from the weaker party, which the weaker party found itself to be financing unless it imported equal amounts of - often overpriced or useless - goods from the stronger party in order to liquidate the clearing balances. Thus Yugoslavia was forced in the 1930s, in order to liquidate huge credit balances with Germany, to accept "enough German aspirins to cover her requirements ten years ahead" (P. Einzig, Bloodless Invasion, 1939, p. 26), and Ghana was compelled in the 1960s to liquidate clearing balances by accepting "enough alarm clocks ... to wake up all of Africa for 10 years" (G.P. Verbit, Trade Agreements for Developing Countries, 1969, p. 101).

60 J.M. Keynes, Collected writings, Vol. 25, 1980, p. 103.

turn to the monetary disorder of the 1930s, but also as a foundation for the subsequent negotiation of a multilateral international trade agreement:

> "There is a logical reason for dealing with the monetary proposals first. It is extraordinarily difficult to frame any proposals about tariffs if countries are free to alter the value of their currencies without agreement and at short notice. Tariffs and currency depreciations are in many cases alternatives. Without currency agreements you have no firm ground on which to discuss tariffs. In the same way plans for diminishing the fluctuation of international prices have no domestic meaning to the countries concerned until we have some firm ground in the value of money... a monetary system gives a firm foundation on which the others can be built. It is very difficult while you have monetary chaos to have order of any kind in other directions".[61]

Keynes emphasized that international monetary rules and legal disciplines were in the national self-interest of all countries:

> "Perhaps the most difficult question to determine is how much to decide by rule and how much to leave to discretion" (either of national governments or of what Keynes termed the "central Management" of the new international monetary organization)... "If the individual members are too free, indiscipline may result and unwarrantable liberties be taken"... "A greater readiness to accept super-national arrangements must be required in the post-war world. If the arrangements proposed can be described as a measure of financial disarmament, there is nothing here which we need be reluctant to accept ourselves or to ask of others. It is an advantage, and not a disadvantage, of the scheme that it invites the member States to abandon that licence to promote indiscipline, disorder and bad-neighbourliness which, to the general disadvantage, they have been free to exercise hitherto."[62]

The IMF Agreement prescribes detailed rules for the national conduct of exchange rate policies, payments associated with current account transactions, and for the convertibility of national currencies. It also provides member states with financial assistance to enable them to correct or avoid temporary payments imbalances without recourse to measures inconsistent with this code of conduct. External financial assistance is thus being used to promote the international rule of law. Under the original par value system, member states were obligated to maintain fixed and uniform rates of exchange for their currency. Under the new Article IV, as amended in 1978, members are free to choose their national exchange arrangements; but "each member undertakes to collaborate with the

61 J.M. Keynes, Collected writings, Vol. 26, 1980, p. 5 f.

62 J.M. Keynes, Proposals for an International Clearing Union, 1943, in: J.K. Horsefield (ed.), The International Monetary Fund 1945-1965, Vol. III, 1969, p. 6 ff (paras. 15, 45).

Fund and other members to assure orderly exchange arrangements and to promote a stable system of exchange rates" (Article IV, section 1). Each member shall notify the Fund of its exchange arrangements (Article IV, section 2), and "the Fund shall exercise firm surveillance over the exchange rate policies of members" (section 3). The Fund's financial assistance is subject to conditions "that will assist members to solve their balance of payments problems in a manner consistent with the provisions of this Agreement and that will establish adequate safeguards for the temporary use of the general resources of the Fund" (Article V, section 3). The "general obligations of members" under Article VIII - inter alia for the avoidance of restrictions on current payments (section 2), the avoidance of discriminatory currency practices (section 3), the convertibility of foreign-held balances (section 4), the furnishing of information on all aspects of national monetary policy and the national balance-of-payments (section 5), and the collaboration with the Fund regarding policies on reserve assets (section 7) - are likewise geared to ensure transparent and rule-oriented monetary and exchange policies. The Fund's objective "to meet the need, as and when it arises, for a supplement to existing reserve assets" by the allocation of special drawing rights (Articles XV to XXV), as well as the Fund's declared "objectives of promoting better international surveillance of international liquidity and making the special drawing right the principal reserve asset in the international monetary system" (Article VIII:7), reflect a concern to meet in a transparent and more rule-oriented manner the long-term global need of member states for the reserve assets with which they support their currencies.

Transparency and rule-of-law determine also the organization, borrowing and lending activities of the World Bank Group, consisting of the International Bank for Reconstruction and Development (IBRD, 1944), the International Finance Corporation (IFC, 1956), the International Development Association (IDA, 1960) and the International Centre for the Settlement of Investment Disputes (ICSID, 1965). Just as, according to the former director of the Legal Department of the IMF, "international monetary law, in a sufficiently comprehensive and systematic form to justify recognition of it as a separate province of public international law, came into existence on December 27, 1945"[63] with the entry into force of the IMF Agreement, the strengthening of the rule of law in international finance and development has been a major contribution of the World Bank:

63 J. Gold, Legal and Institutional Aspects of the International Monetary System, Vol. II, IMF 1984, p. 724.

> "Over four decades, the World Bank has pioneered new legal concepts and contributed to legal advancements on various levels: the establishment of international and domestic development institutions; the international law governing financial operations in the field of development; the promotion of the rule of law in foreign direct investments in developing countries; and the establishment of development institutions and legal infrastructures in developing countries."[64]

The 1944 Agreement establishing the IBRD has served as a model for the establishment of numerous other international and national finance and development institutions. The World Bank's lending operations are always based on widely standardized loan agreements, development credit agreements or guarantee arrangements which are governed by public international law and put all borrowers on an equal footing. All these agreements are registered with and published by the United Nations pursuant to Article 102 of the UN Charter. The World Bank's success as the world's most important borrower on international capital markets may "be attributed, among other causes, to a number of legal provisions in its Articles of Agreement, and to the legal design of its borrowing instruments and policies".[65] Especially through the financing, investment and technical assistance activities of the IFC, through the provision of facilities for conciliation and arbitration of foreign investment disputes by the ICSID, and through the 1985 World Bank Convention establishing the Multilateral Investment Guarantee Agency (MIGA), the World Bank Group has contributed to a more favourable investment climate in developing countries through the promotion of the rule of law. The "internationalization" of the World Bank's loan and guarantee agreements, as well as of foreign investment agreements subjected to ICSID's jurisdiction, pursues objectives similar to those of the GATT's dispute settlement procedures: to set up a framework of substantive and procedural rules of international law and of quick and inexpensive third party adjudication designed to protect not only the foreign investors from foreign government interferences contrary to international law, but also the defendant state from the more "power-oriented" traditional means of international dispute settlement, such as diplomatic protection, retorsions and reprisals.

---

64 See: H.G. Petersmann, The World Bank's Contribution to the Law of International Finance and Development (1944-1984), in: Archiv des Völkerrechts 1985, pp. 241 ff, 242.

65 See: H.G. Petersmann (note 64), p. 252 ff.

C) The Principle of the Use of Non-discriminatory and Proportionate Policy Instruments

Under the gold standard until 1914, the voluntarily accepted "rules of the game" (e.g. gold as full legal tender, unrestricted exchange of other means of payment into gold, free coinage of gold, free import and export of gold) subjected the money, fiscal, credit and exchange policies of governments and central banks to a severe common discipline (e.g. determination of a country's money supply by the amount of its gold reserves), which enabled stable exchange rates, free convertibility of currencies and quasi-automatic adjustments of balance-of-payments deficits. Even though the gold standard was entirely a matter of national law, the self-imposed linkage of the national currency with gold forced the national governments and central banks to conduct their money and credit policies in a manner consistent with the maintenance of a multilateral liberal trade and payments system. The interwar period showed that, once these self-imposed national disciplines and the ensuing "depolitisation" of national economic policies as well as of the international division of labour were no longer respected, an efficient international division of labour with freedom of payments at stable exchange rates could no longer be maintained without internationally agreed legal disciplines for the use of non-discriminatory and less-distortive instruments of monetary policy. Just as GATT law ranks the various trade policy instruments according to their economic efficiency and promotes a market-conforming multilateral trading system, the law and policies of the IMF are aimed at promoting the use of less-distortive monetary policy instruments in order to reestablish a multilateral payments and trade system with stable exchange rates and free convertibility of currencies:

- Under the original par value system, Article IV committed member states to the use of unitary fixed rates of exchange of their currency consistent with the generally agreed economic policy objectives of price stability, high levels of employment and real income, and a sustainable balance-of-payments position. Under the new Article IV, as amended in 1978, "each member undertakes... to promote a stable system of exchange rates" and "shall endeavor to direct its economic and financial policies toward the objective of fostering orderly economic growth with reasonable price stability". The Fund has given more precision to the obligations of Article IV by the adoption of the following three specific principles for the guidance of national exchange rate policies:

"A. A member shall avoid manipulating exchange rates or the international monetary system in order to prevent effective balance of payments adjustment or to gain an unfair competitive advantage over other members.

B. A member should intervene in the exchange market if necessary to counter disorderly conditions which may be characterized inter alia by disruptive short-term movements in the exchange value of its currency.

C. Members should take into account in their intervention policies the interests of other members, including those of the countries in whose currencies they intervene."[66]

- As regards the exchange practices of member states, no member that has accepted the "general obligations" of Article VIII "shall, without the approval of the Fund, impose restrictions on the making of payments and transfers for current international transactions" (section 2) nor "engage in, or permit any of its fiscal agencies... to engage in, any discriminatory currency arrangements or multiple currency practices..., except as authorized by this Agreement or approved by the Fund" (section 3). Article XIV provides for transitional arrangements for members not yet able to accept the obligations of Article VIII for freedom of current payments and convertibility of currencies. Members remain free, however, to regulate and control international capital movements provided that the controls do not restrict current payments or transfers (Article VI:3).

- The Fund's financial assistance to overcome temporary balance-of-payments difficulties without resort to mutually harmful trade and payments restrictions is conditional on the adoption of adjustment policies "that will assist members to solve their balance of payments problems in a manner consistent with the provisions of this Agreement and that will establish adequate safeguards for the temporary use of the general resources of the Fund" (Article V:3). The aim of this "principle of conditionality" is "to help members to attain, over the medium term, a viable payments position in a context of reasonable price and exchange rate stability, a sustainable level and growth rate of economic activity, and a liberal system of multilateral payments".[67] The Fund's policy of conditionality attaches much importance to the attainment and maintenance of appropriate price incentives (e.g. as regards exchange rates, interest

66 Decision No. 5392 (77/63), in: IMF, Selected Decisions, 9th ed. 1981, p. 11 f.

67 M. Guitian, Fund Conditionality, Evolution of Principles and Practices, IMF 1981, p. 3.

rates, or prices of goods and services of special importance to the economy) because, "as long as the economic decisionmaking process needs to be based on the principle and the accurate measurement of the opportunity cost of scarce resources, prices are relevant for all economies (regardless of their particular lines of organization) and for all decision makers (whether in the private or the public sectors)".[68]

- Under the original par value system of Article IV, a member state could change the par value of its currency normally only if the Fund concurred that the proposed change was "necessary" to "correct" a "fundamental disequilibrium" of the balance-of-payments. The underlying objective was to promote exchange rate stability and to discourage transitory, excessive or inadequate exchange rate changes. The new Article IV allows each member to choose its exchange arrangements (e.g. floating exchange rates) and to determine the external value of its currency under those arrangements. But the principles adopted by the Fund for the guidance of exchange rate policies continue to be aimed at the promotion of realistic and stable exchange rates,[69] without which production costs in different countries could not be compared and an efficient worldwide division of labour with mutual gains from trade could hardly become effective.

The World Bank has granted loans and development credits to more than 120 member countries. Its stringent loan conditions (see Articles III, IV of the IBRD Agreement) have ensured the productive use of the Bank's financial resources in the common interest of the Bank and its borrowers (see Article III:4,v) and have contributed to the fact that the World Bank has so far (1987) never incurred a financial loss on any of its loans. In accordance with the principle of project lending (Article III:4,vii), the loans and development credits are assigned to well-prepared development projects with a high priority in the development programs of the borrower country.

---

68 M. Guitian (note 67), p.10. The welfare-reducing effects of distortions of the prices of goods, services, capital and labour are emphasized also by the World Bank, see R. Agarwala, Price Distortions and Growth, World Bank Staff Paper No. 575, 1984.

69 For details see M. Guitian (note 67), p. 10 ff.

D) The Principle of Protection of Property Rights

The law of the GATT, the IMF and the World Bank Group is ultimately designed to increase legal certainty for transnational trade transactions, payments and investments. All these economic transactions involve contractual arrangements and exchanges of property rights. The exporting country usually cannot unilaterally protect the rights of its national traders and investors in foreign jurisdictions. International agreements, such as GATT, the IMF Agreement and the World Bank Agreements, contain mutually beneficial commitments among exporting and importing countries to treat international economic transactions in a predictable and rule-oriented manner and, thereby, to protect the property rights of those engaged in international trade and investments.

This function of public international economic law to protect the property rights of those engaged in international economic transactions is reflected in many provisions of the IMF Agreement. The prohibition in Article VIII:2,a to "impose restrictions on the making of payments and transfers for current international transactions" implies, for instance, that a member state may not restrict the ability of its residents to make payments in domestic or foreign currency to non-residents in settlement of current international transactions. Property rights are also protected through the pivotal role played by the IMF in the financing, renegotiating and restructuring of foreign debts and in the promotion by the World Bank Group of foreign investments in developing countries. Both the IMF and the World Bank have to use their funds on a revolving basis and, hence, have to ensure their productive use and orderly repayment by borrowing countries. Other foreign public and private funds for the indebted capital-importing countries are also not unlimited and are, just like the capital flight from many of these countries, highly dependent upon credible and legally stable investment conditions in these countries. Yet many of these countries suffer from weak traditions of protection of property rights, from unstable national investment conditions, and from broad discretionary government powers for bureaucratic controls and market interventions. In such a situation, international legal commitments may offer a more credible means of reducing domestic investment insecurity and of limiting the national government discretion compared to purely national commitments, which can be easier changed by subsequent governments.

For instance, the private arrangements negotiated in the "London Club" and the government arrangements negotiated in the "Paris Club" of creditors on the rescheduling of foreign public debts have often been made conditional on the acceptance by the debtor country of an IMF stand-by arrangement and of the economic conditions attached to the use of the Fund's financial resources. The World Bank has (up to 1986) never had to declare a borrower country in default. This seems to have been due not only to the "cross-reference clauses" and "cross-default clauses" incorporated into the World Bank's loan and guarantee agreements, which entitle the Bank to suspend the disbursement of already approved loans of a defaulting borrower. Another important reason is also the "internationalization" of these agreements which, as obligations governed by public international law, are endowed with a somewhat higher standing in the domestic decision-making processes of the borrowing governments. The International Center for the Settlement of Investment Disputes (ICSID), by providing international arbitration and conciliation mechanisms for investment disputes between states and foreign investors, protects investors from governmental interferences that violate international law, and offers additional investment security which the host country might be unable to create unilaterally through purely national measures. The 1985 World Bank Convention establishing the Multilateral Investment Guarantee Agency (MIGA) envisages international guarantees for direct foreign investments, equity investments and other forms of "eligible investments" (see Article 12, e.g. licensing and franchising agreements, management and service contracts) against a large number of non-commercial risks (see Article 11), such as government restrictions on the transfer and convertibility of profits, expropriation, breach of legal commitments, war and civil disturbance.[70] Like GATT, IMF and ICSID, MIGA can be seen as an agreement on mutual self-restraint among exporting and importing countries seeking to promote the common interest in legal certainty and in protection of property rights and to avoid mutually self-destructive policies. The international legal guarantees by MIGA and the institutional framework provided by MIGA for continuous policy cooperation among capital-exporting and capital-importing countries are likely to increase the actual ability of host countries to improve their domestic investment climate and to attract badly needed additional financial resources.

70 The text of the Convention establishing MIGA is reproduced in: International Legal Materials 1985, p. 692 ff.

E) The Principle of National Economic Sovereignty

The right of each state to regulate the national currency, trade and investments within the national jurisdiction has always been considered an essential element of state sovereignty. Prior to the entry into force of the IMF Agreement in 1945, there were few international treaties - such as the 1865 treaty between Belgium, France, Italy and Switzerland establishing the Latin Monetary Union - limiting the national freedom to create money and to establish, maintain or change its internal or external value.[71] In 1929, the Permanent International Court of Justice declared that "it is indeed a generally accepted principle that a State is entitled to regulate its own currency";[72] the Court's statement seemed to imply "that the State was not subject to legal restraint in applying this principle" and "that states incurred no international responsibility because of the way they conducted their monetary policies, whatever might be the effects on other states".[73] The "rules" underlying the international gold standard were never laid down in precise terms, and were not considered to be part of international law.[74]

The monetary experience of the 1930s demonstrated that, even if the disciplines of the gold standard were no longer observed, the actual ability of countries to pursue independent monetary and exchange policies was very limited. The large number of competitive devaluations of national currencies between 1931 and 1936 showed, for instance, that the exchange rate of a currency (i.e. its price in terms of other currencies) could not be unilaterally determined if there are mutually offsetting depreciations of other currencies. And in an interdependent international economy, exchange rates can have a strong influence on investments, asset values, production, trade and employment in many countries. The 1936 Tripartite Monetary Agreement between France, the United Kingdom and the USA and, above all, the 1944 IMF Agreement were based on this insight that national "monetary sovereignty" could no longer be secured in a realistic sense without an agreed international code of conduct for the national monetary and exchange policies.

71 On the legal aspects of the creation of money and of the establishment, maintenance and change of its internal and external value see: S.A. Silard, Money and Foreign Exchange, in: Zweigert/Drobnig et alii (eds.), International Encyclopedia of Comparative Law, Vol. XVII, Chapt. 20, 1975, pp. 3-81.

72 Case Concerning the Payment of Various Serbian Loans Issued in France, Permanent International Court of Justice, Collection of Judgments, Series A, No. 20/21, 1929, p. 44.

73 J. Gold (note 41), p. 2.

74 See: International Currency Experience: Lessons of the Inter-War Period, League of Nations, 1944.

The provisions of the IMF Agreement regulating exchange rates, financial assistance and convertibility strike a balance between, on the one side, the principle that exchange rates and convertibility are a two-ended relationship and therefore properly matters of international concern; and, on the other side, the authority retained by member states to take the final decision on their own national monetary and exchange policies. Under the original Article IV, exchange rates were fixed in agreement with the IMF (sections 1,a and 5,e) and remained subject to international scrutiny in the IMF; but only a member state was entitled to propose a change in the par value of its currency (section 5,b). The Fund was not entitled to object if a proposed change remained within 10 per cent of the initial par value (section 5,c), and even an "unauthorized change" of par value was deemed not to be in violation of Article IV if certain conditions were satisfied (section 6). The new Article IV, as amended in 1978, permits each member state to choose its exchange arrangements and to determine the external value of its currency without a requirement of prior or subsequent agreement with the Fund. In its surveillance over the exchange rate policies of members, the Fund "shall respect the domestic social and political policies of members, and ... shall pay due regard to the circumstances of members" (Article IV:3,b).

The IMF Agreement also leaves it to each member state to decide whether it wants to accept the obligations of convertibility in Article VIII or to maintain restrictions on payments and transfers for current international transactions under the transitional arrangements in Article XIV. The "obligation to collaborate regarding policies on reserve assets" (Article VIII:7) notwithstanding, IMF member states retain also broad freedom as regards their national policy with respect to reserve assets. The stand-by arrangements for the financial assistance of the Fund are treated not as international agreements but as a decision of the Fund, to which the borrowing member's letter of intent setting forth its adjustment programme is annexed; as a consequence, departures from the adjustment programme are not breaches of international law, and the borrowing member is protected from the charge that it has subjected important areas of policy to the legal authority of the Fund.[75] Similarly, countries introducing import restrictions under GATT Article XII to safeguard the balance-of-payments shall not be required to withdraw or modify such restrictions on the ground that a change in their domestic economic policies would render unnecessary such restrictions (Article XII:3,d of GATT).

75 See: J. Gold, The Legal Character of the Fund's Stand-By-Arrangements and Why it Matters, IMF 1980.

There are no basic conflicts of interests between the Bretton Woods institutions and their member states. Both the IMF and the World Bank were designed to serve the interests of their members. Both have a strong self-interest in ensuring the most productive use of their financial assistance and in maintaining the creditworthiness of their borrowers. Thus, the World Bank Agreement explicitly prescribes that "the Bank shall act prudently in the interests both of the particular member in whose territories the project is located and of the members as a whole" (Article III:4,v). And "the Bank shall make arrangements to ensure that the proceeds of any loan are used only for the purposes for which the loan was granted, with due attention to considerations of economy and efficiency and without regard to political or other non-economic influences or considerations" (Article III:5,b of the IBRD Agreement). When the member country in whose territory the project is located is not itself the borrower, the member country concerned must guarantee the repayment of the loan (see Article III:4,i); thus, the Bank makes no loans without the consent of the member country in whose territory the project is located. Similarly, the World Bank is allowed to borrow money only with the approval of the member in whose market the funds are raised, as well as of the member in whose currency the loan is denominated (see Article IV:1,b). And in no case shall "the Bank and its officers... interfere in the political affairs of any member; nor shall they be influenced in their decisions by the political character of the member or members concerned. Only economic considerations shall be relevant to their decisions, and these considerations shall be weighed impartially in order to achieve the purposes stated in Article I" (Article IV:10).

4. Constitutional Functions of Multilateral International Institutions and Procedures: The Example of the "Bretton Woods System"

In a globally integrated world economy composed of more than 170 sovereign states, international economic law is important not only as a set of substantive rules but also as a set of procedures. In a decentralized international rule system where compliance rests essentially on consent, procedural rules and multilateral institutions are necessary for the maintenance of the consensus on the substantive rights and obligations, for the application of the rules and the identification of the common interest in new situations, for the settlement of disputes and for the elaboration of additional new rules. The "constitutional function" of substantive international economic rules, namely to constitute long-term legal restraints on mutually harmful domestic policies, cannot remain effective without an appropriate procedural and institutional framework for day-to-day politics. Procedural and institutional rules are also necessary to ensure that the international institutions do not exceed and abuse their limited delegated powers. Procedural rights for private participation in international decision-making processes (e.g. in ICSID arbitration proceedings) and for the enforcement of the international rules through domestic courts (see Articles X:3,b of GATT, VIII:2,b of the IMF Agreement, 54:1 ICSID Convention) can strengthen and "anchor" an effective application of international economic rules within the domestic economic, political and legal systems.

A) The Bretton Woods Agreements as "Living Constitutions" and "Legal Systems"

The IMF Agreement and the IBRD Agreement provide not only for mutually consistent sets of general international monetary and financial rules of unlimited duration, but also for the establishment of separate international organizations possessing international legal personality and similar institutional structures (inter alia, a Board of Governors as plenary and major decision-making organ, the Executive Board of Directors, and the "Managing Director" of the IMF and the "President" in case of the Bank).[76] While the 1944 "United Nations Monetary and Financial Conference" at Bretton Woods had on its agenda only the negotiation of the agreements creating the IMF and the World Bank, Resolution VII of the Final Act of this conference recognized that it would not be possible to achieve all the purposes set out in Article I of the IMF Agreement without a complementary third agreement establishing an International Trade Organization. Specifically the conference recommended:

> "To the participating Governments that, in addition to implementing the specific monetary and financial measures which were the subject of this Conference, they seek, with a view to creating in the field of international economic relations conditions necessary for the attainment of the purposes of the Fund and of the broader primary objectives of economic policy, to reach agreement as soon as possible on ways and means whereby they may best:
>
> 1) reduce obstacles to international trade and in other ways promote mutually advantageous international commercial relations;

76 For details see: J. Gold, The Relationship Between the International Monetary Fund and the World Bank, in: J. Gold (note 40), Vol. II, pp. 453 ff.

> 2) bring about the orderly marketing of staple commodities at prices fair to the producer and consumer alike;
>
> 3) deal with the special problems of international concern which will arise from the cessation of production for war purposes; and
>
> 4) facilitate by cooperative effort the harmonization of national policies of Member States designed to promote and maintain high levels of employment and progressively rising standards of living".[77]

The 1948 Havana Charter for an International Trade Organization was never ratified. But its regulatory functions were partially assumed by the 1947 General Agreement, which had been negotiated at the same 1946 and 1947 meetings which prepared the Havana Charter. Since the failure of the Havana Charter to materialize, the General Agreement, originally conceived as an interim agreement incorporating the results of the 1947 negotiations on tariff liberalization, has gradually evolved into a worldwide multilateral trade agreement of unlimited duration and into the central international trade organization constituting the "third pillar" of what is generally considered together to form the "Bretton Woods system". The complementarity of the functions, jurisdictions, regulations and policies of the IMF, the World Bank and GATT are recognized also in their constituent agreements (see, e.g., Articles I of the IMF Agreement; I, II:1 of the IBRD Agreement; XII, XIV, XV, XXXVI of the GATT).[78]

Multilateral agreements among states establishing international organizations are often referred to as "constitutions". The reason for this is that such agreements differ from ordinary treaties in several respects. They not only regulate rights and obligations among states, but they also constitute new subjects of international law and regulate their functions, powers and structures. Their long-term objectives, general framework rules, open membership, proper organs with legislative and administrative powers of their own, separate legal personality as well as responsibility in international law, often enable these agreements to function like "living constitutions",[79] the interpretation and legal evolution of which are likely to change over time in response to changes in international relations. The more frequent the original agreements are being amended and further developed by supplementary agreements, the more their contractual nature

77 Proceedings (above note 54), p. 941.

78 On the relationships between the IMF and GATT see the publications by J. Gold (above notes 54 and 76) and E.U. Petersmann (note 53).

79 See: H.G. Schermers, International Institutional Law, 1980, p. 565.

may be gradually modified by "constitutional" and institutional elements. With increasing international economic interdependence, the international institutions and international economic rules are also likely to become increasingly important instruments and frameworks of national policy-making. Today, many national economic policy objectives can no longer be achieved without active participation and cooperation within GATT and the IMF. And due to the incorporation into domestic law of the "primary" and "secondary" treaty law of these international economic organizations, the domestic monetary and foreign trade law in many countries has become dependent upon their continued membership in GATT and the IMF.

Even though the purposes (Article I) and the institutional structure of the IMF (Article XII) have been essentially maintained since the 1940s, the regulatory and financial functions of the Fund have undergone basic changes. The first amendment of the IMF Agreement, which took effect on 28 July 1969, created the Special Drawing Rights (SDR) as a supplement to existing reserve assets and entrusted the allocation of SDRs as a new function to the IMF. The second amendment, which entered into force on 1 April 1978, thoroughly revised the IMF Agreement following the breakdown of the par value system and modified a considerable number of Articles, such as those dealing with exchange arrangements, SDRs and gold, and the financial operations of the Fund. In addition to these formal amendments, the Fund has used numerous other techniques for adapting its legal norms to changing circumstances, such as its powers to "adopt such rules and regulations as may be necessary or appropriate to conduct the business of the Fund" (Article XII:2,g), or the powers to take decisions, make recommendations or issue guidelines in connection with its regulatory, supervisory, and financial activities.[80] The explicit recognition in the IMF Agreement that "the Fund shall be guided in all its policies and decisions by the purposes set forth in this Article" (Article I), and that the powers of the Fund must be exercised in a manner according with "the international monetary system" (see Articles IV:2,c VIII:7, XXII), have increased the disposition to find legal solutions under the Articles also for newly arising monetary problems and to construe the IMF Agreement from a teleological perspective as a comprehensive legal system.[81] As a result, the Fund's jurisdiction is seen as being coextensive with the "international monetary system", and "the range of matters that is accepted as

80 See: J. Gold (note 41), pp. 17-26.

81 On the "international monetary system" as a legal concept see: J. Gold, Developments in the International Monetary System, the IMF and International Monetary Law since 1971, in: J. Gold, Vol. II (note 40), pp. 17, 22 ff.

bearing on the balance of payments, and therefore properly of concern to the Fund, has increased steadily, with the result that the distinction between international and domestic policies, with the exclusion of the Fund from the consideration of domestic policies, has now disappeared to a large extent".[82]

The legal evolution of the World Bank and the considerable expansion of its financial and other developmental activities (e.g. the financing of "structural adjustment programs" of developing countries with balance-of-payments problems in addition to the traditional project lending) are likewise illustrative of an impressive capacity to deal with new challenges. The IBRD Agreement was amended only once, in 1965, to permit the Bank to lend to the IFC (Article III:6). The comprehensive regulatory powers of the Board of Governors, inter alia to increase the capital stock of the Bank and to "adopt such rules and regulations as may be necessary or appropriate to conduct the business of the Bank" (Article V:2,b), provided the legal basis for numerous other adjustments of the law of the Bank in response to changing circumstances. But the most important legal and institutional adaptations to changing needs were achieved through separate multilateral agreements initiated by the World Bank and leading to the establishment of the IFC in 1956, the IDA in 1960, ICSID in 1966, and the MIGA in 1987.[83] This legal technique of concluding supplementary side-agreements among interested member states dealing with specific problem matters, successfully practised also in the context of the GATT Tokyo Round, had the advantage of avoiding a formal amendment of the IBRD Agreement and of leaving it to each individual IBRD member state to decide whether it wants to participate in the additional agreements. Membership in IFC and IDA is open only to member countries of the IBRD, and the institutional structures and procedures of the three legally distinct organizations are closely interrelated. For instance, while the IFC has its own staff, the IDA and the IBRD are managed by the same staff and apply the same project criteria.

The General Agreement was originally conceived as an interim-agreement incorporating the results of the tariff liberalizations negotiated in 1947 at Geneva. The intention was to suspend Part II of the General Agreement on the entry into force of the Havana Charter (see Article XXIX of GATT), and to bring the remaining parts of the General Agreement definitively into force as a complement of the Havana Charter. In spite of the non-ratification of the Havana

---

82 J. Gold, Vol. II (note 40), p. 449.

83 For details see: H.G. Petersmann (note 64), pp. 244 ff.

Charter, the General Agreement was never put into force (see Article XXVI) and continues to be applied "provisionally" through the 1947 GATT Protocol on Provisional Application as well as subsequent Protocols of Accession. Yet, both the qualification of the application of the General Agreement as "provisional" and the "grandfather clause", according to which Part II of the General Agreement is to be applied only "to the fullest extent not inconsistent with existing legislation", appear to have lost almost all legal significance.[84] Since the inclusion of GATT Article XXVIII **bis** in 1955, which provides for regular tariff negotiations directed to the substantial reduction of trade barriers in the context of GATT, the General Agreement has gradually evolved from a short-term reciprocal tariff agreement into a worldwide multilateral framework agreement of unlimited duration covering, in principle, all tariff and non-tariff trade barriers.

As a consequence of its drafting history, the General Agreement does not include provisions on the establishment of an international trade organization or of organs other than the CONTRACTING PARTIES acting jointly (Article XXV:1).[85] Since it became clear in 1950 that the Havana Charter would not be ratified and there would be no International Trade Organization established under it, the GATT CONTRACTING PARTIES acting jointly have gradually endowed the General Agreement with all organs typical of an international organization: the CONTRACTING PARTIES as the plenary and highest body with comprehensive regulatory, administrative, deliberative and quasi-judicial competences; the Council of Representatives as the executive organ acting on behalf of the CONTRACTING PARTIES between their regular annual sessions; the GATT Committee on Trade and Development; the GATT Consultative Group of 18; a large number of other standing GATT Committees (e.g. on balance-of-payments restrictions, subsidies, antidumping, tariff concessions, customs valuation, import licensing, technical barriers to trade, government procurement); numerous temporary working parties and panels of dispute settlement; and the GATT Secretariat, headed by the GATT Director-General. The decisions establishing these GATT institutions were regularly based upon Article XXV:1, under which the GATT CONTRACTING PARTIES have the general power to take joint action not only "for the purpose of giving effect to those provisions of this Agreement which involve joint action", but also "generally with a

---

84 For details see: E.U. Petersmann, The EEC as a GATT Member, in: Hilf/Jacobs/Petersmann (note 17), p. 26 f.

85 See Article XXV:1, second sentence: "Wherever reference is made in this Agreement to the contracting parties acting jointly, they are designated as the CONTRACTING PARTIES."

view to facilitating the operation and furthering the objectives of this Agreement". Even though decisions of the CONTRACTING PARTIES can be taken by a majority of the votes cast, except as otherwise provided for in this Agreement (see Article XXV:4), decisions and other resolutions of all GATT bodies are regularly adopted on the basis of consensus. The pragmatic establishment of all institutions necessary for the effective operation of the General Agreement and for the furthering of its objectives has gradually transformed the General Agreement into the central worldwide trade institution possessing all essential characteristics of an international organization.

The competences conferred upon the CONTRACTING PARTIES in Article XXV, as well as in numerous more specific GATT provisions (e.g. Articles XII:4, XVI:5, XIX:3, XXIII:2, XXIV:7), are very broad. The scope of competences is sometimes (e.g. in Articles XXV:1, XXXVIII:1) explicitly related to the objectives of the General Agreement which, in turn, are drafted in very broad terms encompassing "relations in the field of trade and economic endeavour" and "the substanial reduction of tariffs and other barriers to trade and the elimination of discriminatory treatment in international commerce" (GATT preamble). Moreover, Article XXIX:1 of GATT commits the contracting parties to observe the general economic policy principles of the Havana Charter which refer also to matters such as fair labour standards (Article 7), foreign investments (Article 11), restrictive business practices (Articles 46 ff) and trade in services (Article 53). Articles XXXVI, XXXVIII:1 require the contracting parties to collaborate jointly to further the trade and economic development of less-developed countries. The GATT CONTRACTING PARTIES have actually used their competences not only for the administration of the existing GATT framework of rights and obligations and for the conclusion of international agreements between GATT and other states (e.g. Switzerland) and other international organizations (e.g. the IMF). But they have also used GATT as a forum for debates and negotiations on matters other than trade liberalization, such as the recommendation of principles for foreign investments, disposal of surplus products and of strategic stocks, or freedom of contract in transport insurance.[86] Numerous additional agreements on trade and related matters (e.g. subsidies, government procurement) have been negotiated in the context of GATT.[87] In 1964, the GATT CONTRACTING PARTIES established an "In-

86 See the detailed references to this GATT practice in: E.U. Petersmann (note 12), under Article XXV. See further: F. Roessler, The Competence of GATT, in: Journal of World Trade Law 1987, pp. 73 ff.

87 The various agreements are listed in: Status of Legal Instruments, GATT, 1983.

ternational Trade Center" charged with assisting developing countries in promoting their exports; in 1967, the GATT CONTRACTING PARTIES and the United Nations agreed to transform the International Trade Center into a "joint subsidiary organ".[88]

In a 1979 GATT Decision on "Action By the CONTRACTING PARTIES On The Multilateral Trade Negotiations", the CONTRACTING PARTIES reaffirmed "their intention to ensure the unity and consistency of the GATT system, and to this end they shall oversee the operation of the system as a whole and take action as appropriate".[89] The decision reflects the evolution of GATT law into a comprehensive "GATT-MTN-system".[90] At the same time, the CONTRACTING PARTIES adopted by means of consensus various additional decisions negotiated during the GATT Tokyo Round, which amounted to an informal amendment of Articles I, XII and XVIII sections A, B and C GATT.[91] Given the practical difficulties of ensuring the requirements of formal GATT amendments pursuant to Article XXX, not only side-agreements among a limited number of interested GATT contracting parties but also carefully negotiated and generally agreed GATT decisions may therefore substitute for formal amendments in the text of the General Agreement. The GATT most-favoured-nation obligations require that also trade benefits provided under collateral agreements among a limited number of interested contracting parties must be extended to all other GATT parties.[92]

B) The Bretton Woods Agreements as Institutional Framework for Multilateral Supervision, Negotiations and Dispute Settlement

An important regulatory function of the Bretton Woods Agreements is to provide an international forum for a continuous process of multilateral supervision

---

88 See: G.M. Engblom, International Trade Centre UNCTAD/GATT, in: R. Bernhardt (ed.), Encyclopedia of Public International Law, Instalment 5 (1983), pp. 183 ff.

89 Text in: BISD 26th Supplement, GATT 1980, p. 201.

90 See J.H. Jackson, The Birth of the GATT-MTN System: A Constitutional Appraisal, Law and Policy in International Business 1980, pp. 21 ff.

91 Texts in: BISD 26th Supplement, GATT 1980, pp. 203-210.

92 In November 1968, the GATT Director-General gave a ruling, in response to a request from the Antidumping Committee, that the parties to the GATT Antidumping Agreement have a legal obligation under GATT Article I to apply the benefits granted under the Antidumping Agreement in their trade with all GATT contracting parties, see doc. L/3149.

of national economic policies, for multilateral negotiations and for expeditious settlement of questions of interpretation as well as of international disputes.

The implementing rules adopted by the IMF require the Managing Director to report to the Executive Board any case in which it appears to him that a member state is not fulfilling obligations under the IMF Agreement.[93] Members of the Board of Governors and of the Executive Board may place any matter, including complaints and disputes, on the agenda for any meeting of their respective organs. Apart from the period of floating exchange rates between the breakdown of the par value system after 15 August 1971 and the entry into force of the second amendment of the IMF Agreement on 1 April 1978, specific breaches of IMF obligations by individual members have been rare.[94] Member states have made only few formal complaints to the IMF against another member state. The Fund has made sparing use of the various financial and other remedies (e.g. "representations" to a member, publication of a report made to a country, denial of benefits, suspension of rights) which the Fund is authorized to apply in response to breaches of obligations or to other undesirable conduct by a member state. In order to meet its obligation to exercise firm surveillance over the exchange rate policies of members (see Article IV:3,b), the Fund has adopted principles and procedures for exercising surveillance and conducts regular consultations with members. The stand-by arrangements and performance criteria for the use of the Fund's financial resources also offer many possibilities of protecting the Fund's resources and of exercising surveillance without need for adverse publicity and censorious formal sanctions. The violation of an obligation by one member state does not entitle other member states to resort to self-help by disregarding their obligations vis-à-vis the violator.

The infrequency of formal complaints, disputes and "sanctions" in IMF practice are indicative of the "constitutional function" of IMF rules to commit governments to the use of transparent, non-discriminatory and economically efficient exchange, monetary and economic policies in their own national self-interest. The devaluation of a national currency, austerity measures in order to reduce national payments imbalances and inflation, and the resultant domestic price increases are often resented by the general public and are viewed as a sign of political failure. National stabilization programs are therefore often stymied by domestic political forces. In such a situation, the international IMF obligations

93 By-Laws, Rules and Regulations, 36th Issue, IMF 1979, pp. 44, 62 (rules K-1, S-1).

94 J. Gold (note 40), p. 26.

can legally, politically and economically strengthen governments in implementing market-conforming exchange rates and necessary monetary and fiscal restraints. They can act as a legal constraint on the abuse of discretionary government powers for market-distorting policies benefiting special interests and "distributional coalitions" (M. Olson). The conditional financial assistance by the IMF can extend the politically painful domestic adjustment processes over a longer period of time and thereby promote the political feasibility of domestic stabilization policies. As Haggard has pointed out, the Fund can serve as an "external lobbyist" for welfare-increasing but politically unpopular policies and "might be equally useful as an enemy on which austerity can be blamed even as it is - albeit haltingly - pursued".[95]

What has been said of the institutional constraints, legal disciplines and financial assistance of the IMF, applies similarly to the World Bank Group. The central task of the World Bank Group consists in promoting the economic development of its borrowing countries. In order to depoliticize disputes, all loan and guarantee agreements of the World Bank provide for their submission, in case of controversies, to international arbitration to the exclusion of any other remedy. Decisions of the arbitration tribunal are to be by majority vote and are final and legally binding. Yet, the arbitration provisions in the World Bank's almost 3000 loan and guarantee agreements appear never to have been invoked.[96] And despite its policy of not rescheduling or renegotiating the financial terms of its loan and credit agreements, the World Bank has so far (1987) never incurred a financial loss on any of its loans and credits. Both the Bank and its borrowers share a common interest in the most productive use of the loans. The World Bank's affiliates IFC, ICSID and MIGA, on the one hand, and the host countries of foreign investments, on the other, also have a common interest in improving the investment climate in developing countries through the promotion of the rule of law and of the credit-standing of the capital-importing countries. Several hundred investment agreements include clauses submitting investment disputes to the jurisdiction of ICSID, which is considered advantageous to both host states (e.g. agreed exclusion of "diplomatic protection" by the investor's home state, judicial enforceability of pecuniary arbitral awards by the courts of ICSID member states) as well as to private investors (e.g. certainty of independent and speedy international arbitration, reduction of political invest-

95 S. Haggard, The Politics of Adjustment: Lessons from the IMF's Extended Fund Facility, in: International Organization 1985, pp. 505, 534.

96 H. Golsong, International Bank for Reconstruction and Development, in: R. Bernhardt (note 88), pp. 58, 63.

ment risks). Like ICSID, the World Bank's Convention establishing MIGA can also be seen as an international "anchoring" and legal definition of the national self-interest of countries in the pursuit of transparent, non-discriminatory and welfare-increasing investment policies in accordance with the rule of law.

The amendments of the General Agreement agreed upon at the 1955 Review Session of the GATT CONTRACTING PARTIES, including the addition of Article XXVIII **bis** on tariff negotiations and of Article XVI:B on the prohibition of export subsidies, reflected the transformation of the General Agreement from a reciprocal tariff agreement into a permanent multilateral framework of regular trade negotiations and multilateral dispute settlement. As tariffs have become successively liberalized during the various "GATT Rounds", the emphasis - especially in the GATT "Tokyo Round" (1973-1979) and in the 1986 Ministerial Declaration launching the GATT "Uruguay Round" - has shifted from the objective of further tariff liberalizations to the negotiation of additional legal disciplines for trade-distorting economic policies (e.g. subsidies, government procurement) and non-tariff barriers to trade in goods and services (e.g. insufficient protection of intellectual property rights).[97] In compliance with the 1979 GATT "Understanding Regarding Notification, Consultation, Dispute Settlement and Surveillance", the GATT Council began in 1980 to hold twice a year special meetings "to conduct a regular and systematic review of developments in the trading system" with "particular attention... to developments which affect rights and obligations under the GATT (and) matters affecting the interests of less-developed contracting parties".[98] Additional regular surveillance activities are carried out by various other GATT organs, including the Committee on Trade and Development, the Committee on Balance-of-Payments Restrictions, the Committees established under the various GATT Tokyo-Round Agreements, the Textiles Surveillance Body, and the Textiles Committee's Sub-Committee on Adjustment.[99] By increasing the accountability of governments for their trade policies and by requiring governments publicly to explain and defend their trade restrictions, international surveillance can promote transparent, non-discriminatory and welfare-increasing trade policy-making, especially if national

97 See, e.g.: Ministerial Declaration on the Uruguay Round, GATT Activities 1986, GATT 1987, pp. 15 ff.

98 Paragraph 24 of the Understanding, in: Texts (note 28), p. 204.

99 See: R. Blackhurst, Strengthening GATT Surveillance of Trade-Related Policies, in: E.U. Petersmann/M. Hilf (eds.), The New GATT Round of Multilateral Trade Negotiations, 1988, pp.123, 131 ff.

trade policy-makers "use" the international trade organizations as an "ally" for offsetting domestic protectionist pressures from special interest groups.[100]

Participation in the so far 8 "GATT Rounds", as well as in the trade agreements resulting from these multilateral trade negotiations, is voluntary. Yet, most GATT contracting parties consider it advantageous to participate actively in such multilateral trade negotiations. In the Tokyo Round, for instance, 77 of the then 84 GATT contracting parties, as well as 29 non-contracting parties, notified the GATT of their desire to participate in these trade negotiations. The publicity and political significance of worldwide comprehensive trade negotiations, and their enlarged scope for mutually advantageous bargains, make it politically easier for governments to take a comprehensive approach to their national trade policy and to resist sectoral protectionist pressures incompatible with the multilateral "standstill" and "rollback" commitments undertaken at the outset of GATT Rounds[101] as well as with the negotiating objective of a comprehensive "package deal".[102] The additional export opportunities made possible through multilateral trade negotiations act as an incentive for export industries actively to support reciprocal trade liberalization, and can help to offset the protectionist pressures from import-competing producers.

The General Agreement contains some 30 provisions obligating contracting parties to hold bilateral and multilateral consultations on restrictive trade measures in specific instances (e.g. Articles VI:7, XII:4, XVI:1, XIX:2, XXII, XXIII:1, XXVIII), or providing for other multilateral procedures that can be used for the settlement of disputes (e.g. Articles XII:4, XIX:3, XXIII:2, XXIV:7, 10, XXV:5, XXVIII:4). Between 1948 and 1990, more than 150 formal complaints were instituted under the central dispute settlement provision of Article XXIII GATT.[103] A large number of additional complaints were dealt with in consultations under Article XXII GATT.[104] Since 1980, some 20 formal complaints have

---

100 See: H. Hauser, International Trade Policy, in: Aussenwirtschaft 1986, pp. 395, 399; M. Henderson, The OECD as an instrument of national policy, in: International Journal 1981, pp. 793-814.

101 See Part I.C on "Standstill and Rollback" of the 1986 Ministerial Declaration (note 97), p. 5.

102 On the Uruguay Round of GATT see: E.U. Petersmann, The Mid-Term Review Agreements of the Uruguay Round, in: German Yearbook of International Law 32 (1989), pp. 280-322.

103 For chronological and country-lists of these disputes see the GATT Analytical Index (note 15) under Article XXIII.

104 For a survey see the GATT Analytical Index under Article XXII. Many of these consultations were not notified to the GATT.

been submitted under the dispute settlement provisions of the various MTN Agreements concluded at the end of the GATT Tokyo Round in 1979.[105] More than 90 per cent of the altogether more than 70 working party and panel reports under Article XXIII have been adopted and implemented. And even in the case of the four panel reports (relating to Spanish restrictions on soyabean oil, Canadian restrictions on the sale of gold coins, EEC production subsidies on canned fruit, and EEC tariff preferences for citrus products) not adopted under Article XXIII, the complaining party withdrew its complaint or agreed on a settlement of the dispute.

GATT practice confirms that international trade conflicts in GATT are often only a reflection of prior domestic conflicts in national policy formation between the trade policy commitments under GATT and domestic pressures for protectionist rule-departures for the benefit of special interests. Thus, "tacit collusion" among the disputing governments can rather often be seen in GATT dispute settlement decisions leading to the confirmation of legal interpretations that were espoused by the "losing" government itself in the national policy deliberations prior to the dispute; the "losing" government then gladly avails itself of the GATT dispute settlement decision in order to resist domestic protectionist pressures. And there are also instances showing that GATT dispute settlement procedures can occur more rapidly than domestic judicial proceedings on the very same issue. In the 1977 case "suspension of customs liquidation by the United States",[106] for instance, the GATT working party, established at the request of Japan, confirmed within only three weeks the legal interpretation shared also by the US government that a prior decision by the US Customs Court was inconsistent with Article VI:4 of GATT; this GATT ruling successfully assisted the appeal lodged by the US government itself to the US Court of Customs and Patent Appeals, which then repealed the lower court decision in compliance with the GATT ruling.

More than 90 per cent of all complaints under GATT Article XXIII are "violation complaints", i.e. complaints in which the applicant country asserts "the failure of another contracting party to carry out its obligations under this Agreement" (Article XXIII:1,a) and requests the withdrawal of the measures concerned. The "Agreed Description of the Customary Practice of the GATT in the Field of Dispute Settlement", adopted in 1979, confirms this right to specific

105 For a survey see the GATT Analytical Index under Article XXIII, section 34.

106 BISD 24th Suppl, GATT 1978, p. 134.

performance of GATT obligations by stating that "in the absence of a mutually agreed solution, the first objective of the CONTRACTING PARTIES is usually to secure the withdrawal of the measures concerned if these are found to be inconsistent with the General Agreement. The provision of compensation should be resorted to only if the immediate withdrawal of the measure is impracticable and as a temporary measure pending the withdrawal of the measures which are inconsistent with the General Agreement".[107] The terms of reference regularly request panels to examine the complaint "in the light of the relevant GATT provisions", and virtually all GATT panels focus on this legal examination of the compatibility of the disputed measures with GATT law. Most of the GATT dispute settlement decisions under Article XXIII have led to the withdrawal of those measures which were found to be inconsistent with GATT law, and have contributed to the "rule of law" in international trade. By promoting "rule-oriented" rather than "power-oriented" trade policies and dispute settlements, GATT law and its enforcement through the GATT dispute settlement procedures protect GATT contracting parties from protectionist pressures not only by foreign governments but also by domestic pressure groups. In spite of their lack of "political clout" (inter alia also due to their reduced GATT commitments and their political dependence on the voluntary Generalized System of Preferences), also small developing GATT contracting parties have successfully used Article XXIII in order to enforce their GATT rights and, for instance, to resist protectionist pressures placed upon them for the "voluntary" acceptance of export restraints.[108]

Following the precedent set by numerous bilateral trade agreements concluded before World War II, GATT Article XXIII admits also "non-violation complaints", i.e. complaints whenever "any contracting party should consider that any benefit accruing to it directly or indirectly under this Agreement is being nullified or impaired or that the attainment of any objective of the Agreement is being impeded as the result of ... (b) the application by another contracting party of any measure, whether or not it conflicts with the provisions of this Agreement, or (c) the existence of any other situation" (Article XXIII:1, b, c). The drafting history indicates that these "non-violation complaints" were mainly designed to protect the mutual balance of advantages resulting from the reci-

107 BISD 26th Suppl, GATT 1980, p. 216.

108 See, for instance, the successful complaints in 1978 by Hong Kong against Norway (BISD 27S/119) or in 1979 by Chile against the EEC (BISD 27S/98) against discriminatory import restrictions imposed after the refusal by these developing countries to accept "voluntary export restraints".

procal trade negotiations and from the "schedules of concessions" (Article II) not only against trade restrictions specifically prohibited in the substantive GATT provisions, but also against other kinds of "nullification or impairment". GATT contracting parties were considered to be entitled not only to the observance by other contracting parties of the express legal GATT obligations, but also to a larger kind of balance of rights and obligations and commercial opportunities deriving therefrom.

The GATT CONTRACTING PARTIES have only cautiously used this "common law jurisdiction" on a case-by-case basis in order to prevent the circumvention of tariff concessions through governmental measures not prohibited by the General Agreement and, thereby, to preserve the balance of the original exchange of concessions. Apart from the right to the observance and specific performance of GATT provisions, including the right to compensation in case of direct withdrawal of tariff concessions (Article XXVIII), the only other "benefit accruing under this Agreement" in terms of Article XXIII:1, recognized so far by the CONTRACTING PARTIES, has been the "reasonable expectation" (bona fide) that the competitive advantages deriving from tariff concessions under Article II of GATT will also not be nullified or impaired by the concession-granting country in an indirect way through the subsequent introduction of a governmental measure, not inconsistent with the General Agreement, which upsets the competitive relationship between the bound "concession product" and directly competitive products from other origins and which could not be reasonably anticipated by the complaining party at the time of the tariff negotiations.[109] A case in point is a 1985 panel report on a complaint by the United States, which found that the unforeseeable introduction of EEC production aids for certain canned fruit had nullified or impaired benefits accruing to the US from prior tariff concessions granted by the EEC on these products under Article II.[110] There are important procedural and substantive differences between "violation complaints" and "non-violation complaints": A violation of a GATT rule is presumed to have adverse competitive effects on other contracting parties ("prima facie nullification or impairment") and entails a legal obligation to withdraw the illegal measure. By contrast, a "non-violation complaint" implies a more far-reaching burden of proof on the part of the complaining party (e.g. demonstration of "reasonable expectations" and subsequent "upsetting of com-

109 For a survey of the GATT practice relating to "non-violation complaints" since the Chilean complaint in 1950 against certain Australian subsidies, see the GATT Analytical Index (note 15) under Article XXIII.

110 See GATT document L/5778.

petition"). And the CONTRACTING PARTIES may only recommend, but not prescribe in a legally binding manner, the withdrawal of the distorting but lawful measure; if the recommendation to remove the competitive distortion is not followed, they may only authorize the adversely affected contracting party to suspend the application of equivalent GATT obligations or concessions towards the country that has impaired the tariff concessions.

5. The "Constitutional Dilemma" of Liberal International Trade Rules

A) Liberal International Trade Rules as a Self-imposed "Constitutional Restraint" on the Government Powers to Restrict Individual Freedoms of Trade

Chapter VII has attempted to show that, for a number of reasons, liberal international trade rules can serve "constitutional functions" for the interpretation and application of the domestic foreign trade laws of GATT contracting parties:

(a) The legal GATT obligations for the use of transparent, rule-oriented, non-discriminatory and proportionate instruments of taxation and economic regulation, for "due process" and judicial protection of individual rights not only correspond to basic constitutional principles of liberal democracies. But they give precision to and extend these liberal principles in the trade policy area and are often much more comprehensive than the autonomously adopted foreign trade regulations of GATT member countries and of the EEC (see below chapter IX.3.D).

(b) The interpretation and application of domestic foreign trade regulations in compliance with the self-imposed international GATT obligations would considerably enlarge the individual rights of domestic importers, exporters, producers and consumers. Observance of the GATT principle of transparent policy-making would increase the scope for democratic participation in trade policy decision-making processes and for judicial protection of individual rights. Observance of the GATT requirements for rule-oriented trade policies would considerably increase the predictability and legal certainty of international trade transactions and reduce international transaction costs. Respect for the GATT guarantees of non-discriminatory market access enlarges the individual freedom of choice and real income of domestic consumers and enables domestic traders and producers to buy and sell goods in the best foreign markets. The GATT requirements for the use of market-conforming, less-distortive trade policy instruments promote undistorted competition and non-discriminatory treatment and render the abuse of private and public economic power (e.g. domestic cartelization) more difficult. The admission by the European Court of Justice of direct actions (pursuant to Article 173 paragraph 2 of the EEC Treaty) by exporters, related importers and domestic producers participating in antidumping and countervailing duty proceedings[111] illustrates also that the incorporation of the detailed GATT guarantees of "due process" and individual procedural rights (e.g. to be heard) into domestic antidumping, countervailing and other foreign trade regulations have enabled domestic courts considerably to extend the judicial protection of individual rights against executive misuses of trade policy powers or manifest errors of appraisal.

(c) The mutually agreed GATT obligations can serve "constitutional functions" not only in respect of the individual rights of those engaged in international trade but also in respect of the objective principles of liberal constitutions. They legally define the national "public interest" in a liberal and rule-oriented use of the various trade policy instruments and legally limit the discretionary trade policy powers of governments accordingly. They promote a democratic "government by discussion" and enlarge the scope for parliamentary and judicial review of executive trade policies. The GATT prohibitions of mutually harmful trade policy instruments tend to depoliticize international trade relations and to protect governments from power-oriented trade policies of foreign governments. The GATT obligations for the use of market-conforming trade policy instruments (i.e. non-discriminatory tariffs) further promote and protect the international price mechanism, on the proper functioning of which the modern integrated "open economies" strongly

111 See notably the 1979 Ballbearings cases 113/77 (ECR 1979, 1185) and 118-121/77 (ECR 1979, 1277, 1303, 1337), the 1981 Alusuisse case (ECR 1981, 3463), the first Allied case of February 1984 (joined cases 239 and 275/82, ECR 1984, 1005) and the Timex case of March 1985 ECR 1987 1923-1974 relating to antidumping procedures. As regards countervailing duty proceedings, see the Fediol case 191/82 (ECR 1983, 2913). For a discussion of these cases see below chapter IX.4.E.

depend.[112] By requiring domestic producers to adjust to import compe-tititon, they promote and depoliticize also domestic competition and specify the legal admissibility and conditions of the use of import restrictions for purposes of income redistribution among domestic groups. The liberal international GATT obligations can thereby serve as a counterweight to the various asymmetries in the domestic political representation of the liberal trading interests of consumers and the protectionist self-interests of import-competing producers.

B) Not All International Rules Serve Constitutional Functions

The "constitutional function" of liberal international trade rules derives from the fact that they enlarge and protect individual rights, limit the abuse of discretionary government powers and provide for the reciprocal application of constitutional principles of liberal democracies in the trade policy area in a mutually agreed manner. Many international rules do not share this liberal and long-term constitutional function, for instance bilateral or sectoral short-term arrangements (e.g. for textiles and steel) restricting individual freedoms of trade, allowing arbitrary trade discrimination and trade distortions, or implementing non-transparent "grey area trade restrictions" designed to circumvent the multilateral GATT legal disciplines and to escape domestic parliamentary and judicial review.

Hence, there is a need for distinguishing in the "constitutional analysis" long-term, non-discriminatory international rules aimed at "market integration" from short-term, discriminatory rules aimed at "market organization" (see above chapter II.3). Liberal international trade, monetary and investment rules serve as a substitute for domestic constitutional rules by restraining government powers to tax and restrict transnational economic transactions in a discriminatory and welfare-reducting manner. International market integration intensifies domestic competition and, thereby, reduces the need for government interventions in the domestic economy. Liberal international economic rules admit decentralized decision-making by governments and private economic agents and use "policy competition" among governments as a discovery procedure, thereby

112 For a detailed explanation of this point see: J. Tumlir, GATT Rules and Community Law, in: Hilf/Jacobs/Petersmann (note 17), pp. 1 ff.

"promoting multiple search and experimentation, encapsulating errors, and thus safeguarding the possibility of nations learning from each other".[113]

C) Inadequate Constitutional "Checks and Balances" at the International Level: The Risk of Intergovernmental Collusion

Democratic constitutionalism proceeds from the historical experience that government powers are likely to be abused unless their exercise is legally constrained by long-term constitutional rules for the separation and only limited delegation of government powers. The historical record of past and present trade mercantilism clearly confirms this assumption that trade politicians have hardly ever exercised discretionary trade policy powers in a manner maximizing national economic welfare. Like Adam Smith's discovery that a spontaneous and efficient market order at the **national** level depends on an appropriate structure of "laws and institutions", a liberal international trade order and undistorted international competition cannot be achieved without appropriate **international** legal and institutional restraints. A major conclusion of the analysis in Part II of the "new protectionism" was, however, that there are neither at the international nor at the domestic level sufficient constitutional "checks and balances" effectively limiting the discretionary trade policy powers to the use of transparent, non-discriminatory and welfare-increasing trade policy instruments. An ever increasing number of VERs, VRAs and OMAs have been negotiated among government executives (including the EC Commission) at the international level restricting individual freedoms and property rights without effective parliamentary and judicial review.

Just as the theory of public choice has demonstrated that national democratic processes do not sufficiently constrain governments to implementing the "national public interests", also international rules, procedures and institutions can be abused by politicians to pursue special interests at the expense of national welfare. The conversion of the numerous "grey area restrictions" and VERs, often bilaterally negotiated and agreed in secrecy without transparent procedures and without public discussions, into lawful import tariffs pursuant to GATT Article XIX would frequently require tariff rates of several hundred percent, which would be unlikely to find a political majority in national parliaments. The circumvention of the multilateral GATT obligations for the public choice of trans-

113 J. Tumlir, International Economic Order: Rules, Cooperation and Sovereignty, in: P. Oppenheimer (ed.), Issues in International Economics, 1980, pp. 1, 12.

parent, non-discriminatory and least-distortive trade policy instruments through bilateral international arrangements can be viewed as collusion among executives at the expense of national welfare, serving to hide the costs of concessions to domestic pressure groups. Adam Smith's observation - that "people of the same trade seldom meet together, even for merriment and diversion, but the conversation ends in a conspiracy against the public, or in some contrivance to raise prices"[114] - appears to be applicable also to many other instances of international short-term policy coordination among governments. One author has concluded that:

> "International organization can be and is abused, and the cause is not an occasional lack of virtue among politicians but a systematic built-in tendency toward collusion at the expense of the citizens. Such collusion is not only undesirable in itself. There is also the danger that it discredits and crowds out unambiguously desirable forms of international cooperation: agreements to remove non-market obstacles to market interdependence in the field of international trade and capital movements."[115]

There are many reasons why discretionary "policy coordination" at the international level tends to increase the political weight of the executive branches of governments at the expense of democratic control. For instance, participation in international meetings, mutual approval of each other's policies at such meetings, or internationally agreed "reasonable departures" from the general international rules enable the participating policy-makers to increase their prestige, to shirk domestic responsibility for unpopular measures, to "sell" such policies as part of an international agreement, to protect themselves against superior performance of foreign governments, and to stifle political criticism at home.[116] The sheer distance of international agencies abroad, the frequent confidentiality of international negotiations, language barriers and other information barriers are further impediments to effective democratic control of current international policy processes.[117] Additional "constitutional problems" arise whenever international organizations (e.g. the EEC) are used for the implementation of redistributive policies without democratic legitimation (e.g. the EC's support for "cri-

---

114 A. Smith, The Wealth of Nations, 1776 (1976), p. 144.

115 See R. Vaubel, A public choice approach to international organization, in: Public Choice, 1986, pp. 39, 53.

116 See R. Vaubel (note 115), p. 44 f.

117 See K. Kaiser, Transnational relations as a threat to the democratic process, in: International Organization 1971, pp. 706-720.

sis cartels", subsidies, minimum prices, production quotas, trade restrictions, and agricultural excess production). Hence, as Hayek emphasized already in 1944:

> "What we need and can hope to achieve is not more power in the hands of irresponsible international economic authorities, but, on the contrary, a superior political power which can hold the economic interests in check, and in the conflict between them can truly hold the scales, because it is itself not mixed up in the economic game"... "The powers which must devolve on an international authority are not the new powers assumed by the states in recent times, but that minimum of powers without which it is impossible to preserve peaceful relationships, i.e. essentially the powers of the ultra-liberal 'laissez-faire' state. And even more than in the national sphere, it is essential that these powers of the international authority should be strictly circumscribed by the Rule of Law"... "This division of power would inevitably act at the same time also as a limitation of the power of the whole as well as of the individual state"... "It is, in fact, one of the main advantages of federation that it can be so devised as to make most of the harmful planning difficult while leaving the way free for all desirable planning. It prevents, or can be made to prevent, most forms of restrictionism"... "An international authority which effectively limits the powers of the state over the individual will be one of the best safeguards of peace. The international Rule of Law must become a safeguard as much against the tyranny of the state over the individual as against the tyranny of the new super-state over the national communities".[118]

D) Inadequate "Domestic Law Effects" of International Obligations

General international law and most international treaties leave it to each individual state concerned to decide autonomously on the validity, rank and direct applicability of international rules within the domestic legal system. International trade agreements are usually addressed to "states" or "contracting parties" and set out rules for the conduct of governments or obligations requiring the achievement of a specified result. The international rules assert supremacy over municipal law in the sense that, at the level of international law, "a party may not invoke the provisions of its internal law as justification for its failure to perform a treaty" (see Article 27 of the 1969 Vienna Convention on the Law of Treaties) or another obligation of public international law. But, even though the purpose of international trade agreements frequently is to coordinate or unify domestic trade regulation and to specify and protect the rights of those engaged in international trade, the international trade agreements usually leave it to each contracting party to decide on how to "ensure... the conformity of its laws, regulations and administrative procedures with the provisions of this Agree-

118 F.A. v.Hayek, The Road to Serfdom, 1944, pp. 172, 173, 175.

ment".[119] There are hardly any international trade agreements explicitly requiring the **direct** applicability of precise and unconditional international legal obligations by domestic citizens and domestic courts.

Non-compliance by legislative, administrative or judicial organs with international obligations entails the international responsibility of the state or of the "contracting party" concerned. GATT law explicitly spells out that the GATT obligations of each contracting party must be observed also by the "regional and local governments and authorities within its territory" (Article XXIV:12) as well as by "state enterprises" (Article XVII) and "restrictions made effective through state-trading operations" (see the interpretative note to Articles XI, XII, XIII, XIV and XVIII). The subdivision of powers and duties within the state is usually without importance for the international responsibility of the state as a whole arising from non-compliance with international obligations, unless the international agreement includes rules to the contrary (for instance in the "federal state clause" in GATT Article XXIV:12). But the breach of international obligations as such does not entail an automatic abrogation of the internal rules in conflict with the international obligations. Even precise and unconditional international obligations, which leave no discretion for their domestic implementation, can become "self-executing" and "directly applicable" by individuals at the municipal level only insofar as they become part of the municipal law system and their direct applicability by domestic authorities and individuals is recognized by the respective domestic legal system.

The "domestic law effects" of international legal rules within the legal order of a state always depend on a rule of domestic law. In "dualist" legal systems, the international rules must be transformed into municipal ones in order to become applicable to the legal relations of the citizens with each other and with their national government. This act of transformation can be organized once and forever by the municipal law system (e.g. by a constitutional provision whereby rules of general international law binding on the state are automatically transformed into municipal rules). Or the act of transformation of the international into a municipal rule can take place on an **ad hoc** basis (e.g. transformation of international treaty rules through an act of parliament). If, as in most Commonwealth countries, the international GATT obligations were never transformed nor incorporated as such into municipal law, the international obligations cannot provide a direct cause of action. While domestic statutes in the same

119 Standard formula used in the final clauses of the various 1979 Tokyo Round Agreements, see: The Texts of the Tokyo Round Agreements, GATT 1986, pp. 47, 75, 97, 144.

subject area might be construed by domestic courts with reference to international treaty obligations, national legislation will prevail over the international obligations in case of inconsistency between the two.

The "monist" assertion of the supremacy of international law even within the municipal sphere is often coupled with the argument that both international and domestic law are ultimately concerned with the conduct and welfare of individuals. Just as, from a democratic perspective, people establish governments with limited powers in order to protect and promote their equal individual rights and welfare, the international law rules for the peaceful coexistence and cooperation of sovereign states, if validly accepted by the government concerned, can be viewed as a self-imposed restraint voluntarily agreed as a condition of the proper functioning of the municipal legal systems. Since World Wars I and II, a large number of national constitutions explicitly stipulate that the generally recognized rules of international law are a valid part of the domestic legal system[120] and that international legal obligations may create individual rights to be protected by domestic courts.[121] Also international law itself includes an ever increasing number of rules providing for individual rights not only of foreigners but of all citizens within the jurisdiction of the contracting parties, and granting individuals access to international tribunals or other international instances.

Yet, even though states are no longer perceived as the sole subjects of international rules and international obligations are recognized as binding constituent parts of the domestic legal systems of many states, in most states the rule continues to obtain that international treaty obligations can be validly overriden in municipal law by subsequent national legislation.[122] Moreover, in a number of countries (such as France and the United Kingdom) the courts follow the executive in matters of interpretation of international treaties and exercise judicial

---

120 See, for instance, Article 4 of the German Constitution of 1919, Article 25 of the German Basic Law of 1949, Article 10 of the Italian Constitution of 1947, Article 8 of the Austrian Constitution of 1920, Article 9 of the Spanish Constitution of 1931, Article 55 of the French Constitution of 1958.

121 See, for instance, Articles 25 and 100 II of the German Basic Law of 1949, and for a survey: I. Brownlie, Principles of Public International Law, 3rd edition, 1979, p. 53.

122 This seems to be true also in states like Italy, where the international GATT obligations were directly applied by domestic courts because the implementing legislative act was considered a **lex specialis** overriding **leges generales**, whether prior or posterior, unless the Parliament expressly declares that it wants to derogate the international obligation, See: C. Mastellone, Comment on Cases Nos. 266 and 267-269/81 of the European Court of Justice, in: Common Market Law Review 1983, pp. 559, 570.

self-restraint vis-à-vis political "acts of state" ("actes de gouvernment").[123] Especially in the field of GATT law, individuals often lack effective means to enforce the liberal international trade rules if the governments are unwilling to comply with them. The foreign trade policy of most states continues to be shaped by the governmental assertion of a "sovereign power" to tax and restrict the foreign trade transactions of domestic citizens also in a manner inconsistent with international treaty obligations.

123 See: E.U. Petersmann, Act of State Doctrine, Political Question Doctrine and Judicial Control of Foreign Affairs Powers, in: Jahrbuch des Oeffentlichen Rechts 1976, pp. 587-620 (in German).

FOURTH PART: POSSIBILITIES OF "CONSTITUTIONALIZING" FOREIGN TRADE POLICY AND FOREIGN TRADE LAW IN CONSTITUTIONAL DEMOCRACIES

"The effective limitation of power is the most important problem of social order... To limit this power was the great aim of the founders of constitutional government in the seventeenth and eighteenth centuries. But the endeavour to contain the powers of government was almost inadvertently abandoned when it came to be mistakenly believed that democratic control of the exercise of power provided a sufficient safeguard against its excessive growth. We have since learnt that the very omnipotence conferred on democratic representative assemblies exposes them to irresistible pressure to use their power for the benefit of special interests, a pressure a majority with unlimited powers cannot resist if it is to remain a majority. This development can be prevented only by depriving the governing majority of the power to grant discriminatory benefits to groups or individuals".

F.A. von Hayek[1]

"A constitution is not intended to embody a particular economic theory, whether of paternalism and the organic relation of the citizen to the state or of "laissez faire". It is made for people of fundamentally differing views."

Justice Oliver Holmes[2]

Part I of this study showed that voluntary trade transactions take place only because there exist mutual gains from trade as a result of possible exchanges of goods and services. The mutually beneficial international division of labour emerged in a decentralized manner as a legally stratified "spontaneous order". It was further shown that the economic, legal and policial reasons for liberal trade

1 F.A. v.Hayek, The Political Order of a Free People, 1979, p. 128.

2 From the dissenting opinion of Justice O. Holmes in the US Supreme Court decision in Lochner v. New York, 198 US 45 (1905).

and rule of law are even more valid **among** sovereign nations than they are **within** nations.

Part II explained why - just as markets are rarely perfect and require general legal rules and government interventions in order to achieve "efficient" outcomes - also government policies are rarely perfect and can supply "public goods" (such as liberal trade and rule of law) only if the exercise of all government powers is restrained through long-term constitutional rules and institutional "checks and balances". The "new protectionism" was described as "government failure" not only on the economic ground that, as widely recognized today, "import protection is never the best form of intervention in principle".[3] But the public choice of non-transparent, discriminatory and disproportionately harmful trade policy **instruments**, and the apparent contrast between the declared policy objective of trade liberalization and the actual increase in non-tariff trade barriers imposed by OECD countries,[4] also appear to indicate that the discretionary trade policy powers are often no longer effectively limited by constitutional restraints. Governments feel free to tax and restrict the transnational trade transactions of their citizens. The dangers from majoritarianism (e.g. in the US Congress) and from the erosion of individual liberty in certain trade policy areas call for more appropriate constitutional arrangements. The "constitutional failure" seems due in particular to the inadequate legal regulation of the various asymmetries in the political organization and representation of the interests of producers, investors, traders and consumers as well as to the inadequate constitutional "checks and balances" on the exercise of foreign policy powers. A distinct legal expression of this "constitutional failure" was seen in the fact that both the national constitutional rules for the public choice of transparent, non-discriminatory and proportionate policy instruments as well the multilaterally accepted, reciprocal international GATT obligations for the public choice of transparent, non-discriminatory and proportionate trade policy instruments are increasingly

3 World Development Report 1987, World Bank 1987, p. 7, with an explanation of why other forms of government intervention (such as subsidies) can correct "market failures" more efficiently and with less social costs.

4 For a recent survey and analysis see again the World Development Report (note 3), pp. 10, 133 ff: "Since World War II, tariffs in industrial countries on most manufactures have fallen so far that they are no longer significant barriers to trade. But recent years have seen a resurgence of protection in the form of non-tariff barrirs. The proportion of North American and European Community imports affected by various nontariff restrictions has risen by more than 20 percent from 1981 to 1986"..."Instead of tariffs, which are now very low, the main instrument of recent protection has been the nontariff barrier. It contravenes widely accepted principles of nondiscrimination and transparency in measures to restrict trade-principles which remain sound".

being disregarded by means of non-transparent, mutually harmful "grey area trade restrictions" without effective parliamentary review and without due process and judicial protection of individual rights.

Part III described how long-term international legal obligations for the use of transparent, non-discriminatory and proportionate policy instruments can serve "constitutional functions" by legally defining, giving precision to and extending the corresponding principles of national constitutional laws to the ever more important foreign trade sectors of national economies. It explained why general legal restraints on the government powers to tax and restrict transnational trade transactions are necessary for the equal protection of individual rights and national welfare and why they are more likely to be accepted by governments on a reciprocal, multilateral basis at the level of international law than unilaterally at the level of national law (see also below chapter IX.3.B). But it also pointed to the risk of "intergovernmental collusion" aimed at circumventing domestic constitutional principles, and referred to the various reasons for the often inadequate "domestic law effects" of the self-imposed international legal obligations within domestic legal systems.

Part IV inquires into the constitutional problem of how the mutually supplementary national and international liberal rules can be made more effective so that they can actually achieve their declared policy objectives and their important economic, political and legal regulatory functions for the modern integrated "open economies". This inquiry proceeds from the premise (described in Part I) that an international division of labour requires legal rules defining and protecting the ownership, use and transferability of the various factors of production, goods and services, and that the rules impinge on the efficient use of the resources, on the costs of doing business and of economic transactions enabling a welfare-increasing international division of labour. The historical evolution in a number of European countries of economic laws protecting private ownership and commercial freedoms from arbitrary government confiscation, taxation and regulation is instructive of the "constitutional nature" of the economic rules that characterize most of today's industrial market economies. The economic and political decentralization since the late Middle Ages prompted the towns and commercial interests to offer resistance to the medieval rulers and led to the creation of representative bodies which conceded additional taxes and government revenue in exchange for commercial freedoms and economic rights of merchants, towns and the landed gentry. In England, the private and commercial interests represented in the parliament finally achieved victory over the kings in the seventeenth century. From then on, economic freedoms and property rights became more secure, the division of labour and capital markets developed rapidly and, in the view of many economists,[5] the changed legal conditions (e.g. new forms of incorporation and limited liability of firms) and reduced transaction costs have helped the subsequent industrial revolution.

Chapter VIII starts at this point in time and begins with a brief discussion and refutation of the view, then prevailing even among the liberal founding fathers of the ideas of "democratic constitutionalism" during the seventeenth century (such as Locke and Montesquieu), that rule of law and democracy are incompatible with the particular requirements of foreign policy (VIII.1). It then examines successively the extent to which foreign affairs powers, notably trade policy powers, have been limited through national constitutional rules in the liberal eighteenth century constitution of the United States (VIII.2), in the liberal nineteenth century constitution of Switzerland (VIII.3), and in the liberal twentieth century constitution of the Federal Republic of Germany (VIII.4). The comparative analysis confirms that the respective national constitutions were meant to constitute limited government powers also in the field of foreign affairs. The international GATT and IMF rules rest on the same liberal principles which underlie American, Swiss and German constitutional law (VIII.5.A). Moreover, the self-imposed international GATT and IMF obligations constitute examples of "vertical separation of powers" and "functional federalism" because these international legal restraints on the national discretionary foreign economic policy powers are in several respects more precise and comprehensive than the corresponding principles of the autonomous national foreign trade and monetary laws (VIII.5.B). But the multilaterally agreed international trade, monetary and investment rules cannot remain effective over time unless they are placed into a "constitutional framework" subjecting the interpretation, application and observance of the international rules to a more effective system of "checks and balances" notably by domestic parliaments and courts (VIII.5.C).

Chapter IX concludes that the necessary "constitutionalization" of the discretionary trade policy powers of governments (including the EC executives) might be achieved best by incorporating liberal international trade rules into the domestic constitutional systems of trading countries. Even though international economic and legal integration do not require uniformization, there are clear limits to international private law as a technique for legal integration (IX.1).

5 See, for example, the World Development Report 1987 (note 3 above), p. 61f; D.C. North, Institutions, Economic Growth and Freedom: An Historical Introduction, 1986.

And there are also a number of important political and legal reasons why the necessary constitutional restraints on the discretionary trade policy powers are unlikely to be achieved unilaterally at the national level of domestic laws (IX.2). Yet, in the words of the economist W. Röpke, "a good order on the national level is required to assure a working order also on the international level".[6] Moreover, "it was the original purpose of the GATT - and of the broader concepts of multilateralism, or of international economic cooperation - to strengthen governments against the particularist pressures emanating from national economies".[7] The customs union law of the EEC was based on a strict implementation and observance of GATT Article XXIV by the legislative, executive and judicial bodies within the EEC and illustrates that a "constitutional approach" can achieve an effective implementation of the international GATT obligations in a manner extending the individual freedoms and other fundamental rights of European traders, producers and consumers accross national frontiers (IX.3). The "progressive constitutionalization" of German foreign trade law - from the international customs union treaty establishing the German Customs Union (1834 - 1866) up to the EEC Treaty and the international GATT obligations as an "integral part of the Community legal system" - offers another historical example of using liberal international trade rules for "constitutionalizing" domestic foreign trade laws (IX.4.B). GATT law has also served as an important instrument for the harmonization of the foreign trade law of the EEC (IX.4.C). The various "domestic law effects" of liberal international trade rules could be strengthened, inter alia, by more detailed international and domestic rules specifically regulating the participation of domestic parliaments, courts and individual citizens in the domestic application of liberal trade rules (IX.A, D, E, F). Since internationalism and liberalism must begin at home, liberal international trade rules should be incorporated into domestic legislation and protected by domestic courts for the benefit of the individual rights of domestic citizens.

6 W. Röpke, International Order and Economic Integration, 1959, p. 16.

7 International Trade 1982-83, GATT 1983, at p. 21; see also: W.B. Carmichael, National Interest and International Trade Negotiations, in: The World Economy 1986, pp. 341 ff.

VIII. FOREIGN AFFAIRS AND FOREIGN TRADE IN THE NATIONAL CONSTITUTIONS OF LIBERAL DEMOCRACIES: A COMPARATIVE LEGAL ANALYSIS OF THE CONSTITUTIONS OF THE UNITED STATES, SWITZERLAND AND GERMANY

1. Are Rule of Law and Democracy Incompatible with Foreign Policy?

A) Reasons Advanced in Support of the Incompatibility Hypothesis

The rule of law idea proceeds from the assumption that the equal rights of the citizens and the admissible objectives, scope and exercise of government powers should be legally defined through long-term general rules; government institutions should be entrusted with only limited discretionary powers and be mutually restrained through "checks and balances" so as to ensure the highest possible degree of adherence to the rules. Democratic politics should further be made with the participation of a broad variety of interests and in a transparent manner before a public sufficiently well-informed to draw the appropriate conclusions at the next election.

According to a long tradition of political arguments, described already by Thucydides and later defended by supporters not only of monarchical absolutism (e.g. Machiavelli, Bodin, Hobbes) but also of liberal democracies (e.g. Locke, Montesquieu, Tocqueville),[8] there is an inherent incompatibility between the requirements of foreign policy and the ideals of rule of law and democratic decision-making. In the words of Locke:

> "what is to be done in reference to foreigners, depending much upon their actions, and the variations of designs and interests, must be left in great part to the prudence of those who have this power committed to them, to be managed by the best of their skill, for the advantage of the Commonwealth".[9]

The main reasons advanced in support of the perception of foreign policy as "high policy", permanently confronted with exceptional situations which require

8 See: Ch.R. Beitz, Political Theory and International Relations, 1979, pp. 13 ff.

9 J. Locke, Two Treatises of Civil Government, 1690, Vol.II, Chpt, XII, quoted from P.G. Richards, Parliament and Foreign Affairs, 1967, p. 16.

conducting foreign policy in a non-democratic manner unconstrained by stringent legal requirements, are the following:

a) A first argument (e.g. by Locke) is that foreign policy decisions have to react to foreign events and often result from international bargaining processes, in which the national bargaining position may be weakened by openness and internal disunity and which may be conducted best in secrecy by "professionals" who know the adversary and know how to bargain. National parliaments have little influence on these international bargaining processes, and parliamentary debates "will normally involve only retrospective examination of the consequences of irrevocable decisions already implemented".[10] Hence, "the sovereign right of parliament to change such an agreement or to stop its implementation is, in fact, mainly theoretical because of the costs that such actions might entail".[11]

b) A second argument traditionally invoked in support of the incompatibility hypothesis is that foreign policy questions involve the nation's security and integrity and that these "supreme interests" are too important to be left to democratic politics which often tends to avoid unpleasant choices (e.g. military expenditures) and may lead to irrational foreign policy decisions.[12]

c) A third line of argument is that the implications of foreign policy questions for the individual citizen are often remote, indirect and obscure so that most people and also parliamentarians tend to give little attention to foreign policy issues and leave them to "the experts".

10 I. Brownlie, Parliamentary Control over Foreign Policy in the United Kingdom, in: A. Cassese (ed.), Parliamentary Control over Foreign Policy, 1980, p. 4.

11 K. Kaiser, Transnational Relations as a Threat to the Democratic Process, in: International Organization 1971, pp. 706, 713 f.

12 For a critical discussion of this argument see: K. Goldmann/S. Berglund/G. Sjösted, Democracy and Foreign Policy, 1986, pp. 2 f, 14 ff.

B) Foreign Policy as Domestic Policy: Why Rule of Law and Democracy are Necessary in the Trade Policy Area

After the outbreak of World War I, brought about by a diplomatic game of which most people had been unaware and leading to the slaughtering of millions of people, the British member of parliament A. Ponsonby wrote:

> "When a small number of statesmen, conducting the intercourse of nations in secrecy, have to confess their inability to preserve good relations, it is not an extravagant proposal to suggest that their isolated action should be supplemented and reinforced by the intelligent and well-informed assistance of the peoples themselves". Even though the people would not always be right, "if they are wrong, they will then suffer for their own folly and pay for their own mistakes, instead of, as now, sacrificing themselves for the faults and errors of the few men who have neglected to confide in them". "Information is the indispensable preliminary to control", and "public discussion is the best means of educating a people".[13]

The historical experience with World War II, again triggered by the "power-oriented" foreign policies of authoritarian governments, and the decentralized, "rule-oriented" economic and political European integration since World War II have further put into doubt the assertion by "foreign policy establishments" that the ideals of rule of law and democracy are incompatible with the special requirements of foreign policy. The proponents of a rule-oriented, democratic exercise of foreign policy criticize, in particular, the misleading and authoritarian premisses of the incompatibility hypothesis:

a) As a result of the increasing international integration and interdependence, the differences between domestic and foreign policy are diminishing. Bargaining, complexity and remoteness are characteristic also of many domestic policy processes, and many foreign policy objectives (such as trade liberalization) can be promoted through unilateral measures.

b) In liberal democracies, the allegedly "supreme foreign policy interest" of the citizens cannot be determined in an authoritarian manner without democratic discussion and participation by representative assemblies and the citizens. There are many examples (such as Germany's Ostpolitik, Switzerland's referendum on the accession to the UN, or the open discussion in the USA on the American participation in the war in

13 A. Ponsonby, Democracy and Diplomacy, 1915, pp. 7 f, 29, 116.

Vietnam) that better information and public discussion can stimulate a widespread interest in foreign policy issues and can increase the influence of parliaments on important foreign policy choices. The distribution and balance of foreign policy powers between the legislature and the executive vary from country to country (e.g. the US Senate being at one extreme and the British House of Commons at the other), and seem to be influenced more by domestic constitutional traditions than by alleged necessities of foreign policy. Empirical evidence also suggests that totalitarian governments disregarding human rights and rule of law in domestic politics frequently act aggressively also in foreign politics, and that democratic principles are the most effective method of making peaceful change possible.

c) The classical perception of international relations as a permanent struggle for power is no longer adequate for the modern "age of integration". Today, most states continuously cooperate on the basis of hundreds of bilateral and multilateral international agreements and organizations, and the national gains from "rule-oriented" cooperation have become much more important than short-term benefits from "power-oriented" foreign policies. In many fields of international "market integration", private enterprises, central banks and domestic courts have become the most important agents. Many "foreign policy issues", traditionally managed by foreign ministries, have been "depoliticized" through general legislation, or the responsibility has been shifted to other ministries (see, for instance, the final authority of the German Minister of Economic Affairs for most issues of European economic integration policy).

d) In an increasing number of countries, the jurisprudence and jurisdiction recognize that the foreign affairs powers and treaty powers must be exercized in conformity with the national constitutions and are subject to judicial review by domestic courts.[14] Economic theory likewise emphasizes that in the modern "open economies" (such as the EEC and EFTA countries), in which the foreign trade sector accounts for a large part of the gross domestic product, many "foreign economic issues" involve at the same time important domestic policy issues. Hence, if rule of law

14 See the survey by L. Wildhaber, Treaty-Making Power and Constitution, 1971, pp. 344, 354 ff.

and democracy are not maintained in the conduct of foreign policy, they will be difficult to maintain also in many areas of domestic policy.

The above-mentioned arguments in support of rule-oriented, democratic decision-making about "foreign policy" are valid also for the specific case of trade policy. The historical experience of the German customs union (1834-1871) as well as of the customs union of the EEC illustrates a number of additional reasons for the "legalization" and "judicialization" of transnational relations, notably that "foreign trade" can be regulated in a more efficient, more democratic and more depoliticized manner through long-term, general legal rules and their judicial protection than through discretionary executive trade policies:

e) Trade transactions are carried out through contracts and the transfer of property rights and give rise to conflicts among the short-term interests of traders, sellers and buyers (e.g. in case of trade in counterfeit goods, dumping and subsidies) which must be reconciled through long-term national legal rules and international agreements protecting the freedoms and property rights of domestic citizens in foreign jurisdictions.

f) The various trade policy instruments operate by taxing domestic citizens, restricting their individual freedoms, interfering in their property rights (e.g. existing contracts), by distorting or limiting domestic competition, or by granting (indirect) subsidies. They require long-term legal rules in order to ensure the equal protection of individual rights and to commit governments to the use of transparent, non-discriminatory and proportionate policy instruments.

g) The trade policy objectives of market-conforming prices, exchange rates and fair competition, recognized in GATT and IMF law, likewise depend on general long-term rules (e.g. prohibitions of restraints of competition and of business activities with adverse "external effects") rather than on discretionary short-term government interventions.

h) The various asymmetries in the traditionally weak political representation of the general free trade interests of domestic consumers, compared to the more easily and more effectively organized protectionist group interests, need to be corrected through legal rules and procedural safeguards of "due process". The welfare-reducing and redistributive effects of trade restrictions call for legal safeguards against the particular risks of "government failure" in the trade policy area.

2. Foreign Affairs and Foreign Trade in a Liberal Eighteenth Century Constitution: The Constitution of the United States

A) The Objective of Democratic Constitutionalism: "Sovereignty of the People" and Constitutional Limitation of all Government Powers

Historically, the chief aim of the framers of the American Constitution was to protect individual freedom through permanent constitutional rules constituting and limiting all government powers and subjecting their exercise to the supremacy of the Constitution. The fundamental rights of the people were recognized as being prior to government. The government powers were, therefore, not a source of the individual rights and were constitutionally limited and essentially confined to the task of promoting individual rights and providing those "public goods" that people cannot provide for themselves through private markets. The American concept of "popular sovereignty" was clearly stated in the preamble of the US Constitution ("We the people of the United States...do ordain and establish this Constitution for the United States of America"). And during the controversy over the ratification of the constitution, when the omission of a formal Bill of Rights was the major issue, A. Hamilton and other framers argued "that the Constitution is itself, in every rational sense, and to every useful purpose, a Bill of Rights".[15]

The very purpose of the addition to the Constitution of a formal Bill of Rights in 1791 was to place these fundamental rights even more clearly beyond the reach of majoritarian politics and to protect them as legal principles to be applied by the courts. This was made explicit in the Ninth Amendment ("The enumeration in the Constitution of certain rights shall not be construed to deny or disparage others retained by the people") and in the Tenth Amendment ratified in 1791 ("The powers not delegated to the United States by the Constitution, nor prohibited by it to the States, are reserved to the States, or to the People"). Both amendments had been inserted into the Constitution to make clear that the federal government had been established with only limited, enumerated powers and that the Bill of Rights had been enacted as an additional protection of the rights **retained** by the people into which the government is not to interfere. The

15 See, e.g.: L.W. Levy, Bill of Rights, in: L.W. Levy (ed.), Essays on the Making of the Constitution, 1987, 258 ff, 263; H.J. Abraham, Freedom and the Court. Civil Rights and Liberties in the United States, 1988, pp. 3 ff.; E.F. Cooke, A Detailed Analysis of the Constitution, 4th edition 1975, p. 109.

listing of the powers conferred upon the government (notably in Article I, section 8) and the constitutional limitation of the powers also of the legislature reflected the strong disapproval by the framers of the US Constitution of the British Parliament's claim in 1766 to "unlimited and unlimitable parliamentary sovereignty" in the sense that the representative assembly was not only the highest but also an unlimited authority which could pass any law it saw fit and was not bound to observe any general rules not of its own making.[16]

The founders of the US Constitution thus limited both the "popular will" as well as all government powers by the constitutional commitment to general principles designed to secure the rule of law and overall consistency of all government regulations. As proclaimed in the Declaration of Independence (1776), governments were seen to derive "their just powers from the consent of the governed", and the "consent of the governed" was not identified with legislative majority rule because constitutional government is by definition limited government. The US Congress was established **not** as an omnipotent legislator but with limited powers subject to institutional "checks and balances" (e.g. judicial review and the possibility of a "presidential veto" of proposed legislation). As in the case of the English Parliament up to the seventeenth century, the main function of Congress was seen in the control of the executive and in general legislation conforming to the constitutional rules without interfering into the "private sovereignty" retained by the people. The US Constitution was perceived **not** as the source of all other law applicable within the United States but rather as a formal agreement on the highest principles for the good organization of limited government, the powers of which are subject to limits residing in the fundamental, inalienable rights of the citizens. The people and the individual were considered to be free only if the government was not.[17]

---

16 See M.J.C. Vile, Constitutionalism and the Separation of Powers, 1967, p. 158, who describes the gradual loss of the original conception of democratic constitutions and the arrogation of arbitrary powers by the English Parliament. For a critical discussion and refutation of the assumptions underlying Blackstone's doctrine of parliamentary sovereignty, notably that "the nation did not need to be protected against its own will" (J. St. Mill, On Liberty, 1859, Everyman Edition p. 67) and that democratic procedures and parliamentary control made it possible to dispense with other constitutional limitations on government powers, see F.A. v.Hayek (note 1), p. 3 ff.

17 That the legal distinction between "government" (as an organization with limited powers) and "society", notwithstanding their numerous interrelationships, can contribute to the protection of individual freedom and "private sovereignty" has been rightly emphasized also with regard to German constitutional law e.g. by E.W. Böckenförde, Die Verfassungstheoretische Unterscheidung von Staat und Gesellschaft als Bedingung der individuellen Freiheit, 1973, p. 35 ff.

B) Constitutional Restraints on the Foreign Relations Powers

The US Constitution does not mention the term "foreign affairs". Nor does it delegate a "power to conduct foreign relations" to the federal government. The Constitution confers on the Congress the power to tax and spend (including for foreign affairs), to regulate commerce with foreign nations, to define offenses against the law of nations, and to declare war. And the Constitution allocates to the President the power to appoint ambassadors, to make treaties (with the consent of the Senate), and to be the commander in chief. But this constitutional blueprint for the governance of foreign affairs, which has never been formally amended in respects relevant for foreign affairs over the past 200 years, is incomplete. And the constitutional allocation of foreign affairs (notably the President's treaty-making power) does not conform to a strict division between "legislative powers" and "executive powers". Since, according to a famous dictum by Justice Hughes, "the Constitution is what the judges say it is", and the Supreme Court has not said much about the constitutional scope and distribution of powers over foreign affairs, many issues relating to constitutional restraints on the foreign relations powers have been resolved only **ad hoc** without a final decision in principle.

Many of the provisions of the Constitution apply equally to domestic and foreign affairs. For instance, the limitations of government powers in favour of the individual in the Bill of Rights, added by amendment immediately after the Constitution came into force, "apply to the conduct of foreign as well as domestic affairs".[18] However, according to the 1936 Supreme Court decision in "US v.Curtiss-Wright Export Corp.",[19]

> "the broad statement that the federal government can exercise no powers except those specifically enumerated in the Constitution, and such implied powers as are necessary and proper to carry into effect the enumerated powers, is categorically true only in respect of our internal affairs"..."the investment of the federal government with the powers of external sovereignty did not depend upon the affirmative grants of the Constitution. The power to declare and wage war, to conclude peace, to make treaties, to maintain diplomatic relations with other sovereignties, if they had never been mentioned in the Constitution, would have vested in the federal government as necessary concomitants of nationality"..."we are dealing not alone with an authority vested in the President by an exertion of legislative power, but with such an authority plus the delicate, plenary and exclusive power of the President as the sole organ of the federal government in the

18 L. Henkin, Foreign Affairs and the Constitution, 1972, pp. 26, 253 f.

19 299 US 304 (1936).

> field of international relations - a power which does not require as a basis for its exercise an act of Congress, but which, of course, like every other governmental power, must be exercised in subordination to the applicable provisions of the Constitution. It is quite apparent that if, in the maintenance of our international relations, embarrassement...is to be avoided and success for our aims achieved, congressional legislation which is to be made effective through negotiation and inquiry within the international field must often accord to the President a degree of discretion and freedom from statutory restriction which would not be admissible were domestic affairs alone involved."

Despite frequent criticism of this decision and notably of its assumption of inherent presidential powers over foreign relations derived from sovereignty rather than from the Constitution,[20] this decision has become the foundation of subsequent decisions and has far-reaching constitutional implications. In particular, the limitation of the "enumeration of powers doctrine" to "domestic affairs" means that foreign affairs powers are not "enumerated powers". Moreover, the court finding that Congress might exercise greater latitude in delegating power to the President over foreign affairs than in delegating discretion to him over internal matters raises doubts as to what extent the constitutional blueprint of "separation of powers" - the exercise by Congress of "all legislative powers herein granted" (Article I), of "executive power" by the President (Article II), and of "judicial power" by independent courts (Article III) - can be used as a justiciable guideline for the distribution among the federal branches of the undifferentiated bundle of "foreign affairs powers" derived from sovereignty.[21]

Today, the most controversial issues of the foreign affairs powers continue to arise in connection with the operation of the constitutional principles of "separation of powers" and "checks and balances" in foreign affairs. In the 1952 decision "Youngstown Sheet & Tube Co.v.Sawyer",[22] the Supreme Court refused to uphold President Truman's seizure of steel mills in order to avert a strike which he said might dangerously reduce the supply of munitions for the Korean war;

---

20 For a criticism of this theory see: Henkin (note 18), p. 22 f; Berger, The Presidential Monopoly of Foreign Relations, Michigan Law Review 1972, pp. 26 ff, according to whom the "inherent power theory" circumvents the manifest intention of the framers of the Constitution to create a federal government of limited, enumerated powers and defeats their purpose to condition presidential action in the field of foreign relations on congressional participation."

21 Henkin (note 18), p. 27, infers from various Supreme Court decisions that "it seems to have been assumed that they are distributed 'naturally', those that are 'legislative in character' to Congress, those 'executive' to the President, with apparently also a judicial foreign affairs power lodged in the federal courts".

22 343 US 579 (1952).

the Court found that such Presidential authority could be derived neither from an act of Congress nor from the Constitution itself. In the 1981 decision in "Dames & Moore v. Regan",[23] the Supreme Court upheld President Carter's orders transferring certain blocked Iranian assets under US jurisdiction by giving a broad reading to the scope of presidential authority delegated by Congress in the International Emergency Powers Act, taking into account also the congressional acquiescence in past cases where a President had negotiated the settlement of international claims. As regards the congressional trade policy powers "to regulate commerce with foreign nations" and "to lay and collect duties" (Article I, section 8), the decision in "US v. Guy W.Capps, Inc." by the US Court of Appeals[24] referred also to the principle of separation of powers for its finding that "the power to regulate foreign commerce is vested in Congress, not in the executive or the courts", and that an executive agreement on the restriction of Canadian potato exports into the USA

> "was void because it was not authorized by Congress and contravened provisions of a statute dealing with the very matter to which it related"..."The executive may not by-pass congressional limitations regulating such commerce by entering into an agreement with the foreign country that the regulation be exercised by that country through its control over exports. Even though the regulation prescribed by the executive agreement be more desirable than that prescribed by congressional action, it is the latter which must be accepted as the expression of national policy".

There are also a number of court decisions where the separation of powers principle was used in support of **executive** trade policy powers and in order to prevent the Congress from abdicating its functions by delegating broad discretionary powers to the executive with no criterion specified for its use. In "Consumers Union of U.S., Inc. v. Kissinger",[25] the US Court of Appeals held that the question of congressional preemption is not pertinent to executive negotiations of "voluntary" export restraints: "There is no potential for conflict between exclusive congressional regulation of foreign commerce - regulation enforced ultimately by halting violative importations at the border - and assurances of voluntary restraint given to the Executive".[26]

---

23 453 US 654 (1981).

24 US Court of Appeals, Fourth Circuit, 204 F.2d 655 (1953).

25 US Court of Appeals, District of Columbia, 506 F.2d 136 (1974).

26 See above chapter VI.2.A.b for a critical discussion of this court decision and the more persuasive dissenting opinion of judge Leventhal.

Several court decisions have held that "a constitutional delegation of powers requires that Congress enunciate a policy or objective or give reasons for seeking the aid of the President. In addition the act must specify when the powers conferred may be utilized by establishing a standard or intelligible principle which is sufficient to make it clear when action is proper".[27] The constitutional limits on delegation of legislative authority, notably the unconstitutionality of the frequently used congressional oversight device of a "legislative veto" requiring the President to report to Congress action taken pursuant to a delegated authority and permitting Congress or one House thereof to veto the action within a certain time limit, were further clarified in the Chadha case.[28] In this case, the Supreme Court invalidated a "legislative veto" by the House of Representative because that legislative act did not conform to the constitutional structure under which legislation is to be adopted (e.g need for both Houses of Congress to participate in enacting legislation, right of Congress to participate in enacting legislation, right of the President to veto legislative action in which case a two-thirds vote in each House is required to enact legislation); in the words of the court, "Congress must abide by its delegation of authority until that delegation is legislatively altered or revoked", and the effect of the existing legislation cannot be altered by a legislative act which was not taken by both Houses and was not presented to the President (thereby depriving him of his veto right)".[29]

The preceding analysis suggests that the judicial interpretation of the constitutional doctrines of "separation of powers", "limited delegation of powers" and "checks and balances" no longer provides unambiguous guidelines for the distribution and exercise of foreign affairs and trade policy powers in the United States. There appear also to be no other agreed guiding principles for reducing

---

27 Star-Kist Foods, Inc. v. US, Court of Customs and Patent Appeals, 275 F.2d 472 (1959).

28 Immigration and Naturalization Service v. Chadha, 462 US 919 (1983). On the non-delegation doctrine in US constitutional law see: S.A. Barber, The Constitution and the Delegation of Congressional Power, 1975.

29 For an analysis of the effect of the Chadha decision on the various US trade acts providing for "legislative vetoes" and on the tightening of the reins by Congress in the Trade and Tariff Act of 1984 see: H.H. Koh, Congressional Controls on Presidential Trade Policymaking after I.N.S. v. Chadha, in: New York University Journal of International Law and Politics 1986, pp. 1189 ff.; Jackson/Davey, Legal Problems of International Economic Relations, 2nd ed. 1987, p. 112, point out that the Chadha decision does not appear to affect the other important congressional oversight device of "fast track procedures", used in 1979 to implement the Tokyo Round agreements into US law and in 1985 to implement the US-Israel Free Trade Agreement, under which the President is authorized to negotiate international trade agreements the implementation of which remains subject to congressional approval in the form of a statute that could be vetoed by the President.

the uncertainty of the constitutional principles for this "twilight zone" as regards foreign affairs. In the words of Professor Henkin,

> "the foreign relations powers appear not so much 'separated' as fissured, along jagged lines indifferent to classical categories of governmental power: some powers and functions belong to the President, some to Congress, some to the President-and-Senate; some can be exercised by either the President or the Congress, some require the joint authority of both"..."Delegations by Congress to the President have been extensive and constant and 'Curtiss-Wright' tells us that in foreign affairs the principle of separation does not bar them. The special checks are also modified"...[30]

Presidents have achieved an undisputed, sometimes exclusive "foreign affairs power", but its scope and delimitation towards the commerce power of Congress remain uncertain.[31] Notably in the field of foreign trade law, some of the international trade agreements concluded by the President (including GATT) have domestic effect as law in the United States. But the precise borderlines between the presidential and congressional trade policy powers and the scope of other constitutional restraints on trade policy-making (e.g. those resulting from the Bill of Rights) will often need to be clarified by the courts or by congressional legislation.

C) Individual Rights and Foreign Affairs

The US Constitution begins with the words: "We the people of the United States, in order to form a more perfect union, establish justice, insure domestic tranquility, provide for the common defense, promote the general welfare, and secure the blessings of liberty to ourselves and our posterity, do ordain and establish this Constitution for the United States of America." The Articles of the Constitution mention the individual only infrequently and view him as a beneficiary of the constitutional limitation, enumeration and separation of government powers rather than as a subject of new constitutional "rights". During the Constitutional Convention and subsequent ratification debates, the proposal of an explicit bill of rights had been rejected on several grounds: the enumeration

30 L. Henkin (note 18), p. 32.

31 For a detailed analysis see L. Henkin (note 18), pp. 44 ff, 69 ff, as well as: L. Henkin, Foreign Affairs and the Constitution, in: Foreign Affairs 1987, pp. 284-310.

of specific rights could adversely affect the many other inalienable human rights and recognized common law liberties; and a bill of rights was believed unnecessary because the federal government was given only limited, enumerated powers without authority to diminish fundamental liberties.[32] Alexander Hamilton expressed this then prevailing constitutional theory in the "Federalist Papers" in the following words: "The people surrender nothing; and as they retain everything, they have no need of particular reservations".[33] When the Bill of Rights was added to the Constitution in 1789/91, it was explicitly made clear that "the enumeration in the Constitution of certain rights shall not be construed to deny or disparage others retained by the people" (Amendment IX). The Bill of Rights provisions do not "grant" the people their rights and are not the source of the legal existence and protection of their individual liberties; they only take account of them[34] and protect these "inalienable" liberties, viewed as existing independent of and antedating the Constitution, by the constitutional limitations imposed on the exercise of government powers.

What these other "natural rights" are can be authoritatively determined only by Congress and the courts. Just as the meaning of many constitutional provisions has changed over the years, the interpretation of these constitutional guarantees of not specifically enumerated liberties in a broad sense - such as the admonition in the Fifth and Fourteenth Amendment that no person shall be deprived of "life, liberty or property without due process of law", which has its origin in chapter 39 of the Magna Carta of 1215 - may change in response to changing circumstances. The Supreme Court, for instance, has recognized that the "unlisted rights" to engage in political activity, the right to privacy and the right to travel freely within the United States were protected under the Ninth Amendment; with regard to the right to travel abroad, the Supreme Court has held that, "if that liberty is to be regulated, it must be pursuant to the law-making functions of the Congress".[35] While it is possible that the courts might utilize the Ninth Amendment also in cases involving individual rights in foreign trade and other foreign relations, this does not seem likely given the judicial self-restraint vis-à-vis economic liberties other than rights relating to property (due process of

32 See: B.H. Siegan, Economic Liberties and the Constitution, 1980, pp. 13, 15, 29; Levy (above note 15), pp. 266, 282.

33 A. Hamilton, number 84 of the Federalist Papers, quoted from Siegan, p. 29.

34 See the examples from the Bill of Rights in: L. Henkin (note 18), p. 484. Only the Thirteenth Amendment on "freedom from slavery" seems to confer a new individual freedom.

35 Kent v. Dulles, 357 US 116, 129 (1958).

law, just compensation, uniform taxation) and personal liberty (such as freedom of speech, press, religion, assembly, right to indictment by grand jury, trial by jury, right to counsel, freedom from unreasonable search and seizures, freedom from self-incrimination).[36]

Thus, even though the US Constitution was established to "secure the blessings of liberty" (preamble), the US Court of Customs and Patent Appeals held in "US v. Yoshida International, Inc." that "no one has a vested right to trade with foreign nations".[37] And also Congress replaced the words "right to export" contained in the first draft of the Export Administration Act of 1979 by the word "ability to export" so as to avoid the law being "misconstrued" as denoting a constitutionally protected, legally enforceable right to export free from government restriction.[38] Hence, in accordance with the original conception of the Constitution to support individual rights principally by assuring good government, private foreign trade transactions are likely to be protected more through "objective" constitutional principles and procedures than through recognition of "subjective" individual freedoms of trade. For instance, exports covered by existing contracts are constitutionally protected against retroactive government interferences by the constitutional prohibitions on **ex post facto** laws and on impairment of contract obligations (Article I, sections 9 and 10).[39] And aggrieved American importers, exporters, manufacturers and consumers are protected under the "due process of law" requirement of the Fifth Amendment also in transnational transactions and have the constitutional right to challenge the methods used to calculate and impose customs duties and the propriety of antidumping and countervailing duties before impartial, properly appointed members of the judiciary.[40]

While the Supreme Court's "Curtiss-Wright" decision exempted foreign affairs from the rigors of the constitutional "limited delegation" requirement, the Supreme Court recognized nonetheless that the President's foreign affairs powers

---

36 See: B.H. Siegan, (note 32).

37 526 F.2d 560 (1975).

38 Senate Reports No. 169, 96th Congress, 3rd Session, 1,3 (1979).

39 See the "contract sanctity clause" in section 6 of the Export Administration Amendments Act of 1985, in: ILM 1985, pp. 1369 ff.

40 "Substantive due process" requires not only that government restrictions "shall not be unreasonable, arbitrary or capricious, and that the means selected shall have real and substantial relation to the object sought to be attained" (Nebbia v. New York, 291 US 502, 525, 1934) but protects also a person's liberty, for instance the right to travel abroad (see Kent v. Dulles, 357 US 116, 129, 1958).

"of course, like every other governmental power, must be exercised in subordination to the applicable provisions of the Constitution".[41] And in a later case the Court confirmed:

> "Broad as the power in the National Government to regulate foreign affairs must be, it is not without limitation. The restrictions confining Congress in the exercise of any of the powers expressly delegated to it in the Constitution apply with equal vigor when that body seeks to regulate our relations with other nations".[42]

Professor Henkin therefore concludes from the case-law that "nothing in the Constitution suggests that the rights of individuals in respect of foreign affairs are different from what they are in relation to other exercises of governmental power"..."Nor is any particular exercise of foreign affairs power exempt from limitations in favor of individual rights"..."In principle, the Bill of Rights limits foreign policy and the conduct of foreign relations as it does other federal activities".[43]

D) The Courts in Foreign Affairs

The judiciary Article III and the doctrine of judicial review, established in the famous case Marbury vs. Madison (1803), of the constitutionality also of acts of the legislature are the hallmark of American constitutional law. But the courts have developed an armory of reasons for avoiding judicial decisions on delicate foreign affairs issues: The courts have considered themselves bound by executive assertions of immunity; they will give great weight to interpretations of treaties and determinations of international law by the executive branch; they have declared certain foreign policy issues to be non-justiciable "political questions"; they have exercised judicial self-restraint also towards foreign "acts of state"; and federal courts will hear only a "case or controversy" that is not moot and has been brought to the court by a petitioner with "standing" to make a "justiciable" claim in an actual case against an available defendant.[44] The courts have also tolerated wider delegations of discretionary powers in the foreign affairs area, where Congress "must of necessity paint with a brush broader than that it cu-

---

41 US v. Curtiss-Wright Export Corp., 299 US 304, at p. 320 (1936).

42 Perez v. Brownell, 356 US 44,58 (1958).

43 Henkin (note 18), pp. 252, 253, 254, 269 ff (as regards the almost identical constitutional safeguards for individual rights against infringement by the States).

44 For a survey of the pertinent case-law see Henkin (note 18), pp. 205 ff.

stomarily wields in domestic areas",[45] even though the Chadha case may have compelled Congress to define future delegations of discretion to the executive branch more carefully with justiciable standards.

The Supreme Court, in the 1918 case "Oetjen v. Central Leather Co.", still held that "the conduct of the foreign relations of our Government is committed by the Constitution to the Executive and Legislative - 'the political' - Departments of the Government, and the propriety of what may be done in the exercise of this political power is not subject to judicial inquiry or decision".[46] But the Supreme Court has made it clear in "Baker v. Carr" that "it is error to suppose that every case or controversy which touches foreign relations lies beyond judicial cognizance".[47] The latter decision identified as qualifying for judicial reticence those questions which have one or more of the following elements:

> "a textually demonstrable constitutional commitment of the issue to a coordinate political department; or a lack of judicially discoverable and manageable standards for resolving it; or the impossibility of deciding without an initial policy determination of a kind clearly for nonjudicial discretion; or the impossibility of a court's undertaking independent resolution without expressing lack of the respect due coordinate branches of government; or an unusual need for unquestioning adherence to a political decision already made; or the potentiality of embarrassment from multifarious pronouncements by various departments on one question."

As regards the "act of state doctrine", the Supreme Court has said that it is not required by international law, by the political question doctrine, or by anything in the Constitution, but is rather an expression of "the strong sense of the Judicial Branch that its engagement in the task of passing on the validity of foreign acts of state may hinder rather than further this country's pursuit of goals both for itself and for the community of nations as a whole in the international sphere".[48]

This kind of "federal judge-made law"[49] has influenced the constitutional system for foreign relations. But the "Hickenlooper Amendment" to the Foreign Assistance Act, sometimes also called "Sabbatino Amendment" or "rule of law Amendment" because it mandated courts to modify the judicial "Sabbatino

45 Zemel v. Rusk, 381 US 1,17 (1965). See also Curtiss-Wright, 299 US, at 320 (1936).

46 246 US 297, 302 (1918).

47 369 US, 186, 211 (1962).

48 Sabbatino v. Banco Nacional de Cuba, 376 US 398 (1964).

49 L. Henkin (note 18).

doctrine" (i.e. the judicial recognition of foreign acts of state done within the foreign country even if they violate international law) and requested the courts to decide suits concerning foreign expropriation of US assets "on the merits giving effect to the principles of international law", demonstrated also that the role of the judiciary in foreign affairs and the justiciability of foreign policy issues can be influenced by congressional legislation.[50] A case in point is the US Trade Agreements Act of 1979, which has considerably extended the justiciability and judicial review of antidumping and countervailing duty proceedings.[51] Yet, in "Banco Nacional de Cuba v. Farr",[52] a US district court - while affirming the constitutionality of the Hickenlooper Amendment's repeal of the judicial abstention requirement of the act of state doctrine - left open "whether there might be a constitutional compulsion that the courts accept the direction of Congress even as to issues the Court has held to be nonjusticiable because they are 'political questions'".

E) The Constitution and International Law: The Fragility of GATT Law as Part of US Domestic Law

Foreign policy powers are increasingly being exercized through the conclusion of international agreements rather than through unilateral national acts. Since liberal international trade agreements are designed to protect the freedoms and property rights not only of foreign but also of domestic traders, the constitutional provisions on the observance and incorporation of international legal obligations can contribute to the protection of individual rights in foreign relations.

According to Article VI, clause 2, of the Constitution,

> "This Constitution, and the Laws of the United States which shall be made in pursuance thereof, and all treaties made, or which shall be made, under the authority of the United States, shall be the supreme law of the land; and the judges in every State shall be bound thereby..."

50 See: Franck/Bob, The Return of Humpty-Dumpty: Foreign Relations Law after the Chadha Case, in: AJIL 1985, pp. 912, 958; E.U. Petersmann, Act of State Doctrine, Political Question Doctrine and Judicial Review of Foreign Relations Powers, in: Jahrbuch des öffentlichen Rechts 1976, pp. 587, 598, 612 ff.

51 See: E.A. Vermulst, Antidumping Law and Practice in the United States and the European Communities, 1987, pp. 121 ff.

52 243 F. Supp. 957 (S.D.N.Y. 1965, affirmed 383 F.2d 166 (2d Circuit 1967).

In the "Paquete Habana" case, the Supreme Court construed this "supremacy clause" to mean that

> "International law is part of our law, and must be ascertained and administered by the courts of justice of appropriate jurisdiction, as often as questions of right depending upon it are duly presented for their determination. For this purpose, where there is no treaty, and no controlling executive or legislative act or judicial decision, resort must be had to the customs and usages of civilized nations..."[53]

The US Constitution does not explicitly confer on any branch of the government a power to violate international law. An early Supreme Court decision emphasized that a treaty is obligatory "on all, as well on the Legislative, Executive and Judicial Departments...as on every individual of the nation".[54] Yet, the Supreme Court has on several occasions upheld acts of Congress inconsistent with international treaty obligations,[55] and international treaties are generally held to be subordinate to the Constitution; they are considered to have the same status in US law as an act of Congress and, therefore, to be supreme in relation to prior domestic law. Hence, in case of conflict between an international treaty obligation and a statute, either the "lex posterior"-rule or the "lex specialis"-rule apply depending on the circumstances. The executive and the courts are therefore constitutionally obligated to give effect to international treaty obligations even in the face of an earlier act of Congress to the contrary, unless there is a "controlling" later act of Congress.

Customary international law is likewise recognized to be law of the United States without any express "incorporation" and is to be given effect by the courts when it is "self-executing".[56] Like an international treaty, customary international law is inferior to the US Constitution but has the same status as an act of Congress.[57] Congress is recognized to have the power to enact legislation inconsistent with an established principle of customary law. The President, by contrast, is required by his "executive power" to take care that the law and international legal obligations be faithfully executed (Article II, section 3) and, in general, appears to lack independent constitutional authority to violate interna-

---

53 175 US 677, 700 (1900).

54 Ware v. Hylton, 3 US (3 Dall.), 199, 272 (1796).

55 For instance, in the "Chinese Exclusion Case", 130 US 581, 602 f (1889), see: L. Henkin, The President and International Law, in: AJIL 1986, pp. 930, 931.

56 See: L. Henkin (note 55), p. 932; L. Henkin (note 18), p. 221.

57 See Henkin (note 55), p. 933.

tional legal obligations until they have been terminated under international law or are superseded by an intervening act of Congress or presidential action authorized by such an act.[58]

In the words of the Supreme Court, "treaties must continue to operate as part of our municipal law, and be obeyed by the people, applied by the judiciary and executed by the President, while they continue unrepealed".[59] Can it be inferred herefrom that the international GATT obligations for non-discriminatory market access and for the use of transparent, non-discriminatory and proportionate trade policy instruments can operate as an effective legal restraint on the trade policy powers of the US government? The answer to this question is negative for several reasons. The attempt by US Secretary of State Cordell Hull after World War II to replace the "laissez-faire for governments", characteristic for the national trade policies of most states during the period between World Wars I and II, by an agreed system of multilaterally agreed, complementary international and national legal constraints on the government powers to tax and regulate foreign trade[60] could never be fully implemented even within US domestic law in several respects:

a) At the 1946 preparatory conference in London, for instance, the US delegation had still requested that the contemplated multilateral trade agreement

> "should deal with these subjects in precise detail so that the obligations of member governments would be clear and unambiguous. Most of these subjects readily lend themselves to such treatment. Provisions on such subjects, once agreed upon, would be self-executing and could be applied by the governments concerned without further elaboration or international action".[61]

---

58 On this controversial issue see notably L. Henkin (note 55), p. 936, and J.P. Paust, The President Is Bound by International Law, in: AJIL 1987, pp. 377 ff, 387: "The President has no...constitutional power to violate a treaty or law".

59 Chew Heong v.United States, 112 US 536, 563 (1884).

60 For a description of Cordell Hull's "international treaty strategy" see: J. Tumlir, Protectionism. Trade Policy in Democratic Societies, 1985, pp. 25f; I.M. Destler, American Trade Politics: System Under Stress, 1986, pp. 12 ff; E.U. Petersmann, Strengthening the Domestic Legal Framework of the GATT Multilateral Trade System: Possibilities and Problems of Making GATT Rules Effective in Domestic Legal Systems, in: Petersmann/Hilf (eds.), The New GATT Round of Multilateral Trade Negotiations, 1988, pp. 51 ff.

61 UN Doc. EPCT/C.II/PV.2 (1946), p. 8.

Under US law, the self-executing international obligations of a multilateral trade treaty approved by the US Senate, or of an executive agreement authorized or subsequently approved by Congress, would have become part of the domestic law of the United States with a legal rank superior to prior federal legislation and to all state law, past and future.[62] And also the "non-self-executing obligations" of a multilateral trade agreement could have become part of US federal law through congressional implementing legislation or an act of the executive (e.g. an executive order, a regulation, or a proclamation). The international obligations would not have limited the legal power of Congress to enact subsequent law overriding the domestic legal effect of the international obligations, and might thus not have prevented occasional statutory violations of GATT obligations by the Congress (such as the quantitative restrictions on agricultural trade prescribed in the 1954 enactment of section 22(f) of the Agricultural Adjustment Act of 1933 as well as in the 1964 and 1979 Meat Import Acts, the 1971 enactment of the DISC export subsidies, the 1974 revision of the US escape clause legislation disregarding some requirements of GATT Article XIX, certain conditional MFN provisions deviating from GATT Article I in the 1979 Trade Agreements Act, or the so-called Wine Equity Act incorporated in the Trade and Tariff Act of 1984).[63] But a congressional ratification of the envisaged multilateral trade agreement as a self-executing treaty under US law might have prevented the long-standing political hostility of Congress toward "the Executive Agreement known as the General Agreement on Tariffs and Trade".[64] And, if effectively protected through congressional implementing legislation as well as by domestic courts, self-executing international treaty obligations might also have served as a more effective legal constraint on the increasingly frequent congressional actions introducing, threatening, authorizing or tolerating trade restrictions in violation of GATT obligations.

---

62 On the status of international obligations in US domestic law see also: R.E. Hudec, The Legal Status of GATT in the Domestic Law of the United States, in: Hilf/Jacobs/Petersmann (eds.), The European Community and GATT, 1986, pp. 188 ff.

63 On these and other US federal statutes contradicting GATT requirements see R.E. Hudec (note 62), p. 239 f.

64 The quotation formed part of a famous disclaimer in various congressional trade acts between 1951 and 1958 renewing the trade negotiating authority of the President contained in section 350 of the Reciprocal Trade Agreements Act of 1934 (e.g. section 10 of the Trade Agreements Extension Act of 1951).

Due to the non-ratification of the Havana Charter as well as of the GATT by Congress, GATT was concluded by the USA as a mere "executive agreement" subject to a "grandfather clause" allowing the maintenance of pre-existing mandatory legislation inconsistent with Parts II and III of GATT. While most US courts appear to assume that the General Agreement is self-executing, both Jackson and Hudec conclude that the General Agreement is a non-self-executing agreement under US law.[65] Only GATT Articles I to XXXV have entered US federal law by means of presidential proclamations based on section 350 of the Reciprocal Trade Agreements Act of 1934, as extended in 1945, with a legal rank, at least of Articles III to XXXV GATT, inferior to all federal statutory law. As part of federal law, GATT law is generally considered to be directly applicable and superior only to state law. As regards the 1979 Tokyo Round Agreements, section 3 of the Trade Agreements Act of 1979 explicitly states that no provision of the Tokyo Round Agreements shall have self-executing effect under US law nor "be construed as creating any private right of action of remedy for which provision is not explicitly made under this Act or under the laws of the United States".[66] In conclusion, GATT law can hardly be said to have effectively restrained the broad constitutional and political powers of Congress to tax and regulate the foreign trade transactions of US citizens in a non-transparent, discriminatory and particularly harmful manner in contravention of the GATT obligations for transparent, non-discriminatory and least-distortive trade policy-making.

b) The mercantilist perception of the liberal GATT obligations as a potential risk, and of individual rights of domestic traders as a favour granted by Congress, is reflected not only in deliberate statutory violations of GATT law, congressional threats of such violations, in the congressional denial of a self-executing character of the 1979 Tokyo Round Agreements, and in the congressional care to prevent a direct applicability by individuals of the often precise and unconditional prohibitions of trade restrictions set out in the Tokyo Round Agreements. It has contributed to at least three additional trends in US foreign trade legisla-

65 R.E. Hudec (note 62), pp. 195 ff; J.H. Jackson, The General Agreement on Tariffs and Trade in United States Domestic Law, Michigan Law Review 66 (1967), pp. 249, 290-292.

66 See section 3(f), U.S.C. 2503(f).

tion that have further weakened the effectiveness of the international GATT obligations in US domestic law:

Firstly, the increasing tendency to disregard the constitutional requirement of limited delegation of powers by granting extensive discretionary trade policy powers to the executive branch unconstrainted by precise substantive guidelines or by other effective legal restraints on their discretionary exercise. As Hudec commented: "The more that trade policy measures are made subject to such discretionary powers, and especially when those powers are exercised behind closed doors, as is often the case, the less it can be said that GATT obligations are effective as a matter of domestic law".[67]

Secondly, the explicit statutory authorization, to be found in virtually all recent US trade acts (e.g. in the 1979 Trade Agreements Act with regard to the domestic implementation of the 1979 GATT Agreements on Government Procurement and Technical Barriers to Trade), of executive trade restrictions in violation of GATT rules.[68]

Thirdly, congressional acquiescence in, and political support of, discretionary executive "grey area trade restrictions" (e.g. export restraint arrangements for Japanese automobiles) that are neither authorized by US domestic law nor by GATT law and further undermine the GATT legal system for non-discriminatory trade competition.[69] Given the broad powers of the US President to legally override the domestic law effects of the international GATT obligations with few, if any, effective parliamentary and judicial controls on the exercise of the executive trade policy discretion, it appears hardly possible to conclude that GATT law operates as an effective legal constraint on the exercise under US domestic law of the discretionary trade policy powers of the US President.

c) As regards judicial review of discretionary trade policy decisions, Hudec's recent analysis of US court decisions arrived at the conclusion

67 R.E. Hudec (note 62), p. 241.

68 R.E. Hudec (note 62), p. 231 ff.

69 See: R.E. Hudec (note 62), p. 244, and for a case study: M.W. Lochmann, The Japanese Voluntary Restraint on Automobile Exports: An Abandonment of the Free Trade Principles of the GATT and the Free Market Principles of United States Antitrust Laws, in: Harvard International Law Journal 27 (1986), pp. 99-157.

that the courts "have given constitutional approval to these broad delegations of authority, they have been reluctant to curb regulatory practices at the margins of the law, and they have almost invariably deferred to the judgment of the Executive Branch as to whether statutory criteria have been met - often finding that the courts simply have no power at all to inquire into these matters".[70] Various delegated trade policy powers of the US President (e.g. for trade restrictions on agricultural and textile products, trade restrictions for national security reasons or during "a time of national emergency", withdrawal of tariff preferences for developing countries, retaliation against "unreasonable" behaviour of foreign trading partners) and various administrative trade restrictions erected outside the import relief laws (e.g. voluntary export restraints, the "trigger price mechanism" for steel imports) have been held by the courts to be for all practical purposes free from justiciable legal restraints.[71] US courts appear to have never sustained a private claim that a GATT obligation prevailed over a provision of US federal law. Courts have been willing to interpret federal law in conformity with the GATT obligations of the USA, but the case-law suggests that, in case of conflict, "federal law always prevails over a conflicting GATT obligation, regardless of which was later and regardless of whether the PPA (Protocol on Provisional Application) reservation applies".[72] Effective judicial review of trade restrictions is available in technical, "rule-oriented" areas such as customs valuation and antidumping procedures, which are administered according to detailed rules. But in the more politicized and more discretionary "high policy tracks", such as escape clause actions under GATT Article XIX (as implemented in section 201 of the 1974 US Trade Act) or export restrictions under GATT Article XXI (as implemented in the 1979 US Export Administration Act), the courts seem to consider import and export transactions of domestic citizens as a privilege rather than as an individual right to be protected by the courts.

The conclusion to be drawn from this brief survey is thus a mixed one. The "Cordell Hull strategy" has been successful in bringing about rather effective national and international legal constraints on the national go-

70 R.E. Hudec (note 62), p. 241.

71 See: R.E. Hudec (note 62), pp. 244 ff.

72 R.E. Hudec (note 62), p. 211.

vernment power to tax foreign trade transactions through tariffs and similar charges: US tariffs have been liberalized from the Smoot-Hawley average of 60 per cent to around 5 per cent today; the implementation in US domestic law of the international GATT rules on tariff matters (e.g. customs valuation, antidumping and countervailing duty proceedings) has contributed to an increasing "legalization" of trade policy-making by means of tariffs; and the substantive and procedural standards agreed upon in the pertinent GATT rules have also enabled an effective judicial protection of domestic citizens vis-à-vis the government powers to tax foreign trade transactions. But the "Cordell Hull Strategy" has operated much less successfully in respect of non-tariff trade barriers. Neither the legislative nor the judicial branches of the US government appear willing to effectively enforce in US domestic law the comprehensive GATT legal disciplines on the **trade policy powers to regulate foreign trade through non-tariff barriers**, which the executive branch has voluntarily accepted at the international level of GATT law on behalf of all the branches of the government of the United States.

F) Conclusions: The Need to Make the Existing Constitutional Restraints on Trade Policy Powers More Precise and Effective

The preceding survey of the US constitutional system for foreign affairs leads to the following three conclusions:

a) The constitutional guarantees of limited government, separation and only limited delegation of powers, judicial review and protection of individual rights are recognized, at least in principle, to be applicable also to the government powers to tax and restrict the transnational trade transactions of US citizens. Yet, these constitutional principles are much less stringently applied in the regulation of transnational economic relations compared with purely domestic economic regulations.

b) The general international GATT obligations, which were negotiated at the initiative of the USA in order to prevent a recurrence of the discretionary trade protectionism of the inter-war period and are applicable to about 80 per cent of US trade with more than 120 countries, often include more precise, more liberal and more justiciable obligations for the use of transparent, non-discriminatory and proportionate trade policy instruments compared with US constitutional law and with the numerous US Tariff Acts, Trade Acts, Trade Agreement Acts, Agricultural Acts and other sectoral or specific trade regulations restricting foreign trade transactions in respect of certain countries, products, prices or quantities of traded goods. Yet, the self-imposed international GATT obligations do not appear to operate as an effective legal constraint on the discretionary legislative and executive trade policy powers of the US government. Nor are they effectively enforced by US courts against legislative and executive trade restrictions inconsistent with GATT law. The lack of adequate **national** constitutional safeguards for a transparent, non-discriminatory and proportionate exercise of the discretionary government powers to tax and restrict the trade transactions of domestic citizens does not appear to be effectively compensated by the incorporation of GATT law into US legislation and by its judicial protection against the use of non-transparent, discriminatory and disproportionately harmful trade policy instruments.

c) The framers intended the Constitution and the judiciary to be safeguards also against disproportionate interferences into economic liberties and property rights.[73] Nothing in the Constitution indicates that the individual rights of US citizens shall be less effectively protected vis-à-vis the exercise of the trade policy powers of the US government than in respect of other purely domestic regulatory powers. During the years between 1789 and 1937, the Supreme Court examined federal and state laws dealing with economic and social matters and, relying on the doctrine of substantive due process (under either the Fifth or Fourteenth Amendment), declared many unconstitutional because they deprived a plaintiff of property or contract rights or economic liberty without due process of law.[74] Beginning with the case "West Coast Hotel Co. v. Parrish" in 1937[75] and definitively with the 1941 case "Olsen v.

73 This has been shown in the study by B.H. Siegan (note 32), who notes: "The Framers expected the federal judiciary to exercise judicial review insofar as civil liberties were concerned, primarily to secure property and other economic interests" (p. 318). See also J.A. Dorn/H.G. Manne (eds.), Economic Liberties and the Judiciary, 1987, e.g. the contribution by J.A. Dorn, Judicial Protection of Economic Liberties, pp. 1-26.

74 See the case-law described in part II of B.H. Siegan's study, pp. 110 ff.

75 300 US 379 (1937).

Nebraska",[76] the Court adopted far less exacting standards of review of economic legislation and discontinued the judicial doctrine of "economic due process".[77] Since this demise of substantive due process, the Court upheld economic and social legislation unless it was found devoid of all rationality or violated intellectual, political or other specially protected liberties. This current stance of the courts and the resultant dichotomy between the judicial protection of intellectual and political liberties, on the one side, and of economic liberties, on the other side,[78] adversely affect not only the large number of people for whom the freedom to pursue economic opportunities and to engage freely in a trade or profession is among the most important liberties. But, as more than 50 studies mentioned by Siegan have shown with regard to domestic economic regulation and as modern economics has demonstrated also with regard to foreign trade restrictions, they have often resulted in a reduction of social welfare at large and in an arbitrary redistribution of income from consumers to the regulated groups. The lack of judicial review of whether economic regulation is a suitable and proportionate means for the achievement of an important governmental objective is characteristic also for the exercise of foreign trade policy powers. It has further weakened the transnational exercise of individual rights and has contributed to the fact that economic competition is increasingly replaced by political competition where "losers in the economic arena seek relief from legislators who have the power to make them winners".[79]

---

76 313 US 236 (1941); see also Lincoln Federal Labor Union v. Northwestern Iron & Metal Co, 335 US 525 (1949).

77 See: B.H. Siegan, pp. 184 ff.

78 See: B.H. Siegan, pp. 248 ff, and F.A. v.Hayek, The Constitution of Liberty, 1960, e.g. pp. 32 ff, for a criticism of the judicial differentiation among the marketplace of ideas and the marketplace of goods and services which are closely interrelated. For many people, economic concerns tend to outweigh political ones.

79 B.H. Siegan (note 32), p. 331.

3. Foreign Affairs and Foreign Trade in a Liberal Nineteenth Century Constitution: The Constitution of Switzerland

A) Foreign Affairs in the Swiss Constitution

According to Article 2 of the Federal Constitution of the Swiss Confederation of 1874, "the aim of the Confederation is to preserve the outward independence of the fatherland, to maintain internal peace and order, to protect the freedom and the rights of the confederates and to promote their common prosperity".[80] This enumeration of constitutional objectives, the provision in the Constitution for broadly defined foreign policy powers, their distribution among the executive (see Article 102, paras. 8 and 9) and the legislative branches of the federal government (see Article 85, paras. 5 and 6), and the explicit recognition of international treaties as part of domestic law to be observed by the courts (Article 113) follow a pattern similar to the corresponding provisions of the US Constitution.

The Swiss Constitution deals, however, not only with the "classical" foreign affairs matters such as the right to declare war and to make peace (Articles 8, 85 para. 6), the conclusion of international treaties with foreign states (Articles 8, 9, 85 para. 5, 89 para. 3), the federal army and common defense (Articles 18 to 22 **bis**, 85 para. 6, 102 para. 9), and the general foreign relations powers of the Federal Council which "shall watch over the external interests of the Confederation, particularly its international relations, and shall be in charge of external affairs generally" (Article 102, para. 8).[81] In contrast to the US Constitution, the Swiss Constitution mentions also more specific foreign policy objectives such as "the preservation of the independence and neutrality of Switzerland" (Articles 85 para. 6, 102 para. 9) and the imposition of only "the lowest possible import duties" and "export duty rates as moderate as possible" (Article 29). This explicit constitutional requirement of a liberal foreign trade policy is a corollary of the constitutional guarantees for "freedom of trade and industry" (Article 31) and reflect the important insight that external and internal government policies in-

80 For an unofficial English translation of the Swiss Constitution of 1874, as amended, see: Blaustein/Flanz (eds.), Constitutions of the Countries of the World, Vol. XV, 1982.

81 For a detailed account of the distribution of competences between the Confederation and the Cantons in the field of foreign affairs, as well as of the foreign policy competences between the various organs of the Confederation, see: J. Monnier, Les Principes et les Règles Constitutionnels de la Politique Etrangère Suisse, in: Zeitschrift für Schweizerisches Recht, Vol. 105 (1986), pp. 107-247.

teract in many ways and must be mutually consistent in order to fully achieve their goals. The about 100 formal amendments of the Swiss Constitution since 1874 have added further constitutional provisions dealing with specific foreign policy issues, such as explicit constitutional provisions for federal powers "to enact rules concerning precautionary measures of economic defense of the country as well as concerning measures for safeguarding the supply of the country with vital goods and services, given serious situations of shortage that the economy cannot cope with on its own" (Article 31 **bis**, para. 3,e), to adopt foreign economic policy measures departing from the "freedom of trade and industry" (Article 31 **quinquies**), and to conclude "agreements of international law that provide for the entry into an international organization" or "involve a multilateral unification of law" (Article 89, para. 3).

As in the case of the national constitutions of most states, the provisions of the Swiss Constitution for the conduct of foreign policy focus on the regulation of the domestic procedures and competences. The substantive guidelines and foreign policy objectives spelled out in the Constitution remain vague, rudimentary and open enough to allow flexible responses to continuously changing international relations and to often unforeseen developments abroad. The Federal Council and the Federal Assembly are the principal actors for the conduct of foreign policy. The Cantons retain specified rights to conclude certain treaties and maintain official intercourse with foreign states (see Articles 9 and 10). And certain international agreements, as well as the entry into international organizations of collective security or supranational entities, are to be submitted to the people for approval or rejection under the conditions specified in the Constitution (Article 89). This "democratization" of the decision-making processes on foreign policy has been further strengthened by the constitutional protection of individual rights (e.g. freedom of trade) and the participation of Switzerland in international agreements on the liberalization of transnational relations (e.g. the free trade area agreements of Switzerland with the EFTA countries and the EEC).

B) Explicit Constitutional Protection of Freedom of Trade and Industry

Article 31 of the Swiss Constitution of 1874 stipulates:

> "(1) Freedom of trade and industry is guaranteed throughout the territory of the Confederation, subject to such limitations as are contained in the Federal Constitution and the legislation enacted under its authority".

"(2) Cantonal regulations concerning the exercise of trade and industry and the taxes on such activities remain unaffected. However, such regulations shall not depart from the principle of freedom of trade and industry except where the Federal Constitution provides otherwise. Cantonal monopolies are likewise excepted."

This explicit constitutional guarantee of freedom of trade and industry was a reaction to the mercantilistic privileges and restraints of the guilds during the 19th century and appears to be unique compared to other national constitutions. The US Constitution does not explicitly guarantee economic liberty and protects the "freedom of enterprise" and other economic liberties only indirectly in the due process clauses of the Fifth and Fourteenth Amendments. In France (in 1791), Switzerland (1798), Prussia (in 1810) and various other European states during the 19th century, the termination of the mercantile systems of guilds and the legal protection of the freedom of trade came about through legislative acts.[82] But also in the 20th century, hardly any other European country seems to have included an explicit guarantee of freedom of trade equivalent to Article 31 into its national constitution. Nor do the international human rights covenants explicitly recognize an individual freedom in the sense of Article 31.

The Swiss courts recognize that Article 31 protects all private economic activities of Swiss citizens including the production, trade, sale and purchase of goods and services of a monetary value: Article 31 "protège donc toute activité économique privée tendant à la production d'un gain et exercée à titre professionel, soit toute activité déployée par une personne dans un but lucratif".[83] The courts and legal doctrine further recognize that Article 31 serves several functions both as an individual right as well as an objective constitutional principle with specific federal and economic policy functions.[84]

a) Freedom of Trade as an Individual Right

Freedom of trade and commerce is constitutionally protected as an individual right to the free choice and exercise of any kind of professional and other eco-

82 See: P. Saladin, Grundrechte im Wandel, 3rd edition, 1982, p. 211 f, who notes that the English common law included effective guarantees of freedom of industry already in the 18th century. The Swiss Constitution of 1848 did not include a federal guarantee of freedom of trade.

83 Federal Court Decisions (BGE) Vol. 103, I, a, p. 259, 262.

84 See P. Saladin (note 82), pp. 216 ff, and J.P. Müller/S. Müller, Grundrechte, Besonderer Teil, 1985, p. 313.

nomic private activity with a lucrative purpose at any place in Switzerland.[85] "Trade and industry" are construed to mean participation in economic markets as supplier or demander of goods or services, including imports, exports and related payments,[86] regardless of whether the gainful activities are being exercised independently, dependently, professionally or only occasionally. The freedom of trade and industry protects thus also the free movement of persons, services and capital as well as freedom of contract as constitutive elements of the free choice and exercise of one's professional and other economic, private activities.[87] As an individual right, the freedom of trade and industry can be invoked by private natural and juridical persons not only of Swiss nationality but, to a limited extent,[88] also of foreign nationality. It limits the regulatory powers of all federal as well as cantonal government organs, notwithstanding the only limited judicial review of federal legislation.[89]

According to the Federal Court, the freedom of trade and industry does not confer individual rights to claim governmental contributions or the supply of other governmental grants.[90] This case-law has met with increasing criticism in the legal doctrine and has been mitigated in more recent decisions of the Federal Court.[91] Economic and legal doctrine rightly emphasize that the exercise of professional and other economic freedoms and the maintenance of non-discriminatory competition depend on the governmental supply of "public goods" such as contract law, company, competition, environment, social, monetary and for-

---

85 See: Federal Court Decision Vols. 100, I, a, p. 174; 103, I, a, pp. 259 ff; 106, I, a, p. 363.

86 See: L. Schürmann, Wirtschaftsverwaltungsrecht, 2nd edition, 1983, p. 27 f.

87 See L. Schürmann (note 86), p. 28, who is, however, of the view that private consumers are not protected by Article 31 (p. 31). This view seems to be shared by the Federal Court (Federal Court Decisions Vol. 103, I, a, p. 401) but appears doubtful since the freedom to consume (e.g. free choice of books) is an important determinant of the real income and personal development of each individual. See: Ch.-A. Junod, Liberté économique et protection des consommateurs, in: Festschrift für H. Huber, 1981, pp. 385 ff. On the constitutional protection of freedom of contract see P. Saladin (note 82), p. XLIV.

88 See: Federal Court Decisions Vol. 108, I, a, p. 148 f.

89 A. Grisel, La "réserve" de l'administration face au législateur et au juge, in: D. Dicke/Th. Fleiner-Gerster (eds.), Staat und Gesellschaft, Festschrift für L. Schürmann, 1987, p. 37 ff, 55, has rightly pointed out that the administration does not benefit from a "réserve" based on a constitutional principle.

90 Federal Court Decisions Vol. 104, I, a, p. 95: "die Grundrechte ... vermitteln keinen Anspruch auf positive Leistungen des Staates".

91 In 1976, the Court recognized a right to the use of public ground (Federal Court Decisions Vol. 101, I, a, p. 479). In Federal Court Decisions Vol. 107, I, a, p. 307 relating to freedom of opinion and of information, the Federal Court further qualified its previous case-law.

eign trade laws and administrative implementing acts. If, for instance, the government imposes quantitative restrictions on the importation of cheap foreign goods or promotes the sale of domestic goods by means of export subsidies, Article 31 must be construed as a legal basis for an individual right of Swiss traders and producers to the non-discriminatory access to the limited number of import licences and export subsidies and, for instance if the refusal of the import licence or export subsidy amounts to an arbitrary discrimination, possibly for an individual right to the granting of an import licence or export subsidy.

b) Freedom of Trade as an Objective Constitutional Principle and Institutional Guarantee

From the beginning, Article 31 pursued two additional objectives besides protecting individual economic liberty: First, to limit the regulatory powers of the cantons in order to protect freedom of trade among the cantons and the economic integration within the Federation.[92] And, second, to guarantee a federal economic system based on free competition. The Federal Court has decided in a large number of judgments that the constitutional freedom of trade and industry guarantees a "system of free competition" prohibiting governmental economic restrictions whose sole purpose is to protect certain producers from fair competition by others. Article 31

> "consacre le régime de la libre concurrence. Cela signifie en première ligne qu'on ne peut interdire à une personne l'exercice d'une profession ou d'une industrie pour le seul motif qu'elle ferait concurrence à des entreprises existantes, leur enlèverait des clients, diminuerait leurs recettes ou rendrait même leur exploitation impossible."[93]

Other Federal Court decisions have said that Article 31 presupposes non-discriminatory competition and prohibits governmental interferences and distortions of competition designed to protect certain producers or to direct economic activities in a planned manner.[94] Freedom of trade and industry is thus protec-

---

92 See the report of the Federal Council explaining the need for the 1874 Constitution in: Bundesblatt 1870, II, pp. 672, 673.

93 Federal Court Decisions Vol. 80, I, pp. 121, 126. See also Vol. 52, I, p. 293 ff, 300.

94 See Federal Court Decisions 86 I, p. 273 ff; Vol. 88, I, pp. 231, 236: "la libera concorrenza, che è implicita nella libertà di commercio, presuppone l'uguaglianza di trattamento e quindi il divieto di creare vantaggi a favore di alcuni et a detrimento di altri"; 102, I, a, p. 116: "Eine Verletzung von Art. 31 BV ... liegt vor, wenn eigentumsbeschränkende Massnahmen der Kantone unter dem Deckmantel der Raumplanung einen Eingriff in den wirt-

ted not only as an individual freedom but also as an institutional guarantee of an economic system based on non-discriminatory competition as a decentralized, liberal means of maximizing both individual as well as social welfare.[95]

Yet, as P. Saladin has criticized, the federal economic legislation and the Federal Court's case-law relating to the institutional guarantee of undistorted competition appear ambiguous. Various federal laws and court cases seem to have attributed more importance to the preservation of existing economic structures than to dynamic competition. Article 31 is construed as **not** protecting competitors from trade-distorting government subsidies and public procurement practices; and the general constitutional requirements of a legislative basis and of proportionality of executive restraints of the freedom of trade have not been consistently observed with regard to Article 31.[96]

c) Constitutional Bases for Governmental Limitations of Freedom of Trade

The legal determination of the scope of application of Article 31 must take into account its different individual and institutional functions: the protection of the individual right to the free development of one's professional and other personal economic activities, on the one side, and the public interest in a uniform federal economic system based on non-discriminatory competition, on the other side. Moreover, Article 31 has to be construed as part of the overall constitutional order with due regard to the large number of additional constitutional provisions authorizing government regulations of the economic order.

Article 31 stipulates explicitly that "Freedom of trade and industry is ... subject to such limitations as are contained in the Federal Constitution and the legislation enacted under its authority". In particular Articles 31 **bis** and 31 **quinquies**

schaftlichen Wettbewerb bezwecken, um bestimmte Gewerbezweige oder Betriebsformen vor Konkurrenz zu schützen oder in ihrer Existenz zu sichern".

95 See Federal Court Decisions Vol. 45, I, p. 347, 357 f: "Von dem Gedanken getragen, dass grundsätzlich die freie Entfaltung der individuellen wirtschaftlichen Kräfte und der sich daraus ergebende Wettbewerb aus dem Gesichtspunkt der allgemeinen Volkswohlfahrt die zweckmässigste Ordnung des Wirtschaftslebens darstellt, gewährt er (Article 31) dem Einzelnen als persönliches Freiheitsrecht die Befugnis, seine persönlichen Fähigkeiten und materiellen Mittel auf dem wirtschaftlichen Gebiet ungehindert zur Geltung zu bringen, soweit diese Betätigung nicht gegen die höheren Interessen der Volksgemeinschaft verstösst".

96 See P. Saladin (note 82), pp. 224 f, 247, 300 ff, 324, 331, 355, 367, 404. For instance, a legislative authorization ("formeller Gesetzesvorbehalt") of executive restraints of the individual freedom of trade is required by the Court only "as a rule" (Federal Court Decisions Vol. 80, I, p. 350 ff).

of the Constitution are recognized to provide broad constitutional authority for governmental limitations of trade and industry. Article 31 **bis**, as amended in 1947 and 1980, reads:

> "(1) Within the limits of its constitutional powers, the Confederation shall take measures to promote the general welfare and the economic security of its citizens.
>
> (2) While promoting the general interest of the Swiss economy, the Confederation may enact regulations on the exercise of trade and industry and take measures in favour of specific economic sectors or professions. In so doing, it must respect the principle of freedom of trade and industry, subject to the provisions of paragraph 3.
>
> (3) If the common interest justifies it, the Confederation is entitled, in departing, as needed, from principles of free trade and industry, to enact rules:
>
> a. to preserve important economic sectors or professions whose existence is threatened as well as to promote the professional qualifications of persons exercising an independent activity in those sectors or professions;
>
> b. to maintain a sound peasant population, ensure agricultural productivity and consolidate rural landownership;
>
> c. to protect regions the economy of which is threatened;
>
> d. to prevent economically or socially harmful effects of cartels and similar groupings;
>
> e. concerning precautionary measures of economic defense of the country as well as concerning measures for safeguarding the supply of the country with vital goods and services, given serious situations of shortage that the economy cannot cope with on its own.
>
> (4) Regulations under headings a and b shall be enacted only if the economic sectors or professions to be protected have taken such measures to help themselves as can be reasonably expected of them.
>
> (5) Federal legislation enacted under paragraph 3, headings a and b, shall promote the development of organisations based on mutual assistance."

Article 31 **quinquies**, as amended in 1978, adds, inter alia:

> "(1) The Confederation takes measures for a balanced economic development, particularly in order to prevent and combat unemployment and inflation. It cooperates with the Cantons and economic organizations.

> (2) Concerning measures in the domains of money and credit, public finance, and foreign economic relations, the Confederation may, if necessary, depart from principles of economic freedom of trade and industry. It may require the enterprises to form tax-privileged reserves for job creation. After release of such reserves, the enterprises decide freely on their use within the limits of the legal application purposes.
>
> (3) For the establishment of their budgets, Confederation, Cantons and municipalities take into account the requirements of the economic situation...
>
> (4) The Confederation takes into account the uneven economic development of particular areas of the country.
>
> (5) The Confederation conducts the data collections necessary for policies of economic development."

Article 31 **sexies**, inserted in 1981, adds:

> "(1) The Confederation takes measures to protect consumers while safeguarding the general interests of the national economy and respecting the freedom of trade and industry.
>
> (2) Consumer organizations benefit, within the limits of the legislation on unfair competition, from the same rights as vocational and economic associations."

These and other constitutional provisions illustrate that the Constitution reserves broad regulatory powers to the federal legislator to limit the freedom of trade and industry also in the field of foreign trade. Legislative restraints of the freedom of trade and industry must, however, balance the various constitutional values against each other and must, in particular, meet the various constitutional "balancing principles" such as: (a) the legislative restraints must be capable of and necessary for attaining their constitutionally recognized objective; (b) their social benefits must remain proportionate in relation of their social costs; and (c) the social cost-benefit-relationship should be regulated by the legislator in a manner maximizing the positive and minimizing the negative social effects.[97] Governmental restraints of the freedom of trade and industry must have

---

97 The latter aspect of the proportionality requirement, which is recognized in the pertinent German literature (see, e.g., H.H. v. Arnim, Staatslehre der Bundesrepublik Deutschland, 1984, p. 215f), seems to be often overlooked in the Swiss literature, see: Y. Hangartner, Zur Konzeption der Handels- und Gewerbefreiheit, in: Dicke/Fleiner-Gerster (note 89), pp. 117, 123ff.

a constitional basis and their limits must be determined by the democratic legislator himself.[98]

The case-law of the Federal Court has attributed a high value to the freedom of trade and industry compared to other constitutional principles allowing restraints of or, in the words of Article 31 **bis**, "departures" from the freedom of trade and industry. But the Federal Court has also emphasized that Article 31 cannot assert primacy over other constitutional provisions:

> "Les différentes normes constitutionnelles doivent être coordonnées et non subordonnées, à moins que le constituant lui-même n'ait institué un ordre hiérarchique déterminé" ... "le recourant voudrait donner la prééminence à la liberté du commerce et de l'industrie sur les autres dispositions de la constitution et restreindre aux prescriptions de police au sens étroit la faculté pour les cantons de déroger à cette liberté au sens de l'art. 31 al. 2 Cst. Mais rien ne justifie une telle prééminence, comme l'admet généralement la doctrine".[99]

The Federal Court recognizes that the preservation of freedom of trade - both as an individual right as well as an institutional guarantee of free competition - requires a framework of general legal rules. The Federal Court has therefore recognized in numerous decisions that general government regulations for reasons of security, social policy or also for economic reasons (e.g. cartel legislation) do not necessarily conflict with the freedom of trade and industry.[100] The Court rightly emphasizes the importance of the constitutional requirement of non-discrimination (Article 4 of the Constitution) for the equal protection of the individual freedoms of trade and for non-discriminatory competition as a constitutional objective and principle:

> "Une mesure administrative est incompatible avec l'article 31 Cst. si elle entrave le libre jeu de la concurrence en frappant inégalement les commerçants d'une même branche.

98 In this sense: Y. Hangartner (note 97), p. 125. See also P. Saladin (note 82), p. XLVIII f. Different views are expresed as to whether the constitutional basis must be explicit and unambiguous (in this sense L. Schürmann, note 86, p. 118) or whether implied, but "correctly construed" constitutional powers are sufficient (see Y. Hangartner, Grundzüge des Schweizerischen Staatsrechts, Vol. II, 1982, p. 149).

99 Federal Court Decisions Vol. 99, I, a, p. 620f. According to F. Gygi, Wirtschaftsverfassungsrecht, 1981, pp. 16f, 42f, the Swiss Constitution does not guarantee an "economic constitution of freedom of trade and industry", as many Swiss lawyers assert (e.g. Ch.-A. Junod, note 87 above), but only an "economic constitution for economic policy"

100 For a survey of this case-law see P. Saladin (note 2), pp. XLII ff, 234 ff, and F. Gygi, Wirtschaftspolitik aus verfassungsrechtlicher Sicht, in: Zeitschrift für Schweizerisches Recht 1981, p. 229 ff.

> L'intervention doit être aménagée de telle sorte qu'elle ne mette pas ceux qu'elle vise en état d'infériorité par rapport à leur concurrents directs, c'est-à-dire ceux qui s'adressent au même public pour satisfaire les mêmes besoins".[101]

The Federal Court has for a long time attributed a "supra-private value" ("une valeur supraprivée") to free competition as a decentralized coordinating mechanism for private economic decisions, which is economically more efficient, legally more liberal and politically more difficult to abuse than coordination through private cartels or administrative directives.[102] The more recent case-law of the Federal Court appears, however, to have become more tolerant towards cartelistic restraints proceeding from the economically doubtful assumption that private restraints of competition may be beneficial not only for the cartelists themselves but also for the society at large.[103] A similar "protectionist producer bias" is reflected in the Court's recent case law according to which Article 31 protects "toute activité économique privée tendant à la production d'un gain et exercée à titre professionnel", including freedom of contract, yet not the freedom to consume in spite of the explicit constitutional provisions designed to protect consumers.[104]

The sweeping constitutional amendments since 1947 authorizing almost all kinds of government interventions into the economy, including "measures in favour of specific economic sectors or professions" (Article 31 **bis**), appear to have considerably weakened the traditional constitutional protection of freedom of trade and industry.[105] Article 31 **bis** has been used as a constitutional basis also for comprehensive foreign trade restrictions, especially on agricultural trade.[106] Article 31 **quinquies**, introduced into the Constitution in 1978, has granted an additional blanket authorization for "departures" from the freedom

---

101 Federal Court Decisions vol. 78, I, pp. 298, 303: See also the more recent judgment in vol. 109, I, a, p. 122, where the Court said that cantonal measures must not interfere into free competition ("libre concurrence").

102 Federal Court Decisions Vol. 94, II, p. 339

103 See Federal Court Decisions Vol. 98, II, 377 and, for instance, R. Zäch, Geschlossene oder Offenen Schweizerische Wirtschaftsverfassung?, in: Dicke/Fleiner-Gerster (above note 89), pp. 131, 135; P. Saladin (note 82), p. 224 f.

104 See Federal Court Decisions Vol. 102, I, a, p. 122, and P. Saladin (note 82), p. XLVI.

105 According to L. Schürmann (note 86), p. 16, the constitutional amendments of 1947 have confirmed a comparatively high rank of the freedom of trade and industry.

106 See F. Gygi note 99), p. 143, and the detailed account of Swiss foreign trade restrictions on agricultural goods in: K. Weber, Die Schweizerische Aussenhandelsgesetzgebung, 1975, pp. 156 ff, 169 ff.

of trade in the field of foreign economic relations. An even broader delegation of powers, not specified by substantive and procedural restraints, is provided for in Article 1 of the 1982 Swiss Federal Law on Foreign Economic Measures:

> "To the extent that foreign measures or extraordinary conditions abroad influence the exchange of goods, services and payments of Switzerland in a manner affecting essential Swiss economic interests, the Federal Council may, as long as circumstances require,
>
> a) introduce controls, licences, restrictions or prohibitions for the importation, exportation and transit of goods and services;
>
> b) regulate payments with specified countries and, if appropriate, impose levies in order to offset price or monetary distortions in the exchange of goods, services and payments".[107]

This seemingly unlimited delegation of competences from the Federal Assembly to the Federal Council to regulate, restrict or prohibit the transnational trade and payments transactions of Swiss citizens points to another "constitutional dilemma": Not only the traditional substantive constitutional guarantees in Articles 29 and 31 for freedom of foreign trade, but also the procedural constitutional safeguards (such as separation and only limited delegation of powers) no longer appear to operate as effective constitutional restraints on the executive taxation and restriction of importers, exporters, producers and consumers engaged in foreign trade. The numerous constitutional authorizations of government interventions into the "spontaneous order" of market competition (see Articles 31 **bis, quinquies** and **sexies**, 34 **ter**, 38, 39) confer broad discretionary regulatory powers to the democratic legislator subject to only limited judicial review (see Article 113, para. 3). The self-imposed international GATT and EFTA obligations of Switzerland for the use of transparent, market-conforming, non-discriminatory and proportionate trade policy instruments appear to be more precise and more comprehensive than the autonomous regulations in Swiss law of how the national constitutional principles of transparent democratic policy-making, use of low tariffs (Article 29), non-discrimination and proportionality must be observed in the field of foreign trade policy.

107 Bundesgesetz über Aussenwirtschaftliche Massnahmen of 25 June 1982, Systematische Sammlung des Bundesrechts 946.201 (unofficial translation by this author).

C) Other Constitutional Restraints on the Foreign Affairs Powers

a) The Policy Goals of Article 2

Article 2 of the Constitution stipulates, inter alia, that "the aim of the Confederation is to preserve the outward independence of the fatherland". This constitutional objective reflects the centuries-old history of the gradual formation of the Swiss Confederation and of its legal protection against threats from abroad. The neutrality of Switzerland, even though recognized in various legal instruments since the "Acte portant reconnaissance et garantie de la neutralité perpétuelle de la Suisse et de l'inviolabilité de son territoire" signed by various states in 1815, is mentioned only in Articles 85 (section 6) and 102 (section 9) but not in Article 2 of the Constitution.

The Federal Council has defined the term "outward independence" in the narrow sense of "protection of the actual existence of Switzerland as independent state and its recognition as sovereign member of the community of states".[108] An isolationist interpretation of the requirement to protect the "outward independence" would be inconsistent with the simultaneous requirement of Article 2 "to protect the freedom and the rights of the confederates and to promote their common prosperity"; for, the economic welfare of a small country and the effective protection of the rights of its citizens abroad in foreign jurisdictions depend on international economic and legal integration securing access to foreign markets and supplies.[109] The constitutional objectives set out in Article 2 supplement therefore those of Articles 29 and 31 on liberal customs duties and freedom of trade. The permantent neutrality of Switzerland is a long-standing political axiom of Swiss foreign policy, but it is controversial whether it is also constitutionally mandated;[110]as a principle of public international law, it does not stand in the way of liberal, non-discriminatory foreign trade pursuant to multilateral international agreements such as GATT and regional customs unions or free trade areas admitted under GATT Article XXIV.

108 See the Report on the Accession of Switzerland to the UNO, in: Bundesblatt 1982, I, pp. 504, 543.

109 See: W. Kälin, Verfassungsgrundsätze der schweizerischen Aussenpolitik, in: Zeitschrift für Schweizerisches Recht, 1986, S. 249 ff, 290 f.

110 On the divergent views in Swiss legal doctrine on this issue see, for instance, W. Kälin (note 109), p. 294, 330; J. Monnier (note 81), pp. 121 ff.

The principles of "solidarity", "universality" and "disponibilité" (in the sense of readiness and willingness to contribute to the solution of international problems) are also declared principles of Swiss foreign policy.[111] But they are not mentioned in the Swiss constitution and, arguably, are not required by Article 2 of the Constitution.[112] They have served as political guiding principles for various national laws of Switzerland (e.g. the 1976 federal law on international economic development aid). They are fully consistent also with the objectives of mutually beneficial, non-discriminatory liberal trade in conformity with international agreements such as GATT.

b) Constitutional Rule-of-Law Requirements

The "legality principle" of Swiss constitutional law means in a broad sense that all legislative, executive and judicial government powers must be exercised in conformity with the law. It includes the constitutional requirements of the primacy of constitutional law over other national laws, of the primacy of lawful legislation over administrative regulations ("Gesetzesvorrang", "suprématie de la loi"), and of the need for a legislative authorization ("Gesetzesvorbehalt, "réserve de la loi") of executive interferences into individual rights.

According to the case-law of the Federal Court, the constitutional principle of legislative reservation of powers ("Gesetzesvorbehalt") applies not only to direct interferences into individual rights ("Eingriffsverwaltung"), but also to the granting and administration of certain public services whenever they impact on the equal rights of domestic citizens ("Leistungsverwaltung").[113] Yet, it remains controversial in Swiss legal doctrine whether the constitutional principle of legislative reservation of powers applies to the executive foreign affairs powers and to what extent the legislative authorizations need to be specified in the field of foreign policy.[114] Another interrelated question is whether the constitutional requirement of a legislative authorization necessitates in all cases a formal parliamentary act ("formeller Gesetzesbegriff") or whether other legal rules of a

---

111 See: W. Kälin (note 109), pp. 298-347; Monnier (note 81), pp. 126-134.

112 See, however, W. Kälin, at pp. 334, 383, according to whom these principles have become Swiss customary constitutional law with the same rank as Article 2 of the Constitution.

113 See notably the "Wäffler case" in Federal Court Decisions Vol. 103, I, a, pp. 380 ff.

114 See G.C. Haas, Verfassungsrechtliche Aspekte der Schweizerischen Aussenwirtschaftspolitik, 1989, pp. 22 et seq.; Th.G. Borer, Das Legalitätsprinzip und die Auswärtigen Angelegenheiten, 1986, pp. 373 et seq.; Th.Cottier, Die Verfassung und das Erfordernis der gesetzlichen Grundlage, 1983.

general and abstract nature (e.g. constitutional rules, parliamentary or executive regulations, international treaties, customary law) may suffice ("materieller Gesetzesbegriff").

In addition to the long-standing customs legislation (Federal Customs Law of 1925, as amended) and agricultural legislation (Federal Law on the Promotion of Agriculture and on the Preservation of the Peasant Class of 1951, as amended), the Federal Assembly has enacted an increasing number of general laws regulating export risk guarantees (Federal Law on Export Risk Guarantees of 1958), foreign investment risks (Federal Law on Investment Risk Guarantees of 1970), production of and trade in war materials (Federal Law on War Materials of 1972), and other foreign economic policy measures (e.g. Federal Law on Foreign Economic Policy Measures of 1982) including development aid (Federal Law of 1976 on International Development Cooperation and Humanitarian Aid). International agreements ratified by Switzerland are valid and applicable within Switzerland like federal laws (see below under d) and are also considered as a sufficient legal basis for governmental implementing measures.

This legislative regulation of "foreign" affairs is to be welcomed for a number of reasons. In view of the ever increasing economic, political and legal international integration, it is no longer possible to draw a neat dividing line between "domestic" and "foreign" policy matters. Most "domestic" policy matters can become a matter of international cooperation, and many "foreign" policy actions are implemented not only in the forms of international law and diplomacy but give rise also to domestic implementing measures and to repercussions on domestic citizens. Especially for the citizens of a small country, its "external" relations are often no less important than purely "internal" relations. This is true in particular for the international division of labour through trade, where a number of constitutional reasons would seem to necessitate a legislative basis for executive restraints or distortions of transnational trade transactions of Swiss citizens:

aa) According to the original constitutional concept of Article 29 - which corresponds to the present GATT principle of "tariffs only" - trade policy should be conducted by means of tariffs to be regulated in general federal customs legislation. Only under "extraordinary conditions" should the Confederation be authorized to resort to "temporary special measures" (see Article 29, paragraph 2).

bb) Article 31 of the Constitution likewise explicitly stipulates that "freedom of trade and industry is guaranteed .... subject to such limitations as are contained in the Federal Constitution and the legislation enacted under its authority".

cc) Governmental restraints or distortions of foreign trade transactions interfere with the individual freedoms of trade of Swiss citizens and with the constitutional requirements of equal treatment (Article 4) and non-discriminatory competition (Article 31).

dd) The international GATT obligations of Switzerland set out detailed rules for, in principle, all trade policy instruments. There are no specific "foreign policy reasons" why national trade regulations should, or could, not likewise be laid down in general legislative rules. The free trade area agreements concluded by Switzerland with the EEC and EFTA countries have also proven that international trade, in spite of its continous dynamic change, is amenable to and requires general long-term rules.

ee) Since governmental restraints or distortions of foreign trade transactions redistribute income among national groups in a manner reducing the potential national economic welfare, such redistributive value decisions call for democratic legitimation through parliamentary acts, transparent discussions and procedural guarantees enabling the participation of all affected groups.

c) Protection of Individual Rights in Foreign Affairs

Swiss courts and legal doctrine recognize that all government powers are legally bound by the constitution and by the rule of law. The constitutional guarantees of individual rights limit also the exercise of the foreign affairs powers, even though the extent of this constitutional protection may differ from that in purely national affairs because of the limited scope of application of certain individual rights and because of the particular "international" nature of the transnational exercise and protection of individual rights.[115] In a liberal democracy, the constitutional guarantees of individual rights constitute and determine the "public interest". The Swiss constitution does not allow a definition of the national "foreign policy interest" without regard to, or in opposition to, the individual rights

115 See: W. Kälin (note 109), p. 352.

of Swiss citizens; nor is it allowed to treat the latter as mere objects of the government.[116]

The constitutional protection of individual rights in foreign affairs serves individual as well as "institutional" functions:

aa) As individual guarantees of personal freedom, economic liberty, property rights, equal treatment, substantive and procedural "due process",[117] individual rights limit the scope of government powers also in the field of foreign affairs and protect Swiss citizens and other individuals subject to Swiss jurisdiction from certain disproportionate governmental restraints that cannot be justified by a prevailing public interest. Thus the federal government and legal doctrine recognize that the constitutional guarantees of equal protection (Article 4), freedom of trade (Article 31) and of other individual rights limit, for instance, the scope of the treaty-making powers and of the power to regulate the internal implementation of foreign policy acts (e.g. a trade embargo).[118]

bb) As objective principles of Swiss constitutional law, the constitutionally guaranteed individual rights commit the government to protect and promote individual rights also in transnational relations. Thus the Federal Court recognizes that international treaty obligations must be construed in conformity with the constitutional guarantees of individual rights.[119] And foreign demands for extradition, for legal assistance, for the enforcement of foreign judgments, or for the supply of war materials (see Article 11 of the 1972 Swiss War Materials Act) must be turned down if their implementation would result in a violation of national and international human rights.[120]

cc) The governmental respect for individual rights in foreign affairs entails a largely decentralized regulation and order of transnational relations. The citizens themselves, through their transnational exercise of individual rights, must

---

116 On this "constitutive function" of individual rights as "the foundation of government" (preamble of the Bill of Rights of Virginia of 12 July 1776) see P. Saladin (note 82), pp. 292 ff.

117 For a survey of the various individual rights which are explicitly or implicitly protected under Swiss constitutional law see: P. Saladin (note 82); J.P. Müller/S. Müller (note 84); Y.Hangartner, Grundzüge des Schweizerischen Staatsrechts, Band II: Grundrechte, 1982; U. Häfelin/W. Haller, Schweizerisches Bundesstaatsrecht, 2nd ed. 1988, pp. 325 ff.

118 See: W. Kälin (note 109), pp. 354 ff.

119 See: Federal Court Decisions Vol. 102, I, a, pp. 40 ff

120 See the examples and references to the pertinent Swiss statutes by W. Kälin (note 109), p. 361 f.

be the main agents of international political, economic and social integration. The individual rights as institutional gurantees commit the government to the creation of a liberal framework of national and international rules and institutions protecting international cooperation against both "government failures" and "market failures". The national and international human rights guarantees promote the mutual consistency and complementarity of national and international law as well as decentralized processes of peaceful change, continuous adjustment and a welfare maximizing division of labour.

d) Respect for International Law

The Swiss Constitution does not clearly define the relationship between international law and Swiss law. According to the established practice of Swiss courts and legal doctrine, rules of public international treaty law and customary law binding upon Switzerland are a valid part of Swiss law without any need for the "transformation" or specific "incorporation" of the international rules concerned.[121] As regards the internal rank of international rules within the Swiss legal system, the Federal Court has treated the human rights guarantees of the European Convention on Human Rights as constitutional guarantees.[122] Swiss courts and legal doctrine recognize the primacy of international law over Swiss law and the legal obligation of all government organs to act in conformity with international law. Federal law inconsistent with international law is generally not considered to be void ipso iure. Swiss practice attempts to avoid such conflicts by construing national law in conformity with international law or by not applying or repealing national rules inconsistent with international obligations.[123] The Federal Court has, however, recognized the possiblity of deliberate, valid deviations by the Swiss legislator from international legal obligations.[124]

---

121 On this Swiss practice see: J.P. Müller/L. Wildhaber, Praxis des Völkerrechts, 2nd edition, 1982, pp. 103 ff. A recent Swiss Federal Court decision concludes (Federal Court Decisions Vol 102, I, a, pp. 317,329): "In matters of extradition as in other areas, international treaties take precedence over national law, even if they are prior to national law; in case of a contradiction between the provisions of the law and those of a treaty, the latter take precedence over the former; the provision of the law are only applicable for the points that have not been expressly or implicitly regulated by the treaty".

122 See: Federal Court Decisions Vol. 101, I, a, p. 67.

123 For details see: Y. Hangartner, Grundzüge des Schweizerischen Staatsrechts, Vol.I, pp. 44, 200; W. Kälin, Der Geltungsgrund des Grundsatzes "Völkerrecht bricht Landesrecht", in: Die Schweizerische Rechtsordnung in ihren internationalen Bezügen, 1988, pp.45 ff.

124 Federal Court Decisions Vol. 99, I, b, p. 39. For a criticism of this court decision see: E.U. Petersmann, Die Verfassungsentscheidung für eine völkerrechtskonforme Rechtsordnung

The question of the internal validity and legal rank of international obligations must be distinguished from the question of their direct applicability by the judiciary and private citizens. According to the Federal Court, in Switzerland

> "an international treaty approved by the Federal Assembly acquires legal force by the exchange of the instruments of ratification and becomes, **ipso facto**, an integral part of the federal legal order. If the provisions of this international treaty are directly applicable, that is to say sufficiently clear and precise to serve as the basis of a decision in a particular case, they are binding not only upon the authorities but upon individuals as well. Purely programmatic provisions, those that regulate a matter only in outline form, leaving the Contracting State a large power of discretion or decision, or those that simply lay down guidelines and are not intended for the Administration or judicial authorities but for the legislator, lack the required precision".[125]

Directly applicable ("self-executing") are notably precise and unconditional prohibitive rules which do not presuppose additional implementing rules and regulate or protect individual rights. Even if the international rules do not explicitly prescribe their direct applicability within the domestic legal systems, they may be capable of being directly applied and the domestic legal system concerned (e.g. the constitutional guarantees of individual rights in Switzerland) may require their direct applicability for the benefit of the citizens. Article 113, section 1 of the Swiss Constitution prescribes, inter alia, that the "Federal Court shall ... adjudicate... complaints concerning the violation of the constitutional rights of citizens as well as individual complaints concerning the violation of ... international treaties". This constitutional recognition of the function of international treaties to protect indiviual rights suggests that precise and unconditional international treaty obligations protecting individual rights should be presumed to be directly applicable in Swiss law.

---

als Strukturprinzip der Schweizer Bundesverfassung, in: Archiv des Öffentlichen Rechts, 1990.

125 Federal Court Decisions Vols. 105, II, p. 49; 100, I, b, p. 230; 98, I. b, p. 387.

125a See A. Auer, La juridiction constitutionelle en Suisse, 1983, pp. 59 ff, and for a differentiated recent analysis: W. Kälin Verfassungsgerichtsbarkeit in der Demokratie, 1987, pp. 160 ff.

D) Lack of Judicial Control over Foreign Policy Decisions and Federal Legislation

Article 113, section 3 of the Swiss Constitution is widely construed to exempt federal legislation from judicial review[125a]. Moreover, similar to, and influenced by, the English "act of state doctrine", the US "political question doctrine" and the French legal doctrine of non-justiciable "actes de gouvernement", Swiss law exempts also certain foreign policy acts from judicial review.[126] Article 110,a of the 1943 federal law on the organization of the federal judiciary explicitly declares inadmissible administrative court actions against "decisions relating to the internal or external security of the country, to the neutrality, to diplomatic protection and in the field of other foreign affairs".[127] The explanation of this provision by the Swiss Federal Council[128] and the comprehensive review of foreign trade restrictions by Swiss courts[129] suggest that foreign trade restrictions are, at least in principle, not exempt from judicial review by Swiss courts.

This is confirmed also by Article 113, section 3 (and the corresponding Article 114, section 3, relating to the Federal Administrative Court) of the Swiss Constitution, according to which "the Federal Court shall apply the laws and generally binding decrees adopted by the Federal Assembly, as well as the international treaties approved by this Assembly". In the case of individual complaints concerning the constitutional freedom of foreign trade (Articles 29 and 31), the Federal Court should therefore apply also the often precise and unconditional GATT prohibitions of foreign trade restrictions. Cantonal, intercantonal and federal executive regulations - but not federal "laws and generally binding decrees" in the sense of Article 113 of the Constitution - could therefore be declared void by the Federal Court if they were found to be inconsistent with precise and unconditional prohibitions of international trade agreements. Yet, the Federal Court has so far refrained from directly applying GATT rules.[130] While the Court has recognized the direct applicability of the non-discrimination requirement in Article 16 of the EFTA Agreement, it has refused to apply directly

126 See: G. Müller, Reservate staatlicher Willkür - Grauzone zwischen Rechtsfreiheit, Rechtsbindung und Rechtskontrolle, in: Festschrift für H. Huber, 1981, pp. 110, 121 ff.

127 Systematische Sammlung des Bundesrechts SR 173.110 (translation by this author)

128 See: Bundesblatt 1965, II, p. 1306

129 See: the detailed survey by K. Weber (note 106), pp. 303 ff. See: also W. Kälin, Das Verfahren der staatsrechtlichen Beschwerde, 1984, pp. 106 ff.

130 See: Federal Court Decisions Vol. 112, Ib, p. 183.

the trade and competition rules in Articles 13, 20 and 23 of the Free Trade Area Agreement between Switzerland and the EEC; a recent decision by the Court has held that the non-application of the procedural provisions in Articles 16 and 17 of Protocol No. 3 to the free trade area agreement between Switzerland and the EEC amounted to a violation of the procedural rights which Swiss law grants to importers under Article 4 of the Constitution and under Swiss administrative law.[131]

Due to the lack of judicial control over federal legislation and over the constitutionality of international agreements, the Federal Court cannot review the constitutionality of legislative foreign trade and agricultural restrictions, for instance whether less restrictive or less distortive legislative trade restrictions would have been possible and more proportionate.[132] Many Swiss foreign trade laws delegate broad discretionary regulatory powers to the executive branch and thereby further reduce the scope for judicial review.[133] The Federal Court must observe international agreements. But the Court has been criticized, with good reason, for its "judicial protectionism" in the "Omo case"[134] where the Court refused to apply directly precise and unconditional obligations of the free trade agreement between Switzerland and the EEC in contrast to the EC Court of Justice which directly applied and enforced similar provisions in the free trade agreements between the EEC and EFTA countries.[135] The Court's argument that the treaty prohibitions of quantitative restrictions are addressed to the Swiss legislator and to the Swiss administration and may not be invoked by individuals against the Swiss trade mark law of 1890, appears indeed formalistic in the light of the Swiss Federal Court's earlier case law recognizing the direct applicability of EFTA treaty provisions[136] and in view of the precise and unconditional prohibitions of the free trade area agreement with the EEC committing the "contracting parties" (i.e. not only the executive but also the legislative and judicial government organs) to refrain from tariffs, quantitative restrictions and "any measure likely to jeopardize the fulfilment of the objectives of the Agreement" (Article 22).

---

131 See: Federal Court Decisions Vol. 98, Ib, p. 385; 105, II, p. 49; 104, II, p. 175; 111, Ib, p.323.

132 See: the various Court cases discussed by K. Weber (above note 106) pp. 16-19.

133 See: K. Weber (note 106), pp. 16, 30, 320 f.

134 See: Federal Court Decisions Vol. 105, II, p. 49.

135 See: O. Jacot-Guillarmod, Judicial protectionism: legal fate or political challenge to free trade in Europe? in: EFTA Bulletin 4/1985, pp 8 ff.

136 Federal Court decisions Vol. 98, I, b, p. 385.

The Swiss Federal Council has, for its part, recognized in a 1984 report on relations with the EEC that a "harmonious development of case law (of European Supreme Courts) constitutes an important contribution to the realisation of the objectives of the Free Trade Agreements".[137] Just as the constitutional guarantee of freedom of trade in Article 31 is recognized to confer justiciable individual rights on traders and producers, precise and unconditional international treaty prohibitions extending this freedom of trade across national frontiers should likewise be recognized to serve the interests and individual rights of domestic citizens.

4. Foreign Affairs and Foreign Trade in a Liberal Twentieth Century Constitution: The Basic Law of the Federal Republic of Germany

A) Human Rights as Foundations of All Government Powers

The Constitution of the Federal Republic of Germany, the Basic Law of 23 May 1949, is strongly influenced by the traumatic experiences with the preceeding political totalitarianism in Nazi Germany as well as by certain "constitutional failures" of the German constitution of 1919. The "Weimarer Rechtsverfassung" of 1919 had entrusted the democratic legislator with the power to restrict, modify or even suspend all constitutional guarantees. The Basic Law of 1949 demonstratively turned away from this concept of "relative democracy" and legal positivism ("Gesetz ist Gesetz") towards the constitutional commitment to inalienable human rights binding all government powers and to the constitutional guarantee of a "free democratic basic order", the basic principles of which cannot be amended even by the democratic legislator according to the so-called "eternity clause" of Article 79, section 3. This constitutional recognition of inalienable human rights (Article 1), the detailed enumeration of substantive and procedural fundamental rights (e.g. in Articles 2 to 20, 33, 38, 101, 103, 104) and the additional protection of basic rights through objective constitutional principles (such as separation of powers) and institutional "checks and balances" (e.g. the Federal Constitutional Court) were influenced by the liberal constitutional traditions notably of US constitutional law. But the special constitutional

137 Bundesblatt 1984, I, pp. 464 ff, 474. In its 1988 report on the position of Switzerland in the process of European integration, the Federal Council also confirmed that the free trade area agreement obligates all the government organs of the "contracting parties" (Bundesblatt 1988, II, pp. 233 ff., 331).

safeguards for a "free democratic basic order" (see Articles 10, 18, 21, 91) and the Basic Law's constitutional guarantees of human rights as "the basis and foundation of government" (Virginia Bill of Rights, 1776) go in several respects beyond those of US constitutional law, notably as regards the constitutional restraints on the foreign relations power.

a) The Constitutional Guarantee of a "Free Democratic Basic Order"

The American and European liberal constitutions in the tradition of the American and French Human Rights Declarations of 1776, 1789 and 1791 differ in their enumerations of individual basic rights (e.g. in the US Bill of Rights of 1791 and in the preamble of the French Constitutions of 1946 and 1958) and in their protection of these rights through objective constitutional principles (e.g. of separation of powers or through the "principes généraux du droit" developed by the French Conseil d'Etat).[138] According to the German Federal Constitutional Court, the constitutional guarantee of a "free democratic basic order" not only protects the fundamental rights set out in the Basic Law as subjective rights and as objective guarantees. It also guarantees objective constitutional principles designed to protect equal freedoms and democracy, such as sovereignty of the people, separation of powers, responsibility of the government, the precedence of parliamentary legislation over acts of the administration, the independence of the courts, the multiple political parties system and the equal opportunity of all political parties, including the right to form and exercise a political opposition.[139] The Federal Constitutional Court has consistently held that "the Basic Law is a value-bound order, which recognizes the protection of freedom and human dignity as the ultimate object of all law".[140] This is most clearly recognized in Article 1 on "Protection of human dignity":

> "(1) The dignity of man shall be inviolable. To respect and protect it shall be the duty of all state authority.
>
> (2) The German people therefore acknowledge inviolable and inalienable human rights as the basis of every community, of peace and of justice in the world.

---

138 For a comparative survey see: A. Bleckmann, Allgemeine Grundrechtslehren, 1979, p. 7 ff.

139 See: Bundesverfassungsgericht Entscheidungen Vols. 2, p. 1 ff; 5, p. 85 ff; 12, p. 45 ff; 44, p. 125 ff.

140 Bundesverfassungsgericht Entscheidung Vol. 12, pp. 45, 51 (unofficial translation by the author). For an unofficial English translation of the Basic Law see: Blaustein/Flanz (eds.), Constitutions of the Countries of the World (note 80), Vol. VI, pp. 43 ff.

(3) The following basic rights shall bind the legislature, the executive and the judiciary as directly enforcable law".

The constitutional supremacy of the fundamental rights is likewise reflected in Article 2 on "Rights of liberty" and Article 3 on "Equality before the law", notably in the interpretation by the Federal Constitutional Court of Article 2, section 1 ("Everyone shall have the right to the free development of his personality in so far as he does not violate the rights of others or offend against the constitutional order or the moral code") as a general, comprehensive guarantee of individual freedom of action in all its personal, economic and other manifestations.[141] The "supremacy clause" of Article 1, section 3, the interpretation of Article 2, section 1 as an individual right to be free from unconstitutional government restraints, the large number of additional specific guarantees of substantive and procedural fundamental rights enumerated in the Basic Law, notably the constitutional guarantees of "the essential content of a basic right" (Article 19, section 2) and of the availability of judicial review "should any person's right be violated by public authority" (Article 19, section 4), and the constitutional prohibition in Article 79, section 3 of "amendments of... the basic principles laid down in Articles 1 and 20"[142] add up to a comprehensive system of subjective and objective constitutional guarantees designed to safeguard and reconcile the fundamental rights of the individual with those of others and with the "public interests" of the community.[143]

b) The Fundamental Rights as Constitutive Elements of the "Public Interest"

The Basic Law constitutes limited government powers and rejects the idea of omnipotent government powers. The constitutional supremacy of the funda-

141 Such a broad interpretation of the constitutional guarantee of personal freedom has been recognized neither by the US Supreme Court nor by the Swiss Federal Court, see e.g. P. Saladin (note 82), pp. XXIX, 230 ff.

142 Article 20 on "Basic principles of the Constitution" reads: "(1) The Federal Republic of Germany is a democratic and social federal state. (2) All state authority emanates from the people. It shall be exercised by the people by means of elections and voting and by specific legislative, executive and judicial organs. (3) Legislation shall be subject to the constitutional order; the executive and the judiciary shall be bound by law and justice. (4) All Germans shall have the right to resist any person or persons seeking to abolish that constitutional order, should no other remedy be possible."

143 For a recent survey in English language of the Basic Law's "fundamental rights system" see: C. Starck, Constitutional Definition and Protection of Rights and Freedoms, in: C. Starck (ed.), Rights, Institutions and Impact of International Law according to the German Basic Law, 1987, pp. 19-61.

mental rights implies that, as it was formulated in an earlier draft of Article 1 of the Basic Law, "the state exists for the sake of the people, not the people for the sake of the state". Not only the constitutional guarantees of individual rights directly binding the executive, judicial as well as legislative branches of government, but also the institutional and organizational rules of the Basic Law are designed to safeguard the freedoms and other rights of individuals.[144] The individual human being with his personal interests, preferences and needs must be the starting point and ultimate object of all government activities. The "state" as such no longer possesses a constitutionally recognized separate value of its own (such as "la gloire de l'état"),[145] nor are there constitutionally recognized "specific state interests" independent from the individual interests of the citizens.[146] The government officials must serve as trustees of the interests of all the citizens and not of their own interests or of certain group interests only.[147]

This rejection by the German Basic Law of an intrinsic value of the "state" as such, and also of political parties and private associations as such in spite of their important role for the effectuation of individual rights,[148] has far-reaching legal implication. Thus the distinction between "private" and "public" interests does not relate to different subjects of the interests but both refer to the individuals protected by the fundamental rights guaranteed in the Basic Law. The distinction between the "public interest" of its citizens, or between "the state" and "the society", refers rather to the different institutions and procedures for the determination and pursuit of the same individual interests. Even though it has often been unduly neglected in the extensive German legal literature on the distinction between "the state" and "the society",[149] the arguments of the classical economic, political and legal liberals (such as Locke, Smith and St.Mill) in favour of equal freedoms and property rights were always based on the constitu-

---

144 See: Bundesverfassungsgericht Entscheidungen Vol. 21, pp. 362, 372

145 See: K. Stern, Das Staatsrecht der Bundesrepublik Deutschland, Vol. I, 2nd edition, 1984, p. 571.

146 See: H.H. von Arnim, Staatslehre der Bundesrepublik Deutschland, 1984, p. 173: "es gibt keine spezifischen Staatsinteressen. Der Staat hat vielmehr die Interessen der vom Grundgesetz verfassten menschlichen Gemeinschaft wahrzunehmen. Der Staat - das sind wir ... Der Staat des Grundgesetzes ist der Staat seiner Gesellschaft. Die Verfolgung irgendwelcher anderer Interessen als der der Menschen wäre illegitim".

147 See: H.H. von Arnim (note 146), p. 129 f.

148 See: H.H. von Arnim (note 146), p. 133 f.

149 See, e.g.: E. Grabitz, Freiheit und Verfassungsrecht, 1976, and the criticism of Grabitz' portrayal of "laissez-faire liberalism" by A. Bleckmann (note 138), pp. 219-226

tional assumption that a maximization of individual and social economic welfare through undistorted competition, or the improvement of "public opinion" through a transparent discussion and an open "market in ideas", could be achieved only in a framework of "laws and institutions" (A.Smith) supplied and protected by the government. The separation of legislative, executive and judicial government powers, the representation of the people through a freely elected parliament, the constitutional requirement of "general legislation" (Article 19 section 1) as a safeguard of equal rights and legal certainty, the legal primacy of constitutional law over legislation, and of legislation over administrative acts, the constitutional requirement of a legislative authorization of executive interferences into individual rights, and the guarantees of independent judicial review are all constitutional principles designed to protect and effectuate the equal rights of the citizens.

The German courts and legal doctrine recognize therefore that the fundamental rights of the Basic Law provide not only actionable subjective rights but at the same time also objective guarantees.[150] In the words of the Federal Constitutional Court:

> "According to their history and their present contents, the fundamental rights are primarily individual rights, human and civil rights which aim to protect concrete, particularly endangered spheres of human freedom. The function of the fundamental rights as objective guarantees lies in the strengthening of their binding force but, nevertheless, flows directly from the primary function of the fundamental rights as subjective guarantees, which the secondary function as objective guarantees should always heed and not try to undermine".[151]

The Federal Constitutional Court has also recognized that the effectuation of fundamental rights often depends on supplemetary procedural and institutional guarantees and that the state may be under a constitutional obligation to promote the implementation of fundamental rights through appropriate organiza-

150 For a survey of the various functions as "defensive rights", political and social "participatory rights", "institutional guarantees", "constitutional value decisions", "objective norms", "constitutional programms", etc., and of the correlative government obligations see Bleckmann (note 138), pp. 155 ff.

151 Bundesverfassungsgericht Entscheidungen Vol. 50, pp. 290, 337.

tional and procedural rules.[152] The "public interest" and the "private interests" are therefore interrelated and both designed to protect the fundamental rights of the citizens. The Basic Law frequently empowers the legislature to define limits to a number of fundamental rights which explicitly provide for a legislative reservation of power (Gesetzesvorbehalt).[153] But, since the legislature itself is also bound to the fundamental rights by the supremacy clause of Article 1, the inherent limits of the fundamental rights and the "objects of legal protection" (Rechtsgüter) justifying legislative restraints of individual rights must ultimately always be derived from the Constitution itself.[154]

The necessary balancing among the various fundamental rights for the delimitation of their respective constitutional limits must respect the constitutional requirements of suitability, necessity and proportionality of fundamental rights restrictions: the restriction in question must be capable of achieving the constitutionally admissible objective;[155] it must not be more restrictive than necessary;[156] and the means must be proportionate in relation to the ends pursued.[157] In carrying out its judicial review of laws, the Federal Constitutional Court has also examined the legislator's factual determinations and has required the legislator to amend a statute if the legislator's factual predictions have proved to be wrong after some time.[158]

The legislative determination of the constitutional limits of the fundamental rights must further take into account that decentralized steering mechanisms, based upon the free execise of individual freedoms and property rights in the

---

152 See, e.g., Bundesverfassungsgericht Entscheidungen Vol. 53, pp. 30, 64 ff. (proceedings for obtaining the permission to operate a nuclear power plant); Vol. 41, pp. 251, 265 (measures for maintaining order in school).

153 On the diverse forms of "legislative reservations of powers" in the fundamental rights guarantees of the German Basic Law see: Starck (note 143), p. 26 f.

154 See: K. Hesse, Grundzüge des Verfassungsrechts der Bundesrepublik Deutschland, 1967, p. 123: Denn "wie die grundrechtlichen Freiheitsgewährleistungen durch die Verfassung begründet werden, so können auch die Grenzen dieser Gewährleistungen ihre Grundlage allein in der Verfassung finden".

155 See, for instance, Bundesverfassungsgericht Entscheidungen Vol. 16, pp. 147, 181.

156 See, for instance, Bundesverfassungsgericht Entscheidungen Vol. 39, pp. 156, 165.

157 See, for instance, Bundesverfassungsgericht Entscheidungen Vol. 28, pp. 264, 280; 29, pp. 221, 235. Some authors (e.g. H.H. von Arnim, note 146, p. 215) require also an additional economic cost-benefit analysis in order to ensure the public choice of economically efficient governement measures.

158 See: Bundesverfassungsgericht Entscheidungen vol. 25, pp. 1, 13; 50, pp. 290, 335; 57, pp. 139, 161 f.

framework of appropriate "laws and institutions" (e.g. private contracts, collective bargaining, undistorted economic and political competition), may enable a more liberal and a more welfare-increasing coordination of the diverse individual self-interests with the common long-term "public interest" than the various governmental instruments and procedures for promoting the "public interest".[159] Thus the constitutional requirement of a "free basic democratic order" is legitimized also by the expectation that transparent democratic decision-making processes are more likely to produce "just" decisions in the "common interest".[160] Appropriate decision-making procedures enabling the participation and protection of all constitutionally recognized interests in the decision-making process concerned, are a constitutionally required condition of public legislative, executive and judicial decisions as well as of the use of decentralized societal decision-making processes for the pursuit of public goods.[161]

B) The "Constitutionalization" of the Foreign Relations Power

More than the previous German Constitutions of 1871 and 1919 and than most foreign national constitutions, the Basic Law attempts to ensure the basic constitutional functions of protecting individual rights, constituting limited government powers, and of organizing the state in a manner promoting integration and a liberal order, also in respect of the constitutional authority of the government to conduct relations with other states. This is evidenced, inter alia, (a) by the constitutional protection of individual rights in foreign affairs, (b) by the constitutional requirement of separation and only limited delegation of foreign affairs powers, and (c) by the comprehensive judicial review of the exercise of the foreign affairs powers. It is further illustrated by the internal validity, rank and direct applicability of public international law within the Federal Republic of Germany and the constitutional decision of the Basic Law in favour of international integration (C).

---

159 See on this important subject: H.H. von Arnim, Gemeinwohl und Gruppeninteressen, 1977, who emphasizes the insufficient representation of certain "general interests" (e.g. of consumers and taxpayers) in decentralized decision-making processes and the need for correcting these biases in decision-making processes through procedural and institutional rules.

160 See: M. Kriele, Das demokratische Prinzip im Grundgesetz, in: Veröffentlichungen der Vereinigung der deutschen Staatsrechtslehrer, Vol 29, pp. 46, 52, 58, 107 f.

161 For the necessary qualifications of this constitutional requirements, see: H.H. von Arnim (note 146), pp. 195 ff.

a) Constitutional Protection of Individual Rights in Foreign Affairs: Freedom of Foreign Trade as a Constitutional Guarantee

Articles 1, section 3, and 20, section 3 of the Basic Law make it clear that the fundamental rights guarantees are directly binding on all state activities including the foreign relations power, regardless of whether the latter is exercised by means of international agreements or unilateral international acts or by means of domestic implementing legislation, executive regulations or judicial decisions. For internationally integrated "open states" like the Federal Republic of Germany, in which more than 25 per cent of the gross national product come from foreign trade, the transnational exercise of individual freedoms and of other basic rights is no less important than their purely domestic exercises. The "serving function" of the government for the benefit of its citizens may be viewed as even more necessary in transnational relations because the individual access to foreign countries and markets and the effectuation of individual rights across national frontiers often depend on the conclusion of intergovernmental agreements on the reciprocal liberalization of national barriers and on the mutual protection of individual rights of foreign citizens.

Paragraph 1, section 1, of the German Law on Foreign Economic Relations of 1961 (Aussenwirtschaftsgesetz)[162] reads:

> "(1) In principle trade and commerce with foreign economic areas is free as to goods, services, capital, payments or other economic transactions as well as to transactions between residents in foreign assets and gold (= Foreign Economic Transactions). Applicable are the restrictions contained in this Law or prescribed by ordinance based on this Law."

Paragraph 2, section 2, adds:

> "(2) Restrictions are to be limited as to character and extent to the minimum necessary to achieve the purpose stipulated in the empowering legislation. They are to be formulated in such a way as to interfere as little as possible with the liberty of economic activities. Restrictions may affect existing contracts only if the purpose to be achieved would otherwise substantially be endangered."

Paragraph 3, section 1, further stipulates:

162 An English translation of this law is to be found in: U.R. Siebel, German restrictions on Capital Transactions with Foreigners, 1973, p. 41 ff.

> "(1) In case this Law or an ordinance based on this Law stipulates that transactions or deals require an authorization, this authorization has to be granted if it can be expected that the purpose of such provision would not or only insignificantly be endangered by the execution of such transaction or deal. In other cases the authorization can be granted if the general economic interest in the implementation of such transactions or deal is greater than the impairment of the stipulated purpose which would be the consequence of such implementation."

It is generally recognized that the principle of freedom of foreign economic transactions laid down in § 1 of the German Law on Foreign Economic Relations has constitutional rank and is protected by the constitutional guarantees of freedom of trade and profession (Article 12 of the Basic Law), property (Article 14) and by the general right to the free development of one's personality (Article 2), which includes also freedom of contract, of competition and of other economic liberties to the extent they are not already protected by the more specific fundamental rights guarantees of the Basic Law.[163] In parallel to the German Law on Trades and Occupations (Gewerbeordnung) which was first enacted in 1869 and proclaims in its § 1 the general freedom of business and industrial establishment subject to the conditions and regulations set out in the Law, the Foreign Economic Relations Law of 1961 was designed to confirm the constitutional guarantees of freedom of transnational economic relations and to regulate the substantive and procedural conditions for its possible restriction.[164] In spite of the various legislative reservations of power set out in § 1 of the Law, the inherent limits and admissible legislative or executive restraints of the freedom of foreign economic relations can be derived ultimately only from the constitution itself.[165]

The explicit requirements in § 2 of the Foreign Economic Relations Law to limit any restrictions "to the minimum necessary to achieve the purpose stipulated in the empowering legislation" and to formulate the restrictions "in such a way as to interfere as little as possible with the liberty of economic activities", just like the requirement in § 3 as to the granting of authorizations, are also only

163 See: Bundesverfassungsgericht Entscheidungen Vol. 12, p. 294 and H.P. Ipsen, Aussenwirtschaft und Aussenwirtschaftspolitik, 1967, pp. 50 ff; E. Putzier, Die Ermächtigungen des Aussenwirtschaftsgesetzes, 1987, p. 15 f, with further references.

164 See: the official explanation of the purpose of the Foreign Economic Relations Law in the pertinent parliamentary report (Bundestagsdrucksache Nr. 1285) reproduced in: H.F. Schulz, Aussenwirtschaftsrecht, Kommentar, 1966, pp. 157, 160 ff.

165 See: H.P. Ipsen (note 163), p. 50 ff.

legislative concretizations of the constitutional principles of proportionality and reasonableness of governmental restraints of individual rights.

The constitutional rank and character of the freedom of foreign trade is further reflected in the fact that the Foreign Economic Relations Law deliberalty refrains from authorizing certain government interferences into foreign economic relations. Thus the Foreign Economic Relations Law deliberately does not grant any authority to the Federal Government to restrict foreign trade and payments for balance-of-payments reasons,[166] or to interfere into existing contracts[167] or into already granted authorizations in a manner amounting to an expropriation of property rights.[168]

Article 1, section 3 of the Basic Law prescribes the binding effect of the basic rights on all government organs without differentiating as to whether the exercise of the basic rights engenders effects inside or outside the Federal Republic of Germany and whether the government exercises domestic or "foreign policy" powers. The mere fact that the exercise of the individual freedom of trade entails the choice of foreign (rather than domestic) trading partners and a transfer of goods, services or payments across the national frontiers is, in principle, no reason for according less constitutional protection under Articles 2, 12 and 14 of the Basic Law to the freedom to engage in foreign trade as compared to

166 The temporary cash-deposit obligation introduced in 1971 in order to counter the massive inflow of foreign capital into Germany following the "Smithsonian Agreement" on the realignment of the major currencies (see E.U. Petersmann, Zum Rechtswandel des IMF-Paritätensystems, in: Wirtschaftsrecht 1974, pp. 119, 136 ff; E. Ott, Geldeinfuhr und Bardepot, 1980) necessitated an amendment of the foreign Economic Relations Law. The text of the newly introduced para. 6,a clearly indicates that it serves conjunctural policy reasons (i.e. protection of the "overall economic equlibrium") rather than foreign trade policy reasons. The constitutionality, especially of the maintenance of the temporary cash-deposit requirement beyond 1973, has remained controversial (see E. Ott, p. 19 ff, 132 ff, and H.J. Hahn,, Bardepot und Währungsrecht, in: Verwaltung im Dienste von Wirtschaft und Gesellschaft, Festschrift für L. Fröhler, 1980, pp. 413, 431 ff.)

167 On the German practice of exempting existing contracts from politically motivated international trade embargos and, in the case of the 1962 NATO embargo on exports of steel pipes to the USSR, of compensating the German firms in conformity with Article 14, section 3 of the Basic Law for the damage suffered from the retroactive interferences into existing contracts see: E.U. Petersmann, Internationale Wirtschaftssanktionen als Problem des Völkerrechts und des Europarechts, in: Zeitschrift für Vergleichende Rechtswissenschaft 1981, pp. 1, 3 ff. with further references).

168 See: E.U. Petersmann, Rechtsprobleme der deutschen Interimsgesetzgebung für den Tiefseebergbau, in: ZaöRV 1981, pp. 267, 302 ff, with further references; K.W. Ebert, Rechtliche Beschränkungen des Technologietransfers im Aussenwirtschaftsverkehr, 1986, pp. 228 ff.

the freedom of purely domestic trade.[169] The actual scope of protection of the fundamental rights guarantees in foreign affairs, for instance of the individual right to diplomatic protection abroad[170] or of individual rights adversely affected by the conclusion of an international agreement,[171] can be determined only with due regard to the particular circumstances of each case.[172]

The Foreign Economic Relations Law recognizes in various provisions that specific foreign policy considerations may justify restrictions on transnational economic transactions which may be constitutionally inadmissible in respect of purely domestic economic transactions. According to § 5, "Legal transactions and other dealings within the scope of foreign economic transactions can be restricted in order to allow the fulfilling of international agreements which have received the consent of the legislative bodies in the form of a federal law".[173] And, pursuant to § 1 section 2, the freedom of foreign economic transactions "is without prejudice as to ... legal provisions passed by supranational authorities to which parts of sovereign rights have been transferred."

Thus, the customs union law and the foreign trade law of the EEC have superseded and in part displaced the autonomous national foreign trade law of the Federal Republic of Germany.[174] For example in respect of certain VERs and VRAs, European Community law has even been used as a legal basis for foreign trade restrictions inconsistent with GATT law which would have been inadmis-

---

169 See: H.P. Ipsen (note 163) p. 52 and Bundesverfassungsgericht Entscheidungen Vol. 6, pp. 36, 42 where the Federal Constitutional Court recognized that Article 2, section 1, of the Basic Law protects also the freedom to leave the Federal Republic of Germany

170 See, e.g., E. Klein, Diplomatischer Schutz und grundrechtliche Schutzpflicht, in: Die Oeffentliche Verwaltung 1977, p. 704 ff.

171 See, e.g., R. Bernhardt, Bundesverfassungsgericht und Völkerrechtliche Verträge, in: Bundesverfassungsgericht und Grundgesetz, 1976, Vol. II, p. 154 ff.

172 See, e.g., M. Schröder, Zur Wirkkraft der Grundrechte bei Sachverhalten mit grenzüberschreitenden Elementen, in: Festschrift Schlochhauer, 1981, pp. 137 ff.; A. Bleckmann Grundgesetz und Völkerrecht, 1975, pp. 241 ff; R. Geiger, Grundgesetz und Völkerrecht, 1985, pp. 171 ff.

173 For a survey of the use of this provision see J. Linde, Aussenwirtschaftsgesetz und zwischenstaatliche Vereinbarungen, 1970

174 See, e.g.: E. Hornung, Die Zulässigkeit von Einfuhrbeschränkungen nach dem Aussenwirtschaftsgesetz und ihre Vereinbarkeit mit dem Europäischen Gemeinschaftsrecht, 1982; J.F. von Fürstenwerth, Ermessensentscheidungen im Aussenwirtschaftsrecht, 1985; A. Vollbrecht, Warenverkehrslenkung nach dem Aussenwirtschaftsgesetz im Rahmen des Europäischen Gemeinschaftsrecht, 1987.

sible under the German Foreign Economic Relations Law.[175] Certain politically motivated foreign trade embargos (e.g. in the context of the Coordinating Committee for East-West-trade = COCOM) continue to be based on, and implemented through, the national foreign trade laws of the EEC member states.[176] Under the broad authority in § 7 of the Foreign Economic Relations Law, "legal transactions and other dealings within the scope of foreign economic transactions can be restricted in order to (1) assure the security of the Federal Republic of Germany, ... or (3) avoid significant disturbances of the foreign relations of the Federal Republic of Germany". Yet, there are serious doubts expressed in German legal literature as to the constitutionality and legal validity of this authorization on the ground of its vagueness and, arguably, inconsistency with the constitutional requirement of limited delegation of powers and of specification of "the content, purpose and scope of the authorization so conferred ... in such law" (Article 80, section 1 of the Basic Law).[177]

b) Separation and only Limited Delegation of Foreign Relations Powers

Like the US and Swiss Constitution, the Basic Law neither mentions the "foreign relations power" as a term of art nor perceives it as a "fourth state function" separate from the three classical legislative, executive and judicial government functions. The constitutional government authority to conduct and regulate international relations and to address the consequences of those relations is divided "horizontally" among the various federal organs (Articles 24, 59) as well as "vertically" between the Federation and the "Länder" (Article 32). The constitutionally guaranteed autonomy of the communes (Article 28) and the freedoms of the citizens to exercise their fundamental rights across the national frontiers imply a further decentralisation of the foreign relations of the Federal Republic of Germany.[178]

---

175 See: E.U. Petersmann, Verfassungsrechtliche Grundprobleme bei der rechtlichen Regelung der Instrumente der Handelspolitik, in: H.W. Kruse (ed.) Zölle, Verbrauchssteuern, Europäisches Marktordnungsrecht, 1988, pp. 5, 20 ff.

176 For details see E.U. Petersmann (above note 167)

177 Paragraph 7, section 1 is considered to be unconstitutional by H.P. Ipsen (note 16), pp. 41 ff. and Linde (note 173), pp. 87 ff.

178 See: U. Fastenrath, Auswärtige Gewalt im Offenen Verfassungsstaat, in A. Dittmann/M. Kilian (eds.), Kompetenzprobleme der Auswärtigen Gewalt, 1982, pp. 1 ff; U. Beyerlin, Federal Aspects of the Foreign Relations Power in the Federal Republic of Germany, in: R. Bernhardt/U. Beyerlin (eds.), Reports on German Public Law and Public International Law, 1986, pp. 3 ff.

In principle, "relations with foreign states shall be conducted by the Federation" (Article 32, section 1). This basic rule is interpreted in a wide sense empowering the Federation to conduct relations with all subjects of international law (see also Article 87, section 1 on the federal foreign service for the conduct of diplomatic and consular relations). International treaties affecting the particular conditions of a Land are also within the treaty-making power of the Federation which only has to consult the Länder concerned in advance (Article 32, section 2). The foreign policy powers of the Federation under Articles 32 and 59 do not, however, modify the distribution of implementing powers pursuant to Articles 83 ff. of the Basic Law. With the consent of the federal government, the Länder may conclude treaties with foreign states in the field of their own exclusive competences to legislate (Article 32, section 3).[179] In the "Lindauer Arrangement" of 14th November 1957 between the Federation and the Länder, the federal government has undertaken an obligation to obtain the prior consent of the Länder if an international treaty is going to affect their exclusive legislative powers.[180]

On the level of the Federation, the Basic Law distributes the foreign relations powers between the various executive, legislative and judicial government branches. Article 59, section 1 gives the authority to represent the Federation in its international relations to the Federal President:

> "(1) The Federal President shall represent the Federation in its international relations. He shall conclude treaties with foreign states on behalf of the Federation. He shall accredit and receive envoys."

The President's foreign affairs powers are, however, constitutionally limited by Article 58 according to which "orders and decrees of the Federal President shall require for their validity the countersignature of the Federal Chancellor or of the appropriate Federal Minister". In practice, the President has delegated most of his foreign affairs powers to either the Federal Chancellor or various federal ministers. The Federal President may refuse to ratify an international treaty if he considers the treaty to be inconsistent with substantive or procedural provisions of the Basic Law; but he may not refuse the ratification or the publication of the consenting act of the legislature merely on grounds of political considera-

179 A list of 31 such agreements is reproduced by U. Fastenrath (note 178), pp. 43 ff.

180 For the text and application of the Lindauer Arrangement see K. Stern (note 145), pp. 693 ff. On the participation of the German Länder in the various foreign policy decision-making processes see: R. Hrbek, Die Beteiligung der Deutschen Länder an den innerstaatlichen Beratungen und Entscheidungen in EG-Angelegenheiten, 1988.

tions because this would interfere with the substantive foreign policy powers of the Chancellor (Article 65) and of the legislature (Article 59, section 2).[181]

The foreign relations power is therefore often described as a "combined power" resting mainly with the Federal Government (Article 62 ff), the Federal Parliament (Bundestag) and the Federal Council (Bundesrat) composed of members of the governments of the Länder. According to Article 59, section 2:

> "(2) Treaties which regulate the political relations of the Federation or relate to matters of federal legislation shall require the consent or participation, in the form of a federal law, of the bodies competent in any specific case for such federal legislation. As regards administrative agreements, the provisions concerning the federal administration shall apply mutatis mutandis."

Moreover, according to Article 24, section 1:

> "(1) The Federation may by legislation transfer sovereign powers to inter-governmental institutions."

The Federal Constitutional Court has held in one of its early decisions that "foreign and trade policy" are in principle executive matters within the competence of the Federal Government:

> "In the parliamentary democracy, legislation is on principle reserved to parliament and government and administration are allocated to the Executive. The latter applies also to the conduct of foreign and trade policy... The legal presumption speaks in favour of the exclusiveness of these explicitly established competences of the Government... The Federal Parliament cannot take over these functions of the government unless government functions have been explicitly allocated to it. Such an exceptional competence of the Legislature within the realm of the Executive has been provided for in Article 59, section 2 of the Basic Law within precisely circumscribed limits".[182]

A recent Constitutional Court decision has confirmed that unilateral foreign policy decisions regulating the political relations of the Federation or relating to matters of federal legislation (in the case concerned the stationing of Pershing 2 missiles with nuclear heads in the territory of the Federal Republic of Germany) are within the competence of the executive and do not require the con-

181 See: B.O. Bryde, Commentary on Article 82 of the Basic Law in: I. von Münch (ed.), Grundgesetz-Kommentar, Vol. III, 2nd ed., 1983, Article 82, nos 2 ff.; A. Bleckmann (note 172), p. 213 f.

182 Bundesverfassungsgericht Entscheidungen Vol. 1, p. 394 (translated into English by the author). In a similar sense: Bundesverfassungsgericht Entscheidungen Vol. 2, p. 379.

sent or participation by the Federal Parliament (analogous to Article 59, section 2) unless specifically stipulated in the Basic Law (e.g. in Article 115, a, concerning the determination of the "state of defence" by the Federal Parliament).[183] Apart from its power of authorizing or refusing the conclusion of international treaties in the sense of Article 59, section 2, the Federal Parliament has accordingly no power of legally comitting the Federal Government to a certain conduct of foreign affairs. Thus the Federal Parliament cannot force the Federal Government to negotiate, to conclude or to refrain from denunciating international treaties and, pursuant to § 82 of the rules of procedure of the Bundestag, has no power to alter the text of a draft treaty, on the acceptance or rejection of which it has to decide.[184] Nor does it follow from the principle of democracy (Article 20, section 1) that the Bundestag has to decide on all politically vital questions which could affect the state as a whole.[185] According to the Federal Constitutional Court, the limitation of the foreign policy powers of the Bundestag and Bundesrat in Article 59, section 2 is an expression of the functional and organizational distinction and separation of legislative, executive and judicial government powers in the Basic Law (see Article 20, section 2) and is predicated on the assumption that the Federal Government disposes of the best personal and organizational means for the current conduct of foreign affairs.[186]

Yet, even outside the field of the "mixed" treaty-making and supranational integration powers, the conduct of foreign affairs is no longer a monopoly of the executive branch of the Federal Government. Many foreign policy decisions depend for their effectiveness on parliamentary implementation by legislation or on the parliamentary appropriation of funds, on the support by other federal organs (such as the German Central Bank and the federal courts), on the legislative and administrative implementation by the Länder (e.g. in the field of international trade rules on subsidies) and on the participation by the citizens themselves and by non-governmental institutions (e.g. the DIN Institute which plays a central role in the harmonization of technical standards in Germany). And, vice versa, private business practices (e.g. dumping) and administrative practices of local authorities (e.g. in the field of government procurement) may have a

183 Bundesverfassungsgericht Entscheidungen Vol. 68, pp. 1, 84 ff.

184 But the Bundestag may exercise its political control function (e.g. by electing another Chancellor pursuant to Article 67 of the Basic Law) and can oblige the Federal Government to make certain reservations, see R. Geiger (note 172), pp. 155 f.

185 Bundesverfassungsgericht Entscheidungen Vol. 49, pp. 89, 124 f; 68 pp. 87 f.

186 Bundesverfassungsgericht (note 183) at p. 86

strong impact on the foreign trade relations and trade policy of the Federal Republic of Germany.[187]

The broad foreign relations powers of the Federal Government can also not dispense from the constitutional requirement (e.g. in Articles 12 and 14 of the Basic Law) that executive foreign trade and economic restrictions taxing or limiting the individual freedoms and property rights of German citizens need a legislative basis. The "dual nature" of many foreign policy measures (e.g. of a trade embargo) as both an external measure vis-à-vis foreign states and simultaneously an internal measure vis-à-vis the domestic citizens illustrates that the "foreign policy" powers of the legislature may go well beyond those spelled out in Articles 59, section 2, and 24, section 1, of the Basic Law. The German legal doctrine has therefore rightly emphasized that the explicity established "foreign policy" powers of the Federal Parliament should not be construed too narrowly as exceptions to a comprehensive executive prerogative in the field of foreign policy.[188] Even the Federal Government's predominant role with regard to unilateral foreign policy decisions in the forms of international law and diplomacy is subject to important exceptions.[189] It seems therefore more appropriate to follow the prevailing view in German legal doctrine, which accords also with the prevailing views in Swiss and US constitutional law doctrine,[190] to characterize the "foreign relations powers" as "mixed" and in part "combined" powers that necessitate the constant cooperation of the legislative, executive and judicial government organs no less than in most areas of domestic policy-making.[191]

187 On the continued existence of a national "German trade policy" in the broader context of the common commercial policy of the EEC see G. Abel, Die Bundesrepublik Deutschland als GATT-Mitglied und EG-Mitglied, in: M. Hilf/E.U. Petersmann, GATT und Europäische Gemeinschaft, 1986, pp. 73, 75.

188 See: E. Menzel, Die auswärtige Gewalt der Bundesrepublik, in: Veröffentlichungen der Vereinigung Deutscher Staatsrechtslehrer 12 (1953), pp. 179, 194 ff, 220; R. Bernhardt (note 171), as p. 179, with further references

189 For instance in respect of the determination of the "state of defence" reserved to the legislature in Article 115, a of the Basic Law. See also C. Tomuschat, Die Aufwertung der Deutschen Mark, 1970, according to whom the revaluation of the German Mark, decided upon by the Federal Government in 1969, was legally void due to lack of a sufficient legislative authorization and a governmental ordinance conforming to Articles 80, 82 of the Basic Law.

190 See: Th.Borer (note 114 above), pp. 419 ff, with further references

191 This is without prejudice to the convincing decision of the Federal Constitutional Court (above note 183 at pp. 2, 83 ff.) that the principle of democracy or the political importance of foreign policy decisions are not a sufficient basis for disregarding the explicit allocation and distribution of legislative and executive competences in Articles 24, section 1 and 59, section 2, of the Basicl Law

The current national decision-making processes in the field of foreign trade and foreign economic policy are characterized by the predominant influence of the Federal Government and of the competent ministries and administrations. The only occasional parliamentary debates on foreign economic policy matters and the infrequent parliamentary initiatives in this field (e.g. participation of members of the Federal Parliament as part of the German delegations to international economic conferences and negotiations)[192] cannot make up for this very limited participation by the Federal Parliament in the formation of foreign economic policy decisions.[193] Yet, the explicit regulation in the Basic Law of parliamentary foreign policy powers only in the field of treaty-making (Article 59, section 2), international integration (Article 24, section 1), the determination of the "state of defence" (Article 115, a) and the conclusion of peace (Article 115, l) cannot imply that foreign policy is exempted from the parliamentary system of government. The parliamentary "informing", "expressive" and "control functions" towards the government (cf. Articles 63 and 67) enable the Bundestag to discuss and pronounce on all foreign policy matters and even to depose the Federal Chancellor (Article 67). The Bundestag has also enacted a large number of general customs, trade, monetary and financial laws which lay down long-term framework rules for the conduct of foreign economic policy.[194]

In conclusion, the allocation and distribution of limited foreign policy powers among the Federal President, the Federal Government, the Bundestag and Bundesrat, the federal courts, the Länder and, increasingly, the European Communities present a complex sytem of separation of powers and of mutual "checks and balances" in the field of foreign policy.

c) Judicial Control of the Foreign Relations Powers

Articles 1, section 3, and 20, section 3 indicate that the Basic Law does not know any constitutionally unlimited government power. Article 19, section 4 guarantees, inter alia:

192 See, e.g.: W. Graf Vitzthum, Parlament und Planung, 1978, pp. 342 ff; H. Steiger, Die Rolle des Parlaments bei der Gestaltung und der Verwirklichung der Aussenpolitik des Staates, in: Viertes Deutsch-Polnisches Juristen Kolloquium, 1979, pp. 15, 35 ff, 71 ff.

193 On the similar situation in Switzerland see Th.Borer (note 114), pp. 423 ff.

194 For a survey see: Hocke/Berwald/Maurer, Aussenwirtschaftsrecht: Gesetze, Verordnungen und Erlasse zum Aussenwirtschaftsrecht mit Kommentar, Loseblattausgabe 1986; Bundesministerium der Finanzen, Vorschriftensammlung für die Finanzverwaltung zum Aussenwirtschaftsrecht, Loseblattausgabe 1987.

> "Should any person's right be violated by public authority, recourse to the court shall be open to him. If jurisdiction is not specified, recourse shall be to the ordinary courts."

The possibility of judicial review of the constitutionality and legality of almost all government regulations is an essential element of the German "Rechtsstaatsprinzip".[195] The Basic Law and the Rules of Procedure of the Federal Constitutional Court enable the Bundesverfassungsgericht to examine the constitutionality of all legislative, executive and judicial measures including the conclusion of international agreements.[196] The Federal Constitutional Court's jurisdiction extends notably also to "complaints of unconstitutionality, which may be entered by any person who claims that one of its basic rights or one of its rights under paragraph (4) of Article 20, under Articles 33, 38, 101, 103 or 104 has been violated by public authority" (Article 93, section 1, § 4,a of the Basic Law). The general courts also exercise their ordinary jurisdiction in foreign relations matters as in domestic matters, deciding cases involving foreign nationals or foreign states and interpreting international agreements, general rules of international law as well as legislation relating to transnational matters. Thus, the civil courts often construe rules of private law (e.g. "ordre public" clauses) in the light of pertinent rules of public international law,[197] and the administrative courts constantly review governmental trade policy measures in the light of European Community law and of German law. Article 100, section 1 of the Basic Law stipulates:

> "If a court considers unconstitutional a law the validity of which is relevant to its decision, the proceedings shall be stayed, and a decision shall be obtained from the Land court competent for constitutioal disputes if a constitution of a Land is held to be violated, or from the Federal Constitutional Court if this Basic Law is held to be violated ..."

This provision applies also to the parliamentary consent in the form of a federal law to international treaties in the sense of Article 59, section 2 of the Basic Law. If a court has doubts as to whether a rule of public international law forms part of German federal law and gives rise to directly applicable rights and obligations of individuals (see Article 25), the court must obtain a preliminary ruling from the Federal Constitutional Court on this question (Article 100, section

195 See: K. Stern (note 145), p. 841 f. See also P. Kunig, Das Rechtsstaatsprinzip, 1986, who convincingly shows that the "Rechtsstaatsprinzip" is a generic term for legal principles and legal consequences following from various specific Articles of the Basic Law.

196 See: R. Bernhardt (note 171), p. 161

197 See: the examples given by F. Pentzlin, Der Universelle Ordre Public im Wirtschaftsrecht als ein Ordnungsprinzip des innerstaatlichen Rechts, 1985, pp. 38 ff., 74 ff.

2). According to Article 177 of the EEC Treaty, the courts may also request a preliminary ruling from the Eruopean Court of Justice on the interpretation of European Community law and the validity of acts of the EC institutions "where such a question is raised before any court or tribunal of a Member State (and) that court or tribunal considers that a decision on the question is necessary to enable it to give judgement". Article 177, section 3 prescribes:

> "Where any such question is raised in a case pending before a court or tribunal of a member state, against whose decisions there is no judicial remedy under national law, that court or tribunal shall bring the matter before the Court of Justice."

In its judicial control of the exercise of the foreign relations power, the Federal Constitutional Court has taken into account that the pertinent national and international legal restraints often confer on the government a broader scope of policy discretion and power of appraisal than in purely domestic matters. Thus, in the field of diplomatic protection, military defence and other foreign policy issues, the Court has frequently examined only whether the Federal Government has exercized its broad foreign policy discretion in a non-arbitrary manner.[198] It has recognized that the limited territorial and personal jurisdiction of the Federal Republic of Germany may justify the use of more flexible legal terms and obligations in the legislative regulation of transnational matters (e.g. compensation for foreign victims of war living abroad) than in purely domestic matters falling under exclusive German jurisdiction.[199] It has also taken into account the frequent need for compromises in international agreements and has therefore accepted the constitutionality of a post-war treaty with France on the status of the Saarland on the ground that, even though the treaty was not fully in line with the requirements of the Basic Law, it was already "closer to the Constitution" in comparison to the prior situation.[200]

The Federal Constitutional Court has recognized the "friendly attitude of the Basic Law towards international law"[201] as reflected in its preamble and Articles 1, 24, 25, 26, 32 and 59, and has striven to interpret German law in conformity

198 Bundesverfassungsgericht Entscheidungen Vol. 68, p. 2; 55, p. 349.

199 Bundesverfassungsgericht Entscheidungen Vol. 56, pp. 1 ff.

200 Bundesverfassungsgericht Entscheidungen Vol. 4, pp. 157, 168 ff. See: also Vol. 12, p. 281; Vol. 18, p. 235.

201 Bundesverfassungsgericht Entscheidungen Vol. 18, pp. 112, 121 ("völkerrechtsfreundliche Grundhaltung des Grundgesetzes").

with international public law and European Community law.[202] Among the large number of international agreements examined by the Federal Constitutional Court, there has so far been only one case relating to the German-Swiss double taxation agreement where the Court has declared unconstitutional and void the consenting federal law in respect of one treaty provision.[203] The Court has emphasized the need for "judicial self-restraint" in its consideration of international matters[204] and has regularly dismissed interlocutory applications for interim injunctions to prohibit the definitive conclusion of an international agreement.[205] Yet, in spite of this self-proclaimed judicial self-restraint, the Court's decision on the treaty of 21 December 1972 between the two German states has ruled on a large number of interpretative questions and has declared these judicial interpretations to belong to the legally binding reasons for judgment ("ratio decidendi").[206] The decisions and ground for judgment of the Federal Constitutional Court are legally binding on all organs of the Federation as well as of the Länder including all courts and administrative bodies (§ 31 of the Law on the Federal Constitutional Court of 1951, as amended).

Like the historically evolved "act of state doctrine" of English courts[207] and the case-oriented "political question doctrine" of US courts,[208] the "judicial self-restraint" of the Federal Constitutional Court has not developed into a systematic constitutional doctrine. Even though such "judicial self-restraint" might often be justifiable (e.g. in order to avoid the international responsibility of the Federal Republic if the Court declares the internal application of an international treaty provision to be unconstitutional), it can hardly claim to be constitutionally re-

202 See notably Bundesverfassungsgericht Entscheidungen Vol. 73, p. 339 as to the relationship between the fundamental rights guarantees of the Basic Law and European Community law, as well as the pertinent recent judgement of April 1987 (reported in: Europarecht 1987, pp. 333 ff., with annotation by M. Hilf, Der Justizkonflikt um EG-Richtlinien: gelöst, in: Europarecht 1988, pp. 1 ff.)

203 Bundesverfassungsgericht Entscheidungen Vol. 30, p. 272. For a survey of the relevant case-law see R. Bernhardt (note 171), pp. 166 ff; H. Steinberger, Entwicklungslinien in der neueren Rechtsprechung des Bundesverfassungsgerichts zu völkerrechtlichen Fragen, in: ZaöRV 1988, pp. 1 ff.

204 Bundesverfassungsgericht Entscheidungen Vols. 35, pp. 257, 262; 36, pp. 1, 14 f.

205 See, e.g.: Bundesverfassungsgericht Entscheidungen Vols. 33, pp. 195, 232; 35, pp. 193, 257, 280; 38, p. 49.

206 For a criticism of this "judicial activism" see R. Bernhardt (note 171), p. 177.

207 For a survey see: F.C. Zeitler, Verfassungsgericht und Völkerrechtlicher Vertrag. Die gerichtliche Kontrolle völkerrechtlicher Akte der Regierung nach deutschem, amerikanischem und englischem Recht, 1974, pp. 51-84, with further references.

208 See: F.C. Zeitler (note 207), pp. 85-119, with further references.

quired by the fundamental principles (e.g. of separation of powers) of the Basic Law.[209] According to the Basic Law, the Federal Constitutional Court can fully control the constitutionality of the exercise of the legally limited foreign affairs powers. Whether the international nature of the case calls for a different interpretation of constitutional provisions (e.g. of fundamental rights)[210] and whether the broad foreign policy discretion of the government[211] justifies a "judicial self-restraint" in the legal interpretation and judicial enforcement of certain provisions of the Constitution, can be decided only in the light of the concrete constitutional provision at issue and the particular circumstances of each case. Since the "public foreign policy interest" cannot be determined independently from the fundamental rights of the citizens,[212] there are hardly any convincing reasons for granting less judicial protection to individual rights in transnational affairs than in domestic affairs.[213]

C) The Constitutional Decision in Favour of International Integration

The US Constitution, the Swiss Constitution, the Constitution of the German Reich of 1871 and the Weimar Constitution of 1919 do not include as many provisions explicitly referring to international law and international cooperation

---

209 See: F.C. Zeitler (note 207), pp. 144 f., 178 f.; E.U. Petersmann (above note 50), p. 616 f; R. Bernhardt (note 171), p. 186. But see also Bundesverfassungsgericht Entscheidungen Vol. 55, pp. 349, 367 f.: "... ist es für die Wahrung der Interessen der Bundesrepublik Deutschland von erheblicher Bedeutung, dass sie auf internationaler Ebene mit einer einheitlichen Stimme auftritt, wahrgenommen von den zuständigen Organen der auswärtigen Gewalt. Im Hinblick hierauf obliegt den Gerichten grösste Zurückhaltung, etwaige völkerrechtlich fehlerhafte Rechtsauffassungen dieser Organe als Ermessensfehler zu bewerten."

210 See, e.g.: Bundesverfassungsgericht Entscheidungen Vols. 18 pp. 112 ff.; 29, pp. 183 ff.; 31, 58 ff.; M. Schröder (note 172), pp. 138 ff.

211 See: Bundesverfassungsgericht Entscheidungen Vol. 40, pp. 141, 178; "Die Weite des Ermessens im auswärtigen Bereich hat ihren Grund darin, dass die Gestaltung auswärtiger Verhältnisse und Geschehensabläufe nicht allein vom Willen der Bundesrepublik Deutschland bestimmt werden kann, sondern vielmehr von Umständen abhängig ist, die sich ihrer Bestimmung entziehen ..."

212 See above chapter VIII.4.A.b and C. Tomuschat, Der Verfassungsstaat im Geflecht der Internationalen Beziehungen, in: Veröffentlichungen der Vereinigung der Deutschen Staatsrechtslehrer 36 (1978), pp. 7, 21

213 See M. Schröder (note 172), pp. 144 who shows that there are only very few cases in which the Federal Constitutional Court seems to have construed the fundamental rights guarantees of the Basic Law more restrictively in transnational affairs than in domestic affairs. See also the more recent Federal Constitutional Court decisions (e.g. in Vol. 63, pp. 332, 337 f.) discussed by R. Geiger (note 172), pp. 332, 337 f., who gives also a survey of the pertinent court procedures for appeals by individuals or by the various government organs on constitutional issues relating to foreign affairs powers.

as the Basic Law of 1949. Apart from the various constitutional provisions regulating the competences of the Federation, the Länder and of the various government organs in foreign affairs (e.g. Arts. 32, 59, 115, a, b, e), mention is to be made in particluar of the following provisions of the Basic Law:

- the Preamble expresses, inter alia, the German people's "resolve to preserve their national and political unity and to serve the peace of the world as an equal partner in a united Europe";

- in Article 1, section 2, "the German people... acknowledge inviolable and inalienable human rights as the basis of every community, of peace and of justice in the world";

- pursuant to Article 9, section 2, "associations, the purposes or activities of which conflict with ... the concept of international understanding, are prohibited";

- according to Article 24, "(1)The Federation may by legislation transfer sovereign powers to intergovernmental institutions." "(2)For the maintenance of peace, the Federation may enter a system of mutual collective security; in doing so it will consent to such limitations upon its rights of sovereignty as will bring about and secure a peaceful and lasting order in Europe and among the nations of the world." "(3)For the settlement of disputes between states, the Federation will accede to agreements concerning international arbitration of a general, comprehensive and obligatory nature";

- Article 25 states that "The general rules of public international law shall be an integral part of federal law. They shall take precedence over the laws and shall directly create rights and duties for the inhabitants of the federal territory";

- Article 26 prescribes that "(1)Acts tending to and undertaken with the intent to disturb the peaceful relations between nations, especially to prepare for aggressive war, shall be unconstitutional. They shall be made a punishable offence." "(2)Weapons designed for warfare may not be manufactured, transported or marketed except with the permission of the Federal Government. Details shall be regulated by a federal law";

- Article 100, section 2 provides that, if there are doubts in a court proceeding as to whether a rule of public international law forms part of German federal law and whether it engenders directly applicable rights and obligations of the individual, the court shall request a preliminary ruling from the Federal Constitutional Court.

The Federal Constitutional Court and German legal doctrine perceive these various provisions not only as a deliberate turning away from "national legal autarky" but also as an expression of a "friendly tendency of the Basic Law towards international law",[214] a "constitutional decision of the Basic Law in favour of international cooperation"[215] and as a "constitutional principle of endeavouring to make the national legal order agree with the international legal order".[216] The incorporation of public international law into German law and the constitutional requirement "to serve the peace of the world as an equal partner in a united Europe" also reflect a constitutional decision in favor of international economic, political and legal integration.[217]

a) Validity, Rank and Direct Applicability of International Law in the Federal Republic of Germany

The Basic Law seeks to ensure the widest possible harmony of public international and German law without taking a position on the theoretical problem of whether international and municipal law have to be understood as parts of one legal order based on one common source ("monism") or of separate legal orders requiring special provisions in order to be brought into a reciprocal relationship

---

214 Bundesverfassungsgericht Entscheidungen Vol. 6, pp. 309, 362; 18, pp. 112, 121; 31, pp. 58, 75.

215 K. Vogel, Die Verfassungsentscheidung des Grundgesetzes für eine internationale Zusammenarbeit, 1964.

216 R. Bernhardt (note 171), p. 159 f. ("Das Streben nach Uebereinstimmung von internationaler und nationaler Rechtsordnung als Verfassungsprinzip").

217 A. Bleckmann, Die Völkerrechtsfreundlichkeit der Deutschen Rechtsordnung, in: Die Oeffentliche Verwaltung, 1979, pp. 309 ff., rightly notes "dass das Grundgesetz in verstärkter Rückbesinnung auf die in den vorherigen deutschen und in den demokratischen westlichen Verfassungen zum Ausdruck gelangenden Werte ein Gegenmodell zu den totalitären Diktaturen des Nationalsozialismus und des Ostblocks aufstellen wollte" ... "in dem doppelten Sinne der verstärkten Durchsetzung gemeinsamer westlicher Werte und der bewussten Abkehr von bestimmten anderen Verfassungsmodellen" (p. 310).

("dualism"). The Basic Law lays down different rules for the "incorporation"[218] of "treaties which regulate the political relations of the Federation or relate to matters of federal legislation" (Article 59, section 2, first sentence),[219] "administrative agreements" (Article 59, section 2, second sentence),[220] and "general rules of public international law" (Article 25).[221]

As regards international treaties, the international law principle of "pacta sunt servanda" implies not only the rule that treaties are binding upon the parties, but also an obligation to execute them in good faith.[222] The choice of the method of implementation of international law on the national level is within the competence of each state unless the international treaty prescribes a specific mode of domestic implementation. The provision in Article 59, section 2 of the Basic Law that "Treaties which regulate the political relations of the Federation or relate to matters of federal legislation shall require the consent or participation, in the form of a federal law, of the bodies competent in any specific case for such federal legislation", serves several functions: it secures the parliamentary "control function" vis-à-vis the treaty-making power of the executive in respect of political treaties and of other treaties requiring implementing legislation;[223] it shall also induce the legislature to take in due time, prior to the entry

218 This term is used here in a neutral sense for all forms of implementing international obligations in the domestic sphere (e.g. "transformation" by enactment of internal legislation or "adoption" by declaring international rules applicable internally without changing their international nature and content).

219 According to the Federal Constitutional Court, a "political treaty" in the sense of Article 59, section 2, is a treaty which affects the existence, territorial integrity, independence, political position or weight of the Federal Republic in the international community (Bundesverfassungsgericht Entscheidungen Vol. 1, pp. 372, 381). A treaty "relates to matters of federal legislation" if its domestic implementation requires legislation by the Federation or by the Länder (Vol. 1, pp. 372, 388).

220 This term is usually defined in a negative way as referring to all international treaties not covered by the first sentence of Article 59, section 2, i.e. treaties which are neither a "political treaty" nor require domestic implementing legislation.

221 The term "general rules" comprises both general customary public international law as well as general principles of public international law (in the sense of Article 38, section 1, c of the Statute of the ICJ) binding on the Federal Republic of Germany, see: Bundesverfassungsgericht Entscheidungen Vols. 23, pp. 288, 317; 31, pp. 145, 177.

222 See Article 26 of the Vienna Convention on the Law of Treaties. The Permanent Court of International Justice, in its Advisory Opinion on the exchange of Greek and Turkish Populations (PCIJ Series B No. 10, 1925), has even affirmed a general duty to bring internal law into conformity with obligations under international law.

223 Even though the rules of procedures of the Bundestag do not allow parliamentary proposals of amendments of the draft agreement, the Bundestag may adopt non-binding resolu-

into force of the international agreement, all measures necessary for the domestic implementation of the treaty obligations; the legislative act of assent further authorizes the Federal President to ratify the treaty and provides for the incorporation of the treaty into the national legal system once the treaty has entered into force for the Federal Republic of Germany.

Whether the legislative act of assent "transforms" the international obligations into German Law, as held by the Federal Constitutional Court in some decisions,[224] or whether it only declares them applicable internally without changing their character as international law, as held by the Constitutional Court in more recent decisions as well as by the prevailing ("moderately dualist") German legal doctrine,[225] has no relevance for their internal legal rank and force of a federal law. But the different theories of "transformation" and "adoption" may have an impact on the interpretation and continued internal validity of the incoporated rules in case of termination or denunciation of the international treaty.[226] While the Federal Constitutional Court seems to have been of the view in a number of cases that only directly applicable treaty rules become part of the national legal order,[227] a more convincing view is to admit that - in general - the whole treaty is incorporated into the national legal order without destruction of the synallagmatic relationship between the directly applicable and the other treaty provisions; the question of its internal legal validity should not be unnecessarily linked to the separate question of the direct applicability of treaty provisions because the separation of "transformable" and "non-transformable" treaty provisions may have negative effects on the interpretation of treaty provisions by national courts.[228]

---

tions and recommend reservations relating to the agreement, see K. Stern (note 145), p. 504 f.

224 See e.g., Bundesverfassungsgericht Entscheidungen Vol. 6, pp. 290, 294; 15, pp. 337, 348; 30, pp. 272, 284. The more recent court decision in Vol. 46, pp. 342, 362 referred, however, to an "order of application" in respect of Article 59, section 2.

225 See, e.g.: R. Bernhardt (note 171), p. 172, with further references; H. Steinberger (note 203), p. 4.

226 For instance, the act of "transformation" may be construed as enlarging the addressees of the incorporated rule, modifying its content and basing its validity on national law so that the rule loses its connection with the international treaty.

227 See: Bundesverfassungsgericht Entscheidungen Vol. 29, pp. 348, 360.

228 In this sense A. Bleckmann (note 172), pp. 279 ff.; M. Hilf, General Problems of Relations between Constitutional Law and International Law, in: Starck (note 143), pp. 177, 14; K.J. Partsch, International Law and Municipal Law, in: R. Bernhardt (ed.), Encyclopedia of Public International Law, Instalment 10 (1987), pp. 238, 248.

International treaties incorporated into German law pursuant to Article 59, section 2, have the internal rank of the incorporating act. International treaties incorporated through federal legislation prevail over pre-existing legislation under the principle of lex posterior derogat legi priori. They may prevail also over subsequent legislation under the principle of lex specialis derogat legi generali because it must be presumed under the Basic Law that the legislator had no intention of unilaterally repudiating the international treaty obligation and of abrogating its domestic validity.[229] Administrative agreements in the sense of Article 59, section 2, share the internal rank of the implementing executive ordinances.[230]

Regulations and decisions of "supra-national" international organizations become effective in German Law on the basis of the federal law which has "transferred" such law-making powers to the international organization concerned in conformity with Article 24 of the Basic Law. Decisions by non-supranational organizations have to be incorporated by an act of either the legislature or the executive, depending on which institution would be competent to adopt a corresponding rule of national law.[231] The general rules of public international law take, according to Article 25 of the Basic Law, precedence over the federal laws and the laws of the Länder, but do not override constitutional law.[232]

Article 25 of the Basic Law further prescribes that "the general rules of public international law ... shall directly create rights and duties for the inhabitants of the federal territory". This provision reflects the fact that most rules of public international law, even if formally addressed to governments only, are ultimately designed to regulate individual rights (e.g. of foreign or domestic workers, producers, investors, traders, refugees, soldiers etc.). Article 25 entitles "the inhabitants of the federal territory" to request the observance and, if possible, direct application of general rules of public international law by the government organs concerned. They may also enter a complaint of unconstitutionality on the ground that government restrictions are inconsistent with Article 25 and do

229 See: M. Hilf (note 228), p. 19; G. Ress, Wechselwirkungen zwischen Völkerrecht und Verfassung bei der Auslegung völkerrechtlicher Verträge, Berichte der Deutschen Gesellschaft für Völkerrecht 23 (1982), pp. 20 ff.

230 On the various kinds of administrative agreements and implementing modalities see O. Rojahn, commentary on article 59, in: I. v.Münch, Grundgesetzkommentar, Vol. 2, 1976, p. 680 f.

231 See: M. Hilf (note 228), p. 187 f.; R. Geiger (note 172), p. 200.

232 See: Bundesverfassungsgericht Entscheidungen Vol. 37, pp. 271, 279; 23, pp. 288, 316.

therefore not form part of the "constitutional order" in the sense of Article 2, section 1.[233]

b) The Supranational Option of the Basic Law

According to Article 24 of the Basic Law, "the Federation may by legislation transfer sovereign powers to intergovernmental institutions" (section 1) and, "for the maintenance of peace, ... may enter a system of mutual collective security; in doing so it will consent to such limitations upon its rights of sovereignty as will bring about and secure a peaceful and lasting order in Europe and among the nations of the world" (section 2). "For the settlement of disputes between states, the Federation will accede to agreements concerning international arbitration of a general, comprehensive and obligatory nature" (section 3).

Article 24 reflects the German people's "resolve .. to serve the peace of the world as an equal partner in a united Europe" (preamble of the Basic Law) and is widely perceived as one of the fundamental decisions and constitutional guidelines of the Basic Law without precedent in any previous German Constitution. Similar to the various "supranational clauses" in several constitutions of other EEC member states,[234] Article 24 acknowledges the need for new forms of intergovernmental cooperation and provides a "supranational option"[235] not only for economic and political but also for military and legal international integration of the Federal Republic. It endows the legislature with a comprehensive "integration power" enabling it to "transfer" sovereign powers to intergovernmental institutions which, by virtue of their constituent treaties and the transfer of powers pursuant to Article 24, are competent to enact "secondary supranational law" with supremacy over German law[236] and with direct ("self-executing")

---

233 Bundesverfassungsgericht Entscheidungen Vol. 23, pp. 288, 300.

234 See: Article 25 of the Belgian Constitution, Article 20 of the Danish Constitution, Article 28 of the Greek Constitution, Article 29 of the Irish Constitution, Article 8 of the Constitution of Portugal, Article 93 of the Spanish Constitution, as well as the more general provisions in Articles 92-94 of the Dutch Constitution and Article 11 of the Italian Constitution, texts in: Blaustein/Flanz (above notes 80 and 140).

235 K. Stern (note 145) p. 518.

236 See: Bundesverfassungsgericht Entscheidungen Vol. 31, pp. 145, 174: "Art. 24 Abs. 1 GG besagt bei sachgerechter Auslegung nicht nur, dass die Uebertragung von Hoheitsrechten auf zwischenstaatliche Einrichtungen überhaupt zulässig ist, sondern auch, dass die Hoheitsakte ihrer Organe, wie hier das Urteil des Europäischen Gerichtshofs, vom ursprünglich ausschliesslichen Hoheitsträger anzuerkennen sind."

effect for the executive and judicial government organs and individuals of member states.

The Federal Constitutional Court has made clear that "intergovernmental institutions" in the sense of Article 24 are also organizations like "Eurocontrol"[237] and NATO[238] whose "primary" and "secondary" law does not, unlike European Community law, constitute a new autonomous legal order with primacy over the laws of the member states and with directly applicable rules creating rights and obligations for their citizens. The transfer of sovereign powers need not be irrevocable and can take place also in the context of a progressive integration process in conformity with the constituent agreement of the international organization.[239]

The "transfer" of sovereign competences opens the German national legal order to the legal decisions and regulations of the international institution concerned. But this opening is legally limited both by the Basic Law as well as by the limited competences of the international institution as agreed upon (explicitly or implicitly) in its constituent agreement. Article 24 authorizes the transfer not only of legislative, executive and judicial powers of the Federation but also of the Länder which should then adequately participate through the Bundesrat in the adoption of the federal statute pursuant to Articles 24, section 1, and 59, section 2 of the Basic Law.[240] Even though the "statute of transfer" may considerably change the constitutional distribution of competences, it can be adopted

237 Bundesverfassungsgericht Entscheidungen Vol. 58, pp. 1 ff.

238 Bundesverfassungsgericht Entscheidungen Vol. 68, pp. 1, 94: "Art. 24 Abs. 1 GG lässt sich nicht entnehmen, dass eine Uebertragung von Hoheitsrechten immer nur dann vorliegt, wenn einer zwischenstaatlichen Einrichtung die Befugnis zu einem unmittelbaren Durchgriff auf Einzelne eingeräumt wird."

239 Bundesverfassungsgericht Entscheidungen Vol. 58, pp. 1 ff.; 68, pp. 1 f. 93, 97 ff.: "Auch dort, wo nicht schon der Gründungsvertrag selbst den Ablauf eines Integrationsprozesses nach Inhalt, Form und Zeitpunkt festgelegt hat, bedarf es für die einzelnen Vollzugsschritte nicht von vornherein jeweils eines gesonderten Gesetzes im Sinne des Art. 24 Abs. 1 GG. Es ist dort entbehrlich, wo bereits der Gründungsvertrag, dem durch Gesetz zugestimmt worden ist, diesen künftigen Vollzugsverlauf hinreichend bestimmbar normiert hat. Wesentliche Aenderungen des dort angelegten Integrationsprogramms und seiner Vollzüge sind allerdings nicht mehr von dem ursprünglichen Zustimmungsgesetz nach Art. 24 Abs. 1 GG gedeckt."

240 See: C. Tomuschat, Commentary on Article 24, Bonner Kommentar, Second edition 1981, p. 26. On the controversial relationship between Articles 24, section 1, and 59, section 2, see also Stern (note 145), p. 533 f. who sees Article 24, section 1 as a lex specialis. Article 24, section 1 does not subject the federal law to the consent by the Bundesrat, whereas a federal law pursuant to Article 59, section 2 may need the consent by the Bundesrat depending on the contents of the treaty.

by simple majority of the votes cast and does not require the affirmative vote of a two-thirds-majority of the Bundestag prescribed for formal constitutioal amendments according to Article 79, section 2 of the Basic Law. In addition to Article 24, section 1, Article 59, section 2 remains applicable for the conclusion of international agreements providing for the transfer of sovereign powers to intergovernmental institutions.

The main substantive constitutional limitations on the transfer of competences under Article 24, section 1, derive from Article 79, section 3 of the Basic Law, which declares inadmissible any "amendment of this Basic Law affecting the division of the Federation into Länder, the participation on principle of the Länder in legislation, or the basic principles laid down in Articles 1 and 20". The "integration power" granted in Article 24 must not be used for violating the "hard core" of the constitutional guarantees of democracy, rule of law, respect of human rights, judicial protection, "social state" and federalism. This does not mean that the principles and structures of the intergovernmental organization must be identical with those of the Basic Law.[241] Only the basic structure and the very identity of the Basic Law may not be infringed by the supranational agreement.[242] Thus, the German federal law consenting to the Treaties establishing the EC was held to be compatible with the Basic Law notwithstanding the only very limited guarantees in European Community law of separation of powers and of democratic participation through a representative assembly, and the lack of an explicit catalogue of fundamental rights guarantees in European community Law.[243] In its judgment relating to the European Organization for the Safety of Air Navigation (Eurocontrol), the Federal Constitutional Court did not find any infringement of Article 24 but emphasized that "Article 24, section 1 of the Basic Law does not permit to relativize the fundamental rights chapter of the Basic Law without reservation".[244]

The "integration power" provided for in Article 24, section 1 is sometimes also referred to as a "constitutional power" because it authorizes the constitution of a new international organization with limited law-making powers of its own. This terminology is illustrative of the problems of the reciprocal interrelationship between national and international "constitutional law":

241 See: C. Tomuschat (note 240), p. 46.

242 Bundesverfassungsgericht Entscheidungen Vols. 37, pp. 271, 279, 291; 58, pp. 1, 40.

243 See: Bundesverfassungsgericht Entscheidungen Vols. 73, pp. 339 ff; 58, pp. 1 ff.

244 Bundesverfassungsgericht Entscheidungen Vol. 58, pp. 1, 40.

On the one side, the national "integration power" is legally limited by the fundamental principles of the respective national constitutional law (such as Article 79, section 3 of the Basic Law). But the full effectuation of the principles of national constitutional law (e.g. protection of fundamental rights in transnational relations) requires today an "openmindedness" of the national constitution for international integration based on principles common to the various member states and thus no longer fully identical with their respective national concretizations and variations of the principles concerned.

On the other side, the national constitutional principles and the risks of "government failures" also require "constitutionalizing" the regulatory powers of the newly constituted international organizations. This can be achieved in two ways: Either by incorporating the common national constitutional principles into the international integration law, albeit often in only an incomplete manner (e.g. in respect of the principles of separation of powers, parliamentary control and judicial review). Or the observance and effectiveness of the international rules must be protected by supplementary constitutional safeguards and procedural "checks and balances" at the <u>domestic</u> level (e.g. requirements to incorporate the international rules of conduct into domestic legislation, to ensure "due process" in domestic administrative implementing procedures, direct applicability and domestic judicial review of the international rules concerned). In practice, both methods of "constitutionalizing" international integration law are usually combined in varying degrees.

5. Conclusions: The Need for an "International Constitutional Law"

The analysis, in chapter VII, of the constitutional functions of liberal international trade, monetary and investment rules and, in chapter VIII, of the regulation of foreign affairs and foreign trade in the national constitutions of the United States, Switzerland and the Federal Republic of Germany suggest three important conclusions:

A) Liberal International Trade Rules and Democratic Constitutionalism Rest on the Same Liberal Principles

The clear trend, since World War II, to limit the discretionary trade policy powers of governments through self-imposed international rules reflects the widely recognized necessity of extending the fundamental principles of "constitutionalism" (such as limited government and rule of law) to the ever more important trade policy powers of governments and to "constitutionalize" the often mercantilist traditions of domestic foreign trade laws. But a more effective "anchoring" of the liberal international trade and monetary rules within the domestic constitutional systems of liberal democracies is unlikely to be achieved without a better insight into the fact that nondiscriminatory market competition and liberal foreign trade rest on the same value premisses and pursue the same objectives as democratic constitutionalism:[245]

a) Values can be derived only from the individual. Individuals are the best judges of their own welfare and, in order to be able to develop their personal capacities, must be granted the widest possible freedom of choice and of corresponding responsibility (including the right to "trial and error" as a possible means for self-improvement). Since the existence of objective immutable truth remains controversial and uncertain, freedom constitutes an ethical value in itself and not only a possible means to agreed higher political ends (e.g. greater opportunities of knowledge, discovery, production and consumption). Both economic and legal liberalism (e.g. GATT rules) aim at the maintenance and extension of equal freedoms in order to secure individual citizens the maximum freedom of choice (given material constraints).

Central to both economic and legal constitutionalism is the belief that all forms of coercive government intervention should conform to the "rule of law". This means, in particular, that all legislative, executive and judicial government organs should conform to a set of transparent, general, non-discriminatory and long-term principles, rules and procedures. The self-imposed international GATT obligations, for instance, set out transparent, general and non-discriminatory rules of unlimited duration which apply, in principle, to all governmental trade policy measures affecting trade in goods and aim at the maintenance of non-discriminatory trade competition among enterprises acting "solely in accordance with commercial considerations" (see Article XVII of GATT on state-trading enterprises). Both economic and legal constitutional theory emphasize also the need for responsibility of individuals as well as of states for their actions, because responsibility (e.g. of producers to adjust to import competi-

245 On the legal and political tradition of "constitutionalism" see: J.R. Pennock/J.W. Chapman (eds.), Constitutionalism, 1979. For a critical discussion of the value premisses of welfare economics see: C.K. Rowley/A.T. Peacock, Welfare Economics, A Liberal Restatement, 1975, notably pp. 78-102. On "constitutional economics" see in particular R.B. McKenzie (ed.) Constitutional Economics. Containing the Economic Powers of Government, 1984.

tion) influences individual choices in a manner harmonizing individual and social welfare (e.g. as a deterrent for harmful choices for fear of the resultant responsibility). As a decentralized conflict-resolving mechanism, individual responsibility (e.g. legal liability) contributes to reducing the need for government coercion.

b) The inevitable conflicts of freedoms (also within the economic sphere e.g. between freedom of markets and feedom of contract), the need to rank and legally protect freedoms through coercive measures (e.g. protection of property rights as a means of delimiting freedoms and resolving conflicts among them), and the proper domain, rules and procedures for "collective choices" are considered by both economic and legal liberalism as the central constitutional problems. The maintenance and extension of equal freedoms, and of the markets arising from the free exercise of individual freedoms and property rights, require general rules and governments designed to correct "market failures" (such as cartelization and adverse external effects) and to supply "public goods" that are not produced in the open market (e.g. agreed standards of income redistribution and "social justice"). But the presence of market failure is not yet a sufficient condition for government interventions since the "state" does often not act like an efficient, impartial and omniscient servant of the public good. The risks of "government failure" necessitate a "constitution of liberty" (e.g. trade and competition law protecting economic markets, constitutional law protecting political markets) restraining abuses of private and government powers.

c) Just as liberal constitutional theory holds that individual fundamental rights provide the most important determinant of the national "public interest", liberal welfare economics emphasizes that economic development will be maximized if the individual is at the centre of the process. Not only subjective individual welfare but also social welfare depend on the maintenance of individual freedom of the citizens to determine and express their own individual preferences. This individual freedom of choice as well as the social welfare tend to be enlarged by extending the scope of the market and of the price mechanism as a spontaneous information mechanism. The fact that market competition and liberal trade tend to maximize the <u>individual</u> freedom of choice and property rights of the citizens, is not dependent upon any economic theory.[246] But non-discriminatroy market competition tends to maximize also "<u>social</u> welfare" (in the sense of freedom of choice, real income and property rights of all members of society)

---

246 This fact, often misunderstood by lawyers, has been rightly emphasized by A. Bleckmann, Ordnungsrahmen für das Recht der Subventionen, 1984, pp. 27 ff.

and to promote other important objective principles of national constitutional laws, such as democratic "government by discussion" (e.g. determination of production by consumer demand) and limitation of the abuse of power (e.g. competition as an antitrust device).[247] Likewise, non-discriminatory transnational market competition and liberal foreign trade maximize not only the individual freedoms, property rights and non-discriminatory treatment of domestic citizens in transnational relations. They promote simultaneously also important objective principles and goals of national constitutional laws (see, e.g., Articles 29 and 31 of the Swiss Constitution), such as promotion of cheap foreign supplies, non-inflationary economic growth and the public choice of more proportionate, internal policy instruments for whatever economic and social policy objectives a government wants to pursue.

d) Contrary to the frequent slogan of the "indivisibility of freedom", economic liberalism and the national constitutional laws of liberal democracies distinguish between the various kinds of intellectual, political, economic and other freedoms.[248] Also GATT law proceeds from the assumption that at least some of the various economic freedoms (such as freedom of foreign trade and freedom of contract) may be respected in the transnational trade relations also of countries without political or other freedoms (e.g. private ownership of the means of production). Such other freedoms may be mutually complementary or may even condition each other (e.g. freedom of contract and of transferring property rights as conditions for voluntary exchanges through trade).

e) Liberal international trade theory and GATT law are based upon the principle that almost all government interventions into the domestic economy can be made more efficiently and more effectively by internal policy measures rather than trade policy border measures with their harmful distorting effects on domestic prices, competition, consumers and exporters. This "economic theory of optimal intervention" (see above chapter IV.3) has nothing to do with laissez-faire liberalism and corresponds to the "proportionality principle" recognized in the national constitutional laws, e.g. of Switzerland and the Federal Republic of Germany.

---

247 See: A. Bleckmann (note 246) who also concludes rightly "dass die Marktwirtschaft nicht nur die klassischen Freiheiten, sondern vor allem die sozialen Grundrechte, aber auch das Demokratie- und das Rechtsstaatsprinzip maximiert", and according to whom government interventions into the economy must be "market-conforming" (pp. 21 ff.).

248 See: F. Machlup. Liberalism and the Choice of Freedom, in: E. Streissler (ed.), Roads to Freedom: Essays in honour of F.A. v.Hayek, 1969.

The preceding survey suggests that non-discriminatory liberal trade and legal protection of equal freedoms and property rights are two sides of the same coin: On the one side, the legal protection of individual freedoms and property rights gives rise to market competition and to liberal trade because they enable each individual to maximize his individual welfare (e.g. his production and consumption of goods and services) beyond what he could achieve without division of labour. On the other side, market competition and liberal trade are nothing else than the voluntary exercise of individual freedoms by domestic citizens to exchange property rights in a mutually welfare-increasing manner.

B) Liberal International Trade Rules are Equivalent to "Substantive International Constitutional Rules"

The United States, Switzerland and the Federal Republic of Germany are all federal states with written constitutions which reflect the belief of their framers that individual liberties, private property and non-discriminatory liberal trade were safer protected by federal law than by unitary state law. As the history of the elaboration notably of the American and the Swiss Constitution bears out, the framers of the original constitutions sought to limit the economic regulatory powers of the states and to liberalize the economic and trade barriers erected by the states against each other. But it was only in Articles 29 and 31 of the Swiss Constitution that the liberal trade rules were explicitly extended also to the trade relations with third countries.

During the 19th century, trade liberalization among the various German states was progressively achieved in the context of the German Customs Union (Deutscher Zollverein, 1834-1866), through the harmonization of economic legislation in the context of the German Confederation (Deutscher Bund, 1815-1866, e.g. the Commom Commercial Code of 1861), and through the recognition of economic freedoms first in individual states (e.g. Gewerbefreiheit in Pussia since 1806) and then in Article 3 of the 1867 Constitution of the North German Confederation as well as of the 1871 Constitution of the German Reich. This German experience during the 19th century with trade liberalization through customs unions and "confederal arrangements" displays features similar to the progressive trade liberalization after World War II through customs unions and free trade areas among the EEC and EFTA countries. The common historical origins and similar functions of these various liberal international trade rules become apparent if one takes into account that the international GATT rules were strongly influenced by the classical international trade agreements.[249] The customs union provisions of the EEC Treaty (e.g. Articles 12, 30, 36, 95) as well as the free trade area agreements between the EEC and EFTA countries were drafted so as to implement the GATT obligations of the EEC and EFTA countries under GATT Article XXIV. As in the German Zollverein, the liberal international trade rules have brought about an increasing harmonization of national foreign trade laws and, in the EEC, a gradual transformation of the "confederal" into "federal" arrangements establishing centralized trade policy powers enabling common trade legislation with direct effects for the citizens and with primacy over national foreign trade laws.

GATT continues to be an international treaty recognizing the sovereign freedom of each member country to decide autonomously on its national level of trade protection. But, as shown in chapters VII and VIII, the substantive international GATT obligations for the use of transparent, non-discriminatory and proportionate trade policy instruments are more precise and more comprehensive than the corresponding national constitutional principles of transparent policymaking, non-discrimination, proportionality and freedom of trade. The self-imposed international GATT obligations protect and extend individual freedoms and property rights across national frontiers (e.g. individual access to foreign markets) and legally limit the excessively broad trade policy discretion of national legislatures, executives and courts. Whereas, for instance, the non-discrimination requirements of national constitutions tend to prohibit only the discrimination among domestic citizens or residents, the GATT rules prohibit also indirect discriminations and trade distortions among domestic citizens (e.g. competing importers) arising from trade restrictions discriminating among the GATT supplier countries or export markets. Or, whereas the constitutional guarantees of economic liberty in the United States are construed as <u>not</u> protecting the freedom to import and export, the GATT tariff bindings and comprehensive prohibitions of non-tariff trade barriers legally protect individual access to foreign markets and supplies. The national customs, antidumping and other foreign trade laws of GATT contracting parties are based upon the detailed GATT rules and have considerably enhanced legal certainty and judicial review in foreign trade.

The analysis in chapters VII and VIII indicates that the international GATT trading system is gradually evolving into a sort of "confederal legal system" in

249 See, e.g.: H.C. Hawkins, Commercial Treaties and Agreements, Principles and Practice, 1951

which the foreign trade rules at the level of national laws, European Community law and the free trade area agreements between GATT member countries are based on the liberal international GATT rules and interact in many ways. The substantive international GATT prohibitions of trade discrimination (e.g. Articles I, III, XIII) and of non-tariff trade barriers (e.g. Articles II, V, XI:1) are considerably more precise and comprehensive than the often vague regulation of non-tariff trade barriers e.g. in Articles 110-116 of the EEC Traty and in national foreign trade laws. Even the EEC Treaty provisions for the internal customs union (e.g. Articles 30 and 95) are drafted in less precise terms than the corresponding GATT provisions (Articles III, XI:1) and leave open certain questions (such as freedom of transit) that are regulated in detail in GATT law (see Article V). But the substantive international GATT rules are not placed into an effective "constitutional framework" at the international level. Even though the liberal international GATT rules can serve "constitutional functions", their legal effectiveness depends upon supplementary domestic rules, procedures and institutional "checks and balances".

C) The Need to Integrate Liberal International Trade Rules into Domestic Constitutional Systems

Because of the diversity of the national economic, political and legal systems of GATT contracting parties, an enhanced effectiveness of this "layered", overall GATT legal system cannot be realistically expected from "supranational" techniques and international bureaucracies but only from a more effective incorporation of the liberal international GATT rules into the domestic constitutional systems (see chapter IX). Not only from an economic and political perspective but also from a legal point of view must liberalism and internationalism begin at home. For this it is necessary to see that international legal prohibitions of mutually harmfull trade discrimination and of non-tariff trade barriers are of concern not only to the external relations of states but apply also to their internal taxation and economic regulation (see, e.g., GATT Article III on "internal taxation and regulation"). Moreover, the rules not only limit the abuse of government powers but their primary objective is to promote and protect access to foreign markets, due process and judicial review for the benefit of all domestic citizens (importers, exporters, competitors, producers, consumers, taxpayers). As shown in Chapters VII and VIII, the national and international legal limitations of government powers pursue the same constitutional objectives and supplement each other:

a) From the national perspective, the American, Swiss and German constitutions constitute limited government powers also in respect of foreign affairs. The substantive constitutional restraints - such as the guarantees of fundamental rights, non-discrimination and proportionality - are recognized to apply also to the foreign affairs powers, notwithstanding the need for differentiating depending on whether the foreign affairs powers are exercised in the forms of national law vis-à-vis the domestic citizens or by means of international agreements or unilateral international acts addressed to foreigners abroad and to foreign governments. Many freedoms (e.g. access to foreign markets) and other constitutional guarantees can, however, be effectively protected in transnational relations only by means of reciprocal obligations among states. The constitutional guarantees of nondiscriminatory treatment can be considerably enlarged through international agreements protecting domestic traders also from the trade-distorting effects resulting from discriminations among supplier countries and among export markets. There is a striking parallelism between the declared objectives of the international GATT and IMF rules, on the one side, and those of the autonomous national foreign trade and monetary laws of the OECD contries, on the other side. Moreover, the international GATT obligations for non-discriminatory market access and for the public choice of transparent, non-discriminatory and proportionate trade policy instruments are considerably more precise and more comprehensive than the often vaguely circumscribed autonomous national foreign trade laws of states (e.g. the Swiss Federal Law on Foreign Economic Measures of 1982 or the German Federal Law on Foreign Economic Relations of 1961).

b) From the international perspective, the liberal international trade and monetary obligations are, however, not placed into a "constitutional framework" protecting the "public interest" in the observance of these welfare-maximizing international rules from the "rent-seeking" pressures of protectionist interest groups. Viewed from the point of view of Article 16 of the French Constitution of 1789 - according to which "Toute société, dans laquelle la garantie des droits n'est pas assurée, ni la séparation des pouvoirs déterminée, n'a point de constitution" - the international trade and monetary rules lack an "international constitution". Nor are the procedural constitutional safeguards and institutional "checks and balances" of the national legal systems - such as parliamentary legislation and control, separation and only limited delegation of trade policy powers, judicial protection of individual rights - effectively applied to the foreign trade policy area.

As long as international trade relations and international economic law continue to be misconceived from a mercantilist perspective as the result of struggles for economic advantages reflecting the "rapport de force" among countries, the "power-oriented" insistence on "sovereign freedom" (e.g. to disregard the international GATT obligations) and on broad executive foreign policy discretion will impede attempts to "constitutionalize" foreign trade policymaking. Yet, the "constitutional problem" remains that the risks of "government failure" are even greater in foreign affairs than in domestic affairs. The same political prevalence of "rent-seeking" protectionist group interests which is recognized to require procedural and institutional safeguards in domestic economic affairs (e.g. an independent central bank protecting the public interest in monetary stability from group interests in inflationary monetary policies, autonomous antitrust authorities protecting the public interest in undistorted competition from protectionist group interests), requires also constitutional restraints on the broad discretionary foreign economic policy powers of governments.

c) General long-term international legal restraints on discretionary trade policy powers can help to keep legislative coalitions and protectionist group interests within constitutional bounds. The successful meshing of the mutually complementary international and national "constitutional requirements" for the use of transparent, non-discriminatory and proportionate policy instruments, especially in the 24 OECD countries with liberal democracies which account for more than 60 % of world trade, appears to be the most important "constitutional condition" for an effective legal framework promoting equal freedoms, nondiscriminatory competition and welfare-increasing policy-making in transnational economic relations. In a world economy composed of more than 170 states, the national constitutional guarantees of equal freedoms, nondiscrimination and welfare-increasing policymaking cannot be made effective without complementary international trade, monetary and investment rules. And, vice versa, the multilateral international GATT and IMF obligations for the use of transparent, nondiscriminatory and proportionate trade and monetary policy instruments cannot remain effective over time if their interpretation, applicaiton and observance is left to the discretion of the very same government executives whose broad discretionary powers the rules were designed to restrain. The liberal international rules have to be placed into, and protected by, a "constitutional framework" of institutional "checks and balances" which can be supplied only at the domestic level by extending the national institutional and procedural safeguards of parliamentary legislation and control, limited delegation of powers and judicial protection of individual rights to the self-imposed international liberal trade, monetary and investment rules.[250]

The mutually complementary national and international human rights law as well as European integration law already offer historical examples for such an "international constitutional law" based on vertical separation of powers and a "stratified" liberal international order. In each of the three liberal democracies examined in chapter VIII, equal freedoms, nondiscriminatory competition and a legal-institutional framework designed to avoid both "market failures" as well as "government failures" are recognized to be constitutionally mandated within the national economy. The fundamental rights guarantees of American, Swiss and German constitutional law as well as the constitutional provisions for the incorporation of international law require construing the self-imposed international legal obligations in a manner maximizing the national and international legal guarantees of individual freedoms and property rights.[251] Yet, it is widely not understood, notably by domestic courts, that observance of the self-imposed international GATT obligations for transparent policymaking, nondiscriminatory market access, proportionality of government restrictions, undistorted competition, due process and judicial protection of individual rights maximizes also the fundamental rights guarantees of domestic citizens. Hence, stricter observance of the self-imposed liberal international obligations would assist in achieving the constitutionally mandated task of developing rules and procedures ensuring that the national "public interest" in the conduct of trade policy is pursued and achieved in a manner maximizing the equal fundamental rights of all the citizens rather than the special interests of "rent-seeking" protectionist interest groups.

European Community law has led to a far-reaching modification of German constitutional law via Article 24 of the Basic Law. The economic freedoms and other liberal guarantees of European Community law have legally extended the corresponding national freedoms accross the national frontiers and now form an integral part of the legal systems of the EEC member states.[252] The recognition,

---

250 See: W. Fiedler, Auswärtige Gewalt und Verfassungsgewichtung. Zum Problem des internationalen Verfassungsrechts, in: I. von Münch (ed.), Staatsrecht, Völkerrecht, Europarecht, Festschrift für H.J. Schlochauer, 1981, pp. 57 ff, 69: "Internationales Verfassungsrecht tritt nicht an die Stelle 'nationalen' Verfassungsrechts, es betrifft vielmehr die Gesamtheit der rechtlich bedeutsamen Einwirkungen aus dem internationalen Bereich".

251 On the pertinent international human rights conventions see: P. Sieghart, The International Law of Human Rights, 1984, pp. 24 ff., 252 ff.

252 See: I. Pernice, Grundrechtsgehalte im Europäischen Gemeinschaftsrecht, 1979

by the European Court of Justice, of the direct applicability by domestic courts and by individuals of certain economic freedoms of the EEC's free trade area agreements with the EFTA countries[253] has further extended the individual rights of European citizens and their judicial protection in the foreign trade relations with the EFTA countries. In the foreign trade relations with other states, the national constitutional guarantees of equal freedoms, nondiscriminatory liberal trade and judicial protection of individual rights can likewise be extended through their interpretation in conformity with the more precise and more comprehensive international GATT rules. Since the current "government failure" in the trade policy area is largely due to the incentives for "protectionist rent-seeking" within the prevailing system of discretionary trade policymaking, protecting the rights of traders and consumers interested in liberal trade offers the most promising, democratic way towards a self-enforcing "liberal trade constitution".

253 See: A. Bleckmann, Die unmittelbare Anwendbarkeit der Freihandelsakommen mit den EFTA-Staaten, in: H.G. Koppensteiner (ed.), Rechtsfragen der Freihandelsabkommen der EWG mit den EFTA-Staaten, 1987, pp. 85 ff.

IX. SUMMARY AND CONCLUSIONS: CONSTITUTIONALIZING FOREIGN TRADE POLICY THROUGH LIBERAL INTERNATIONAL RULES AND THEIR INCORPORATION INTO DOMESTIC CONSTITUTIONAL SYSTEMS.

"An international authority which effectively limits the powers of the state over the individual, will be one of the best safeguards of peace. The international Rule of Law must become a safeguard as much against the tyranny of the state over the individual as against the tyranny of the new super-state over the national communities".

F.A. v.Hayek[1]

"... treaties are no longer confined to affairs of State. Yet, by a strange legal anachronism, some States ... still seem to consider that treaties are a matter for governments alone, and fail to take measures to implement even those treaties, such as the European Convention on Human Rights, which are of their very nature appropriate for enforcement in the courts."

F.G. Jacobs[2]

1. International Economic and Legal Integration Do Not Require Uniformization

A) Market Integration through Private Law

Part I of this book has shown that, from a legal perspective, trade and investment transactions consist of the exercise of individual liberties and of agreed exchanges of property rights. Prices only measure the value of these rights. The property rights are voluntarily exchanged only if each party to the trade transac-

1 F.A. v.Hayek, The Road to Serfdom, 1944, p. 175.

2 F.G. Jacobs, Introduction to: F.G. Jacobs/S. Roberts (eds.), The Effects of Treaties in Domestic Law, 1987, p. xxiii.

tion perceives the exchange as value-maximizing for itself and if the exchange of the rights **in rem** and in their exchange value is legally protected through contract law. Likewise, private investments will take place only if the property rights to the proceeds are legally safe. Common resource problems (e.g. overfishing in the High Seas) and adverse external effects (e.g. river pollution) are usually a sign of a lack or inadequate assignment of property rights.

The historical evolution of the contents and assignments of individual freedoms and property rights has been determined not only by their welfare-maximizing properties described by economists, but also because people have valued these individual freedoms in their own right and as means of promoting legal certainty and peaceful change. Foreign trade and investment contracts have contributed to the progressive development of commercial usages and private commercial laws serving the common interests of traders in legal certainty and reduced transaction costs. The ancient laws of the Greek cities, Roman law, the medieval "revival" of the Roman law of the Corpus Juris Justinianeum leading to a "common law of Europe" ("gemeines Recht", "jus commune") commented upon by scholars and applied by courts in much of continental Europe until the great national legal codifications,[3] and especially the medieval law merchant as a particular jus mercatorum and customary law applied also by governmental authorities: all included particular rules promoting international trade transactions and transnational economic and legal integration through private law. From about the 17th century, however, international trade and market integration through uniform private commercial law were increasingly hampered by the political emergence of nation-states with centralized, absolute government powers, national codifications of economic law and mercantilist government interventions into the domestic economy and foreign trade.[4]

The evolution of modern postmercantilist trade theory and trade law can be classified into three stages:[5]

3 See H. Coing, Die Ursprüngliche Einheit der Europäischen Rechtswissenschaft, 1968; M. Cappelletti (ed), New Perspectives for a Common Law of Europe, 1978. As the English common law claimed precedence over "repugnant" statutory law until the "Glorious Revolution of 1688" proclaimed the supremacy of the enactments of Parliament (see the celebrated Dr. Bonham 's Case of 1610, 8 Coke 's Reports 118a, 77 ER 652), so on much of the European continent the jus civile of the Empire and the jus canonicum of the Church claimed to be the law of the highest universal authorities with preeminence vis-à-vis conflicting local statutory law until the opposite rule ("lex municipii vincit legem generalem in loco") eventually prevailed.

4 See above chapter II.3 and 5.

5 See W.M. Corden, Trade Policy and Economic Welfare, 1974, pp. 2ff.

- In the first stage, during the 19 th century and under the influence of the economic theories of "absolute advantages" (Adam Smith, 1723-1790) and "comparative advantages" (David Ricardo, 1772-1823) of trading nations, the gains from trade came to be appreciated leading to a gradual liberalisation of the mercantilist trade regulations and to the Europeen free trade system (1860-1914) based essentially upon international market integration through private law, liberal national trade and monetary legislation (e.g. prescribing the convertibility of national currencies into gold and prohibiting most non-tariff trade barriers) and bilateral long-term trade agreements interlinked through unconditional most-favoured-nation commitments.

- In the second stage, roughly between the first and the second world wars, more and more qualifications to laissez-faire and complete free trade were developed, promoting in many European countries the establishment of large government bureaucracies for the administration of economic policy, an ever increasing public sector, the "politicisation" of the economy, governmental restrictions on transnational commercial transactions and notably discriminatory non-tariff trade barriers.

- In the third stage, the period since World War II, "the link between the case for free trade and the case for laissez-faire has been broken" on the ground that foreign trade restrictions or distortions are hardly ever an "optimal policy" for correcting "domestic distortions" of the economy and promoting the national economic welfare.[6] The main policy recommendation underlying this "economic theory of optimal government intervention" is that, whatever national economic policy objectives a government decides to pursue, domestic internal instruments of government intervention (such as tax laws, antitrust laws or production subsidies) can almost always achieve the national economic policy objectives in a more efficient and more effective manner than governmental foreign trade restrictions with their market-distorting and welfare-reducing side-effects. This economic ranking of trade and monetary policy instruments also underlies the postwar GATT and IMF Agreements which prohibit only the use of non-transparent, discriminatory and disproportionately harmful instruments of trade and monetary policy without impinging upon the national freedom of each member country to intervene into its domestic economy, to decide on the value of its national currency and to protect its domestic producers by means of trade tariffs.[7]

---

6 See M. Corden (note 5) and above chapter IV.3.

7 For details see above chapters I.4, III.3, IV.3, V.1, VII.2 and 3.

With the eighteenth century Enlightenment, economic, political and legal liberalism and the individualizing view of society began to become preponderant. In the American Declaration of Independence (1776), the US Constitution (1787/89) and the Bill of Rights (1791), just as in the French "Déclaration des Droits de l'Homme" (1789), the state was now clearly conceived to be composed of and established by individuals with the limited task of promoting their individual and common ("public") interests. One of the major discoveries of Adam Smith's "Inquiry into the Nature and Causes of the Wealth of Nations" (1776) was that the economic welfare of England was mainly due to its legal guarantees of individual freedoms, property rights and private, self-interested market competition under the rule of law:

> "That security which the laws in Great Britain give to every man that he shall enjoy the fruits of his own labour, is alone sufficient to make any country flourish, notwithstanding ... twenty other absurd regulations of commerce... The natural effort of every individual to better his condition, when suffered to exert itself with freedom and security, is so powerful a principle, that it is alone, and without any assistance, not only capable of carrying on the society to wealth and prosperity, but of surmounting a hundred impertinent obstructions with which the folly of human laws too often incumbers its operations."[8]

The liberal economic arguments in favour of equal freedoms, protection of private property rights and private competition, like the complementary reasons given by political and legal liberalism in favor of individual rights and rule of law, offered also a theory of "governmental-political failure" that strongly influenced the constitutional-legal reforms which have taken place in North America and Europe since the 18th century.[9]

The economic, political and legal liberalism of the 18th century had largely emerged in reaction to previous historical experiences with political absolutism and economic mercantilism of the European nation-states. The historical revival of a "new mercantilism" during the 1930s and again since about the 1970s[10] prompted a new liberal counterreaction further analyzing the conditions under which private competition and private law could contribute to a welfare-maximizing division of labour both within and among countries. The various neolibe-

8 A. Smith, An Inquiry into the Nature and the Causes of the Wealth of Nations (Liberty Classics 1976), Book IV, chapter V, p. 540.

9 See above chapters V.4, VIII.2.A and VIII.3.B.

10 See above chapters V.2 and 4.

ral theories of "Ordo-liberalism"[11] and "constitutional economics"[12] criticize the widespread belief in the "macroeconomic management" of "welfare states" not only on economic grounds but also for its "constitutional ignorance" and totalitarian, undemocratic premisses: If values can be derived only from individuals and governments are established only for the purpose of promoting the interests of individuals, then equal individual freedoms and private markets are a precondition for revealing individual preferences and for enabling governments to determine the "public interest". Democratic economic, political and legal (sub)systems must therefore be evaluated in terms of the comparative ease with which they enable individual citizens to exercise their individual fundamental rights and to engage in voluntary exchanges, contracts, trades, political discussions and social decisionmaking processes. Supra-individualistic conceptions of national welfare and of economic efficiency independent of the market processes through which individual choices are exercised, the proffering of policy advice by neoclassical economists (such as J.M. Keynes) as if democratic governments can manipulate the economy as benevolent despots without political and constitutional constraints, or the implied assumption that government officials will invariably use their powers to serve only the public interest, are being criticized as inconsistent with the individualistic values and practical experiences of liberal economies and democracies.[13]

Already the classical economists acknowledged the existence of "market failures" (such as the risk of cartelization and the need for the governmental supply of "public goods") and recognized that markets tend to reconcile individual and social interests only if property rights are well defined.[14] Resources with badly defined or non-existent property rights (e.g. clean air) tend to be overused and may induce the private production of goods with larger social costs than benefits. The economic and legal "property rights theory"[15] has, however, shown that such harmful "external effects" (e.g. the factory smoke which has harmful effects on those occupying neighbouring land) can often be avoided by a reassignment

---

11 See above chapter III.4.A.

12 See, e.g. : J.D. Gwartney/R.E. Wagner (eds.), Public Choice and Constitutional Economics, 1988; R.B. McKenzie (ed.), Constitutional Economics, 1984.

13 See, for instance: J.M. Buchanan/J. Burton/R.E. Wagner, The Consequences of Mr. Keynes, 1978.

14 See above chapter IV.1.

15 For good surveys of the literature see: A. Schüller (ed.), Property Rights und ökonomische Theorie, 1983; A.I. Ogus/C.G. Veljanowski (eds.), Readings in the Economics of Law and Regulation, 1984, pp. 53 ff.

of private property rights, the introduction of liability rules and decentralized bargaining without further government intervention. The European Court of Justice's interpretation of the EEC Treaty prohibitions of tariffs and non-tariff trade barriers as directly applicable individual rights has also demonstrated that the governnmental supply of "public goods", such as trade liberalization and open markets, can be promoted by the recognition of individual freedoms and property rights. Like the economic market mechanisms themselves, individual rights and private law as the legal means for market exchanges serve therefore important economic functions for the production of both private as well as public goods and the promotion of both individual as well as social economic welfare.[16]

B) Divergent National Choice of Law Rules, Jurisdiction Rules, Recognition and Enforcement Rules as Barriers to Trade and Investment

Transnational trade transactions are exposed to a particularly high degree of uncertainty because they involve sellers and buyers in different countries and the goods or services have to be supplied accross national frontiers. The uncertainty often entails higher trade and investment costs compared to purely domestic transactions, and may act as an investment and trade barrier. The private contractual arrangements on the sale, carriage, delivery and payment of the goods or services are usually governed by a specific national legal system. According to the almost universally recognized principle of party autonomy, the parties are free to choose, either expressly or implicitly, the applicable law (lex contractus) governing the formation, validity, interpretation and performance of their contract. Such a choice of law by the parties will be respected in principle in most countries of the world and "endeavours to obviate the unpredictable findings of unforseeable tribunals and to consolidate the contract under one law while negotiation is in course".[17]

In the absence of an express or implied choice of law clause, the proper law of the contract must be determined according to objective criteria e.g. by the court which has been seized of a dispute relating to the contract. Unfortunately, there is little international consensus on these criteria, for instance whether the applicable law should be the law of the party who is to furnish the characteristic performance, or the law at the place of performance, or that at the place of conclu-

16 See also B. Rebe, Privatrecht und Wirtschaftsordnung, 1978.

17 E. Rabel, The Conflict of Laws: A Comparative Study, Vol. 2, 1960, p. 365.

sion of the contract, or the law which the parties are presumed to have intended to apply. Each state can decide for itself

- the conditions under which the proper law of international contracts must be determined and may be governed by its own law (choice of law);
- the conditions under which its national courts are competent to entertain suits which have contacts with more than one legal system (jurisdiction of courts);
- and the conditions under which foreign judgments will be recognized and enforced.

Most states do not consider it as adequate that international commercial transactions with contacts to several legal systems are invariably governed by their own national law and courts. They have therefore developed special national conflict of law rules (also called "private international law" in spite of its national character) which often differ from country to country and are subject to national public policy exceptions excluding the application of foreign laws that are inconsistent with the public policy of the forum state. The lack of uniformity of the national conflict of law rules implies that the parties to international commercial transactions often remain uncertain as to where an action relating to the performance of their contract may be brought, which law the court will apply, and whether a judgment will be recognized and enforced outside the country where it was rendered. The jurisdiction of national courts and the court procedures are, on principle, also determined by the lex fori.[18] Moreover, many states have provided for "long-arm statutes" enabling plaintiffs to bring an action even if the parties and their dispute have little or no contact with the forum state (e.g. if the existence within the jurisdiction of assets belonging to a non-resident defendant is recognized as a ground for jurisdiction);[19] this may then induce the disputant parties to a strategy of "forum shopping", i.e. of selecting a national court on the ground that the national law, applicable under the forum's private international law, is perceived to favour the party concerned. "Forum shopping"

18 See U. Drobnig, Private International Law, in: R. Bernhardt (ed.), Encyclopedia of Public International Law, Instalment 10, 1987, pp. 330, 333.

19 An example of an "exorbitant" rule of jurisdiction is Article 14 of the French Civil Code which provides that any French national may sue a foreigner in the French courts.

is also encouraged by the remarkable "homeward trend"[20] of courts, i.e. the noticeable regularity with which courts have found that the applicable law is the law of the forum. Additional uncertainties inherent in national conflict of law rules are due to the problems of ascertaining foreign law. A national court, faced with the problem of ascertaining the content of foreign law to which a choice of law rule may refer, will find this often time-consuming, costly and difficult particularly if the foreign law belongs to a different system of law, is written in a language unfamiliar to the court, or is obscure in respect of the pertinent legal issue. The courts of some countries (notably in common law countries) treat foreign law as a "fact" and leave it to the parties to plead and prove the application of foreign law; the courts in other countries (e.g. in some EEC countries) raise at least certain issues **ex officio** and acquire information about the foreign law either alone or with the cooperation of the parties.[21]

C) Harmonization of International Private Law through International Treaties

The uncertainties caused by the divergent national choice of law rules, jurisdiction rules, recognition and enforcement rules are widely seen as a barrier to international trade transactions which require predictability as to the applicable law and as to where an action may be instituted.[22] The very purpose of trade liberalization is to induce a substantial growth of contractual trade transactions accross national frontiers. The increasing international economic integration is therefore likely to increase also the number of international disputes and the need to resolve these disputes in a uniform way.

The widely recognized need for uniform rules on choice of law, jurisdiction, recognition and enforcement of foreign judgments has given rise to a large number of bilateral and multilateral agreements, partly promoted by international

20 See, e.g.: P. Hay/O. Landol/R. Rotunda, Conflict of Laws as a Technique for Legal Integration, in: Cappelletti/Seccomble/Weiler (eds.), Integration Through Law, Vol. 1, Book 2, 1986, pp. 161, 164 f.

21 See P. Hay/O. Landol/R. Rotunda (note 20), pp. 174 ff.

22 See, e.g., the reports by M. Giuliano/P. Lagarde on the Convention on the Law Applicable to Contractual Obligations (OJ EC No. C 282, 31 October 1980, pp. 1 ff) and by Jenard on the Convention of 27 September 1968 on Jurisdiction and the Enforcement of Judgments in Civil and Commercial Matters (OJ No. C 59, 5 March 1979, pp. 1 ff).

institutions such as the Hague Conference of Private International Law[23] and the European Community pursuant to Article 220 of the EEC Treaty.[24] The hazards of relying on the divergent national conflict of law rules are further reduced by what is sometimes called an international "lex mercatoria", i.e. the elaboration of standard clauses and standard form contracts which are widely agreed upon by parties to international commercial transactions and uniformly applied by arbitration bodies and whose use is systematically promoted by international institutions such as the UN Commission for International Trade Law (UNCITRAL) and the International Chamber of Commerce.[25] There also exists today a multiplicity of international organizations, agreements and model laws aiming at the unification of the substantive national commercial laws e.g. in the fields of bills of exchange and cheques, protection of intellectual property, transport law and the law of sales.[26] The unification of substantive law rules, especially when they apply to internal as well as international relationships, is, however, often much more difficult to achieve compared to the simpler process of unification of conflict of law rules.[27]

D) Sovereignty and the Limits of International Private Law as a Technique for Legal Integration and "Policy Integration"

The modern integrated world economy is composed of more than 170 sovereign states with differing national economies, policies and legal systems. The international law principle of the "sovereign equality of states" (Article 2 of the UN Charter) implies a right of states to diversity, which promotes competition in ideas as well as among national policies and thereby "multiple search and experimentation, encapsulating errors, and thus safeguarding the possibility of na-

---

23 See A. Dyer, Hague Conventions on Private International Law, and A. Dyer, Hague Conventions on Civil Procedure, in: R. Bernhardt (ed.), Encyclopedia of Public International Law, Instalment 9, 1986, pp. 147 ff, 151 ff.

24 See the Convention on Jurisdiction and the Enforcement of Judgments in Civil and Commercial Matters of 1968 (O.J. No. L 304, 30 Oct. 1978, p. 36), concluded in implementation of Article 220 of the EEC Treaty, as well as the 1980 Rome Convention on the Law Applicable to Contractual Obligations (O.J. No. L 266, 9 Oct. 1980, p. 1), which will introduce uniform choice of law rules for contracts.

25 See above chapter II.5.A.

26 For a survey see: H. Kötz, Unification and Harmonization of Laws, in: R. Bernhardt (ed.), Encyclopedia of Public International Law, Instalment 10, 1987, pp. 513 ff.

27 See P. Hay/O. Landol/R. Rotunda (above note 20), p. 169 f.

tions learning from each other".[28] But virtually all theories of international law and of national constitutional law recognize the legally limited and relative nature of state sovereignty in the sense of internal self-government and external independence from superior government power, yet subject to international law.[29] These inherent legal limitations of national sovereignty derive mainly from two sources: first, the recognition of inherent and inalienable human rights in national constitutional laws as well as in international law; and, second, the principle of the primacy of public international law over national law, reflected in various international law principles (such as "pacta sunt servanda") and recognized also in many national constitutions (e.g. in Articles 24 and 25 of the German Basic Law of 1949), which entails an increasing legal limitation of national sovereignty. But states remain in principle free to decide on whether they want to accept international treaty obligations or to accede to international organisations. As the Permanent Court of International Justice has affirmed in the "Wimbledon case", such auto-limitations of state sovereignty through international law are emanations from and not violations of sovereignty: "The Court declines to see in the conclusion of any Treaty by which a State undertakes to perform or refrain from performing a particular act an abandonment of its sovereignty. No doubt, any convention creating an obligation of this kind places a restriction upon the exercise of the sovereign rights of the State, in the sense that it requires them to be exercised in a certain way. But the right of entering into international engagements is an attribute of State sovereignty".[30]

In addition to the inherent national and international legal limitations of state sovereignty, the actual "political sovereignty" of states - in the sense of a society's capacity to make collective decisions that can effectively realize their chosen objectives - is increasingly being reduced also by the factual constraints imposed on national public policies as a result of the worldwide interdependence and integration of the modern open national economies whose welfare depends to an increasing extent on their active participation in the international division of labour. It is no longer possible to maximize the national gains from the interna-

28 J. Tumlir, International Economic Order: Rules, Cooperation and Sovereignty, in: P. Oppenheimer (ed.), Issues in International Economics, 1980, at p. 12.

29 See: L. Wildhaber, Sovereignty and International Law, in: Macdonald/Johnston (eds.), The Structure and Process of International Law: Essays in Legal Philosophy, Doctrine and Theory, 1983, pp. 425, 429; E.U. Petersmann, Sovereignty, International Law and the United Nations Code of Conduct on Transnational Corporations, in: D. Dicke (ed.), Foreign Investment in The Present and a New International Economic Order, 1987, pp. 310, 315ff.

30 The S.S. Wimbledon, PCIJ Ser.A, no. 1 (1923), at p. 25.

tional division of labour through liberal trade, monetary and investment policies and, at the same time, to maintain complete national policy autonomy. Hence, there is a constant tension between the "territorial sovereignty" and reserved "domestic affairs" of states, on the one side, and the transterritorial effects of their national economic policies (especially monetary and trade policies) and transnational business activities, on the other side. Since the exports of goods, services or capital from one country are the imports of another country, states cannot unilaterally guarantee the rights of their own national traders, producers, migrant workers or investors in foreign jurisdictions. Nor can they unilaterally determine the value of their national exchange rate, which is not only one of the most important prices in the national economy but at the same time an international relationship between national economies. Also many other national economic policy decisions by one state (e.g. to grant an export subsidy) can be rendered ineffective by countervailing measures of other states (e.g. by imposing countervailing duties on subsidized imports). Hence the need to supplement the efforts directed at international "market integration" by measures aimed at "policy integration" or policy coordination.

The above considerations illustrate also the limits of private international law as a technique for legal integration. The legal and business uncertainty resulting from the diversity of the national conflict of law rules and from the existing possibilities for bringing an action on an international contract in more than one country cannot be eliminated by any one country alone. Nor could an internationally agreed harmonization of the national conflict of law rules eliminate all the uncertainties inherent e.g. in the ascertainment and application of foreign laws. Harmonisation of the substantive commercial laws of the major trading countries will be even more difficult to achieve. National courts may also deny the recognition and application of foreign law on grounds of national public policy or pursuant to fundamental principles and rules of the "international ordre public"[31] serving essential common interests of the international community. Thus the German Federal Constitutional Court, in the case of a Spanish divorcee, denied the application of the foreign law, applicable under German conflict of law rules, because it would lead to results incompatible with the fundamental rights guarantees of the German Basic Law.[32] Especially Anglo-American courts have often declined to recognize and apply foreign exchange controls,

---

31 See: G. Jaenicke, International Public Order, in: R. Bernhardt (ed.), Encyclopedia of Public International Law, Instalment 7, 1984, pp. 314 ff.

32 Bundesverfassungsgericht, Decision of 4 May 1971, Vol. 31, p. 58.

export restrictions, expropriations and other foreign public laws by resort to an alleged principle that the courts of the forum will not apply foreign public law and will not assist in the extraterritorial implementation of foreign public law provisions which serve the public interest of another state. Even though the so-called principle of the inapplicability **a priori** of foreign public law is not based on cogent reasons and may greatly impede international cooperation, states retain freedom under general international law to recognize or not foreign acts of state.[33] The conclusion of international treaties waiving recourse to national public policy exceptions in economic matters, such as Article VIII: 2, 6 of the IMF Agreement with regard to exchange controls and Articles X: 3, XX of the GATT with regard to foreign trade controls, may therefore prove to be the most effective method for coordinating national public economic laws and their judicial application.

The harmonisation of international private law, albeit necessary for the legal security and predictability required by the worldwide international trade in goods and services, contributes also little to the "constitutional task" of "policy integration" and coordination of the divergent national macroeconomic and sectoral government interventions into the modern "mixed economies". Especially the increasing attempts at liberalizing international trade in services have revealed the fact that the mere liberalisation of border barriers or even the granting of national treatment are often not enough to achieve the aim of liberal trade unless the rules on the free movement of goods and services are supplemented by policy coordination (e.g. in the field of competition policy as regards monopoly rights of national suppliers of certain services) and approximation of public economic laws (e.g. as regards reciprocal recognition of professional requirements, coordination of sectoral economic regulations).[34]

---

33 As to the limits of this national freedom see: W. Meng, Recognition of Foreign Legislative and Administrative Acts, in: R. Bernhardt (above note 26), pp. 348 ff.

34 See on these aspects, e.g.: C.D. Ehlermann/G. Campogrande, Rules on Services in the EEC: A Model for Negotiating World-Wide Rules?, in: E.U. Petersmann/M. Hilf (eds.), The New GATT Round of Multilateral Trade Negotiations, 1988, pp. 481 ff.

2. The Need to Constitutionalize Discretionary Trade Policy Powers and Why This Cannot Be Fully Achieved Unilaterally at the National Level

A) Discretionary Trade Policy Powers to Tax and Restrict the Trade Transactions of Domestic Citizens Require Constitutional Restraints

The national constitutional law of most states has evolved in response to the historical grievances and experiences with "market failures", "government failures" and "constitutional failures" of earlier times. Most principles of national constitutional laws reflect social learning processes about the importance in specific policy areas of certain general values, principles, rules and institutions. Thus the emphasis placed, for instance, by Jean Bodin (1530-1596) in France and Thomas Hobbes (1588-1679) in England on the importance of the governmental "sovereign" monopoly of the use of force and the governmental task of securing peace and order were in part a reaction to the previous civil wars in France and England. The later constitutional demands - e.g. by Charles de Montesquieu (1689-1755) for separation of powers, by John Locke (1632-1704) and John Stuart Mill (1806-1873) for the recognition of inalienable human rights, by Abbé Sieyès (1748-1836) in France and Edmund Burke in England (1729-1797) for parliamentary democracy, or by I. Kant (1724-1804) for general and abstract rules of law - were in part attempts to better protect individual liberties against earlier abuses of domestic government powers. The modern constitutional demands for social justice evolved in response to the social problems experienced during the times of laissez-faire liberalism and industrialization since the second half of the 19th century. And the inclusion of constitutional provisions (e.g. Article 109 section 2 of the German Grundgesetz, adopted in 1967) for an anticyclical exercise of the governmental taxing, spending and borrowing powers came about in response to the economic recessions experienced in the early 1930s and again in 1966/67. Yet, as shown in chapters V, VI and VIII of this book, there continue to be very few national constitutions which include explicit, specific constitutional restraints on the government powers to tax and regulate the transnational trade transactions of their citizens.

The concept of a limiting constitution grew up in England in response to the abuses of "monarchical absolutism" and its claim to stand above legislation ("legibus absolutus"). The chief aim of liberal constitutionalism was to limit the abuse of government powers by means of two constitutional devices: Recognition of inalienable human rights; and the separation and only limited delegation of government power on the legislature, the judiciary and the executive subject to the rule of law. Over the past 200 years, this liberal constitutional objective - that the representative government of a free people must itself be governed by long-term constitutional rules - has only gradually become accepted in the liberal democracies of Europe. The century following the American and French revolutions was in many European countries still characterized by a "process of absolutization of the nation-state".[35] It was only during the second half of the 19th century that the constitutional limitation of the executive powers of the "political branch" and its independent control by the legislative branch became institutionally accepted in France, Germany, Italy and a number of other states of continental Europe. And it was only during the 20th century in the aftermath of World Wars I and II and after the historical experience of the potential tyranny of constitutionally unconstrained governments that the judicial control of the constitutionality of the exercise of the legislative powers has become accepted in a growing number of European states (such as Austria, Germany, Greece, Italy, Israel, Portugal, Spain and Sweden) and Japan.[36] These processes of "constitutionalization" of government powers developed gradually, as witnessed by the history of judicial review over administrative acts in the 19th century, and continue to progress in the present, as illustrated by the acceptance of judicial review by the European Court of Human Rights and the EC Court of Justice in all the EC member states.

The analysis of the "new protectionism" in Part II of this book has attempted to show that the liberal constitutional postulates of equal freedoms, rule of law, separation and only limited delegation of powers are far from being achieved in the trade policy area. For instance, the "enumerated powers" principle of the US Constitution and the corresponding principle of "compétence d'attribution" of European Community law have prevented neither the US Congress nor the EC Council from taxing and restricting the transnational trade transactions of their citizens also by means of discriminatory and disproportionately harmful trade policy instruments inconsistent with international law.[37] And the non-transparent, discriminatory taxation and limitation of American and European citizens by discretionary "grey area trade restrictions", imposed by the US Executive and

35 M. Cappelletti, Foreword to: Cappelletti/Seccombe/Weiler (eds.), Integration Through Law, Vol. 1, Book 1, 1986, p. VIII.

36 See: M. Cappelletti/D. Golay, The Judicial Branch in the Federal and Transnational Union: Its Impact on Integration, in: Cappelletti/Seccombe/Weiler (above note 20), pp. 261, 272.

37 See above chapters V. 2 and VI. 2.

the EC Commission in violation of their self-imposed international GATT obligations,[38] eludes effective judicial control by US courts and European courts, respectively.[39]

Part II further listed the economic, political and legal reasons for the national self-interest in liberal trade[40] and the political and legal asymmetries in domestic decision-making processes about trade policy, which explain why trade is not free and why trade liberalization meets with strong political resistance especially from import-competing producers.[41] Part II concluded that the "new-protectionism" is a sign not only of "government failure" but also of "constitutional failure" in the sense that the "grey area trade protectionism" is due mainly to inadequate rules for the "constitution" of trade policy powers and procedures for trade policymaking, just as "market failures" are often due to inadequate property rights and competition rules.[42] From this followed another conclusion, described in Part II as the "need for taming the mercantilist Leviathan through constitutional rules".[43] The main reasons why the exercise of discretionary trade policy powers requires no less constitutional restraints than the exercise of other government powers of taxation and economic regulation, were listed as follows:[44]

First, there is a strong need to protect individual rights in the trade policy area. Voluntary trade transactions are an exercise of individual freedoms and property rights and take place only if each party perceives the trade transaction to increase its individual welfare.[45] Import restrictions tax and restrict these individual freedoms and reduce the individual economic welfare of the trading partners concerned (e.g. in terms of the individual "freedom to choose" and real income of consumers). Selective import restrictions also distort non-discriminatory competition among domestic traders in the importing country. All import restrictions further redistribute income among domestic groups by taxing dome-

---

38 On the GATT-inconsistency see the detailed analysis in: E.U. Petersmann, Grey Area Trade Policy and the Rule of Law, in: Journal of World Trade 1988, pp. 23-44.

39 See above chapters V. 2 and VI. 2.

40 See above chapter V. 1 and chapters I. 2 and III. 3.

41 See above chapters V. 3 and VI. 3.

42 See above chapter VI. 4.

43 See above chapter V. 5.

44 See above chapter V. 5.

45 See above chapters I. 2 and 3.

stic consumers and enabling import-competing producers to raise their prices and to collect "protection rents".[46] The current "grey area trade policy" and "protectionist biases" in domestic decisionmaking procedures about trade policy[47] also disregard the individual procedural rights in a liberal democracy to "due process", such as individual access by adversely affected citizens to transparent proceedings and to judicial review of administrative decision-making processes which interfere into their equal rights.

Second, there is a strong need to define legally the national self-interest in liberal trade and rule of law in the trade policy area. This is so not only for economic reasons, for instance because foreign trade, which now accounts on average for 20 to 30 percent of the gross domestic product of GATT contracting parties, has proven to be the most dynamic engine of economic growth in many countries and trade restrictions almost always reduce the national economic welfare of the restricting country.[48] No less important are the legal and political reasons, notably the fact that open markets and liberal trade under the rule of law extend the equal freedoms of domestic citizens across national frontiers and promote also international political cooperation and decentralized peaceful change.[49] If, in liberal democracies, constitutional values must be derived from the individual citizens and the object of democratic politics is the furtherance of their equal individual rights and interests, then the governmental pursuit of the "public interest" depends necessarily on democratic political procedures, including freedom to choose and open markets, which enable individuals to express their preferences and to participate in collective decisionmaking processes. Enlarging individual freedoms through open markets carries a positive democratic value in itself. Without democratic processes through which values (preferences, interests) can be expressed, governments cannot democratically determine what is the "best" one from among several political options.[50] Hence, the constitutional need to prescribe the use of transparent and non-discriminatory policy instruments and procedures in all areas of government policy including trade policy. Because trade policy is characterized by conflicts among producer and consumer interests and because the protectionist self-interests of the relative small number of import-competing producers are politically easier to organize than

46 See chapter V. 3. A.

47 See chapter VI. 3.

48 See above chapters III. 3, IV. and V. 1.

49 See above chapter VII. 2.

50 See, e.g., J. Buchanan, Liberty, Market and State, 1986, p. 250.

the dispersed consumer interests,[51] there is also a constitutional need in liberal democracies to design political procedures in a manner reducing conflicts among the majority interests (e.g. the consumer interests in cheaper, better or a larger variety of imported goods) and the minority interests (e.g. producer interests in adjustment assistance vis-à-vis import competition) to the maximum possible.

Third, there is a strong need to limit the discretionary trade policy powers which are an invitation to well-organized, protectionist interest groups to influence the exercise of government discretion for the benefit of their special interests.[52] A democracy based on individual liberty and effective political equality can be secured over time only if all government powers are constitutionally constrained. Since the conflicts between the liberal trade interests of consumers and of the national economy at large can be reconciled with the protectionist self-interests of import-competing producers without recourse to welfare-reducing import restrictions,[53] the constitutional principle of proportionality of government restrictions of individual rights, as well as the above-mentioned democratic functions of the proportionality requirement, call for constitutional restraints on the discretionary trade policy powers and for the protection of freedom of trade. Without such constitutional restraints, the current democratic procedures risk to be "captured" by the better organized producer interests at the expense of the consumer interests leading to an even larger "politicization" of transnational trade at the expense of private freedoms and competition.[54] Another important reason for constitutionally restraining the admissible range of trade policy decisions follows from the economic proposition that the allocation of resources, the production, choice and distribution of goods can be most efficiently determined by the citizens themselves through market competition rather than through governments.[55] This does not necessarily require constitutional free trade guarantees similar to Articles 9, 12, 30 and 34 of the EEC Treaty or an explicit constitutional recognition of the ordering principle of market competition. But the experience from past and present mercantilism calls for a constitutional recognition that government restrictions of the transnational exercise of individual freedoms and property rights are no less subject to the constitutional guarantees

51 See above chapter VI. 3.

52 See above chapter V. 3. A.

53 See above chapter IV. 3.

54 On this "capture theory" see above chapter V. 3. A.

55 See above chapters I. 2, III. 3, IV and V. 1.

of publicness, nondiscrimination, proportionality and judicial review than government restrictions of purely domestic exercises of e.g. freedom of trade and property rights.

Fourth, the above-mentioned arguments in favour of constitutionally protecting the transnational exercise of economic freedom and constitutionally restraining the governmental trade policy discretion further call for legislative rules regulating the transparent, nondiscriminatory and proportionate use of the various trade policy instruments in more detail. The spread of "grey area trade restrictions" no longer transparent to the public, without any specific legislative basis and without parliamentary control and judicial protection of individual rights,[56] has illustrated the lack of effective constitutional restraints on trade politics and the political asymmetries in "interest-determined" rather than "rule-oriented" decisionmaking processes about trade policy. This empirical evidence of "government failure" is in line with the predictions of "public choice theory" that periodically elected trade politicians and trade bureaucrats have strong self-interests in exchanging trade protection for political support by protectionist interest groups.[57] The necessary "legislative choice" among the various alternative trade policy instruments is greatly facilitated by the almost worldwide economic consensus on the economically optimal ranking of the various trade policy instruments[58] and by its legal recognition in the multilaterally agreed GATT obligations which rank the various economic and trade policy instruments in almost the same order as economic theory suggests[59] and legally commit member countries to observe these principles in their domestic trade legislation and administration. But in order to remain effective over time, the constitutional guarantees and necessary legislative choices for the use of transparent, nondiscriminatory and proportionate trade policy instruments (such as tariffs and production subsidies) must be supplemented by procedural guarantees of "due process" and judicial protection of the individual freedom of foreign trade so that "separation of powers" - in the classical sense of constitutional limitation and mutual "checks and balances" of every governmental power - can actually be brought about.

---

56 See above chapters V. 2 and 4.

57 See above chapter V. 3.

58 See above chapter IV. 3.

59 See above chapter VII. 2.

B) Impediments to Constitutionalizing Trade Policy Unilaterally at the National Level

Why is it that hardly any national constitution explicitly protects the freedoms and property rights of its citizens across national frontiers (e.g. freedom of foreign trade)? Why do most national constitutions regulate only a few institutional and procedural aspects of the governmental foreign affairs powers (e.g. the procedures for the conclusion of international treaties, for the declaration of wars and for other diplomatic acts) without explicitly subjecting their discretionary exercise to the constitutional guarantees of fundamental rights and judicial review?

The discussion of the need to constitutionalize the discretionary trade policy powers of governments inevitably leads to the question of how the proposed constitutional, legislative and judicial reforms could actually be implemented. This question can obviously not be answered without due regard to the existing rules and institutions within which "public choices" are made. These existing rules, procedures and self-interests of the "public choosers" reveal a number of considerable impediments to constitutionalizing trade policy unilaterally at the national level.

a) The Political Insistence on "External Sovereignty" and on Foreign Policy Discretion

Most national constitutions focus on the constitutional task of "nation-building" and "internal integration". The federal constitutions of the United States, Switzerland and Germany, analyzed in chapter VIII, were each proceded by confederal arrangements among the respective component states. And in the history of each of these federal states, just as in the history of many other federal states, the external political environment provided a major incentive for the gradual progress of national unification. The widespread support during the 18th and 19th centuries of the "incompatibility hypothesis" described above in chapter VIII. 1, namely the belief in the incompatibility of democracy and rule of law with the requirements of foreign policy, was enhanced by the classical "international law of coexistence"[60] since the Peace Treaties of Westphalia (1648) up to World War II, which recognized war as a lawful means of settling certain

60 On the distinction between the "international law of coexistence" and the "international law of cooperation" see: W. Friedmann, The Changing Structure of International Law, 1964, pp. 60 ff.

international disputes and limited itself largely to regulating the modalities of coexistence between legally equal sovereign states by imposing on them essentially passive obligations of non-interference into,and respect for, the jurisdiction of other states.

Many 18th and 19th century constitutions are accordingly characterized by an "introverted" and vis-à-vis third countries "defensive constitutional attitude" and insistence on "external sovereignty". Thus it was mentioned in chapter VIII that the preambles of both the US Constitution and the Swiss Constitution refer to the intent of providing "for the common defense" (US Constitution) and of "strengthening the alliance of the Confederates and of maintaining and furthering the unity, strength and honour of the Swiss nation" (Swiss Constitution). The Swiss Constitution emphasizes in its Article 2 that "The aim of the Confederation is to preserve the outward independence of the fatherland" (etc.); according to Article 8 "The Confederation alone has the right to declare war and to make peace, as well as to conclude alliances and treaties, especially customs and commercial treaties, with foreign states".

Since World War II, "nearly 40 percent of the world's population now lives within polities that are formally federal, while another third live in polities that utilize federal arrangements in some way".[61] One characteristic feature of federal constitutions, as shown in chapter VIII, is the transfer of most foreign affairs powers to the federal level which is considered to be "best" suited for exercising them most effectively. Whereas, with regard to internal matters, federalism is widely seen as a constitutional safeguard of "vertical" separation of powers and as a decentralized form of government offering addititonal means of democratic control, the constitutional regulation of the federal foreign affairs powers tends to reflect the search for unity ("speaking with one voice") and for combined strength vis-à-vis third countries.[62] This is true not only in areas such as defense and security. The united external posture is reflected likewise in the generally broad interpretation of the international treaty-making powers of the federations as well as of their treaty-implementing powers which, in most federations (with the exception notably of Canada and to some extent Germany), even exceed the internal distribution of legislative competences among the federation

61 D.J. Elazar (ed.), Federalism and Political Integration, 1979, Introcuction at p. 3.

62 K.C. Wheare, Federal Government, 1963, concludes that "it is usually assumed that the foreign relations of a federation will be controlled predominantly, if not exclusively, by the general government of the whole territory" (p. 169).

and the constituent states.[63] Also this unitary element of the federal foreign relation powers is influenced by the international environment and international law which treats states generally as unitary actors and only rarely takes account of the internal structure of federations by means of "federal clauses".[64]

The comparative analysis in chapter VIII has revealed still another feature of the constitutional regulation of national foreign relations powers, namely the broad foreign policy discretion reserved to the legislative and executive branches of government and respected by domestic courts. The US Constitution includes a few provisions protecting the states against abuses of discretionary trade policy powers, notably in Article I, section 9 according to which "No tax or duty shall be laid on articles exported from any state" (para. 5), and "No preference shall be given by any regulation of commerce or revenue to the ports of one State over those of another" (para. 6). But the US Constitution does not explicitly protect the individual freedom of foreign trade of the citizens, and the US Congress and the courts seem to consider access to foreign markets as a privilege rather than as an individual right.[65] Since the abandonment by the Supreme Court in the 1930s of the judicial review of "substantive economic due process", the law-making powers of Congress in economic and trade policy matters appear to elude effective substantive constitutional constraints.[66]

The Swiss Constitution of 1874, concluded at the time of the European free trade system, is unique in respect of its explicit constitutional safeguards of liberal trade both within the Federation and with third states.[67] But the constitutional guarantee of low import and export duties (Article 29), which in the 19th century was equivalent to a constitutional guarantee of liberal access to foreign markets because non-tariff trade barriers hardly existed, has largely lost its constitutional significance due to subsequent constitutional amendments which grant broad discretionary powers to the federal government for the introduction

63 See Cappelletti /Seccombe /Weiler, General Introduction to : Cappelletti /Seccombe /Weiler (above note 35), p. 52.

64 See Kos-Rabcewicz-Zubkowski, Federal Clause, in: R. Bernhardt (above note 26), pp. 162 ff.

65 See above chapter VIII. 2. C.

66 See above chapter VIII. 2. B, E and F, and T. Sandalow, The Expansion of Federal Legislative Authority, in: T. Sandalow/E. Stein (eds.), Courts and Free Markets, 1982, pp. 50 ff.

67 See above chapter VIII. 3. B.

or maintenance of non-tariff trade barriers without judicial control of federal legislation.[68]

The 1949 Basic Law of the Federal Republic of Germany was described in chapter VIII as a new type of liberal 20th century constitution based upon a comprehensive fundamental rights catalogue that protects also transnational exercises of individual rights,[69] a rather developed "constitutionalization" of the foreign relations power supplemented by a liberal foreign trade legislation and judicial protection of individual freedom of foreign trade,[70] and an explicit constitutional decision in favour of international integration.[71] Its "constitutional approach" to economic regulation is perhaps best reflected in its explicit constitutional restraints on the public taxing, borrowing and spending powers, which add up to a "tax constitution" protecting not only the parliamentary prerogative to tax but also the constitutional requirements of the completeness and balanced nature of the budget (Article 110), for instance by constitutional requirements of parliamentary authorization of public loans (Article 115) whose repayment could necessitate subsequent tax increases and whose admissible amount is constitutionally limited to the sum of public investment expenditures generating future income.[72] The constitutional guarantees of freedom of foreign trade (Articles 2, 12, 14) have become supplanted and considerably enlarged by the directly applicable EEC Treaty guarantees of the free movement of goods, services, persons and payments among the 12 EEC member states[73] as well as by the free trade agreements of the EEC with the EFTA states which are recognized to form an "integral part of the European Community legal system".[74] Yet, the EEC Treaty's regulation of the common commercial policy powers of the EEC (Articles 110-116) remains regrettably vague and transfers broad dis-

68 See above chapter VIII. 3. B. c and D.

69 See above chapter VIII. 4. A.

70 See chapter VIII. 4. B.

71 See chapter VIII. 4. C.

72 See: P. Kirchhof, The Public Debt, Democratic Principles and the Rule of Law, in: D.Ch.Dicke (ed.), Foreign Debts in the Present and in a New International Economic Order, 1986, pp. 339, 342 ff.

73 See notably: I. Pernice, Grundrechtsgehalte im Europäischen Gemeinschaftsrecht, 1979, pp. 68 ff.

74 See: H.G. Koppensteiner (ed.), Rechtsfragen der Freihandelsabkommen der EWG mit den EFTA-Staaten, 1987, notably the contribution by A. Bleckmann, Die unmittelbare Anwendbarkeit der Freihandelsabkommen mit den EFTA-Staaten im Rechtsraum der EWG, at pp. 85 ff.

cretionary trade policy powers to the EC executives without parliamentary review and without effective judicial control of "grey area trade restrictions" in violation of GATT law.[75]

b) The Persistence of Mercantilist Doctrine

The above-mentioned trend in national constitutional laws as well as in European Community law towards a united foreign posture and broad discretionary trade policy powers is influenced also by the widespread persistence of mercantilist thinking. The mercantilist view that nations gain from export promotion and from import restrictions because they enhance a "favourable" balance of payments and enlarge domestic production and employment, entails a nationalistic, "power-oriented" view of international economic relations as a struggle among rival countries for export markets and balance of trade surpluses.[76] Because mercantilists tend to view the economy as a static "zero sum game", in which "what is given to someone, has to be taken away from somebody else" (J.B. Colbert, French finance minister under Louis XIV and founder of "Colbertism"), they tend to emphasize the need for discretionary government powers and for government interventions in foreign economic policy, and are inclined to subject the observance of international treaty obligations ("concessions") to strict insistence on reciprocity (see Article 55 of the current French Constitution of 1958).

Even though no serious economist today still accepts the mercantilist ideas of economic gain and loss, the mercantilist views of selling (earning) as economically beneficial and buying (spending) as costly are intuitively appealing and continue to influence foreign trade policy and foreign trade law.[77] Moreover, both mercantilists and liberals agree on the increasing importance of trade policy powers because, in an integrated world economy where 20-30 percent of a country's income derive from its foreign trade, "a government's own trade policy decisions are the most important determinant of its economic welfare".[78] Even GATT law uses the mercantilist notion of "trade concessions" (Articles II. XXVIII), places strong emphasis on "reciprocity" of trade liberalization at home

75 See above chapter VI. 2. B.

76 On the mercantilist doctrines see above chapter V. 4.

77 See the examples given and critically discussed by R.E. Hudec, Developing Countries in the GATT Legal System, 1987, pp. 138 ff.

78 Hudec (note 77), p. 159.

and abroad (Article XXVIII bis), and has endorsed the legal claims by developing countries that non-reciprocal trade liberalization (Article XXXVI: 8) and national freedom to restrict and distort foreign trade (e.g. Article XVIII) are instruments of preferential treatment of developing countries.[79] By contrast, the liberal economic proposition that trade distortions cause economic loss to all countries affected by them because they induce a less productive use of domestic resources than would be possible under liberal trade, is intellectually more difficult to understand. In the words of Paul Samuelson, the Ricardian theory of comparative advantage, i.e. the demonstration that trade is mutually profitable even when a country can produce every commodity at lower costs than its trading partners, is perhaps the "one proposition in all of the social sciences which is both true and non-trivial".[80]

c) The Asymmetries in Domestic Decisionmaking Processes about Trade Policy

Chapter V. 3 on "Why Trade is not free and why trade liberalization meets resistance" listed the major political explanations of trade protectionism, especially: the protectionist self-interests of import-competing producers; the various reasons why producer interests are politically easier to organize than consumer interests; the relatively stronger political influence of import-competing producers than of domestic consumers on domestic decision-making processes about trade policy; the "public choice" explanation of why trade politicians and trade bureaucracies depend on domestic political support and pursue their own interests (e.g. in terms of votes, reelection, power and career prospects) by "supplying" trade protection in exchange for political support in the "political market for protectionism"; and the "conservative social welfare function" which reflects a broad political consensus for preventing sudden, drastic income losses and unemployment in import-competing industries. Chapter VI. 3 further extended this economic-political analysis by empirical and legal descriptions of the insufficient procedural guarantees in US domestic laws as well as in European Community

---

79 For a critical discussion of these views see Hudec (note 77), pp. 127 ff, and E.U. Petersmann, International Trade Order and International Trade Law. Economic and Legal Issues of Integrating Developing Coutries into the Multilateral Trading System, in: Th.Oppermann/E.U. Petersmann (eds.), Reforming the International Economic Order, 1987, pp. 201, 217 ff.

80 Quoted from G.M. Meier, International Economics, 1980, at p. 28, who presents a readily understandable exposition of the theory of comparative advantage at pp. 17 ff.

law for the public choice of transparent, non-discriminatory and proportionate trade policy instruments.

Are constitutional reforms and restraints of discretionary trade policy powers possible at all since the existing asymmetries in domestic decisionmaking processes about trade policy are likely to obstruct also such constitutional reforms? Can Adam Smith's attack on mercantilism in "The Wealth of Nations" and the subsequent, gradual transition in England from mercantilism to liberal trade, with the hallmark of the House of Common's repeal of the protectionist corn laws in 1846, be taken as historical proof of the "power of ideas" over special interests? The brief historical account of past and present trade mercantilism in chapter V. 4 referred already to various historical studies arguing that England's shift to a liberal trade policy might have been less influenced by A. Smith's liberal trade theory than by the then powerful political coalition of liberal trade interests in the National Anti-Corn Law League of 1838 to 1846.[81] The comparative legal study in chapter VIII of the federal constitutional laws of the United States, Switzerland and Germany indicates an important "constitutional experience" in this respect: Effective trade liberalization among the states of the American Confederation of 1777/81, among the Cantons of the Swiss Confederation of 1848, among the states belonging to the German Confederation of 1815 to 1866 (Deutscher Bund), and also among the member States of the EEC was achieved only following the adoption of the federal constitutions in the United States in 1787/89, in Switzerland in 1874, the 1867 Constitution of the North German Confederation (Norddeutscher Bund) followed by the 1871 Federal Constitution in Germany, and the "pre-federal constitution" of the EEC Treaty of 1957. Each time, with the exceptions of the 1867 and 1871 German constitutions which consolidated the trade liberalisation already achieved in the previous German Customs Union (Deutscher Zollverein), a major motive for the adoption of these federal constitutions was to overcome the trade protectionism among the constituent states through mutually agreed prohibitions of trade barriers within the confederation[82] or their progressive elimination among the EEC member states.

81 See above chapter V. 4 (at footnote 53) and C.K. Rowley/R. D. Tollison, Rent-Seeking and Trade Protection, in: Aussenwirtschaft 1986, pp. 303, 321 ff.

82 See above chapter VIII. 2. A and VIII. 3. B.

d) The "Public Good"-Character of a Liberal International Trader Order

A liberal international trade order is a "public good" in the sense that it cannot be produced as a "private good" in private markets and it benefits all trading countries even including those "free-riding" countries which do not contribute to the "production" of a liberal international trade order by dismantling their own national trade barriers.[83] It was shown in chapter VII. 1. D above that, for a number of economic and political reasons, "international public goods" can be provided without "international governments" most effectively through international agreements among the major (trading) countries. For a number of reasons, the biased national political and legal structures favoring protectionist "rent-seeking" and government interventions into transnational trade transactions are more likely to be overcome through agreement on liberal rules at the international rather than at the national level.

3. Constitutional Functions of Liberal International Economic Rules

A) Liberal International Agreements Can Serve Constitutional Functions: In Constitutional Democracies Liberal International Trade Rules Must Be Constitutionally Presumed to Protect Individual Rights

Part III described the constitutional functions of liberal international trade and monetary rules not only on the international level among states but also for the interpretation and "constitutionalization" of the domestic foreign trade laws in constitutionally limited democracies. As shown in chapter VIII, a major purpose of the framers of the US Constitution as well as of the Swiss and German Constitutions of the 19th century was to bar the states from establishing barriers to domestic trade and from unduly interfering with economic liberties and property rights. The framers of the US Constitution "did believe that individual liberties, private property and private enterprise were safer under federal auspices".[84] The texts of the US and the Swiss Constitution make it explicitly clear that the constitutions were established by "the people" and "granted" limited powers of government designed "to protect the freedom and the rights of the

83 See above chapter VII. 1. D.

84 B.H. Siegan, The Economic Constitution in Historial Perspective, in: R. McKenzie (above note 12), pp. 39 ff, 50.

confederates and to promote their common prosperity" (Article 2 of the Swiss Constitution). During the constitutional convention of 1787, James Madison and other "founding fathers" repeatedly warned against unlimited democracy and unlimited majority rule which could lead to a majoritarian tyranny unless the powers of government were constitutionally limited.[85] Because J. Madison saw the state's only legitimate function in securing the fundamental individual rights "retained by the people" (Ninth Amendment), he declared himself to be "in favor of a bill of rights, provided it be so framed as not to imply powers not meant to be included in the enumeration".[86] These democratic, constitutional functions of the Bill of Rights of 1789 were well described in the Supreme Court's opinion in West Virginia State Board of Education v. Barnette in the following terms:

> "The very purpose of a Bill of Rights was to withdraw certain subjects from the vicissitudes of political controversy, to place them beyond the reach of majorities and officials and to establish them as legal principles to be applied by the Courts. One's right to life, liberty, and property, to free speech, a free press, freedom of worship and assembly, and other fundamental rights may not be submitted to vote; they depend on the outcome of no elections."[87]

The comparative analysis of American, Swiss and German constitutional law in chapter VIII showed the historial impact of US constitutional law on the framers of the Swiss Constitution of 1874 and the German Grundgesetz of 1949. Also Swiss and German constitutional law recognize unwritten, inalienable human rights guarantees and the "protective function" of their respective constitution to limit the government and to protect individual rights.[88] The explicit recognition in the Swiss Constitution and in the German Basic Law of economic liberties reflected the Madisonian belief that also economic policies could be improved best by improving the basic rules within which private and public economic agents act, rather than by relying on the good intentions of government agents using their powers under the pressures of majoritarian and interest-group politics. The recognition of the applicability of the fundamental rights guarantees to the exercise of the governmental trade policy powers[89] is based on the

---

85 For a historical account see: J.A. Dorn, Public Choice and the Constitution: A Madisonian Perspective, in: Gwartney/Wagner (above note 12), pp. 57-97.

86 Letter by J. Madison to Th.Jefferson dated 17 October 1788, quoted from Dorn (note 85), at p. 73.

87 319 US 624, 638 (1943).

88 See above chapter VIII. 3. B and 4. A.

89 See above chapter VIII. 2. C, 3 C, c, and 4, B, a.

same liberal insight that government powers are limited in nature and most "trade policy problems" can be solved best by protecting the equal freedoms and property rights of domestic citizens.

The characteristic difference between a "federal order" and an "international" or "confederal" order is usually seen in the fact that "the federal order is confronted with two potential classes of subjects: the states and the people(s)".[90] According to this view, the central federal government partially replaces the state governments in a direct governmental relationship with the people and the states are no longer considered as sovereign subjects within the area of federal competence; by contrast, an international organization or the confederal government in a confederation must reach individual citizens only through the constituent polities.[91] Such a perception appears inconsistent not only with the increasing number of international agreements and organizations - such as the European Communities, EFTA, the European Court and Commission of Human Rights or the World Bank's International Center for the Settlement of Investment Disputes - which protect individual rights by means of directly applicable international rules and procedures.[92] The "mediatization" of the individual and of his human rights appears even more doubtful from the perspective of liberal constitutional democracies with limited government powers designed to secure individual rights.

If humans are born free and the acknowledged task of democratic constitutions and of constitutionally limited governments is to protect the free exercise of individual rights under the rule of law, then voluntarily accepted international obligations to protect individual freedom of trade in transnational trade transactions must be constitutionally presumed to protect the individual rights of domestic citizens. This constitutional law presumption is valid independently of the various other economic and legal arguments to the same effect, for instance that trade liberalization benefits the liberalizing country itself and that "the fact that the courts of one of the parties consider that certain stipulations in the agreement are of direct application whereas the courts of the other party do not recognize such direct application is not in itself such as to constitute a lack of

90 Cappelletti/Seccombe/Weiler (note 63), at p. 26.

91 See Cappelletti/Seccombe/Weiler (note 63), pp. 27, 123.

92 See J.A. Frowein/S. Schulhofer/M. Shapiro, The Protection of Human Rights as a Vehicle of Integration, in: Cappelletti/Seccombe/Weiler (eds.), Integration through Law, Vol. 1, Book 3, 1986, pp. 231 ff.

reciprocity in the implementation of the agreement".[93] The constitutional principle of limited delegation of powers applies also to the foreign economic relations powers of constitutionally limited governments, even if this constitutional limitation is explicitly recognized in the foreign trade and economic legislation of only a few countries, such as in the 1961 German Law on Foreign Economic Relations.[94]

B) Why It Can Be Easier to Agree on and Specify Liberal Principles for Foreign Trade in Reciprocal International Agreements Rather than in National Laws

A federal order contributes to the protection of individual rights by distributing governmental powers both "vertically" between the federal and state levels as well as "horizontally" amongst the legislative, executive and judicial branches of the federal and state governments. The vertical division of competences and decentralization of government powers enhances also the local participation of citizens in, and their democratic control over, the exercise of government powers.

The painful European experiences with the concentration and "absolutization" of government powers prompted various proposals during and after World War II for extending the federal principle to international order so as to create a "stratified international legal order", whose different "legal layers" and "vertical" divisions of government powers could act as a multiple limitation and separation of government powers. In his influential book "The Road to Serfdom" of 1944, Hayek concluded, for instance, that:

> "the principle of federation is the only form of association of different peoples which will create an international order without putting an undue strain on their legitimate desire for independence. Federalism is ... nothing but the application to international affairs of democracy, the only method of peaceful change man has yet invented. But it is a democracy with definitely limited powers."[95]

These and other proposals for an extension of "the federal principle of organization" to the international level perceived federalism as a means of promoting

93 Case 104/81 (Kupferberg), Judgment by the European Court of Justice of 26 October 1982, E.C.R. 1982, pp. 3641 ff (para. 18).

94 See above chapter VIII. 4. B.

95 F.A. v.Hayek, The Road to Serfdom, 1944, pp. 172 ff. In a similar sense see: L. Robbins, Economic Planning and International Order, 1937, pp. 240 ff.

"power-sharing" and decentralized, participatory forms of constitutionally limited government. They did not propose establishing new centralized supranational governments at the international level. The "federal principle" was rather seen as a means of guarding against abuses of power by strengthening the overall national and international legal system through the "anchoring" of basic constitutional principles in public international law. These international agreements would have to respect the autonomy and "sovereign equality" (Article 2 UN Charter) of states and would, therefore, have to be confined essentially to internationally agreed prohibitions, freedoms and corresponding obligations of both states and individuals.

Why is it that, after World War II, many states have agreed at the international level to international obligations on the liberalization of foreign trade and the protection of individual freedoms which their respective national constitutions did not explicitly guarantee? Why is it rational for a sovereign state to consent to international "rules of the game" which guarantee the access of its citizens to foreign markets and protect their rights in foreign jurisdictions? Why do governments find it easier to accept international "constitutional" rules behind a "veil of uncertainty",[96] for instance after a cataclysm such as World War II, where their future positions are difficult to predict? It is submitted that governments voluntarily accept liberal international trade obligations not only because there are reciprocal political gains from such "legal exchanges", just as there are economic gains from free trade. But there are also various domestic political considerations, indicated above in chapter IX. 2, which may make it easier even for a constitutionally limited democratic government to commit itself to liberal principles for foreign trade in reciprocal international agreements at the international level rather than unilaterally at its national level in its own national foreign trade laws:

a) The confidentiality, remoteness and international political significance of multilateral trade negotiations, such as those of GATT, can assist governments in escaping, or in overcoming, the protectionist pressures from domestic groups interested in broad government discretion for redistributive trade restrictions, and in colluding as a sort of "intergovernmental cartel" for trade liberalization.

96 On the importance of the aspect of uncertainty in "constitutional choices" see J. Buchanan/G. Tullock, The Calculus of Consent: Logical Foundations of Constitutional Democracy, 1962, pp. 81 ff.

b) Given the widespread political preference for foreign policy discretion and the mercantilist misperception of trade policy, legal restraints on discretionary trade policymaking may appear politically easier to accept on a multilateral and reciprocal basis than as a unilateral "concession".

c) Reciprocal international legal guarantees of access to foreign markets mobilize political support from free trade interests in the domestic political debate, notably from domestic export industries whose access to foreign markets cannot be secured unilaterally by the exporting country alone. The reciprocity principle underlying international trade negotiations (see Article XXVIII bis of GATT) ensures that the protectionist self-interests of import-competing industries will be confronted with the liberal trade interests of importers and export industries, both at home in national decisionmaking as well as in the reciprocity negotiations at the international level.[97]

d) Even though each country benefits economically first and most from reducing its own trade barriers, joint multilateral trade liberalization reduces the mutual adjustment costs and the risks of trade diversion.

e) International legal obligations hold a higher legal rank than ordinary domestic legislation or administrative regulations in many domestic legal systems (e.g. in European Community law and Japanese law). International legal obligations for the public choice of transparent, non-discriminatory and least-distortive trade policy instruments can thereby increase the political weight of domestic trade politicians and the political influence of liberal trade interests in domestic decisionmaking processes.

f) Long-term international legal obligations protecting governments and their peoples from the continuous domestic protectionist pressures make thus economic and legal sense. As Hudec put it: "Liberal trade policy would not fare very well if every new generation of officials were permitted to rethink the case for free trade, especially if they had to do so in the process of resolving ad hoc problems one-by-one as they come

97 This argument is elaborated by F. Roessler, The Rationale for Reciprocity in Trade Negotiations under Floating Carrencies, in: Kyklos 1978, pp. 258 ff; H. Hauser, Foreign Trade Policy and the Function of Rules for Trade Policy Making, in: D. Dicke/E.U. Petersmann (eds.), Foreign Trade in the Present and in a New International Economic Order, 1988, p. 18 ff.

> across the desk".[98] And, as M.Corden pointed out: "it is possible to resist these (protectionist) pressures once when the rules are made, but not continously".[99]

Governments depend upon domestic political support and, in the trade policy area, have often become "prisoners of their domestic pressure groups"[100] due to the numerous "protectionist biases" in domestic decisionmaking processes about trade policy. Long-term liberal international trade obligations strengthen domestic political support for liberal trade policies, act as a deterrent on "rent-seeking" protectionist lobbying and change the incentive structures and political-legal constraints within which trade politicians and trade bureaucracies must act at home.[101]

C) The Overlooked Paradox: Liberal International Trade Rules Enlarge Individual Rights and the Principles of Constitutional Democracies

The historical experience of the inter-war period and the failure of the various economic world conferences, convened during the 1920s and 1930s, to reconstruct the liberal pre-war trading system[102] made it evident to many states that "laws and institutions", which Adam Smith had shown to be necessary for "economic order" to exist at the national level, were a prerequisite of economic order also at the international level. The 1944 Bretton Woods Conference, the 1946 London, the 1947 Geneva and 1948 Havana Conferences showed also a worldwide willingness to take on a "constitutional attitude" in the sense of an understanding of the difference between choosing long-term basic rules and acting within those rules.[103] At least the US delegation, then the driving force in these worldwide negotiations, explicitly requested that the international treaty prohibitions of tariffs and non-tariff trade barriers should be "precise", "clear",

98 Hudec (above note 77), p. 163.

99 W.M. Corden, On Making Rules for the International Trading System, in: R.M. Stern (ed.), US Trade Policies in a Changing World Economy, 1987, pp. 413, 418.

100 V. Curzon-Price, Industrial and Trade Policy in a Period of Rapid Structural Change, in: Aussenwirtschaft 1986, pp. 201 f.

101 See H. Hauser, Domestic Policy Foundation and Domestic Policy Function of International Trade Rules, in: Aussenwirtschaft 1986, pp. 171 ff.

102 For an account of these various conferences by one of the participants see: W.E. Rappard, Post-War Efforts for Freer Trade, 1938.

103 For a historical account of these conferences by the then head of the US delegation see: C. Wilcox, A Charter for World Trade, 1949.

"unambiguous" and "self-executing" so that they "could be applied by the governments concerned without further elaboration or international action".[104] This proposed "constitutional design" was strongly influenced by the United States' own domestic "constitutional experience" with its protectionist Smoot-Hawley Tariff Act of 1930 and the Reciprocal Trade Agreements Act of 1934, which had demonstrated that protectionist legislation introduced by temporary congressional coalitions could trigger a world-wide crisis and that, even if governments correctly perceived their national self-interest in liberal trade, a liberal international trade order would not develop spontaneously.[105]

Chapter VII.1 attempted to explain why the difficulties of voluntarily agreeing on a "constitution of liberty" at the international level among a large number of sovereign states are similar to the problems of "constitutional choice" at the national level. Just as self-interested individuals can transform the "Hobbesian war" into mutually beneficial cooperation by securing their equal rights through long-term constitutional rules, so states can protect their "sovereign equality" and transform "beggar-my-neighbour policies" into international cooperation through liberal international rules and prohibitions of mutually harmful policies. At least some of the founders of the post-war international economic order were fully aware of this need for an "international economic and legal constitution".[106] And they were also aware of the fact, analyzed in more detail above in chapter III. 3 and 4 and VII. 5, that "in logic and in practice, freedom of international trade depends upon the preservation of freedom in domestic life"[107] and "a good order on the national level is required to assure a working order also on the international level".[108]

Chapter VII.2 explained in detail that the liberal international trade rules of GATT law are an expression and mutually agreed concretization of the principles of transparent and rule-oriented policymaking, non-discrimination, proportionality, fair competition, "due process", judicial protection of individual rights,

104 UN Doc. EPCT/C.II/PV. 2 (1946) p. 8. The full text of the quotation is reproduced above in chapter VIII. 2. E.

105 See, e.g.: C. Wilcox (note 103), pp. 6 ff, 34 ff.

106 See, e.g., C. Wilcox' book on a "Charter for World Trade" (above note 103), who notes at p. 195: "Voluntary agreement for mutual advantage has always been the method by which order has been established in international affairs. There seems to be no reason why this method should not be applied to international trade". See further above chapter III. 3 and 4.

107 C. Wilcox (note 103), at p. 34.

108 W. Röpke, International Order and Economic Integration, 1959, p. 16.

and national freedom (sovereignty) to decide autonomously on the national level of tariff protection as well as on transparent, temporary safeguard measures against imports injuring domestic producers. These "constitutional functions" are no more obvious than in the customs union law of the EEC, whose prohibitions of tariffs and non-tariff barriers within the EEC are in part literally based on the corresponding GATT prohibitions and have been construed by the EC Court of Justice as directly applicable individual freedoms across national frontiers. Chapter VI. 2 showed that the principles of transparency, rule of law, non-discrimination, proportionality, due process, judicial protection of individual rights and national sovereignty are at the same time basic legal principles recognized in the constitutional law of the United States as well as in European Community law and in the constitutional traditions of the EEC member states.

The insight - that liberal international trade rules agreed among states with different national economic and legal systems can define and enlarge individual freedoms and other constitutional principles of liberal democracies - appears, at first sight, paradoxical from the national perspective of a liberal democracy. The brief analysis of the foreign trade laws and practices of the United States and the EEC (chapter VI. 2) showed that this insight is widely disregarded by domestic legislative, administrative and judicial bodies, which seem to act on the assumption that one's own domestic constitutional guarantees of equal freedoms, non-discrimination and proportionality are more precise than the allegedly vague GATT rules. It may therefore be useful to briefly illustrate that even the "general principles" of European Community law, derived by the EC Court of Justice from the common constitutional traditions of the EC member states, are less comprehensive in the foreign trade policy area than the pertinent GATT principles.

D) An Illustration: Comparing the "General Principles" of the Administrative Law of the EEC with the Foreign Trade Law of GATT

Unlike GATT law, the EEC Treaty provisions on the common commercial policy (Articles 110-116) do not explicitly require the use of transparent, non-discriminatory and proportionate trade policy instruments. Nor does the EEC Treaty contain any specific rules, such as those of GATT law, on non-tariff trade barriers vis-à-vis third countries. Even the EEC Treaty provisions on the progressive liberalization of tariffs and non-tariff trade barriers within the EEC leave open many legal issues (such as freedom of transit or the meaning of "measures having an equivalent effect to quantitative restrictions") which have been explicitly dealt with in great detail e.g. in GATT Articles III, V and XI: 1. The foreign trade law of the EEC has been elaborated in the "secondary" Community law, enacted by the EC Council and the EC Commission, and continues to be supplemented to a large extent by the national foreign trade laws of the 12 EEC member states. These national foreign trade laws, more than many other areas of national administrative laws, are strongly influenced by national legal and political traditions and differ in many respects.

The foreign trade regulations by the EC Council, to the extent they lay down general rather than sectoral rules for the regulation of foreign trade, have regularly been adopted with explicit reference to and in implementation of the pertinent GATT obligations of the EEC. This is true, e.g., for the following Council regulations:

- Council Regulation (EEC) No. 950/68 of 28 June 1968 on the Common Customs Tariff,[109] and numerous subsequent Council regulations amending the Common Customs Tariff, serve, inter alia, the explicit objective of implementing GATT tariff bindings under Article II GATT. Likewise, Council Regulation (EEC) No. 1224/80 of 28 May 1980 on the valuation of goods for customs purposes[110] is expressly designed to bring the EEC's customs valuation system into conformity with the 1979 GATT Agreement on Implementation of Article VII.
- Council Regulation (EEC) No. 288/82 of 5 February 1982 on common rules for imports[111] proceeds from the directly applicable principle that "importation into the Community ... shall be free and therefore not subject to any quantitative restrictions", without prejudice to certain precisely specified exceptions (Article 1, para. 2). It sets out provisions for the adoption of protective measures pursuant to GATT Articles XIX to XXI "with due regard for existing international obligations" (preamble, Article 16) and also transposes "the provisions of the Agreement on import licensing procedures signed within the framework of GATT ... into Community law" (preamble).

109 O.J.L 172 (Spec. Ed. 1968 I p. 275). The Common Customs Tariff is published annually in a consolidated form in the Official Journal of the EC to incorporate changes which have been made in the interim.

110 O.J. 1980, L 134/1 (31. 5. 80).

111 O.J. 1982, L 35/1 (9. 2. 82).

- Council Regulation (EEC) No. 2603/69 establishing common rules for exports[112] starts from the likewise directly applicable "Community principle that exports to third countries are not subject to any quantitative restriction, subject to the exceptions provided for in this Regulation" (preamble). Its exceptions for export restrictions take account of the relevant GATT provisions (Articles XI: 2, XX) and emphasize that "any protective measures necessitated by the interests of the Community should be adopted with due regard for existing international obligations" (preamble).

- Council Regulation (EEC) No. 2176/84 of 23 July 1984 on protection against dumped or subsidized imports from countries not members of the EEC[113] states expressly that "these rules were adopted in accordance with existing international obligations, in particular those arising from Article VI of the GATT, from the Agreement on Implementation of Article VI of the GATT (1979 Anti-Dumping Code) and from the Agreement on Interpretation and Application of Articles VI, XVI and XXIII of the GATT (Code on Subsidies and Countervailing Duties)" (preamble). The Regulation permits "the adoption of special measures (only) where this does not run counter to the Community's obligations under the GATT" (preamble).

- Council Regulation (EEC) No. 2641/84 of 17 September 1984 on the strengthening of the common commercial policy with regard in particular to protection against illicit commercial practices[114] prescribes that "the Community must act in compliance with its international obligations" (preamble) and may take only "commercial policy measures ... which are compatible with existing international obligations and procedures" (Article 10, para. 3).

In addition to these general "framework regulations", however, the EC Council and the EC Commission have adopted a very large number of sectoral, country-specific or product-specific foreign trade regulations (e.g. every year more than 3000 regulations for agricultural and steel products) which sometimes openly depart from the general GATT principles incorporated into these "framework

112 O.J. 1969, L 324/25 (27. 12. 69).

113 O.J. 1984, L 201/1 (30. 7. 84). The revised new text of the Regulation of 11th July 1988 is published in: O.J. 1988, L 209/1 (2.8.1988).

114 O.J. 1984, L 252/1 (20. 9. 84).

regulations" e.g. by introducing quantitative restrictions discriminating against a single GATT member country in violation of GATT Articles XI, XIII[115] or discriminatory quantitative export restrictions in violation of GATT Articles XI, XIII.[116] In the altogether more than 800 cases brought to the European Court of Justice against various agricultural and steel regulations, the EC Court of Justice has acknowledged a large degree of discretion of the EC institutions in deciding on objectives and means of interventionist policies. The Court also refrained from examining the "GATT consistency" of these regulations and their consistency with the above-mentioned "framework regulations" for trade policy. The Court rather attempted to limit and control the exercise of the EC's trade policy discretion by referring to the general principles of the administrative law of the EC, which the Court derives either directly from European Community law itself (e.g. the principle of non-discrimination), or indirectly from the "general principles common to the laws of the member states" as a source of Community law, or from the general principles in international agreements concluded by the EEC and its member states.

A comparison of these general principles of the administrative law of the EC, as construed by the EC Court of Justice, with the general principles of the foreign trade rules of GATT law shows that the pertinent GATT principles and rules are comparatively more precise, more liberal and more comprehensive with regard to certain trade policy problems:

a) Transparent Policymaking and Rule of Law

GATT law commits contracting parties to use transparent and predictable trade policy instruments (i.e. tariffs) and to publish promptly all their trade regulations prior to their enforcement "in such a manner as to enable governments and traders to become acquainted with them" (Article X: 1). Moreover, temporary safeguard measures must be taken, if at all, subject to transparent proce-

115 See, e.g., Case 112/80 - Dürbeck I, - E.C.R. 1980, p. 1095 (import restrictions on Chilean apples in contravention of Article XIII GATT); Case 245/81 - Edeka AG v. Federal Republic of Germany - E.C.R. 1982, p. 2745 (import restrictions on preserved mushrooms from South Korea in contravention of Article XIII GATT). The inconsistency between the import restrictions on Chilean apples with Article XIII GATT was formally established by the GATT Council (BISD 27 S/98). In both above-mentioned judgments, the Court did not take account of the infringement of Article XIII GATT.

116 See the numerous "voluntary restraint agreements" (VRAs) concluded by the EEC, e.g.: Council Regulations (EEC) Nos. 3708 - 3713/85 of 10 December 1985 on the restriction of the export of certain steel products to the United States, in: O.J. 1985, L 355 (31. 12. 1985).

dures on the import side (Articles VI, XIX) so that they can be exposed to parliamentary and judicial review in the importing country. The basic requirement of GATT law to conduct trade policy in a transparent and rule-oriented manner on the basis of a few, rather simple general principles is but a reflection of the national constitutional principles of limited government, legal certainty and rule of law.

The foreign trade law of the EEC does not explicitly confine the trade policy power of the EEC to the use of transparent and lawful trade policy instruments. But the EC Court of Justice's recognition of GATT law as a "integral part of the Community legal system" with primacy over secondary Community law[117] implies an obligation under Community law to act in conformity with the self-imposed international GATT obligations.

In the case-law of the EC Court of Justice, the principle of legal certainty has played an important role and has been applied as a general principle of Community law in various different contexts.[118] In the trade policy area, the Court has invoked it, inter alia, as a legal limitation on the Community powers to enact or amend rules or withdraw individual rights with retroactive effect,[119] to impose financial charges or apply tariff classification criteria which are not "clear and precise",[120] to disregard certain time limits,[121] or to unduly interfere into acquired rights and legitimate expectations of individuals.[122] But the Court has also decided in many cases "that the principle of respect for legal certainty, important as it may be, cannot be applied in an absolute manner",[123] notably if the uncertainties in international markets and the possibility of trade policy in-

---

117 On the status of international agreements concluded by the EEC, including GATT law, as an "integral part of the Community legal system" see: E.U. Petersmann, International and European Foreign Trade Law, in: Common Market Law Review 1985, pp. 441, 452 ff.

118 For general surveys of the case-law see notably: H.G. Schermers, Judicial Protection in the European Communities, 3rd ed. 1983, pp. 45 ff; P. Pescatore, Les Principes Généraux du Droit en tant que Source du Droit Communautaire, in: FIDE, The General Principles Common to the Laws of the Member States as a Source of Community Law, 1986, pp. 17, 26 ff.

119 See the comprehensive and nuanced case-law cited by H.G. Schermers (note 118), pp. 51 ff, and P. Pescatore (note 118), pp. 27 ff.

120 See P. Pescatore (note 118), pp. 28, 32.

121 See H.G. Schermers (note 118), pp. 47 ff.

122 See H.G. Schermers (note 118), pp. 50 - 59.

123 Cases 42 and 49/59 (Second Snupat Case), ECR 1961, p. 87.

terventions were predictable.[124] The legal uncertainties created by this case-law have largely reduced the role of the principle of legal certainty in the trade policy area to, in the words of Judge Pescatore, a role of a "bonne à tout faire".[125]

The "constitutional problem" derives from the fact that international markets are inherently unstable and that the very function of general international trade rules is to create legal certainty and to reduce uncertainties and resultant transaction costs. The Court has explicitly recognized this function of the foreign trade law of the EEC by deciding:

> "The Council, having adopted a general regulation with a view to implementing one of the objectives laid down in Article 113 of the Treaty, cannot derogate from the rules laid down in applying those rules to specific cases without interfering with the legislative system of the Community and destroying the equality before the law of those to whom the law applies".[126]

Yet, the Court, having recognized GATT law as an "integral part of the Community legal system"[127] and notwithstanding the explicit incorporation of the basic GATT obligations into most of the generally applicable foreign trade regulations of the EC, has acknowledged an almost unlimited discretion of the EC institutions to introduce and amend price and quantitative regulations for individual products (notably agricultural and steel products), to restrict imports and exports in a discriminatory manner inconsistent with GATT law, and to utilize more than any other GATT contracting party unpublished "grey area trade restrictions" which are often administered abroad in the exporting country without any judicial protection of the adversely affected EC citizens.[128] In the Edeka case, for instance, the German importer was told by the Court that the almost total prohibition of mushroom imports, imposed by the EC Commission against the GATT member country Korea in manifest violation of Article XIII, was not contrary to the protection of legitimate expectation because the EC institutions enjoyed discretionary trade policy powers to restrict traditional trading relations

124 See the cases discussed by P. Pescatore (note 118), p. 31, 38 f.

125 P. Pescatore (note 118), p. 33.

126 Case 113/77 - NTN Toyo Company - ECR 1979, 1185, para. 21.

127 See: E.U. Petersmann (above note 117).

128 See the list of some 135 unpublished VERs in the GATT Publication "Review of Developments in the Trading System", 1987, pp. 99 ff., more than the half of which protect the EEC market. On the inconsistency of these agreements with GATT Articles XI and XIII see: E.U. Petersmann, Grey Area Trade Policy and the Rule of Law, in: Journal of World Trade Law 1988, pp. 23 - 44.

in violation of GATT law.[129] And, according to Pescatore,[130] there has so far never been any case before the Court where private plaintiffs could sucessfully invoke their "legitimate expectations" vis-à-vis discretionary trade interventions by the EC institutions. According to the "GATT case law" of the Court, the rule of law in international trade, as protected by GATT law, may not be relied upon by EC citizens.[131]

b) Non-Discriminatory Treatment

Governmental trade discrimination among supplier countries or among export markets often entails discrimination also among domestic traders which have entered into trade relations with these countries. Thus, in the above-mentioned Edeka case, the German importer complained that he had been placed at a disadvantage in relation to other competing importers because the discriminatory import restrictions had cut off his traditional supplies of mushrooms from Korea and, due to the EC Commission's transfer of Korea's traditional market shares to Chinese suppliers of mushrooms, had artificially improved the competitive position of his competitors which traditionally imported mushrooms from China.

The Court of Justice has recognized in the Edeka judgment that:

> "The prohibition of discrimination contained in the second subparagraph of Article 40 (3) of the treaty is merely a specific enunciation of the general principle of equality which is one of the fundamental principles of Community law. That principle means that like situations should not be treated differently unless such different treatment is objectively justified".[132]

The Court has also recognized that the prohibition of discrimination operates as a fundamental protection against distorting interventions into competition and that Community measures provoking disturbances in the competitive capacity of undertakings must be considered discriminatory.[133] Also Article 112 of the EEC

129 Case 245/81 - Edeka - ECR 1982, pp. 2745 ff, at p. 2758.

130 P. Pescatore (note 118), at p. 38.

131 For a critical survey of this "GATT case-law" see: E.U. Petersmann, Application of GATT by the Court of Justice of the European Communities, in: Common Market Law Review 1983, pp. 397 - 437.

132 Case 245/81 - Edeka - ECR 1982, p. 2745.

133 For a survey of this case-law see: M. Herdegen, The Relation between the Principles of Equality and Proportionality, in: Common Market Law Review 1985, pp. 683, 685 f.

Treaty recognizes as a basic objective of the foreign trade law of the EEC "to ensure that competition between undertakings of the Community is not distorted".

Yet, whenever traders within the EEC instituted legal proceedings against discriminatory import restrictions imposed by the EC Commission in manifest violation of the EEC's GATT obligations for the non-discriminatory administration of trade restrictions, the Court of Justice of the European Communities has disregarded the precise and unconditional GATT prohibitions of trade discrimination. In the Dürbeck I case, the Court even declared a discriminatory import restriction on Chilean apples as compatible with Community law although the GATT Council had decided in a legally binding manner in a GATT dispute settlement proceeding instituted by Chile that the import restrictions had violated the non-discrimination requirements of GATT Article XIII.[134] Since the precise and unconditional GATT prohibitions of trade discrimination (Articles I,III,XIII) have been recognized by the Court to form an "integral part of the Community legal system" and are designed to protect non-discriminatory trade competition in the interest of the EC citizens, it is to be regretted that the Court tolerates numerous trade restrictions and distortions as being compatible with the EEC principles of non-discriminatory treatment even though they are in manifest violation of the international GATT prohibitions of trade discrimination.

c) Proportionality of Restrictions

The principle of proportionality is one of the basic premises of both GATT law as well as Community law. GATT law does not require any contracting party to give up the pursuit of any economic or social policy goal. It only limits the use of non-transparent, discriminatory and particularly harmful instruments for achieving such goals. GATT law ranks the various trade policy instruments according to their respective economic efficiency in almost the same order as economic theory suggests; the more trade-distorting and non-transparent the trade policy instruments are, the more stringent are the legal GATT constraints on their use.[135]

---

134 Case 112/80 - Dürbeck I - ECR 1981, pp. 1095 ff. On the GATT inconsistency see: E.U. Petersmann (note 131), at p. 410.

135 See above chapter VII. 2. D for details.

The principle of proportionality has been recognized also as a general principle of European Community law.[136] The general legal requirement that the means used by the authorities must be in proportion to their purpose and must restrict the freedoms recognized in Community law as little as possible, has been applied by the EC Court of Justice in the field of foreign trade law, for instance, with regard to the authorization of protective measures under Article 115 of the EEC Treaty,[137] the setting of threshold prices for agricultural products,[138] the loss of deposits for import certificates if proof of importation had not been furnished in time,[139] and the resort to import restrictions under the safeguard clauses of the EEC's agricultural market organizations.[140] Yet, regrettably, the case-

136 P. Pescatore (above note 118) remarks that the principle of proportionality is among the most frequently invoked principles of Community law (p. 19).

137 See the Chinese Mushroom Case 62/70 (E.C.R. 1971, 909, 910) in which the Court supported the application that the Commission had violated the principle of proportionality by using its power to authorize protective measures under Article 115 of the EEC Treaty for blocking an import of a minimal quantity: "the Commission, by extending the authorization at issue to an application relating to a transaction which was insignificant in terms of the effectiveness of the measure of commercial policy proposed by the Member State concerned and which in addition had been submitted at a time when the principle of the free circulation of goods applied unrestrictedly to the goods in question, has exceeded the limit of what is necessary within the meaning of Article 115" ... (consideration 15).

138 See the Werhahn Case 63 - 69/72 (E.C.R. 1973, 1250, 1251), in which the applicant alleged that the principle of proportionality had been infringed as a result of the setting of an excessively high level of threshold prices for durum wheat. The Court found that "it does not seem that the Council in its assessment of the level of the threshold price, went beyond what might be considered necessary for achieving the object of the aid system for durum wheat" (considerations 18 - 20).

139 See the Buitoni Case 122/78, in which the Court found that the principle of proportionality was violated by a provision that provided for the loss of a deposit for a certificate of import if traders, who had actually imported, failed to furnish the necessary proof thereof (E.C.R. 1979, 685, considerations 20 - 23). In Case 66/82 - Fromançais SA - E.C.R. 1983, 395, the Court examined the proportionality of the forfeiture of a security and specified the proportionality principle in the following terms: "In order to establish whether a provision of Community law is consonant with the principle of proportionality it is necessary to establish, in the first place, whether the means it employs to achieve its aim correspond to the importance of the aim and, in the second place, whether they are necessary for its achievement".

140 See the Wünsche Case 345/82, in which the Court held that the principle of proportionality justified the use by the EC Commission of additional import levies rather than of more restrictive import quotas or prohibitions as safeguard measures even though the pertinent EEC regulation provided only for the suspension or complete refusal of import licenses or the introduction of minimum prices as safeguard measures (E.C.R. 1984, 1995, considerations 22 - 25). In Cases 41 - 44/70 - International Fruit Company - E.C.R. 1971, 426, the Court had already decided that the Commission, if it is authorized to introduce safeguard measures which suspend imports from third countries completely, may also apply less restrictive safeguard measures.

law of the Court of Justice has not taken into account the pertinent legal GATT obligations of the EEC and their economic rationale in interpreting the proportionality principle in the foreign trade law of the EEC. For example, even though the general foreign trade regulations of the EEC explicitly require the EEC to act in conformity with its "existing international obligations" and GATT Articles XI, XIII, XIX clearly prohibit discriminatory quantitative trade restrictions as the least transparent and most distorting protective instrument, the EC Court of Justice has held the EC Commission to be competent not only to introduce discriminatory import restrictions in manifest violation of GATT law[141] but also to negotiate "voluntary export restraints" administered abroad in the exporting country without transparent procedures or judicial review and sometimes supplemented by additional import controls within the EEC.[142] The Court's invocation of the Community law principle of proportionality as a legal justification of this least transparent, costliest, discriminatory and internationally illegal form of import protection curtailing the individual rights of adversely affected European traders and consumers, reveals a highly legalistic reasoning

141 See, for instance, the above-mentioned Dürbeck Case 112/80 (note 134) where the inconsistency of the discriminatory import restrictions of the EEC with GATT Article XIII had been formally established in a GATT Panel Report adopted by the GATT Council (BISD 27S/98) prior to the judgment by the Court. In the above-mentioned Edeka Case 245/81 (note 132), the manifest inconsistency with GATT Article XIII of discriminatory import restrictions against the GATT contracting party South Korea was again ignored by the Court which held: "It cannot be said that it (= the EC Commission) exceeded the limits of its discretionary power by almost totally prohibiting imports from Taiwan and South Korea, countries which did not agree to such a voluntary restraint, in favour of imports originating in the People's Republic of China which did accept an agreement of voluntary restraint" (E.C.R. 1982, p. 2757).

142 See the Dürbeck- and Edeka-cases referred to above (notes 132 and 134), in which the Court acknowledged that "the Commission's attempt, before adopting coercive measures, to obtain the agreement of supplier countries on a voluntary restriction of their exports to the Community cannot be regarded as being unacceptable from the point of view of Community law since it demonstrates the Community's effort to refrain from adopting coercive measures unless all else fails" (E.C.R. 1982, p. 2757). The Court's decision - apart from ignoring the GATT-inconsistency of VERs, their particular economic harmfulness and their regular introduction at the request (threat) of the importing country in order to obviate even more harmful alternative safeguard measures - appears unrealistic in respect of its assumption that VERs are "voluntary" and less "coercive" for domestic citizens than alternative import restrictions which are, at least, transparent and subject to procedural guarantees and judicial review. The frequent characterization of VERs as a unilateral measure taken by the exporting country is likewise not convincing because VERs are usually negotiated with the importing country (EEC) and often supplemented by supervisory measures (e.g. automatic import licenses) in the importing country (see, e.g. , Commission Regulation EEC No. 873/83 of 12 April 1983 introducing a system of automatic authorization of imports of products subject to a VER negotiated with South Korea, O.J. L 96/8 of 15 April 1983).

without regard to economic analysis, the international GATT obligations of the EEC and the individual rights of European citizens.

d) Judicial Protection of Individual Rights

GATT law already includes numerous substantive and procedural rules for the domestic administration and judicial review of both trade policy border measures as well as internal trade policy measures. For instance, "each contracting party shall administer in a uniform, impartial and reasonable manner all its laws, regulations, decisions and rulings" and "shall maintain, or institute ...., judicial, arbitral or administrative tribunals or procedures for the purpose, inter alia, of the prompt review and correction of administrative action relating to customs matters" (Article X: 3). The various Tokyo Round Agreements on customs valuation, import licensing, antidumping and countervailing duty proceedings, technical barriers to trade, subsidies and government procurement set out additional rules and procedures for the "due" exercise of the various trade policy instruments.[143] Due to the gradual liberalization of tariffs and other trade policy border measures, the GATT rules for the liberalization and regulation of internal trade restrictions and policy measures have taken on increasing importance. A major objective of GATT law is that trade in goods, once they have crossed customs frontiers, is not further distorted by other discriminatory government restrictions. For instance, "the products of the territory of any contracting party imported into the territory of any other contracting party shall be accorded treatment no less favourable than that accorded to like products of national origin in respect of all laws, regulations and requirements affecting their internal sale, offering for sale, purchase, transportation, distribution of use" (Article III: 4). Accordingly, "the products of the territory of any contracting party imported into the territory of any other contracting party shall not be subject, directly or indirectly, to internal taxes or other internal charges of any kind in excess of those applied, directly or indirectly, to like domestic products" (Article III: 2), and "no contracting party shall establish or maintain any internal quantitative regulation relating to the mixture, processing or use of products in specified amounts or proportions which requires, directly or indirectly, that any specified amount or proportion of any product, which is the subject of the regulation, must be supplied from domestic sources "(Article III: 5).

---

143 For a survey see: E.U. Petersmann, Strengthening the Domestic Legal Framework of the GATT Multilateral Trade System, in: E.U. Petersmann/M. Hilf (eds.), The New GATT Round of Multilateral Trade Negotiations, 1988, pp. 33, 79 ff.

The EEC Treaty does not contain any equivalent, precise rules on the use of non-tariff trade barriers in the foreign trade relations of the EEC. The generally applicable framework regulations laying down the "secondary" foreign trade law of the EEC are, for the most part, explicitly based on and implement the pertinent GATT obligations of the EEC. In more than a dozen judgments, the Court has referred to GATT rules in view of interpreting or testing the validity of Community provisions on customs matters,[144] safeguard measures,[145] freedom of transit,[146] antidumping and antisubsidy rules ,[147] actions for compensation for damages[148] or the nature of free trade area agreements with EFTA countries.[149] While the Court has rightly pointed out that, in the intra-Community relations among the EC member countries, the context and functions of Community law may warrant a more liberal interpretation of Community rules com-

144 See, for instance: Case 14/69 - Markus & Walsh - E.C.R. 1969, 349 (the Court found that the terms of a Community regulation on the sugar market conformed to the relevant GATT tariff bindings and were therefore valid); Case 92/71 - Interfood - E.C.R. 1972, 231 (the Court determined the tariff classification of "fruit containing added sugar" in the common customs tariff by reference to principles underlying GATT provisions); Case 9/73 - Schlüter - E.C.R. 1973, 1157 (the incorporation of GATT commitments into the common customs tariff confers rights upon individuals); Case 79/77 - Kühlhaus - E.C.R. 1978, 821 (the Court expresses doubts as to whether it is appropriate to apply monetary compensatory amounts to imports under a GATT tariff quota providing for exemption from import-levy): Case 90/77 - Stimmung - E.C.R. 1978, 1000 (the Court rejects the plaintiff's contention that levies and monetary compensatory amounts on imported beef are inconsistent with GATT tariff bindings, by saying that the Commission's explanations drawn from GATT have "not been refuted by the applicant").

145 See Case 112/80 - Dürbeck I - E.C.R. 1981, 1095 (a challenge brought against the validity of a discriminatory safeguard measure restricting the importation of Chilean apples was dimissed by the Court by relying on the misleading information supplied by the EC Commission that a GATT Panel had found the import restrictions not to infringe Articles I or II of the GATT - the violation of GATT Article XIII confirmed by the GATT Panel was not taken into account by the Court); Case 245/81 - Edeka - E.C.R. 1982, 2745 (the plaintiff's argument that the almost total prohibition of imports from South Korea was contrary to GATT Article XIII and to the Community law principle of the protection of legitimate expectation, was rejected by the Court).

146 Case 226/81 - SIOT - E.C.R. 1983, 731 (the Community law principle of freedom of transit within the Community was defined in terms close to, but apparently less liberal than, Article V of GATT).

147 The most recent judgments relate to the "Ballbearings II" Cases, e.g. Case 258/84, ECR (1987) p. 1923-1974.

148 See Case 11/81 - Dürbeck II - E.C.R. 1982, 1251 (the Court disregarded the arguments of the plaintiff that the GATT-inconsistency of the discriminatory safeguard measures against Chilean apples entailed the liability of the EEC to compensate the damage suffered by the complaining importer as a result of these protective measures).

149 See Case 270/80 - Polydor - E.C.R. 1982, 329 (the nature of the free-trade agreement with Portugal was defined by the Court by referring to GATT Article XXIV).

pared to identically worded GATT rules,[150] the Court has also construed Community rules (e.g. the freedom of transit) in a less liberal manner than the corresponding GATT provisions.[151] Notably the 1979 GATT Antidumping Agreement has contributed to a considerable "legalization" and "judicialization" of the discretionary antidumping practices of the EEC which, because they have reduced the scope for abuse of government discretion and have increased transparency and predictability of antidumping proceedings, "can be praised unreservedly".[152] Thus, in the five "Ballbearings I" cases of 1979, the first EC Court decisions relating to antidumping law, the Court took into account the pertinent GATT rules and was highly critical of the lack of procedural safeguards in EEC antidumping proceedings (the Commission had refused to inform the complaining exporters of any details relating to the calculation of the alleged dumping margins and injury).[153] As in response to the judicial criticism, the then existing Antidumping Regulation 459/68 was amended to provide for improved rights for defendants in antidumping proceedings and to bring the EC antidumping law more into conformity with the pertinent GATT rules. The new EEC Antidumping Regulation 3017/79[154] incorporated , inter alia, the changes agreed upon in the 1979 GATT Antidumping Code (e.g. the specific rules to determine causation of injury) and further improved the procedural rights of participants in EEC antidumping proceedings.

In a series of subsequent judgments, the Court further improved the individual rights in antidumping proceedings by ruling, inter alia, that certain business secrets submitted by applicants to support their application had to be treated confidentially,[155] that complainants had a right to judicial review as to whether the Commission had disregarded their procedural rights even if the complainants had not been named in the regulation at issue,[156] that also exporters had a right

150 See Case 270/80 above (note 149).

151 See the Court's definition of freedom of transit in Community law in Case 226/81 above (note 146) and the seemingly less qualified freedom of transit guaranteed in Article V of GATT.

152 So the conclusion of the thorough analysis by E.A. Vermulst, Antidumping Law and Practice in the United States and the European Communities, 1987, at p. 15.

153 Case 113/77 - NTN Toyo Bearing Co. and others vs. Council - ECR 1979, p. 1185.

154 OJ No. L 339, 1979, p. 1.

155 Case 236/89 - Celanese Chemical Corp. vs. Council - ECR 1982, p. 1183.

156 Case 191/82 - FEDIOL vs. Commission - ECR 1983, p. 2913 (relating to a countervailing duty proceeding).

to appeal when affected by an antidumping measure,[157] that the Commission must give all interested parties sufficient information on the dumping and injury issues in question so that the parties can ascertain whether the Commission had made accurate factual determinations,[158] and that the EC Council is required to make findings on the record so that the parties and the EC Court of Justice may review them.[159] The increasing number of antidumping cases decided by the EC Court of Justice are widely seen not only as a welcome judicial limitation on the broad trade policy discretion of the EC executives in antidumping proceedings. They also illustrate the contribution which detailed international GATT rules and procedures can make to the promotion of "due process" and individual rights in the domestic administration of foreign trade regulations.

4. The Need to Incorporate Liberal International Rules into Domestic Constitutional Systems

Chapter VII. 1 showed that, just as individuals voluntarily agree to market exchanges and commercial contracts only if they perceive the exchange and contract to be in their individual self-interest, governments tend to participate voluntarily in international agreements only if they perceive the agreed rules to be in their national self-interest. Even though governments often pursue conflicting interests, they enter international agreements such as GATT because they offer mutual gains through cooperation.

Chapter VII. 1 also emphasized the important distinction between the choice of long-term constitutional rules and choices within these rules.[160] Agreements on long-term rules have to be prepared from behind a "veil of uncertainty" (J.Buchanan) because the rules to be chosen are expected to remain in existence over a long time period; hence, participants will find it difficult to identify their long-term self-interests and are more prepared to accept general criteria such as equity, fairness and justice. By contrast, agreement on policy alternatives or "result-oriented" market-sharing within the rules may be more difficult to attain because they affect more directly and more visibly public and private interests which are then likely to oppose the agreement. This then raises the

157 Cases 239 and 275/82 - "Allied I" - ECR 1984, 1005.

158 Case 264/82 - Timex v. Commission - ECR 1985, p. 849.

159 Case 53/83 - "Allied II" - ECR 1985, 1621.

160 See J. Buchanan, Freedom in Constitutional Contract, 1977, pp. 287 ff.

question: How to enforce the long-term constitutional rules among sovereign states which do not accept any external enforcement process imposed on them against their will? How to achieve an international "self-enforcing" constitution? How to prevent the current political processes and pressures "pragmatically" eroding and changing the long-term agreed rules?

Chapter VII. 5 referred to the inadequate constitutional "checks and balances" at the international level and to the resultant risks of intergovernmental collusion and piecemeal adjustments gradually undermining the constitutional system, as illustrated by the bilaterally agreed "grey area trade policies" and their "pragmatic" toleration by the GATT contracting parties. Chapter VIII then showed that, even in liberal constitutional democracies, the existing constitutional restraints at the national level are not effectively applied and judicially enforced vis-à-vis the discretionary foreign trade policy powers of governments as well as of the EC institutions. Chapter VIII. 5 concluded from this analysis that the only promising strategy for "constitutionalizing" the discretionary trade policy powers of governments consists of integrating the liberal international trade rules into the domestic constitutional systems. Chapter VIII. 5. A and B ended on the optimistic argument that such a "constitutional strategy" should be acceptable in liberal constitutional democracies (and has been applied within the EEC) because the liberal international trade rules and democratic constitutionalism rest on the same liberal principles, namely that governmental (trade) policies should be designed to maximize the equal freedoms and property rights of the citizens and enlarge the potential for satisfying individual's preferences.

The remainder of this chapter elaborates on the various possibilities of rendering the international and domestic constitutional restraints on discretionary trade policymaking more effective by incorporating the liberal international trade rules (of GATT and of the various free trade area agreements of the EEC and EFTA countries) into the domestic constitutional systems.

A) The Need for More Detailed International Rules Regulating the "Domestic Law Effects" of Liberal International Trade Obligations

The analysis of the constitutional and foreign trade laws of the United States, Switzerland and Germany in chapter VIII showed the limited "domestic law effects" of GATT law within these countries: In each of these countries the General Agreement is considered to be binding under international law and to have become part of the respective federal legal systems. In Switzerland and in Germany, the General Agreement is considered to have the internal rank of a federal law with primacy over previous legislation ("lex posterior derogat legi priori"); even though the courts have acknowledged that subsequent legislation may overrule the domestic law effects of GATT on the ground of the "lex posterior" - rule, the courts do not lightly assume such a legislative intention and tend to construe subsequent legislation in conformity with existing treaty obligations ("lex posterior specialis non derogat legi generali"). But, notwithstanding the fact that the GATT prohibitions of trade discrimination (Articles I, III, XIII) and of non-tariff trade barriers (Articles II to XI: 1) are drafted in more precise and more detailed language than the corresponding provisions of the EEC and EFTA agreements and explicitly provide for their protection by domestic courts (Article X: 3), both Swiss and German courts consider the General Agreement to be, in the words used by German courts,[161] a "mere trade agreement" and a "framework for the conduct of trade policy" because the GATT contracting parties did not intend, according to the courts, to create self-executing provisions directly applicable by domestic courts and individuals.

The analysis of the "GATT case law" of US courts in chapter VIII. 2. D showed that a number of US courts have directly applied certain precise and unconditional GATT prohibitions and have declared municipal ordinances (e.g. on "buy American policies") to be invalid on the ground of "violation of GATT law". But it was indicated that there are also court decisions denying the self-executing character e.g. of Article III of GATT. And all US courts seem to hold that, due to the lack of congressional ratification of the General Agreement which was concluded by the US President as an "executive agreement" in terms of US law, GATT law is inferior to US federal law, prior and subsequent, within the United States.

The discussion of the "constitutional dilemma of liberal international trade rules" (chapter VII. 5) had mentioned that general international law leaves it to each individual state to decide for itself how to implement its international legal obligations within its domestic legal system. The "domestic law effects" of international legal obligations within the domestic legal system of a state will always depend on a rule of domestic law and, in most states, of domestic constitutional law. Even if domestic law, for instance in the United States and Switzerland, recognizes the "automatic validity" within the domestic legal system of internatio-

161 See the judgment of the Tax Court of Hamburg of 29 October 1969, reported in: American Journal of International Law 1971, pp. 627 ff; see also the criticism of this judgment by S.A. Riesenfeld, at pp. 548 ff, in the same journal.

nal treaties binding on the state without any need for an additional legislative act of "incorporation" or "transformation" of the international agreement into the domestic legal system, the domestic law effects depend on recognition by domestic law. But international law usually "requires the application of treaties in all circumstances";[162] the international treaty obligations require a result to be achieved and the different government branches assume joint international responsability to that end. Hence, if the General Agreement and free trade area agreements prohibit "each contracting party" from using certain discriminatory and non-tariff trade barriers because of their mutually harmful effects, these often precise and unconditional treaty obligations refer not only to the executive but also to the legislative and judicial government branches.[163] And because these self-imposed international legal restraints on the abuse of discretionary trade policy powers tend to maximize the equal freedoms, property rights and economic welfare of domestic citizens, the domestic constitutional guarantees of equal freedoms and property rights justify a presumption in favour of the direct application of these liberal international trade rules by domestic administrations and courts.[164]

The above-mentioned arguments in favour of direct application of liberal international trade rules by the domestic courts of liberal democracies are unlikely to become generally accepted in the near future. The same reasons (indicated above in chapter IX. 2) which impede the strict application of the national constitutional restraints to the domestic exercise of discretionary trade and foreign policy powers, are likely to impede also the willingness of domestic courts to enforce liberal international treaty obligations against their own governments. In addition, there are also a number of widespread legal doctrines working against the domestic judicial review of the observance of liberal international trade rules, notably:

a) the "dualist" legal systems and traditions of a number of Commonwealth, Scandinavian and other countries, where international treaties continue to be considered as a matter for the government alone, binding the state as against the other contracting parties, and are usually not incorporated as such into domestic law thus preventing individuals

162 F. Jacobs (above note 2), p. XXIV.

163 This is rightly emphasized by O. Jacot-Guillarmod, Judicial Protectionism: Legal fate or political challenge to free trade in Europe?, in: EFTA Bulletin 4/85, pp. 8, 11.

164 See above chapter IX. 3. A.

from invoking the provisions of international treaties in domestic courts;[165]

b) the widely held view of national courts and academic writers that the self-executing or directly applicable nature of international treaty provisions depends on the intent of the contracting parties, which is generally dubious and differs from party to party, rather than upon the objective contents and functions of the international obligations and upon the national constitutional law of the country concerned (e.g.: Is the international treaty obligation precise and unconditional enough to be directly applied by a domestic court? Does it require legislative implementing legislation or reserve executive implementing discretion excluding the direct judicial application? Does its judicial application protect individual rights recognized under the domestic constitutional law?);[166]

c) the also widely held view of domestic courts in many countries, including the United States (see above chapter VIII. 2. D and E) and Switzerland (see above chapter VIII. 3. D), that courts should not meddle with "high foreign policy" and should attribute more importance to the foreign policy discretion of the foreign policy "experts" and of the "parliamentary sovereign" than to the constitutional guarantees of individual rights of domestic citizens in foreign affairs.

The "constitutional problem" remains that transnational trade and financial transactions of private citizens, notwithstanding their ever increasing importance, continue to be regulated and progressively liberalized mainly by international agreements concluded among governments. The strict implementation of the liberal international trade rules suffers from political and legal asymmetries: The individuals whose rights are being protected are not themselves parties to

165 F. Jacobs (note 2) observes that the main difference between "monist" and "dualist" legal systems lies not so much in the presence or absence of Parliamentary participation as in the question whether it is the treaty itself, or the incorporating legislation, which is law applied by the courts (p. XXVI).

166 As here: S.A. Riesenfeld, The Doctrine of Self-Executing Treaties and GATT: A Notable German Judgment (above note 161), who concludes (p. 550): "Although the doctrine looking to the intent of the parties is widely supported by practice and theory, it seems much more reasonable to consider the self-executing or executory nature of international conventions a matter depending primarily upon the constitutional law of each nation rather than upon a dubious intent of the parties. Consequently in the United States a treaty ought to be deemed self-executing if it: (a) involves the rights and duties of individuals; (b) does not cover a subject for which legislative action is required by the Constitution; and (c) does not leave discretion to the parties in the application of the particular provision".

the international treaties; and the governments whom the treaties oblige to protect individual rights often give in to the strong protectionist pressures from domestic interest groups in exchange for political support. Hence, the need to change the legal restraints and incentive structures in a manner promoting domestic political support for and observance of international trade agreements by all government organs. For this it is important to recognize that the traditional perception of "international" law as the law of the external relations of states is misleading because most international agreements, such as the GATT obligations for the liberalization of national trade barriers, are to be implemented within the member states concerned and purport to regulate the conduct of the various branches of governments for the benefit of their own citizens. The main regulatory function of liberal international trade rules, such as those of GATT, is less contractual (such as the legal "binding" of reciprocal tariff concessions pursuant to Article II) than "legislative": to restrict the discretionary trade policy powers of governments through general long-term rules promoting legal certainty, individual freedoms and due process, and enabling thereby domestic traders, producers and consumers to maximise their individual welfare through trade.

From the point of view of international law, there are no obstacles to negotiating international provisions requiring governments to incorporate certain rules into domestic legislation, specifying the domestic forms and procedures for the administration of such trade rules, or stipulating the availability of domestic judicial review. The need for such international rules in international commercial relations is illustrated by the large number of international obligations in the area of international private commercial law requiring specific legislative, executive or judicial actions, for instance in the 1964 Hague Convention relating to a uniform law on the international sale of goods or in the 1968 European Convention on jurisdiction and enforcement of civil and commercial judgments.[167] The frequent disregard by national legislatures, administrations and courts for

---

167 Numerous international conventions, especially those on international private and commercial "uniform law", require the contracting parties to take specifically determined implementing actions by legislative, executive or judicial organs (e.g. to reproduce in its legislation the actual text of the uniform law annexed to the international convention in question). Failure to carry out these implementing acts (e.g. to incorporate certain rules in domestic law) then entails international responsibility for breach of the treaty. It is well settled also in GATT practice that state responsibility can be generated by acts or omissions by all state organs, including the judiciary and the domestic courts (see, for instance, the 1977 GATT Working Party report on suspension of customs liquidation by the USA, which concerned a GATT complaint by Japan against the USA relating to a judgment of the US Customs Court that was inconsistent with GATT Article VI: 4, BISD 24S/134).

the international GATT obligations confirms that the traditional GATT approach of leaving the domestic implementation of GATT rules to the national discretion of governments, and the traditional trade policy approach in most countries of bestowing governments with broad discretionary powers to tax and restrict the foreign trade transactions of their citizen, cannot secure welfare-maximizing trade policies. The reason is that, as Hauser put it, "the power to use regulations on a discretionary basis is an invitation to special interest groups to use the political process for their purposes. This applies for purely domestic regulations as well as for border controls".[168]

B) The Progressive Constitutionalization of German Foreign Trade Law through Liberal International Trade Rules

The practical experiences, analyzed in chapter VIII, of the United States, Switzerland and Germany with the "constitutionalization" of discretionary trade and foreign policy powers offers important insights. In each instance, the trade regulatory powers of the constituent states (cantons) were legally subjected to general long-term rules on the federal level. The historical experience, since the 19th century, of economic and legal integration through customs union law in Germany appears particularly illustrative of how liberal international trade rules can contribute to constitutionalizing discretionary trade policy powers.

a) Freedom of Internal Trade through Customs Union Law and "Cooperative Federalism"

An essential feature of the federal structure of Germany not only under the Basic Law of 1949, but already since the establishment of the German Confederation (Deutscher Bund, 1815 - 1866), continues to be its "cooperative system which enables problems to be solved in a manner which does not necessarily involve recourse to central decision-making".[169] The common trade regulation foreseen in Article XIX of the German Confederation Act of 1815 was progressively achieved in the framework of an international customs union treaty of 1833 establishing the German Zollverein, a common customs area without in-

168 H. Hauser (note 97), p. 27.

169 J.A. Frowein, Integration and the Federal Experience in Germany and Switzerland, in: Cappelletti/Seccombe/Weiler (note 35), pp. 573, 574; Feuchte, Die bundesstaatliche Zusammenarbeit in der Verfassungswirklichkeit der Bundesrepublik Deutschland, Archiv des öffentlichen Rechts 1973, pp. 473 ff.

ternal customs duties and with common customs legislation which gradually became the catalyst for German economic and political unification. In addition to exercising its exclusive legislative competences for tariff and customs legislation and to monitoring member state compliance with this legislation, the Zollverein became a party to 28 international trade agreements promoting a further unification of foreign trade law for the whole of the customs union.[170] The Federal Diet of the German Confederation promoted economic and legal integration also through unification and harmonisation of economic legislation, notably the Common Regulation on Negotiable Instruments of 1848 and the Common Commercial Code of 1861.

From 1806, Prussia and some other German states began to introduce individual freedom of industrial activities (Gewerbefreiheit) for their own citizens. But only Article 3 of the 1867 Constitution of the North German Confederation (Norddeutscher Bund) proclaimed for the first time a federal guarantee for every citizen of a member state to take up residence, to engage in industrial activities and to exercise the rights of a citizen in any other member state. This individual freedom of trade and industry, later incorporated into Article 3 of the 1871 Federal Constitution of the German Reich and regulated in more detail in the 1867 Law on the Free Movement of Persons and the 1869 Law on the Freedom of Industrial Activities, was another important step towards the economic and legal integration of Germany. But, while the German Supreme Court (Reichsgericht) was authorized under the 1871 Constitution to control the compatibility of state legislation with federal law, the court had no jurisdiction to declare federal legislation null and void.

From 1867 to 1871, the North German Confederation and the southern German states were members of a revised customs union which was then described as "a federal state for customs matters" (Zoll-Bundesstaat) in view of its powers to enact directly applicable customs legislation with priority over the member state laws and to conclude trade agreements with foreign countries.[171] The 1871 Federal Constitution further expanded the federal legislative competences in economic matters. A constitutional amendment of 1873 introduced a federal competence for civil law in general, thus enabling the elaboration of the German Civil Code that entered into force on 1 January 1900. Since the 1919 Federal Constitution, the federal legislative competence extends to almost all economic

170 For details see: J.A. Frowein (note 169), p. 577; E.R. Huber, Deutsche Verfassungsgeschichte seit 1789, Vol. 1, 1957, pp. 796 ff.

171 See E.R. Huber (note 170), Vol. 3 (1963), at p. 635.

matters. This is now explicitly recognized in Article 74, section 11 of the 1949 Basic Law: "Concurrent legislative powers shall extend to ... the law relating to economic matters (mining, industry, supply of power, crafts, trades, commerce, banking, stock exchanges and private insurance)". But the German Länder participate in the exercise of these federal legislative powers through the Federal Council (Bundesrat) and, according to Article 83 of the Basic Law, "the Länder shall execute federal laws as matters of their own concern in so far as this Basic Law does not otherwise provide or permit". A further separation and constitutional limitation of economic regulatory powers derives from the comprehensive fundamental rights guarantees in Articles 1 to 19 of the Basic Law and from the strong position of the Federal Constitutional Court which, between 1949 and 1980,declared 111 federal statutes unconstitutional.[172] Thus, "participatory federalism", horizontal and vertical distribution of powers and institutional "checks and balances" continue to be characteristic elements of German federalism.

b) National Constitutional Protection of Freedom of Foreign Trade

The progressive trade liberalization among the German states since the time of the German Zollverein and the conclusion of a large number of international trade agreements by this customs union (or by Prussia on behalf of the Zollverein) contributed also to the liberalization of foreign trade during the second half of the 19th century. But it was only after the experience of the inter-war period and World War II that the discretionary foreign trade policy powers were considerably limited by national constitutional law. As described above in chapter VIII. 4, Article 1 of the German Basic Law of 1949 proclaims that the sole function of the State consists in the promotion and protection of the dignity and human rights of man. Economic liberty, freedom of contract, the freedom to choose and carry out a profession, private property and the freedom to engage in foreign commerce are protected by the constitution as individual rights (Arts. 2, 12, 14). Accordingly, the Law on Foreign Economic Relations (Aussenwirtschaftsgesetz = AWG) of 1961 declares in its section 1: "In principle trade and commerce with foreign Economic Areas are free as to goods, services, capital, payments or other economic transactions as well as to transactions between residents in foreign assets and gold". If, therefore, "in case this Law or an ordinance based on this Law stipulate that transactions or deals require an authorization then this authorization has to be granted if it can be expected that the

172 See J.A. Frowein (note 169), p. 590.

purpose of such provision would not or only insignificantly be endangered by the execution of such transaction or deal" (section 3 AWG).

It is recognized that the constitutional guarantees of economic liberties and private property (including contractual rights, import licences and a business firm's capability to operate) protect also transnational economic transactions. A taking is permissible only if done "for the public good" by means of a law that specifies itself the kind and extent of compensation (Art. 14 para. 3). Accordingly, restrictions on foreign economic relations "may affect existing contracts only if the purpose to be achieved would otherwise significantly be endangered" (section 2 para. 2 AWG). Existing contracts are regularly given special treatment in case of trade restrictions adopted by the German Government and, in principle, may not be affected retroactively without granting of compensation for unforeseeable damage suffered therefrom. Revocation of a licence is allowed only under specified conditions and may entail an obligation to grant compensation (cf. section 30 AWG).

None of the constitutional liberties and individual rights may ever be changed in its essence (Art. 19 para. 2). Hence, foreign trade restrictions "are to be limited as to character and extent to the minimum necessary to achieve the purpose stipulated in the empowering legislation. They are to be formulated in such a way as to interfere as little as possible with the liberty of economic activities ... Restrictions have to be abolished as soon and insofar as the reasons which necessitated their introduction are no longer relevant" (section 2 paras. 2 and 3 AWG).

The Constitution prescribes that Parliament may delegate law-making powers only through a legislative act that determines "subject-matter, purpose and extent of the delegated authority" in the authorizing act itself (Art. 80). The German foreign trade legislation authorizes the executive branch to restrict foreign commerce by regulation only in specific ways, under specified circumstances and for specified objectives. For instance, foreign trade restrictions are permitted only in the form of licences or prohibitions but not by means of government orders to act, with the exception of the authority delegated to the Government in 1971 to introduce a cash deposit requirement for credits raised abroad to counteract threats to domestic economic stability (section 61 AWG). The delegated law-making powers appear more precisely circumscribed in German foreign trade legislation than in United States foreign trade laws, and do not authorize the executive branch deliberately to violate binding international law (e.g. GATT obligations). As a result of the limited delegation of powers, the Government is legally barred from applying various kinds of foreign trade restrictions, such as certain expropriating interferences in existing contracts and certain foreign exchange restrictions. All government regulations restricting foreign economic relations are to be submitted to Parliament without delay, and Parliament may request their immediate removal within four months after their promulgation (section 27, para. 2 AWG).

The Constitution guarantees individual access to the courts and judicial reviewability of all government restrictions of individual freedoms and other rights (Art. 19 para. 1). German courts do not recognize a "political question" or "act of State"-doctrine and review foreign trade laws, restrictions and other government measures in foreign affairs more closely than United States courts. But the courts do concede a substantive degree of foreign policy discretion, and generally decline to substitute their judgment for that of the Parliament or of the Government when the latter exercise their discretion within the limits of the law.

The constitutional guarantees of individual freedoms and property rights, limited delegation of power, proportionality of government action and judicial review thus appear to protect rather effectively those engaged in the foreign trade of Germany, and thereby also the national self-interest in liberal and non-discriminatory trade competition. Deliberate violations of GATT obligations, "grey area trade policy measures" such as "Voluntary Export Restraints" (VERs), or the unilateral use of trade restrictions to achieve foreign policy goals are hardly ever resorted to by the German Government. The trade protection afforded to German producers may nonetheless be explained in terms of "rent-seeking" pressures from protectionist domestic interest groups.[173] Even though international agreements, such as GATT and the IMF Agreement, are recognized to form part of German law with the rank of a federal parliamentary act, the German courts have declined a right of private plaintiffs directly to invoke GATT obligations in national courts so as to invalidate certain German trade restrictions.[174] The reason given for this denial of "direct applicability" of GATT provisions is that GATT provides, in the view of the courts, only a "framework

173 Cf. H.H. Glissmann/F.D. Weiss, On the Political Economy of Protection in Germany, World Bank Staff Working paper No. 427, 1980.

174 Cf. M. Hilf, The Application of GATT within the Member States of the European Community, with Special Reference to the Federal Republic of Germany, in: Hilf/Jacobs/Petersmann (eds), The European Community and GATT, 1986, pp. 153, 157 f.

for foreign trade policies".[175] Thus, foreign trade relations with countries other than EEC and EFTA states continue to be perceived by many German courts from a political perspective, warranting judicial deferrence to the political discretion of the government, rather than in terms of protecting individual traders and non-discriminatory competition from discriminatory trade restrictions in violation of GATT rules.

c) The "Communitarization" of German Foreign Trade Law through the Customs Union Law of the EEC

According to the Court of Justice of the EC, "the EEC Treaty has created its own legal system ... which became an integral part of the legal systems of the Member States and which their courts are bound to apply".[176] Moreover, "Community law not only imposes obligations on individuals but is also intended to confer upon them rights. These rights arise not only where they are expressly granted by the Treaty, but also by reason of obligations which the Treaty imposes in a clearly defined way upon individuals as well as upon the Member States and upon the institutions of the Community".[177] The autonomy and uniformity of Community law with respect to national law, its supremacy over the national laws (including constitutional law) of Member States, its direct effect in and status as part of the national legal systems, and the direct applicability of precise and unconditional rules of Community law by private subjects have become generally recognized "constitutional principles" of Community law. The wide aims and far-reaching powers of the three European Communities notwithstanding, it is also acknowledged that the European Communities, unlike states and like international organizations, possess merely limited derived powers ("compétence d'attribution"). As explicitly stated in the EEC Treaty, the activities of the Community shall include those "provided in this Treaty" (Article 3), and "each institution shall act within the limits of the powers conferred upon

175 German tax courts have ruled in a series of judgments that "GATT... obligated the contracting parties to observe the envisaged commercial policy, but... did not establish any legal norms which reach directly and immediately into the legal sphere of the citizens of the member nations" (see the judgment of 29 October 1969 by the Tax Court of Hamburg, reported in: American Journal of International Law 1971, pp. 627-631). The reasons given by these courts appear superficial and overlook the fact that many GATT rules prohibit trade discrimination (e.g. Arts. I: 1, III, V: 5, XIII) and certain trade barriers (e.g. Arts. V: 3, XI: 1) in a more precise manner than the corresponding EEC Treaty provisions (e.g. Arts. 30, 34, 95) that are recognized as being directly applicable by adversely affected individuals.

176 Case 6/64 - Costa v. ENEL - (1964) E.C.R. 585.

177 Case 26/62 - van Gend en Loos - (1963) E.C.R. 1, 10.

it by this Treaty" (Article 4). Mainly due to the case-law of the Court of Justice, the various interrelated treaties establishing the Communities and the various subsequent amendments of the Community treaties have evolved into a comprehensive "European constitutional law" comprising also basic rules of international law, general principles of European Community law, as well as guarantees of human rights, including guarantees of individual economic liberties and property rights.[178]

The "common market" (Article 2) - based on the "five freedoms" for the movement of goods, services, persons, payments and capital, on non-discrimination and a system promoting undistorted competition - and the three common policies for agriculture, foreign trade and transport constitute the main elements of the substantive community law of the economy set out in the EEC Treaty. The Court of Justice of the EC has construed the EEC Treaty prohibitions of customs duties and charges having equivalent effect (Article 12), of quantitative restrictions and all measures having eqivalent effect (Articles 30 and 34), the prohibitions of discriminatory taxes (Article 95) and of other kinds of discrimination (e.g. Articles 7, 119), the freedom of movement for workers (Article 48), the freedom of establishment (Article 52), the freedom of payments (Article 106), as well as other general principles of Community law (e.g., freedoms of contract, of profession, of competition, protection of property rights and other human rights, principles of legal certainty and fair administration of the law) as conferring directly applicable individual rights to be protected by the courts.[179] This "constitutional interpretation" has considerably extended and strengthened the individual guarantees of economic liberties, property rights and non-discriminatory competition of European producers, workers, investors, traders, buyers and sellers across national frontiers.

The "anchoring" of individual rights in European Community law provides a "second line of constitutional entrenchment".[180] It legally implements the economic proposition that economic liberties and rule of law among states are no less advantageous than within states. The general principles of "rule of law", "de-

178 See: R. Bernhardt, The sources of Community law: the Constitution of the Community, in: Thirty Years of Community law, EC 1983, pp. 69-82.

179 For an analysis of this case-law of the Court see, e.g.: I. Pernice, Grundrechtsgehalte im Europäischen Gemeinschaftsrecht, 1979; A. Bleckmann, Die Bindung der Europäischen Gemeinschaft an die Europäische Menschenrechtskonvention, 1986.

180 See J. Tumlir, International Economic Order and Democratic Constitutionalism, in: ORDO Vol. 34 (1983), p. 80.

mocracy", "free competition" and "proportionality" of government restraints of individual freedoms, which the Court has recognized as part of European Community law subject to the exceptions and regulatory powers provided for in the Community treaties (e.g. for steel, agricultural and nuclear products), may even be construed as "constitutive principles" of a neo-liberal "economic constitution" based on the "common market" among the 12 EC member states.[181] The EEC Treaty provisions for the common agricultural policy (Articles 85-99), approximation of laws (Articles 100-102), economic policy (Articles 103-109), the common commercial policy (Articles 110-116), social policy (Articles 117-128) and association policy (Articles 131-136, 238) reserve a broad discretion of the EC institutions for economic regulation. But the exercise of these wide regulatory powers must pay due regard to, and be balanced against, the constitutional guarantees of individual freedoms and "the institution of a system ensuring that competition in the common market is not distorted" (Article 3, f), into which they must not unnecessarily interfere. As predicted by v. Hayek in 1944, the "pre-federal" limitation and "vertical" division of powers between the Communities and their member states "inevitably act ... as a limitation of the power of the whole as well as of the individual state".[182] The EEC Treaty obligates each member state to "abstain from any measure which could jeopardise the attainment fo the objectives of this Treaty" (Article 5), and the EEC Treaty obligations for "free trade" and "undistorted competition" among the 12 EC member states can be judicially enforced by the EC "market citizens" against the governments of EC member states.

d) "Constitutional Failure" of the EEC Treaty Provisions on the Common Commercial Policy?

In contrast to the detailed rules of the EEC Treaty on trade liberalization and competition within the Community and in contrast also to the comprehensive foreign trade regulations of GATT law, the EEC Treaty deals with the "common commercial policy" in only seven Articles (Articles 110-116), two of which are concerned with the transitional period (Articles 111, 112). Exchange rate policies were left to the national competence of Member States even without provision for their coordination (Article 107). The few Articles on the common commercial policy are vague in substance and have rightly been criticized as

181 See e.g.: M. Zulegg, Demokratie und Wirtschaftsverfassung in der Rechtsprechung des Europäischen Gerichtshofs, in: Europarecht 1982, pp. 21 ff.

182 F.A. v.Hayek (note 1), p. 173.

"poorly drafted".[183] The objectives of the autonomous tariff policy (Article 29), of the common agricultural policy (Article 39) and of the commercial policy (Article 110) hardly indicate the priorities among the juxtaposed aims and appear to elude effective judicial control over whether, for instance, the EEC's agricultural market organizations "ensure that supplies reach consumers at reasonable prices" (Article 39(e)) and do not go beyond the objective of merely "stabilizing imports or exports" (Article 40, para. 3) by systematically displacing foreign products inside and outside the EEC. The trade policy powers for industrial goods (Articles 28, 113) and agricultural goods (Articles 28, 43, 113) constitutie exclusive Community competences for trade in goods and services[184] without limiting this unprecedented delegation of powers by specifying the "uniform principles" (Article 113) on which the common commercial policy shall be based.

The Treaty provisions on trade policymaking do not mention participation or control by the European Parliament,[185] with the exception of Article 43 on the common agricultural policy which provides that the Council shall decide on a proposal from the Commission after consultation of the Parliament (Article 43). Trade restrictions are decided upon by the Council or by the Commission in the form of regulations (Article 189) which, since they apply to future imports and affect an unlimited number of persons, usually cannot be challenged by private parties through direct actions before the Court of Justice (Article 173, para. 2).[186] The EC Commission has instituted numerous infringement proceedings

183 U. Everling, "Die gemeinsame Handelspolitik", in: Les relations extérieures de la Communauté Européenne unifiée, (Institut d'études juridiques européennes de la Faculté de droit de l'Université de Liège, 1969) pp. 187, 201; C.D. Ehlermann, "The scope of Article 113 of the EEC Treaty", in: Etudes de droit des Communautés Européennes - Mélanges offerts à P.H. Teitgen (1984), pp. 145, 147.

184 See, C.D. Ehlermann (note 183), pp. 147-157; P. Gilsdorf, Die Grenzen der Gemeinsamen Handelspolitik, 1988.

185 See, Article 113 and the safeguard clauses in the EEC's various foreign trade regulations, which usually authorize the Commission to undertake investigations and preliminary measures whereas the final decision on antidumping duties, countervailing duties or "protection against illicit commercial practices" is to be taken by the Council. Council Regulation (EEC) No. 288/82 on common rules for imports authorizes the Commission to decide on protective measures, but the decision taken by the Commission may be overruled by the Council (Art. 15). The European Parliament does not participate in the decision-making about safeguard measures.

186 See, however, the recent judgments by the Court with regard to anti-dumping and anti-subsidy proceedings in which the Court has recognized not only a right of foreign producers and exporters but also of related importers and competing producers within the EEC to bring direct actions under Article 173 against anti-dumping and anti-subsidy determina-

against EEC states (Article 169) for breaches of "internal" Community law, but neither the Commission nor the EEC states have ever resorted to the Court for judicial review of foreign trade restrictions which had been introduced by the EEC or by individual EC states in contravention of GATT rules. While the Court has accepted that GATT law forms part of Community law, it has, up to 1988, always refrained from reviewing the observance of the GATT rules on non-discrimination and undistorted competition by the EEC. Only in its judgment of 22 June 1989, the Court has acknowledged for the first time that - since Council Regulation No 2641/84 on the strengthening of the common commercial policy conferred on private operators the right to invoke GATT provisions in their complaint to the EC Commission - those operators were entitled to apply to the Court to review the legality of the Commission decision applying those GATT provisions.[187]

e) The "Communitarization" of the International GATT Rights and Obligations of the EEC States: A Third Line of "Constitutional Entrenchment"?

Historically, the scarce wording of the EEC Treaty provisions on the common commercial policy is to be explained, inter alia, by the fact that all EEC states were members of the GATT and of the International Monetary Fund at the

tions. In Case 191/82 - Fediol v. Commission [1983] E.C.R., p. 2913, the Court ruled, inter alia: "Regulation No. 3017/79 acknowledges that undertakings and associations of undertakings injured by subsidization practices on the part of non-member countries have a legitimate interest in the initiation of protective action by the Community. It follows that undertakings and associations of undertakings in the Community, which have made an application to the Commission under Article 5 of the said regulation for the initiation of an anti-subsidy proceeding, may not be refused the right to put before the Court any matters which would facilitate a review as to whether the Commisssion has observed the procedural guarantees granted to complainants by Regulation No. 3017/79 and whether or not it has committed manifest errors in its assentment of the facts, has omitted to take into consideration any essential matters of such a nature as to give rise to a belief that subsidization is taking place or has included in the reasons on which its decision is based considerations amounting to a misuse of powers". See also Joined Cases 239/82 and 275/82 - Allied Corporation v. Commission, E.C.R. 1984 p. 1005. The principles of these judgments should be applicable, mutatis mutandis, also with regard to the procedural guarantees and individual rights granted to private complainants in Council Regulation (EEC) No. 2641/84 of 17 September 1984 on the strengthening of the common commercial policy with regard in particular to protection against illicit commercial practices (O.J. 1984 L 252/1) as well as in Council Regulation (EEC) No. 288/82 of 5 February 1982 on common rules for imports (O.J. 1982 L 35/1).

187 Case 70/87 - Fediol v. Commission - E.C.R. 1987 (not yet reported).

time the EEC Treaty was negotiated.[188] The Treaty admits (Article 234) and presupposes (e.g. Article 110) the continuing membership in these worldwide trade and monetary organizations. It also enjoins "the Commission to ensure the maintenance of all appropriate relations with the organs of the United Nations, of the specialized agencies and of the General Agreement on Tariffs and Trade" (Article 229).

All 12 EEC member states were contracting parties of GATT before their membership in the EEC. Germany acceded to GATT upon entry into force of the Torquay Protocol to the GATT of 21 April 1951, which it signed on 1 September 1951 and put into force on 1 October 1951. The acceptance had been authorized by the German federal parliament (Bundestag) in an Act of 10 August 1951, and the Torquay Protocol, the GATT itself, subsequent amendments to GATT, and the various GATT protocols of tariff concessions were all incorporated into German law by means of federal acts promulgated in the federal law gazette "with the force of law". Like all GATT contracting parties, Germany applies the GATT "provisionally". But this "provisional application" has meanwhile lost its transitional nature and no longer differs significantly from the legal status which would result from the entry into force and a "definitive" application of the GATT.[189] By its statutory incorporation into German law, GATT law received the legal status of a federal act taking precedence over prior inconsistent legislation, but being inferior to subsequent inconsistent federal legislation according to the rule "lex posterior derogat legi priori". Under Article 31 of the German Basic Law, GATT law has priority over any law of the German states ("Länder") and municipalities. Following a decision of the Federal Finance Court in 1959, German Courts have consistently declined to directly apply and enforce GATT rules invoked by private persons before the courts.[190] The Agreement on the International Monetary Fund entered into force for Germany on 14 August 1952 - again "with the force of law" and with the status of a federal act in German law - and, to the extent as provided for in Article VIII: 2, b of the IMF Agreement, has been directly applied by German courts.

Articles 110 - 116 EEC Treaty have conferred exclusive powers on the EEC for a common commercial policy comprising all measures regulating foreign trade

188 See: Ernst/Beseler, in: Groeben/Boeckh/Thiesing/Ehlermann (eds.), Kommentar zum EWG-Vertrag, Vol. I, 3rd ed., Commentary on Article 113, p. 1912.

189 See: E.U. Petersmann, The EEC as GATT Member - Legal Conflicts between GATT law and European Community law, in: Hilf/Jacobs/Petersmann (note 174), pp. 23, 26 f.

190 See, above notes 174 and 175.

in goods and services.[191] According to the Court of Justice of the EC, the General Agreement has become legally binding upon the EEC "in so far as under the EEC Treaty the Community has assumed the powers previously exerrcised by member states in the area governed by the General Agreement".[192] The full "substitution of the Community for the member States in relation to commitments under GATT took place on 1 July 1968, following the introduction of the Common Customs Tariff", when "the Community ... assumed its full powers in relation to the sphere covered by GATT".[193] "Since so far as fulfilment of the commitments provided for by GATT is concerned, the Community has replaced the member States, the mandatory effect, in law, of these commitments must be determined by reference to the relevant provisions in the Community legal system and not to those which gave them their previous force under the national legal system".[194] From this it follows that, as in the case of international agreements concluded by the EEC pursuant to Article 228 of the EEC Treaty, GATT law has become an "integral part of the Community legal system".[195] By contrast, since Article 105 EEC Treaty provides only for the coordination of the national monetary policies and the EEC has neither internally nor externally assumed the obligations entered into by all EEC member states under the IMF Agreement, it appears that the latter obligations have not become an "integral part" of Community law.[196]

The transformation, since 1 July 1968, of GATT law into an "integral part of the Community legal system" has strengthened the legal effects of GATT law within the EEC in various ways. According to the principles established by the Court in

191 See above (note 184).

192 Cases 21-24/72 - International Fruit Company E.C.R. (1972) 1226, para. 18.

193 Cases 267-269/81 - SPI/SAMI - E.C.R. (1983) 801, para. 17.

194 Case 38/75 - Nederlandse Spoorwegen - E.C.R. (1975) 1450, para. 16.

195 This appears to be generally acknowledged today, even though the formula of an "integral part of the Community legal system" - first used by the Court of Justice in relation to the Association Agreement with Greece (Case 181/73-Haegeman - 1974 E.C.R. 449, 460) and subsequently also in relation to other international agreements concluded by the EEC (e.g. Case 104/81 - Hauptzollamt Mainz v. Kupferberg - 1982 E.C.R. 3641, 3622) - does not explicitly appear in the "GATT case-law" of the Court, who treats GATT law nonetheless as Community law in the sense of Article 177 of the EEC Treaty; see: U. Everling, The Law of the External Economic Relations of the European Community, at p. 94, and C.D. Ehlermann, Application of GATT Rules in the European Community, p. 132, in: Hilf/Jacobs/Petersmann (above note 174).

196 See: E.U. Petersmann, Commentary on Article 234 EEC Treaty, in: Groeben/Boeckh/Thiesing/Ehlermann (eds.), Kommentar zum EWG-Vertrag, 3rd edition, 1983, Vol. II, p. 1150 f.

the International Fruit Company case and in the Kupferberg case, which are valid also for GATT law,[197] fulfilment of GATT obligations by the Community institutions and EC member states has become an obligation also under European Community law and "not only in relation to the non-member country concerned but also and above all in relation to the Community which has assumed responsibility for the due performance of the agreement".[198] As international treaty law binding on the EEC, GATT law is subordinate to the treaties establishing the Communities but takes precedence over "secondary" Community law enacted by the Community institutions. "It follows from the Community nature of such provisions that their effect in the Community may not be allowed to vary according to whether their application is in practice the responsibility of the Community institutions or the Member States and, in the latter case, according to the effects in the internal legal order of each Member State which the law of that State assigns to international agreements concluded by it. Therefore, it is for the Court, within the framework of its jurisdiction in interpreting the provisions of agreements, to ensure their uniform application throughout the Community".[199] GATT law therefore constitutes a yardstick for the legality and the validity not only of secondary Community law but also of all national law of EC member states. Due to the exclusive Community competence in the field of the common commercial policy, EC member states can no longer lawfully adopt national commercial policy measures (e.g. national trade restrictions in violation of GATT rules, national withdrawal from GATT) unless they have been authorized under Community law to do so.[200] And the adoption by the EEC of new legal GATT obligations becoming an "integral part" of Community law may be construed, under certain circumstances, as automatically amending existing provisions of the foreign trade law of the Communities and their member states.[201]

As an "integral part of the Community legal system", GATT law can effectively serve as a "third line of constitutional entrenchment" of legal guarantees for non-discriminatory foreign trade competition. The legal priority of international

---

197 C.D. Ehlermann (note 195), p. 132: "Although the GATT is not strictly speaking an agreement concluded under Article 228 (1), it ranks with international accords binding by virtue of that provision".

198 Case 104/81 (note 195), p. 3662.

199 Case 104/81 (note 195), p. 3663.

200 See Case 41/76 - Donckerwolcke v. Procureur de la République - (1976), ECR 1921, 1937.

201 See C.D. Ehlermann (note 195), p. 132 f, who rightly observes: "A formal amendment of existing secondary legislation is still highly desirable even where the only aim is to prevent conflict, simply in the interests of clarity and certainty in the law".

law binding on the EEC over secondary Community legislation, as well as over national legislation, recognized by the Court of Justice in the Third International Fruit Company case,[202] implies a far-reaching "constitutional constraint" on the commercial policy powers of the EEC and its member States: GATT law is binding on the EEC and its member states not only on the level of public international law, but also as an "integral part" of Community law restraining the EEC institutions as well as individual EC member states from lawfully introducing trade restrictions in violation of GATT law. Regardless of whether this voluntarily accepted "constitutional restraint" of the "sovereign power to violate an international treaty" is subject to legal exceptions[203] or not,[204] it is an important "supranational feature" of European Community law that goes beyond the traditional sovereign power retained by states under their domestic laws to enact national legislation considered lawful within their respective national jurisdiction even if it violates binding international law. This long-term constitutional constraint on the EEC institutions' use of non-transparent, discriminatory and mutually harmful trade policy instruments in violation of GATT law does not impose any "sacrifice" or burden on the EEC. Under GATT law, the EEC remains free to decide autonomously on its own level of trade protection, to withdraw tariff concessions (Article XXVIII), and to introduce trade restrictions for economic and other purposes in conformity with the numerous, generously drafted safeguard clauses of GATT law (e.g. Articles VI, XI:2, XVII to XXI). From the point of view of Community law, the GATT obligations for the use of transparent, nondiscriminatory and proportionate trade policy instruments can serve as a needed "constitutional constraint" on the broad discretionary trade policy powers of the EC executives and as a "constitutional substitute" for the insufficient parliamentary and judicial control of these regulatory powers.

---

202 Cases 21-24/72 ECR 1219.

203 See E.U. Petersmann (note 189), p. 55, who argues that the consensual practice (1973-1978) of floating exchange rates in contravention of Article IV IMF Agreement and the practical difficulties of formally amending the General Agreement (cf. Article XXX GATT) are illustrative of the possibility of very exceptional situations, in which a deviation from an international GATT obligation, unanimously agreed by the Council pursuant to the procedures of Article 235 EEC Treaty, might "prove necessary to attain, in the course of the operation of the common market, one of the objectives of the Community and this Treaty has not provided the necessary powers" (Article 235). But such an exceptional situation should not be lightly assumed to exist, for GATT law leaves all contracting parties, including the EEC, an almost unconstrained freedom to achieve any economic or political policy objective through transparent, lawful and efficient policy instruments.

204 See Hilf (note 174), p. 162, according to whom "the institutions of the Community ... do not have the power to deviate from obligations of international law".

C) GATT Law as an Agent for the Harmonization and "Judicialization" of Foreign Trade Law: The Case of Antidumping Law

The historical experience with economic and legal integration in the United States, Switzerland, Germany and the EEC indicates that confederal and federal arrangements for the establishment of customs unions, the unification of economic legislation, and the protection of economic freedoms and fundamental rights played a decisive role in the gradual liberalization of both internal and external trade. In the field of foreign trade law, the federal legislative competences (e.g. of the USA and the EEC) comprised federal competences for the implementation and administration e.g. of customs matters, import licenses, import relief laws and export subsidies. But in many federal states (such as Canada, Germany and Switzerland), important foreign trade regulations continue to be executed also by state administrative authorities and federal legislation needs to be supplemented by state regulations (e.g. in areas such as government procurement, technical barriers to trade, taxation and subsidies). In the EEC, most of the foreign trade regulations of the EEC are to be implemented by the national administrations of the member states.

After World War II, the economic legislation in many states has become increasingly "interventionist" and "particularistic" due to the emergence of "social welfare states" and government interventions into almost all areas of the national economies. The current GATT negotiations on the liberalization of trade in services reveal how densely regulated many national services sectors have become (e.g. transportation, banking, insurances, telecommunications). As the judiciary in many countries has either exercised judicial self-restraint in the review of the constitutionality of economic legislation (e.g. in the United States since the late 1930s, see above chapter VIII.2.F) or is constitutionally barred from reviewing federal legislation (e.g. in Switzerland, see above chapter VIII.3.D), the effective "economic constitution" in many countries has become what the national legislature determines it to be.[205]

National foreign trade legislation has been a remarkable exception to the above-mentioned trends. As a result of the detailed GATT rules for customs matters (e.g. customs valuation, fees and formalities connected with importation and exportation, antidumping and countervailling duties) and the comprehen-

205 See J. Buchanan (note 160), p. 292: "In matters of economic policy, the effective American constitution is what Congress determines it to be; the judiciary adopts a hands-off attitude here".

sive GATT prohibitions of non-tariff trade barriers, the national foreign trade laws of most GATT member countries have become more transparent, less discriminatory, more liberal and increasingly harmonized. Within the EEC, the Community regulations on the common customs tariff, on customs valuation procedures, import licenses, common rules for imports and exports, antidumping and countervailing duties, safeguard measures, tariff preferences, procedures for the award of public supply contracts or for the introduction and implementation of technical regulations and standards were regularly adopted in implementation of the international GATT rules concerned.[206] Foreign trade law has thereby become the area in which harmonization and approximation of national economic legislation could be achieved more successfully than in most other fields of European integration.

This important role of liberal international trade rules as an engine for the harmonization and "judicialization" of foreign trade laws, which are traditionally strongly influenced by national features and particularities, may be briefly illustrated by the example of antidumping law. Even though the concept of "dumping" (broadly defined as the selling of a product on a foreign market at a price below that charged on the domestic market) is deceptively simple and the number of countries actively using antidumping duties continues to be limited, antidumping law has developed into one of the most complex and controversial fields of national and international trade law for a number of reasons:

- national antidumping laws were progressively enacted - first in Canada (1904) followed by New Zealand (1905), Australia (1906), South Africa (1914), the USA (1916/21), the United Kingdom (1921) and an increasing number of other countries[207] - and still display numerous differences;

- the attempt at coordinating the divergent national laws and practices through GATT Article VI and the 1967 GATT Agreement on Implementation of Article VI had only limited success because of, inter alia, GATT's "grandfather clause", exempting preexisting mandatory legislation, and the US Congress' refusal to incorporate certain 1967 Code provisions into US antidumping legislation;

206 See above chapter IX.3.D. Most texts are reproduced in: E. Völker / J. Steenbergen, Leading Cases and Materials on the External Relations Law of the EC, 1985.

207 See: E.A. Vermulst (note 152), pp. 697 ff. For a collection of texts see: Antidumping and Countervailing Measures Legislation. Loose-leaf collection of texts, GATT 1987.

- the 1979 GATT Agreement on Implementation of Article VI gave more precision to some terms (such as "material injury", "causation" and "industry") but still includes certain principles which leave considerable discretion to the importing countries and have led to divergent policies by their investigating authorities; and
- even though the 1979 Antidumping Code has been continuously further developed through the deliberations and recommendations of the GATT Antidumping Committee and is currently being reexamined in the context of the Uruguay Round of multilateral GATT negotiations, there are a number of new kinds of antidumping measures (e.g. against "input dumping" and "subassembly dumping") which are widely criticized as being protectionist and inconsistent with GATT law.

Price differentiation in national and international markets is a widely used business practice. Dumping, in the sense of international price discrimination by private firms, is neither **per se** undesirable nor prohibited as such. The international regulation has always addressed the "dumping problems" from the perspective of the importing countries by regulating and limiting the protective measures that may be taken against dumped imports. The first antidumping laws of Canada (1904), New Zealand (1905), Australia (1906) and South Africa (1914) did not make the admissibility of antidumping duties contingent upon a previous showing that dumping had caused injury to the domestic industry producing the like product.[208]

It was only in 1921, that three countries (Australia, the United Kingdom and the USA) enacted antidumping legislation which made injury a prerequisite for imposition of antidumping duties. This injury requirement enabled domestic customs administrations "to refrain from interference with all dumping whose benefit to the customer is not clearly offset in part at least by an injury, actual or prospective, to ... industry".[209]

The various studies initiated by the League of Nations in the 1920s, including a "Memorandum on Dumping" written for the League by Prof. Viner in 1926,[210] did not bring about an approximation of the divergent national antidumping laws. Article VI of the 1947 General Agreement set out the first international

208 See: J. Viner, Dumping: A Problem in International Trade, 1966 edition, pp. 192 ff.

209 Viner (note 208), at p. 263.

210 Reprinted in Viner (above note 208).

multilateral rules for the harmonization of national antidumping rules. Yet, because the General Agreement was applied subject to the "grandfather clause" of the Protocol of Provisional Application and many national antidumping laws antedated the General Agreement, a comparative study by the GATT secretariat of the antidumping laws in 20 GATT member countries (of which only 8 had actually used their laws) revealed a large number of differing national practices and interpretations in respect of GATT Article VI.[211] Moreover, GATT Article VI did not regulate antidumping procedures, and some of its substantive terms were opaque. In the GATT Kennedy Round of multilateral trade negotiations (1963-1967), a more precise "Agreement on the Implementation of Article VI" was therefore elaborated which entered into force on 1 July 1968 after having been signed by 17 countries.

The 1967 Antidumping Agreement established detailed procedural and more precise substantive requirements for national antidumping laws and excluded the further recourse to the "GATT grandfather clause" by the parties to the Antidumping Agreement. But the US Congress refused to implement the Code provisions into domestic law. This non-implementation of the 1967 Antidumping Code in US domestic legislation and the elaboration of additional GATT rules on subsidies and countervailing duties during the GATT Tokyo Round of multilateral trade negotiations (1973-1979) were among the major reasons for the elaboration of the 1979 "Agreement on Implementation of Article VI of GATT" which also changed certain substantive provisions (notably on "causation", "material injury" and "industry") and entered into force on 1 January 1980.

The provisions of the 1979 Antidumping Agreement were incorporated into the domestic legislation of 24 GATT member countries plus the EEC and have made an important contribution to further harmonizing and improving domestic antidumping rules and procedures. In addition, the creation of the Antidumping Code Committee under Article 14 of the Agreement has provided an international forum for the regular examination of national antidumping practices and has led to the adoption of a number of agreed interpretations and important Committee recommendations. The antidumping rules have thereby been continuously further developed. The current Uruguay Round of multilateral GATT negotiations (1986-1990) has again led to multilateral negotiations aimed at incorporating the various Antidumping Committee recommendations into the text of the Agreement, reinforcing existing disciplines and adapting the Code to new

211 GATT, Antidumping and Countervailing Duties, 1958; see also: Report of the Group of Experts, Antidumping and Countervailing Duties, GATT 1961.

regulatory problems that have become apparent in national antidumping practices.

The total of approximately 600 antidumping proceedings, initiated during the period from 1980 to 1986 in the United States and the EEC,[212] illustrates the continuing importance of antidumping law. In the EEC, antidumping measures are the trade protection measures most frequently resorted to by EC authorities. During the 1970s, the majority of EEC antidumping proceedings were terminated by means of unpublished price-revision undertakings of the exporting firms without official determination of the existence of dumping or injury; and the separate antidumping procedures of the European Coal and Steel Community have been used mainly as a means of putting pressure on third countries to enter into voluntary export restraint arrangements,[213] the inconsistency of discriminatory governmental quantitative trade restrictions with GATT Article XIII notwithstanding. The 1979 GATT antidumping provisions have not only induced the EC Commission to establish, at least provisionally, the existence of dumping and injury before accepting voluntary price undertakings. But they have also contributed to the important role played by the EC Court of Justice, since its first "Ballbearings judgments" in antidumping matters in 1979,[214] in bringing about more transparency and judicial control of EEC antidumping proceedings. It was mainly because of the detailed procedural guarantees for traders and producers involved in antidumping proceedings, incorporated from the 1979 GATT Antidumping Agreement into the EEC antidumping regulations, that the EC Court of Justice considerably liberalized the admissibility standards for direct actions by private producers, exporters and related importers under Article 173 of the EEC Treaty.[215]

Under Article 173 para. 2 of the EEC Treaty, "Any natural or legal person may, under the same conditions, institute proceedings against a decision addressed to

---

212 A chronological list of EEC antidumping proceedings is reproduced in: I. Van Bael/J.F. Bellis, International Trade Law and Practice of the European Community. EEC Antidumping and other Trade Protection Laws, 1985, pp. 221-246. A similar list is to be found also in the annex to: J.F. Beseler/A. N. Williams, Antidumping and Antisubsidy Law: The European Communities, 1986.

213 See Van Bael/Bellis (note 212), pp. 129, 134.

214 See above note 153.

215 See above chapter IX.3.D,d and, for detailed analyses of the Court decisions in antidumping matters: E.A. Vermulst (note 152), pp. 254-274; Van Bael/Bellis, pp. 127 ff; J.K. Lockett, EEC Antidumping Law and Trade Policy After Ballbearings II, in: Northwestern Journal of International Law and Business, 1987, pp. 365 ff.

that person or against a decision which, although in the form of a regulation or a decision addressed to another person, is of direct and individual concern to the former." In conformity with its earlier ruling that the aim of Article 173 EEC Treaty is "to ensure the legal protection of individuals in all cases in which they are directly and individually concerned by a Community measure - in whatever form it appears - which is not addressed to them",[216] the Court has held, for example in the Timex-case,[217] that a regulation imposing a definitive antidumping duty was "legislative in nature and scope" inasmuch as it applied to "traders in general", yet at the same time it constituted a decision of direct and individual concern to the applicant who was "one of those traders" to which the antidumping duties applied and who had participated in the antidumping proceedings. The EC Court of Justice applied the same considerations, and extended thereby private parties' right of action, also in countervailing duty proceedings[218] and enterprises directly involved in state aid proceedings (Article 92 of the EEC Treaty)[219] because, as the Court stated in the recent COFAZ case, "where a regulation accords applicant undertakings procedural guarantees entitling them to request the Commission to find an infringement of Community rules, those undertakings should be able to institute proceedings (i.e. before the Court) in order to protect their legitimate interests".

The incorporation of the detailed procedural rules of the 1979 GATT Antidumping and Subsidy Codes into Council Regulations (EEC) Nos. 3017/79, 1580/82, 2176/84 and 2423/88 on protection against dumped or subsidized imports from countries not members of the EEC[220] has contributed to the gradual recognition of a now comprehensive system of procedural rights and judicial review in antidumping, countervailing duty and state aid cases. The Court has recognized the admissibility of direct actions under Article 173 EEC Treaty by foreign exporters, related Community importers and Community producers.[221]

216 Case 69/69 - Alcan v. Commission - ECR 1970, pp. 385, 393.

217 Case 264/82 - Timex v. Council and Commission - ECR 1985, p. 849. On the same subject see also the "Allied I" and "Allied II" cases above in notes 157 and 159.

218 See the Fediol case above in note 156.

219 Case 169/84 - COFAZ v. Commission - ECR (1986) 319-417.

220 The texts are published in: OJ No. L 339 (31.12.1979), p. 1; No. L 178 (22.6.1982), p. 9; No. L 201 (30.7.1984), p. 1; No L 209 (2.8.1988) p. 1.

221 See: K. Hailbronner/v.Heydebrand u.d. Lasa, Der gerichtliche Rechtsschutz im Antidumping- und Antisubventionsrecht der EWG, in: Recht der Internationalen Wirtschaft 1986, pp. 889 ff, who rightly critize the Court's discriminatory treatment of unrelated importers

In the Fediol case,[222] the Court announced it would review: whether the Commission had observed the procedural safeguards granted to complainants by the basic regulation; whether the Commission had committed manifest errors in its assessment of the facts; whether the Commission had neglected to consider essential matters; or whether the Commission had abused its powers. The Timex-case and Allied II-case[223] also established the important principle that the EEC institutions are required to make findings on the record and to give all interested parties sufficient information so that the parties and the Court can ascertain whether or not the Commission made accurate determinations.

In the area of procedural reforms, the GATT antidumping rules and the "judicialization" of EC antidumping law have no doubt curbed the scope for protectionist abuses of the broad discretionary trade policy powers of the EC Commission acting as police officer, prosecutor and judge in antidumping proceedings.[224] It remains to be seen whether the EC Court of Justice will also act as a more neutral arbiter of the **substantive** antidumping rules and, in spite of its disappointing "Ballbearings II"-judgments of 7 May 1987 in which the Court refrained from reviewing certain substantive legal problems because they related to "complex economic situations",[225] will contribute in future cases also to curbing the existing scope for protectionist abuses of the substantive EEC antidumping rules.

---

who may so far invoke the EC Court of Justice only via the preliminary ruling procedure under Article 177 which has several disadvantages.

222 See above note 156 at p. 2935.

223 See above notes 158 and 159.

224 See J. Bourgeois, the former head of the EC antidumping division, in: EC Antidumping Enforcement - Selected Second Generation Issues, in: Fordham Corp. Law Institute 1985, pp. 563 ff, who notes that EEC antidumping cases are progressively becoming more "adjudicative-like processes," a trend to which he ascribes four factors (see p. 586): A first factor is the way in which the procedure itself is organized in line with the requirements of the 1979 GATT Antidumping Code, which is itself indebted to U.S. models. A second factor is the presence of trade laywers (sic), who have a natural tendency to change their clients into litigants. A third factor is the change of heart of the Court of Justice that has opened the door to judicial review. A fourth factor is the growing proportion of cases leading to the imposition of anti-dumping duties rather than price undertakings. Such cases are more contentious and the corresponding decisions need to be drafted more rigorously.

225 For a critical review of these judgments (above note 147) see: Lockett (above note 215), whose careful comparison of US and EC court cases comes to the conclusion: "in the United States, there is meaningful substantive judicial review of the implementation of antidumping policies and laws; in the EEC, at least based upon present indications, there is none" (at p. 401).

The "dialectic" evolution of national and international antidumping law over the past 80 years illustrates the interdependence between national and international economic law: National laws not only influence and limit the development of international rules, but also, conversely, international rules may serve as an engine for changing and "constitutionalizing" national laws, e.g. by legally limiting the admissible degree and use of national trade protection measures. Another example of this interrelationship between national constitutional structures and international economic rules - the long-standing hostility of the US Congress towards "the executive agreement called GATT" and the congressional opposition to domestic implementation of the 1967 GATT Antidumping Agreement negotiated by the US executive - is analyzed in the following section, albeit from a different perspective.

D) The Need to Involve Domestic Legislatures: The "Fast Track Procedure" in the US Trade Acts of 1974 and 1988

The separation and only limited delegation by the US Constitution of legislative, executive and judicial powers of the US federal government has resulted in constant tension between Congress and the executive in the field of foreign trade policy and law.[226] Following the traumatic experience of the protectionist Smoot-Hawley Tariff Act of 1930, Congress delegated authority to the President in the Reciprocal Trade Agreements Act of 1934 to enter into international trade agreements on the reciprocal reduction of tariffs and to implement those agreements without further reference to Congress. But the negotiation and acceptance by the United States of the GATT under this authority (as renewed in 1945), without further reference to Congress, was for several decades resented by members of Congress who refused to recognize GATT as an international agreement validly accepted by the United States. On many occasions, Congress reminded the President of its constitutional power to "regulate commerce with foreign nations" and to "pay and collect taxes, duties, imposts" (Article I, section 8 US Constitution), and "this history of congressional hostility to the GATT has affected U.S. international trade relations and its relationship to the GATT over the years".[227]

226 See above chapter VIII.2 and J.H. Jackson in: J.H. Jackson / J.V. Louis / M. Matsushita, Implementing the Tokyo Round. National Constitutions and International Economic Rules, 1984, pp. 140 ff.

227 J.H. Jackson (note 226), at p. 145.

The conclusion by the US President of the GATT as an executive agreement in terms of US constitutional law (rather than as a "treaty" requiring a two-thirds affirmative vote by the US Senate) and the ever increasing role of GATT as the central international trade organization resulted in a **de facto** shift of trade policy powers to the President. One occasion, described by one close observer as "one of the great fiascos of United States trade policy",[228] where Congress reminded the executive branch of the congressional trade policy powers, arose after the conclusion of the GATT Kennedy Round negotiations when Congress refused to authorize acceptance of the 1967 GATT Agreement relating to chemicals, to implement the 1967 Antidumping Agreement provisions into domestic law, and to renew the presidential authority (expired in 1967) under the 1962 Trade Expansions Act to negotiate for reductions in tariffs.[229]

When the US Trade Act of 1974[230] finally renewed the President's negotiating authority in view of the GATT Tokyo Round negotiations, sections 102 and 151 of the Trade Act subjected the presidential negotiating authority for the reduction of non-tariff trade barriers to a particular "fast track procedure". These procedures required the President to consult with the key congressional committees before entering into any trade agreement, to notify the Congress of his intention to enter into such an agreement, and to submit any such agreement to the Congress together with a draft of an implementing bill and a statement of any administrative action proposed to implement such an agreement. The "fast track procedure" further modified the procedures for the congressional authorization of the President to approve and implement the international agreements into US domestic law. Section 151 required the automatic discharge of an implementing bill or approval resolution from committee consideration, prohibited any amendments to the bill, and limited the floor considerations in the House and the Senate so that, within a reasonable period, Congress would have to act on the negotiation result. This "fast track procedure" and the close collaboration between Congress, the President and private business sectors during the Tokyo Round negotiations were the main reasons why the 1979 GATT Tokyo Round Agreements were approved and implemented by Congress in the same year.[231]

---

228 J.H. Jackson, US-EEC Trade Relations: Constitutional Problems of Economic Interdependence, in: Common Market Law Review 1979, at p. 470.

229 See: J. Evans, The Kennedy Round in American Trade Policy, 1971, pp. 299 ff; J.H. Jackson (note 226), p. 146.

230 Public Law 93-618, approved on 3 January 1975, 19 USC 2101-2487, 88 Stat. 1978.

231 See: J.H. Jackson (note 226), pp. 152 f, 159 ff, 169 ff.

The "fast track procedure", which was also adopted in section 3(c) of the 1979 Trade Agreements Act and in the 1988 Omnibus Trade and Competitiveness Act providing trade negotiating authority to the President for the GATT Uruguay Round negotiations,[232] is widely seen as an important "means of accommodating the interests of both the executive branch in its international dealings and the Congress with its responsiveness to constituents".[233] The legal regulation of the relationship between the legislative and the executive government branches is of central importance not only for the United States in view of the constitutional limitations of the international treaty-making powers of the executive. It is of "constitutional significance" also for other countries for a variety of reasons:

a) As shown above in chapters VII and IX.3, multilateral international legal obligations for the use of transparent, non-discriminatory and proportionate trade policy instruments serve constitutional functions for the protection of equal freedoms and property rights in transnational trade transactions. Because their adoption or change is rather of a "legislative" than of an administrative nature, they should be approved by parliaments and/or incorporated into domestic implementing legislation.

b) The "constitutional dilemma" of the international trading system based upon GATT, namely that many general GATT rules have been allowed to erode as a result of "pragmatic" piecemeal adjustments and "protectionist collusion" among government executives, offers additional political arguments to the effect that the long-term basic international rules (e.g. the non-discrimination principle) cannot be protected effectively over time if their observance and "management" by national executives is not controlled by national legislatures and courts.

c) Economic, political and legal theory provides strong and convincing arguments for a "deregulation" of governmental trade restrictions in favor of individual freedoms and for legal limitations of executive trade policy discretion because the latter is an incentive for "rent-seeking" domestic interest groups to lobby for a protectionist exercise of the trade policy

232 Trade Agreements Act of 1979, Public Law 96-39, approved 26 July 1979, 93 Stat. 144; Omnibus Trade and Competitiveness Act, Public Law 100-418, approval 23rd August 1988, 102 Stat. 1107.

233 J.H. Jackson (note 226), p. 166.

discretion. The detailed legislative regulation, notably by the US Congress, of the conditions under which antidumping duties and other import relief measures may be adopted by the executive, has promoted legal certainty and a quasi-adjudicatory approach to antidumping proceedings as well as to other discretionary restrictions of transnational trade transactions of domestic citizens. More transparent, general and precise trade policy rules are more likely to be achieved through long-term "constitutional choices" and legislative improvements in the basic rules than through the current trade policy processes and executive "management" of foreign trade.

d) The widespread decay of the constitutional doctrine of limited delegation of powers was shown to be a major legal cause of grey area trade protectionism.[234] Transparent and possibly educative parliamentary discussions, legislative determination of general nondiscriminatory (trade) policy rules and more precisely circumscribed delegations of limited (trade) policy powers to the executive are constitutionally mandated requirements of liberal democracies in order to make the (foreign trade) law predictable and capable of guiding the behavior of domestic citizens.

e) The scope of judicial review depends on the existence of precise legislative rules and guidelines restraining the executive trade policy discretion. As chapter IX.4 C has attempted to show, the EC Court's judicial protection since 1979 of individual rights in antidumping proceedings was essentially prompted by the fact that the detailed GATT antidumping rules had been incorporated in the EEC's antidumping regulations. Since the internationally agreed requirements for the use of transparent, non-discriminatory and proportionate trade policy instruments are precise, unconditional and go far beyond the general domestic constitutional principles of legal certainty, non-discrimination, proportionality and individual freedom of trade, the national legislatures should clearly instruct the courts to construe the domestic constitutional guarantees of freedom of trade, non-discrimination and proportionality in conformity with the voluntarily accepted international obligations.

234 See above chapters V.5, VI.3.D and VI.4.

E) The Need to Involve Domestic Courts: The "Constitutionalization" of the Customs Union Law of the EEC by the EC Court of Justice as a Precedent?

The comparative analysis in chapter VIII of judicial review of foreign trade restrictions in the United States, Switzerland and Germany had shown that, in the field of transnational trade, the national courts tend to enforce the constitutional guarantees of individual rights, non-discrimination, proportionality, limited delegation of power, and judicial review of discretionary government restrictions in a much less stringent manner than in the field of purely domestic trade restrictions. And it was emphasized that there are hardly any convincing economic, political or legal reasons why the judicial protection of these constitutional guarantees vis-à-vis the domestic exercise of government powers should be less effective only because the trading partner resides abroad rather than within the national economy. This even more so as the national constitutional guarantees of economic liberty are not restricted to the choice of domestic trading partners.

Chapter VIII further pointed out that - even though the GATT is recognized to form part of the federal legal system in the United States, Switzerland and Germany and prescribes precise obligations as to the use of tariffs and non-tariff trade barriers - the courts have so far refrained from examining the "GATT conformity" of federal trade restrictions. Only a few US courts have applied GATT rules, and this only in respect of trade restrictions adopted by states or municipalities. But chapter VIII mentioned also that, for instance, Swiss courts have directly applied the non-discrimination requirement of Article 16, para. 1 of the EFTA Convention.[235] The EC Court of Justice has directly applied the prohibition of fiscal discrimination in Article 21 of the free trade area agreement EEC-Portugal[236] as well as in Article 3 of the free trade area agreement EEC-Spain,[237] and the prohibition of measures having equivalent effect to quantitative restrictions in Article 14, para. 2 of the free trade area agreement EEC-Portugal.[238] Even though the EC Court, in its case "Les Rapides Savoyards", de-

235 Banque de Crédit International v. Conseil d'Etat du Canton de Genève, BGE Vol. 98 I b 385 (1972).

236 Case 104/81 - Kupferberg I - ECR 1982, p. 3641.

237 Case 253/83 - Kupferberg II - ECR, 157.

238 Case 270/80 - Polydor - ECR 1982, p. 329 (the EC Court construed Article 14, however, less stringently than the corresponding Article 30 of the EEC Treaty).

cided on 12 July 1984,[239] emphasized the need for reciprocity in respect of the mutual recognition of the determination of origin by the customs administrations of the exporting countries in EEC-EFTA trade relations, the Court also emphasized that "the fact that the courts of one of the parties consider that certain stipulations in the agreement are of direct application whereas the courts of the other party do not recognize such direct application, is not in itself such as to constitute a lack of reciprocity in the implementation of the agreement".[240]

Chapter IX.3.D recalled and illustrated the often overlooked "paradox" that the international GATT obligations for the use of transparent, non-discriminatory and proportionate trade policy instruments are considerably more precise and comprehensive than the corresponding principles of the foreign trade laws of the EEC and of GATT member countries. Chapter IX.3.D.d and 4.C showed by the example of antidumping law that the incorporation of GATT antidumping rules into the antidumping law of the EEC and the judicial interpretation of the EEC antidumping law in conformity with GATT obligations have considerably improved the rule of law and the judicial protection of individual rights in antidumping proceedings. The direct application by the EC Court of Justice of the prohibitions of tariffs, non-tariff trade barriers and trade discrimination in the EEC Treaty and in the free trade area agreements between the EEC and the EFTA countries even more clearly illustrates the potential contribution of liberal international trade rules to the judicial protection of individual rights and non-discriminatory competition. The "constitutional principles" of European Community law - such as the direct applicability of the freedoms of trade, services, persons and payments, the autonomy, supremacy and direct effect of Community law, the judicial protection of unwritten fundamental rights and general principles of Community law, or the doctrines of the exclusive and preemptive nature of Community competences - were all established through the "constitutional jurisprudence" of the EC Court of Justice. Without this progressive process of "judicial constitutionalization" of European Community law, "we would hardly be able to speak of a Community as we know it today; substantive achievements would be perhaps no more than, say, those of the GATT".[241]

How can a stricter judicial control of the constitutional limitations of governmental trade policy powers be attained? In European Community law, the "con-

239 Case 218/83, ECR 1984, p. 3105.

240 Case 104/81 (above note 236), para. 18.

241 Cappelletti/Seccombe/Weiler (note 63), at p. 31.

stitutional jurisprudence" by the EC Court of Justice was enhanced by the fact that the EC treaties established authorities with clearly limited functions and powers; the lack of effective parliamentary review of these Community powers entailed that effective judicial protection of individual rights by the EC Court of Justice could to some extent "compensate" the lack of parliamentary control and democratic legitimation of Community law. In view of the different national legal systems of the EC countries (notably in respect of judicial protection of individual rights), the principle of the uniformity of Community law likewise required an active role of the EC Court of Justice. A strong judicial review by the EC Court of Justice was also called for by the inadequate separation of legislative and executive powers among the EC executives, whose close collaboration make it unlikely that, for instance, the EC Commission would ever attack before the EC Court of Justice a trade restriction adopted by the EC Council as inconsistent with GATT obligations.[242]

By contrast, the federal states analyzed in chapter VIII are based upon **constitutions** (rather than treaties) establishing democratically controlled governments and courts which have perceived their judicial role vis-à-vis the federal foreign affairs powers in a different manner, as described in chapter VIII. In the United States, for instance, the constitutional separation of legislative, executive and judicial government powers has prompted the courts to exercise judicial self-restraint vis-à-vis discretionary foreign policy and trade policy decisions. Chief Justice Marshall's justification in the landmark case Marbury v. Madison[243] of the judicial power to declare an act of Congress void - namely, that judges must be bound to enforce the constitution against conflicting ordinary law if the constitution is to be "higher law" - does not exclude that the courts respect the broad foreign policy discretion left to the democratically legitimated legislative and executive government branches by the vague constitutional regulation of the foreign affairs powers. Yet, if international treaty obligations validly accepted by the United States are recognized to be binding and to protect legally the individual rights of US citizens: Why should precise self-imposed legal restraints of the discretionary trade policy powers not be treated by the courts as legally meaningful for the interpretation of US foreign trade law?

In Switzerland, the Swiss courts assert judicial review only of cantonal laws vis-à-vis federal law; there is no judicial review of federal legislation because a judi-

242 This is unlikely because the EC Council adopts regulations on the basis of proposals by the EC Commission.

243 5 U.S. (1 Cranch), p. 137 (1803).

cial invalidation of parliamentary federal legislation is considered to be incompatible with the constitutional principle of democracy.[244] While the landmark decision of the German Reichsgericht of 4 November 1925 and the 1929 amendment of the Austrian Constitution introduced judicial review of the constitutionality of legislation in Germany and Austria, most other European countries continued to recognize parliamentary supremacy until World War II and rejected judicial review of legislation on the ground that the interpretation of the often vague national constitutions should be left to the national parliament as the elected representative of the democratic will. It was only after the historical experience before and during World War II of the potential tyranny of constitutionally unconstrained governments, that the movement toward constitutionalism was revived and the need for judicial control of legislation recognized in an increasing number of European countries.[245]

The fact that in several EEC member states (such as Belgium, England, France, the Netherlands and Luxembourg) national courts still have no power to review the constitutionality of parliamentary legislation, has not prevented the EC Court of Justice from reviewing the "constitutionality" of EC regulations, decisions and directives and to develop an ever more comprehensive "constitutional jurisprudence" based upon the "common constitutional traditions" of the EC member states.[246] Since its Third International Fruit Company Case,[247] the EC Court of Justice has consistently recognized that

> "the jurisdiction of the Court, as laid down in Article 177 of the EEC Treaty, to give rulings on the validity of measures adopted by the institutions of the Community cannot be limited by the grounds on which the validity of these measures may be contested. It therefore extends to all grounds capable of invalidating those measures".[248]

However, the Court made its examination of the compatibility of Community law with a provision of international law subject to two conditions: (a) "the Community must first of all be bound by that provision", and (b) "where the invalidity is relied upon before a national court, it is also necessary that that provi-

244 See above chapter VIII.3.D and W. Kälin, Verfassungsgerichtsbarkeit in der Demokratie, 1987, p. 23.

245 For details see: Cappelletti/Golay (note 36), pp. 271 ff.

246 See the various contributions to: J. Schwarze (ed.), Der Europäische Gerichtshof als Verfassungsgericht und Rechtsschutzinstanz, 1983; W. Grewe/H. Rupp/H. Schneider (eds.), Europäische Gerichtsbarkeit und nationale Verfassungsgerichtsbarkeit, 1981.

247 Joined Cases 21-24/72, ECR 1972, p. 1219.

248 Ibidem (note 247), at p. 1219.

sion of international law should be capable of conferring rights on citizens of the Community which they can invoke before the courts".[249] In respect of GATT, the EC Court concluded that GATT law has become binding on the EEC but that "the great flexibility of its provisions, in particular those conferring the possibility of derogation, the measures to be taken when confronted with exceptional difficulties and the settlement of conflicts between the contracting parties" exclude the direct application of GATT provisions by EC citizens before the courts.[250]

The EC Court's case-law in respect of international agreements is generally interpreted as meaning that rules of international treaty law and of general international law binding on the EC are subordinate to the EC treaties but take precedence over "secondary" Community law enacted by the EC institutions. In the words of the former Director-General of the EC Commission legal service: "Rules of international law binding on the Community therefore constitute a yardstick for the legality and validity of such secondary legislation".[251] The "constitutional problem" seems to be related primarily to the doctrine of "direct effect", described by the former judge Pescatore with good reason as "an infant disease of Community Law".[252]

The "constitutional problem" must not be obfuscated by the Court's "GATT case-law". Several authors have convincingly shown that the Court's arguments against "direct effects" of GATT rules reflect a sad ignorance of GATT law and appear to have been motivated more by a political "non possumus"[253] in view of the political opposition by all EC executives and member state executives to judicial enforcement of GATT rules.[254] Since the EC treaties are **treaties** (rather than constitutions) establishing democratically not effectively controlled institutions with limited legislative and executive powers subject to judicial review: Why are precise and unconditional international legal prohibitions of harmful trade restrictions, which limit the discretionary trade policy powers of the EC executives and protect and enlarge the equal freedoms and property rights of

249 Ibidem (note 247), at p. 1219.

250 Ibidem (note 247), p. 1228.

251 C.D. Ehlermann (note 195), at p. 131.

252 P. Pescatore, The Doctrine of "Direct Effect": An Infant Disease of Community Law, in: European Law Review 1983, pp. 155 ff.

253 P. Pescatore (note 252), at p. 177.

254 See for a detailed criticism of this GATT case-law, with references to the pertinent literature: E.U. Petersmann (above notes 117 and 131).

EC citizens, so openly disregarded by the EC Court of Justice in proceedings instituted by private citizens before national courts?[255] If the purpose of all government regulations in a constitutional democracy must be to promote the equal rights of the citizens: Should precise and unconditional internationally agreed freedoms of trade and international obligations to grant judicial protection of individual rights (see GATT Article X:3) not be presumed to confer individual rights[256] and, quite apart from the doctrines of "direct effect" and "invocability", be observed and implemented also in the interpretation and application of domestic law? Where does the EEC Treaty authorize the EC institutions to limit the individual freedoms of trade in manifest violation of their self-imposed international legal obligations?

The "constitutionalization" of the **internal** freedoms of trade of Community law by their judicial interpretation and protection as individual rights of a "higher law status" still needs to be supplemented by a "constitutionalization" of the trade policy powers of the EC institutions. In one of its early "constitutional landmark cases", the van Gend en Loos judgment, the Court has recognized that:

> "Community law not only imposes obligations on individuals but is also intended to confer upon them rights which become part of their legal heritage. These rights arise not only where they are expressly granted by the Treaty, but also by reason of obligations which the Treaty imposes in a clearly defined way upon individuals as well as upon the Member States and upon the institutions of the Community".[257]

This judicial recognition of the EC citizens as legal subjects of Community law and the Court's recognition of "higher law" in the form not only of unwritten fundamental rights and general constitutional principles of Community law but also of international law forming "an integral part of Community law", point the direction for the necessary constitutional and judicial limitations of the Community's trade policy powers to tax and restrict the individual rights of EC citi-

---

255 While it seems to be generally recognized that the EC Court of Justice would apply and enforce GATT rules in "direct actions" instituted by EC institutions or EC member states, it is still an open question whether the Court's denial of "direct applicability" of GATT rules applies only to "indirect actions" under Article 177 of the EEC Treaty or also to "direct actions" by private citizens (e.g. under Article 173). For the new Fediol case of 1989 see note 187 above.

256 In this sense above chapter IX.3.A.

257 Case 26/62, ECR 1963, p. 1.

zens. Two other important "constitutional considerations" have been pointed out by former Advocate-General Verloren van Themaat:[258]

- quite apart from the doctrines of "direct applicability" and "direct effect", the general principles of legal certainty and "estoppel" should be recognized to imply "that the Community cannot rely on either its regulations or other measures on foreign trade in a conflict with a private party, as far as these regulations or other measures violate unconditional and sufficiently clear GATT provisions or MTN agreements. This might be considered a logical consequence of the recognition of these provisions and agreements as binding for the Community;"

- since the numerous different trade policy instruments are to a large extent interchangeable as measures of trade protection, "they should be submitted to the same or equivalent institutional procedural and substantive general legal principles; only then can a meaningful application of a principle of proportionality become possible."

If the EC Court of Justice and e.g. the German courts had examined the "direct applicability" of GATT provisions not in a generic manner in the light of preconceived ideas about the nature of trade policy, but by reading the text of the individual prohibitions invoked (as suggested by Article 31 of the Vienna Convention on the Law of Treaties), they would have noticed that the GATT prohibitions of trade discrimination (Articles I, III, XIII) and of non-tariff trade barriers (e.g. Articles II, XI:1) are not only precise and unconditional but they also apply in principle to **all** the various, interchangeable trade policy instruments. An interpretation of the foreign trade law of the EEC in conformity with GATT law would have avoided the paradoxical inconsistencies e.g. that the Community law principles of non-discrimination are construed in the field of **industrial** goods as prohibiting safeguard measures inconsistent with the non-discrimination requirements of GATT law,[259] but in the field of **agricultural** goods as

---

258 P. Verloren van Themaat, Possibilities for National Measures of Implementation to Strengthen the Legal Quality of International Rules on Foreign Trade, in: D. Dicke/E.U. Petersmann (above note 97), pp. 51 ff.

259 The safeguard clause in Article 16 of the Council Regulation (EEC) No. 288/82 of 5 February on common rules for imports (O.J. L 35/1, 9.2. 1982) only admits import restrictions "with due regard for existing international obligations" and has always been applied so far in conformity with the non-discrimination requirements of GATT Articles I, XIII and XIX.

permitting safeguard measures violating the non-discrimination requirements of GATT law.[260]

F) The Need to Involve Individual Citizens: A "Self-Enforcing Constitution" Depends upon Protection of Individual Rights

Adam Smith valued liberty as an attribute of the "laws and institutions" that are necessary to maximize individual and social economic welfare. He criticized the "impertinence and presumption in kings and ministers to pretend to watch over the economy of private people", as well as the impudence of monopolists to portray and push through their selfish self-interests as "public interests", because he could show that the mercantilist trade restrictions had diminished rather than increased individual and social economic welfare.[261] Individual liberty, private property and general rules of law would enable a largely "spontaneous market order" allowing men with many different values and purposes to cooperate together freely and to their mutual benefit because, in following their own interest, each would be guided by market competition to further the aims also of many others. Adam Smith's theory of justice was "rule-oriented" but not "rights-based": Even though he emphasized the need for a "protective state" and for the governmental supply of "public goods", his general assumption was that the "system of natural liberty" under the rule of law would promote not only individual but also social economic welfare and justice.[262]

The "constitutional choice" of the framers of the US Constitution of a constitutionally limited democracy was strongly influenced by Adam Smith's utilitarian justification of economic liberty and rule of law. Thus, James Madison, sometimes described as "The Founding Father",[263] stated in a speech in the First Congress on 9 April 1789:

> "I own myself the friend to a very free system of commerce, and hold it as a truth, that commercial shackles are generally unjust, oppressive, and impolitic; it is also a truth, that if industry and labor are left to take their own course, they will generally be direc-

260 See the cases referred to above in note 142 and: J. Sack, The Commission's Powers under the Safeguard Clauses of the Common Organizations of Agricultural Markets, in: Common Market Law Review 1983, pp. 757 ff.

261 See above chapter V.4.

262 See above chapter V.4 and 5 and: J.M. Buchanan, The Justice of Natural Liberty, in: G. O'Driscoll (ed.), Adam Smith and Modern Political Economy, 1979, pp. 117 ff.

263 R.A. Rutland, James Madison: The Founding Father, 1987.

> ted to those objects which are the most productive, and this in a more certain and direct manner than the wisdom of the most enlightened Legislature could point out ... All are benefitted by exchange, and the less this exchange is cramped by Government, the greater are the proportions of benefit to each."[264]

But the enumeration of the objectives of the US Constitution in its preamble - inter alia, to "secure the blessings of liberty to ourselves and our posterity" - clearly expresses the much broader perception of the framers of the US Constitution which valued liberty directly as an unalienable "natural right" and not so much on the ground of its instrumental role for promoting economic welfare. Political and legal liberalism ever since have defended equal liberties and decentralized market mechanism (e.g. "markets in ideas", freedom to vote in "political markets") more for their political than their economic properties, notably for their ability to reduce the need for government interferences into individual rights: As long as individual rights are well-defined and legally protected, private property and self-interested competition tend to ensure not only that valued resources are allocated to their most highly valued uses but also that the liberty of individuals, who are presumed to be the only democratically legitimate source of evaluation, will be maximized.[265] While self-interested individuals will voluntarily agree to long-term constitutional rules because such agreements protect and enlarge their individual rights, just as voluntary commercial agreements enlarge their economic freedom of choice, the aim, "value" and "justice" of constitutional rules and democratic governments were seen to consist in the furtherance of equal personal liberty and property rights under the rule of law.

The liberal premise that the state's only legitimate function is to secure the inalienable rights of the citizens and that government powers are therefore essentially limited to those necessary to protect these individual rights, contributed to the view of the framers of the US Constitution that the limited powers of the federal government made the inclusion into the Constitution of a Bill of Rights "unnecessary". James Madison, in a letter to Thomas Jefferson dated 17 October 1788, wrote that "the rights in question are reserved by the manner in which the federal powers are granted"; "there is great reason to fear that a positive declaration of some of the most essential rights could not be obtained in the requisite latitude", and "the limited powers of the federal government and the jealousy of

---

264 Quoted from: J.A. Dorn, Government, the Economy and the Constitution, in: The Cato Journal 1987, pp. 283 ff.

265 See, e.g.: J.M. Buchanan, Towards the Simple Economics of Natural Liberty, in: Kyklos 1987, pp. 3 ff; J. Gray, v.Hayek on Liberty, 1984, pp. 60 ff, 76, 78.

the subordinate governments afford a security which has not existed in the case of the state governments".[266] But Madison later became a leading advocate of a Bill of Rights, and the decreasing effectiveness of the "enumerated powers principle" of the US Constitution as a delimitation of federal power appears to have vindicated this change of mind.

The rise of interventionist welfare states since World War II has been influenced by the "constructivist" belief that economies and societies can be "steered" and manipulated at will by benevolent governments. The classical liberal insight that open markets under the rule of law tend to maximize also individual rights as well as the progress and use of knowledge and that governments can hardly know anything about the "public good" unless people are free to express their individual preferences in open markets, continues to be ignored also in much of the literature on national and international economic law. Chapter V of this book has described the "new mercantilism" as an example of "government failure" because the governmental use of transparent, non-discriminatory and proportionate trade policy instruments in compliance with the constitutional laws of liberal democracies and their mutually agreed GATT obligations could solve the modern trade and adjustment problems in a more democratic, lawful and economically efficient manner. But chapter VI also showed that this "government failure" was not so much due to "political failure" of politicians and bureaucrats, who depend on domestic political support and are hardly ever free to act like "benevolent dictators", but is rather due to "constitutional failures" and inadequate rules for the "constitution" of trade policy powers and procedures for trade policymaking.

Chapter VII then pointed out that liberal international trade rules are not an end in themselves, but a means to protect and enlarge individual freedoms (e.g. to buy and sell goods in the best international markets) and to commit governments to the use of transparent, non-discriminatory and proportionate policy instruments. Even though GATT law does not contain a "Bill of Rights", it has effectively protected and enlarged individual rights by applying liberal principles of constitutional law and internationally agreed objective legal standards to the government powers to tax and restrict the trade transactions of domestic citizens. The comparative analysis of American, Swiss and German constitutional law in chapter VIII confirmed these "constitutional functions" of liberal international trade rules by showing that the national constitutional guarantees of

266 Quoted from: J.A. Dorn, Public Choice and the Constitution: A Madisonian Perspective, in: Gwartney/Wagner (note 12), pp. 57, 73.

equal freedoms, non-discrimination, transparent and proportionate policy-making were meant to restrain also the government powers to tax and restrict the **trans**national exercises of individual rights. But chapter VIII illustrated also that, for various reasons, these national constitutional guarantees are observed much less effectively in the field of "foreign" trade transactions than in purely domestic transactions.

Chapter IX, after having described the potential and the limits of market integration through private law, then elaborated in more detail the main "constitutional hypothesis" of this book: In **trans**national economic transactions, liberal international trade rules and negotiations can give more precision to the often vague national constitutional principles of transparent policymaking, nondiscrimination, proportionality, due process and economic liberty and can strengthen the domestic incentive structures for the "constitutionality" of trade policy processes. But liberal international trade rules can perform "constitutional functions" only if they have the character of general, non-discriminatory long-term rules and only to the extent that they actually restrict governments in the use of discretionary policy instruments.[267] Chapter IX.3.D and 4.C concluded that the international GATT rules had been most successful in furthering the harmonization of domestic foreign trade and administrative law in areas such as customs and antidumping law where the judicial protection of individual rights enabled adversely affected citizens to oppose protectionist abuses.

The "constitutional reconstruction" needed to "constitutionalize" discretionary trade policy powers must therefore begin at home by recognizing that there are no convincing legal, political and economic reasons for restricting individual rights to the choice of **domestic** trading partners and for not ensuring effective judicial protection of individual rights and rule of law in **trans**national trade transactions. In both American and European integration, the judicial protection of individual rights has played a pivotal integrational role and, by enabling domestic citizens to enforce their freedom of trade against protectionist abuses, has mobilized "the vigilance of individuals concerned to protect their rights".[268] But just as individuals can secure and retain their domestic freedoms only through long-term constitutional rules, they can legally secure their free and non-discriminatory access to **foreign** markets only through liberal **international** rules among trading countries. Because these liberal international trade rules

267 Above chapters VII.5 and VIII.5.

268 Case 26/62 - van Gend en Loos - ECR 1963, p. 10.

protect and enlarge the individual rights and the observance of the domestic constitutional guarantees of liberal democracies, they should be incorporated into domestic legislation and individual citizens should be entitled to invoke these international liberties before domestic courts. The constitutional lawyer should recognize freedom of trade as a basic individual right and should not misunderstand it as a mere "economic theory". That this is true not only for the individual choice of domestic trading partners within a constitutional democracy but also for transnational trade transactions with foreign trading partners, is the main thesis of this book and, as the historical experience of European integration teaches, is the most important prerequisite of the necessary "constitutionalization" and "democratization" of governmental foreign trade restrictions.

PUPIL 1

Foreign Debts in the Present and a New International Economic Order
ed. by Detlev Chr. Dicke, 1986, (2nd ed. 1987), XII-364 p.

PUPIL 2

Foreign Investment in the Present and a New International Economic Order
ed. by Detlev Chr. Dicke, 1987, XII-358 p.

PUPIL 3

Constitutional Functions and Constitutional Problems of International Economic Law
by Ernst-Ulrich Petersmann, 1991, LII-464 p.

PUPIL 4

Foreign Trade in the Present and a New International Economic Order
by Detlev Chr. Dicke and Ernst-Ulrich Petersmann, 1988, XII-428 p.

PUPIL 5

Fundamental Principles Governing the International Economic Order
by Detlev Chr. Dicke and Thomas Oppermann, 1991.

PUPIL 6

Liberalization of Services and Intellectual Property in the Uruguay Round of GATT
ed. by Giorgio Sacerdoti, 1990, XIV-258 p.

PUPIL 7

Adjudication of international Trade Disputes
ed. by Günther Jaenicke und Ernst-Ulrich Petersmann, 1991, app. 350 p.

For Product Safety Concerns and Information please contact our EU representative GPSR@taylorandfrancis.com
Taylor & Francis Verlag GmbH, Kaufingerstraße 24, 80331 München, Germany

www.ingramcontent.com/pod-product-compliance
Lightning Source LLC
LaVergne TN
LVHW011102300926
849160LV00008B/253

* 9 7 8 0 3 6 7 1 5 4 2 7 1 *